Measurement and Assessment in Teaching

SEVENTH EDITION

Robert L. Linn
University of Colorado

Norman E. Gronlund
University of Illinois

Merrill,
an imprint of Prentice Hall

Upper Saddle River, New Jersey   Columbus, Ohio

Library of Congress Cataloging-in-Publication Data

Linn, Robert L.

   Measurement and assessment in teaching / Robert L. Linn, Norman E. Gronlund.—7th ed.

     p. cm.

   Rev. ed. of: Measurement and evaluation in teaching / Norman E. Gronlund, Robert L. Linn.

   Includes bibliographical references and index.

   ISBN 0-02-348261-3

   1. Educational tests and measurements. I. Gronlund, Norman Edward, 1920- II. Measurement and evaluation in teaching. III. Title.

LB3051.L545   1995

371.2'6—dc20   94-9006

                                                     CIP

Cover art: Paul Klee, *Castle and Sun* (Private collection)
Editor: Kevin M. Davis
Developmental Editor: Carol S. Sykes
Production Editor: Mary Harlan
Text Designer: Anne Flanagan
Cover Designer: Anne Flanagan
Production Manager: Deidra M. Schwartz
Illustrations: Carlisle Communications, Ltd.

This book was set in Garamond by Carlisle Communications, Ltd.

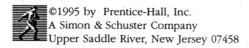©1995 by Prentice-Hall, Inc.
A Simon & Schuster Company
Upper Saddle River, New Jersey 07458

Printed in the United States of America
10 9 8 7 6 5 4 3

ISBN 0-02-348261-3

Prentice-Hall International (UK) Limited, London
Prentice-Hall of Australia Pty. Limited, Sydney
Prentice-Hall of Canada Inc., Toronto
Prentice-Hall Hispanoamericana, S.A., Mexico
Prentice-Hall of India Private Limited, New Delhi
Prentice-Hall of Japan Inc., Tokyo
Simon & Schuster Asia Pte. Ltd., Singapore
Editora Prentice-Hall do Brasil, Ltda., Rio de Janeiro

Joyce E. Linn
&
Marie A. Gronlund

Preface

Measurement and Assessment in Teaching, Seventh Edition, is intended to introduce the classroom teacher and prospective teacher to those elements of measurement and assessment that are essential to good teaching. The main theme throughout the book is that the assessment of learning plays an important role in the instructional process and that its effectiveness depends largely on the ability to construct and select tests and assessments that provide valid measures of learning outcomes.

The seventh edition has been substantially revised to reflect major changes that have occurred in educational testing and assessment since the last edition. Some of the more significant changes include (1) the introduction of a new chapter on the use of performance-based assessment procedures to measure complex achievement (chapter 10), (2) the reorganization of the chapters to bring a fuller array of assessment procedures (e.g., observation, peer appraisal, and self-report) together with more formal tests and assessments, (3) the revision of the chapter on objectives to reflect new understandings of learning and cognition, (4) the revision and updating of the discussion of validity to reflect the importance of the consequences of the uses and interpretations of the results of tests and assessments in judging validity, (5) the addition of material on reliability that is appropriate for performance-based and other types of assessments requiring the use of judgmental scoring, (6) the revision of the concluding chapter to reflect current trends and issues in externally mandated tests and assessments, and (7) the updating of material on published tests to reflect new editions and new approaches to assessment.

The book was designed for the introductory course in educational measurement and assessment, at either the undergraduate or graduate level, and assumes no previous knowledge of measurement or statistics. The writing is direct, and numerous examples are used throughout the book to illustrate important concepts and approaches to testing and assessment. Statistical concepts are introduced only where necessary for understanding and discussion and then the emphasis is on interpretation rather than computation. A section on elementary statistics is provided in

Appendix A for those who want to understand how to obtain the statistical results discussed.

As with earlier editions, the focus of the book is best described by a list of general learning outcomes that should result from its use:

1. An understanding of the role of measurement and assessment in the instructional process.
2. The ability to define instructional goals and objectives in ways that facilitate the construction of appropriate tests and assessments.
3. An understanding of the concepts of validity and reliability and their role in the construction, selection, interpretation, and use of tests and assessments.
4. The ability to construct classroom tests and assessments that measure a variety of learning outcomes (from simple to complex).
5. The ability to obtain assessment information from classroom observations, peer appraisals, and self-reports.
6. The ability to administer tests and assessments properly and to use their results effectively (with due regard to the necessary precautions).
7. The ability to interpret test and assessment results properly (with full awareness of their meaning and the ever-present error of measurement).
8. An understanding of both the potentialities and the limitations of the various test and assessment procedures used in the school.
9. An understanding of how tests and assessments can contribute to effective marking and reporting system and to improved instructional decisions.
10. The ability to interpret and use the results of published tests properly and to select the ones that are most appropriate for a given purpose.
11. An understanding of trends and issues in the use of externally mandated tests and assessments.

These understandings and abilities are most likely to be attained when reading the book is supplemented by other experiences. In the Student Exercise Manual, available for use with this book, each chapter contains specific learning outcomes and numerous related test items and problems that are intended to help you understand and apply measurement concepts. In addition, or instead, textbook reading can be accompanied by practical projects in construction of tests and assessments, in scoring and analysis of results, in selection of tests and other assessment procedures, and in the interpretation of test and assessment results. In any event, practical application of the material will enhance learning and contribute to competence in using measurement skills.

This book was completed while Robert Linn was a Fellow at the Center for Advanced Study in the Behavioral Sciences. He is grateful for the support provided for this fellowship by the Spencer Foundation.

Our special thanks to the individuals who reviewed the sixth edition of the book and to those who reviewed the draft revisions of this edition and provided many valuable suggestions:

❏ Susan M. Brookhart, Duquesne University

❏ Donald J. Brown, California State University–Hayward

❏ Jim Flaitz, University of Southwestern Louisiana

❏ Betty E. Gridley, Ball State University

❏ Carl J. Huberty, University of Georgia

❏ Robert M. Jones, University of Houston–Clear Lake

❏ Robert W. Lissitz, University of Maryland

❏ Robert F. McMorris, SUNY at Albany

❏ Stephanie Salzman, Idaho State University

❏ Hoi Suen, Pennsylvania State University

❏ Kinnard White, University of North Carolina–Chapel Hill

We also thank the publishers who generously permitted use of their copyrighted materials. We are also grateful for the patience and support of our wives and for the valuable help of the Merrill editorial staff.

R.L.L.
N.E.G.

Contents in Brief

Contents

Chapter 10
Measuring Complex Achievement:
Performance-Based Assessments   237

Chapter 11
Assessment Procedures: Observational Techniques,
Peer Appraisal, and Self-Report   265

Chapter 12
Assembling, Administering, and Appraising
Classroom Tests and Assessments   299

PART I
The Measurement and Assessment Process

CHAPTER 1
The Role of Measurement and Assessment in Teaching

Assessment of student learning requires the use of a number of techniques for measuring student achievement. But assessment is more than a collection of techniques. It is a process, a systematic process, that plays a significant role in effective teaching. It begins with the identification of learning goals and ends with a judgment concerning the extent to which those goals have been attained.

A common image evoked by the mention of educational measurement and assessment is that of paper-and-pencil tests—especially standardized, multiple-choice tests. The image is hardly surprising. Most students, particularly those educated in the United States, have had considerable experience with a variety of standardized tests before entering college. Standardized tests have also played a prominent role in discussions of the state of education in the United States and in the educational reform initiatives of the past decade. Standardized tests have been the focus of intense controversy because of charges that they are biased against minorities and females, and that they drive instruction in undesirable ways by an overemphasis on low-level skills. Given the importance of standardized testing for educational policy makers, and the issues and controversies that surround it, it is essential that teachers understand the technology of standardized testing, its uses and abuses.

But measurement and assessment include much more than standardized tests. Students spend considerably more time taking teacher-constructed tests and tests selected by teachers from materials furnished by publishers than they do taking standardized tests. But even the addition of teacher-constructed and teacher-selected tests leaves us with an incomplete picture of the domain of measurement and assessment. Formal assessments of student worksheets, homework assignments, projects, and term papers further expand the concept of the domain, but still leave it incomplete because many of the assessments that are critical to the moment-by-moment classroom activities are informal.

Informal classroom observation guides many instructional decisions. For example, oral questioning of students may indicate the need for a complete review of the material; class discussion may reveal misunderstandings that must be corrected on the spot; interest in a topic may suggest that more time should be spent on it than originally planned. Similarly, in observing individual students, a teacher decides that Sandra needs help in writing a complete paragraph, that Bill needs more practice in doing mathematics problems, that Juan and Betty should be given remedial work in reading, and that Maria should be encouraged to read more challenging books.

Instructional decisions such as these are made continually during the process of teaching. Some are based on students' oral responses, some on the actual performance of a skill, others on a student's quizzical look, tone of voice, or physical behavior. All are based on the teacher's moment-by-moment observations. Although these observations are informal, they play an indispensable role in effective teaching.

Tests and other procedures for measuring student learning are not intended as replacements for the teacher's informal observations and judgments. Rather, they are intended to complement and supplement the teacher's informal methods of obtaining information about students. The teacher is still the observer and decision maker. Measurement and assessment procedures merely provide more systematic, objective evidence on which to base instructional decisions.

INSTRUCTIONAL DECISIONS REQUIRING ASSESSMENT DATA

Numerous decisions made by teachers require them to supplement their informal observations of students with more systematic measures of aptitudes, achievement, and personal development. It would not be feasible to make an exhaustive list of all such decisions, but it is possible to identify some of the more common ones. The following list of questions illustrates some of the major instructional decisions teachers are likely to encounter during the course of their teaching. Examples of the types of measurement and assessment procedures that might be most helpful in answering the questions are included in parentheses.

1. How realistic are my teaching plans for this particular group of students? (Scholastic aptitude tests, past record of achievement.)

2. How should the students be grouped for more effective learning? (Teacher-constructed tests, past record of achievement, observation.)

3. To what extent are the students ready for the next learning experience? (Pretests of needed skills, past record of achievement.)

4. To what extent are students attaining the learning goals of the course? (Teacher-constructed tests, class projects, oral questioning, observation.)

5. To what extent are students progressing beyond the minimum essentials? (Teacher-constructed tests, general achievement tests, class projects, observation.)

6. At what point would a review be most beneficial? (Periodic quizzes, oral questioning, observation.)

7. What types of learning difficulties are the students encountering? (Diagnostic tests, observation, oral questioning, student conferences.)

8. Which students should be referred to counseling, special classes, or remedial programs? (Scholastic aptitude tests, achievement tests, diagnostic tests, observation.)

9. Which students have poor self-understanding? (Self-ratings, student conferences.)

10. Which school grade should be assigned to each student? (Review of portfolio of all assessment data.)

11. How effective was my teaching? (Achievement tests, students' ratings, supervisors' ratings.)

This list of questions highlights the need for various types of information in teaching, but instructional decisions are not so neatly ordered. There are always numerous sub-questions to be answered and an overlap among the various decisions. Many different types of assessment data might be useful in a particular situation. The teaching–learning process involves a continuous and interrelated series of instructional decisions concerning ways to enhance student learning. Our main point here, however, is that the effectiveness of the instruction depends to a large extent on the nature and quality of the information on which the decisions are based.

ASSESSMENT, TEST, AND MEASUREMENT

The terms *assessment, test,* and *measurement* are easily confused because all may be involved in a single process. **Assessment** is a general term that includes the full range of procedures used to gain information about student learning (observations, ratings of performances or projects, paper-and-pencil tests) and the formation of value judgments concerning learning progress. (The term *assessment* as used in this edition is similar to the use of the term *evaluation* in the last edition, but with greater emphasis on realistic and complex types of performance tasks.) A **test** is a particular type of assessment that typically consists of a set of questions administered during a fixed period of time under reasonably comparable conditions for all students. **Measurement** is the assigning of numbers to the results of a test or other type of assessment according to a specific rule (e.g., counting correct answers or awarding points for particular aspects of an essay). The specific meaning of each term is summarized in the following box.

Assessment is a much more comprehensive and inclusive term than measurement or testing. The term *measurement* is limited to quantitative descriptions of students; that is, the results of measurement are always expressed in numbers (e.g., Mary correctly solved 35 of the 40 arithmetic problems). It does not include

TERMINOLOGY

Assessment: Any of a variety of procedures used to obtain information about student performance. Includes traditional paper-and-pencil tests as well as extended responses (e.g., essays), and performances of authentic tasks (e.g., laboratory experiments). Assessment answers the question "How well does the individual perform?"

Test: An instrument or systematic procedure for measuring a sample of behavior by posing a set of questions in a uniform manner. Because a test is a form of assessment, tests also answer the question "How well does the individual perform—either in comparison with others or in comparison with a domain of performance tasks?"

Measurement: The process of obtaining a numerical description of the degree to which an individual possesses a particular characteristic. Measurement answers the question "How much?"

qualitative descriptions (e.g., Mary's work was neat) nor does it imply judgments concerning the worth or value of the obtained results. Assessment, on the other hand, may include both quantitative descriptions (measurement) and qualitative descriptions (nonmeasurement) of students. In addition, assessment always includes value judgments concerning the desirability of the results. Figure 1.1 shows the comprehensive nature of assessment and the role of measurement and nonmeasurement techniques in the assessment process. As noted in the diagram, assessment may or may not be based on measurement; when it is, it goes beyond simple quantitative descriptions.

GENERAL PRINCIPLES OF ASSESSMENT

Assessment is an integrated process for determining the nature and extent of student learning and development. This process will be most effective when the following principles are taken into consideration.

   1.   Clearly specifying what is to be assessed has priority in the assessment process.   The effectiveness of assessment depends as much on a careful description of what to assess as it does on the technical qualities of the assessment procedures used. Thus, specification of the characteristics to be measured should precede the selection or development of assessment procedures. When assessing student learning, this means clearly specifying the intended learning goals before selecting the assessment procedures to use.

   2.   An assessment procedure should be selected because of its relevance to the characteristics or performance to be measured.   Assessment procedures are frequently selected on the basis of their objectivity, accuracy, or

FIGURE 1.1
The assessment process

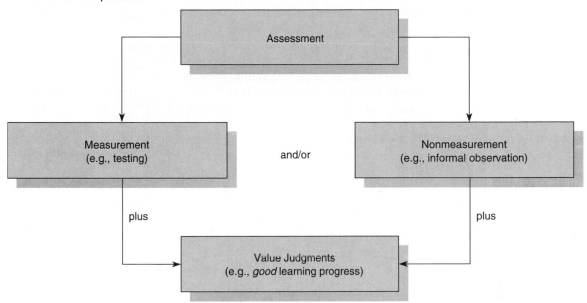

convenience. Although these criteria are important, they are secondary to the main criterion: Is this procedure the most effective method for measuring the learning or development to be assessed? Every procedure is appropriate for some uses and inappropriate for others. In assessing student achievement, for example, we need a close match between the intended learning goals and the types of assessment tasks used. If the development of the ability to organize ideas and write a well-integrated composition is a learning goal, then a multiple-choice test on the mechanics of writing would be a poor substitute for assessments based on analyses of student writing under a variety of conditions (e.g., in-class essay tests, writing projects, and term papers).

   3. Comprehensive assessment requires a variety of procedures.   No single type of instrument or procedure can assess the vast array of learning and development outcomes emphasized in a school program. Multiple-choice and short-answer tests of achievement are useful for measuring knowledge, understanding, and application outcomes, but essay tests and other written projects are needed to assess the ability to organize and express ideas. Projects that require students to formulate problems, accumulate information through library research, or collect data (e.g., through experimental observations or interviews) are needed to measure certain skills in formulating and solving problems. Observational techniques are needed to assess performance skills and various aspects of student behavior. And self-report techniques are useful for assessing interests and attitudes. A complete picture of student achievement and development requires the use of many different assessment procedures.

   4. Proper use of assessment procedures requires an awareness of their limitations.   Assessment procedures range from very highly developed measuring instruments (e.g., standardized aptitude and achievement tests) to rather crude assessment devices (e.g., observational and self-report techniques). Even the best educational and psychological measuring instruments yield results that are subject to various types of measurement error.

Sampling error is one common problem in educational and psychological measurement. An achievement test may not adequately sample a particular domain of instructional content. An observational instrument designed to assess a student's social adjustment may not sample enough behavior for a dependable index of this trait. Fortunately, sampling error can be controlled through careful application of established measurement procedures.

A second source of error is caused by chance factors influencing assessment results, such as guessing on objective tests, subjective scoring on essay tests, errors in judgment on observation devices, and inconsistent responding on self-report instruments (e.g., attitude scales). Because of these problems, students just a few points apart on an educational assessment should not be considered to be different. In fact, no score on an educational or psychological assessment should be treated as a totally accurate measurement of the characteristic in question. Through the careful use of assessment procedures we are able to keep these errors of measurement to a minimum.

The incorrect interpretation of measurement results constitutes another major source of error. Users of educational assessments sometimes interpret results as more precise than they are, or as an indication of characteristics beyond those the assessment is designed to measure. For instance, scholastic aptitude scores are sometimes interpreted as measures of innate abilities rather than modifiable abilities, or as a measure of general personal worth rather than as a limited measure of verbal and numerical reasoning. Misinterpretation of test results is all too common, but it can be controlled by careful attention to what the test actually measures and how accurately it does so.

These limitations of assessment procedures do not negate the value of tests and other types of assessments. A healthy awareness of the limitations of assessment instruments makes it possible to use them more effectively. Keep in mind that the cruder the instrument, the greater its limitations and, consequently, the more caution required in its use.

5.   *Assessment is a means to an end, not an end in itself.*   The use of assessment procedures implies that some useful purpose is being served and that the user is clearly aware of this purpose. To blindly gather data about students and then file the information away is a waste of both time and effort. Assessment is best viewed as a process of obtaining information on which to base educational decisions.

ASSESSMENT AND THE INSTRUCTIONAL PROCESS

The main purpose of classroom instruction is to help students achieve a set of intended learning goals. These goals should typically include desired changes in the intellectual, emotional, and physical spheres. When classroom instruction is viewed in this light, assessment becomes an integral part of the teaching-learning process. The intended learning outcomes are established by the instructional goals, the desired changes in students are brought about by the planned learning activities, and the students' learning progress is periodically assessed by tests and other assessment devices. While the interdependent nature of teaching and learning is beyond dispute, the interdependent nature of teaching, learning, and assessment is less often recognized. The statements in "Measurement and Assessment—Essential Components of Effective Teaching" attest to the fact that leaders in the advancement of teaching as a profession recognize the critical role of assessment as an integral part of effective teaching. The interdependence of these three facets of education can be clearly seen in the following steps included in the instructional process.

Identifying Instructional Goals

The first step in both teaching and assessment is determining the learning outcomes to be expected from classroom instruction. How should students think and act when they complete the learning experience? What knowledge and understanding should the students possess? What skills should they be able to display? What interests and attitudes should they have developed? What changes in habits of thinking, feeling, and doing should have taken place? In short, what specific changes are we striving for, and what are students like when we have succeeded in bringing about these changes?

Preassessing the Learners' Needs

When the instructional goals have been clearly specified, it is usually desirable to make some assessment of the learners' needs in relation to the learning outcomes to

---

Measurement and Assessment—Essential Components of Effective Teaching

The Holmes Group (an organization of major universities working on the reform of teacher education): "Professional teachers" are described as "skilled diagnosticians of children's learning needs." They are expected to "interpret the understandings students bring to and develop during lessons . . . [and to] identify students' misconceptions and question their surface responses that mask true learning."

National Board of Professional Teaching Standards (a group created to provide certification of highly accomplished professional teachers): "Teachers are responsible for managing and monitoring student learning. The teachers we intend to recognize know how to create, enrich, maintain, and alter instructional settings to capture and sustain student interest. They use many methods to measure student growth and understanding."

Sources: From *Tomorrow's Teachers: A Report of the Holmes Group* by The Holmes Group, 1986, East Lansing, MI: The Holmes Group; and *Questions and Answers* by the National Board of Professional Teaching Standards, 1991, Washington, DC: The National Board of Professional Teaching Standards.

be achieved. Do the students possess the abilities and skills needed to proceed with the instruction? Have the students already developed the skills and understanding intended? Assessing students' knowledge and skill at the beginning of instruction enables us to answer such questions. This information is useful in planning work for students who lack the prerequisite skills and in modifying our instructional plans to fit the needs of the learners.

Providing Relevant Instruction

Relevant instruction takes place when course content and teaching methods are integrated into planned instructional activities designed to help students achieve the intended learning outcomes. During this instructional phase, measurement and assessment provide a means of monitoring learning progress and diagnosing learning difficulties. Thus, periodic assessment during instruction provides a type of feedback-corrective procedure that aids in continuously adapting instruction to group and individual needs.

Assessing the Intended Learning Outcomes

The final step in the instructional process is to determine the extent to which the learning objectives were achieved by the students. This is accomplished by using tests and other types of assessments that are specifically designed to measure the intended learning outcomes. Ideally, the instructional goals will clearly specify the desired changes in students and the assessment instruments will provide a relevant measure or description of the extent to which those changes have taken place. Matching a range of assessment procedures to the intended learning outcomes, with particular emphasis on those that are judged to be most important, is basic to effective classroom assessment and will receive considerable attention in later chapters.

Using the Results

Student assessment is often regarded as being essentially for the benefit of teachers and administrators. This attitude overlooks the direct contribution assessment can make to students. Properly used assessment procedures can contribute directly to improved student learning by (1) clarifying the nature of the intended learning outcomes, (2) providing short-term goals to work toward, (3) providing feedback concerning learning progress, and (4) providing information for overcoming learning difficulties and for selecting future learning experiences. Although these purposes are probably best served by the periodic assessment during instruction, the final assessment of intended outcomes also should contribute to these ends.

Information from carefully developed tests and other types of assessments also can be used to improve instruction. Such information can aid in judging (1) the appropriateness and attainability of the instructional goals, (2) the usefulness of the instructional materials, and (3) the effectiveness of the instructional methods. Thus, assessment procedures can contribute to improvements in the teaching-learning process itself, as well as contributing directly to improved student learning.

Assessment results are, of course, also used for assigning marks and reporting student progress to parents. The systematic use of a wide range of assessment procedures provides an objective and comprehensive basis for reporting on each student's learning progress. In addition to marking and reporting, assessment results also are used in the school for various administrative and guidance functions. They are useful in curriculum development, in aiding students with educational and vocational decisions, and in assessing the effectiveness of the school program. The simplified instructional model shown in Figure 1.2 summarizes the basic steps in the instructional process and illustrates the interrelated nature of teaching, learning, and assessment.

FIGURE 1.2
Simplified instructional model

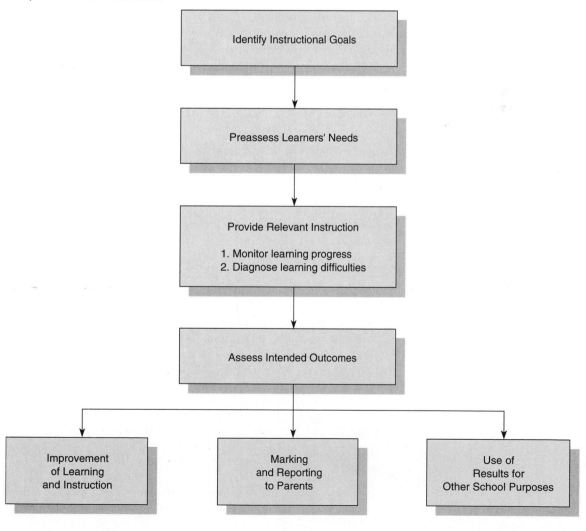

TYPES OF ASSESSMENT PROCEDURES

The assessment process may include a wide variety of procedures. These may be classified and described in many different ways, depending on the frame of reference used. Here we shall present those bases for classification that are most useful for understanding and using assessment procedures in teaching. Although the categories are not discrete, they provide a good general overview of assessment procedures and a useful introduction to some basic terms. The specific procedures used in classroom assessment will be described and illustrated in later chapters.

Maximum Performance versus Typical Performance

Tests and other types of assessments may be placed in two broad categories on the basis of the nature of the measurement. These have been labeled by Cronbach (1990) as *measures of maximum performance* and *measures of typical performance*. In the first category are those procedures used to determine a person's abilities. Procedures of this type are concerned with how well individuals perform when they are motivated to obtain as high a score as possible. In short, the assessment results indicate what individuals can do when they put forth their best effort. Aptitude and achievement tests are included in this category. A distinction between these two types of tests is commonly made in terms of the use of the results rather than of the qualities of the tests themselves. An aptitude test is primarily designed to predict success in some future learning activity, while an achievement test is designed to indicate degree of success in some past learning activity. Because some tests may be used for both purposes, however, it is obvious that the difference is mainly a matter of emphasis. For example, an algebra test designed to measure achievement at the end of the course also may be used to predict success in future mathematics courses. Such overlapping of function prevents distinct classification, but the terms *aptitude* and *achievement* provide useful designations for discussions of measures of ability.

The second category in this classification of procedures includes those designed to reflect a person's typical behavior. Procedures of this type are concerned with what individuals *will* do rather than what they *can* do. Methods designed to assess interests, attitudes, adjustment, and various personality traits are included in this category. Here the emphasis is on obtaining representative responses rather than high scores. Although this is an extremely important area in which to appraise students, assessments of typical behavior are fraught with difficulties. Inadequacy of testing instruments in this field has led to wide use of interviews, questionnaires, anecdotal records, ratings, and various other self-report and observational techniques. None of these techniques alone provides an adequate appraisal of typical behavior, but the combined results of a number of them enable the teacher to make fairly accurate judgments concerning student progress and change in these areas.

Fixed-Choice Tests and Complex-Performance Assessments

The format of tests and assessments has been the subject of considerable debate and controversy in recent years. The multiple-choice test item has been the most widely used format on standardized tests used in the United States for more than half a century. Multiple-choice and other variations of fixed-choice test items (e.g., true-false, matching) are highly efficient because students can respond to a relatively large number of questions in a brief period of time and the responses can be machine scored. Objective scoring, high reliability for a given period of time, and cost effectiveness are major advantages of this technique.

Although fixed-choice tests have always had their critics, several perceived weaknesses of this testing format have attracted widespread attention in recent years. Of particular concern are the beliefs that: (1) fixed-choice tests tend to overemphasize factual knowledge and low-level skills at the expense of higher-order problem solving and conceptual skills and (2) such tests drive instruction in ways that are inconsistent with current understandings of cognition and learning that emphasize the importance of engaging students in the construction of knowledge and their own understandings rather than the accumulation of discrete facts and procedural skills (Resnick and Resnick, 1992).

With the 1990s has come a groundswell of support for a quite different approach to measurement and assessment, one which relies on extended tasks and the analysis of complex student performances. The tasks are intended to closely reflect long-term instructional goals and require students to solve problems of importance outside the confines of the classroom, or to perform in ways that are valued in their own right. Written essays are one example of a complex-performance task that reflects the instructional goal of effective communication more than a fixed-choice test could. Other examples include open-ended mathematics problems requiring extended responses, laboratory experiments in science, oral presentations, projects, and exhibitions of student work.

Fixed-choice tests and complex-performance assessments represent two ends of a continuum. Tests requiring the construction of short answers fall between the extremes. Even an essay test may not be a complex-performance assessment if students are allowed only a brief period to respond, have no choice of topic, and no chance to revise.

Performance assessments are frequently referred to as "authentic assessments" to emphasize that they assess performance while students are engaged in problem solving and learning experiences that are valued in their own right, not just as a means of appraising student achievement. However, not all performance assessments are "authentic" in the sense that they engage students in solving real problems.

Performance assessments are more time-consuming to administer and score than fixed-choice tests. Human judgment is a critical part of scoring and requires a high degree of expertise and training. Fixed-choice tests and complex-performance assessment, as well as a range of intermediate techniques, are useful for assessing student achievement. As will be highlighted in subsequent chapters, a full range of assessment procedures is needed, and the particular mix must be carefully tailored to the purposes of the assessment and to its impact on teaching and learning.

Placement, Formative, Diagnostic, and Summative Assessment

Tests and other assessment procedures can also be classified in terms of their functional role in classroom instruction. One such classification system follows the sequence in which assessment procedures are likely to be used in the classroom (Airasian and Madaus, 1972). These categories classify the assessment of student performance in the following manner:

1. *Placement assessment:* To determine student performance at the beginning of instruction.
2. *Formative assessment:* To monitor learning progress during instruction.
3. *Diagnostic assessment:* To diagnose learning difficulties during instruction.
4. *Summative assessment:* To assess achievement at the end of instruction.

Each of these types of classroom assessment typically requires instruments specifically designed for the intended use.

Placement Assessment.   Placement assessment is concerned with the student's entry performance and typically focuses on questions such as the following: (1) Does the student possess the knowledge and skills needed to begin the planned instruction? For example, does the beginning reader have the necessary reading readiness skills, or does the beginning algebra student have a sufficient command of essential arithmetic concepts? (2) To what extent has the student already developed the understanding and skills that are the goals of the planned instruction? Sufficient levels of comprehension and proficiencies might indicate the desirability of skipping certain units or of being placed in a more advanced course. (3) To what extent do the student's interests, work habits, and personality characteristics indicate that one mode of instruction might be better than another (e.g., group instruction versus independent study)? Answers to questions like these require the use of a variety of techniques: records of past achievement, pretests on course objectives, self-report inventories, observational techniques, and so on. The goal of placement assessment is to determine for each student the position in the instructional sequence and the mode of instruction that is most beneficial.

Formative Assessment.   Formative assessment is used to monitor learning progress during instruction. Its purpose is to provide continuous feedback to both student and teacher concerning learning successes and failures. Feedback to students provides reinforcement of successful learning and identifies the specific learning errors that are in need of correction. Feedback to the teacher provides information for modifying instruction and for prescribing group and individual work. Formative assessment depends heavily on specially prepared tests for each segment of instruction (e.g., unit, chapter). Tests and other types of assessment used for formative assessment are most frequently teacher made, but customized tests made available by publishers of textbooks and other instructional materials also can serve this function. Observational techniques are, of course, also useful in monitoring student progress and identifying learning errors. Because formative assessment is directed toward improving learning and instruction, the results are typically not used for assigning course grades.

Diagnostic Assessment.   Diagnostic assessment is a highly specialized procedure. It is concerned with the persistent or recurring learning difficulties that are left unresolved by the standard corrective prescriptions of formative assessment. If a student continues to experience failure in reading, mathematics, or other subjects, despite the use of prescribed alternative methods of instruction, then a more detailed diagnosis is indicated. To use a medical analogy, formative assessment provides first-aid treatment for simple learning problems and diagnostic assessment searches for the underlying causes of those problems that do not respond to first-aid treatment. Thus, diagnostic assessment is much more comprehensive and detailed. It involves the use of specially prepared diagnostic tests as well as various observational techniques. Serious learning disabilities also are likely to require the services of educational, psychological, and medical specialists. The aim of diagnostic assessment is to determine the causes of persistent learning problems and to formulate a plan for remedial action.

Summative Assessment.   Summative assessment typically comes at the end of a course (or unit) of instruction. It is designed to determine the extent to which the instructional goals have been achieved and is used primarily for assigning course grades or for certifying student mastery of the intended learning outcomes. The techniques used in summative assessment are determined by the instructional goals, but they typically include teacher-made achievement tests, ratings on various types of performance (e.g., laboratory, oral report), and assessments of products (e.g., themes, drawings, research reports). Although the main purpose of summative assessment is grading, or the certification of student achievement, it also provides information for judging the appropriateness of the course objectives and the effectiveness of the instruction.

Norm-Referenced and Criterion-Referenced Measurement

How the results of tests and other assessment procedures are interpreted also provides a method of classifying these instruments. There are two basic ways of interpreting student performance. **Norm-referenced** interpretation describes the performance in terms of the relative position held in some known group (e.g., typed better than 90 percent of the class members). **Criterion-referenced** interpretation describes the specific performance that was demonstrated (e.g., typed 40 words per minute without error). When interpretations are confined to the attainment of a specific objective (e.g., capitalized all proper nouns) they are sometimes called objective referenced. This is a type of criterion-referenced interpretation, but it does not cover as broad a domain of tasks as that typically used in criterion referencing. These concepts are defined more specifically in the accompanying box.

Norm-referenced interpretations might be based on a local, state, or national group, depending on the use to be made of the results. Using national norms, for example, we might describe a student's performance on a vocabulary test as equaling or exceeding that of 76 percent of a national sample of sixth-graders. Criterion-referenced interpretations can be made in various ways. For example, we can (1) describe the specific learning tasks a student is able to perform (e.g., counts from 1 to 100), (2) indicate the percentage of tasks a student performs correctly (e.g., spells 65 percent of the words in the word list), or (3) compare the test performance to a set standard and make a mastery/nonmastery decision (e.g., answers correctly at least 80 percent of the items measuring identification of the main idea in paragraphs). Although a standard of mastery can be used in making one type of criterion-referenced interpretation, it is not an essential element of criterion-referenced testing, as illustrated in the first two examples.

Although the term *percent* was used in illustrating both types of interpretation, it was used in a distinctly different way each time. The norm-referenced interpretation indicated the student's relative standing in a norm group by noting the percentage of students in the group who obtained the same, or a lower, score (called a percentile score). The criterion-referenced interpretation focused on the percentage of items answered correctly (called a percentage-correct score). Although many types of scores are used in testing, the distinction between the percentile score and the percentage-correct score is a significant one because it illustrates the basic difference between a norm-referenced interpretation and a criterion-referenced interpretation.

TERMINOLOGY

Norm-Referenced Test: A test designed to provide a measure of performance that is interpretable in terms of an individual's *relative standing in some known group*.

Criterion-Referenced Test: A test designed to provide a measure of performance that is interpretable in terms of a *clearly defined and delimited domain of learning tasks*.

Other terms that are less often used but have meanings similar to criterion referenced: *objective referenced, content referenced, domain referenced,* and *universe referenced*.

Strictly speaking, "norm referenced" and "criterion referenced" refer only to the method of interpreting the results. These distinct types of interpretation are likely to be most meaningful and useful, however, when tests (and other assessment instruments) are specifically designed for the type of interpretation to be made. Thus, it is legitimate to use the terms *criterion referenced* and *norm referenced* as broad categories for classifying tests and other assessment procedures.

Tests that are specifically built to maximize one type of interpretation are impossible to identify merely by examining the test itself (see "Comparison of Norm-Referenced Tests and Criterion-Referenced Tests"). It is in the construction and use of the tests that differences can be noted. An identifying feature of norm-referenced tests is the selection of items of average difficulty and the elimination of items that all students are likely to answer correctly. This procedure provides a wide spread of scores so that discrimination among students at various levels of achievement is possible. This is useful for decisions based on relative achievement, such as selection, grouping, and relative grading. By contrast, criterion-referenced tests include items that are directly relevant to the learning outcomes to be measured, without regard to whether the items can be used to discriminate among students. No attempt is made to eliminate easy items or alter their difficulty. If the learning tasks are easy, then test items will be easy. The goal of the criterion-referenced test is to obtain a description of the specific knowledge and skills each student can demonstrate. This information is useful for planning both group and individual instruction.

These two types of tests are best viewed as the ends of a continuum, rather than as a clear-cut dichotomy. As shown in the following continuum, the criterion-referenced test emphasizes description of performance and the norm-referenced test emphasizes discrimination among individuals.

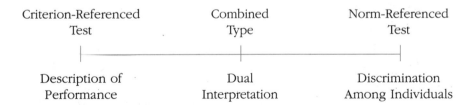

Criterion-Referenced Test	Combined Type	Norm-Referenced Test
Description of Performance	Dual Interpretation	Discrimination Among Individuals

In an attempt to capitalize on the best features of both, test publishers have attempted to make their norm-referenced tests more descriptive, thus allowing for both norm-referenced and criterion-referenced interpretations. Similarly, test publishers have added norm-referenced interpretations to tests that were specifically built for criterion-referenced interpretation. The use of dual interpretation with published tests seems to be an increasing trend that will move many tests more toward the center of the continuum. Although this involves some compromises in test construction and some cautions in test interpretation, the increased versatility may contribute to more effective test use.

Comparison of Norm-Referenced Tests (NRTs) and Criterion-Referenced Tests (CRTs)*

Common Characteristics of NRTs and CRTs

1. Both require specification of the achievement domain to be measured.
2. Both require a relevant and representative sample of test items.
3. Both use the same types of test items.
4. Both use the same rules for item writing (except for item difficulty).
5. Both are judged by the same qualities of goodness (validity and reliability).
6. Both are useful in educational assessment.

Differences Between NRTs and CRTs

Remember, differences are only a matter of emphasis.

1. NRT: Typically covers a *large* domain of learning tasks, with just a few items measuring each specific task.
   CRT: Typically focuses on a *delimited* domain of learning tasks, with a relatively large number of items measuring each specific task.
2. NRT: Emphasizes *discrimination* among individuals in terms of relative level of learning.
   CRT: Emphasizes *description* of what learning tasks individuals can and cannot perform.
3. NRT: Favors items of average difficulty and typically omits very easy and very hard items.
   CRT: Matches item difficulty to learning tasks, without altering item difficulty or omitting easy or hard items.
4. NRT: Interpretation requires a clearly defined group.
   CRT: Interpretation requires a clearly defined and delimited achievement domain.

*When each is built to maximize its type of interpretation.

SUMMARY OF ASSESSMENT CATEGORIES

A summary of the basic ways of describing classroom tests and other assessment procedures is presented in Table 1.1. Further discussion of these assessment categories will be encountered in later chapters.

TABLE 1.1

Describing classroom assessment procedures

Basis for Classification	Type of Assessment	Function of the Assessment	Illustrative Instruments
Nature of Assessment	Maximum performance	Determines what individuals *can do* when performing at their best.	Aptitude tests, achievement tests
	Typical performance	Determines what individuals *will do* under natural conditions.	Attitude, interest, and personality inventories; observational techniques; peer appraisal
Form of Assessment	Fixed-Choice Test	Efficient measurement of knowledge and skills, indirect indicator	Standardized multiple-choice test
	Complex-Performance Assessment	Measurement of performance in contexts and on problems valued in their own right	Hands-on laboratory experiment, projects, essays, oral presentations
Use in Classroom Instruction	Placement	Determines prerequisite skills, degree of mastery of course goals, and/or best mode of learning.	Readiness tests, aptitude tests, pretests on course objectives, self-report inventories, observational techniques
	Formative	Determines learning progress, provides feedback to reinforce learning, and corrects learning errors.	Teacher-made tests, custom-made tests from textbook publishers, observational techniques
	Diagnostic	Determines causes (intellectual, physical, emotional, environmental) of persistent learning difficulties.	Published diagnostic tests, teacher-made diagnostic tests, observational techniques
	Summative	Determines end-of-course achievement for assigning grades or certifying mastery of objectives.	Teacher-made survey tests, performance rating scales, product scales
Method of Interpreting Results	Criterion referenced	Describes student performance according to a specified domain of clearly defined learning tasks (e.g., adds single-digit whole numbers).	Teacher-made tests, custom-made tests from test publishers, observational techniques
	Norm referenced	Describes student performance according to relative position in some known group (e.g., ranks tenth in a classroom group of 30).	Standardized aptitude and achievement tests, teacher-made survey tests, interest inventories, adjustment inventories

Other Descriptive Terms

Some of the terms used to describe tests that are presented here as contrasting types are really the ends of a continuum (e.g., speed versus power tests).

Informal versus Standardized Tests.   Informal tests are those constructed by classroom teachers, whereas those designed by test specialists and administered, scored, and interpreted under standard conditions are called standardized tests.

Individual versus Group Tests.   Some tests are administered on a one-to-one basis using careful oral questioning (e.g., individual intelligence test), whereas others can be administered to a group of individuals.

Mastery versus Survey Tests.   Some achievement tests measure the degree of mastery of a limited set of specific learning outcomes, whereas others measure a student's general level of achievement over a broad range of outcomes. Mastery tests typically use criterion-referenced interpretations and survey tests tend to emphasize norm-referenced interpretations, but some criterion-referenced interpretations also are possible with carefully prepared survey tests.

Supply versus Selection Tests.   Some tests require examinees to supply the answer (e.g., essay test), whereas others require them to select the correct response from a given set of alternatives (e.g., multiple-choice test).

Speed versus Power Tests.   A speed test is designed to measure the number of items an individual can complete in a given time, whereas a power test is designed to measure level of performance under ample time conditions. Power tests usually have the items arranged in order of increasing difficulty.

Objective versus Subjective Tests.   An objective test is one on which equally competent examinees will obtain the same scores (e.g., multiple-choice test), whereas a subjective test is one where the scores are influenced by the opinion or judgment of the person doing the scoring (e.g., essay test).

SUMMARY

Measurement and assessment play an important role in the instructional program of the school. They provide information that can be used in a variety of educational decisions. The main emphasis in classroom assessment, however, is on decisions concerning student learning and development.

From an instructional standpoint, **assessment** may be defined as a systematic process of determining the extent to which instructional objectives (i.e., intended learning outcomes) are achieved by students. The assessment process includes both measurement procedures (e.g., tests) and nonmeasurement procedures (e.g., informal observation) for describing changes in student performance as well as value judgments concerning the desirability of the changes.

The process of assessment is likely to be most effective when guided by a set of general principles. These principles emphasize the importance of (1) clearly specifying what is to be assessed, (2) selecting assessment procedures in terms of their relevance, (3) using a variety of assessment procedures, (4) being aware of their limitations, and (5) regarding assessment as a means to an end, and not an end in itself.

The interrelated nature of teaching, learning, and assessment can be seen in the following sequential steps in the instructional process: (1) preparing instructional objectives, (2) preassessing learners' needs, (3) providing relevant instruction (monitoring learning progress and diagnosing difficulties), (4) assessing the intended learning outcomes, and (5) using the assessment results to improve learning and instruction. In addition to the direct contribution testing and assessment make to classroom instruction, they also play an important role in marking and reporting, curriculum development, educational and vocational guidance, and assessing the effectiveness of the school program.

The vast array of assessment procedures used in the school can be classified and described in many different ways. The following are especially useful designations for describing the various procedures:

Nature of the Assessment

1. Maximum performance (what a person can do).
2. Typical performance (what a person will do).

Format of Assessment

1. Fixed-choice test (student selects response to question from available options).
2. Complex-performance assessment (student constructs extended response or performs in response to complex task).

Use in Classroom Instruction

1. Placement assessment (measures entry behavior).
2. Formative assessment (monitors learning progress).
3. Diagnostic assessment (identifies causes of learning problems).
4. Summative assessment (measures end-of-course achievement).

Method of Interpreting the Results

1. Norm referenced (describes student performance in terms of the relative position held in some known group).
2. Criterion referenced (describes student performance in terms of a clearly defined and delimited domain of learning tasks).

Other terms used to describe tests and other assessment instruments include the following contrasting types:

❑ Informal and standardized
❑ Individual and group

❑ Mastery and survey
❑ Supply and selection
❑ Speed and power
❑ Objective and subjective

LEARNING EXERCISES

1. List several instructional decisions and explain how each can be improved by the use of tests and other types of assessments.

2. Describe the meaning of the following terms: assessment, test, measurement.

3. Why is it necessary to specify what is to be assessed before selecting or constructing an assessment instrument?

4. Give an example of a measure of maximum performance and a measure of typical performance. Of what value is this distinction?

5. What are some of the perceived advantages and disadvantages of fixed-choice tests relative to complex-performance assessments?

6. Classify each of the following by indicating whether it refers to placement assessment, formative assessment, diagnostic assessment, or summative assessment.
   a. An end-of-course test used to assign grades.
   b. A test of arithmetic skills on the first day of algebra.
   c. An assessment in science used to assess learning progress.
   d. A device for observing and recording reading errors.

7. List the similarities and differences between criterion-referenced measurement and norm-referenced measurement. For what purposes is each most useful?

8. Which of the following represents a criterion-referenced interpretation and which a norm-referenced interpretation?
   a. Mary's reading score placed her near the bottom of the class.
   b. Chan defined 90 percent of the science terms correctly.
   c. Mike can identify all of the parts of a sentence.
   d. Teresa surpassed 85 percent of the sixth-graders on the arithmetic test.

9. How would you distinguish between each of the following?
   a. Informal test and standardized test.
   b. Individual test and group test.
   c. Mastery test and survey test.
   d. Supply test and selection test.
   e. Speed test and power test.
   f. Objective test and subjective test.

10. From your past school experiences, list some examples of inadequate or inappropriate use of tests or other assessment instruments. For each example, describe how the action or situation should have been handled.

REFERENCES

Airasian, P. W. & Madaus, G. J. (1972). Functional types of student evaluation. *Measurement and Evaluation in Guidance, 4,* 221–233.

Cronbach, L. J. (1990). *Essentials of psychological testing* (5th ed.) New York: Harper and Row.

Resnick, L. B. & Resnick, D. P. (1992). Assessing the thinking curriculum: New tools for educational reform. In B. R. Gifford & M. C. O'Connor (Eds.), *Changing assessments: Alternative views of aptitude, achievement and instruction* (pp. 37–75). Boston: Kluwer Academic Publishers.

FURTHER READING

Bloom, B. S., Madaus, G. J., & Hastings, J. T. (1981). *Evaluation to improve learning*. New York: McGraw-Hill. Chapter 4, "Summative Evaluation," Chapter 5, "Diagnostic Evaluation," and Chapter 6, "Formative Evaluation" provide a comprehensive treatment of these evaluation types.

Cronbach, L. J. (1990). *Essentials of psychological testing* (5th ed.). New York: Harper & Row. Chapter 2, "Varieties of Tests and Test Interpretations," describes tests of maximum performance and typical performance, computer use in testing, and the features of psychometric and impressionistic testing.

Nitko, A. J. (1984). Defining "Criterion-referenced test." In R. A. Berk (Ed.), *A guide to criterion-referenced test construction*. Baltimore: Johns Hopkins University Press. A comprehensive review of the various meanings of criterion referencing.

Linn, R. L. (1992). Measurement in Education. In *Encyclopedia of Educational Research* (Vol 3, pp. 798–805). New York: Macmillan. Provides a historical overview of educational measurement and sources of information about educational measurement, and discusses uses of and approaches to educational measurement.

CHAPTER 2

Instructional Goals and Objectives: Foundation for Assessment

What types of learning outcomes do you expect from your teaching? Knowledge? Understanding? Applications? Thinking skills? Performance skills? Attitudes? Clearly, defining desired learning outcomes is the first step in good teaching. It is also essential to the assessment of student learning. Sound assessment requires relating the assessment procedures as directly as possible to intended learning outcomes.

Instructional goals and objectives play a key role in both the instructional process and the assessment process. They serve as guides for both teaching and learning, communicate the intent of the instruction to others, and provide guidelines for assessing student learning. These major purposes are illustrated in Figure 2.1.

During the late 1980s and early 1990s there have been numerous attempts, as part of national and state educational reform efforts, to rethink the major goals of instruction. This rethinking was epitomized by publication of the *Curriculum and Evaluation Standards* by the National Council of Teachers of Mathematics (1989). The NCTM standards have served as a model for other content areas working to establish new curriculum standards. With the encouragement and support of foundations and the federal government, national efforts to establish subject-matter standards were initiated in a variety of areas, including English, science, history, geography, social studies, civics, foreign languages, and the arts. A key characteristic of these efforts is that they seek to establish more ambitious instructional goals for all students.

The NCTM standards illustrate what are called *content standards* in the federal Goals 2000: Educate America Act of 1994. The first two NCTM standards for Grades

FIGURE 2.1
The purposes of instructional goals and objectives

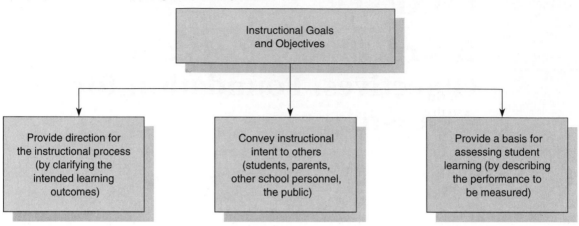

1 to 4 are shown in the accompanying "Guidelines" box. Although these brief standards are described in more detail in the NCTM's publication, they are general descriptions of the knowledge, skills, and understandings that should be taught. They provide a broad framework from which more specific curriculum guidelines, instructional materials, and assessments may be developed.

A number of states and districts provide more detailed curriculum guidelines and associated instructional materials. Such guidelines and materials specify the types of performance students are expected to demonstrate at the end of the instructional sequence (e.g., unit or course). Describing intended learning outcomes in performance terms is the main function of properly stated instructional goals and objectives. This clarification of what students should be learning and how the learning is to be expressed not only aids the teacher but also helps others understand the focus of the instruction. Some states and districts are beginning to emphasize the importance of learning outcomes to the process of education by developing guidelines for outcomes-based education and tying graduation requirements to the attainment of learning goals.

Our interest in this book, of course, is in the usefulness of instructional goals objectives for assessing student learning. As noted in Chapter 1, effective assessment depends as much on a clear description of what is to be assessed as on a determination of how to assess. Thus, before we develop or select tests and other assessment instruments to measure student learning, we need to clearly specify the intended learning outcomes. That is the main function of well-stated instructional goals and objectives.

GUIDELINES

National Council of Teachers of Mathematics: Curriculum and Evaluation Standards

NCTM Standard 1: Mathematics as Problem Solving

In Grades K–4, the study of mathematics should emphasize problem solving so that students can

❑ use problem-solving approaches to investigate and understand mathematical content;

❑ formulate problems from everyday and mathematical situations;

❑ develop and apply strategies to solve a wide variety of problems;

❑ verify and interpret results with respect to the original problem;

❑ acquire confidence in using mathematics meaningfully.

NCTM Standard 2: Mathematics and Communication

In Grades K–4, the study of mathematics should include numerous opportunities for communication so that students can

❑ relate physical materials, pictures, and diagrams to mathematical ideas;

❑ reflect on and clarify their thinking about mathematical ideas and situations;

❑ relate their everyday language to mathematical language and symbols;

❑ realize that representing, discussing, reading, writing, and listening to mathematics is a vital part of learning and using mathematics.

Source: *Curriculum and Evaluation Standards* (pp. 23 & 26) by National Council of Teachers of Mathematics, 1989, Reston, VA: National Council of Teachers of Mathematics. Copyright 1989 by the National Council of Teachers of Mathematics. Reprinted by permission.

INSTRUCTIONAL OBJECTIVES AS LEARNING OUTCOMES*

Instructional goals and objectives are sometimes stated in terms of actions to be taken. Thus, we might have a statement like this:

> Demonstrate to students how to use the microscope.

Although this statement clearly indicates what the teaching activity is, it is less clear about intended learning outcomes and does not point very explicitly to the type of

---

*Some of the material in this chapter was adapted from Gronlund, N.E. (1995). *How to write and use instructional objectives* (5th ed.). Upper Saddle River, N.J.: Prentice Hall.

student assessment that would be most appropriate. Literally, the objective will have been achieved when the demonstration has been completed—whether the students have learned anything or not. A better way to state objectives is in terms of what we expect students to be able to do at the end of instruction. After demonstrating how to use the microscope, for example, we might expect students to be able to demonstrate skill in using the microscope to identify features of a cell.

A statement such as this directs attention to the students and to the types of performance they are expected to exhibit as a result of the instruction. Thus, our focus shifts from the teacher to the student and from the learning experiences to the learning outcomes. This shift in focus makes clear the intent of our instruction and sets the stage for assessing student learning. Well-stated outcomes make clear the types of student performance we are willing to accept as evidence that the instruction has been successful.

When viewing instructional objectives in terms of learning outcomes, it is important to keep in mind that we are concerned with the *products* of learning rather than with the *process* of learning. Figure 2.2 makes three important points about the role of instructional objectives in teaching–learning situations.

First, objectives establish direction, and when they are stated in terms of learning outcomes, they go beyond knowledge of the specific course content. Note the distinction between "study of " and "knowledge of " cell structures. The content (study of cell structure) is more aptly listed under process because it is the vehicle through which objectives (knowledge of parts of cell, and so on) are attained.

Second, consider the varying degrees of dependence that the products ("knowledge," "skill," and "ability") have on the course content. "Knowledge of parts of cell" is the most closely related to the specific content of a biology course. "Skill in using microscope" and "ability to write accurate reports of scientific observations," relate to a greater variety of course content that could be used to achieve the same objectives.

The third point illustrated by the diagram is the degree to which objectives vary in complexity. The first learning outcome, "knowledge of parts of cell," is specific, is easily attained, and can be measured readily by a short answer or fixed-response paper-and-pencil test. The last learning outcome, "ability to write accurate reports of scientific observations," is rather general, is unlikely to be attained completely in a single course, and requires judgmental analysis of student performances.

FIGURE 2.2
The relationship of learning experience to learning outcomes

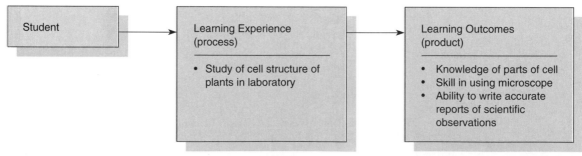

Student → Learning Experience (process)
- Study of cell structure of plants in laboratory

→ Learning Outcomes (product)
- Knowledge of parts of cell
- Skill in using microscope
- Ability to write accurate reports of scientific observations

FROM OVERLY SPECIFIC OBJECTIVES TO THE THINKING CURRICULUM

The predominant approach to the development and construction of tests during the past several decades has relied upon behavioral psychology. Behavioral psychology provided a framework to analyze learning outcomes in small steps and specific skills. Learning was conceptualized as being quite hierarchical, with higher-order skills dependent on a linear development based on a foundation of lower-level, "essential skills". This decomposition of desired outcomes into small steps allowed for a high degree of specificity of learning outcomes. (For an elaboration of these points, see Shepard, 1991.)

Highly specific objectives enabled the construction of very precise test objectives. When coupled with the notion of linear learning hierarchies, specific objectives provided a natural basis for developing "criterion-referenced mastery tests". The behavioral objectives used to construct mastery tests were typically concerned with relatively simple knowledge and skill outcomes. This made it possible to analyze each intended learning outcome in considerable detail and to describe the expected student performance in very specific terms. The objective to "add whole numbers," for example, might be further defined by a list of specific tasks such as the following:

❑ Add two single-digit numbers with sums of ten or less (2 + 5).
❑ Add two single-digit numbers with sums greater than ten (6 + 8).
❑ Add three single-digit numbers with sums of ten or less (2 + 4 + 3).
❑ Add three single-digit numbers with sums greater than ten (7 + 5 + 9).
❑ Add two two-digit numbers without carrying (21 + 34).
❑ Add two two-digit numbers with simple carrying (36 + 27).
❑ Add two two-digit numbers with carrying into nine (57 + 48).
❑ Add two or more three-digit numbers with repeated carrying (687 + 839).

With mastery objectives like these, it was frequently possible to specify a large representative sample of the specific responses expected of the students at the end of instruction. The learning tasks were then placed in sequential order so that they could be systematically taught and tested until mastery was achieved, as shown in Figure 2.3.

FIGURE 2.3
Learning tasks in sequential order

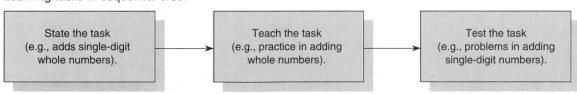

This procedure of stating specific tasks and then teaching and testing them one-by-one has been used in individualized instruction, in training programs, and in areas of classroom instruction that stress simple learning outcomes (e.g., basic skills). The limited nature of the objectives and the detailed specification of the learning tasks enhance the use of criterion-referenced interpretation.

Although this approach to test specification and construction continues to be used by some, the learning theory on which it is based has been strongly challenged in recent years by researchers focusing on learning and cognitive development. Cognitive research has discredited the notion that basic skills must be learned before higher-level thinking, reasoning and problem solving skills can be learned. According to cognitive research and theory, effective learning even at the most elementary levels of reading and arithmetic requires the active involvement of students in constructing meaning by thinking and reasoning. (For a more complete discussion see Resnick and Resnick, 1992.)

This cognitive research perspective of learning has several implications for assessment. First, the types of instructional objectives associated with the perspective are concerned with the more complex learning outcomes (e.g., understanding, problem solving, reasoning, thinking skills, application to authentic problem situations outside of school). Second, the perspective suggests the need for more comprehensive tasks that involve extended periods of time. Third, tasks need to be presented in a meaningful context, that is, they need to involve "authentic" problems.

Resnick and Resnick (1992) used an example from the assessment of writing to illustrate the distinction between the approaches to assessment that are compatible with the behavioral and cognitive perspectives. From either perspective it could be readily agreed that the ability to edit one's own work is an important part of writing. An analysis of the specific skills involved might lead to the development of a test where students were presented with written material and asked to identify errors and choose possible corrections. As Resnick and Resnick note, such a test might be useful for identifying copyediting skills, but would not foster the skills involved in writing and revising one's own work because it would not involve actual "crafting [of] phrases and sentences to convey intended meaning" (Resnick and Resnick, 1992; p. 6). Thus, the cognitive perspective leads to the use of written essays where students write rough drafts, review their drafts, and revise.

The cognitive research perspective also has implications for assessments in other content areas. In reading it encourages the use of authentic texts (e.g., complete short stories, or informational pieces) rather than the use of short segments consisting of a paragraph or two written specifically for the test. In mathematics it encourages the application of problems with real-world content (e.g., the collection and analysis of data to determine the best location of a store). In science it encourages the use of performance-based tasks involving active experimentation and analysis of results. In social studies it encourages the analysis of documents and the interpretation of historical events.

The above description identifies two ends of a continuum running from highly specific objectives (e.g., addition of two-digit integers or identify details that are explicitly stated in text) to much more general learning goals (e.g., relate physical materials and diagrams to mathematical ideas or read complicated text with understanding). In practice, neither extreme is apt to be entirely satisfactory as a guide to the development or selection of assessments. The former leads to an overemphasis on disconnected, low-level skills and factual knowledge. The latter remains at too general a level to provide adequate guidance for the development or selection of assessments that will have desirable measurement properties. Thus, in practice, an intermediate framework is needed to guide the development of assessments.

Types of Learning Outcomes to Consider

Although the cognitive research perspective is useful in forcing attention on broader educational goals that need to be addressed in the development or selection of an assessment, those general goals need to be supplemented by more systematic thinking about the types of learning outcomes that would provide evidence that the goals are being achieved. It is useful, for this reason, to classify learning outcomes under a few general headings. Any such classification is necessarily arbitrary, but it serves several useful purposes. It indicates types of learning outcomes that should be considered; it provides a framework for classifying those outcomes; and it directs attention toward changes in student performance in a variety of areas.

The following list of types of outcomes delineates the major areas in which instructional objectives might be classified. The more specific areas under each type should not be regarded as exclusive; they are merely suggestive of categories to be considered. For a different set of categories, see the lists of outcomes in Appendix E.

1. Knowledge
   1.1. Terminology
   1.2. Specific facts
   1.3. Concepts and principles
   1.4. Methods and procedures

2. Understanding
   2.1. Concepts and principles
   2.2. Methods and procedures
   2.3. Written material, graphs, maps, and numerical data
   2.4. Problem situations

3. Application
   3.1. Factual information
   3.2. Concepts and principles
   3.3. Methods and procedures
   3.4. Problem-solving skills

4. Thinking skills
   4.1. Critical thinking
   4.2. Scientific thinking

5. General skills
    5.1. Laboratory skills
    5.2. Performance skills
    5.3. Communication skills
    5.4. Computational skills
    5.5. Social skills
6. Attitudes
    6.1. Social attitudes
    6.2. Scientific attitudes
7. Interests
    7.1. Personal interests
    7.2. Educational interests
    7.3. Vocational interests
8. Appreciations
    8.1. Literature, art, and music
    8.2. Social and scientific achievements
9. Adjustments
    9.1. Social adjustments
    9.2. Emotional adjustments

Taxonomy of Educational Objectives

A useful guide for developing a comprehensive list of instructional objectives is the *Taxonomy of Educational Objectives*. This is a detailed classification of objectives, similar in form to the classification system used for plants and animals. It attempts to identify and classify all possible educational outcomes. The system first divides objectives into the following three major areas:

1. *Cognitive Domain:* Knowledge outcomes and intellectual abilities and skills.
2. *Affective Domain:* Attitudes, interests, appreciation, and modes of adjustment.
3. *Psychomotor Domain:* Perceptual and motor skills.

Each of the three domains is subdivided into categories and subcategories. The major categories in the cognitive domain, for example, are knowledge, comprehension, application, analysis, synthesis, and evaluation. These categories begin with relatively simple knowledge outcomes and proceed through increasingly complex levels of intellectual ability. This pattern of classification is characteristic of all three of the domains.

The *Taxonomy* is primarily useful in identifying the types of learning outcomes that should be considered when developing a comprehensive list of objectives for classroom instruction. One need not use the terminology of the taxonomies when stating learning outcomes, but a review of the various taxonomy categories will aid in the development of a more complete list. The broad range of learning outcomes covered in the *Taxonomy* provides assurance that important types of learning are

GUIDELINES

Begin with a Simple Framework

Starting with a simple framework (Knowledge, Understanding, Application) will help move from factual information to more complex learning outcomes, as illustrated in the following examples:

K = Knowledge

U = Understanding

A = Application

    Each of these categories can be expanded with skills and affective outcomes as needed.

Reading

K: Knows vocabulary.

U: Reads with comprehension.

A: Reads to obtain information to solve a problem.

Writing

K: Knows the mechanics of writing.

U: Understands grammatical principles in writing.

A: Writes to communicate for a specific purpose.

Math

K: Knows the number system and basic operations.

U: Understands math concepts and processes.

A: Uses mathematics to solve problems.

Science

K: Knows terms and facts.

U: Understands scientific principles.

A: Applies principles to new situations.

Social Studies

K: Knows factual information about social issues.

U: Understands causes of social issues.

A: Applies critical thinking skills to social issues.

not overlooked. Appendix E provides a detailed summary of the *Taxonomy* categories and a list of the original sources from which the summaries were derived. In addition to detailed descriptions of the categories in each domain, illustrative instructional objectives from a variety of content areas are presented, as well as lists of verbs that are useful in stating objectives for student performance.

Other Sources for Lists of Objectives

Illustrative instructional objectives for various grade levels and subject-matter areas may be obtained from the following sources.

1.   Methods books.   Most books on methods of teaching discuss objectives, present examples, and cite references to other sources of objectives in various instructional areas.

2.   Yearbooks and subject-matter standards publications of educational organizations.   The yearbooks (and other publications dealing with subject-matter standards) of organizations such as the National Council of Teachers of English, the National Council of Teachers of Mathematics, the National Council for the Social Studies, and the National Science Teachers Association provide an excellent resource.

3.   Encyclopedia of Educational Research.   This publication typically contains an article on each major teaching area, which includes references to sources of instructional objectives.

4.   Curriculum frameworks and guides.   Many local and state curriculum frameworks or guides contain lists of instructional objectives.

5.   Test manuals.   The manuals accompanying published tests frequently contain lists of objectives that were used in constructing the tests.

6.   Banks of objectives.   There are various banks of objectives and relevant test items maintained by some organizations and test publishers. See Appendix C for addresses of some objectives banks.

In using objectives from these various sources, it is important that the ones selected be relevant to the local instructional program. Selected objectives will most likely need to be reworded. Many of them will not be stated as intended learning outcomes or in performance terms. Published lists of objectives are probably most useful for obtaining ideas concerning possible outcomes and for assessing the completeness of a prepared list.

Criteria for Selecting Appropriate Objectives

Our emphasis throughout this section has been on the role of the classroom teacher in the process of selecting instructional objectives. We have deliberately avoided discussions concerning which objectives should receive priority at various grade levels and in various subject matter areas. This is a decision for school boards, administrators, curriculum committees, and individual teachers. Our aim has been to clarify how to identify those instructional objectives that will be most useful for teaching and assessment purposes.

In preparing a list of instructional objectives for a particular course, the teacher is faced with the problem of determining the adequacy of the final list of objectives. The following questions will serve as criteria for this purpose (see Figure 2.4):

1.   Do the objectives include all important outcomes of the course? Knowledge objectives are seldom neglected. However, objectives in the area of understanding, application, thinking skills, attitudes, and the like tend to be slighted unless special efforts are made to consider them. Objectives derived mainly from the methods of instruction and the social experiences of the students are also easily overlooked.

2.   Are the objectives in harmony with the general goals of the school? The objectives developed by individual teachers must be consistent with the general goals of the school in which they are used. For example, if independent thought, self-direction, and effectiveness of communication are highly valued in the school, these outcomes should be reflected in the teachers' objectives. Similarly, objectives inconsistent with these valued outcomes should be omitted from the list. Part of the difficulty of applying this criterion is that the goals of the school are seldom explicitly stated.

3.   Are the objectives in harmony with sound principles of learning? Because objectives indicate the desired outcomes of a series of learning experiences, they should be consistent with sound principles of learning. That is, they should (1) be appropriate to the age level and experiential background of the students (principle of readiness), (2) be related to the needs and interests of the students (principle of motivation), (3) reflect learning outcomes that are most permanent (principle of retention), and (4) include learning outcomes that are most generally applicable to various specific situations (principle of transfer).

4.   Are the objectives realistic in terms of the abilities of the students and the time and facilities available?   First attempts at identifying objectives for a particular course frequently result in an impressive but unattainable list of outcomes. Thus, the final list of objectives should be reviewed in light of the abilities of the group members, the time available for achieving the objectives, and the adequacy of the facilities and equipment available. It is usually better to have a limited set of clearly defined, attainable objectives than a long list of nonfunctional goals.

Make Allowance for Unanticipated Learning Outcomes

No matter how carefully a set of instructional objectives has been selected for a course, there are likely to be some unanticipated effects of the instruction. These effects may be desirable or undesirable, and the majority of them are likely to fall into the affective area. For example, as a result of instruction, students may become more dependent or more independent, more conforming or more creative, more critical of printed material or more uncritical, more positive in their self-concept or

FIGURE 2.4
Summary of criteria for selecting
the final list of objectives

more negative, and more interested in the subject or less interested. Outcomes of this nature are easily overlooked because they are more likely to result from the method of instruction than from the content of instruction.

In addition to these more global changes, specific classroom activities may create a need for focusing on outcomes that were not prespecified. An accident in the chemistry laboratory, for example, may indicate a need for special instruction in safety. Similarly, an unanticipated student interest in the metric system may create a need to modify instruction in a mathematics class, or an unforeseen international crisis may alter social studies instruction. Thus, although instructional objectives provide a useful guide for instruction, teachers need to be flexible enough in their teaching and testing to allow for unplanned events and unanticipated learning outcomes.

METHOD OF STATING INSTRUCTIONAL OBJECTIVES

In preparing a list of instructional objectives for a course of study, we have two immediate goals in mind. One is to create as complete a list of objectives as possible. This is most likely to occur if we follow the procedures for selecting objectives described in the previous section. The other goal is to state the objectives so that they clearly indicate the learning outcomes that we expect from our instruction.

The task of stating instructional objectives can be simplified if we constantly keep in mind that we are listing intended outcomes of teaching–learning situations. We are not describing what we intend to do during instruction but are listing the expected results of that instruction. The point of orientation, then, is the student and the types of performance that the student should demonstrate at the end of the teaching–learning experience.

Stating objectives in terms of learning outcomes rather than the learning process is easier said than done. Most of us are so concerned with course content and the ongoing process in the classroom that we find it difficult to concentrate on the results of instruction. The very nature of teaching conditions us to focus our attention on the learning process. But we can shift this focus if we continually ask ourselves: What should the students be able to do at the end of the course or unit of study that they could not do at the beginning? As we attempt to answer this question—always in terms of knowledge, understanding, skills, attitudes, and the like—we will find that the students' terminal performance has, almost automatically, become the center of focus. We are then in a much better position to state our instructional objectives in terms of learning outcomes.

How to Obtain a Clear Statement of Instructional Objectives

A list of objectives for a course or unit of study should be detailed enough to convey the intent of the instruction, yet general enough to serve as an effective overall guide in planning for teaching and assessment. You can do this most easily by defining your objectives in two steps: (1) stating the general objectives of instruction as intended learning outcomes and (2) listing under each objective a sample of the

Stating Objectives as Learning Outcomes

Don't state them in terms of

1. teacher performance (e.g., "Teach students key concepts").
2. learning process (e.g., "Student learns meaning of concepts").
3. course content (e.g., "Student studies geometric figures").
4. two objectives (e.g., "Student knows and understands concepts").

State them in terms of student performance at the end of instruction.

1. "Knows the meaning of concepts."
   1.1 "Identifies a definition of the concept."
   1.2 "Identifies the concept that fits a given description."
   1.3 "Matches the concept to a picture" (e.g., geometric figures).
   1.4 "Differentiates between the concept and a second concept."
   1.5 "Applies the concept to an everyday situation."

specific types of performance that students should be able to demonstrate when they have achieved the objective (Gronlund, 1991). This procedure should result in statements of general objectives and specific learning outcomes like the following:

1. Understands scientific principles.
   1.1. Describes the principle in own words.
   1.2. Identifies examples of the principle.
   1.3. States tenable hypotheses based on the principle.
   1.4. Uses the principle in solving novel problem.
   1.5. Distinguishes between two given principles.
   1.6. Explains the relationship between two given principles.

The expected learning outcome is concerned with understanding, and the general objective starts right off with the verb *understands*. There is no need to add such repetitious material as "the students should be able to demonstrate that they understand." Keeping the statement free of unnecessary words and starting with a verb help to focus on the intended outcome. There are several things to remember about the specific learning outcomes listed beneath the general objective.

First, each statement begins with a verb. Here, however, the verbs are specific and indicate definite, observable responses; that is, responses that can be seen and assessed by an outside observer. These verbs—*describes, identifies, states, uses, distinguishes,* and *explains*—state specific learning outcomes in terms of observable student performance. See Appendix E for more verbs that state specific learning outcomes in the cognitive, affective, and psychomotor areas. Terms such as these clarify what the students will do to demonstrate their *understanding.* Vague terms like *realizes, sees,* and *believes* are less useful in defining objectives because they describe internal states that can be expressed by many different types of overt behavior.

Second, the list of specific learning outcomes is merely a sample of the many specific ways that an *understanding of scientific principles* might be shown. A student who achieved this objective probably could demonstrate many other responses. Because it would be impractical to list all of the specific types of performance that denote understanding, an attempt is made to obtain a *representative sample*. This yields an operational definition of the general objective, yet keeps the overall list of objectives and specific learning outcomes within manageable proportions.

Finally, it should be noted that the specific learning outcomes are free of specific course content. Rather than listing the scientific principles the students are to understand, they specify the types of student performance acceptable as evidence of understanding. Keeping the statements free of specific course content makes it possible to use the same list of learning outcomes with various units of study. Each unit of study will indicate the principles to be understood, and the list of specific learning outcomes will indicate how the students are expected to demonstrate their understanding. As we shall see in Chapter 5, a table of specifications is a convenient means of relating the learning outcomes to the various content areas for evaluation purposes.

Stating the General Instructional Objectives

One problem in stating the general instructional objectives is selecting the proper level of generality. The objectives should be specific enough to provide direction for instruction but not so specific that instruction is reduced to training. When we state our major objectives in general terms, we provide for the integration of specific facts and skills into complex response patterns. General statements also give the teacher greater freedom in selecting the methods and materials of instruction. The "understanding of scientific principles," for example, may be achieved through lecture, discussion, demonstration, group problem-solving activity, laboratory work, or some combination of these methods. Similarly, the objective may be achieved through the use of different textbooks or various other types of instructional material. Stating the general objectives at this level provides a focus for instruction, but does not restrict the teacher to a particular instructional method or a given set of instructional materials.

The following list of general instructional objectives shows the desired level of generality:

❑ Knows basic terminology.
❑ Understands concepts and principles.
❑ Relates concepts to everyday observations.
❑ Applies principles to new situations.
❑ Interprets charts and graphs.
❑ Demonstrates skill in critical thinking.

❏ Writes a well-organized theme.

❏ Appreciates poetry.

❏ Demonstrates scientific attitude.

❏ Evaluates an experiment's adequacy.

The verbs at the beginning of each statement are general enough to encompass a range of specific learning outcomes. A sample of specific outcomes would need to be added before these general statements would be useful guides for teaching and assessment. Note that each statement contains a single objective (e.g., *not* "Knows and understands"), and that each statement is relatively free of course content.

The degree of generality may, of course, vary somewhat with the period of instruction for which the list is being prepared. The objectives for a brief unit of instruction are likely to be more specific than those for an entire course of study. In either case, however, selecting eight to twelve general instructional objectives will usually provide a list that is both manageable and suitable.

Stating the Specific Learning Outcomes

As stated earlier, each general instructional objective must be defined by a sample of specific learning outcomes to clarify how students can demonstrate that they have achieved the general objective. Unless the general objectives are further defined in this manner, they will not provide adequate direction for teaching or testing.

Statements of specific learning outcomes for a general objective will be easier to write and will more clearly convey instructional intent if each statement begins with an action verb that indicates definite, observable responses (e.g., *identifies, solves, communicates*). Such statements specify the types of student performance acceptable as evidence that the general instructional objective has been achieved. This assumes, of course, that each specific learning outcome is directly relevant to the general objective it is defining. A statement like "Writes the textbook definition of a principle" would be appropriate for listing under "Knows principles," but not under "Understands principles." For the latter objective, we would need a statement that goes beyond the recall of information, because understanding implies some novelty in the response. Here, a statement like "Explains the principle in own words" or "Applies the principle to solve an applied problem" would be more relevant.

A major problem in defining general instructional objectives is deciding how many specific learning outcomes to list under each objective. It is obvious that a fixed number cannot be specified. Simple knowledge and skill outcomes typically require fewer statements than complex ones. Because it is usually impossible or impractical to list all possible student responses for each general objective, the sample should be as representative as possible. In most cases there is not much advantage in listing more than seven or eight specific learning outcomes for each objective; four or five statements are probably more common. As a general guide, enough learning outcomes should be listed for each objective to show the typical performance of students who have satisfactorily achieved the objective.

The following general objectives and specific learning outcomes illustrate a satisfactory level of specificity for stating the intended learning outcomes:

1. Understands the meaning of concepts.
    1.1. Explains the concept in own words.
    1.2. Identifies the meaning of a concept in context.
    1.3. Differentiates between proper and improper instances of a concept.
    1.4. Distinguishes between two similar concepts on the basis of meaning.
    1.5. Uses a concept to explain an everyday event.

2. Demonstrates skill in critical thinking.
    2.1. Distinguishes between fact and opinion.
    2.2. Distinguishes between relevant and irrelevant information.
    2.3. Identifies fallacious reasoning in written material.
    2.4. Identifies the limitations of given data.
    2.5. Formulates valid conclusions from given data.
    2.6. Identifies the assumptions underlying conclusions.

In addition to illustrating the desired degree of specificity, these statements are good examples of content-free objectives. As noted earlier, both the general objectives and the specific learning outcomes should be kept free of specific content so that they can be used with various units of study. In stating our specific learning outcomes, we are attempting to describe what types of student performance represent each general objective—not what specific content the students are to learn.

Keeping the specific learning outcomes content-free is, of course, a matter of degree. In some cases all we can do is modify our statements so that they apply to a wider range of course material. The following statements illustrate ways to improve specific learning outcomes in this regard:

EXAMPLES   *Poor:*   Distinguishes between a square and a rectangle.

Better: Distinguishes among geometric shapes.

Poor: Describes the main characters in *Silas Marner.*

Better: Describes the main characters in the story.

If we used the first version of each of these specific learning outcomes, we would have to write new statements for each identification, comparison, or description we wanted our students to make. The better versions can be used with various areas of content, thus freeing us from the repetitive writing of objectives as new subject matter is considered. Specific learning outcomes should specify the *types of reactions* the students are to make to the content, not identify the content itself.

In some cases it may be desirable or necessary to consult reference books and other relevant materials for the types of performance that might represent an objective. When defining such complex outcomes as critical thinking, literary appreciation, and scientific attitude, for example, a review of the literature can be very useful. Although you may not find a detailed list of the specific components of each outcome, even general descriptions of the concepts will aid in defining relevant types of performance. In any event, resist the temptation to omit complex outcomes simply because they are difficult to define.

Clarification of Verbs Used in Specific Learning Outcomes

Because the action verb is a key element in stating the specific learning outcomes, the selection and clarification of these verbs play an important role in obtaining a clearly defined set of instructional objectives. Ideally, we would like each verb (1) to convey clearly our instructional intent and (2) to specify precisely the student performance we are willing to accept as evidence that the general objective has been attained. Some verbs convey instructional intent well (e.g., *identifies*); others are more effective at specifying the student responses to be observed (e.g., *labels, encircles, underlines*). When it is necessary to choose between these two types of verbs, it is best to select those that most clearly convey instructional intent and then, if necessary, clarify further the expected student responses in one of the following ways:

1. Add a third level of specificity to the list of objectives.
2. Define the action verbs used in the specific learning outcomes.
3. Use sample test items to illustrate the intended outcomes.

These procedures are probably most useful as guides to test construction and for communicating your intended learning outcomes to others.

The meaning of each specific learning outcome can be further clarified by listing some of the tasks students are expected to perform to demonstrate achievement of the outcome. This would provide three levels for each instructional objective as follows:

1. Comprehends the meaning of written material.
    1.1. Identifies the main thought in a passage.
        1.11 Underlines the topic sentence.
        1.12 Selects the most appropriate title for the passage.
        1.13 Writes the main theme of the passage.

Adding a third level of specificity, like this, might be useful for clarifying some learning outcomes. The specific tasks describe how students will indicate that they can "identify the main thought in a passage." But our intended outcome is still identifying the main thought. Underlining, selecting, and writing are simply responses we are willing to use as indicators of the "ability to identify." Thus, although the third level may be a desirable transition between specific learning outcomes and relevant test items, these specific responses are not instructional outcomes in their own right (i.e., we are not interested in teaching students how to underline, select, and write, but how to identify). This third level of specificity highlights one of the advantages of using levels of objectives rather than a list of specific tasks to describe the intended outcomes of instruction. With levels, we are less likely to confuse the intended outcomes of instruction with the indicators of those outcomes.

Summary of Steps for Stating Instructional Objectives

The final list of objectives for a course or unit should include all important learning outcomes (e.g., knowledge, understanding, skills, attitude) and should clearly convey how students are expected to perform at the end of the learning experience. The following summary of steps (Gronlund, 1995) provides guidelines for obtaining a clear statement of instructional objectives:

I. Stating the general instructional objectives.
    1. State each general objective as an intended learning outcome (i.e., students' terminal performance).
    2. Begin each general objective with a verb (e.g., *knows, applies, interprets*). Omit "The student should be able to. . . ."
    3. State each general objective to include only one general learning outcome (e.g., not "Knows and understands").
    4. State each general objective at the proper level of generality (i.e., it should encompass a readily definable domain of responses). Eight to twelve general objectives will usually suffice.
    5. Keep each general objective sufficiently free of course content so that it can be used with various units of study.
    6. Minimize the overlap with other objectives.
II. Stating the specific learning outcomes.
    1. List beneath each general instructional objective a representative sample of specific learning outcomes that describe the terminal performance students are expected to demonstrate.
    2. Begin each specific learning outcome with an action verb that specifies observable performance (e.g., *identifies, describes*).
    3. Make sure that each specific learning outcome is relevant to the general objective it describes.
    4. Include enough specific learning outcomes to describe adequately the performance of students who have attained the objective.
    5. Keep the specific learning outcomes sufficiently free of course content so that the list can be used with various units of study.
    6. Consult reference materials for the specific components of those complex outcomes that are difficult to define (e.g., critical thinking, scientific attitude, creativity).
    7. Add a third level of specificity to the list of outcomes, if needed.

This procedure for stating objectives does not include the conditions under which the achievement of learning outcomes will be demonstrated (e.g., open book, diagrams will be provided) or the standards for evaluating performance (e.g., 90 percent correct). Although some teachers may want to add such information to each objective, there are advantages in stating the conditions and standards separately from the objectives. In many cases, the same conditions and standards apply to all objectives being assessed at a given time, and thus a statement like the following may be sufficient for an entire set of objectives:

EXAMPLE   Student performance will be determined under closed book conditions, but all needed formulas will be provided. Hand calculators may be used.

A statement such as this will prevent the repetitious writing of the same conditions and standards for each objective and also avoid rewriting the list of objectives each time the conditions or standards are changed. We may, for example, use the same objectives for different units of study (e.g., knows term, understands principles, applies principles) but want to vary the conditions and standards to suit the nature and complexity of the material studied. We may also wish to modify the conditions or standards to match a particular group of students. Thus, limiting the statements of objectives to concise descriptions of desired student performance and stating the conditions and standards separately as needed seem to be desirable for most classroom instruction. The time saved from writing instructional objectives over and over can usually be well spent on other instructional activities.

SUMMARY

Instructional goals and objectives provide the foundation for both instruction and assessment of student learning. To achieve this purpose, they should not be so specific that they fractionalize learning and emphasize relatively simple knowledge and skill outcomes. Nor should they be as broad and general as the goals described for state and national programs. For both instruction and assessment purposes, an intermediate framework is needed. We are describing one that is readily adaptable to the complex learning outcomes suggested by cognitive research.

Instructional objectives make clear what learning outcomes we expect from our teaching. They describe our instructional intent in terms of the types of performance students are expected to demonstrate as a result of instruction. A convenient means of preparing instructional objectives is to follow a two-step process: (1) State the general instructional objectives as intended learning outcomes. (2) Define each general objective with a list of specific learning outcomes that describe the observable responses that the learners will be able to make when they have achieved the general objective.

When instructional objectives are viewed as learning outcomes and are defined in performance terms, numerous types of intended outcomes might be included. In addition to the more obvious knowledge outcomes, those in the areas of understanding, application, thinking skills, performance skills, attitudes, interests, appreciation, and adjustment should also be considered. Suggestions for objectives in these and other areas may be obtained from Appendix E, *Taxonomy of Educational*

Objectives, from various published sources, and from objectives banks that have been prepared for national distribution. External sources should be used as aids only. Instructional objectives usually are most relevant when teachers develop their own lists, as these take into account the unique features of the local school and community.

The adequacy of the list of objectives for a particular course can be judged by the extent to which it (1) includes all important outcomes of the course, (2) is in harmony with the school's general goals, (3) is in harmony with sound principles of learning, and (4) is realistic in terms of the students' abilities and the time and facilities available.

No matter how comprehensive a set of instructional objectives may be, there are likely to be some unanticipated outcomes of instruction. Thus, teachers should be alert to this possibility during instruction and should take these unplanned effects into account when assessing the learning outcomes of a course.

The task of stating instructional objectives is simplified if we keep in mind that we are making a list of intended outcomes of instruction, stated in terms of the types of performance the students are expected to demonstrate at the end of the teaching–learning experience. The procedure for stating the objectives for a particular course includes the following steps:

1. State each general instructional objective as an intended learning outcome that encompasses a readily definable domain of student responses. Each general objective should begin with a verb (e.g., *knows, understands, applies*), contain only one general learning outcome, and be relatively content-free. Typically, eight to twelve general objectives will suffice.

2. List beneath each general instructional objective a representative sample of specific learning outcomes stated in terms of student performance. Each should begin with an action verb (e.g., *identifies, describes*), be relevant to the general objective, and be relatively free of course content so that it can be used with various units of study.

Instructional objectives will require the least rewriting and function most effectively if the conditions and standards of performance are stated separately.

LEARNING EXERCISES

1. What are some of the advantages of stating instructional objectives as learning outcomes?

2. Give examples of how ultimate objectives (e.g., good citizenship) might be stated as immediate objectives.

3. Make a list of multiple-course objectives (e.g., study skills) that might be emphasized in your teaching area.

4. Using the summary of steps for stating instructional objectives as a guide, restate each of the following as general instructional objectives.
   a. To learn the basic terms in the unit.
   b. Be familiar with the laboratory procedures.
   c. Can show how to write a well-organized paragraph.
   d. Increases ability to read with comprehension.

5. Using the summary of steps for stating instructional objectives as a guide, restate each of the following as specific learning outcomes.
   a. Sees the importance of following safety practices.
   b. Realizes the correct way to spell technical terms.
   c. Is aware of the proper use of laboratory equipment.
   d. Learns the symbols on a weather map.

6. List some of the unplanned effects of instruction (i.e., unanticipated outcomes) that might occur in one of your teaching areas. Which ones would you include in your assessment of student learning? Why?

7. What arguments would you present for and against including the conditions of measurement and the desired standard of performance in each stated objective?

8. For a unit of instruction in one of your major teaching areas, prepare a list of general instructional objectives and specific learning outcomes following the procedures suggested in this chapter.

REFERENCES

Gronlund, N. E. (1995). *How to write and use instructional objectives* (5th ed.). New York: Macmillan.

National Council of Teachers of Mathematics. (1989). *Curriculum and evaluation standards for school mathematics.* Reston, VA: National Council of Teachers of Mathematics.

Resnick, L. B. & Resnick, D. P. (1992). Assessing the thinking curriculum: New tools for educational reform in B. R. Gifford & M. C. O'Connor (Eds.), *Changing assessments: Alternative views of aptitude, achievement, and instruction* (pp. 37–75). Boston: Kluwer Academic Publishers.

Shepard, L. A. (1991). Psychometricians' Beliefs About Learning. *Educational Researcher, 20* (7), 2–16.

FURTHER READING

Bloom B. S., Madaus G. J., & Hastings J. T. (1981). *Evaluation to improve learning.* New York: McGraw-Hill. See Appendix A for a condensed version of the *Taxonomy of Educational Objectives.*

Gronlund, N.E. (1995). *How to write and use instructional objectives* (5th ed.). Upper Saddle River, N.J.: Prentice Hall. A brief guide describing the step-by-step procedures for stating instructional objectives and for using them in teaching, testing, and assessment. Presents illustrations of instructional objectives, lists of action verbs, and a checklist for evaluating instructional objectives.

National Council of Teachers of Mathematics. (1989). *Curriculum and Evaluation Standards for School Mathematics.* Reston, VA: National Council of Teachers of Mathematics. Provides an excellent illustration of general statements of instructional goals, sometimes referred to as subject-matter standards, content standards, or curriculum standards.

CHAPTER 3
Validity

When constructing or selecting assessments, the most important questions are: (1) To what extent will the interpretation of the scores be appropriate, meaningful, and useful for the intended application of the results? and (2) What are the consequences of the particular uses and interpretations that are made of the results?

Assessments take a wide variety of forms, ranging from the familiar multiple-choice or other type of fixed-response test to extended observations of performance. They also serve a variety of uses in the school. For example, assessment results might be used to identify student strengths and weaknesses, to plan instructional activities, or to communicate progress to students and parents; achievement tests might be used for selection, placement, diagnosis, or certification; aptitude tests might be used for predicting success in future learning activities or occupations; and appraisals of personal–social development might be used to better understand learning problems or to evaluate the effects of a particular school program. But regardless of the type of assessment used or how the results are to be used, all assessments should possess certain characteristics. The most essential of these are *validity, reliability,* and *usability.*

Validity refers to the adequacy and appropriateness of the interpretations made from assessments, with regard to a particular use. For example, if an assessment is to be used to describe student achievement, we should like to be able to interpret the scores as a relevant and representative sample of the achievement domain to be measured. If the results are to be used to predict students' success in some future activity, we should like our interpretations to be based on as good an estimate of future success as possible. If the results are to be used as a measure of students' reading comprehension, we should like our interpretations to be based on evidence that the scores actually reflect reading comprehension and are not distorted by irrelevant factors. Basically, then, validity is always concerned with the specific use of assessment results and the soundness of our proposed interpretations of those results. As we shall see later in the chapter, however, this does not mean that validation procedures can be matched to specific assessment uses on a one-to-one basis.

In recent years, our understanding of *validation* has also come to include an evaluation of the adequacy and appropriateness of the uses that are made of assessment results. This expanded view of validity leads to a focus on the consequences of particular uses of assessment results. For example, if a state- or district-mandated test led teachers to ignore important content not covered by the test, that consequence would need to be taken into account in judging the validity of that test use (Messick, 1989).

Reliability refers to the *consistency* of assessment results. If we obtain quite similar scores when the same assessment procedure is used with the same students on two different occasions, we can conclude that our results have a high degree of reliability from one occasion to another. Similarly, if different teachers independently rate student performances on the same assessment task and obtain similar ratings, we can conclude that the results have a high degree of reliability from one rater to another. Like validity, reliability is intimately related to the type of interpretation to be made. For some uses, we may be interested in asking how reliable our assessment results are over a given period of time and, for others, how reliable they are over different samples of the same behavior. In all instances in which reliability is being determined, however, we are concerned with the *consistency* of the results, rather than with the *appropriateness of the interpretations* made from the results (validity).

The relation between reliability and validity is sometimes confusing to persons who encounter these terms for the first time. Reliability (consistency) of measurement is needed to obtain valid results, but we can have reliability without validity. That is, we can have consistent measures that provide the wrong information or are interpreted inappropriately. The target-shooting illustration in Figure 3.1 depicts the concept that *reliability is a necessary but not sufficient condition for validity.*

FIGURE 3.1
Reliability (consistency) is needed to obtain valid results (but one can be consistently "off target").

Target 1

Target 2

Target 3

Kit ("Bullseye") Carson
(reliable and valid shooting)

Bill ("Scattershot") Henry
(unreliable and invalid shooting)

Jack ("Rightpull") Armstrong
(reliable but invalid shooting)

In addition to providing results that possess a satisfactory degree of validity and reliability, an assessment procedure must meet certain practical requirements. It should be economical from the viewpoint of both time and money; it should be easily administered and scored; and it should produce results that can be accurately interpreted and applied by available school personnel. These practical aspects of an assessment procedure all can be included under the heading of usability. The term **usability,** then, refers only to the *practicality* of the procedure and says nothing about the other qualities present.

NATURE OF VALIDITY

When using the term *validity* in relation to testing and assessment, there are a number of cautions to be borne in mind.

1. Validity refers to the *appropriateness of the interpretation of the results* of an assessment procedure for a given group of individuals, not to the procedure itself. We sometimes speak of the "validity of a test," for the sake of convenience, but it is more correct to speak of the validity of the interpretation and use to be made from the results.

2. Validity is a *matter of degree;* it does not exist on an all-or-none basis. Consequently, we should avoid thinking of assessment results as valid or invalid. Validity is best considered in terms of categories that specify degree, such as high validity, moderate validity, and low validity.

3. Validity is always *specific to some particular use or interpretation.* No assessment is valid for all purposes. For example, the results of an arithmetic test may have a high degree of validity for indicating computational skill, a low degree of validity for indicating arithmetical reasoning, a moderate degree of validity for predicting success in future mathematics courses, and essentially no validity for predicting success in art or music. Thus, when appraising or describing validity, it is necessary to consider the specific interpretation or use to be made of the results. Assessment results are never just valid; they have a different degree of validity for each particular interpretation to be made.

4. Validity is a *unitary concept.* The conceptual nature of validity has typically been described for the testing profession in a set of standards prepared by a joint committee made up of members from three professional organizations that are especially concerned with educational and psychological testing and assessment. In the most recent revision of the *Standards for Educational and Psychological Testing* (American Psychological Association, 1985), the traditional view that there are several different types of validity has been discarded. Instead, validity is viewed as a unitary concept based on various kinds of evidence.

5. Validity involves an *overall evaluative judgment.* It requires an evaluation of the degree to which interpretations and uses of assessment results are justified by supporting evidence and in terms of the consequences of those interpretations and uses.

There are many ways of accumulating evidence to support or challenge the validity of an interpretation or use of assessment results. Traditionally, the ways of accumulating evidence have been grouped together in one of three categories (content-related, criterion-related, and construct-related evidence). These three categories of evidence are important considerations in arriving at an overall evaluation of the degree of validity of any given interpretation of scores on a test or other assessment procedure. But these traditional categories do not take into account that the consequences of uses and interpretation of assessment results also influence validity. Hence, it is better to think of four interrelated considerations—content, assessment-criterion relationships, construct, and consequences—in evaluating validity rather than a list of distinct validation methods.

MAJOR CONSIDERATIONS IN ASSESSMENT VALIDATION

Four major considerations for validation are briefly described in Table 3.1. The strongest case for validity can be made when evidence is obtained regarding all four considerations in Table 3.1. That is, interpretations and uses of assessment results are

TABLE 3.1
Major considerations in validation

Consideration	Procedure	Meaning
Content	Compare the assessment tasks to the specifications describing the task domain under consideration.	How well the sample of assessment tasks *represents* the domain of tasks to be measured.
Test–Criterion Relationship	Compare assessment results with another measure of performance obtained at a later date (for prediction) or with another measure of performance obtained concurrently (for estimating present status).	How well performance on the assessment *predicts* future performance or *estimates* current performance on some valued measures other than the test itself (called a *criterion*).
Construct	Establish the meaning of the assessment results by controlling (or examining) the development of the assessment, evaluating the relationships of the scores with other relevant measures, and experimentally determining what factors influence performance.	How well performance on the assessment can be interpreted as a meaningful measure of some characteristic or quality.
Consequences	Evaluate the effects of use of assessment results on teachers and students. Both the intended positive effects (e.g., increased learning) and possible unintended negative effects (e.g., narrowing of instruction, drop out of school) need to be evaluated.	How well use of assessment results accomplishes intended purposes and avoids unintended effects.

likely to have greater validity when we have an understanding of (1) the assessment content and the specifications from which it was derived, (2) the relation of the assessment results to other significant measures, (3) the nature of the characteristic(s) being measured, and (4) the consequences of the uses and interpretations of the results. However, for many uses of a test or an assessment, it is not practical or necessary to have evidence dealing with all four considerations. For example, it is not practical to expect that a teacher would provide evidence that a classroom assessment designed to measure student learning is related to other significant measures. In this case, the primary concern would be content, but some of the analyses of the meaning of the scores (construct considerations) and possible effects on student motivation and learning (consequence considerations) would be relevant.

Similarly, in using a scholastic aptitude test to predict future success in school, test–criterion relationships would be of major interest. But we would also be concerned about the appropriateness of the content, possible irrelevant factors (not part of the construct) that influence test performance (e.g., motivation, test anxiety, test-taking skills), and possible unintended consequences of uses of predictions. Thus, content, construct, and consequence considerations would be relevant. One consideration is likely to be of primary importance, but the other three are useful for a fuller understanding of the meaning of the assessment results and, therefore, contribute to the validation of our interpretations.

Although there are many other considerations that are relevant to validity, our discussions of *content, test–criterion relationships, construct,* and *consequence* considerations will focus on those procedures that are most useful in practical educational settings.

CONTENT CONSIDERATIONS

Content considerations are of special importance when we wish to describe how an individual performs on a domain of tasks that the assessment is supposed to represent. We may, for example, expect students to be able to spell the 200 words on a given list. Because a 200-word spelling test is too time-consuming, we may select a sample of 20 words to represent the total domain of 200 spelling words. If Margaret correctly spells 80 percent of these 20 words, we would like to be able to say that she can probably spell approximately 80 percent of the 200 words. Thus, we would like to be able to generalize from the student's performance on the *sample* of words in the test to the performance that the student would be expected to demonstrate on the domain of spelling words that the test represents.

The validity of the interpretation that a test score implies that the student can probably spell a given percentage of words in the whole domain depends on a number of considerations that go beyond the question of content. For example, construct considerations, such as the assumption that Margaret was trying to do her best, that she did not copy her neighbor's spelling words, and that she understood the teacher's pronunciation of the words, influence the validity of the interpretation that she can spell a given fraction of the words. Here, however, our concern is with the extent to which our 20-word test constituted a *representative sample* of the 200 words. In this instance, we can obtain a fairly representative sample of spelling words by simply starting with our 200-word list and selecting every tenth word. Having thus assured ourselves that we have a reasonably representative sample, we would have good support for the desired interpretation in terms of content considerations. As we shall see shortly, judging how adequately an assessment samples a given domain of achievement is usually much more complex than in this simple example, particularly when the learning outcomes involve more complex understandings or integrated performances.

The essence of the content consideration in validation, then, is determining the adequacy of the sampling of the content that the assessment results are interpreted to represent. More formally, *the goal in the consideration of content validation is to determine the extent to which a set of assessment tasks provides a relevant and representative sample of the domain of tasks about which interpretations of assessment results are made.* In classroom assessment, the domains of achievement tasks are determined by the curriculum and instruction, and assessment development involves (1) clearly specifying the domain of instructionally relevant tasks to be used to measure student achievement and (2) constructing or selecting a representative set of assessment tasks. Thus, to obtain a valid measure of learning outcomes, we proceed from the instruction (what has been taught) to the achievement domain (what is to be measured) and finally to the assessment itself (a representative sample of relevant tasks). As shown in Figure 3.2, content considerations in validation require a judgment that all three are in close harmony.

FIGURE 3.2
Content considerations in the assessment of classroom achievement

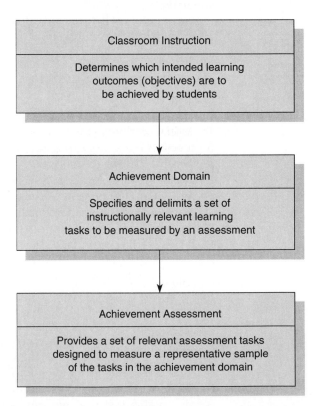

Classroom Instruction

Determines which intended learning outcomes (objectives) are to be achieved by students

Achievement Domain

Specifies and delimits a set of instructionally relevant learning tasks to be measured by an assessment

Achievement Assessment

Provides a set of relevant assessment tasks designed to measure a representative sample of the tasks in the achievement domain

Rigorous judgments regarding validity based on content considerations should not be confused with *face validity,* which refers only to the appearance of the assessment. Based on a superficial examination of the tasks, does the assessment appear to be a reasonable measure? A simple example can be used to make a clear distinction between making validity claims based on rigorous consideration of content definitions and the adequacy of sampling of tasks and making claims based on face validity (i.e., on the basis of appearance). If we are giving an arithmetic test to a young child, we might phrase an item as follows: "If you had a ten-foot piece of *string* and you cut it in half, how long would the two pieces be?" If the test was to be given to carpenters, we would substitute the word *board* for string in this item. Similarly, for plumbers we would use the word *pipe* and for electricians the word *wire.* The problem remains the same, but by phrasing it in appropriate terms, it appears more relevant to the test taker (i.e., it has greater face validity). The validity of interpretations of our arithmetic test scores would not be determined by how the test looked, however, but rather by how well it sampled the domain of arithmetic tasks important to each group (i.e., children, carpenters, plumbers, and electricians). Thus, our arithmetic test may provide an adequate measure of content for one group but not another, even though the items were phrased in terms appropriate to each group. Although a test should look like an appropriate measure to obtain the cooperation of those taking the test, face validity should not be considered a substitute for more rigorous evaluation of content definitions and sampling adequacy.

Content Considerations in Assessment Development to Enhance Validity

Content issues are typically considered during the development of an assessment. It is primarily a matter of preparing detailed specifications and then constructing an assessment that meets these specifications. Although there are many ways of specifying what an assessment should measure, one widely used procedure in constructing achievement tests uses a two-way chart called a *table of specifications.* We shall use a brief form of it here to help clarify the process of content validation in preparing classroom assessments. More elaborate tables of specifications and other types of specifications will be described and illustrated in Chapter 5.

Table of Specifications. The learning outcomes of a course or curriculum may be broadly defined to include both subject matter content and instructional objectives. The former is concerned with the topics to be learned and the latter with the types of performance students are expected to demonstrate (e.g., knows, comprehends, applies). Both of these aspects are of concern in defining content domain and assuring adequate sampling from it. We should like any assessment of achievement that we construct to produce results that represent both the content areas and the objectives we wish to measure, and the table of specifications aids in obtaining a sample of tasks that represents both.

TABLE 3.2
Sample table of specifications

Content Area	Instructional Objectives			
	Knows Concepts	Comprehends Concepts	Applies Concepts	Total
Air Pressure	4	8	4	16
Air Temperature	4	4	4	12
Humidity and Precipitation	8	12	4	24
Wind	4	4	4	12
Clouds	8	12	0	20
Fronts	4	8	4	16
Total	32	48	20	100

A table of specifications, in a very simple form, is presented in Table 3.2 to show how such a table is used in test development. The percentages in the table indicate the relative degree of emphasis that each content area and each instructional objective is to be given in the test. Thus, if a 25-item classroom test is to measure a representative sample of subject-matter content, 16 percent of the items (i.e., 4 items) should be concerned with air pressure, 12 percent with air temperature, 24 percent with humidity and precipitation, 12 percent with the wind, 20 percent with the clouds, and 16 percent with fronts. Similarly, if the test is to measure a representative sample of the instructional objectives, 32 percent of the items (i.e., 8 items) should measure knowledge of concepts, 48 percent should measure comprehension of concepts, and 20 percent should measure application of concepts. This, of course, implies that the emphasis on knowledge, comprehension, and application for each content area will follow the percentages in the table of specifications. For example, 4 percent of the test items (i.e., a single item) concerned with air pressure should measure knowledge of concepts, 8 percent should measure comprehension of concepts, and 4 percent should measure application of concepts.

As noted earlier, the specifications describing the achievement domain to be measured should be in harmony with what was taught. Thus, the weights assigned in this table reflect the emphasis that was given during instruction. For example, comprehension outcomes received more emphasis than either knowledge or application outcomes in the instruction and therefore were given almost as much weight in the table as the other two categories combined. The table, then, indicates the sample of instructionally relevant learning tasks to be measured, and the more closely the test items correspond to the specified sample, the greater the likelihood of obtaining a valid measure of student learning.

The test items and other kinds of assessment tasks must function as intended if valid results are to be obtained. Test items and assessment tasks may function improperly if they contain inappropriate vocabulary, unclear directions, or some other defect. Similarly, tasks designed to measure understanding and application may measure only the simple recall of information if the solutions to the problems have been directly taught during instruction. In short, a host of factors can influence the intended function of the tasks and thus the validity of the assessment results. Much of what is written in this book concerning the construction of classroom assessments is directed toward producing valid measures of achievement.

Content Considerations in Test Selection

Evidence obtained from an analysis of content domain definition and content coverage (sampling adequacy) is also of concern when selecting published achievement tests. When test publishers prepare achievement tests for use in the schools, they pay special attention to content. Their test specifications, however, are based on what is commonly taught in many different schools. Thus, a published test may or may not fit a particular school situation. To determine whether it does, it is necessary to go beyond the title of the test and to examine what the test actually measures. How closely does the test content correspond to the course content and the curriculum and instructional goals in the *local instructional program*? Does the test provide a balanced measure of the intended learning outcomes, or are some areas overemphasized and others neglected? These are the types of questions that need to be asked. A published test may provide more valid results for one school program than for another, depending on how closely the set of test tasks matches the achievement to be measured.

The same types of specifications used in preparing classroom assessments can be used in selecting published tests. The detailed descriptions of course content and instructional objectives and the relative emphasis to be given to each can help us determine which of several published tests is most relevant to our particular situation. It is simply a matter of examining the items in each test and comparing them to our test specifications. The test that provides the most balanced measure of the specified achievement domain is the one that will produce the most valid results. Many test publishers include a detailed description of their test specifications in the test manual. Although this makes it easier to judge the potential validity of the test results, there is no substitute for examining the test tasks themselves and judging how validly they measure the intended learning outcomes in the local instructional program.

Content Considerations in Other Areas

Although content considerations are of primary interest in assessing achievement, they are also of interest in other areas. For example, examining the content of a scholastic aptitude test aids in understanding the meaning of the scores and provides some evidence concerning the types of prediction for which it might be best suited. Similarly, when constructing or selecting an attitude scale, we are interested in how adequately the items cover those attitudinal topics included in the domain to be measured. In the same manner, an interest inventory should include samples of items that adequately represent those aspects of interest we wish to measure. In these and other situations, the content validation procedure is essentially the same as that in testing and assessment of achievement. It is a matter of analyzing the content and tasks included in the measuring instrument and the domain of outcomes to be measured and judging the degree of correspondence between them.

TEST–CRITERION RELATIONSHIPS

Although few teachers will conduct studies relating assessment results to other measures, it is important to understand the use of test–criterion relationships in evaluating validity. Understanding how test–criterion relationships are analyzed, for example, will help in evaluating the use of standardized tests to make predictions of student performance in other settings.

Although performance assessments can be used to predict performance on a *criterion measure* (e.g., grades in subsequent years), traditional paper-and-pencil tests are more commonly used. That is so, in part, because tests are often viewed as predictors for more complicated outcome measures (e.g., success in college, or success on the job). Complex performance-based assessments are more likely to be evaluated in terms of considerations of content, construct, and consequences than by their relationships to a criterion measure. Hence, we will limit our attention in this section to tests, recognizing that the approaches could also be used to relate results from other types of assessment procedures to criterion measure.

Whenever test scores are to be used to predict future performance or to estimate current performance on some valued measure other than the test itself (called a **criterion**), we are especially concerned with evaluating the relationship between the test and the criterion. For example, reading readiness test scores might be used to *predict* students' future achievement in reading, or a test of dictionary skills might be used to *estimate* students' current skill in the actual use of the dictionary (as determined by observation). In the first example, we are interested in prediction and thus in the relationship between the two measures over an extended period of time. This procedure for obtaining evidence of validity calls for a *predictive validation study.* In the second example, we are attempting to estimate present status and thus we are interested in the relationship between two measures obtained concurrently. A high relationship in this case would show that the test of dictionary skills is a good indicator of actual skill in using a dictionary. This procedure for obtaining evidence of validity calls for a *concurrent validation study.* In the *Standards for Educational and Psychological Testing* (American Psychological Association, 1985) both the predictive and concurrent designs have been subsumed under the more general category, criterion-related validation. This appears to be a desirable arrangement because the method of determining and expressing validity is the same in both cases. The major difference resides in the time period between the two obtained measures, as illustrated in Figure 3.3.

The focus of both types of studies shown in Figure 3.3 is on determining the extent to which test performance is related to some other valued measure of performance. As noted earlier, the second measure of performance (called a criterion) may be obtained at some future date (when we are interested in predicting future performance) or concurrently (when we are interested in estimating present

FIGURE 3.3
Studies of types of test–criterion relationships (based on time difference only)

Predictive Validation Study

Concurrent Validation Study

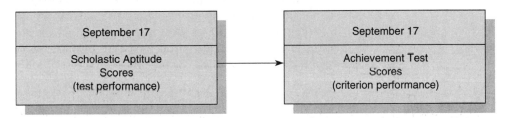

performance). First, let us examine the use of test–criterion relationships from the standpoint of predicting success in some future activity.

Predicting Future Performance

Suppose that Mr. Young, a junior high school teacher, wants to determine how well the scores from a scholastic aptitude test will predict success in his seventh grade mathematics class. Because the scholastic aptitude test is administered to all students when they enter junior high school, these scores are readily available to Mr. Young. His biggest problem is deciding on a *criterion* of successful achievement in mathematics. For lack of a better criterion, Mr. Young decides to use a comprehensive departmental examination that is administered to all seventh-grade math sections at the end of the school year. It is now possible for Mr. Young to determine how well the scholastic aptitude test scores predict success in his mathematics class by comparing the students' scholastic aptitude test scores with their scores on the departmental examination. Do those students who have high scholastic aptitude test scores also tend to have high scores on the departmental examination? Do those who have low scholastic aptitude test scores also tend to have low scores on the departmental examination? If this is the case, Mr. Young is inclined to agree that the scholastic aptitude test scores tend to be reasonably accurate in predicting achievement in this mathematics class.

In our example, Mr. Young merely inspected the scholastic aptitude and achievement test scores to determine the agreement between them. Although this may be a desirable preliminary step, it does not provide a very precise notion of the degree of relationship between the aptitude test scores and the scores on the comprehensive departmental examination, nor does it provide a very good way of communicating the results. The degree of relationship can be described more precisely by statistically correlating the two sets of scores. The resulting *correlation coefficient* provides a numerical summary of the degree of relationship between the two sets of scores. A correlation coefficient provides a concise, quantitative summary of the relationship for anyone who has learned to understand and interpret this statistical measure. Scores on the scholastic aptitude test also can be converted to predicted achievement scores by means of a *regression equation.*

Communication of the meaning of the relationship also can be facilitated by the use of a graphical presentation of the results in the form of a *scatterplot* or by the use of an *expectancy table.* The construction of scatterplots (also known as scattergrams or scatter diagrams) and the calculation and interpretation of correlation coefficients and regression equations are described and illustrated in Appendix A. In this chapter, we confine our discussion to the use and interpretation of these indicators of relationship within the context of criterion-related validation. The construction and interpretation of expectancy tables and regression equations also will be described here.

Correlation

In order to illustrate the use of correlation coefficients and scatterplots in studies of test–criterion relationships, let us consider the exact scores that Mr. Young's students received on both the scholastic aptitude test (predictor) and the departmental examination in mathematics (criterion). This information is provided in the first two columns of Table 3.3. By inspecting these two columns of scores as Mr. Young did, we see that the high scores in Column 1 tend to match the high scores in Column 2. This comparison is difficult to make, however, because the sizes of the test scores in the two columns are different.

The agreement of the two sets of scores can be more easily seen if the test scores are converted to ranks. This has been done in Columns 3 and 4 of Table 3.3. Note that the student who was first on the aptitude test ranked third on the departmental examination; the student who was second on the aptitude test ranked fourth on the departmental examination; and so on. Comparing the ranks of the students on the two tests, as indicated in Columns 3 and 4 of Table 3.3, gives us a fairly good picture of the relationship between the two sets of scores. From this inspection we know that students who had a high standing on the aptitude test also had a high standing on the departmental examination and that students who had a low standing on the aptitude test also had a low standing on the departmental examination. Our inspection of Columns 3 and 4 also shows us, however, that the relationship between the students' ranks on the two tests is not perfect, that there is some shifting in rank from one test to another. Our problem now is how we can express the degree of relationship between these two sets of ranks in meaningful terms. This is where the scatterplot and the correlation coefficient become useful.

A scatterplot of the pairs of scores for the twenty students in Mr. Young's class is shown in Figure 3.4. Each dot represents the two scores that were obtained by an

TABLE 3.3
Test scores and test-score ranks for twenty junior high school students

	1	2	3	4
Pupil	Fall Aptitude Score	Spring Arithmetic Score	Aptitude Rank	Arithmetic Rank
Sandra	119	77	1	3
Bob	118	76	2	4
Maria	116	72	3	6
Susan	115	67	4	8
Bill	112	82	5	1
Carl	109	63	6	10
Laura	108	60	7	12
Chang	106	78	8	2
Jane	105	69	9	7
Karl	104	49	10	18
Jim	102	48	11	19
Frank	100	58	12	14
Karen	98	56	13	16
Joan	97	57	14	15
Carlos	95	74	15	5
June	94	62	16	11
John	93	46	17	20
George	91	65	18	9
Alice	90	59	19	13
Martin	89	54	20	17

individual student. The dots that correspond to the scores received by three of the students (Sandra, Carlos, and John) are labeled (see Appendix A for another example and details on the construction of a scatterplot). The scatterplot immediately shows us two important facts about the relationship between scores on the aptitude test administered in the fall and student performance on the comprehensive departmental examination in the spring. First, students such as Sandra, who score well above average in the fall, usually do better than average on the comprehensive examination in the spring, while most students who score well below average in the fall also score below average in the spring (e.g., John). Second, there are some notable exceptions. Carlos, for example, ranked fifteenth out of twenty on the fall aptitude test, but he obtained the fifth highest score on the comprehensive examination in the spring. Although both facts (that there is a relationship and that it is imperfect) also could be seen from studying the scores in Table 3.3, the scatterplot provides an efficient summary and makes it clear that some of the exceptions to the statement that there is a relationship between the two sets of scores are substantial.

The relationship seen in Figure 3.4 still has not been quantified. For this we need to obtain a **_correlation coefficient,_** a statistical summary of the relationship

FIGURE 3.4
Scatterplot of test scores for twenty junior high school students (scores shown in Table 3.3)

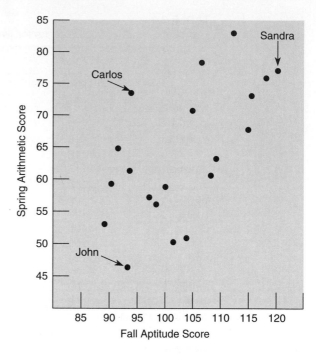

between the scores on the two tests. The correlation coefficient we shall use is known as the *Pearson product–moment correlation coefficient,* and is denoted by *r.* Procedures for calculating this coefficient are described in Appendix A. Here we shall focus on its meaning.

When the procedures for calculating a product–moment correlation coefficient are applied to the scores for the twenty students in Mr. Young's class we find that $r = .58$. This correlation coefficient is a statistical summary of the degree of relationship between the two sets of scores in Mr. Young's data. It indicates the extent to which the fall aptitude test scores (predictor) are predictive of the spring mathematics test scores (criterion). This type of correlation coefficient, called a ***validity coefficient,*** indicates the correlation between a test and a criterion measure. (A criterion-related validation study should be based on a larger number of cases than the twenty students used here, but we are simply explaining what a validity coefficient is and how to interpret it.) The validity coefficient is not a measure of the validity of the test use or interpretation because, as has already been emphasized, content, construct, and consequences are also important to the overall evaluative judgment of validity.

How good is Mr. Young's validity coefficient of .58? Should Mr. Young be happy or disappointed with this finding? Is this aptitude test a good predictor of future performance in mathematics? Unfortunately, there are no simple and straightforward answers to such questions.

The following correlation coefficients indicate the extreme degree of relationship possible between variables:

1.00 = perfect positive relationship
.00 = no relationship
−1.00 = perfect negative relationship

Because Mr. Young's validity coefficient is .58, we know that the relationship is positive but substantially less than perfect. The closer a validity coefficient is to 1.00, the greater accuracy in predicting from one variable to another. A coefficient of −1.00 would also indicate perfect prediction from one variable to another, but in educational measurements we are most commonly concerned with positive relationships.

The three scatterplots in Figure 3.5 show in schematic form how Mr. Young's validity coefficient of .58 compares with correlations of 0.00 and 1.00. Each dot on the scatterplot indicates an individual score's position on both the predictor and the criterion. Thus, with a correlation of 1.00, each individual falls at the same position on both measures, providing a perfect prediction. At the other extreme, with a correlation of .00, an individual's score on the predictor tells us nothing about the criterion score. At each score level on the predictor, some individuals have high criterion scores, some have low criterion scores, and others fall in between. There is simply no basis for predicting. The scatterplot for a correlation of about .60 indicates that high predictor scores *tend* to go with high criterion scores and that low predictor scores tend to go with low criterion scores, but the relationship is far from perfect. As the size of a correlation coefficient increases, the dots on a scatterplot move in the direction of the diagonal series of dots shown for a perfect positive correlation (1.00), indicating increased prediction efficiency.

Another way of evaluating Mr. Young's validity coefficient of .58 is to compare it with the validity coefficients obtained from other methods of predicting performance in mathematics. If this validity coefficient is larger than those obtained with other prediction procedures, Mr. Young will continue to use the scholastic aptitude test as the best means available to him for predicting his students' arithmetic performance. Thus, validity coefficients are large or small only in relation to one another. When prediction is important, we shall always consider more favorably the

FIGURE 3.5

Scatterplots illustrating different degrees of positive relationship between a predictor and a criterion

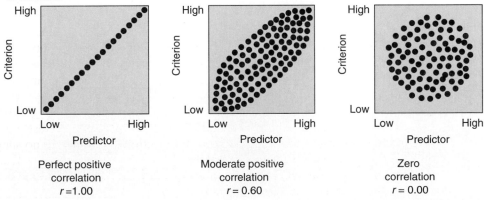

| Perfect positive correlation $r=1.00$ | Moderate positive correlation $r=0.60$ | Zero correlation $r=0.00$ |

test with the largest validity coefficient. But in this regard, even aptitude tests with rather low validity may be useful if they are the best predictors available and if the predictions they provide are better than chance.

Estimating Present Performance

Up to this point we have emphasized the role of test–criterion relationship in predicting future performance. Although this is probably its major use, there are times when we are interested in the relation of test performance to some other current measure of performance. In this case, we obtain both measures at approximately the same time and correlate the results. This is commonly done when a test is being considered as a replacement for a more time-consuming method of obtaining information. For example, Mrs. Brown, a biology teacher, wondered if an objective test of study skills could be used in place of the elaborate observation and rating procedures she was currently using. She felt that if a test could be substituted for the more complex procedures, she would have much more time to devote to individual students during the supervised study period. An analysis of the specific student characteristics on which she rated the students' study skills indicated that many of the procedures could be stated in the form of objective test questions. Consequently, she developed an objective test of study skills that she administered to her students. To determine how adequately the test measured study skills, she correlated the test results with ratings of the students' study skills she obtained through arduous observation. The resulting correlation coefficient of .75 indicates considerable agreement between the test results and the criterion measure and validates Mrs. Brown's test of study skills.

Factors Influencing Correlation Coefficients

A number of factors influence the size of correlation coefficients, including validity coefficients. Knowing these factors can help with the interpretation of a particular correlation coefficient—one we have computed ourselves or one found in a test manual. Some of the basic factors to consider are shown in Figure 3.6. In general, larger correlation coefficients are obtained when the characteristics measured are

FIGURE 3.6
Some basic factors influencing the size of correlation coefficients

more alike (e.g., correlating scores from two reading tests), the spread of scores is large, the stability of the scores is high, and the time span between measures is short. As we move along the continuum toward the other end of the scale on any of these factors, the correlation coefficients tend to become smaller. Thus, a small predictive validity coefficient might be explained, in part, by any one of the factors shown on the right side of Figure 3.6 or, more commonly, by some combination of them.

Expectancy Table

How well a test predicts future performance or estimates current performance on some criterion measure also can be shown by directly plotting the data in a twofold chart like the one shown in Figure 3.7. Here, Mr. Young's data (from Table 3.3) have been tabulated by placing a tally showing each individual's standing on both the fall aptitude scores and the spring mathematics scores. For example, Sandra scored 119 on the fall aptitude test and 77 on the spring math test, and so a tally representing her performance was placed in the upper right-hand cell. The performance of all other students on the two tests was tallied in the same manner. Thus, each tally mark in Figure 3.7 represents how well each of Mr. Young's 20 students performed on the fall and spring tests. The total number of students in each cell and in each column and row is also indicated.

The expectancy grid shown in Figure 3.7 can be used as an expectancy table simply by using the frequencies in each cell. The interpretation of such information is simple and direct. For example, of those students who scored above average on the fall aptitude test, none scored below 65 on the spring mathematics test, 2 out of 5 scored between 65 and 74, and 3 out of 5 scored between 75 and 54. Of those who scored below average on the fall aptitude test, none scored in the top category on the spring mathematics test, and 4 out of 5 scored below 65. These interpretations are limited to the group tested, but from such results one might make predictions concerning future students. We can say, for example, that students who score above average on the fall aptitude test will probably score above average on the spring mathematics test. Other predictions can be made in the same way by noting the frequencies in each cell of the grid in Figure 3.7.

FIGURE 3.7
Expectancy grid showing how scores on the fall aptitude test and spring arithmetic test are tallied in appropriate cells (from data in Table 3.3)

Fall Aptitude Scores	Spring Arithmetic Scores				
	45–54	55–64	65–74	75–84	Totals
Above Average (over 110)			// 2	/// 3	5
Average (95–110)	// 2	〢卌 5	// 2	/ 1	10
Below Average (below 95)	// 2	// 2	/ 1		5
Totals	4	7	5	4	20

More commonly, the figures in an expectancy table are expressed in percentages, which can be readily obtained from the grid by converting each cell frequency to a percentage of the total number of tallies in its row. This has been done for the data in Figure 3.7 and the results are presented in Table 3.4. The first row of the table shows that of the 5 students who scored above average on the fall aptitude test, 40 percent (2 students) scored between 65 and 74 on the spring math test, and 60 percent (3 students) scored between 75 and 84. The remaining rows should be read in a similar manner. The use of percentages makes the figures in each row and column comparable. Our predictions then can be made in standard terms (that is, chances out of 100) for all score levels. Our interpretation is apt to be a little clearer if we say that Maria's chances of being in the top group on the criterion measure are 60 out of 100 and that Ron's are only 10 out of 100 than if we say that Maria's chances are 3 out of 5 and that Ron's are 1 out of 10.

Expectancy tables take many different forms and may be used to show the relation between various types of measures. The number of categories used with the predictor, or criterion, may be as few as two or as many as seem desirable. Also, the predictor may be any set of measures useful in predicting, and the criterion may be course grades, ratings, test scores, or whatever other measure of success is relevant. For example, expectancy tables are frequently used in predicting the grade-point averages of college freshmen by combining data from high school grades and an admissions test such as the Scholastic Aptitude Test (SAT) or the American College Testing Program's ACT. An example of such an expectancy table is shown in Table 3.5.

When interpreting expectancy tables based on a small number of cases, like Mr. Young's class of twenty students, our predictions should be regarded as highly tentative. Each percentage is based on so few students that we can expect large fluctuations in these figures from one group of students to another. It is frequently possible to increase the number of students represented in the table by combining test results from several classes. When we do this, our percentages are, of course, much more stable, and our predictions can be made with greater confidence. In any event, expectancy tables provide a simple and direct means of indicating the predictive value of test results.

TABLE 3.4

Expectancy table showing the relation between fall aptitude scores and spring arithmetic scores

Fall Aptitude Scores	Percentage in Each Score Group on Spring Arithmetic Test			
	45–54	55–64	65–74	75–84
Above average (Over 110)			40	60
Average (95–110)	20	50	20	10
Below average (Below 95)	40	40	20	

Note: Data from Figure 3.7.

TABLE 3.5
Expectancy table for predicting
college grade-point average
from test scores

	Probability of a Grade-Point Average of at Least		
Test Score	1.0 (D Ave.)	2.0 (C Ave.)	.3.0 (B Ave.)
51 to 60	.99+	.93	.72
41 to 50	.98	.80	.53
31 to 40	.91	.68	.35
21 to 30	.75	.53	.22

Regression Equations

Regression equations provide a way of converting the scores obtained on a test into predicted criterion scores. In its simplest form, the scores on a test, X, are multiplied by a constant, b, known as the *regression coefficient,* and another constant, a, called the *intercept,* is added to the result. The result is a *predicted* or *estimated criterion score,* Y. That is,

$$\hat{Y} = a + b\ (X)$$

The caret (^) is used to distinguish the predicted criterion score from the one actually observed, Y. Procedures for computing the regression coefficient and intercept are explained in Appendix A. Here, we focus on the interpretation.

The regression coefficient for predicting the math achievement tests from the aptitude test scores for the twenty students in Mr. Young's class is

$$\hat{Y} = -1.91 + .64\ (X)$$

or

Predicted Mathematics Score = -1.91 + .64 times Aptitude Score

In Table 3.3 it can be seen that Alice has an aptitude score of 90. Her predicted mathematics score is 55.7 (-1.91 + .64 × 90). Alice actually got a score on the mathematics test of 59. That is, she did better on the mathematics test than was predicted by the regression equation.

The regression equation corresponds to the diagonal line shown in Figure 3.8. The scatterplot is the same as the one in Figure 3.4, but the *regression line* has been added. The arrows going from the aptitude score of 90 to the regression line and then from the regression line to the vertical axis corresponding to the mathematics test scores illustrate how the prediction for Alice can be obtained graphically. The fact that the dot corresponding to Alice's scores is above the regression line indicates that she did better than was predicted from her score on the aptitude test score. Some students, like Alice, do better than predicted from the regression equation while others, like Laura, do worse than predicted. Overall, however, the average of the predicted mathematics scores is the same as the average of the actual math scores. Thus, there is a balancing out of math scores that are higher than predicted with those that are lower than predicted.

FIGURE 3.8

Regression line for predicting spring mathematics scores from fall aptitude scores (scores shown in Table 3.3)

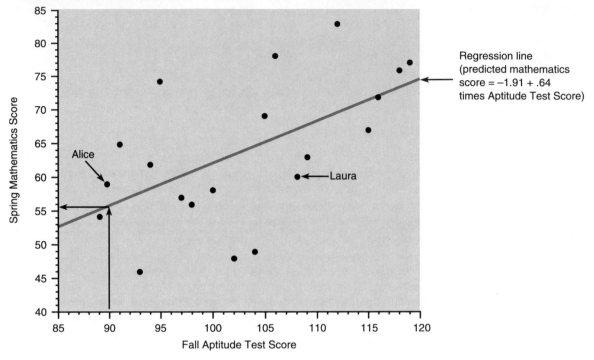

The "Criterion" Problem

In a criterion-related validation study, a major problem is obtaining a satisfactory criterion of success. Remember that Mr. Young used a comprehensive departmental examination as the criterion of success in his seventh-grade mathematics class, and that Mrs. Brown used her own ratings of the students' study skills. In each instance, the criterion of success was only partially suitable as a basis for test validation. Mr. Young recognized that the departmental examination did not measure all of the important learning outcomes that he aimed at in teaching mathematics. There was not nearly enough emphasis on problem solving or arithmetic reasoning; the interpretation of graphs and charts was sadly neglected; and, of course, the test did not evaluate the students' attitudes toward arithmetic (which Mr. Young considered to be extremely important). Likewise, Mrs. Brown was well aware of the shortcomings of her rating of students' study skills. She sensed that some students "put on a show" when they knew they were being observed, and that other students were probably overrated on study skills because of their high achievement in class work. Despite these recognized shortcomings, both Mr. Young and Mrs. Brown found it necessary to use these criterion measures because they were the best available.

The plights of Mr. Young and Mrs. Brown in finding a suitable criterion of success for test validation are not unusual. For most educational purposes, there is no entirely satisfactory criterion of success. Those used tend to be lacking in comprehensiveness and in most cases produce results that are less stable than those of the test being validated. The lack of a completely satisfactory criterion measure makes content and construct considerations all the more important.

CONSTRUCT CONSIDERATIONS

The analysis of content and investigations of test–criterion relationships thus far described provide validity evidence that is directly applicable to specific practical test uses. The review of the content domain and sampling helps us determine how well test or assessment scores represent a given domain of tasks and is especially useful in both the preparation and evaluation of all types of assessment of achievement. The relationship between a test and a criterion measure indicates how well test scores predict or estimate performance on that criterion measure. In addition to these more specific and immediately practical uses, we usually wish to interpret test and assessment results in terms of more general individual characteristics. These characteristics may be labeled in a variety of ways (e.g., skills, accomplishments, abilities, psychological traits, personal qualities), but regardless of the label, they involve some inference about the person that goes beyond the factual statement that he or she obtained a given score on a particular test or assessment. For example, rather than speak about a student's score on a particular mathematics test or how well it predicts grades in future mathematics courses, we might want to infer that the student possesses a certain degree of mathematical reasoning ability. This provides a broad general description of student performance that has implications for many different uses.

Whenever we wish to interpret assessment results in terms of some individual characteristic (e.g., reading comprehension, mathematics problem-solving ability), we are concerned with a *construct*. A ***construct*** is an individual characteristic that we assume exists in order to explain some aspect of behavior. Mathematical reasoning is a construct and so are reading comprehension, understanding of the principles of electricity, intelligence, creativity, and such personality characteristics as sociability, honesty, and anxiety. These are called constructs because they are theoretical constructions that are used to explain behavior. When we interpret assessment results as a measure of a particular construct, we are implying that there is such a construct, that it differs from other constructs, and that the results provide a measure of the construct that is little influenced by extraneous factors. Verifying such implications is the task of construct validation.

There is an important advantage in being able to interpret performance on assessments in terms of psychological constructs. Each construct has an underlying set of expectations and previously studied relationships that can be brought to bear in describing and predicting a person's behavior. If, for example, we say a person has good reading comprehension, or is sociable, we know what type of behavior might be expected in various specific situations.

Construct validation may be defined as the process of determining the extent to which performance on an assessment can be interpreted in terms of one or more constructs. Although construct validation has been commonly associated with theory building and theory testing (Cronbach & Meehl, 1955), it also has implications for the practical use of assessment results. Whenever an assessment is to be interpreted as a measure of a particular construct, the various types of evidence useful for construct validation should be considered during its development or selection. This will almost certainly include consideration of content and may include consideration of test–criterion relationships, but a variety of other types of evidence are also relevant. The most appropriate types of evidence will be dictated by the particular construct to be measured.

In general, the process of construct validation involves (1) identifying and describing, by means of a theoretical framework, the meaning of the construct to be measured; (2) deriving hypotheses regarding performance on an assessment from the theory underlying the construct; and (3) verifying the hypotheses by logical and empirical means. Construct validation takes place primarily during the development and tryout of a test or an assessment and is based on an accumulation of evidence from many different sources. When selecting a published test that presumably measures a particular construct, such as mathematical reasoning or reading comprehension, the test manual should be examined to determine what evidence is presented to support the validity of the proposed interpretations.

An illustration of some types of evidence that might be used in the construct validation of an assessment of mathematical reasoning is shown in Figure 3.9. Although other types of studies could be added, this listing is sufficient to clarify the variety of types of evidence needed to support the claim that the assessment scores can be interpreted as measures of mathematical reasoning. Notice that considerations of both content and test–criterion relationships are included, along with other comparisons and correlations. No single type of evidence is sufficient, but the accumulation of various types of evidence helps describe what the assessment measures and how the scores relate to other significant variables. This clarifies the meaning of the assessment performance and aids in determining how validly mathematical reasoning is being measured.

In theory building and theory testing, the accumulation of evidence for construct validation may be endless. As new data are gathered, both the theory and the test or assessment are likely to be modified, and the testing of hypotheses continues. For the practical use of test and assessment results, however, we need to employ a more restricted framework when considering construct validation. During the development and selection of tests and assessments, our focus should be on the types of evidence that it seems reasonable to obtain, giving special attention to those data that are most relevant to the types of interpretations to be made. We can thus increase our understanding of what the assessment measures and how validly it does so without becoming involved in an endless task of data gathering.

Methods Used in Construct Validation

Construct validation depends on logical inferences drawn from a variety of types of data. As noted earlier, analyses of content and criterion relationships provide partial support for our interpretations, but this must be supplemented by various studies

FIGURE 3.9
Some types of evidence used in construct validation

that further clarify the meaning of the assessment results. Although it is impossible to describe all of the specific procedures that might be used in construct validation, the following exemplify some of the more commonly used methods.

1. Defining the domain or tasks to be measured. The specifications should be so well-defined that the meaning of the construct is clear and it is possible to judge the extent to which the assessment provides a relevant and representative measure of the task domain. If a single construct is being measured, the tasks should evoke similar types of responses and be highly interrelated.

2. *Analyzing the mental process required by the assessment tasks.* The mental process called forth by the assessment tasks can be determined both by examining the test tasks themselves or by administering the tasks to individual students and having them "think aloud" as they perform the tasks. Thus, examination of the items in a reading comprehension test may indicate that literal comprehension is emphasized, with relatively few items devoted to inferential comprehension. Similarly, a review of the requirements for performance of a laboratory task in science may reveal that there is a substantial emphasis on accurate recording of results, but too little emphasis on the conceptual integration of the laboratory results with theory or everyday experiences. Such judgments can be checked by administering the tasks to individual students and having them explain how they obtain their responses. In the example in Figure 3.9, "thinking aloud" may verify that the tasks call for the intended reasoning process, or it may reveal that most problems can be solved by a simple trial-and-error procedure.

3. *Comparing the scores of known groups.* In some cases it is possible to predict that scores will differ from one group to another. These may be age groups, trained and untrained, adjusted and maladjusted, and the like. For example, level of achievement generally increases with age (at least during childhood and adolescence). Also, it is reasonable to expect that performance on an assessment will differ for groups that have received different amounts of instruction in the subject matter of the assessment and that scores on adjustment inventories will discriminate between groups of adjusted and maladjusted individuals. Thus, a prediction of differences for a particular test or assessment can be checked against groups that are known to differ and the results used as partial support for construct validation.

4. *Comparing scores before and after some particular learning experience or experimental treatment.* We would like our assessments to be sensitive to some types of experiences and insensitive to others. Certainly, we would like assessments of student achievement in a given subject matter area to improve during the course of instruction. On the other hand, we would not like them to be influenced by such factors as student anxiety. Thus, both a demonstration of increases in performance following instruction and a demonstration that performance was affected little by a treatment designed to reduce student anxiety would both lend support to the construct validity of the assessment.

5. *Correlating the scores with other measures.* The scores of any particular assessment can be expected to correlate substantially with the scores of other measures of the same or a similar construct. By the same token, lower correlations would be expected to be obtained with measures of a different ability or trait. For example, we would expect rather high correlation between two scholastic aptitude tests, but much lower correlation between a scholastic and a musical aptitude test. Similarly, we would expect student performances on two assessments of writing to have substantially higher correlations with each other than either would have with an assessment in mathematics. Thus, for any given test or assessment, we would predict higher correlations with like tests and assessments and lower correlations with unlike tests and assessments. In addition, we might also predict that the assessment scores would correlate with various practical criteria. Scholastic aptitude scores, for example, should correlate satisfactorily with school grades, scores on performance in chemistry, and other measures of achievement in chemistry. This latter type of evidence is, of course, obtained by studies of test–criterion relationships. Our interest here, however, is not in the immediate problem of prediction, but rather in using these correlations to support the claim that the test measures scholastic aptitude or that the assessment measures understanding of chemical principles. As indicated earlier, construct validation depends on a wide array of evidence, including that provided by the other validation procedures.

In construct validation, our interest is not limited to the construct the assessment was designed to measure. Any factor that might influence the results is of legitimate concern. For example, we might ask how much the scores on a reading test depend on speed of reading or to what extent scores on a mathematical reasoning assessment with tasks involving lengthy written descriptions of the problem and requiring extended student responses are influenced by reading and writing ability. Broadly conceived, construct validation is an attempt to account for the differences in assessment results. During the development of an assessment, an attempt is made to rule out extraneous factors that might distort the meaning of the scores, and follow-up studies are conducted to verify the success of these attempts. The aim is to clarify the meaning of student performance by identifying the nature and strength of all factors influencing the scores on the assessment.

Construct validation is important to all types of testing and assessment—achievement, aptitude, and personal/social development. Whether constructing or selecting an assessment, the meaning of the resulting scores is dependent on the care with which the assessment was constructed and the array of evidence supporting the types of interpretations to be made. Construct validation is emphasized in most recent discussions of validity in the technical and theoretical literature, in part, because, as we have seen, it subsumes considerations of content and criterion relationships and, in part, because meaning is crucial in our uses and interpretations of the scores. The latter point was stressed by Messick, who stated, "The meaning of the measure, and hence its construct validity, must always be pursued—not only to support test interpretation but also to justify test use" (Messick, 1989, p. 17).

CONSIDERATION OF CONSEQUENCES

Messick (1989) has argued persuasively that an overall judgment regarding the validity of particular uses and interpretations of assessment results requires an evaluation of the consequences of those uses and interpretations. Assessments are intended to contribute to improved student learning. The question is, do they? And, if so, to what extent? What impact do assessments have on teaching? What are the possibly negative, unintended consequences of a particular use of assessment results?

The expansion of the concept of validity to include consideration of the consequences of use and interpretation of assessment results has been especially important in the recent movement toward more authentic, performance-based approaches to assessment. A number of proponents of these alternative forms of assessment have argued that a heavy reliance on multiple-choice tests, especially in situations where students and teachers are being held accountable for results, has had a number of unintended negative effects. They argue that the high stakes associated with test results lead teachers to focus narrowly on what is on the test while ignoring important parts of the curriculum that are not covered by the test.

In some instances a single form of a standardized test—that is, a single set of multiple-choice questions—is used year after year in a state or school district. In such a situation the narrowing may be worse than simply focusing on the domain of skills that the test is intended to measure. It may lead to teaching the specific content of the test items. This not only would be an undesirable narrowing of what is taught, but would be likely to inflate test scores and change the meaning of the results, possibly changing the construct measured from problem solving to memorization ability.

Although the negative effects are most serious where high stakes are attached to the results obtained on a single test form used year after year, the concern about consequences is not limited to such situations. Distortions of instruction could be expected even if a new test form were used each year, because of lack of alignment of the test to the learning objectives emphasized in the curriculum. For example, a curriculum that emphasized problem solving and conceptual understanding could be undermined by holding teachers accountable for student scores on a test that emphasized low-level skills and factual knowledge. Drill and practice on the skills and facts emphasized on the test might raise scores, but would not facilitate achievement of the primary learning goals.

Considerations of consequences are equally important for performance-based assessment. It is just as important to attend to both the intended positive effects and the possible unintended negative effects for performance-based assessments as it is for standardized, multiple-choice tests. For both types of assessment, consequences are directly related to the stakes that are attached to the results. As the stakes increase for teachers or students, so too should the demands for evidence regarding consequences of the uses and interpretations of results.

An adequate consideration of consequences needs to include both intended consequences (e.g., contributes to learning, increases student motivation) and unintended consequences (e.g., narrows the curriculum, increases the number of high school dropouts). Consequences are particularly important where assessment results are used to make high-stakes decisions regarding individuals (e.g., retention in grade, assignment to a remedial instructional program, or the award of a high school diploma).

The use of an assessment to retain students in grade is not recommended, but it is a way in which assessments are sometimes used and may be used to illustrate the impact of consequences on the overall validation. An analysis of consequences of the use of an assessment for retention in grade should seek evidence that students who are retained are generally better off than they would have been if they had not been retained. Such evidence might come from a comparison of the subsequent achievement and attitudes of students just below and just above the minimum score required for advancement in grade. A positive finding would require that students who were just below the cut score, and therefore retained in grade, eventually out-performed their counterparts who were just above the cut score and therefore promoted in grade. The opposite finding would provide evidence that the use of assessment to retain students had negative consequences and would contribute to a judgment that grade retention was not a valid use of this assessment. It would also be important to compare the long-term results such as dropout rates and eventual graduation rates. For a classroom assessment, studies of consequences would obviously be much less elaborate. Indeed, considerations of consequences would generally be limited to a logical analysis of likely effects.

Teachers have an excellent vantage point for considering the likely effects of assessments. First, they know the learning objectives that they are trying to help their students achieve. Second, they are quite familiar with instructional experiences that the students have had. Third, they have an opportunity to observe students while they are working on an assessment task and to talk to students about their performances. This first-hand awareness of learning objectives, instructional experiences, and students can be brought to bear on an analysis of the likely effects of assessments by systematically considering questions such as the following.

1. Do the tasks match important learning objectives? WYTIWYG, what you test is what you get, has become a popular slogan. Despite the fact that it is an over-simplification, it is a good reminder that assessments need to reflect major learning outcomes. Problem-solving skills and complex thinking skills requiring integration, evaluation, and synthesis of information are more likely to be fostered by assessments that require the application of such skills than by assessments that require students merely to repeat what the teacher has said or what is stated in the textbook.

2. Is there reason to believe that students study harder in preparation for the assessment? Motivating student effort is a potentially important consequence of tests and assessments. The chances of achieving this goal are improved if students have a clear understanding of what to expect on the assessment, know how the results will be used, and believe that the assessment will be fair.

3. Does the assessment artificially constrain the focus of students' study? If it is judged important to be sure that students can solve a particular type of mathematics problem, for example, then it is reasonable to focus an assessment on that type of problem. However, much will be missed if such an approach is the only mode of assessment. In many cases the identification of the nature of the problem may be at least as important as facility with application of a particular formula or algorithm. Assessments that focus only on the latter skills are not likely to facilitate development of problem identification skills.

4. Does the assessment encourage or discourage exploration and creative modes of expression? Although it is important for students to know what to expect on an assessment and have a sense of what to do to prepare for it, care should be taken to avoid overly narrow and artificial constraints that will discourage students from exploring new ideas and concepts.

FACTORS INFLUENCING VALIDITY

Numerous factors tend to make assessment results invalid for their intended use. Some are rather obvious and easily avoided. No teacher would think of measuring knowledge of social studies with a mathematics assessment. Nor would a teacher consider measuring problem-solving skills in third-grade arithmetic with an assessment designed for seventh graders. In both instances, the assessment results would obviously be invalid. The factors influencing validity are of this same general nature but much more subtle in character. For example, a teacher may overload a social studies test with items concerning historical facts, and thus the scores are less valid as a measure of achievement in social studies. Or a third-grade teacher may select appropriate arithmetic problems for an assessment but use vocabulary in the problems and directions that only the better readers are able to understand. The arithmetic assessment then becomes, in part, a reading assessment and reduces the validity of the results for their intended use. These examples show some of the more subtle factors influencing validity to which the teacher should be alert, whether constructing classroom assessments or selecting published ones.

Factors in the Test or Assessment Itself

A careful examination of test items and assessment tasks will indicate whether the test or assessment appears to measure the subject-matter content and the mental functions that the teacher is interested in assessing. However, any of the following factors can prevent the test items or assessment tasks from functioning as intended and thereby lower the validity of the interpretations from the assessment results. The first four factors are equally applicable for assessments with tasks requiring extended student performances and traditional tests. The last six factors apply most directly to tests with fixed-choice or short-answer items that are scored right or wrong.

   1. Unclear directions. Directions that do not clearly indicate to the student how to respond to the tasks and how to record the responses will tend to reduce validity.

   2. Reading vocabulary and sentence structure too difficult. Vocabulary and sentence structure that are too complicated for the students taking the assessment will result in the assessment's measuring reading comprehension and aspects of intelligence, which will distort the meaning of the assessment results.

   3. Ambiguity. Ambiguous statements in assessment tasks contribute to misinterpretations and confusion. Ambiguity sometimes confuses the better students more than it does the poor students.

   4. Inadequate time limits. Time limits that do not provide students with enough time to consider the tasks and provide thoughtful responses can reduce the validity of interpretations of results. Rather than measuring what a student knows about a topic or is able to do given adequate time, the assessment may become a measure of the speed with which the student can respond. For some content (e.g., a typing test), speed may be important. However, most assessments of achievement should minimize the effects of speed on student performance.

5. Inappropriate level of difficulty of the test items. In norm-referenced tests, items that are too easy or too difficult will not provide reliable discrimination among students and will therefore lower validity. In criterion-referenced tests, the failure to match the difficulty specified by the learning outcome will lower validity.

6. Poorly constructed test items. Test items that unintentionally provide clues to the answer will tend to measure the students' alertness in detecting clues as well as mastery of skills or knowledge the test is intended to measure.

7. Test items inappropriate for the outcomes being measured. Attempting to measure understanding, thinking skills, and other complex types of achievement with test forms that are appropriate only for measuring factual knowledge will invalidate the results.

8. Test too short. A test is only a sample of the many questions that might be asked. If a test is too short to provide a representative sample of the performance we are interested in, its validity will suffer accordingly.

9. Improper arrangement of items. Test items are typically arranged in order of difficulty, with the easiest items first. Placing difficult items early in the test may cause students to spend too much time on these and prevent them from reaching items they could easily answer. Improper arrangement may also influence validity by having a detrimental effect on student motivation. This influence is likely to be strongest with young students.

10. Identifiable pattern of answers. Placing correct answers in some systematic pattern (e.g., *T, T, F, F* or *A, B, C, D, A, B, C, D*) will enable students to guess the answers to some items more easily, and this will lower validity.

In short, any defect in the construction of the test or assessment that prevents it from functioning as intended will invalidate the interpretations to be drawn from the results. Much of what is written in the following chapters is directed toward helping teachers improve the validity of their interpretations of test scores and other assessment results.

Functioning of Tasks and Teaching Procedures

In assessing achievement, the ways in which tasks function cannot be determined merely by examining the form and content of the assessment. For example, the following task may appear to measure arithmetical reasoning if examined without reference to what the students have been taught:

EXAMPLE   Ken learned that 60 percent of the graduates from his high school are admitted to community colleges, 30 percent are admitted to public four-year colleges or universities, and 10 percent are admitted to private four-year colleges or universities. Since these percentages add up to 100, Ken reasons that he is sure to get admitted to some college or university. Explain, possibly with the use of a diagram, what is wrong with Ken's reasoning.

However, if the teacher has taught the solution to this particular problem before giving the assessment, the task now will measure no more than memorized knowledge. Similarly, assessments of understanding, critical thinking, and other complex learning outcomes will provide valid measures in these areas only if the tasks function as intended. If the students have previously been taught the solutions to the particular problems included in the assessment, or have been taught mechanical steps for obtaining the solutions, the assessment results cannot be considered valid indicators of the achievement of the more complex mental processes.

Factors in Administration and Scoring

The administration and scoring of an assessment may also introduce factors that have a detrimental effect on the validity of the interpretations from the results. In the case of teacher-made assessments, such factors as insufficient time, unfair aid to individual students who ask for help, cheating, and the unreliable scoring of student performances tend to lower validity. In the case of published tests, failure to follow the standard directions and time limits, giving students unauthorized assistance, and errors in scoring similarly contribute to lower validity. For all types of assessments, adverse physical and psychological conditions at the time of the assessment may also have a negative effect.

Factors in Student Responses

In some instances, invalid interpretations are caused by personal factors influencing a student's response to the assessment situation rather than to any shortcomings in the test instrument or its administration. Some students may be bothered by emotional disturbances that interfere with their performance. Others may be frightened by the assessment situation and thereby are unable to respond normally, and still others may not be motivated to put forth their best effort. These and other factors that restrict and modify students' responses in the assessment situation will obviously distort the results.

Nature of the Group and the Criterion

Validity is always specific to a particular group. An arithmetic test based on story problems, for example, may measure reasoning ability in a group at an early stage of instruction and a combination of simple recall of information and computation skill in a more advanced group. Similarly, scores on a science assessment may be accounted for largely by reading comprehension in one group and by knowledge of facts in another. What an assessment measures may be influenced by such factors as age, gender, ability level, educational background, and cultural background. Thus, in appraising reports of validity included in test manuals or other sources, it is important to determine the nature of the validation group. How closely it compares in significant characteristics with the group of students we wish to assess determines how applicable the information is to our particular group.

As shown in Figure 3.6, correlations between a test and a criterion will be smaller when (1) the characteristics measured by the test and the criterion are less alike, (2) the spread of scores is smaller, (3) the stability of scores is lower, and (4) the time span between measures is longer. Of these factors, probably the most frequently overlooked is the nature of the criterion being predicted. This is unfortunate, because knowing the specific nature of the criterion can help evaluate test–criterion correlations. For example, scores on a mathematics aptitude test are likely to provide a more accurate prediction of achievement in a science course in which quantitative problems are stressed than in one in which they play only a minor role. Likewise, we can expect scores on a critical thinking test to correlate more highly with grades in social studies courses that emphasize critical thinking than in those that depend largely on the memorization of the factual information. These examples simply illustrate the general rule that test–criterion correlations are influenced by the similarity between the performance measured by the test and the performance represented in the criterion. Thus, both need to be examined carefully for a full understanding of the relationship.

Because validity information varies with the group tested and the composition of the criterion measures used, published validation data should be considered highly tentative. Whenever possible, the validity of the test results should be checked in the specific local situation.

SUMMARY

The most important quality to consider when constructing or selecting an assessment procedure is *validity,* which refers to the meaningfulness and appropriateness of the uses and interpretations to be made of assessment results. When assessing validity, keep in mind that validity is a quality of the interpretation of the results rather than of the assessment itself, that its presence is a matter of degree, that it is always specific to some particular interpretation or use, and that it is a unitary concept.

Although validity is a unitary concept, it involves the consideration of several kinds of evidence. Considerations of content, test–criterion relationships, construct, and consequences all can contribute to the meaning of a set of results; validity is strongest when evidence to support all four of these considerations is present.

An analysis of the content of an assessment should evaluate the appropriateness of the content domain and determine the extent to which the assessment tasks provide a relevant and representative sample of the domain of content under consideration. Content considerations are especially important when validating achievement testing, or constructing classroom tests and assessments. Written specifications for the assessment should define a domain of instructionally relevant tasks and then tasks that provide a representative sample of the domain should be constructed or selected. Content considerations are also important when selecting published achievement tests. Here, the crucial question is how well the test measures the content and objectives of the local instructional program. The same types of test specifications used in constructing classroom tests can aid in selecting published tests.

Studies of the extent to which test performance is related to some other valued measure of performance (called a criterion) also contribute to the overall evaluation of the validity of a test, especially when the test is used as an indicator of likely performance in other settings (e.g., achieving good grades in college). This may involve studies of how well test scores predict future performance (predictive validation study) or estimate some current performance (concurrent validation study). These validity studies are typically reported by means of a correlation coefficient called a validity coefficient, by use of an expectancy table, or by solving a regression equation that converts test scores to estimated performance on the criterion. Test–criterion relationships are pertinent whenever test results are used to make predictions or substitute for assessment results obtained by more time-consuming methods, but they are of special significance in aptitude testing. Because the meaning of test scores is enhanced by knowing what other measures they relate to, test–criterion relationships are also used in construct validation.

Construct validation is the process of determining the extent to which performance on an assessment can be interpreted in terms of one or more constructs. Construct validation typically includes consideration of content and may include test–criterion relationships as well as several other types of information. The procedure is one of clarifying what is being measured and what factors influence the assessment results, so that performance can be interpreted most meaningfully. This involves both logical analysis and various comparative and correlational studies. Although the accumulation of evidence could be endless, in practical situations we need to focus on the types of evidence that are reasonable to obtain and that are most relevant to the types of interpretations to be made. The more complete the evidence is, the more confident we can be concerning the meaning of the assessment results.

Finally, the consequences of a particular use or interpretation of assessment results are important in arriving at an overall evaluative judgment of the validity of the assessment for that use or interpretation. The evaluation of consequences needs to attend to the anticipated positive effects of a particular use (e.g., enhancing student motivation). It is at least as important, however, to investigate plausible unintended consequences (e.g., increased anxiety, narrowing of instruction). The need of evidence regarding consequences increases as the stakes attached to the assessment results increase.

Many other factors tend to influence the validity of interpretations of tests and assessments. Some of these influences can be found in the test or assessment itself, some in the relationship of teaching to testing and assessment, some in the administration and scoring of the measure, some in the atypical responses of students to the assessment situation, and still others in the nature of the group assessed and in the composition of the criterion measures used. A major aim in the construction, selection, and use of tests and other assessment procedures is to control those factors that have an adverse effect on validity and to interpret the results in accordance with what validity information is available.

This discussion of factors influencing the validity of test and assessment results has shown how pervasive the concept of validity is. Ultimately, it is the users of tests and assessments who must make the final judgment concerning the validity of the uses and interpretations.

LEARNING EXERCISES

1. If a fellow teacher told you that a particular reading test had high validity, what types of questions would you ask?

2. A high-school science teacher prepared a set of assessment tasks to be used in all sections of biology, without consulting the teachers of the other sections. What effect might this have on the assessment's validity? Why?

3. Compare the relative difficulty of determining validity for a norm-referenced survey test in social studies and an assessment of mathematical problem solving. For which one would a table of specifications be most useful? Why?

4. If you wanted to determine the validity of a published achievement test for use in a course you are teaching or plan to teach, what procedure would you follow? Describe your procedure step by step, and give reasons for each step.

5. Define a validity coefficient, and list several factors that will influence its size.

6. Describe how to prepare an expectancy table. What is the advantage of an expectancy table over a validity coefficient for making predictions?

7. The regression equation for predicting freshman grade-point average (GPA) at a local college from the sum of verbal and math scores on the Scholastic Aptitude Test is (SAT V+M):

   predicted GPA = 1.8 + .001 (SAT V+M).

   What are the predicted GPAs for two students with SAT V+M scores of 800 and 1400, respectively? What do these predictions tell you about the test–criterion relationship?

8. What types of evidence might be useful in the construct validation of each of the following?
   a. An assessment of reading comprehension.
   b. An assessment of mathematical reasoning.
   c. A test of creativity.

9. Describe a series of studies that would be useful in evaluating the consequences of a state-mandated high-school graduation test.

10. Describe the steps you would follow to analyze the likely consequences of a series of assessments you developed to measure student progress in using mathematics to solve practical problems.

11. Study the validity sections of a test manual for a published achievement test and a scholastic aptitude test. How does the information differ for these two types of tests? Why?

12. Consult the validity section of the latest edition of *Standards for Educational and Psychological Testing* (see the reading list for this chapter), and review the types of information that test manuals should contain. Compare a recent test manual with the *Standards*.

13. List and briefly describe as many factors as you can think of that might lower the validity of a classroom assessment.

REFERENCES

American Psychological Association. (1985). *Standards for educational and psychological testing.* Washington, D.C.: Author.

Cronbach, L. J., & Meehl, P. E. (1955). Construct validity in psychological tests. *Psychological Bulletin, 52,* 281–302.

Messick, S. (1989). Validity. In R. L. Linn (Ed.), *Educational measurement* (3rd ed.). New York: Macmillan.

FURTHER READING

American Psychological Association. (1985). *Standards for Educational and Psychological Testing.* Washington, D.C.: Author. See the first technical section on test validity for descriptions of basic validation procedures and the nature of validity information to be sought in test manuals.

Anastasi, A. (1988). *Psychological Testing* (6th ed.). New York: Macmillan. Chapter 6, "Validity: Basic Concepts," describes the standard procedures for test validation.

Cronbach, L. J. (1990). *Essentials of Psychological Testing* (5th ed.). New York: Harper & Row. Chapter 5, "Validation," describes and illustrates the procedures of test validation.

Linn, R. L., Baker, E. L., & Dunbar, S. B. (1991). Complex, Performance-Based Assessment: Expectations and Validation Criteria. *Educational Researcher, 20* (8), 15–21. Discusses some priorities in evaluating the validity of complex performance-based assessment.

Messick, S. (1989). Validity. In R. L. Linn, (Ed.), *Educational Measurement* (3rd ed.). New York: Macmillan. Chapter 2 provides a comprehensive and theoretically sophisticated discussion of validity.

Shepard, L. A. (1993). Evaluating Test Validity. *Review of Research in Education, 19,* 405–450. Provides examples of applications of construct validity principles to the evaluation of test use.

CHAPTER 4
Reliability and Other Desired Characteristics

Next to validity, reliability is the most important characteristic of assessment results. Reliability (1) provides the consistency that makes validity possible, and (2) indicates the degree to which various kinds of generalizations are justifiable. The practicality of the evaluation procedure is, of course, also of concern to the busy classroom teacher.

In Chapter 3 we emphasized that validity is the most important consideration in the selection and construction of assessment procedures. First and foremost, we want assessment results to serve the specific uses for which they are intended. Next in importance is reliability, and following that is a host of practical features that can be best classified under the heading, "usability."

NATURE OF RELIABILITY

Reliability refers to the consistency of measurement; that is, how consistent test scores or other assessment results are from one measurement to another. Suppose, for instance, that Miss Jones has just given an achievement assessment to her students. How similar would the students' scores have been had she assessed them yesterday, or tomorrow, or next week? How would the scores have varied had she selected a different sample of tasks? How much would the scores have differed had a different teacher scored it? These are the types of questions with which reliability is concerned. Assessment results merely provide a limited measure of performance obtained at a particular time. Unless the measurement can be shown to be reasonably consistent (that is, generalizable) over different occasions, different raters, or different samples of the same performance domain, we can have little confidence in the results.

We cannot expect assessment results to be perfectly consistent. There are numerous factors other than the quality being measured that may influence assessment results. If a single assessment is administered to the same group twice in close succession, some variation in scores can be expected because of temporary fluctuations in memory, attention, effort, fatigue, emotional strain, guessing, and the like. With a longer time between tests, additional variation in scores may be caused by intervening learning experiences, changes in health, forgetting, and less comparable assessment conditions. If essays or other types of student performances are evaluated by different raters, some variation in scores can be expected due to less-than-perfect agreement among raters. If we use a different sample of tasks in the second assessment, still another factor is likely to influence the results. Individuals may find one assessment easier than the other because it happens to contain more tasks on topics with which they are familiar. Such extraneous factors as these introduce a certain amount of measurement error into all assessment results. Methods of determining reliability are essentially means of determining how much measurement error is present under different conditions. In general, the more consistent our assessment results are from one measurement to another, the less error there will be and, consequently, the greater the reliability.

The meaning of reliability, as applied to testing and assessment, can be further clarified by noting the following general points:

1. Reliability refers to the results obtained with an assessment instrument and not to the instrument itself.   Any particular instrument may have a number of different reliabilities, depending on the group involved and the situation in which it is used. Thus, it is more appropriate to speak of the reliability of the test scores or of the assessment results than of the test or the assessment.

2. An estimate of reliability always refers to a particular type of consistency.   Assessment results are not reliable in general. They are reliable (or generalizable) over different periods of time, over different samples of tasks, over different raters, and the like. It is possible for assessment results to be consistent in one of these respects and not in another. The appropriate type of consistency in a particular case is dictated by the use to be made of the results. For example, if we wish to know what individuals will be like at some future time, constancy of scores over time will be important. On the other hand, if we want to measure an individual's current understanding of certain scientific principles we are apt to be more interested in the consistency of performance across different tasks designed to allow students to apply those principles. Thus, for different interpretations we need different analyses of consistency. Treating reliability as a general characteristic can lead to erroneous interpretations.

3. Reliability is a necessary but not sufficient condition for validity. An assessment that produces totally inconsistent results cannot possibly provide valid information about the performance being measured. On the other hand, highly consistent assessment results may be measuring the wrong thing or may be used in inappropriate ways. Thus, low reliability indicates that a low degree of validity is present, but high reliability does not ensure a high degree of validity. In short, reliability merely provides the consistency that makes validity possible.

4. *Reliability is primarily statistical.* The logical analysis of an assessment will provide little evidence concerning the reliability of the scores. To evaluate the consistency of scores assigned by different raters, two or more raters must score the same set of student performances. Similarly, an evaluation of the consistency of scores obtained in response to different forms of a test or different collections of performance-based assessment tasks requires the administration of both test forms or collections of tasks to an appropriate group of students. Whether the focus is on inter-rater consistency or the consistency across forms or collections of tasks, consistency may be expressed in terms of shifts in the relative standing of persons in the group or in terms of the amount of variation to be expected in an individual's score. Consistency in the first case is reported by means of a correlation coefficient called a reliability coefficient (see "Terminology" box) and in the second case is reported by means of the standard error of measurement. Both methods of expressing reliability are widely used and should be understood by persons responsible for interpreting assessment results.

DETERMINING RELIABILITY BY CORRELATION METHODS

In determining reliability, it would be desirable to obtain two sets of measures under identical conditions and then to compare the results. This procedure is impossible, of course, because the conditions under which assessment data are obtained can never be identical. As a substitute for this ideal procedure, several methods of estimating reliability have been introduced (American Psychological Association, 1985). The methods are similar in that all of them involve correlating two sets of scores, obtained either from the same assessment procedure or from equivalent forms of the same procedure. The correlation coefficient used to determine

TERMINOLOGY

Correlation Coefficient: A statistic that indicates the degree of relationship between any two sets of scores obtained from the same group of individuals (e.g., correlation between height and weight).

Validity Coefficient: A correlation coefficient that indicates the degree to which a measure predicts or estimates performance on some criterion measure (e.g., correlation between scholastic aptitude scores and grades in school).

Reliability Coefficient: A correlation coefficient that indicates the degree of relationship between two sets of scores intended to be measures of the same characteristic (e.g., correlation between scores assigned by two different raters or scores obtained from administrations of two forms of a test).

reliability is calculated and interpreted in the same manner as that used in determining statistical estimates of validity. The only difference between a validity coefficient and a reliability coefficient is that the former is based on agreement with an outside criterion and the latter is based on agreement between two sets of results from the same procedure.

The chief methods of estimating reliability are shown in Table 4.1. Note that different types of consistency are determined by the different methods: consistency over a period of time, over different forms of the assessment, within the assessment itself, and over different raters. The reliability coefficient resulting from each method must be interpreted according to the type of consistency being investigated. Each of these methods of estimating reliability will be considered in further detail as we proceed.

Test–Retest Method

To estimate reliability by means of the test–retest method, the same assessment is administered twice to the same group of students with a given time interval between

TABLE 4.1

Methods of estimating reliability

	Type of Reliability Measure	Procedure
Test–retest method	Measure of stability	Give the same test twice to the same group with any time interval between tests, from several minutes to several years
Equivalent forms method	Measure of equivalence	Give two forms of the test to the same group in close succession
(Test–retest with equivalent forms)	Measure of stability and equivalence	Give two forms of the test to the same group with increased time interval between forms
Split-half method	Measure of internal consistency	Give test once. Score two equivalent halves of test (e.g., odd items and even items); correct correlation between halves to fit whole test by Spearman–Brown formula
Kuder–Richardson method and coefficient *Alpha*	Measure of internal consistency	Give test once. Score total test and apply Kuder–Richardson formula
Inter-rater method	Measure of consistency of ratings	Give a set of student responses requiring judgmental scoring to two or more raters and have them independently score the responses

the two administrations (see Figure 4.1). The resulting assessment scores are correlated, and this correlation coefficient provides a measure of stability; that is, it indicates how stable the assessment results are over the given period of time. If the results are highly stable, those students who are high on one administration of the assessment will tend to be high on the other administration, and the remaining students will tend to stay in their same relative positions on both administrations. Such stability is indicated by a large correlation coefficient. Recall from our previous discussion of correlation coefficients that a perfect positive relationship is indicated by 1.00 and no relationship by 0.00. Measures of stability in the .80 range are commonly reported for standardized tests of aptitude and achievement over occasions within the same year.

One important factor to keep in mind when interpreting measures of stability is the time interval between assessments. If the time interval is short, say a day or two, the constancy of the results will be inflated because students will remember the tasks and their responses to them from the first assessment. If the time interval is long, say about a year, the results will be influenced not only by the instability of the assessment procedure but also by actual changes in the students over that period of time. In general, the longer the interval between the first and second assessments, the more the results will be influenced by changes in the student characteristic being measured, and the smaller the reliability coefficient will be.

The best time interval between assessment administrations will depend largely on the use to be made of the results. Because college admissions test scores may be submitted as part of an application to college several years after the test was taken, stability over several years is quite important. But stability over a long period is neither important nor desirable for an assessment of performance on a unit in a course that is focused on student understanding of certain concepts and readiness to move on to new material. Thus, for some decisions we are interested in reliability coefficients based on a long interval between test and retest; for others, reliability coefficients based on a short interval may be sufficient. The important thing is to seek evidence of stability that fits the particular interpretation to be made.

The test–retest method is unlikely to be relevant for teacher constructed classroom tests, because it is seldom possible or desirable to readminister the same assessment. But in choosing standardized tests, stability is an important criterion. The

FIGURE 4.1
Test–retest method (using same test forms)

Test-Retest

September 25	October 15
Form A	Form A
1. hosidos	1. hosidos
2. hodis osid	2. hodis osid
3. kodsosicos	3. kodsosicos
4. kdosodiso	4. kdosodiso
Score = 82	Score = 86

test manual should provide evidence of stability, indicating the interval between tests and any unusual experiences the group members might have had between testings. Other things (such as validity) being equal, a test shown to possess the type of stability needed to make sound decisions is the best test.

Stability is also an important consideration when using assessment results from school records. When using any assessment result from permanent records, check the date of the assessment and any stability data available to determine whether the results are still dependable. If there is doubt, and the decision is important, a reassessment is in order.

Equivalent Forms Method

The equivalent forms method for estimating reliability uses two different but equivalent forms of an assessment (also called parallel or alternate forms). Equivalent forms are built to the same set of specifications (e.g., test content and difficulty) but are constructed independently. The two forms of the assessment are administered to the same group of students in close succession, and the resulting assessment scores are correlated. This correlation coefficient provides a measure of the degree to which generalizations about student performance from one assessment to another are justified. Thus, it indicates the degree to which the two assessments are measuring the same aspects of behavior.

The equivalent forms method tells us nothing about the long-term stability of the student characteristic being measured. Rather, it reflects short-term constancy of student performance and the extent to which the assessment represents an adequate sample of the characteristic being measured. In assessing achievement, for example, thousands of tasks might be presented in a particular assessment, but because of time limits and other restricting factors, only some of the possible tasks can be used. The tasks included in the assessment should provide an adequate sample of the possible tasks in the area. The easiest way to estimate whether an assessment measures an adequate sample of the content is to construct versions of the assessment that are intended to cover the same domain of content and student skills and correlate the results. A high correlation indicates that the two assessments are providing similar results and, therefore, are probably reliable samples of the general area of content being measured.

The equivalent forms method of estimating reliability is widely used in standardized testing because most standardized tests have two or more forms available. In fact, a teacher should be suspicious of any standardized test that has two forms available and does not provide information about equivalence. The comparability of the results of the two forms cannot be assumed unless such evidence is presented. The equivalent forms method is sometimes used with an interval between the administration of the two forms of the test (see Figure 4.2). Under these test–retest conditions, the resulting reliability coefficient provides a measure of stability and equivalence. This is a more rigorous test of reliability than the test–retest method or equivalent forms method with a short interval between forms, because the stability of the testing procedures, the constancy of the student characteristic being measured, and the representativeness of the sample of tasks

FIGURE 4.2
Equivalent forms method
(without and with a time interval)

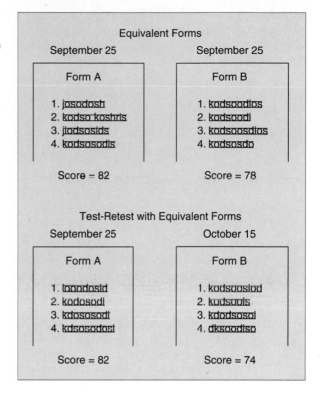

included in the test all are taken into account. Consequently, this is generally recommended as the soundest procedure for estimating the reliability of test scores. As with the ordinary test–retest method, the reliability coefficient must be interpreted in light of the interval between the two forms of the test. For longer time periods, expect smaller reliability coefficients.

Split-Half Method

Reliability can also be estimated from a single administration of a single form of an assessment. The assessment is administered to a group of students in the usual manner and then is divided in half for scoring purposes. The split-half method is easy to implement with a traditional test or quiz consisting of say, ten or more items. To split the test into halves that are equivalent, the usual procedure is to score the even-numbered and the odd-numbered tasks separately (see Figure 4.3). This produces two scores for each student, which, when correlated, provide a measure of internal consistency. This coefficient indicates the degree to which consistent results are obtained from the two halves of the test, and may be thought of as the "half-length test reliability estimate."

Although most often applied with traditional tests containing a sizable number of items, the split-half method is also applicable to assessments consisting of a smaller number of tasks each, or which require a more extended period of time to

FIGURE 4.3
Odd–even scoring for use of split-half methd (odd and even scores are then correlated)

Sum number of odd items correct	Sum number of even items correct	September 25
		Test
Items 1	Items 2	1. nwso rho
3	4	2. nworh orh
5	6	3. Stopey
.	.	4. ta la do
.	.	5. fsttey
.	.	6. odd iteets
Odd score = 40	Even score = 42	Total score = 82

complete. Some limited information can be obtained with as few as two tasks by correlating the scores obtained on one task with those obtained on another. Better information is provided as the number of tasks increases. With a small number of tasks, say four to eight, it is better to divide the tasks into two sets that are judged to be most comparable to each other rather than relying on the more mechanical odd-even method that is appropriate where a larger number of tasks or items is available.

As previously noted, the reliability coefficient is determined by correlating the scores of two half-assessments. To estimate the scores' reliability based on the full-length assessment, the Spearman–Brown formula is usually applied:

$$\text{Reliability on full assessment} = \frac{2 \text{ times correlation between half-assessments}}{1 \text{ plus correlation between half-assessments}}$$

The simplicity of the formula can be seen in the following example, in which the correlation coefficient between scores on the assessment's two halves is .60:

$$\text{Reliability on full assessment} = \frac{2 \times .60}{1 + .60} = \frac{1.20}{1.60} = .75$$

This correlation coefficient of .75, then, estimates the reliability of a full assessment when the half-assessments correlated .60.

The split-half method is similar to the equivalent forms method in that it indicates the extent to which the sample of tasks is a dependable sample of the content being measured. A high correlation between scores on the two halves of an assessment denotes the equivalence of the two halves and consequently the adequacy of the sampling. Split-half reliabilities tend to be higher than equivalent form reliabilities because the split-half method is based on the administration of a single assessment. When two forms of an assessment are administered, even in close succession, more opportunity for inconsistency is introduced (e.g., differences from form to form in attention, speed of work, effort, fatigue, and assessment content).

Because the equivalent forms method takes into account more sources of inconsistency, it provides a more stringent evaluation of reliability.

Kuder–Richardson Method and Coefficient *Alpha*

Another method of estimating the reliability of assessment scores from a single administration is by means of formulas such as those developed by Kuder and Richardson. As with the split-half method, these formulas provide an index of internal consistency but do not require splitting the assessment in half for scoring purposes. One of the formulas, called Kuder–Richardson Formula 20, or KR-20, is applicable only in situations where student responses are scored dichotomously (zero or one), and therefore is most useful with traditional test items that are scored as right or wrong. The KR-20 is based on the proportion of persons passing each item and the standard deviation of the total scores. (A standard deviation is a measure of the spread of scores—see Appendix A.) The generalization of the KR-20 for assessments that have more than dichotomous, right-wrong scores (e.g., each task is scored on a 5-point scale), is called Coefficient *Alpha*. The computation of either KR-20 or Coefficient *Alpha* is rather cumbersome unless information is already available concerning the proportion passing or the standard deviations of scores for individual tasks. However, with the increasing availability of microcomputers and software for scoring and analyzing tests, it is now more feasible to obtain KR-20 and Coefficient *Alpha* estimates of reliability.

But here, our concern is with interpretation of the coefficients rather than the calculations. KR-20 and Coefficient *Alpha* estimates of reliability provide information about the degree to which the items or tasks in the assessment measure similar characteristics. For a test with relatively homogeneous content (e.g., an arithmetic computation test), the reliability estimate generally will be similar to that provided by the split-half method. Indeed, the KR-20 or Coefficient *Alpha* estimate can be thought of as the average of all possible split-half coefficients for the groups tested. This is an advantage when considering an assessment with relatively homogeneous content since the estimate does not depend on the way in which the items are assigned to the two half-tests as in the split-half method. For assessments designed to measure more heterogeneous learning outcomes (e.g., an assessment covering ancient history, the Middle Ages, and modern history) however, the KR-20 or Coefficient *Alpha* estimate will be smaller than that provided by the split-half method and the latter method is to be preferred.

The simplicity of applying the split-half method, the KR-20, or the Coefficient *Alpha* method has led to their widespread use in determining reliability. There are limitations, however, that restrict their value. First, they are not appropriate for speeded assessments—for assessments with time limits that prevent students from attempting every task. If speed is a significant factor in the assessment, reliability estimates will be inflated to an unknown degree. This poses no great problem in estimating the reliability of results from teacher-made assessments, because these are usually designed to allow students adequate time to complete all of the tasks. In the case of standardized tests, however, time limits are seldom so liberal that all students complete the test. Thus, measures of internal consistency reported in test manuals should be interpreted with caution unless evidence is also presented that speed of work is a negligible factor. For speeded tests, reliability obtained by the test–retest or equivalent forms method should be sought.

A second limitation of internal consistency procedures is that they do not indicate the constancy of student response from day to day. In this regard, they are similar to the equivalent forms method without a time interval. Only test–retest procedures indicate the extent to which test results are generalizable over different periods of time.

Inter-Rater Consistency

Judgment is required in scoring student responses to many types of assessments. This is obvious in the case of essay exams, but judgment is also required in scoring responses to open-ended mathematics problems or laboratory exercises in science. Whenever student work is judgmentally scored, it is reasonable to ask whether the same scores would be assigned by another equally qualified judge. Individual classroom teachers seldom have the luxury of having another teacher to independently score examples of student work from their classroom. But there is a growing need to evaluate inter-rater consistency as a result of the increasing numbers of state- and district-mandated assessments that must be judgmentally scored.

Estimation of inter-rater consistency is relatively straightforward. Two or more raters must independently score the performances obtained for an appropriately selected sample of students. Consistency can be evaluated by correlating the scores assigned by one judge with those assigned by another judge. Consistency can also be evaluated by computing the proportion of times that students' performances receive exactly the same scores from a pair of raters and the proportion that are within a single point of each other.

Suppose, for example, that two raters independently scored fifty student essays on a six-point scale. The results of the ratings are summarized in Table 4.2. Rater 1 assigned a score of 6 to five of the essays. For those five essays, Rater 2 assigned a score of 6 to three of them and scores of 4 and 5 to the other two. Thus, each entry in a cell of Table 4.2 shows the number of essays that Rater 1 assigned the score associated with the row, while Rater 2 assigned the score associated with the column of the table. The percentage of exact agreement is obtained by summing the counts where both raters assigned the same score (shown in boldface type), dividing that sum by the total number of essays, and multiplying the result by 100.

Percent exact agreement = 100 × ([3 + 7 + 5 + 4 + 2 + 3]/50) = 48%.

The percentage of times that raters agreed to within one point (all the counts between the two diagonal lines) would be computed in a similar fashion. For this example the percentage of agreement within one score point is 88 percent (100 times [44/50]). One other indicator is the correlation between the two sets of scores, which for the data in Table 4.2 is .80. The level of inter-rater consistency shown in Table 4.2 is high in comparison to levels of consistency generally achieved by independent raters. Even so, six of the fifty students would have their scores fluctuate by 2 points, depending on the person doing the scoring. One way to

TABLE 4.2
Scores assigned to fifty essays
by two independent raters
(Raters 1 and 2)

	Score	1	2	3	4	5	6	Row Total
		Scores Assigned by Rater 2						
	6	0	0	0	1	1	3	5
Scores	5	0	0	1	2	2	3	8
Assigned	4	0	1	2	4	4	1	12
by	3	0	2	5	3	2	0	12
Rater 1	2	1	7	1	0	0	0	9
	1	3	1	0	0	0	0	4
Column Total		4	11	9	10	9	7	50

reduce the influence of raters is to have each performance independently scored by two or more raters and use the average rating. Double scoring is a common practice in situations where judgmentally scored performances have important consequences for individuals.

The percentage of agreement and correlation values indicate the degree to which the relative ordering of responses is consistent from one rater to another. It is possible, however, to have a high correlation, and even a high percentage of agreement, while still having important differences in the overall leniency of the two raters. Where there are disagreements, there is a strong tendency for one rater to consistently give a higher score than the other. Comparisons of the average score assigned by each rater provides a check on differences in leniency. For the example in Table 4.2 the average ratings assigned to the essays are reasonably similar (3.52 for Rater 1 and 3.60 for Rater 2). Thus, there is not cause for concern in this case. The results shown in Table 4.3 (which might have been obtained if Rater 1 had been paired with Rater 3 instead of Rater 2), on the other hand, clearly indicate that Rater 3 is much more lenient than Rater 1, despite the fact that the percentage of exact agreement and the percentage of agreement within one point are the same (48 percent and 88 percent, respectively) for the data in Table 4.3 as they are for the data in Table 4.2.

The evaluation of inter-rater consistency is important to ensure that some students do not receive high scores as the result of rater leniency while others receive low scores because their work was scored by a stringent rater. Average scores assigned by raters to a common set of responses, percentage of agreement, and the correlation between scores assigned by rater pairs all contribute to an overall evaluation of the degree of consistency among different raters.

Achieving a high degree of inter-rater consistency requires the development of consensus among raters regarding the types of performances that are valued. Agreed-upon scoring rubrics and training of raters to use those rubrics with examples of student work are generally required to achieve acceptable levels of inter-rater consistency and ensure that differences in the stringency of rating from one rater to another do not place some students at a disadvantage.

TABLE 4.3
Scores assigned to fifty essays
by two independent raters
(Raters 1 and 3)

		Scores Assigned by Rater 3						
	Score	1	2	3	4	5	6	Row Total
	6	0	0	0	0	0	5	5
Scores	5	0	0	0	0	2	6	8
Assigned	4	0	0	0	3	5	4	12
by	3	0	0	6	4	2	0	12
Rater 1	2	0	5	4	0	0	0	9
	1	3	1	0	0	0	0	4
	Column Total	3	6	10	7	9	15	50

Achieving inter-rater consistency is important for judgmentally scored tasks, but it does not say anything about other types of consistency. For example, a high degree of inter-rater consistency does not guarantee consistency of ratings across tasks. There are other methods of evaluating various types of consistency or generalizability (e.g., across raters, across tasks and over time) simultaneously. Generalizability theory provides the foundation for those methods. That theory is beyond the scope of this book, but a good introduction is provided by Shavelson and Webb (1991).

Comparing Methods

As stated earlier, each of the methods of estimating reliability provides different information concerning the consistency of test results. A summary of this information is presented in Table 4.4, which shows that most methods are concerned with only one or two types of consistency. As its name suggests, the inter-rater method only evaluates the degree of consistency of scores assigned to the same performances by different raters. The test–retest method, without a time interval, takes into account only the consistency of the assessment procedure and the short-term constancy of the response. If a time interval is introduced between the assessments, the constancy of the characteristics of the student from day to day also will be included. However, neither of the test–retest procedures provides information concerning the consistency of results over different samples of tasks, because both sets of scores are based on the same assessment.

The equivalent forms method without a time interval, the split-half method, and the Kuder–Richardson or Coefficient *Alpha* method all take into account the consistency of assessment procedures and the consistency of results over different samples of tasks. Only the equivalent forms method with an intervening time period between tests takes into account all three types of consistency, which is the reason that this measure of stability and equivalence is generally regarded as the most useful estimate of reliability.

TABLE 4.4
Type of consistency indicated by each of the methods for estimating reliability

Method of Estimating Reliability	Type of Consistency			
	Consistency of Testing Procedure	Constancy of Student Characteristics	Consistency over Different Samples of Items	Consistency of Judgmental Scores
Test–retest (immediate)	X	*		
Test–retest (time interval)	X	X		
Equivalent forms (immediate)	X	*	X	
Equivalent forms (time interval)	X	X	X	
Split-half	X		X	
Kuder–Richardson (Coefficient *Alpha*)	X		X	
Inter-rater				X

*Short-term constancy of response is reflected in immediate retest, but day-to-day stability is not shown.

STANDARD ERROR OF MEASUREMENT

If it were possible to assess a student over and over on the same assessment procedures, we would find that the scores would vary somewhat. The amount of variation in the scores would be directly related to the reliability of the assessment procedures. Low reliability would be indicated by large variations in the student's assessment results, and high reliability would be indicated by little variation from one assessment to another. Although it is impractical to administer the same set of assessment tasks many times to the same students, it is possible to estimate the amount of variation to be expected in the scores. This estimate is called the standard error of measurement.

Test manuals for published tests usually list the standard errors of measurement. Thus, all we need to do is take the standard error into account when interpreting individual test scores. For example, let us assume that we have just administered a standardized achievement test battery to a class of fourth-grade students and the results indicate that Mary Smith has a grade equivalent (GE) score of 5.2 on the mathematics test. A grade-equivalent score indicates the grade level that the average student has who has the same number of correct answers as Mary. (See Chapter 14 for a discussion of grade-equivalent scores.) We find in the test manual that the standard error of measurement on the mathematics test is .4. What does the .4 tell us about Mary's mathematics achievement? In general, it indicates the amount of error that must be considered in interpreting Mary's score. More specifically, it provides the limits within which we can reasonably expect to find Mary's true mathematics achievement score. A true score is one that would be obtained if the test were perfectly reliable. If Mary Smith were tested repeatedly under identical conditions and there were no memory, learning, practice, or fatigue effects, 68 percent of her obtained scores would fall within one standard error (.4) of her true score, 95 percent would fall within two standard errors (.8), and 99.7 percent would fall within three standard errors (1.2) (see "Hypothetical Distribution Illustrating the Standard Error of Measurement"). For practical purposes, these limits may be applied to Mary's obtained score of 5.2 to give us the ranges shown in Table 4.5, within which we could be reasonably sure to find her true score.

Although Mary's score of 5.2 indicates that she did better on this particular test than the typical fourth-grade student, the range of scores shows that we cannot be certain that her true score is above that of the average fourth-grade student. One can be quite confident that her true score is somewhere between 4.4 and 6.0 because 95 percent of the observed scores fall within two standard errors of the true score. In interpreting individual test scores, however, the use of one standard error of measurement is more common. Thus, a range of 4.8 to 5.6 typically would be used to describe Mary's test performance.

The standard error of measurement shows why a test score should be interpreted as a band of scores (called a confidence band) rather than as a specific score. With a large standard error, the band of scores is wide, and we have less confidence in our obtained score. If the standard error is small, the band of scores will be narrow and we will have greater confidence that our obtained score is a dependable measure of the characteristic. Viewing an assessment score as a band of scores makes it possible to interpret and use assessment results more intelligently. Apparent differences in scores, between individuals and for the same individual over a period of time, often disappear when the standard error of measurement is considered. A teacher or counselor who is aware of the standard error of measurement realizes that it is impossible to be dogmatic in interpreting minor differences in assessment scores.

The relationship between the reliability coefficient and the standard error of measurement can be seen in Table 4.6, which presents the standard errors of measurement for various reliability coefficients and standard deviations. Notice that as the reliability coefficient increases for any given standard deviation, the standard error of measurement decreases. Thus, large reliability coefficients are associated with small measurement errors in specific test scores, and small reliability coefficients are associated with large measurement errors.

TABLE 4.5
Standard error score bands

Number of Standard Errors	Score Units to Apply to Mary's GE Score of 5.2	Range of Scores
1	0.4	4.8–5.6
2	0.8	4.4–6.0
3	1.2	4.0–6.4

Hypothetical Distribution Illustrating the Standard Error of Measurement

Theoretical Explanation of the Standard Error of Measurement

1. It is assumed that each person has a *true score* on a particular test, a hypothetical value representing a score free of error (true score = 95 on the diagram).

2. If a person could be tested repeatedly (without memory, practice effects, or other changes), the average of the obtained scores would approximate the *true score,* and the obtained scores would *be approximately normally distributed* around the true score (see diagram).

3. From what is known about the normal distribution curve, approximately 68 percent of the obtained scores would fall within one standard error of measurement of the person's true score; approximately 95 percent of the scores would fall within two standard errors; and approximately 99.7 percent of the scores would fall within three standard errors (see "The Normal Curve and the Standard Deviation Unit" in Chapter 17. The standard error of measurement is the standard deviation of the errors of measurement).

4. Although *the true score can never be known,* the standard error of measurement can be applied to a person's obtained score to set "reasonable limits" for locating the true score (e.g., an obtained score of 97 ± 5 = 92 to 102).

5. These "reasonable limits" provide *confidence bands* for interpreting an obtained score. When the standard error of measurement is small, the confidence band is narrow (indicating high reliability), and thus we have greater confidence that the obtained score is near the true score.

TABLE 4.6
Standard errors of measurement
for given values of reliability
coefficient and standard
deviation

	Reliability Coefficient					
SD	.95	.90	.85	.80	.75	.70
30	6.7	9.5	11.6	13.4	15.0	16.4
28	6.3	8.9	10.8	12.5	14.0	15.3
26	5.8	8.2	10.1	11.6	13.0	14.2
24	5.4	7.6	9.3	10.7	12.0	13.1
22	4.9	7.0	8.5	9.8	11.0	12.0
20	4.5	6.3	7.7	8.9	10.0	11.0
18	4.0	5.7	7.0	8.0	9.0	9.9
16	3.6	5.1	6.2	7.2	8.0	8.8
14	3.1	4.4	5.4	6.3	7.0	7.7
12	2.7	3.8	4.6	5.4	6.0	6.6
10	2.2	3.2	3.9	4.5	5.0	5.5
8	1.8	2.5	3.1	3.6	4.0	4.4
6	1.3	1.9	2.3	2.7	3.0	3.3
4	.9	1.3	1.5	1.8	2.0	2.2
2	.4	.6	.8	.9	1.0	1.1

Note: This table is based on the formula SE (Measurement) $= SD\sqrt{1-r}$, where SD is the standard deviation of the assessment scores and r is the reliability coefficient. Reprinted from J. E. Doppelt, *How Accurate Is a Test Score?* Test Service Bulletin, no. 50 (New York: Psychological Corporation).

If the reliability of an assessment procedure and the standard deviation of the assessment scores are known, Table 4.6 can be used to estimate the standard error. In fact, this is the purpose for which the table was developed. All one needs to do to obtain an estimate of the standard error for a given assessment is to enter the column nearest to the reliability coefficient and the row nearest to the standard deviation and read the standard error of measurement from the cell for that row and column. For example, a reliability coefficient of .90 and a standard deviation of 16 would result in a standard error of 5.1, which is obtained by going down the .90 column to the row in which the standard deviation is 16. (See the accompanying "Guidelines" box.)

There are several precautions to keep in mind when using Table 4.6 to estimate the standard error of measurement. First, the reliability coefficient and standard deviation must be based on the same group of persons. Second, entering the table with the reliability coefficient and standard deviation nearest to those in the manual gives only an approximation of the standard error of measurement. Third, the table does not take into account the fact that the standard error of measurement varies slightly at different score levels. Within these limitations, however, Table 4.6 provides a simple and quick method for estimating the standard error of measurement and yields an approximation accurate enough for most practical applications of test results.

So far we have discussed the standard error of measurement and its uses as if the magnitude of measurement errors were always the same regardless of the level of a person's score. Although this is common practice and works well most of the time, the assumption that the standard error of measurement is a constant throughout the score range does not hold up very well for extremely high or extremely low

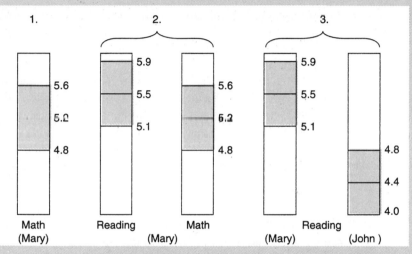

GUIDELINES

Practical Applications of the Standard Error of Measurement in Test Interpretation

A confidence band one standard error above and below the obtained score is commonly used in test profiles to aid in interpreting individual scores and in judging whether differences between scores are likely to be "real differences" or differences caused by chance.

1. *Interpreting an individual score.* The confidence band indicates "reasonable limits" within which to locate the true score (Mary's math score probably falls somewhere between 4.8 and 5.6).

2. *Interpreting the difference between two scores from a test battery.* When the ends of the bands overlap, there is no "real difference" between scores (Mary's scores in reading and math show no meaningful difference).

3. *Interpreting the difference between the scores of two individuals on the same test.* When ends of bands do not overlap, there is a "real difference" between scores (Mary's reading score is higher than John's).

scores. For example, if a multiple-choice test is much too difficult for a student, that student's score is apt to be based almost entirely on the luck he or she has in guessing the correct answers. Likewise, an assessment requiring extended responses to problems that are far too difficult is apt to result in blank or off-task responses. In either case, the standard error for that student will be considerably larger than the standard error for students for whom the test difficulty is more appropriate.

Because the standard errors of measurement tend to be larger for very high and very low scores, some test publishers report standard errors of measurement separately for different ranges of scores. The procedures for estimating standard errors of measurement for different score levels are more complicated, but really no different, except that the numerical value of the standard error used would depend on an individual's test score. This additional information makes it possible to have more accurate score bands for people with extreme scores. Suppose, for example, that for a fourth-grade reading comprehension test, the test manual reported standard errors of measurement for various ranges of GE scores as shown in Table 4.7.

From these results we would recognize that scores indicating performance similar to that of the typical second- or seventh-grade student would be subject to much larger errors of measurement than scores similar to the typical fourth-grade student for whom the test was designed. The wide band for a student with a score of, say, 7.1 (6.3 to 7.9) would warn us that, although the student's performance is clearly well above that of the typical fourth-grade student, we cannot be very precise about how much higher.

The different standard errors by score level also help in selecting the level of a standardized test that will be most appropriate for a particular group of students. For example, if we know that most of the fourth-grade students in a school have scored far below the national average in earlier grades, we would know that the fourth-grade level of the test is apt to be too difficult and will result in large standard errors of measurement. In this case, we could expect that using the level of the test designed for third-grade students would result in scores with smaller standard errors of measurement and, thus, provide more dependable results.

The standard error of measurement has two special advantages as a means of estimating reliability. First, the estimates are in the same units as the assessment scores. This makes it possible to indicate directly the margin of error to allow for when interpreting individual scores. Second, the standard error is likely to remain fairly constant from group to group. This is not true of the reliability coefficient, which is highly dependent on the spread of scores in the group assessed. Because the groups on which reliabilities are reported in test manuals will always differ somewhat from the group to be given the test, the greater constancy of the standard error of measurement has obvious practical value. The main difficulty encountered with the standard error occurs when we want to compare two assessments that use different types of scores. Here the reliability coefficient is the only suitable measure.

TABLE 4.7
Standard errors of measurement by score range

Grade Equivalent Score Range	Standard Error of Measurement
7.0 to 7.9	0.8
6.0 to 6.9	0.6
5.0 to 5.9	0.4
4.0 to 4.9	0.4
3.0 to 3.9	0.5
2.0 to 2.9	0.7

FACTORS INFLUENCING RELIABILITY MEASURES

A number of factors have been shown to affect the conventional measures of reliability. If sound conclusions are to be drawn, these factors must be considered when interpreting reliability coefficients. We have already seen, for example, that speeded tests will produce a spuriously large reliability coefficient with the internal consistency methods of estimating reliability. We have also noted that test–retest reliability coefficients are influenced by the interval between assessments, with shorter intervals resulting in larger reliability coefficients. Although we might want to favor the assessment procedure with the largest reliability coefficient, we would not do so if we recognized that the reported coefficient was inflated by factors irrelevant to the consistency of the measurement procedure. Similarly, we might discount the difference between reliability coefficients reported for two different assessments if the conditions under which they were obtained favored the test with the largest reliability coefficient.

Consideration of the factors influencing reliability not only will help us interpret more wisely the reliability coefficients of standardized tests but also should aid us in constructing more reliable classroom assessments. Although teachers seldom find it profitable to calculate reliability coefficients for the assessments they construct, they should be cognizant of the factors influencing reliability to maximize the reliability of their own classroom assessments.

Number of Assessment Tasks

In general, the larger the number of tasks on an assessment, the higher its reliability will be. This is because a longer assessment will provide a more adequate sample of the behavior being measured, and the scores are apt to be less distorted by chance factors such as special familiarity with a given task or lack of understanding of what is expected on a given task. Suppose that to measure spelling ability, we asked students to spell one word. The results would be patently unreliable. Students who were able to spell the word would be perfect spellers, and students who could not would be complete failures. If we happened to select a difficult word, most students would fail; if the word was an easy one, most students would appear to be perfect spellers. The fact that one word provides an unreliable estimate of a student's spelling ability is obvious. It should be equally apparent that as we add more spelling words to the list, we come closer and closer to a good estimate of each child's spelling ability. Scores based on a large number of spelling words thus are more apt to reflect real differences in spelling ability and therefore to be more stable. By increasing the size of the sample of spelling behavior, therefore, we increase the consistency of our measurement. A longer test also tends to lessen the influence of chance factors such as guessing. For example, on a ten-item true-and-false test, a student might know seven of the items and guess at the other three. A correct guess on all three items would result in a perfect score, and incorrect guesses on all three items would result in only seven correct. This represents a considerable variation in the test score resulting from guessing alone. However, if this same student were taking a test with 100 true-and-false items, the correct guesses would tend to be canceled by incorrect guesses, and the score would be a more dependable indication of actual knowledge.

The fact that a longer assessment tends to provide more reliable results was implied earlier, in our discussion of the split-half method. You will recall that when scores from two halves of a test correlated .60, the Spearman–Brown formula estimated the reliability of the scores for the full-length assessment to be .75. This is equivalent to estimating the increase in reliability to be expected when the number of assessment tasks is doubled.

The relationship of length to reliability poses a problem for assessments that require extended periods of time to be completed, because the critical feature in the length–reliability relationship is the number of tasks, not the amount of assessment time. If each task requires a full class period or even longer to administer, then it is obvious that increases in the number of tasks have a high cost in terms of student time. Nonetheless, if consistency of performance across different tasks intended to assess a common domain of achievement is low, then multiple tasks will be required to achieve adequate levels of reliability.

There are at least two ways in which the extended time periods required for assessment results to achieve adequate reliability may be justified. First, greater time and expense may be justified when the assessment has major consequences for the individuals being assessed or for society (e.g., the licensing of physicians). Second, the devotion of extended periods of time to assessments is justified when the assessments are themselves considered good instructional activities that contribute not only to the measurement of achievement, but directly to student learning. The latter justification is likely to be more relevant for assessments in elementary and secondary schools than the former one.

There is one important reservation in evaluating the influence of the number of tasks on the reliability of the scores: the statements we have been making assume that the assessment will be lengthened by adding tasks of the same quality as those that are already part of the assessment. Adding ten spelling words that are so easy that everyone will get them correct or adding ten spelling words that are so difficult that no one will get them correct will not increase the reliability of the scores on a spelling test. In fact, there would be no influence on the reliability coefficient, because such additions would not influence the standing of students relative to others in the group.

In constructing classroom tests or assigning assessment tasks, it is important to keep in mind the influence of the number of questions or tasks on reliability. If only a small number of questions or tasks can be used (because of time limits, the students' age, or the extended time required to complete each task), then more frequent assessment may be used to obtain a dependable measure of achievement.

In using standardized tests, we should be wary of part-scores based on relatively few items. Such scores are usually low in reliability and of little practical value. Before using such scores, the test manual should be checked for their reported reliabilities. If these are not reported or are very low, the part-scores should be ignored, and only the total test score should be used.

Spread of Scores

As noted earlier, reliability coefficients are directly influenced by the spread of scores in the group assessed. Other things being equal, the larger the spread of scores, the higher the estimate of reliability will be. Because larger reliability coefficients result when individuals stay in the same relative position in a group from one assessment to another, it naturally follows that anything that reduces the possibility of shifting positions in the group also contributes to larger reliability coefficients. In this case, greater differences between the scores of individuals reduce the possibility of shifting positions. Stated another way, errors of measurement have less influence on the relative position of individuals when the differences among group members are large; that is, when there is a wide spread of scores.

This can be easily illustrated without recourse to statistics. Compare the two sets of scores shown in Table 4.8 in terms of the probability that the individuals will remain in the same relative position on a second administration of the assessment. Even a cursory inspection of these scores will show that the persons in Group B are more likely to shift positions on a second administration of the assessment. With a spread of only 10 points from the top score to the bottom score, radical shifts in position can result from changes of just a few points in the scores.

However, in Group A the scores of individuals could vary by several points on a second administration of the assessment, with very little shifting in the relative positions of the group members. The large spread of test scores in Group A makes shifts in relative position unlikely and thus gives us greater confidence that these differences among group members are real.

Objectivity

The objectivity of an assessment refers to the degree to which equally competent scorers obtain the same results. Most standardized tests of aptitude and achievement are high in objectivity. The test items are of the objective type (e.g., multiple choice), and the resulting scores are not influenced by the scorers'

TABLE 4.8
Illustration of score spread

Group A	Group B
95	95
90	94
86	93
82	93
76	92
65	91
60	89
56	88
53	86
47	85

judgment or opinion. In fact, such tests are usually constructed so that they can be accurately scored by trained clerks and scoring machines. When such highly objective procedures are used, the reliability of the test results is not affected by the scoring procedures.

For classroom assessments constructed by teachers or performance-based assessments mandated by states and districts, however, objectivity may play an important role in obtaining reliable measures of achievement. In essay testing and assessments requiring judgmental scoring, the results depend, to some extent, on the person doing the scoring. Different persons get different results, and even the same person may get different results at different times. Such inconsistency in scoring has an adverse effect on the reliability of the measures obtained, for the test scores now reflect the opinions and biases of the scorer as well as differences among students in the characteristic being measured.

The solution is *not* to use only objective tests, or to abandon all methods of assessment that require judgmental scoring. This would have an adverse effect on validity and, as noted earlier, validity is the most important quality of assessment results. A better solution is to select assessment procedures most appropriate for the learning goals being assessed and then make the assessment procedure as objective as possible. In the use of essay tests, for example, objectivity can be increased by careful phrasing of the questions and by a standard set of rules for scoring. Similarly, the objectivity in scoring of science exhibitions can be increased by establishing clear scoring criteria and carefully training raters. Such increased objectivity will contribute to greater reliability without sacrificing validity.

Methods of Estimating Reliability

When examining the reliability coefficients of standardized tests, it is important to consider the methods used to obtain the reliability estimates. In general, the size of the reliability coefficient is related to the method of estimating reliability.

1. Test–retest method	May be larger than with the split-half method if the time interval is short. Coefficients become smaller as the time interval between tests is increased.
2. Equivalent forms method (without time interval)	Coefficients tend to be lower than with the split-half method or the test–retest method using a short time interval.
3. Equivalent forms method (with time interval)	Coefficients become smaller as the time interval between tests is increased.
4. Split-half method (e.g., odd-even)	Provides an indication of the internal consistency of a test. Spuriously high estimates are produced for speeded tests.
5. Kuder–Richardson method (Coefficient *Alpha*)	Typically provides reliability estimates that are smaller than those obtained by the split-half method. These estimates are also inflated by speed.

6. Inter-rater method

Provides an indication of the degree to which similar scores are obtained regardless of who does the rating. Inter-rater consistency can be increased by using well-defined scoring rules and by careful training of raters.

The variation in the size of the reliability coefficient resulting from the method of estimating reliability is directly attributable to the type of consistency included in each method. Recall that the equivalent forms method with an intervening time interval took into account the most sources of variation in the test scores and consequently is a more rigorous method of estimating reliability than test–retest, the use of equivalent forms without an intervening time interval, or internal consistency methods. Thus, smaller reliability coefficients can be expected with this method, and it is unfair to compare such reliability coefficients with those obtained by less stringent methods.

At the other extreme, the larger reliability coefficients typically reported for the split-half method must be accepted cautiously. If speed is an important factor in the testing, split-half reliability coefficients should be disregarded entirely, and other evidence of reliability should be sought.

RELIABILITY OF ASSESSMENTS EVALUATED IN TERMS OF A FIXED PERFORMANCE STANDARD

There are a variety of situations where the primary goal of an assessment is to determine whether performance meets a preestablished standard. Criterion-referenced mastery tests are an example. Typically, such tests are designed to provide the basis for a decision regarding the mastery of a set of essential skills and therefore are frequently pitched at a relatively low level of performance. Comparing performance to a fixed standard rather than to the performance of other students, however, need not limit assessment to the testing of low-level skills and minimum levels of performance. Indeed, in recent years the emphasis has been on establishing high standards of performance for all students.

Regardless of the level of the standard, when we use assessments for the purpose of deciding whether performance meets an established standard, our desire for consistency of measurement is similar to that for norm-referenced tests. Thus, we would like an individual's performance to be consistent from (1) one rater to another; (2) one task to another, when all tasks measure the same learning outcome (internal consistency); (3) one time to another, when the learning outcomes are expected to have a reasonable degree of constancy (stability); and (4) one form of an assessment to another, when the forms are intended to measure the same sample of learning tasks (equivalence). However, the focus is more often on whether the performance meets the standard than on the actual score.

Also, because of the specificity of mastery assessments and their close tie to instruction, they may have a narrower range of scores than is typically produced by norm-referenced measures. The focus on mastery decisions and the smaller variability in scores has led to different approaches in evaluating the reliability of mastery assessments.

Given the emphasis on whether a performance meets or fails to meet a standard, the most natural approach to reliability is to evaluate the consistency with which students are classified as performing above or below the standard. This type of reliability can be readily determined by computing the percentage of consistent decisions as the result of having performances evaluated by different raters or over two equivalent forms of an assessment. Although a number of more complicated approaches have been suggested, the simple calculation of the percentage of people who are consistently classified is the approach that is encouraged by the *Standards* (American Psychological Association, 1985) for tests that are used to make dichotomous decisions with regard to a standard. With only two categories, however, it becomes more important to take into account the level of agreement that would be expected by chance.

Let's assume that we have given two alternate assessments, each consisting of 10 open-ended mathematics tasks, to a classroom group of 30 students. Each task is scored on a four-point scale (ranging from 0 for no response or a response that is off-task to 3 for a solid solution to the problem with adequate justification). Thus, the range of possible scores on each assessment is from 0 to 30 for each alternate assessment. To meet the standard, a student must obtain a score of at least 20. All students obtaining a score of 20 or higher on both assessments are consistently classified as meeting the standard. All students obtaining a score of 19 or lower on both assessments are consistently classified as failing to meet the standard. The remaining students are classified as meeting the standard on one assessment and failing to meet it on the other one. If this latter group of reversals is relatively large, our assessment will obviously be inconsistent in classifying students. The data for such an analysis can be summarized in a two-by-two table like that in Figure 4.4.

By using the information in Figure 4.4, we can compute a percentage of consistency, using the following formula:

$$\% \text{ Consistency Times } 100 = \frac{\text{Meets Standard (both forms)} + \text{Fails to Meet Standard (both forms)}}{\text{Total number in group}}$$

$$\% \text{ Consistency} = \frac{20 + 7}{30} \text{ Times } 100 = 90\%$$

FIGURE 4.4
A classification of thirty students with respect to a fixed performance standard

| | | Assessment B | |
		Fails to meet standard	Meets standard
Assessment A	Meets standard	2	20
	Fails to meet standard	7	1

The 90 percent agreement should be compared to the agreement that would be expected by chance. The latter figure is computed by completing the following steps. (1) Multiply the proportion of students who meet the standard on Assessment A (22 out of 30 = .733) by the proportion of students who meet it on Assessment B (21 out of 30 = .700). This yields (.733 × .700 = .513). (2) Multiply the proportion of students who fail to meet the standard on Assessment A (8 out of 30 = .267) times the corresponding figure for Assessment B (9 out of 30 = .300). This yields (.267 × .300 = .080). (3) Sum the results of Steps 1 and 2, (.513 + .080 = .593). (4) Convert the result of Step 3 to a percentage by multiplying it by 100. This yields 59.3 percent, the level of agreement expected by chance given the passing rates on the two assessments. The observed percent agreement of 90 percent compares favorably to that expected by chance.

Although the percentage of agreement is conceptually simple and easy to compute, it does require two versions of the assessment. This is not a serious shortcoming, however, because assessments designed to determine whether students meet a standard should allow students who fail to meet the standard an opportunity to try again on an alternate set of assessment tasks. It is seldom wise to permit students who do not meet the performance standard on the first attempt to be reassessed with the identical set of tasks. Procedures have been developed to estimate decision consistency based on the administration of a single test form or set of assessment tasks; however, those procedures are relatively complex and are beyond the scope of this textbook (Subkoviak, 1984). Suffice it to say that they are intended to provide approximations to the percentage of agreement based on equivalent forms from data available from the administration of a single set of assessment tasks.

How High Should Reliability Be?

The degree of reliability we demand in our educational assessments depends largely on the decision to be made. If we are going to use assessment results to decide whether to review certain areas of subject matter, we may be willing to use a teacher-made assessment of relatively low reliability. Our decision will be based on the scores of the total group, and variation in individual scores will not distort our decision too much. Even if we do err in our decision, no catastrophe will result. The worst that can happen is that the students will get an unnecessary review of material or they will be deprived of a review that may be beneficial to them. On the other hand, if we are going to use an assessment to decide whether to award a high school diploma or a college scholarship, we should demand the most reliable measurement available. Such decisions have important consequences for the lives of the individuals involved.

It is not only a decision's importance that matters but also whether it is possible to confirm or reverse the judgment at a later time. Decision making in education is seldom a single, final act. It tends to be sequential, starting with rather crude judgments and proceeding through a series of more refined judgments. In the early stages of decision making, low reliability might be quite tolerable because assessment results are used primarily as a guide to further information gathering. For example, on the basis of classroom assessments of questionable reliability, we might decide that some of our students are having such serious learning difficulties that they need special help. This decision can be confirmed or refuted by further assessment with more dependable measures. Opportunities for confirmation and reversal of judgments without serious consequences are almost always present in the early stages of educational decision making. Thus, the important thing when reliability is low or unknown is *not* to treat the scores as if they were highly accurate. Make tentative judgments, seek confirming data, and be willing to reverse decisions when wrong.

Thus, when we ask how high reliability should be, several considerations must be taken into account. How important is the decision? Is it one that can be confirmed or reversed at a later time? How far-reaching are the consequences of the action taken? For irreversible decisions that are apt to have great influence on the lives of individual students, we should make stringent demands on the reliability of the assessments we use. For lesser decisions, especially for those that can be later confirmed or reversed without serious consequences, we should be willing to settle for less reliable measures. Teacher-made tests commonly have reliabilities between .60 and .85, but they are useful for the types of instructional decisions typically made by teachers. Thus, the degree of reliability required depends largely on how confident we need to be about the decision being made. Greater confidence requires higher reliability (see "Reliability Demands and Nature of the Decision").

USABILITY

In selecting assessment procedures, practical considerations cannot be neglected. Assessments are usually administered and interpreted by teachers with only a minimum of training in measurement. The time available for assessment is almost always limited, because assessment is in constant competition with other important activities for time in the school schedule. Likewise, the cost of assessment, although a minor consideration, is as carefully scrutinized by budget-conscious administrators as are other expenditures of school funds. These and other factors pertinent to the usability of assessment procedures must be taken into account when selecting assessment procedures. Such practical considerations are especially important when selecting published tests.

Ease of Administration

If the assessments are to be administered by teachers or others with limited training, ease of administration is an especially important quality to seek. For this purpose, directions should be simple and clear, subtests should be relatively few, and the time needed for administration of the assessment should not be too great. Administering a test with complicated directions and a number of subtests lasting but a few minutes each is a taxing chore for even an experienced examiner. For a person with little training and experience, such a situation is fraught with possibilities for errors in giving directions, timing, and other aspects of administration that are likely to affect

GUIDELINES

Reliability Demands and Nature of the Decision

High reliability is demanded when the

❑ Decision is important.
❑ Decision is final.
❑ Decision is irreversible.
❑ Decision is unconfirmable.
❑ Decision concerns individuals.
❑ Decision has lasting consequences.

> *Example:*   Select or reject college applicants.

Low reliability is tolerable when the

❑ Decision is of minor importance.
❑ Decision making is in early stages.
❑ Decision is reversible.
❑ Decision is confirmable by other data.
❑ Decision concerns groups.
❑ Decision has temporary effects.

> *Example:*   Whether to review a classroom lesson.

results. Such errors of administration can have, of course, an adverse effect on the validity and reliability of the results.

Time Required for Administration

With time for assessment at a premium, we always favor the shorter assessment, other things being equal. But in this case, other things are seldom equal, because reliability is directly related to the length of an assessment. If we attempt to cut down too much on the time allotted to assessment, we may reduce drastically the reliability of our scores. For example, tests designed to fit a normal class period usually produce total test scores of satisfactory reliability, but their part-scores, obtained from the subtests, tend to be unreliable. If we want reliable measures in the areas covered by the subtests, we need to increase our testing time in each area. On the other hand, if we want a general measure in some area, such as verbal aptitude, we can obtain reliable results in 30 or 40 minutes, and there is little advantage in extending the testing time. A safe procedure is to allot as much time as is necessary to obtain valid and reliable results and no more. Between 20 and 60 minutes of testing time for each individual score yielded by a published test is probably a fairly good guide.

Ease of Interpretation and Application

In the final analysis, the success or failure of an assessment program is determined by the use made of the assessment results. If they are interpreted correctly and applied effectively, they will contribute to more intelligent educational decisions. On the other hand, if the assessment results are misinterpreted, misapplied, or not applied at all, they will be of little value and may actually be harmful to some individual or group.

Information concerning the interpretation and use of results of published test results is usually obtained directly from the test manual or related guides. Attention should be directed toward the clarity of score reports, the quality and relevance of norms, and the comprehensiveness of the suggestions for applying the results to educational problems. When the test results are to be presented to students or parents, ease of interpretation and application are especially important.

Availability of Equivalent or Comparable Forms

For many educational purposes, equivalent forms of the same test are often desirable. Equivalent forms of a test measure the same aspect of behavior by using test items that are alike in content, level of difficulty, and other characteristics. Thus, one form of the test can substitute for the other, making it possible to test students twice in rather close succession without their answers on the first testing influencing their performance on the second testing. The advantage of equivalent forms is readily seen in mastery testing, when we want to eliminate the factor of memory while retesting students on the same domain of achievement. Equivalent forms of a test also may be used to verify a questionable test score. For example, a teacher may feel that a scholastic aptitude or achievement test score is spuriously low for a given student and may easily check this by administering an equivalent form of the test.

Many tests also provide comparable forms. Published achievement tests, for example, are commonly arranged in a series that covers different grade levels. Although the content and level of difficulty vary, the tests at the different levels are made comparable by means of a common score scale. Thus, it is possible to compare measurements in Grade 4 with measurements in Grade 6 on a more advanced form of the test. Comparable forms are especially useful in measuring development in the basic skills.

Cost of Testing

The factor of cost has been left to the last because it is relatively unimportant in selecting published tests. The reason for discussing it at all is that it is sometimes given far more weight than it deserves. Testing is relatively inexpensive, and cost should not be a major consideration. In large-scale testing programs where small savings per student add up, using separate answer sheets, machine scoring, and reusable booklets will reduce the cost appreciably. But to select one test instead of another because the test booklets are a few cents cheaper is false economy. After all, validity and reliability are the important characteristics to look for, and a test lacking these qualities is too expensive at any price. The contribution that valid and reliable test scores can make to educational decisions means that such tests are always economical in the long run.

SUMMARY

Next to validity, reliability is the most important quality to seek in assessment results. Reliability refers to the consistency of scores and other assessment results from one assessment to another. In interpreting and using reliability information, it is important to remember that reliability estimates refer to the results of measurement, that different ways of estimating reliability indicate different types of consistency, that a reliable measure is not necessarily valid, and that reliability is strictly a statistical concept. Reliability estimates are typically reported in terms of a reliability coefficient or the standard error of measurement.

Reliability coefficients are determined by several different methods, and each provides a different measure of consistency. The inter-rater method requires that the same set of student performances be scored by two or more raters, and it provides an indication of the consistency of scoring across raters. The test–retest method involves giving the same assessment twice to the same group with an intervening interval, and the resulting coefficient provides a measure of stability. The length of the interval between assessments is determined largely by the use to be made of the results. We are primarily interested in reliability coefficients based on intervals comparable to the periods of time between when the assessment is given and when the scores will be used and interpreted. The equivalent forms method involves giving two forms of an assessment to the same group in close succession or with an intervening time interval. The first assessment yields a measure of equivalence and the second a measure of stability and equivalence. The equivalent forms method provides a rigorous evaluation of reliability because it includes multiple sources of variation in the assessment results. Reliability also can be estimated from a single administration of an assessment, either by correlating the scores on two halves of the assessment or by applying the Kuder–Richardson or Coefficient *Alpha* formulas. Both methods provide a measure of internal consistency and are easy to apply. However, they are not applicable to speeded tests and provide no information concerning the stability of assessment scores from day to day.

The standard error of measurement indicates reliability in terms of the amount of variation to be expected in individual scores. It can be computed from the reliability coefficient and the standard deviation, but it is frequently reported directly in test manuals. The standard error is especially useful in interpreting test scores, because it indicates the band of error (called a confidence band) surrounding each score. It also has the advantage of remaining fairly constant from one group to another.

Reliability estimates may vary in accordance with the length of the assessment, the spread of scores in the group assessed, the difficulty of the assessment tasks, the objectivity of the scoring, and the method of estimating reliability. These factors should be taken into account when appraising reliability information. The degree and type of reliability to be sought in a particular instance depend mainly on the decision being made. For tentative reversible decisions, low reliability may be tolerable. But for final irreversible decisions, we should make stringent demands on the reliability of our measures.

Conventional measures of reliability depend on scores throughout the range and are influenced by the variability among scores. In assessments designed to assess performance in terms of a fixed standard, the classification of students as meeting or failing to meet the standard is the primary concern. Hence, the consistency of classifications for equivalent assessments is most relevant, and the simple percentage of times that consistent decisions are made provides the information needed to evaluate reliability of the decision.

In addition to validity and reliability, it is also important to consider the usability of tests and other assessment procedures, including such practical features as ease of administration, time required, ease of interpretation and application, availability of equivalent or comparable forms, and cost of testing.

LEARNING EXERCISES

1. Define reliability, and describe its importance in assessment.

2. Briefly describe the methods of estimating reliability. Can one method substitute for another? Why or why not?

3. Which method of estimating reliability provides the most useful information for each of the following? Why?
   a. Selecting a scholastic aptitude test for predicting future achievement.
   b. Reassessing students to determine standing relative to a fixed performance standard.
   c. Determining whether a test measures a homogeneous characteristic.
   d. Determining the degree to which essay scores obtained from different raters are affected by differences in the stringency of raters.

4. What effect would the following most likely have on reliability?
   a. Increasing the number of tasks in an assessment.
   b. Removing ambiguous tasks.
   c. Changing from a multiple-choice test to an essay test covering the same material.

5. For which purpose is each of the following most useful? Why?
   a. Reliability coefficient.
   b. Standard error of measurement.

6. Using Table 4.6, determine the standard error of measurement for a set of scores with a standard deviation of 16 and a reliability coefficient of .85.

7. Study the reliability sections of test manuals for a few standardized achievement tests. What types of reliability data are reported? Are these types of data valuable in deciding whether to choose the tests?

8. In the reliability section of the *Standards for Educational and Psychological Testing* (see the reading list for this chapter), review the types of information that test manuals should contain, and then compare a recent test manual with the *Standards*.

9. In reviewing the reliability data in a test manual, a teacher noted the following reliability coefficients:
   a. Correlation of Form A test scores over a one-month interval = .90.
   b. Correlation of Form A with Form B scores over a one-month interval = .85.

c. Correlation of scores based on two halves (odd-even) of Form A = .95.

How would you account for these differences in reliability coefficients (assume that the groups tested were the same)? Which estimate of reli-

ability provides the most useful information? Why?

10. List and briefly describe as many things as you can think of that might be done to increase the reliability of a classroom assessment.

REFERENCES

American Psychological Association. (1985). *Standards for educational and psychological testing.* Washington, D.C.: Author.

Shavelson, R. J., & Webb, N. M. (1991). *Generalizability theory: A primer.* Newbury Park, CA: Sage Publications.

Subkoviak, M. J. (1984). Estimating the reliability of mastery–nonmastery classifications. In R. A. Berk (Ed.), a guide to criterion-referenced test construction (pp. 267–291). Baltimore: Johns Hopkins University Press.

FURTHER READING

Algina, J. (1992). Reliability of measurement. In M. C. Alkin (Ed.), *Encyclopedia of Educational Research* (6th ed.). (pp. 1090–1093). New York: Macmillan. Provides a brief overview of reliability.

American Psychological Association. (1985). *Standards for educational and psychological testing.* Washington, D.C.: Author. See the section on reliability for descriptions of the basic types and for the kind of reliability information to be sought in test manuals.

Anastasi, A. (1988). *Psychological testing* (6th ed.). New York: Macmillan. Chapter 5, "Reliability," describes the various types of reliability coefficients, the standard error of measurement, and the factors influencing reliability.

Cronbach, L. J. (1990). *Essentials of psychological testing* (5th ed.). New York: Harper & Row. Chapter 6, "How to Judge Tests," is an advanced treatment of reliability emphasizing the generalizability of test scores, methods of estimating error, and considerations in interpreting reliability estimates.

Feldt, L. S., & Brennan, R. L. (1989). Reliability. In R. L. Linn (Ed.), *Educational measurement* (3rd ed.). New York: Macmillan. Chapter 3 presents a comprehensive and technically advanced discussion of reliability.

Shavelson, R. J., & Webb, N. M. (1991). *Generalizability theory: A primer.* Newbury Park, CA: Sage Publications. This primer provides an excellent introduction to generalizability, which is an expansion and integration of the reliability issues discussed in this chapter.

PART II

Classroom Tests and Assessments

CHAPTER 5

Planning Classroom Tests and Assessments

Classroom tests and assessments play a central role in the evaluation of student learning. They provide relevant measures of many important learning outcomes and indirect evidence concerning others. They make expected learning outcomes explicit to students and parents and show what types of performances are valued. The validity of the information they provide, however, depends on the care that goes into the planning and preparation of tests and assessments.

The main goal of classroom testing and assessment is to obtain valid, reliable, and useful information concerning student achievement. This requires determining what is to be measured and then defining it precisely so that tasks that evoke the desired performance can be constructed. It also requires specifying the achievement domain in such a manner that the sample of items and assessment tasks will represent the total domain of achievement tasks and the results will be appropriate for the intended instructional uses.

The likelihood of preparing valid, reliable, and useful classroom tests and assessments is greatly enhanced if a series of steps like that shown in Figure 5.1 is followed.

Specific procedures for constructing each of the various types of test items will be described in Chapters 6 through 8. Open-ended essay questions will be discussed in Chapter 9 and other types of performance assessment tasks used for measuring complex achievement will be described in Chapter 10. Chapter 11 will describe the use of observational techniques, peer appraisals, and self-report techniques to assess learning outcomes and student development. Chapter 12 will be concerned with assembling, administering, and appraising classroom tests and assessments. Chapter 13, the last chapter of this section, will describe approaches to marking and reporting.

FIGURE 5.1
Basic steps in classroom testing
and assessment

GOAL
Improved learning
and instruction

8. Using the results

7. Appraising the assessment

6. Administering the assessment

5. Assembling the assessment

4. Preparing relevant assessment tasks

3. Selecting appropriate assessment tasks

2. Developing specifications

1. Determining the purpose of measurement

THE PURPOSE OF CLASSROOM TESTING AND ASSESSMENT

Classroom tests and assessments can be used for a variety of instructional purposes. These can be best described in terms of their location in the instructional process, which closely parallels the types of assessment described in Chapter 1.

Pretesting

Tests and assessments may be given at the beginning of an instructional segment (e.g., unit or course) to determine (1) whether students have the prerequisite skills needed for the instruction (to determine readiness) or (2) to what extent students have already achieved the objectives of the planned instruction (to determine student placement or modification of instruction).

Readiness pretests are typically limited in scope. For example, a pretest in algebra might be confined to arithmetic operations and concepts; a pretest in physics might consist of basic physical concepts or prerequisite skills in algebra; and a pretest in beginning German might be limited to knowledge of English grammar. In addition to being confined to a limited domain, pretest items tend to have a relatively low level of difficulty. Published readiness tests *are* available at the primary school level in the basic skill areas, but most teachers must develop their own readiness pretests. These tests serve as a basis for remedial work or for adaptation of instructional plans.

Pretests for determining the extent to which students have already achieved the objectives of the planned instruction are no different from the tests used to measure the outcomes of instruction. Thus, a test designed to measure final achievement in a course or unit may be given at the beginning to measure entry performance on the objectives. In this case, the final test or assessment should, of course, not be the same test used in pretesting but an equivalent form of it.

Testing and Assessment During Instruction

Tests and assessments given during instruction provide the basis for formative assessment. They are used to monitor learning progress, detect learning errors, and provide feedback to students and teacher. Teachers commonly call these formative tests learning tests, practice tests, quizzes, unit tests, and the like. These tests and assessments typically cover some predefined segment of instruction (e.g., a chapter or particular set of skills) and thus encompass a rather limited sample of learning outcomes. The mix of types of test items and more complex performance assessment tasks needs to be selected with care to ensure that the full range of critical instructional objectives is assessed. Ideally, the tests and assessments will be constructed in such a way that corrective prescriptions can be given for learning objectives that are yet to be achieved. When all students fail a set of items or perform poorly on an extended performance task, a group review may be applicable. When a small number of students have errors, alternative methods of study may be prescribed (e.g., reading assignments, practice exercises, and the like).

Persistent learning difficulties may require the use of diagnostic tests. For this type of testing, a number of test items are needed in each specific area, with some slight variation from item to item. In diagnosing students' difficulties in adding whole numbers, for example, it would be necessary to include addition problems containing various number combinations, some requiring carrying and some not, to pinpoint the specific types of errors being made. Diagnostic testing is a highly specialized area that has been somewhat neglected in educational measurement. There are some published diagnostic tests but these are primarily in the basic skills area. In other areas, teachers have to depend more heavily on the diagnostic features of formative tests or prepare their own diagnostic tests and assessments.

End-of-Instruction Testing and Assessment

At the end of a segment of instruction (e.g., unit or course), our main interest is in measuring the extent to which the intended learning outcomes have been achieved. Although these end-of-instruction tests and assessments are used primarily for summative assessment (e.g., to certify accomplishment or assign grades), they can also serve other functions. End-of-unit tests can be used for feedback to students, assigning of remedial work, and assessing instruction as well as for grading purposes. In fact, they can serve the functions of both formative and summative assessment, and in some cases serve as a pretest for the following unit (e.g., where the units are sequenced, as in math). End-of-course tests provide a broad survey of student learning over all of the intended outcomes of a course. In addition to their use in grading, they can also provide information for evaluating instructional

TABLE 5.1

The basic types of classroom tests and assessments (Source: Adapted from "Functional Types of Student Evaluation" by P. W. Airasian and G. F. Madaus, 1972, *Measurement and Evaluation in Guidance, 4,* pp. 221–233.)

Timing	Before Instruction		During Instruction		End of Instruction
Function	**Readiness**	**Placement**	**Formative**	**Diagnostic**	**Summative**
Focus of measurement	Prerequisite entry skills	Course or unit objectives	Predefined segment of instruction	Most common learning errors	Course or unit objectives
Nature of sample	Limited sample of selected skills	Broad sample of all objectives	Limited sample of learning tasks	Limited sample of specific errors	Broad sample of all objectives
Item difficulty	Typically has low level of difficulty	Typically has wide range of difficulty	Varies with the segment of instruction	Typically has low level of difficulty	Typically has wide range of difficulty
Time of administration	Beginning of course or unit	Beginning of course or unit	Periodically during instruction	As needed during instruction	End of course or unit
Use of results	Remedy entry deficiencies or assignment to learning group	Instructional planning and advanced placement	Improve and direct learning through ongoing feedback	Remedy errors related to persistent learning difficulties	Assign grades, certify accomplishment, or evaluate teaching

effectiveness. A summary of the various types of classroom tests is presented in Table 5.1.

DEVELOPING SPECIFICATIONS FOR TESTS AND ASSESSMENTS

To ensure that classroom tests and assessments measure a representative sample of instructionally relevant tasks it is important to develop specifications that can guide the selection of test items and assessment tasks. When preparing a brief learning test on a limited area (e.g., spelling or capitalization) a simple listing of specific tasks, with an indication of the number of items measuring each task, may suffice. For most testing purposes, however, more elaborate specifications are needed. One device that has been widely used for this purpose is a two-way chart, called a table of specifications (or test blueprint).

Building a Table of Specifications

Building a table of specifications involves (1) preparing a list of instructional objectives, (2) outlining the course content, and (3) preparing the two-way chart. These steps will be illustrated for a weather unit in junior high school science.

Preparing the List of Instructional Objectives. Using the procedure for stating instructional objectives described in Chapter 2, the following list of general objectives and specific learning outcomes was prepared for the weather unit. Although the list is not exhaustive, it illustrates both the method of stating the objectives and the desired amount of detail. If this weather unit was being taught at a lower grade level, our objectives would be defined by fewer and simpler specific learning outcomes; at a higher grade level more complex learning outcomes would be included.

Instructional Objectives for a Weather Unit

1. Knows basic terms.
    1.1. Writes a definition of each term.
    1.2. Identifies the term that represents each weather element.
    1.3. Identifies the term that best fits a given weather description.
    1.4. Matches the term to a picture of the concept.
    1.5. Distinguishes between correct and incorrect uses of the term.
2. Knows weather symbols.
    2.1. Matches each symbol with the weather element it represents.
    2.2. Draws the symbol for each weather element.
    2.3. Identifies the meaning of each symbol.
3. Knows specific facts.
    3.1. Identifies the elements affecting weather.
    3.2. Names the instrument used for measuring each weather element.

3.3. Identifies the unit of measurement used in reporting each weather element.

3.4. Distinguishes between correct and incorrect procedures for determining each weather element.

3.5. Matches the names of each cloud type with a description of its characteristics.

3.6. Identifies the weather conditions associated with each type of front.

4. Understands the influence of factors on weather formation.

4.1. Describes the characteristics of a given weather condition.

4.2. Distinguishes between probable and improbable weather reports.

4.3. Identifies the factors causing a given weather change.

4.4. Predicts future weather from a change in conditions.

4.5. Prepares and delivers to class an oral weather report for another state.

5. Interprets weather maps.

5.1. Describes the weather for a given locality.

5.2. Identifies the different types of fronts shown on a weather map.

5.3. Describes the weather conditions surrounding each front shown on a weather map.

5.4. Identifies the direction of movement for each front shown on a weather map.

5.5. Constructs a weather map using a written description of existing conditions.

6. Measures relevant weather characteristics.

6.1. Measures and records changes in air pressure.

6.2. Measures and records direction and velocity of wind.

6.3. Measures relative humidity.

The list of objectives is limited to those outcomes that can be measured by a classroom test or, as in the case of 4.5, 5.5, and 6, a performance assessment task. It does not include affective outcomes (e.g., demonstrating scientific attitude). A more elaborate evaluation plan for a weather unit might contain a listing of all relevant outcomes with an indication of how each is to be evaluated.

Outlining the Instructional Content.   The second step in preparing a table of specifications is to make an outline of the instructional content. The instructional objectives describe the types of performance the students are expected to demonstrate; the *instructional content* indicates the area in which each type of performance is to be shown. The amount of detail to include in the content outline is somewhat arbitrary, but the outline should be detailed enough to ensure an adequate sampling of content and proper interpretation of the results. The following list of topics and subtopics for a weather unit illustrates an adequate outline for test and assessment preparation.

Content Outline for a Weather Unit

A. Air pressure.

1. Measuring and reporting air pressure.

2. Factors affecting air pressure.

3. Relation to weather changes.

B. Air temperature.
  1. Measuring and reporting air temperature.
  2. Factors affecting air temperature.
  3. Relation to weather formations.
C. Humidity and precipitation.
  1. Measuring and reporting humidity.
  2. Factors affecting humidity.
  3. Forms of precipitation.
  4. Measuring and reporting precipitation.
D. Wind.
  1. Measurement of speed and direction.
  2. Factors affecting speed and direction.
  3. Symbols for reporting speed and direction.
E. Clouds.
  1. Types of clouds.
  2. Characteristics of cloud types.
  3. Factors causing cloud formations.
  4. Relation to weather conditions.
  5. Symbols for cloud types.
F. Fronts.
  1. Types of fronts.
  2. Formation of fronts.
  3. Weather related to fronts.
  4. Symbols for fronts.

Preparing the Two-Way Chart. The final step in building a table of specifications is to prepare a two-way chart that relates the instructional objectives to the instructional content, thus specifying the nature of the sample of test items and assessment tasks. An example of the chart for our junior high weather unit is presented in Table 5.2. This table indicates both the total number of test items and assessment tasks and the percentage allotted to each objective and each area of content. For classroom testing, using the number of items may be sufficient, but the percentages are useful in determining the amount of emphasis to give to each area.

The table is limited to those objectives that can be measured with a classroom test with objective or restricted-response essay items. It excludes those objectives requiring performance (e.g., 4.5, an oral presentation; 5.5, constructing a weather map, and 6.1 through 6.3, using weather instruments). Thus, for comprehensive coverage, the classroom test would need to be supplemented by a set of performance assessment tasks. The relative weight to be given to the results of the performance assessments and the classroom test in the assignment of course grades should be determined in accordance with the relative importance of the objectives. It is critical that important objectives that cannot be assessed by the classroom test be identified, so that plans for assessing the achievement of those objectives can be made. In this example, a simple list of five performance assessment tasks corresponding to instructional objectives 4.5, 5.5, 6.1, 6.2, and 6.3, together with a plan for the relative weight to be given to the scores on those tasks and the classroom test, would suffice.

Table 5.2 was prepared using the following steps.

1. List the general instructional objectives across the top of the table.
2. List the major content areas down the left side of the table.
3. Determine what proportion of the test items should be devoted to each objective and each content area.

The bottom row of Table 5.2 shows that 10 percent of the items are to be devoted to knowledge of basic terms, 15 percent to knowledge of weather symbols, 15 percent to knowledge of specific facts, 40 percent to understanding influence of weather factors, and 20 percent to interpretation of weather maps. Similarly, the column on the far right shows that 20 percent of the items are to be concerned with air pressure, 30 percent with wind, and so on down the column. Typically, these percentages are assigned first, to indicate the relative emphasis to be given to each objective and each content area. The total number of items for each area is then determined. For example, because this is to be a 60-item test, six of the items (10 percent) are to measure knowledge of basic terms and twelve of the items (20 percent) are concerned with air pressure. Thus, the total number of items is computed and listed across the bottom and down the right-hand side of the chart. These numbers are then used as a guide to assign test items to each cell. For example, two items (approximately 33 percent of six) have been assigned to

TABLE 5.2
Table of specifications for a weather unit in junior high school science

Objectives ⟍ Content	Knows			Understands	Interprets	Total Number of Items	Percent of Items
	Basic Terms	Weather Symbols	Specific Facts	Influence of Each Factor on Weather Formation	Weather Maps		
Air pressure	1	2	2	4	3	12	20
Wind	1	2	2	11	2	18	30
Temperature	1	1	2	4	2	10	17
Humidity and precipitation	1	2	1	5	5	14	23
Clouds	2	2	2			6	10
Total number of items	6	9	9	24	12	60	
Percent of items	10	15	15	40	20		100

the cell in the lower left-hand corner, indicating that the test will contain two items measuring knowledge of terms concerning clouds. The assignment of items to each cell is not strictly a matter of following the percentages, however. Some cells may be left blank, as shown in the chart, because items in those areas are inappropriate. Similarly, some cells may receive a larger number of items because the learning tasks for that cell may have received greater emphasis in teaching. Despite these adjustments to the distribution of items, the number of items in the cells of the table should approximate the desired distribution and must add up to the total number of items indicated for each column and row.

The final distribution of items in the table of specifications should reflect the emphasis given during the instruction. Objectives considered more important by the teacher should be allotted more test items. This applies not only to the items within the classroom test but also to performance assessment tasks. The weight given to the performance of such assessment tasks should reflect the importance of the objective. Similarly, areas of content receiving more instruction time should be allocated more test items and assessment tasks. Although the decisions involved in making the table are somewhat arbitrary and the process is time-consuming, the preparation of a table of test specifications, together with a listing of performance assessment tasks needed to supplement the test, is one of the best means for ensuring that the total set of test items and assessment tasks will measure a representative sample of instructionally relevant objectives. As noted in Chapter 3, this provides content-related evidence that the test will provide a valid measure of the intended learning outcomes. The effort that goes into developing specifications also makes it much easier to prepare the test once the plan is developed.

Other Examples of Specifications

Because of its broad coverage, a table of specifications is especially useful in constructing a test or assessment over a unit or course. Here the table ensures that each of the diverse types of learning outcomes will receive appropriate emphasis in the test. Whether a table of specifications is useful in constructing a test over a more limited area, however, depends on the scope of learning outcomes to be covered by the test. If the domain of tasks is very limited, such as "addition of fractions with the same denominator," a table of specifications might be unnecessary. Here we could simply list all, or nearly all, of the specific tasks encompassed by this learning outcome, as follows:

❑ Adds two fractions with same denominator where the answer is less than one ($\frac{1}{3} + \frac{1}{3}$).

❑ Adds two fractions with same denominator where the answer equals one ($\frac{1}{3} + \frac{2}{3}$).

❑ Adds two fractions with same denominator where the answer is greater than one ($\frac{2}{3} + \frac{2}{3}$).

❑ Adds two fractions with same denominator and reduces answer to lowest terms
(⁴⁄₆ + ⁴⁄₆).

❑ Adds more than two fractions with same denominator and reduces answer
(¹⁄₈ + ⁵⁄₈ + ⁶⁄₈).

A list of learning tasks such as this specifies quite clearly the precise nature of the performance involved in "the addition of fractions with the same denominator." We could obtain a fairly representative sample of such tasks by simply constructing five or more items for each task, using various number combinations.

If our arithmetic test were to cover a slightly larger achievement domain, say, "addition of fractions," we might now find a table of specifications quite useful. An illustration of such a table for a fifty-item test is shown in Table 5.3. The use of such a table does not mean, of course, that we should not make the type of detailed breakdown we did for "addition of fractions with the same denominator." Such a detailed listing of tasks aids in teaching, in detecting learning errors, and in constructing test items. The table of specifications, however, supplements such lists by specifying the sample of tasks to be included in the test. As noted earlier, this provides greater assurance that the intended learning outcomes will be measured in a balanced manner.

Using a One-Way Classification System. For tests in some areas, a one-way classification of items may be all that is needed. In planning for a reading test, for example, a list of the reading skills and the number of test items for measuring each skill may be sufficient for specifying what the test is to measure. The content (e.g., passages read) may vary from time to time, but the skill outcomes remain fairly constant. Thus, a master list of skills can be prepared for use with various types of reading material. An example of such a list is presented in Table 5.4.

TABLE 5.3
Table of specifications for a fifty-item test on addition of fractions

Content Area \ Instructional Objectives	Adds Fractions	Adds Fractions and Mixed Numbers	Adds Mixed Numbers	Total Items
Denominators are alike	5	5	5	15
Denominators are unlike (with common factor)	5	5	5	15
Denominators are unlike (without common factor)	6	7	7	20
Total items	16	17	17	50

TABLE 5.4
List of reading comprehension skills and number of items for each specific skill

Reading Skill	Number of Items
Identifies details stated in a passage	10
Identifies the main idea of a passage	10
Identifies the sequence of actions or events	10
Identifies relationships expressed in a passage	10
Identifies inferences drawn from a passage	10
Total number	50

It should be noted that each skill in Table 5.4 is stated in specific performance terms, and that ten items are used to measure each skill. This provides for criterion-referenced interpretation. Although the material to be read is not included in the specifications, it will, of course, need to be carefully selected in terms of interest and readability level. See the "Checklist" box.

CHECKLIST

Reviewing Specifications for Tests and Assessments

	Yes	No
1. Are the specifications in harmony with the purpose of the test or assessment?	____	____
2. Do the specifications indicate the nature and limits of the achievement domain?	____	____
3. Do the specifications indicate the types of learning outcomes to be measured?	____	____
4. Do the specifications indicate the sample of learning outcomes to be measured?	____	____
5. Is the number of test items or assessment tasks indicated for each subdivision?	____	____
6. Are the types of items and tasks to be used appropriate for the outcomes to be measured?	____	____
7. Is the distribution of items and tasks adequate for the types of interpretation to be made?	____	____
8. If sample items or tasks are included, do they illustrate the desired attributes?	____	____
9. Do the specifications, as a whole, indicate a representative sample of instructionally relevant tasks that fits the use to be made of the results?	____	____

████████   # SELECTING APPROPRIATE TYPES OF ITEMS AND ASSESSMENT TASKS

It is common to make a distinction between classroom tests that consist of objective test items and performance assessments that require students to construct responses (e.g., write an essay) or perform a particular task (e.g., measure air pressure). Objective test items are highly structured and require the students to supply a word or two or to select the correct answer from a number of alternatives. They are called objective because they have a single right or best answer that can be determined in advance. Performance assessment tasks, such as essay questions, permit the student to select, organize, and present the answer in essay form. Other types of performance assessment tasks may require the student to use equipment, generate hypotheses, make observations, construct something (e.g., a model), or perform for an audience (e.g., give a speech). For most performance assessment tasks there is not a single right or best response—there may be a variety of responses that are considered excellent. Expert judgment is required to score the performances. There is no conflict between these highly constrained objective items and the much less constrained performance assessment tasks. For some instructional purposes, objective items may be most efficient, whereas for others performance assessments may prove most satisfactory. Each approach should be used where most appropriate, with appropriateness determined by the learning outcomes to be measured and by the advantages and limitations of each approach.

The Objective Test Item

The great variety of different types of objective test items, can be classified into those that require the student to supply the answer and those that require the student to select the answer from a given number of alternatives. These two general classes are commonly further divided into basic types of objective test items, illustrated in the accompanying examples.

EXAMPLES   **Supply Types**

Short answer

What is the name of the author of *Moby Dick*? (Herman Melville)

What is the formula for hydrochloric acid? (HCl)

What is the value of X in the equation $2X + 5 = 9$? (2)

Completion

Lines on a weather map joining points with the same barometric pressure are called (isobars).

The formula for ordinary table salt is (NaCl).

In the equation $2X + 5 = 9$; $X = $ (2).

Selection Types

True–false or alternative response

ⓉF A virus is the smallest known organism.

TⒻ An atom is the smallest particle of matter.

Yes Ⓝⓞ In the equation $2X + 5 = 9$, X equals 3.

Ⓨⓔⓢ No Acid turns litmus paper red.

Matching

(C)	1. And	A Adjective
(D)	2. Dog	B Adverb
(G)	3. Jump	C Conjunction
(F)	4. She	D Noun
(B)	5. Quickly	E Preposition
		F Pronoun
		G Verb

Multiple-choice

In the equation $2X + 5 = 9$, $2X$ means

A   2 plus X.

B   2 minus X.

C   2 divided by X.

Ⓓ   2 multiplied by X.

In which of the following sentences do the subject and verb disagree?

A   When they win, they are happy.

Ⓑ   Politics are hard to understand.

C   The majority is always right.

D   One or the other is to be elected.

In addition to these basic types of objective test items, there are numerous modifications and combinations of types. However, there is little to be gained from listing all the possible variations, as many are unique to particular objectives or subject-matter areas. Some of the more common variations used to measure understanding, thinking skills, and other complex learning outcomes will be illustrated later. An understanding of the principles of test construction, and the principles that apply to each of the specific types of objective test items, should enable teachers to make adaptations that best fit their particular purposes.

The various types of objective test items have one feature in common that distinguishes them from performance assessment tasks: they present students with a highly structured task that limits the type of response they can make. To obtain the correct answer, students must demonstrate the specific knowledge, understanding, or skill called for in the item; they are not free to redefine the problem or to organize and present the answer in their own words. They must select one of several alternative answers or supply the correct word, number, or symbol. This structuring of the problem and restriction on the method of responding contribute to objective scoring that is quick, easy, and accurate. On the negative side, this same structuring makes the objective test item inappropriate for measuring the ability to select, organize, and integrate ideas. To measure such outcomes we must depend on performance assessment tasks.

Since written essays are the most commonly used form of performance assessment tasks it is worth focusing on essay questions before considering other types of performance assessment tasks. The essay question is commonly viewed as one item type. A useful classification, however, is one based on the amount of freedom of response allowed the student. This includes extended-response essay questions, in which students are given almost complete freedom in making their responses, and restricted-response essay questions, in which the nature, length, or organization of the response is limited. These types of essay questions are illustrated as follows:

EXAMPLES   *Extended-response essay questions:*

Describe what you think the role of the federal government should be in maintaining a stable economy in the United States. Include specific policies and programs, and give reasons for your proposals.

Restricted-response essay questions:

State two advantages and two disadvantages of maintaining high tariffs on goods from other countries.

Extended-response essay questions permit students to decide which facts they think are most pertinent, to select their own method of organization, and to write as much as seems necessary for a comprehensive answer. Thus, such questions tend to reveal the ability to evaluate ideas, to relate them coherently, and to express them succinctly. To a lesser extent, they also reflect individual differences in attitudes, values, and creative ability.

Despite the apparent virtues of the extended-response essay questions, they have two weaknesses: (1) they are inefficient for measuring knowledge of factual material because the questions are so extensive that only a small sample of content can be included in any one assessment, and (2) scoring is difficult and apt to be unreliable because the responses include an array of factual information of varying degrees of correctness, organized with varying degrees of coherence, and expressed with varying degrees of legibility and conciseness.

Restricted-response essay questions minimize some of the weaknesses of extended-response essay questions. Restricting the type of response makes it easier to measure knowledge of factual material and reduces somewhat the difficulty of the scoring. On the other hand, the more highly structured task presented by the restricted-response essay questions makes them less effective as a measure of the ability to select, organize, and integrate ideas.

Neither extended-response essay questions nor restricted-response essay questions can serve all purposes equally. The type of essay question to use in a particular situation depends primarily on the learning outcomes to be measured and, to a lesser extent, on such practical considerations as the difficulty of scoring.

Other Types of Performance Assessment

There are many other types of performance assessment tasks. Examples include oral presentations; construction of graphs, diagrams or models; use of equipment or scientific instruments; typing; and playing a musical instrument. Tasks are selected so that the performance corresponds as closely as possible to an important instructional objective.

A distinction can be made between restricted-response performance tasks and extended-response performance tasks. These types are illustrated below.

EXAMPLES *Extended-response performance task*

Prepare a weather report for another state and make an oral presentation of the report to the class using appropriate visual displays.

Restricted-response performance task

Measure and record the relative humidity.

The virtues and limitations of extended- and restricted-response performance tasks are much the same as those listed for extended- and restricted-response essay questions. The freedom provided by the extended response performance task enables students to display such important skills as problem solving, planning, organization, integration, and creativity. Questions of this type also provide an opportunity to observe student performance in more realistic contexts than are possible with objective test items. On the other hand, they are time-consuming to administer and difficult to score.

Restricted-response performance tasks are generally easier to score and require less time than extended-response performance tasks. However, they are generally less suited for measuring the higher-order skills measured by extended-response performance tasks.

Comparative Advantages of Objective Test Items and Performance Assessment Tasks

Both objective test items and performance assessment tasks can provide valuable evidence concerning student achievement. Each has advantages and limitations which make it more appropriate for some purposes than for others. A comparison of the relative merits of objective item tests and performance assessments is presented in Table 5.5.

In considering the comparative advantages of objective-item tests and performance assessments, we must be careful not to fall into either/or thinking;

TABLE 5.5
Comparative advantages of objective tests and performance assessments

	Objective Test	Performance Assessment
Learning outcomes measured	Is efficient for measuring knowledge of facts. Some types (e.g., multiple-choice) can also measure understanding, thinking skills, and other complex outcomes. Inefficient or inappropriate for measuring ability to select and organize ideas, writing abilities, and some types of problem-solving skills.	Is inefficient for measuring knowledge of facts. Can measure understanding, thinking skills, and other complex learning outcomes (especially useful where originality of response is desired). Appropriate for measuring performance on tasks corresponding to important instructional objectives in realistic contexts.
Preparation of questions	A relatively large number of questions are needed for a test. Preparation is difficult and time-consuming.	Only a few tasks are needed for an assessment.
Sampling of course content	Provides an extensive sampling of course content because of the large number of questions that can be included in a test.	Sampling of course content is usually limited because of the small number of tasks that can be included in an assessment.
Control of student response	Complete structuring of task limits student to type of response called for. Prevents bluffing and avoids influence of writing skill, though selection-type items are subject to guessing.	Freedom to respond in own way enables students to display originality and guessing is minimized.
Scoring	Objective scoring.	Judgmental scoring.
Influence on learning	Usually encourages student to develop a comprehensive knowledge of specific facts and the ability to make fine discriminations among them. Can encourage the development of understanding, thinking skills, and other complex outcomes if properly constructed.	Encourages students to concentrate on larger units of subject matter, with special emphasis on the ability to organize, integrate, and express ideas effectively. Essays may encourage poor writing habits if time pressure is a factor (it almost always is).
Reliability	High reliability is possible and is typically obtained with well-constructed tests.	Reliability is typically low, primarily because of inconsistent scoring and limited sample of tasks.

that is, to use either objective items or performance assessment tasks. It is frequently better to use both, with each measuring the particular learning outcomes for which it is best suited. This should also have a desirable influence on student learning, because in preparing for such tests, students must attend to the specific types of learning outcomes measured by objective items as well as the synthesis and integrated performance outcomes measured by performance assessment tasks.

Selecting the Most Appropriate Types of Items and Tasks

A basic principle in selecting the type of test item and assessment task to use is: *Select the item type that provides the most direct measure of the intended learning outcome.* If, for example, the intended learning outcome is writing, naming, listing, or speaking, the task should require the students to supply the answer. If the outcome involves the use of laboratory equipment to solve a problem, nothing short of an actual laboratory performance task will suffice. On the other hand, if the task calls for identifying a correct answer, a selection-type item should be used. In those cases where the specific learning outcome does not make clear which item type to use, selection-type items would be favored because of the greater control over the student's response and the objectivity of the scoring. The following objective-item test was prepared for the weather unit discussed earlier. Note how each type of objective item provides a direct measure of the outcome it was designed to measure.

EXAMPLE   **Short-Answer Items**

Specific Learning Outcome: Writes a definition of each term.

   Directions: Write a one-sentence definition of each of the following terms.

1. Weather
2. Humidity
3. Occluded front

Specific Learning Outcome: Names the instrument used for measuring each weather element.

1. The instrument used to measure the amount of precipitation in a given locality is called a (an) _____ .

Specific Learning Outcome: Lists the characteristics of a given weather phenomenon.

1. List three main characteristics of a hurricane.

Specific Learning Outcome: Measures relative humidity.

1. Use the appropriate instrument to measure the relative humidity and record the value obtained.

Multiple-Choice Items

Specific Learning Outcome: Identifies the units of measurement used in reporting each weather element on a weather map.

1. United States weather maps indicate air pressure in
   - A. inches
   - B. feet
   - C. pounds
   - (D.) millibars

True–False Items

Specific Learning Outcome: Distinguishes between correct and incorrect procedures for determining each weather element.

   T (F) 1. Dew point is determined by cooling a sample of air until it is free of moisture.

   (T) F 2. Ceiling is determined by using balloons that rise at known rates.

Matching Items

Specific Learning Outcome: Matches each weather instrument to the weather element it measures.

   Directions: On the line to the left of each weather element in Column A, write the letter of the weather instrument in Column B that is used for measuring it. Each instrument in Column B may be used once, more than once, or not at all.

Column A	*Column B*
(B) 1. Air pressure	A. Anemometer
(E) 2. Air temperature	B. Barometer
(C) 3. Humidity	C. Hygrometer
(A) 4. Wind velocity	D. Rain gauge
	E. Thermometer
	F. Wind vane

In deciding which selection-type item to use, a common practice is to use the multiple-choice item if it will measure the learning outcome as directly as the other two types. The use of true-false items is typically most valuable in those special instances where there are only two possible alternatives (e.g., distinguishing between correct and incorrect procedures). The matching item is a specialized form of the multiple-choice item and should be used only where a series of homogeneous things are to be related (e.g., dates and events, authors and books, instruments and uses). The multiple-choice item is favored for most other selection-type tasks because the use of four or five alternatives reduces the chances of guessing the answer and provides clues to students' misunderstandings. See Appendix F for other examples of how to relate test items to intended learning outcomes.

Whether a test item or an assessment task actually measures the particular performance called for by a specific learning outcome depends, of course, to a large extent on the skill with which the test item or assessment task is constructed. No amount of skill, however, will enable us to develop a valid test or assessment of achievement if the items or tasks selected for use are inappropriate for measuring the intended outcomes.

CONSIDERATIONS IN PREPARING RELEVANT TEST ITEMS AND ASSESSMENT TASKS

The construction of items and tasks should be preceded by a series of preliminary steps. First, the purpose of the test or assessment should be determined. Second, a set of specifications should be developed. Third, the most appropriate types of test items and performance assessment tasks should be selected. Finally, items and tasks should be constructed in accordance with the specifications developed during the preceding steps. The rules for constructing each type of objective item will be discussed in Chapters 6 through 8, and rules for constructing performance assessments will be discussed in Chapters 9 and 10. Here we shall focus on some of the general considerations involved in preparing relevant objective items and assessment tasks.

Matching Items and Tasks to Intended Outcomes

Classroom tests and assessments are most likely to provide a valid measure of the instructional objectives if the test items and assessment tasks are designed to measure the performance defined by the specific learning outcomes. The process of matching test items and assessment tasks to the learning outcomes to be measured was illustrated earlier. Essentially, it involves fitting each item or task as closely as possible to the intended outcome, as follows:

EXAMPLE *Specific Learning Outcome:* Identifies the function of a given body structure.

Relevant Test Item:

What is the function of the kidneys?

(A) Eliminate waste products.

B Improve the circulation of blood.

C Maintain respiration.

D Stimulate digestion.

Thus, the preparation of relevant test items and assessment tasks means analyzing the performance described in the specific learning outcome (i.e., "Identifies the function of . . .") and constructing a test item or assessment task that calls forth that performance (i.e., "What is the function of . . .?"). Note that the specific learning outcome defines the type of response the student is expected to make, but it does not indicate the specific course content (i.e., kidney) the student is to identify. Keeping the learning outcome free of specific course content makes it possible to key the intended response to various areas of content. For example, students could be asked to identify the function of the heart, the lungs, the muscles, or any other body structure pertinent to the course's content. The desired student performance stated in the specific learning outcome can be keyed to each specific area of content by means of the table of specifications.

In some cases it may be desirable to prepare a general item pattern as an intermediate step between the specific learning outcome and the test item. A general item pattern for our illustrative test item would be as follows:

EXAMPLE   What is the function of. . . ?

An item pattern such as this could be completed by adding the name of any body structure and using it as a short-answer question or by listing appropriate alternatives and using it as a multiple-choice item. Thus, using the item pattern as a guide, we could generate large numbers of relevant test items for this particular learning outcome. This procedure is especially useful when a file of test items is being prepared or when more than one form of the test is needed (e.g., pretesting, post-testing, and retesting).

When item patterns are used as a guide to test construction, they can be arranged by general type of learning outcome:

EXAMPLES   *Knowledge Outcomes*

1. What is the name of . . . ?
2. What is the location of . . . ?
3. What are the characteristics of . . . ?
4. What is the function of . . . ?

Understanding Outcomes

1. What is the reason for . . . ?
2. What is the relationship between . . . ?
3. Which of these is an example of . . . ?
4. Which of these best summarizes . . . ?

Application Outcomes

1. What method would be best for . . . ?
2. What steps should be followed to construct . . . ?
3. Which of these indicates correct application of . . . ?
4. Which of these solutions is correct for . . . ?

Item patterns like these should not, of course, be developed haphazardly. Rather, they should be derived from the specific learning outcomes they represent. Although it usually will not be possible to develop item patterns for all outcomes, listing them will help generate pools of relevant test items. The test construction time saved by using such a list can then be used to construct more effective items for those areas in which general item patterns are not feasible.

Obtaining a Representative Sample of Items and Tasks

A test or assessment, no matter how extensive, is almost always a sample of the many possible test items or tasks that could be included. We expect students to know thousands of facts, but we can test for only a limited number of them; we expect students to develop understanding applicable to innumerable situations, but we can test application to only a limited number of situations; and we expect students to develop thinking skills that will enable them to solve a variety of problems, but we can test their problem-solving ability with only a limited number of problems. In each area of content and for each specific learning outcome, then, we merely select a sample of student performance and accept it as evidence of achievement in that area. We assume that the students' responses to our selected set of items and tasks are typical of what their responses would be to other items and tasks drawn from the same area. This means, of course, that our limited samples must be selected in such a way that they provide as representative a sample as possible in each of the various areas for which the test or assessment is being developed.

Our sampling is most likely to be representative when the preparation of a test or assessment is guided by a carefully prepared set of specifications. Unless a table of specifications, or some similar device, is used as a guide in construction, there is a tendency to overload the test with items measuring knowledge of isolated facts and to neglect more complex learning outcomes. In social studies, for example, it is not uncommon to include a disproportionately large number of items that measure knowledge of names, dates, places, and the like. In science, defining terms and naming structures and functions are commonly overemphasized. In mathematics, computational skill is frequently the only learning outcome measured. In language arts and literature, the identification of parts of speech, literary characters, authors, and the like is frequently too prominent. These learning outcomes are stressed not because we think knowledge of isolated facts is more important than understanding, applications, interpretations, and various thinking skills. Rather, they usually receive undue prominence because we find it easier to construct this kind of test item. Without a carefully developed test plan, ease of construction all too frequently becomes the dominant criterion in constructing test items. As a consequence, the test measures a limited and biased sample of learning tasks, and neglects many learning outcomes of greater importance.

Supplementing objective test questions with performance assessment tasks is one means of ensuring that broader learning objectives are given proper attention. However, it is inefficient to rely only on performance assessments to measure more complex understandings. For this reason, it is important to find ways of constructing objective test items that do more than measure factual knowledge. One approach to this goal of measuring complex achievement is through the use of interpretive exercises. The approach is discussed in detail in Chapter 8.

Number of Items and Tasks.   The number of items and tasks is, of course, an important factor in obtaining a representative sample. The number of items and the number of performance tasks are determined when the set of specifications is built and depend on such factors as the purpose of measurement, the types of test items and assessment tasks used, the age of the students, and the level of reliability needed for effective use of the test or assessment results. Thus, an assessment over a third-grade social studies unit might contain thirty objective items, whereas a survey test over a tenth-grade social studies course might contain more than a hundred objective items and several essay questions. Although there are no hard and fast rules for determining the number of items and tasks, an important consideration from a sampling standpoint is the number of items or tasks devoted to each specific area being measured. We want our tests and assessments to be long enough to provide an adequate sampling of each objective and each content area. As a rule of thumb, it is desirable when constructing a unit test to use at least ten objective test items to measure each specific learning outcome. This number, however, might be lowered to as few as five if the task is extremely limited (e.g., "Adds two single-digit numbers," or, "Capitalizes proper names") and the students are to supply the answers rather than to select them. For a survey test, where the sample of test items typically covers a broad area and emphasis is on the total score, using several objective test items for each specific learning outcome and ten or more for each general objective probably would be sufficient.

Special problems of sampling arise when complex learning outcomes are being measured, because this requires more elaborate objective-type items (referred to as interpretive exercises) and performance assessment tasks. Both interpretive exercises and performance assessment tasks require considerable administration time, but a single test item or assessment task is still inadequate for measuring an intended outcome. One exercise calling for the interpretation of graphs, for instance, is not sufficient to measure adequately the ability to interpret graphs. The nature of the data or the type of graph may be the most influential factor in determining whether it is interpreted properly. When several graphs are used, the effect of such factors is minimized, and we obtain a more representative sample of the ability to interpret graphs.

A similar situation occurs with the use of performance assessment tasks. The performance of any single task depends too heavily on the particular sample of information called for by the task, and thus the only feasible solution is to confine each assessment of complex outcomes to a rather limited area (e.g., graph interpretation, problem solving) and to assess more often. In any event, our aim should be to obtain as representative a sample of student performance as possible in each area to be assessed. Other things being equal, the greater the number of test items or assessment tasks, the greater the likelihood of an adequate sample and the more reliable the results.

Eliminating Irrelevant Barriers to the Performance

When constructing items or assessment tasks, care must be taken to eliminate any extraneous factors that might prevent students from performing their best. If students have achieved a particular learning outcome (e.g., knowledge of terms), we would want them to answer correctly those test items that measure the attainment of that learning outcome. We would be very unhappy (and so would they) if they answered such test items incorrectly merely because the sentence structure was too complex, the vocabulary too difficult, or the type of response called for unclear. These factors, which are extraneous to the central purpose of the measurement, limit and modify the student's responses, and prevent them from showing their true levels of achievement. Such factors are as unfair as determining a person's running ability when an ankle is sprained. Although a measure of running ability would be obtained, the performance would be restricted by a factor we did not intend to include in our measurement.

One way to eliminate factors that are extraneous to the purpose of a measurement is to be certain that all students have the prerequisite skills and abilities needed to make the response. These have been called enabling behaviors because they enable the student to make the response but are not meant to be critical factors in the measurement. That is, they are a necessary but not sufficient condition for responding correctly or performing a task well. Probably the most important enabling behavior in objective testing is reading skill. In written performance assessments, skill in written expression is an additional factor to be considered. In measuring understanding, thinking skills, and other complex learning outcomes, knowledge of certain facts and simple computational skills also might be necessary prerequisites.

In constructing tests and assessments, then, we need to strive for items and tasks that measure achievement of the specific learning outcomes and not differences in enabling behaviors. Differences in reading ability, computational skill, communication skills, and the like should not influence the students' responses unless such outcomes are specifically being measured. The only functional difference between those students who perform well on a task and those who perform poorly should be the possession of the knowledge, understanding, or other learning outcome being measured by the task. All other differences are extraneous to the purpose of the task, and their influence should be eliminated or controlled for valid results.

A special problem in preventing extraneous factors from distorting our test and assessment results is avoiding ambiguity. Objective test items are especially subject to misinterpretation when long, complex sentences are used, when the vocabulary is unnecessarily difficult, and when words that lack precise meaning are used. Thus, from the viewpoint of both level of reading difficulty and preciseness of meaning, the antidote for ambiguity seems to be a careful choice of words and the use of brief, concise sentences. In some cases, ambiguity can be reduced by using pictures or other illustrative material in place of verbal descriptions. When this is done, the illustrative material must, of course, also be carefully checked to make sure it is clear and unambiguous.

An effort should also be made to avoid any racial, ethnic, or gender bias in preparing the test items and performance assessment tasks. The vocabulary and task situations should be acceptable to various racial and ethnic groups and to both males and females, and should be free of stereotyping. For example, in presenting

GUIDELINES

Some Possible Barriers in Test Items and Assessment Tasks

❑ Ambiguous statements
❑ Excessive wordiness
❑ Difficult vocabulary
❑ Complex sentence structure
❑ Unclear instructions
❑ Unclear illustrative material
❑ Racial, ethnic, or gender bias

characters in a story problem, a reading passage, or other test situation, minorities should not be portrayed in stereotypical fashion. Similarly, task situations should not always place males in such traditional roles as athlete, business executive, and professional person and females in such traditional roles as homemaker, teacher, and nurse. A balanced use of different roles for minorities and males and females is necessary if we are to avoid bias as a possible barrier to maximum performance. See the accompanying "Guidelines" box.

Avoiding Unintended Clues in Objective Test Items

Test items should be constructed so that students obtain the correct answer only if they have attained the desired learning outcome. In the preceding principle, we were concerned with those factors that prevent students from responding correctly, even though they have attained the desired learning outcome. Here we are concerned with those factors that enable students to respond correctly, even though they lack the necessary achievement. These are the clues, some rather obvious and some very subtle, that inadvertently creep into test items during construction. They lead the poor achiever to the correct answer and thereby prevent the items from functioning as intended. When test items are short-circuited in this manner, they provide invalid evidence of achievement. Note how *an* provides a clue to the following item:

EXAMPLE   A porpoise is an

    A   plant.

    B   reptile.

    Ⓒ   animal.

    D   bird.

Such clues are not limited to selection-type items, as shown in the following supply-type item:

EXAMPLE   A piece of land that is completely surrounded by water is known as an _____ .

The clue is much less obvious to the person constructing this test item than the clue in our first illustration. To the student taking the test, however, it is readily apparent. The two most plausible answers are *island* and *peninsula*. Because *peninsula* begins with a consonant sound and does not follow the article *an,* it is ruled out as a possibility. This does not imply, of course, that students need to know the rules for good grammatical structure in order to use clues; most clues are analyzed in terms of partial knowledge and hunches. *An peninsula* just does not sound right to the student, so the word *island* is used and the correct answer is obtained.

Leads to the correct answer may also be provided by simple verbal associations. Note how the word *wind* in the following item provides a clue to the answer:

EXAMPLE   Which of the following instruments is used to determine the direction of the wind?

    A   Anemometer.

    B   Barometer.

    C   Hygrometer.

    (D)   Wind vane.

Rather than lead the uninformed to the correct answer, such clues should lead the poor achiever away from the correct answer. In the following item the same clue makes wind vane a plausible (but incorrect) answer for those students who have not learned the uses of the various weather instruments.

EXAMPLE   Which one of the following instruments is used to determine the speed of the wind?

    (A)   Anemometer.

    B   Barometer.

    C   Hygrometer.

    D   Wind vane.

Verbal clues need not be as obvious as these. In fact, the clues that appear in the final version of a test are usually rather subtle, as they are based on partial knowledge and verbal associations not readily apparent to the casual observer. For example, at first glance the following item appears to be free from clues:

EXAMPLE   Which one of the following is used to prevent polio?

    A   Gamma globulin.

    B   Penicillin.

    Ⓒ   Salk vaccine.

    D   Sulfa.

An examination of this item, however, will indicate that the word *vaccine* provides a clue to the answer. All the student needs to know to answer the item correctly is that a vaccine is used to prevent disease. Because most students have been vaccinated at one time or another, they probably possess this partial knowledge needed to make the clue apparent to them. Some students also may have developed a verbal association between *Salk* and *polio* and respond correctly on that basis. In either case, partial knowledge can lead to the correct answer and prevent the item from functioning as intended.

Another type of subtle clue is one based on the words used to qualify statements. For example, true–false statements that include qualifiers such as *sometimes, usually, generally,* and *the like* are most often true, whereas statements containing absolutes such as *always, never, none,* and *only* are most often false. Such words have been called specific determiners. They are difficult to remove from true–false items because true statements generally must be qualified, and false statements frequently must be stated in absolute terms to make them clearly false.

Other common clues in selection-type items include (1) stating correct answers in textbook language or in greater detail than incorrect answers, (2) making correct answers longer than incorrect answers, and (3) placing the correct answers in some identifiable pattern (e.g., *T, F, T, F*). Some of these clues are more likely to be detected by low-achieving students who are desperately searching for some basis for answering.

GUIDELINES

Some Common Clues in Test Items

❑ Grammatical inconsistencies

❑ Verbal associations

❑ Specific determiners (e.g., always)

❑ Phrasing of correct responses

❑ Length of correct responses

❑ Location of correct responses

General Suggestions for Writing Test Items and Assessment Tasks

In preparing a set of test items or assessment tasks, there are some general rules that apply to all types of items or tasks. These will be listed here. The specific rules for writing each item or task type will be described and illustrated in the following chapters.

1. Use your test and assessment specifications as a guide.   The specifications describe the performance to be measured and the sample of learning outcomes to measure. Thus, they serve as an aid for selecting the types of items and tasks to prepare, for writing, and for determining how many items and tasks are needed for each subdomain of achievement.

2. Write more items and tasks than needed.   Preparing more test items and assessment tasks than needed will permit the weaker items and tasks to be discarded during later review. It will also make it easier to match the final set of items and tasks to the specifications.

3. Write the items and tasks well in advance of the testing date. Setting the items and tasks aside for several days and then reviewing them with afresh outlook will reveal any lack of clarity or ambiguity that was overlooked during their preparation. It is frequently surprising how many defects slipped through during the original writing.

4. Write each test item and assessment task so that it calls forth the performance described in the intended learning outcome.   Both during writing and review, compare the task students are asked to perform to the learning outcome the task is designed to measure to make sure the two match.

5. Write each test item and assessment task so that the task to be performed is clearly defined.   Clarity is obtained by carefully formulating the question and instructions, using simple and direct language, using correct punctuation and grammar, and avoiding unnecessary wording.

6. Write each item or task at an appropriate reading level.   Keep the reading difficulty and vocabulary level as simple as possible to prevent these factors from distorting the results. Students' responses should be determined by the performance being measured, not by some factor the item or task was not designed to measure.

7. Write each item or task so that it does not provide help in responding to other items or tasks.   Unless care is taken during writing, one item may provide information that is useful in answering another item. For example, a name, date, or fact inadvertently included in the stem of a multiple-choice item may be called for in a short-answer item in another part of the test.

8. Write each item so that the answer is one that would be agreed upon by experts, or, in the case of assessment tasks, the responses judged excellent would be agreed upon by experts.   This rule is easy to satisfy when measuring factual knowledge but more difficult when measuring complex outcomes calling for the extended essays or other types of performance.

9. Whenever a test item or assessment task is revised, recheck its relevance.   When reviewing items or tasks for appropriateness, clarity, difficulty, and freedom from clues and bias, some revision is often needed. After revising an item or task, check to be sure that it still provides a relevant measure of the intended learning outcome. Even slight changes can sometimes modify the function of an item or a task.

Focusing on Improving Learning and Instruction

The ultimate purpose of testing and assessment is to improve student learning. As you construct classroom tests and assessments, keep in mind the extent to which it is likely to contribute, directly or indirectly, toward this end. Well-constructed classroom tests and assessments should increase both the quantity and quality of student learning.

1. Tests and assessments can have a desirable influence on student learning if attention is paid to the breadth and depth of content and learning outcomes measured.   When we select a representative sample of content from all of the areas covered in our instruction, we are emphasizing to the students that they must devote attention to all areas. They cannot neglect some aspects of the course and do well on the tests. Similarly, when our tests measure a variety of types of learning outcomes, the students soon learn that a mass of memorized factual information is not sufficient. They must also learn to interpret and apply facts, develop deep conceptual understandings, draw conclusions, recognize assumptions, identify cause-and-effect relations, generate hypotheses, solve meaningful problems, and the like. This discourages the students from depending solely on memorization as a basis for learning, and encourages them to develop the use of more complex mental processes.

2. Constructing tests and assessments that measure a variety of learning outcomes should also lead to improved teaching procedures and, thus, indirectly to improved student learning.   As we translate the various learning outcomes into test items and assessment tasks, we clarify our notion of understandings, thinking skills, and other complex learning outcomes. This clarification enables us to plan the learning experiences of students more effectively and increases the degree to which we emphasize understandings, thinking skills, and other complex learning outcomes in our teaching. A well-constructed test or assessment frequently leads to a review of teaching procedures and to the abandonment of those that encourage rote learning.

3. Tests and assessments will contribute to improved teacher–student relations (with a beneficial effect on student learning) if students view the tests and assessments as fair and useful measures of their achievement.   We can make fairness apparent by including a representative sample of the learning outcomes that have been emphasized during instruction, by writing clear directions, by making certain that the intent of each item or task is clear and that each item is free of any type of bias that would prevent a knowledgeable person from performing well, and by providing adequate time limits. Student recognition of usefulness, however, depends as much on what we do with the results of the test or assessment as on the characteristics of the instrument itself. We make the usefulness apparent by using the results as a basis for guiding and improving learning.

SUMMARY

Planning the classroom tests and assessments involves (1) determining the purpose of measurement, (2) developing a set of specifications, (3) selecting appropriate types of test items and assessment tasks, and (4) preparing a set of relevant items and tasks.

Classroom tests and assessments can be used for a variety of instructional purposes, best described in terms of their location in the instructional sequence. There are (1) pretests at the beginning of a course or unit to determine learning readiness, to aid in instructional planning, and to make advanced placements; (2) tests and assessments during instruction to improve and direct student learning and to identify and remedy learning errors; and (3) end-of-instruction tests and assessments used at the end of a course or unit to assign grades, certify accomplishment, or evaluate teaching. Each of these types of classroom testing and assessment places different demands on sampling of items and tasks and the type of interpretation used (i.e., criterion-referenced or norm-referenced).

A sample of student performance is more likely to be representative if a set of specifications is used in planning the test or assessment. Specifications define and delimit the achievement domain to be measured and describe the sample of test items and assessment tasks to be prepared. One form of specifications is a two-way chart called a table of specifications. Building the table involves (1) obtaining the list of instructional objectives, (2) outlining the course content, and (3) preparing the two-way chart that relates the instructional objectives to the course content and specifies the nature of the desired sample or items and tasks. Although a table of specifications is especially useful in preparing summative tests and assessments (because of the broad coverage), it is also useful in preparing some formative tests and assessments. In other cases, however, a test or assessment plan might be limited to a brief list of specific and precisely stated learning outcomes, or it might contain a comprehensive and detailed set of specifications with illustrative sample items or tasks.

The major categories of objective tests or performance assessments may be further subdivided into the following basic types of test items and assessment tasks:

Objective Test

A. Supply type
    1.   Short answer
    2.   Completion

   B. Selection type
      1. True–false or alternative-response
      2. Matching
      3. Multiple choice

Performance Assessment

A. Extended-response

B. Restricted-response

   Objective tests present students with a highly structured task that limits their response to supplying a word, brief phrase, number, or symbol or to selecting the answer from among a given number of alternatives. Performance assessments permit students to respond by selecting, organizing, and presenting ideas or performing in a way they consider appropriate. Objective tests and performance assessments both serve useful purposes in measuring student achievement. The type to use in a particular situation is best determined by the learning outcomes to be measured and by the unique advantages and limitations of each approach. A good practice is to include both objective test items and performance assessment tasks in a comprehensive measurement of student achievement.

   The preparation of a set of relevant test items and assessment tasks involves (1) matching the items and tasks to the learning outcomes as directly as possible, (2) obtaining a representative sample of all intended outcomes, (3) eliminating irrelevant barriers to the answer, (4) preventing unintended clues to the response, and (5) focusing on improving learning and instruction. The rules for constructing each type of objective test item and performance assessment task will be described in the chapters that follow.

LEARNING EXERCISES

1. Describe the nature of a readiness pretest and how the results might be used in teaching.

2. Describe how formative tests/assessments and summative tests/assessments differ.

3. What are the advantages of using a two-way chart when preparing specifications for tests and assessments? For what type of testing and assessment is it most useful? Why?

4. Why is it important for classroom tests and assessments to measure a representative sample of intended learning outcomes?

5. What types of information should be considered during each of the following steps in constructing tests and assessments?

   a. Developing a set of specifications.
   b. Selecting the types of test items and assessment tasks to use.
   c. Writing the test items and assessment tasks.

6. List several learning outcomes that are best measured with objective test items. List several that require the use of performance assessment tasks.

7. List as many specific factors as you can think of that might prevent some students from performing their best even though they possessed the knowledge and skills the item or task was designed to measure.

8. List as many specific factors as you can think of that would enable some students to answer an

objective test item correctly even though they lacked the knowledge the item was designed to measure.

9. Assume that you are going to prepare a brief unit test for a unit of work in a course in your major teaching area. How would you proceed? How would your procedure differ if it were to be an end-of-course summative test or assessment?

FURTHER READING

Gronlund, N. E. (1993). *How to make achievement tests and assessments* (5th ed.). Boston: Allyn & Bacon. Chapters 1 and 2 describe the role of measurement in instruction and provide guidelines on planning achievement tests.

Millman, J., & Greene, J. (1989). The specification and development of tests of achievement and ability. In R. L. Linn (Ed.), *Educational measurement* (3rd ed.). New York: Macmillan. A comprehensive and advanced treatment of test development.

Popham, W. J. (1990). *Modern educational measurement: A practitioner's perspective* (2nd ed.). Englewood Cliffs, NJ: Prentice-Hall. Chapter 9 describes the use of detailed specifications in constructing criterion-referenced tests.

CHAPTER 6

Constructing Objective Test Items: Simple Forms

Each type of test item has its own unique characteristics, uses, advantages, limitations, and rules for construction. In this chapter these characteristics are considered for objective-test forms that typically measure relatively simple learning outcomes: (1) the short-answer item, (2) the true–false item, and (3) the matching exercise.

The preliminary test planning described in the last chapter provides a sound basis for developing classroom tests that can be used for a variety of instructional purposes. The test specifications clarify the sample of achievement to be measured, and the various considerations in test planning form a general framework within which to proceed. The next step is the actual construction of test items. This step is crucial because the validity of a classroom test is ultimately determined by the extent to which the performance to be measured is actually called forth by the test items. Selecting item types that are inappropriate for the learning outcomes to be measured, constructing items with technical defects, or unwittingly including irrelevant clues in the items can undermine all of the careful planning that has gone on before.

The construction of good test items is an art. The skills it requires, however, are the same as those found in effective teaching. Needed are a thorough grasp of subject matter, a clear conception of the desired learning outcomes, a psychological understanding of students, sound judgment, persistence, and a touch of creativity. The only additional requisite for constructing good test items is the skillful application of an array of simple but important rules and suggestions. These techniques of test construction are the topic of this and the next two chapters. The rules for constructing test items, described in these chapters, are applicable to all types of classroom tests.

In this chapter we shall limit our discussion to the simpler forms of objective test items, namely, the (1) short-answer item, (2) true–false or alternative-response item, and (3) matching exercise. These item types are treated together, as their use in classroom testing is largely restricted to the measurement of simple learning outcomes in the knowledge area. The discussion of each item type will be followed by a checklist for reviewing the items.

SHORT-ANSWER ITEMS

The short-answer item and the completion item both are supply-type test items that can be answered by a word, phrase, number, or symbol. They are essentially the same, differing only in the method of presenting the problem. The short-answer item uses a direct question, whereas the completion item consists of an incomplete statement.

EXAMPLES

Short answer

What is the name of the man who invented the steamboat?   (Robert Fulton)

Completion

The name of the man who invented the steamboat is   (Robert Fulton).

Also included in this category are problems in arithmetic, mathematics, science, and other areas, whose solution must be supplied by the student.

Uses of Short-Answer Items

The short-answer test item is suitable for measuring a wide variety of relatively simple learning outcomes. The following outcomes and test items illustrate some of its common uses:

EXAMPLES

Knowledge of terminology

Lines on a weather map that join points of the same barometric pressure are called
                                                                    (isobars).

Knowledge of specific facts

A member of the United States Senate is elected to a term of (6) years.

Knowledge of principles

If the temperature of a gas is held constant while the pressure applied to it is increased, what will happen to its volume?   (It will decrease.)

Knowledge of method or procedure

What device is used to detect whether an electric charge is positive or negative?

(electroscope)

Simple interpretations of data

How many syllables are there in the word Argentina? (4)

In the number 612, what value does the 6 represent? (600)

In the triangle below, what is the number of degrees in each angle? (60)

If an airplane flying northwest made a 180-degree turn, what direction would it be heading? (southeast)

More complex interpretations can be made when the short-answer item is used to measure the ability to interpret diagrams, charts, graphs, and pictorial data.

Even more notable exceptions to the general rule that short-answer items are limited to measuring simple learning outcomes are found in the areas of mathematics and science where the solutions to problems can be indicated by numbers or symbols. The following examples illustrate this use:

EXAMPLES

Ability to solve numerical problems

Milk sells for $.96 a quart and $3.68 a gallon. How many cents would you save on each quart of milk if you bought it by the gallon? (4)

Skill in manipulating mathematical symbols

$$\text{If } \frac{x}{b} = \frac{3}{b-1}, \text{ then } x = \frac{(3b)}{(b-1)}$$

Ability to complete and balance chemical equations

$$Mg + (2)HCl \rightarrow (MgCl_2 + H_2)$$

$$(2)Al + (6)HCl \rightarrow (2AlCl_3 + 3H_2)$$

For outcomes similar to those in these last examples, the short-answer item is clearly superior. The performance described in the learning outcomes is identical with the performance called forth by the test items. To obtain correct answers, students must actually solve problems, manipulate mathematical symbols, and complete and balance equations.

Attempts are sometimes made to measure such problem-solving activities with selection-type test items, commonly resulting in test items that do not function as intended or that measure quite different learning outcomes. In the following multiple-choice items, for example, note how the division problem can be solved by working it backwards (multiplying 2 × 43, or merely 2 × 3) and how in the second problem the value of x can be determined by substituting each of the alternative answers in the equation on a trial-and-error basis. Such problems obviously do not demand the problem-solving behavior we are attempting to measure.

EXAMPLES

$2\overline{)86}$ =

A 41

B 42

Ⓒ 43

D 44

If $\dfrac{x}{4} + \dfrac{x}{16} = 10$, then x equals

A 16

B 24

Ⓒ 32

D 48

Similar difficulties are encountered when we substitute selection items measuring the ability to "recognize balanced chemical equations" for short-answer items measuring the ability to "complete and balance chemical equations." The former task is a simple one requiring little more than a knowledge of arithmetic, but the latter one requires extensive knowledge of chemical reactions and their resulting products.

For large-scale testing programs it is possible to maintain some of the advantages of the supply-type item for mathematics problems that result in numerical answers while still retaining the efficiencies of machine scoring. The grid-in item, for example, was introduced on the Scholastic Assessment Test in the spring of 1994. This item type requires examinees to solve problems and grid in the numerical answer (see example). Obviously, there is no advantage to this type of grid-in item unless the test is administered to a large number of students.

EXAMPLE Five students get scores of 9, 7, 7, 5, and 4 on an eight-item quiz. What is the average score for these five students?

Nevertheless, it is interesting to consider the range of relatively complex mathematical problems that can be posed in a grid-in format. The 1990 Japanese University Entrance Center Examination makes flexible use of grid-in items to present relatively complicated mathematical problems.

EXAMPLE *Directions:* Each problem contains several blanks. Blanks are represented by bracketed, underlined numbers. Each blank must be filled with a single digit or sign. See the method shown in the following examples and answer in the specified space on the answer sheet:

1. {1}, {2}, {3}, {4}, ... each represent values between 0 and 9 or + or – signs. For example, to indicate –8 as the answer to {1}, {2}, mark

{1} ⊝ + 0 1 2 3 4 5 6 7 8 9
{2} – + 0 1 2 3 4 5 6 7 ⑧ 9

2. If the answer is a fraction, reduce the fraction to its lowest terms and indicate the sign in the numerator. For example to indicate –2/9 as the answer to {1}, {2}, /{3}, mark

{1} ⊝ + 0 1 2 3 4 5 6 7 8 9
{2} – + 0 1 ② 3 4 5 6 7 8 9
{3} – + 0 1 2 3 4 5 6 7 8 ⑨

Sample problem

Consider the triangle ABC with coordinates A (0,3), B (–1,0) and C (2,1)

1. The center of the circumscribed circle is

$$\frac{\{1\}}{\{2\}}, \frac{\{3\}}{\{4\}} \qquad \text{answer } \frac{1}{4}, \frac{5}{4}$$

and the radius is

$$\frac{\{5\}\sqrt{\{6\}}}{\{7\}}$$ answer $\dfrac{5\sqrt{2}}{4}$

Also,

$$\sin{<}ABC=\frac{\{8\}}{\{9\}}$$ answer $\dfrac{4}{5}$

and the area of triangle ABC is {10}   answer 4

From these conditions, we know that the radius of the inscribed circle is

$$\frac{\sqrt{\{11\}\{12\}}-\sqrt{\{13\}}}{\{14\}}$$ answer $\dfrac{\sqrt{10}-\sqrt{2}}{2}$

2. If point P moves along the sides of triangle ABC, the maximum value of the distance between the origin O and point P is

    {15}   answer 3

and the minimum value is

$$\frac{1}{\sqrt{\{16\}\,\{17\}}}$$ answer $\dfrac{1}{\sqrt{10}}$

A correctly completed answer sheet for the seventeen bracketed numbers would be as follows:

{1} – + 0 ① 2 3 4 5 6 7 8 9
{2} – + 0 1 2 3 ④ 5 6 7 8 9
{3} – + 0 1 2 3 4 ⑤ 6 7 8 9
{4} – + 0 1 2 3 ④ 5 6 7 8 9
{5} – + 0 1 2 3 4 ⑤ 6 7 8 9
{6} – + 0 1 ② 3 4 5 6 7 8 9
{7} – + 0 1 2 3 ④ 5 6 7 8 9
{8} – + 0 1 2 3 ④ 5 6 7 8 9
{9} – + 0 1 2 3 4 ⑤ 6 7 8 9
{10} – + 0 1 2 3 ④ 5 6 7 8 9
{11} – + 0 ① 2 3 4 5 6 7 8 9
{12} – + ⓪ 1 2 3 4 5 6 7 8 9
{13} – + 0 1 ② 3 4 5 6 7 8 9
{14} – + 0 1 ② 3 4 5 6 7 8 9
{15} – + 0 1 2 ③ 4 5 6 7 8 9
{16} – + 0 ① 2 3 4 5 6 7 8 9
{17} – + ⓪ 1 2 3 4 5 6 7 8 9

Source: L. E. T. Wu (ed.), *Japanese University Entrance Examination Problems in Mathematics.* Washington, DC: The Mathematical Association of America, 1993. pages 1 and 5. Used by permission.

It is clear from this example that grid-in problems requiring complex problem-solving can be constructed, but the approach is only likely to be useful when a test is administered to a large number of students. For classroom use, short-answer problems and extended free-response assessment tasks of the type discussed in Chapters 9 and 10 are likely to provide more information about how students approach such problems and the nature of the difficulties they encounter.

In summary, if the short-answer test item is most effective for measuring a specific learning outcome, it should be used. We should not discard it for selection-type items unless we are fairly certain that the same learning outcomes will be measured. For many of the simpler learning outcomes, such as knowledge of factual information, changing to some form of selection item will not decrease the validity of the measurement and will result in increased objectivity and ease of scoring. For some of the more complex learning outcomes such as those in mathematics and science, however, discarding the short-answer test item may mean a change in the learning outcomes being measured. In deciding whether to use short-answer items or some other item type, our best guide is to follow this principle: Each learning outcome should be measured as directly as possible, and the test-item type most appropriate for the purpose should be used.

Advantages and Limitations of Short-Answer Items

The short-answer test item is one of the easiest to construct, partly because of the relatively simple learning outcomes it usually measures. Except for the problem-solving outcomes measured in mathematics and science, the short-answer item is used almost exclusively to measure the recall of memorized information.

A more important advantage of the short-answer item is that the students must supply the answer. This reduces the possibility that the students will obtain the correct answer by guessing. They must either recall the information requested or make the necessary computations to solve the problem presented to them. Partial knowledge, which might enable them to choose the correct answer on a selection item, is insufficient for answering a short-answer test item correctly.

There are two major limitations that restrict the use of the short-answer test item. One—unsuitability for measuring complex learning outcomes—has already been mentioned. The other is the difficulty of scoring. Unless the question is very carefully phrased, many answers of varying degrees of correctness must be considered for total or partial credit. For example, a question such as "Where was George Washington born?" could be answered by the name of the city, county, state, region, or continent. Although the teacher may have had the name of the state in mind when the question was written, the other answers could not be dismissed as incorrect. But even when this problem is avoided, the scoring is contaminated by the student's spelling ability. If full or partial credit is taken off for misspelled words, the students' test scores will reflect varying degrees of knowledge and spelling skill. If spelling is not counted in the scoring, the teacher must still decide whether misspelled words actually represent the correct answer. We all are familiar with misspellings so bad that it is difficult to determine what the student had in mind. The complications make scoring more time-consuming and less objective than that obtained with selection-type items.

These limitations are less troublesome when the answer is to be expressed in numbers or symbols, as in physical science or mathematics. Here, more complex learning outcomes can be measured, spelling is not a problem, and it is usually easier to write test items for which there is only one correct response.

Suggestions for Constructing Short-Answer Items

The short-answer item is subject to a variety of defects, even though it is considered one of the easiest to construct. The following suggestions will help you avoid possible pitfalls and provide greater assurance that the items will function as intended.

1. *Word the item so that the required answer is both brief and specific.* As indicated earlier, the answer to an item should be a word, phrase, number, or symbol. This can be easily conveyed to the students through the directions at the beginning of the test and by proper phrasing of the question. More difficult is stating the question so that only one answer is correct.

EXAMPLES   *Poor:*   An animal that eats the flesh of other animals is (carnivorous).

     Better: An animal that eats the flesh of other animals is classified as (carnivorous).

The first version of this item is so indefinite that it could be completed with answers such as *the wolf, the lion,* or even *hungry.* Asking the students to classify this type of animal, as called for in the improved version, better structures the problem and defines the type of response required.

2. *Do not take statements directly from textbooks to use as a basis for short-answer items.* When taken out of context, textbook statements are frequently too general and ambiguous to serve as good short-answer items. Note the vagueness of the first version of the following test item, which was taken verbatim from a chemistry textbook:

EXAMPLES   *Poor:*   Chlorine is a (halogen).

     Better: Chlorine belongs to a group of elements that combine with metals to form salts. It is therefore called a (halogen).

Students are most likely to respond to the first version of this test item with the word *gas,* because that is the natural state of chlorine, and there is nothing in the statement to imply that the word *halogen* is wanted. The only students who are apt to supply the intended answer are those who memorized the textbook statements. The revised version measures an important knowledge that is not dependent on the phraseology of the textbook. Such items tend to discourage the students from developing little-understood verbal associations based on textbook language and encourage them to achieve the learning outcomes being measured.

3. A direct question is generally more desirable than an incomplete statement. There are two advantages to the direct-question form. First, it is more natural to the students, as this is the usual method of phrasing questions in daily classroom discussions. This is especially important to elementary students when first exposed to short-answer tests. Second, the direct question is usually better structured and free of much of the ambiguity that creeps into items based on incomplete statements. Just the phrasing of a question requires us to decide what it is we want to know.

EXAMPLES

Poor: John Glenn made his first orbital flight around the earth in _____ (1962).

Better: When did John Glenn make his first orbital flight around the earth? _____ (1962).

Best: In what year did John Glenn make his first orbital flight around the earth? _____ (1962).

The first version of the item could, of course, be completed with *a space capsule, Friendship Seven, space,* and similar answers. Putting it in question form forces us to indicate whether it is the time, place, or method we are interested in knowing. The last version is a refinement that makes the question even more specific and that naturally evolves from a consideration of the *when* aspect of the previous question.

4. If the answer is to be expressed in numerical units, indicate the type of answer wanted. For computational problems, it is usually preferable to indicate the units in which the answer is to be expressed. This will clarify the problem and will simplify the scoring.

EXAMPLES

Poor: If oranges weigh 5 2/3 oz. each, how much will a dozen oranges weigh? _____ (4 lb. 4 oz.).

Better: If oranges weigh 5 2/3 oz. each, how much will a dozen oranges weigh? (4) lb. (4) oz.

Unless the type of unit is specified, as in the revised version, correct answers will include 68 oz., 4 1/4 lb., 4.25 lb., and 4 lb 4 oz. This adds unnecessary confusion to the scoring.

When the problems do not come out even, it is also usually helpful to indicate the degree of precision expected in the answers. For example, specifying that the answers should be "carried out to two decimal places" or "rounded off to the nearest tenth of a percent" makes clear to the students how far to carry their calculations. This will ensure that they reach the degree of precision desired and also prevent them from wasting valuable testing time attempting to achieve a degree of precision not expected.

There are some instances, especially in science, when knowing the proper unit in which the answer is to be expressed and knowing the degree of precision to be expected are important aspects of the learning outcome to be measured. In such cases, the previous suggestions must, of course, be modified.

5.   *Blanks for answers should be equal in length and in a column to the right of the question.* If blanks for answers are kept equal in length, the length of the blank space does not supply a clue to the answer. In the poor version of the following items, the lengths of the blanks restrict the possible answers the students need consider. For the first item they need a long word and for the second item a short one.

EXAMPLES *Poor:* What is the name of the part of speech that connects words, clauses, and sentences?
                                                    (conjunction)

          What is the name of the part of speech that declares, asserts, or predicts something?
                                                       (verb)

     Better: What is the name of the part of speech that connects words, clauses, and sentences?
                                                    (conjunction)

          What is the name of the part of speech that declares, asserts, or predicts something?
                                              _____ (verb)

Placing the blanks in a column to the right of the question makes scoring quicker and more accurate.

6.   *When completion items are used, do not include too many blanks.* If a statement is too mutilated by blanks, the meaning will be lost, and the student will have to guess what the teacher had in mind. Although some mutilated statements seem to measure complex reasoning abilities, such responses are more appropriate as measures of intelligence than achievement.

EXAMPLES *Poor:* (Warm-blooded) animals that are born (alive) and (suckle) their young are called
                                                           (mammals).

     Better: Warm-blooded animals that are born alive and suckle their young are called
                                                           (mammals).

In the revised version, the blank is at the end of the statement so the students are presented with a clearly defined problem before they come to the blank. See the accompanying "Checklist" for a review of the guidelines for constructing short-answer tests.

CHECKLIST		
Reviewing Short-Answer Items		
	Yes	**No**
1. Is this the most appropriate type of item to use for the intended learning outcomes?	_____	_____
2. Can the items be answered with a number, symbol, word, or brief phrase?	_____	_____
3. Has textbook language been avoided?	_____	_____
4. Have the items been stated so that only one response is correct?	_____	_____
5. Are the answer blanks equal in length?	_____	_____
6. Are the answer blanks at the end of the items?	_____	_____
7. Are the items free of clues (such as *a* or *an*)?	_____	_____
8. Has the degree of precision been indicated for numerical answers?	_____	_____
9. Have the units been indicated when numerical answers are expressed in units?	_____	_____
10. Have the items been phrased so as to minimize spelling errors?	_____	_____
11. If revised, are the items still relevant to the intended learning outcomes?	_____	_____
12. Have the items been set aside for a time before reviewing them?	_____	_____

TRUE–FALSE OR ALTERNATIVE-RESPONSE ITEMS

The alternative-response test item consists of a declarative statement that the student is asked to mark true or false, right or wrong, correct or incorrect, yes or no, fact or opinion, agree or disagree, or the like. In each case there are only two possible answers. Because the true–false option is the most common, this item type is most frequently referred to as the true–false test item. Some of the variations, however, deviate considerably from the simple true–false pattern and have their own characteristics. For this reason, some prefer the more general category, alternative-response item. We shall retain the more commonly used true–false designation.

Uses of True–False Items

Probably the most common use of the true–false item is in measuring the ability to identify the correctness of statements of fact, definitions of terms, statements of principles, and the like. For measuring such relatively simple learning outcomes, a single declarative statement is used with any one of several methods of responding.

EXAMPLES

Directions: Read each of the following statements; If the statement is true, circle the T. If the statement is false, circle the F.

Ⓣ   F   1. The green coloring material in a plant leaf is called chlorophyll.

T   Ⓕ   2. The corolla of a flower includes petals and sepals.

Ⓣ   F   3. Photosynthesis is the process by which leaves make a plant's food.

Directions: Read each of the following questions. If the answer is yes, circle the Y. If the answer is no, circle the N.

Ⓨ   N   1. Is 51% of 38 more than 19?

Y   Ⓝ   2. Is 50% of 4/10 equal to 2/5?

Y   Ⓝ   3. If 60% of a number is 9, is the number smaller than 9?

Ⓨ   N   4. Is 25% of 44 less than 12?

One of the useful functions of the true–false item is in measuring the student's ability to distinguish fact from opinion. The following examples illustrate this use:

EXAMPLES

Directions: Read each of the following statements. If the statement is a fact, circle the F. If the statement is an opinion, circle the O.

Ⓕ   O   1. The Constitution of the United States is the highest law of our country.

F   Ⓞ   2. The first amendment to the Constitution is the most important amendment.

Ⓕ   O   3. The fifth amendment to the Constitution protects people from testifying against themselves.

F   Ⓞ   4. Other countries should adopt a constitution like that of the United States.

Directions: Read each of the following statements. If the statement is true, circle the T. If the statement is false, circle the F. If the statement is an opinion, circle the O.

Ⓣ   F   O 1. The earth is a planet.

T   Ⓕ   O 2. The earth revolves around the moon.

T   F   Ⓞ 3. There are intelligent life forms on planets orbiting some distant stars.

These items measure a learning outcome important to all subject-matter areas: if people are to think critically about a topic, they must first be able to distinguish fact from opinion.

All too frequently, true–false tests include numerous opinion statements to which the student is asked to respond true or false. This is extremely frustrating because there is no objective basis for determining whether a statement of opinion is true or false. The student must usually guess what opinion the teacher holds and mark the answers accordingly. This, of course, is undesirable from all standpoints— testing, teaching, and learning. It is much better to have the student identify statements of opinion as such. An alternative procedure is to attribute the opinion to some source, making it possible to mark the statements true or false and measuring knowledge concerning the beliefs held by an individual or the values supported by an organization or institution.

EXAMPLES

Directions: Read each of the following statements. If the statement is true, circle the T. If the statement is false, circle the F.

    T   (F) 1. Franklin D. Roosevelt believed that labor unions interfered with the United States free-enterprise system.

    (T)   F   2. The American Federation of Labor favors the closed shop.

    T   (F) 3. The Supreme Court of the United States supports the principle of equal but separate facilities for the education of different racial groups.

Items like these can become measures of understanding if the opinion statements attributed to an individual or group are new to the student. The task then becomes one of interpreting the beliefs held by the individual or group and applying them to the new situation.

Another aspect of understanding that can be measured by the true–false item is the ability to recognize cause-and-effect relationships. This type of item usually contains two true propositions in one statement, and the student is to judge whether the relationship between them is true or false.

EXAMPLES

Directions: In each of the following statements, both parts of the statement are true. You are to decide whether the second part explains why the first part is true. If it does, circle Yes. If it does not, circle No.

Yes	(No)	1. Leaves are essential	*because*	they shade the tree trunk.
Yes	(No)	2. Whales are mammals	*because*	they are large.
(Yes)	No	3. Some plants do not need sunlight	*because*	they get their food from other plants.

The true–false item also can be used to measure some simple aspects of logic, as illustrated by the following items that were developed for use in a science test:

EXAMPLES   *Directions:* Read each of the following statements. If the statement is true, circle the T; if it is false circle the F. Also, if the converse of the statement is true, circle the CT; if the converse is false, circle the CF. Be sure to give two answers for each statement.

Ⓣ   F   CT   ⒸⒻ   1. All trees are plants.

T   Ⓕ   CT   ⒸⒻ   2. All parasites are animals.

T   Ⓕ   ⒸⓉ   CF   3. All eight-legged animals are spiders.

Ⓣ   F   ⒸⓉ   CF   4. No spiders are insects.

A common criticism of the true–false item is that a student may be able to recognize a false statement as incorrect but still not know what is correct. For example, when students answer the following item as false, it does not indicate whether they know what negatively charged particles of electricity are called; all the answer tells us is that they know they are not called neutrons.

EXAMPLE   T Ⓕ   Negatively charged particles of electricity are called neutrons.

This is a rather crude measure of knowledge, because there is an infinite number of things that negatively charged particles of electricity are *not* called. To overcome such difficulties, some teachers prefer to have the students change all false statements to true. When this is required, the part of the statement it is permissible to change should be indicated.

EXAMPLES   *Directions:* Read each of the following statements. If a statement is true, circle the T. If a statement is false, circle the F and change the underlined word to make the statement true. Place the new word in the blank space after the F.

T   Ⓕ   (electrons) _____   1. Particles of negatively charged electricity are called <u>neutrons</u>.

Ⓣ   F   _____   2. Mechanical energy is turned into electrical energy by means of the <u>generator</u>.

T   Ⓕ   (store) _____   3. An electric condenser is used to <u>generate</u> electricity.

Unless the key words to be changed are indicated, students are liable to rewrite the entire statement. In addition to the increase in scoring difficulty, this frequently leads to true statements that deviate considerably from the original intent of the item. A clever student may even change false statements to true by simply adding *not* in the appropriate place.

Advantages and Limitations of True-False Items

A major advantage of true–false items is that they are efficient. In a given period of time, students can typically respond to roughly three true–false items in the time it takes to respond to two multiple choice items (Ebel & Frisbie, 1991).

Proponents of true–false items like Ebel and Frisbie argue that verbal knowledge is central to educational achievement and that "all verbal knowledge can be expressed in propositions" which can be judged to be true or false (p. 135). They make a strong case for the utility of true–false for measuring a broad range of verbal knowledge.

One advantage cited frequently for true–false items, is, unfortunately, more illusory than real—ease of construction. This has probably resulted from the common practice of taking statements from textbooks, changing half of them to false statements and submitting the product to students as a true–false test. Such test items are often so obvious that everyone gets them correct or so ambiguous that even the better students are confused by them. In short, it is easy to construct poor true–false items. To construct unambiguous true–false items that measure significant learning outcomes, however, requires much skill.

A second advantage attributed to the true–false item is that a wide sampling of course material can be obtained. But this advantage, too, may be more apparent than real. Because a student can respond to many test items in a short period of time, it would be easy to conclude that many areas can be covered. However, many types of subject matter do not lend themselves to true–false type items. True–false statements require course material that can be phrased so that the statements are true or false without qualification or exception. In all subject-matter fields there are areas in which such absolutely true or false statements cannot be made. In some fields, such as the social sciences, practically all significant statements require some qualification. Only relatively trivial statements can be reduced to absolute terms.

One of the most serious limitations of the true–false item is in the types of learning outcomes that can be measured. True–false items are not especially useful beyond the knowledge area. The exceptions to this seem to be distinguishing between fact and opinion and identifying cause-and-effect relationships. These two outcomes are probably the most important measured by this type of item. Many of the learning outcomes measured by the true–false item can be measured more effectively by other forms of selection items, especially the multiple-choice form.

Another factor that limits the usefulness of the true–false item is its susceptibility to guessing. With only two alternatives, a student has a fifty-fifty chance of selecting the correct answer on the basis of chance alone, and because of the difficulty of constructing items that do not contain clues to the answer, the student's chances of guessing correctly are usually much greater than 50 percent. This disadvantage is partially offset by the relatively large number of items that can be answered in a given period of time. Nevertheless, with a typical 100 item true–false test, it is not unusual to have the lowest score above 80. An indeterminate amount of knowledge is reflected in such a score: many of the correct answers can be accounted for by chance or the presence of clues. A scoring formula utilizing a correction for guessing is frequently suggested as a solution for this problem. This formula compensates only chance guesses, however, and does not include those guided by clues. In addition, such a scoring formula favors individuals willing to take a chance. Even when warned that there will be a penalty for guessing, these individuals will continue to guess, using any clues available, and will do better than chance. Cautious students, on the other hand, will mark only those answers they are certain are correct and will omit many items they could have marked correctly using clues and partial information. Thus, the scores tend to reflect personality differences as well as knowledge of the subject.

The great likelihood of successful guessing on the true–false item has effects that are at least as deleterious. (1) The reliability of each item is low, making it necessary to include many items in order to obtain a reliable measure of achievement. (2) The diagnostic value of such a test is practically nil because analyzing a student's response to each item is meaningless.

One last concern that needs to be considered in the design of tests with true–false items is student response sets. As noted earlier, a response set is a consistent tendency to follow a certain pattern in responding to test items. In taking a true–false test, for example, some students will consistently mark "true" those items they do not know, and others will consistently mark them "false." Thus, if there is not a balance between true and false items, a given test will favor one response set over another and introduce an element into the test score that is irrelevant to the purpose of the test.

True–false items are most useful in situations in which there are only two possible alternatives (e.g., right, left; more, less; who, whom; and so on) and special uses such as distinguishing fact from opinion, cause from effect, superstition from scientific belief, relevant from irrelevant information, valid from invalid conclusions, and the like.

Suggestions for Constructing True–False Items

The main task in constructing true–false items is formulating statements free from ambiguity and irrelevant clues. This is extremely difficult, and the only guidance that can be given is a list of things to *avoid* when phrasing the statements.

1.   *Avoid broad general statements if they are to be judged true or false.* Most broad generalizations are false unless qualified, and the use of qualifiers provides clues to the answer.

EXAMPLES   *Poor:*   T   (F)   The president of the United States is elected to that office.

Poor: (T)   F   The president of the United States is usually elected to that office.

In this example, the first version is generally true but must be marked false because there are exceptions, such as when the vice president takes office in event of the president's death. In the second version, the qualifier *usually* makes the statement true but provides a definite clue. Words such as *usually, generally, often,* and *sometimes* are most likely to appear in true statements, and absolute terms such as *always, never, all, none,* and *only* are more apt to appear in false statements. Although the influence of such clues sometimes can be offset by balancing their use in true–false statements, the simplest solution seems to be to avoid the use of broad generalizations that are obviously false or must be qualified by specific determiners.

2. *Avoid trivial statements.*   In an attempt to obtain statements that are unequivocally true or false, we sometimes inadvertently turn to specific statements of fact that fit this criterion beautifully but have little significance from a learning standpoint.

EXAMPLES	*Poor:*	Ⓣ	F	Harry S. Truman was the thirty-third president of the United States.
	Poor:	T	Ⓕ	The United States declared war on Japan on December 7, 1941.

The first item calls for a relatively unimportant fact concerning Truman's tenure as president, and the second item expects the student to remember that the United States did not declare war until December 8. Such items cause students to direct their attention toward memorizing minutiae at the expense of more general knowledge and understanding.

3. *Avoid the use of negative statements, especially double negatives.* Students tend to overlook negative words such as *no* or *not*, and double negatives contribute to the statement's ambiguity. Note the ambiguity in this relatively simple statement, which uses two negatives.

EXAMPLES	*Poor:*	Ⓣ	F	None of the steps in the experiment was unnecessary.
	Better:	Ⓣ	F	All of the steps in the experiment were necessary.

When a negative word must be used, it should be underlined or put in italics so that students do not overlook it.

4. *Avoid long, complex sentences.*   As noted earlier, a test item should indicate whether a student has achieved the knowledge or understanding being measured. Long, complex sentences tend also to measure the extraneous factor of reading comprehension and therefore should be avoided in tests designed to measure achievement.

EXAMPLES	*Poor:*	Ⓣ	F	Despite the theoretical and experimental difficulties of determining the exact pH value of a solution, it is possible to determine whether a solution is acid by the red color formed on litmus paper when it is inserted into the solution.
	Better:	Ⓣ	F	Litmus paper turns red in an acid solution.

As in the preceding example, it frequently is possible to shorten and simplify a statement by eliminating nonfunctional material and restating the main idea. If this is not possible, it may be necessary to change to another item form in order to avoid a complex sentence structure.

5.   *Avoid including two ideas in one statement, unless cause–effect relationships are being measured.* Some difficulties arising from the inclusion of two ideas in one statement are apparent in the following example, which is one of many similar items a teacher actually used in a biology examination. In each instance, the students were asked to judge merely whether the statement was true or false.

EXAMPLE   *Poor:*   T   Ⓕ   A worm cannot see because it has simple eyes.

This item is keyed false because a worm does not have simple eyes. However, when this teacher asked a student why he marked it false, the student said, "Worms *can* see." This demonstrates that students can get items correct with erroneous information. This is so because the first proposition can be true or false, the second proposition can be true or false, and the relationship between them can be true or false. Thus, when students mark the item false, there is no way of determining to which of the three elements they are responding. The best solution to this dilemma seems to be to use only true propositions and to ask the students to judge the truth or falsity of the relationships between them. Such items also might, of course, be divided into two simple statements, each containing a single idea.

6.   *If opinion is used, attribute it to some source, unless the ability to identify opinion is being specifically measured.* Statements of opinion cannot be marked true or false, and it is unfair to expect students to guess how the teacher will score such items, or to respond to opinion statements as statements of fact. Knowing whether some significant individual or group supports or refutes a certain opinion, however, can be important from a learning standpoint.

EXAMPLES   *Poor:*   T   F   Adequate medical care can be best provided through socialized medicine.

         Better: T   Ⓕ   The American Medical Association favors socialized medicine as the best means of providing adequate medical care.

The first version cannot be answered true or false. It may serve a useful purpose in an attitude test, but there is no factual basis on which to decide the truth or falsity of the statement. The second version is clearly false.

7.   *True statements and false statements should be approximately equal in length.* There is a natural tendency for true statements to be longer because such statements must be precisely phrased in order to be absolutely true. This can be overcome by lengthening the false statements through the use of qualifying phrases similar to those found in true statements. Thus, the length of the statement will be eliminated as a possible clue to the correct answer.

8. The number of true statements and false statements should be approximately equal. Constructing a test with an approximately equal number of true statements and false statements will prevent response sets from unduly inflating or deflating the students' scores. You will recall that some students consistently mark statements "true" when in doubt about an answer, whereas others consistently mark them "false." Neither response set should be favored by overloading the test with items of one type.

In honoring this suggestion, the words approximately equal should be given special attention. If a teacher consistently uses exactly the same number, this will provide a clue to the student who is unable to answer some of the test items. The best procedure seems to be to vary the percentage of true statements somewhere between 40 and 60 percent. Under no circumstances should the statements be all true or all false. Students who detect this as a possibility can obtain perfect scores on the basis of one guess.

See the accompanying *Checklist* for questions to use in reviewing true–false items.

CHECKLIST

Reviewing True–False Items

	Yes	No
1. Is this the most appropriate type of item to use?	___	___
2. Can each statement be clearly judged true or false?	___	___
3. Have specific determiners (e.g., usually, always) been avoided?	___	___
4. Have trivial statements been avoided?	___	___
5. Have negative statements (especially double negatives) been avoided?	___	___
6. Have the items been stated in simple, clear language?	___	___
7. Are opinion statements attributed to some source?	___	___
8. Are the true and false items approximately equal in length?	___	___
9. Is there an approximately equal number of true and false items?	___	___
10. Has a detectable pattern of answers (e.g., T, F, T, F) been avoided?	___	___
11. If revised, are the items still relevant to the intended learning outcomes?	___	___
12. Have the items been set aside for a time before reviewing them?	___	___

MATCHING EXERCISES

In its traditional form, the matching exercise consists of two parallel columns with each word, number, or symbol in one column being matched to a word, sentence, or phrase in the other column. The items in the column for which a match is sought are called premises, and the items in the column from which the selection is made are called responses. The basis for matching premises to responses is sometimes self-evident but more often must be explained in the directions. In any event, the student's task is to identify the pairs of items that are to be associated on the basis indicated. For example, the student may be asked to identify important historical events, as in the following illustration:

EXAMPLES   *Directions:* On the line to the left of each United States space event in Column A, write the letter of the astronaut in Column B who achieved that honor. Each name in Column B may be used once, more than once, or not at all.

Column A	*Column B*
(G) 1. First United States astronaut to ride in a space capsule.	A Edwin Aldrin
(E) 2. First United States astronaut to orbit the earth.	B Neil Armstrong
(H) 3. First United States astronaut to walk in space.	C Frank Borman
(B) 4. First United States astronaut to step on the moon.	D Scott Carpenter
	E John Glenn
	F Wally Schirra
	G Alan Shepard
	H Edward White

This matching exercise illustrates an imperfect match; that is, there are more names in Column B than are needed to match each event in Column A. The directions also indicate that an item may be used once, more than once, or not at all. Both of these procedures prevent students from matching the final pair of items on the basis of elimination.

Two other factors are notable in our example. First, the items in the list of premises in Column A are homogeneous, as they all are concerned with important space events. Such homogeneity is necessary if a matching exercise is to function properly. Second, for each premise in Column A there are several plausible responses in Column B. Thus, the incorrect responses serve as attractive choices for those students who are in doubt about the correct answers. Both factors tend to minimize the opportunity for successful guessing.

Uses of Matching Exercises

The typical matching exercise is limited to measuring factual information based on simple associations. Whenever learning outcomes emphasize the ability to identify the relationship between two things and a sufficient number of homogeneous premises and responses can be obtained, a matching exercise seems most appropriate.

It is a compact and efficient method of measuring such simple knowledge outcomes. Examples of relationships considered important by teachers, in a variety of fields, include the following:

Persons .... Achievements
Dates .... Historical Events
Terms .... Definitions
Rules .... Examples
Symbols .... Concepts
Authors .... Titles of Books
Foreign Words .... English Equivalents
Machines .... Uses
Plants or Animals .... Classification
Principles .... Illustrations
Objects .... Names of Objects
Parts .... Functions

The matching exercise has also been used with pictorial materials in relating pictures and words or to identify positions on maps, charts, and diagrams. Regardless of the form of presentation, the student's task is essentially to relate two things that have some logical basis for association. This restricts the use of the matching exercise to a relatively small area of student achievement.

Advantages and Limitations of Matching Exercises

The major advantage of the matching exercise is its compact form, which makes it possible to measure a large amount of related factual material in a relatively short time. This is a mixed blessing, however, as it frequently leads to the excessive use of matching exercises and a corresponding overemphasis on the memorization of simple relationships.

Another advantage often cited for the matching exercise is ease of construction. Poor matching items can be rapidly constructed, but good matching items require a high degree of skill. The correct response for each premise must also serve as a plausible response for the other premises. Any lack of plausibility will reduce the number of possible choices and provide clues to the correct answer. The matching exercise tends to have more irrelevant clues than any other item type, with the possible exception of the true–false item.

The main limitations of the matching exercise are that it is restricted to the measurement of factual information based on rote learning and that it is highly susceptible to the presence of irrelevant clues. Another limitation, somewhat related, is the difficulty of finding homogeneous material that is significant from the viewpoint of our objectives and learning outcomes. For example, we might start out with a few great scientists and their achievements, which we feel all students should know. In order to construct a matching item, it becomes necessary to add the names and achievements of other, lesser-known scientists. Thus, we find ourselves measuring factual information that was not included in our original test plan and that is far less important than other aspects of knowledge we had intended to include. In short, less significant material is introduced into the test because enough significant, homogeneous material is unavailable. This is a common problem in constructing matching exercises and one not easily avoided. One solution is to begin with multiple-choice items, because each item can be directly related to a particular outcome, and to switch to the matching form only when homogeneous material makes the matching exercise a more efficient method of measuring the same achievement.

Suggestions for Constructing Matching Exercises

Although the matching exercise has only limited usefulness in classroom tests, whenever it is used, special efforts should be made to remove irrelevant clues and to arrange it so that the student can respond quickly and without confusion. The following suggestions are designed to guide such efforts:

1.   Use only homogeneous material in a single matching exercise. This has been mentioned before and is repeated here for emphasis. It is without a doubt the most important rule of construction and yet the one most commonly violated. One reason for this is that homogeneity is a matter of degree and what is homogeneous to one group may be heterogeneous to another. For example, let us assume that we are following the usual suggestion for obtaining homogeneity and develop a matching exercise that includes only men and their achievements. We might end up with a test exercise like below.

EXAMPLES

Directions: On the line to the left of each achievement listed in Column A, write the letter of the man's name in Column B who is noted for that achievement. Each name in Column B may be used once, more than once, or not at all.

	Column A	Column B
(A)	1. Invented the telephone.	A. Alexander Graham Bell
(B)	2. Discovered America.	B. Christopher Columbus
(C)	3. First United States astronaut to orbit the earth.	C. John Glenn
(F)	4. First president of the United States.	D. Abraham Lincoln
		E. Ferdinand Magellan
		F. George Washington
		G. Eli Whitney

Although the matching exercise in our example may be homogeneous for most students in the primary grades, the discriminations called for are so gross that students above that level will see it as a heterogeneous collection of inventors, explorers, and presidents. Thus, to obtain homogeneity at higher grade levels, it is necessary to have only inventors and their inventions in one matching exercise, explorers and their discoveries in another, and presidents and their achievements in another. At a still higher level, it may be necessary to limit matching exercises still further, such as to inventors whose inventions are in the same field, in order to keep the material homogeneous and free from irrelevant clues. As we increase the level of discrimination called for in a matching exercise, significant homogeneous material becomes increasingly difficult to obtain. Take inventors, for example. How many significant inventions are there in any one area?

2. Include an unequal number of responses and premises, and instruct the student that responses may be used once, more than once, or not at all. This will make all the responses eligible for selection for each premise and will decrease the likelihood of successful guessing. When an equal number of responses and premises are used and each response is used only once, the probability for guessing the remaining responses correctly is increased each time a correct answer is selected. The odds for correct guessing increase as the list of available responses decreases, and the final response, of course, can be selected entirely on the basis of this process of elimination.

In most matching exercises, imperfect matching can be obtained by including more or fewer responses than premises. In either case, the directions should instruct the student that each response may be used once, more than once, or not at all.

3. Keep the list of items to be matched brief, and place the shorter responses on the right. A brief list of items is advantageous to both the teacher and the student. From the teacher's standpoint, it is easier to maintain homogeneity in a brief list. In addition, there is a greater likelihood that the various learning outcomes and subject-matter topics will be measured in a balanced manner. Because each matching exercise must be based on homogeneous material, a long list will require excessive concentration in one area. From the students' viewpoint, a brief list enables them to read the responses rapidly and without confusion. Approximately four to seven items in each column seems best. There certainly should be no more than ten items in either column.

Placing the shorter responses on the right also contributes to more efficient test taking, as it enables students to read the longer premise first and then to scan rapidly the list of responses.

4. Arrange the list of responses in logical order. Place words in alphabetical order and numbers in sequence. This will contribute to the ease with which the students can scan the responses in searching for the correct answers. It will also prevent them from detecting possible clues from the arrangement of the responses.

EXAMPLES

Directions: On the line to the left of each historical event in Column A, write the letter from Column B that identifies the time period when the event occurred. Each date in Column B may be used once, more than once, or not at all.

	Column A	*Column B*
(B)	1. Boston Tea Party	A. 1765–1769
(A)	2. Repeal of the Stamp Act	B. 1770–1774
(E)	3. Enactment of the Northwest Ordinance	C. 1775–1779
(C)	4. Battle of Lexington	D. 1780–1784
(A)	5. Enactment of Townshend Acts	E. 1785–1789
(B)	6. First Continental Congress	
(E)	7. United States Constitution drawn up	

This matching exercise also demonstrates the use of fewer responses than premises and the desirability of placing the shortest items on the right.

5. *Indicate in the directions the basis for matching the responses and premises.* Although the basis for matching is rather obvious in most matching exercises, there are advantages in clearly stating it. First, ambiguity and confusion will be avoided. Second, testing time will be saved because the student will not need to read through the entire list of premises and responses and then "reason out" the basis for matching.

Special care must be taken when stating directions for matching items. Directions that precisely indicate the basis for matching frequently become long and involved, placing a premium on reading comprehension. For younger students, it may be desirable to give oral directions, put an example on the blackboard, and have the students draw lines between the matched items rather than transfer letters.

6. *Place all of the items for one matching exercise on the same page.* This will prevent the disturbance created by thirty or so students switching the pages of the test back and forth. It also will prevent them from missing the responses appearing on another page and generally adds to the speed and efficiency of test administration.

See the accompanying "Checklist" for a review of all the construction guidelines given here.

CHECKLIST

Reviewing Matching Items

	Yes	No
1. Is this the most appropriate type of item to use?	____	____
2. Is the material in the two lists homogeneous?	____	____
3. Is the list of responses longer or shorter than the list of premises?	____	____
4. Are the responses brief and on the right-hand side?	____	____
5. Have the responses been placed in alphabetical or numerical order?	____	____
6. Do the directions indicate the basis for matching?	____	____
7. Do the directions indicate that each response may be used more than once?	____	____
8. Is all of each matching item on the same page?	____	____
9. If revised, are the items still relevant to the intended learning outcomes?	____	____
10. Have the items been set aside for a time before reviewing them?	____	____

SUMMARY

The construction of classroom tests, like other phases of teaching, is an art that must be learned. It is not enough to have a knowledge of subject matter, defined learning outcomes, or a psychological understanding of the students' mental processes, although all of these are prerequisites. The ability to construct high-quality test items requires a knowledge of the principles and techniques of test construction and skill in their application.

In this chapter we discussed techniques for constructing short-answer items, true–false or alternative-response items, and matching exercises. Although these simple forms of objective test items can be made suitable for measuring understanding, thinking skills, and other complex achievements, considerable skill in item construction is required to go beyond simple knowledge outcomes. Other types of items and tasks are generally more satisfactory for measuring higher-level skills. Thus the primary use of these simple types of items is in measuring knowledge outcomes.

The short-answer item requires students to supply the appropriate word, number, or symbol to a direct question or incomplete statement. It can be used for measuring a variety of simple knowledge outcomes, but it is especially useful for measuring problem-solving ability in science and mathematics. The ease with which short-answer items can be constructed and their relative freedom from guessing favor their use. However, the areas in which they can be effectively used are restricted by the relatively simple learning outcomes measured and by the fact that the scoring can be contaminated by spelling errors. When short-answer items are used, the question must be stated clearly and concisely, be free from irrelevant clues, and require an answer that is both brief and definite. Problems requiring only a number or a symbol for an answer are particularly adaptable to the short-answer form.

The true–false item requires the student to select one of two possible answers. This item type is used for measuring knowledge outcomes when only two alternatives are possible or the ability to identify the correctness of statements of fact is important. It is also adaptable to measuring the ability to distinguish fact from opinion and the ability to recognize cause-and-effect relationships. The use of true–false items is limited by the difficulty of constructing clue-free items that measure significant learning outcomes, the susceptibility of this type to guessing, the low reliability of each item, and the general lack of diagnostic value. When used, special efforts must be made to formulate statements that are free from ambiguity, specific determiners, and clues.

The matching exercises consist of two parallel columns of phrases, words, numbers, or symbols that must be matched. Examples of items included in matching exercises are persons and achievements, dates and historical events, and terms and definitions. The nature of the matching exercise limits it to measuring the ability to identify the relationship between two things. For this restricted use, it is a compact item type that can be used to measure many relationships in a short time. Its limitations include the difficulty of removing irrelevant clues and the difficulty of finding significant homogeneous material. When homogeneous material is available, including more items in one column than in the other, arranging the shorter responses on the right and in logical order, and indicating clearly the basis for matching all will contribute to the effectiveness of the matching exercise.

LEARNING EXERCISES

1. Defend the statement "Short-answer items should not be classified as objective items."

2. How would you handle the scoring of short-answer items when the answers were misspelled?

3. Marking a false statement false does not guarantee that the student knows what is true. How would you handle this problem?

4. You could expect fifty true–false items to have lower reliability than would fifty short-answer items. Why?

5. Under what conditions is it preferable to use a matching item rather than some other item type? When should matching items be avoided?

6. In an area in which you are teaching or plan to teach, construct five short-answer items, five true–false items, and one five-alternative matching exercise. State the objectives being measured by the items.

REFERENCES

Ebel, R. L., & Frisbie, D. A. (1991). *Essentials of educational measurement* (5th ed.). Englewood Cliffs, N.J.: Prentice-Hall.

FURTHER READING

Bloom, B. S., Madaus, G. F., & Hastings, J. T. (1981). *Evaluation to Improve Learning*. New York: McGraw Hill. Chapter 7, "Item Writing and Item Selection," describes the various types of test items and suggestions for writing them. Includes numerous illustrative items and a summary checklist for item writing.

Ebel, R. L., & Frisbie, D. A. (1991). *Essentials of educational measurement* (5th ed.). Englewood Cliffs, N.J.: Prentice-Hall. In Chapter 8, "True–False Test Items," a strong case is made for their use and their construction is described and illustrated.

Gronlund, N. E. (1993). *How to make achievement tests and assessments* (5th ed.). Boston: Allyn & Bacon. Chapter 4 "Writing Selection Items: True–False, Matching, and Interpretive Exercises" describes true–false and matching item construction procedures and provides a number of examples.

CHAPTER 7

Constructing Objective Test Items: Multiple-Choice Forms

Objective test items are not limited to the measurement of simple learning outcomes. The multiple-choice item can measure both the knowledge and understanding levels and is free of many of the limitations of other forms of objective items.

The multiple-choice item is generally recognized as the most widely applicable and useful type of objective test item. It can effectively measure many of the simple learning outcomes measured by the short-answer item, the true–false item, and the matching exercise. In addition, it can measure a variety of complex outcomes in the knowledge, understanding, and application areas. This flexibility, plus the higher quality items usually found in the multiple-choice form, has led to its extensive use in achievement testing.

CHARACTERISTICS OF MULTIPLE-CHOICE ITEMS

A multiple-choice item consists of a problem and a list of suggested solutions. The problem may be stated as a direct question or an incomplete statement and is called the stem of the item. The list of suggested solutions may include words, numbers, symbols, or phrases and are called alternatives (also called choices or options). The student is typically requested to read the stem and the list of alternatives and to select the one correct, or best, alternative. The correct alternative in each item is called the answer, and the remaining alternatives are called distracters (also called decoys or foils). These incorrect alternatives receive their name from their intended function—to distract those students who are in doubt about the correct answer.

Whether to use a direct question or incomplete statement in the stem depends on several factors. The direct-question form is easier to write, is more natural for younger students, and is more likely to present a clearly formulated problem. On the other hand, the incomplete statement is more concise, and if skillfully phrased, it too can present a well-defined problem. A common procedure is to start each stem as a direct question and shift to the incomplete statement form only when the clarity of the problem can be retained and greater conciseness achieved.

EXAMPLES

Direct-question form

In which one of the following cities is the capital of California?

   A   Los Angeles

   Ⓑ   Sacramento

   C   San Diego

   D   San Francisco

Incomplete-statement form

The capital of California is in

   A   Los Angeles.

   Ⓑ   Sacramento.

   C   San Diego.

   D   San Francisco.

In these examples, there is only one correct answer. The capital of California is in Sacramento and nowhere else. All other alternatives are wrong. For obvious reasons, this is known as the correct-answer type of multiple-choice item.

Not all knowledge can be stated so precisely that there is only one absolutely correct response. In fact, when we get beyond the simple aspects of knowledge, represented by questions of the *who, what, when,* and *where* variety, answers of varying degrees of acceptability are the rule rather than the exception. Questions of the *why* variety, for example, tend to reveal a number of possible reasons, some of which are better than the others. Likewise, questions of the *how* variety usually reveal several possible procedures, some of which are more desirable than the others. Measures of achievement in these areas, then, become a matter of selecting the best answer. This type is especially useful for measuring learning outcomes that require the understanding, application, or interpretation of factual information. Care must be taken, however, to be certain that the best answer is one agreed upon by experts, so that the answer can be defended as clearly best.

EXAMPLES   *Best-answer type*

Which one of the following factors contributed most to the selection of Sacramento as the capital of California?

Ⓐ   Central location

B   Good climate

C   Good highways

D   Large population

(or)

Which one of the following factors is given most consideration when selecting a city for a state capital?

Ⓐ   Location

B   Climate

C   Highways

D   Population

What is the most important purpose of city zoning laws?

A   Attract industry

B   Encourage the building of apartments

Ⓒ   Protect property values

D   Provide school "safety zones"

The best-answer type of multiple-choice item tends to be more difficult than the correct-answer type. This is due partly to the finer discriminations called for and partly to the fact that such items are used to measure more complex learning.

USES OF MULTIPLE-CHOICE ITEMS

The multiple-choice item is the most versatile type of test item available. It can measure a variety of learning outcomes from simple to complex, and it is adaptable to most types of subject-matter content. It has such wide applicability and so many uses that many standardized tests use multiple-choice items exclusively. This practice is not recommended for classroom testing. Despite the wide applicability of the multiple-choice item, there are learning outcomes, such as the ability to organize and present ideas, that cannot be measured with any form of selection item. For such skills some form of performance-based assessment is needed (see Chapters 9 and 10).

Because we cannot illustrate all of the uses of the multiple-choice item, we shall show only its use in measuring some of the more common learning outcomes in the knowledge, understanding, and application areas. The measurement of more complex outcomes, using modified forms of the multiple-choice item, will be considered in the following chapter.

Measuring Knowledge Outcomes

Learning outcomes in the knowledge area are so prominent in all school subjects, and multiple-choice items can measure such a variety of these outcomes, that examples can be endless. Here we shall present some of the more typical uses of the multiple-choice form in measuring knowledge outcomes common to most school subjects.

Knowledge of Terminology.   A simple but basic learning outcome measured by the multiple-choice item is knowledge of terminology. For this purpose, students can be requested to show their knowledge of a particular term by selecting a word that has the same meaning as the given term or by choosing a definition of the term. Special uses of a term also can be measured by having students identify the meaning of the term when used in context.

EXAMPLES   Which one of the following words has the same meaning as the word *egress?*

    A   Depress

    B   Enter

    Ⓒ   Exit

    D   Regress

Which one of the following statements best defines the word *egress?*

    A   An expression of disapproval

    Ⓑ   An act of leaving an enclosed place

    C   Proceeding to a higher level

    D   Proceeding to a lower level

What is meant by the word *egress* in the following sentence: "The astronauts hope they can now make a safe egress"?

    A   Separation from the rocket

    B   Reentry into the earth's atmosphere

    C   Landing on the water

    Ⓓ   Escape from the space capsule

Knowledge of Specific Facts.   Another learning outcome basic to all school subjects is the knowledge of specific facts. It is important in its own right, and it provides a necessary basis for developing understanding, thinking skills, and other complex learning outcomes. Multiple-choice items designed to measure specific facts can take many different forms, but questions of the *who, what, when,* and *where* variety are most common. These various types are illustrated in the following examples. Although based on the space program, similar questions could be written in many other subject areas.

EXAMPLES   Who was the first United States astronaut to orbit the earth in space?

    A   Scott Carpenter

    Ⓑ   John Glenn

    C   Virgil Grissom

    D   Alan Shepard

What was the name of the missile that launched the first United States astronaut into orbital flight around the earth?

    Ⓐ   Atlas

    B   Mars

    C   Midas

    D   Polaris

When did a United States astronaut first orbit the earth in space?

    A   1960

    B   1961

    Ⓒ   1962

    D   1963

Where did the *Friendship Seven* capsule land after the first United States orbital flight around the earth?

    Ⓐ   Atlantic Ocean

    B   Caribbean Sea

    C   Gulf of Mexico

    D   Pacific Ocean

Knowledge of Principles.   Knowledge of principles is also an important learning outcome in most school subjects. Multiple-choice items can be constructed to measure knowledge of principles as easily as those designed to measure facts.

EXAMPLES   The principle of capillary action helps explain how fluids

    A   enter solutions of lower concentration.

    B   escape through small openings.

    C   pass through semipermeable membranes.

    Ⓓ   rise in fine tubes.

Which one of the following principles of taxation is characteristic of the federal income tax?

  A   The benefits received by an individual should determine the amount of the tax.

  Ⓑ   A tax should be based on an individual's ability to pay.

  C   All citizens should be required to pay the same amount of tax.

  D   The amount of tax an individual pays should be determined by the size of the federal budget.

Knowledge of Methods and Procedures.   Another common learning outcome readily acceptable to the multiple-choice format is knowledge of methods and procedures. This includes such diverse areas as: knowledge of laboratory procedures; knowledge of methods underlying communication, computational, and performance skills; knowledge of methods used in problem solving; knowledge of governmental procedures; and knowledge of common social practices. In some cases we might want to measure knowledge of procedures before we permit students to practice in a particular area (e.g., laboratory procedures). In other cases, knowledge of methods and procedures may be important learning outcomes in their own right (e.g., knowledge of governmental procedures). The following test items illustrate a few of these uses in different school subjects:

EXAMPLES   Which one of the following methods of locating a specimen under the microscope is most desirable?

  A   Start with the coarse adjustment up, and with your eye at the eyepiece, turn down the coarse adjustment.

  Ⓑ   Start with the coarse adjustment down, and with your eye at the eyepiece, turn up the coarse adjustment.

  C   Start with the coarse adjustment in the center, and with your eye at the eyepiece, turn up and down until you locate the specimen.

To make treaties, the president of the United States must have the consent of the

  A   Cabinet.

  B   House of Representatives.

  Ⓒ   Senate.

  D   Supreme Court.

Alternating electric current is changed to direct current by means of a

  A   condenser.

  B   generator.

  Ⓒ   rectifier.

  D   transformer.

If you were making a scientific study of a problem, your first step should be to

Ⓐ   collect information about the problem.

B   develop hypotheses to be tested.

C   design the experiment to be conducted.

D   select scientific equipment.

We have merely scratched the surface with our examples of multiple-choice items measuring knowledge outcomes. But as you develop items in the particular school subjects you teach, many other uses will occur to you.

Measuring Outcomes at the Understanding and Application Levels

Many teachers limit the use of multiple-choice items to the knowledge area because they believe that all objective-type items are restricted to the measurement of relatively simple learning outcomes. Although it is difficult to go beyond the knowledge level with most of the other types of objective items, the multiple-choice item is especially adaptable to the measurement of more complex learning outcomes. The examples that follow illustrate its use in measuring various aspects of understanding and application.

In reviewing the following items, it is important to keep in mind that such items measure learning outcomes beyond factual knowledge only if the applications and interpretations are new to the students. Any specific applications or interpretations of knowledge can, of course, be taught directly to students as any other fact is taught. When this is done, and the test items contain the same problem situations and solutions used in teaching, it is obvious that the students can be given credit for no more than the mere retention of factual knowledge. To measure understanding and application, an element of *novelty* must be included in the test items. For illustrative purposes, it is necessary to assume that such novelty exists in the examples that follow.

Ability to Identify Application of Facts and Principles.   A common method of determining whether students' learning has gone beyond the mere memorization of a fact or principle is to ask them to identify its correct application in a situation that is new to the student. Application items measure understanding but they also include the ability to transfer learning to situations that have not been previously studied. Thus, the items can be designed to measure understanding at a relatively high level.

EXAMPLES   Which one of the following is an example of a chemical element?

A   Acid

B   Sodium Chloride

Ⓒ   Oxygen

D   Water

Directions: In each of the following sentences circle the word that makes the sentence correct.

            that

1. This is the boy ⟨who⟩ asked the question.
          whom

        ⟨that⟩

2. This is the dog who he asked about.
        whom

Which one of the following best illustrates the principle of capillarity?

(A)   Fluid is carried through the stems of plants.

B   Food is manufactured in the leaves of plants.

C   The leaves of deciduous plants lose their green color in winter.

D   Plants give off moisture through their stomata.

Pascal's law can be used to explain the operation of

A   electric fans.

(B)   hydraulic brakes.

C   levers.

D   syringes.

Which one of the following best illustrates the law of diminishing returns?

A   The demand for a farm product increased faster than the supply of the product.

B   The population of a country increased faster than the means of subsistence.

C   A machine decreased in utility as its parts became worn.

(D)   A factory doubled its labor force and increased production by 50 percent.

Ability to Interpret Cause-and-Effect Relationships.   Understanding can frequently be measured by asking students to interpret various relationships among facts. One of the most important relationships in this regard, and one common to most subject-matter areas, is the cause-and-effect relationship. Understanding of such relationships can be measured by presenting students with a specific cause-and-effect relationship and asking them to identify the reason that best accounts for it.

EXAMPLES   Bread will not become moldy as rapidly if placed in a refrigerator because

(A)   cooling retards the growth of fungi.

B   darkness retards the growth of mold.

C   cooling prevents the bread from drying out so rapidly.

D   mold requires both heat and light for best growth.

An increased quantity of carbon monoxide is produced when fuel is burned in a limited supply of oxygen because

    A   carbon reacts with carbon monoxide.

    Ⓑ   carbon reacts with carbon dioxide.

    C   carbon monoxide is an effective reducing agent.

    D   greater oxidation takes place.

Investing money in common stock protects against loss of assets during inflation because common stock

    A   pays higher rates of interest during inflation.

    B   provides a steady but dependable income despite economic conditions.

    C   is protected by the Federal Reserve System.

    Ⓓ   increases in value as the value of a business increases.

Ability to Justify Methods and Procedures. Another phase of understanding important in various subject-matter areas is concerned with methods and procedures. A student might know the correct method or sequence of steps in carrying out a procedure, without being able to explain why it is the best method or sequence of steps. At the understanding level we are interested in the student's ability to justify the use of a particular method or procedure. This can be measured with multiple-choice items by asking the student to select the best of several possible explanations of a method or procedure.

EXAMPLES   Why is adequate lighting necessary in a balanced aquarium?

    A   Fish need light to see their food.

    B   Fish take in oxygen in the dark.

    Ⓒ   Plants expel carbon dioxide in the dark.

    D   Plants grow too rapidly in the dark.

Why do farmers rotate their crops?

    Ⓐ   To conserve the soil.

    B   To make marketing easier.

    C   To provide for strip cropping.

    D   It removes the brownish yellow color.

Although various aspects of understanding and application can be measured by single multiple-choice items, as shown in the preceding examples, a series of multiple-choice items based on a common set of data is even more adaptable to the measurement of complex achievement. Such items will be illustrated in the next chapter.

ADVANTAGES AND LIMITATIONS OF MULTIPLE-CHOICE ITEMS

The multiple-choice item is one of the most widely applicable test items for measuring achievement. It can effectively measure various types of knowledge and complex learning outcomes. In addition to this flexibility, it is free from some of the common shortcomings characteristic of the other item types. The ambiguity and vagueness that frequently are present in the short-answer item are avoided because the alternatives better structure the situation. In the following examples, note how the vague short-answer item becomes a clear-cut problem.

EXAMPLES   *Poor:*   Lincoln was born in _____ .

Better: Lincoln was born in

> A   Indiana
>
> B   Illinois
>
> Ⓒ   Kentucky
>
> D   Ohio

Your first reaction to the short-answer item might be, "Why not put it in question form to make it clearer?" But even if we ask, "In what state was Lincoln born?" answers such as "poverty" could not be ruled out. In addition to clarifying the specific type of response called for, the multiple-choice item relieves us of the problem of deciding how to score misspelled answers. Although we may be interested in having students spell the names of states correctly, this should be done in a separate spelling test rather than letting it contaminate our measures of achievement.

One advantage of the multiple-choice item over the true–false item is that students cannot receive credit for simply knowing that a statement is incorrect; they must also know what is correct. Note the difference in the following two items:

EXAMPLES   T   Ⓕ   Lincoln was born in 1807.

Lincoln was born in
> A   1805
> B   1807
> Ⓒ   1809
> D   1811

In the true–false version students will receive credit if they mark it false, even if they think Lincoln was born in some year other than 1809. In fact, if a student thought he was born in 1909, it would be marked false and the student would receive a 1-point credit for that response. Because marking statements false does not show that students know what is correct, the resulting scores tend to be inadequate measures of what students have learned. But this problem is not encountered with multiple-choice items because the students must select the correct answer to receive credit. Although the problem also could be resolved by having students change all false statements to true, that procedure is often cumbersome, especially when measuring complex learning outcomes.

Using the best-answer type of multiple-choice item also circumvents a difficulty associated with the true–false item—obtaining statements that are true or false without qualification. This makes it possible to measure learning outcomes in the numerous subject-matter areas in which solutions to problems are not absolutely true or false but vary in degree of appropriateness (e.g., best method, best reason, best interpretation).

One other commonly cited advantage of the multiple-choice item over the true–false item is the greater reliability per item. Because the number of alternatives is increased from two to four or five, the opportunity for guessing the correct answer is reduced, and the reliability is correspondingly increased. The effect of increasing the number of alternatives for each item is similar to that of increasing the length of the test. As was noted in Chapter 6, however, this advantage of the multiple-choice item is partially offset by the fact that roughly three true–false items can typically be responded to in the time it takes to respond to two multiple-choice items.

An advantage of the multiple-choice item over the matching exercise is that the need for homogeneous material is avoided. The matching exercise, which is essentially a modified form of the multiple-choice item, requires a series of related ideas to form the list of premises and alternative responses. In many content areas it is difficult to obtain enough homogeneous material to prepare effective matching exercises. But this problem is avoided with multiple-choice items because each item measures a single idea. Thus, it is possible to measure one or many relationships in a given area when the multiple-choice item is used.

Two other desirable characteristics of the multiple-choice item are worthy of mention. First, it is relatively free from response sets. That is, students generally do not favor a particular alternative when they do not know the answer. Second, using a number of plausible alternatives makes the results amenable to diagnosis. The kind of the incorrect alternatives students select provides clues to factual errors and misunderstandings that need correction.

It is easier to construct high-quality test items in multiple-choice form than in any of the other forms. This does not mean that good multiple-choice items can be constructed without effort. But for a given amount of effort, multiple-choice items will tend to be of a higher quality than short-answer, true–false, or matching-type items in the same area.

Despite its superiority, the multiple-choice item does have limitations. First, as with all other paper-and-pencil tests, it is limited to learning outcomes at the verbal level. The problems presented to students are verbal problems, free from the many irrelevant factors present in natural situations. Also, the applications students are asked to make are verbal applications, free from the personal commitment necessary for application in natural situations. In short, the multiple-choice item, like other paper-and-pencil tests, measures whether the student knows or understands what to do when confronted with a problem situation, but it cannot determine how the student actually will perform in that situation. Second, as with other types of selection items, the multiple-choice item requires selection of the correct answer, and therefore it is not well adapted to measuring some problem-solving skills in mathematics and science or to measuring the ability to organize and present ideas. Third, the multiple-choice item has a disadvantage not shared by the other item types: the difficulty of finding a sufficient number of incorrect but plausible distracters. This problem is especially acute at the early primary level because of the students' limited vocabulary and knowledge in any particular area. Even at this level, however, classroom teachers have been creative in adapting the multiple-choice item to the measurement of newly learned concepts (see Figure 7.1). As students move up through the grade levels and expand their vocabulary, knowledge, and understanding, plausible but incorrect answers become more available. It still takes a touch of creativity, however, to identify and state the most plausible distracters for use in multiple-choice items. This is the task that separates a good test constructor from a poor one. Fortunately, the construction of such items gets easier with experience.

FIGURE 7.1
Illustrative multiple-choice items used at the early primary level. (Directions are given orally.)

SUGGESTIONS FOR CONSTRUCTING MULTIPLE-CHOICE ITEMS

The general applicability and the superior qualities of multiple-choice test items are realized most fully when care is taken in their construction. This involves formulating a clearly stated problem, identifying plausible alternatives, and removing irrelevant clues to the answer. The following suggestions provide more specific maxims for this purpose.

1. *The stem of the item should be meaningful by itself and should present a definite problem.*   Often the stems of test items placed in multiple-choice form are incomplete statements that make little sense until all of the alternatives have been read. These are not multiple-choice items but, rather, a collection of true–false statements placed in multiple-choice form. A properly constructed multiple-choice item presents a definite problem in the stem that is meaningful without the alternatives. Compare the stems in the two versions of the test item in the following examples:

EXAMPLES   *Poor:*   South America

A	is a flat, arid country.
B	imports coffee from the United States.
C	has a larger population than the United States.
Ⓓ	was settled mainly by colonists from Spain.

Better: Most of South America was settled by colonists from

A	England.
B	France.
C	Holland.
Ⓓ	Spain.

Formulating a definite problem in the stem not only improves the stem of the item, but also has a desirable effect on the alternatives. In the preceding example, the alternatives in the first version are concerned with widely dissimilar ideas. This heterogeneity is possible because of the stem's lack of structure. In the second version, the clearly formulated problem in the stem forces the alternatives to be more homogeneous.

A good check on the adequacy of the problem statement is to cover the alternatives and read the stem by itself. It should be complete enough to serve as a short-answer item. Starting each item stem as a direct question and shifting to the incomplete statement form only when greater conciseness is possible is the most effective method for obtaining a clearly formulated problem.

2. *The item stem should include as much of the item as possible and should be free of irrelevant material.*   This will increase the probability of a clearly stated problem in the stem and will reduce the reading time required. The following examples illustrate how the conciseness of an item is increased by removing irrelevant material and including in the stem those words repeated in the alternatives. Notice that to obtain the conciseness of the final version, it is necessary to shift to the incomplete-statement form. The best version provides a slim-trim item that is easily read and focuses directly on the key element in the intended learning outcome.

EXAMPLES

Poor: Most of South America was settled by colonists from Spain. How would you account for the large number of Spanish colonists settling there?

A   They were adventurous.
B   They were in search of wealth.
C   They wanted lower taxes.
D   They were seeking religious freedom.

Better: Why did Spanish colonists settle most of South America?

A   They were adventurous.
B   They were in search of wealth.
C   They wanted lower taxes.
D   They were seeking religious freedom.

Best: Spanish colonists settled most of South America in search of

A   adventure.
B   wealth.
C   lower taxes.
D   religious freedom.

There are a few exceptions to this rule. In testing problem-solving ability, irrelevant material might be included in the stem of an item to determine whether students can identify and select the material that is relevant to the problem's solution. Similarly, repeating common words in the alternatives is sometimes necessary for grammatical consistency or greater clarity.

3. Use a negatively stated stem only when significant learning outcomes require it.   Most problems can and should be stated in positive terms. This avoids the possibility of students' overlooking *no, not, least,* and similar words used in negative statements. In most instances, it also avoids measuring relatively insignificant learning outcomes. Knowing the least important method, the principle that does not apply, or the poorest reason are seldom important learning outcomes. We are usually interested in students' learning the most important method, the principle that does apply, and the best reason.

Teachers sometimes go to ridiculous extremes to use negatively stated items because they appear more difficult. The difficulty of such items, however, is in the lack of sentence clarity rather than in the difficulty of the concept being measured.

EXAMPLES   *Poor:*   Which one of the following states is not located north of the Mason–Dixon line?

     A   Maine

     B   New York

     C   Pennsylvania

     (D)   Virginia

   Better: Which one of the following states is located south of the Mason–Dixon line?

     A   Maine

     B   New York

     C   Pennsylvania

     (D)   Virginia

Both versions of this item measure the same knowledge. But some students who can answer the second version correctly will select an incorrect alternative on the first version merely because the negative phrasing confuses them. Such items thus introduce factors that contribute to the invalidity of the test.

Although negatively stated items are generally to be avoided, there are occasions when they are useful, mainly in areas in which the wrong information or wrong procedure can have dire consequences. In the health area, for example, there are practices to be avoided because of their harmful nature. In shop and laboratory work, there are procedures that can damage equipment and result in bodily injury. And in driver training there are unsafe practices to be emphasized. When the avoidance of such potentially harmful practices is emphasized in teaching, it might well receive a corresponding emphasis in testing through the use of negatively stated items. When used, the negative aspects of the item should be made obvious.

EXAMPLES   *Poor:*   Which one of the following is not a safe driving practice on icy roads?

     A   Accelerating slowly.

     (B)   Jamming on the brakes.

     C   Holding the wheel firmly.

     D   Slowing down gradually.

   Better: All of the following are safe driving practices on icy roads EXCEPT

     A   accelerating slowly.

     (B)   jamming on the brakes.

     C   holding the wheel firmly.

     D   slowing down gradually.

In the first version of the item, the *not* is easily overlooked, in which case students would tend to select the first alternative and not read any further. In the second version, no student would probably overlook the negative element because it is placed at the end of the statement and is capitalized.

4. *All of the alternatives should be grammatically consistent with the stem of the item.*   In the following examples, note how the better version results from a change in the alternatives in order to obtain grammatical consistency. This rule is not presented merely to perpetuate proper grammar usage, however; its main function is to prevent irrelevant clues from creeping in. All too frequently the grammatical consistency of the correct answer is given attention, but that of the distracters is neglected. As a result, some of the alternatives are grammatically inconsistent with the stem and are therefore obviously incorrect answers.

EXAMPLES   *Poor:*   An electric transformer can be used

  A   for storing electricity.

  Ⓑ   to increase the voltage of alternating current.

  C   it converts electrical energy into mechanical energy.

  D   alternating current is changed to direct current.

Better: An electric transformer can be used to

  A   store electricity.

  Ⓑ   increase the voltage of alternating current.

  C   convert electrical energy into mechanical energy.

  D   change alternating current to direct current.

Similar difficulties arise from a lack of attention to verb tense, to the proper use of the articles *a* or *an,* and to other common sources of grammatical inconsistency. Because most of these errors are the result of carelessness, they can be detected easily by carefully reading each item before assembling them into a test. See "How Many Alternatives Should Be Used in Multiple-Choice Items?" for more guidelines on constructing multiple-choice assessments.

5. *An item should contain only one correct or clearly best answer.* Including more than one correct answer in a test item and asking students to select all of the correct alternatives has two shortcomings. First, such items are usually no more than a collection of true–false items presented in multiple-choice format. They do not present a definite problem in the stem, and the selection of answers requires a mental response of *true* or *false* to each alternative rather than a comparison and selection of alternatives. Second, because the number of alternatives selected as correct answers varies from one student to another, satisfactory scoring methods are more cumbersome than most teachers are likely to want to use or have to explain to students.

How Many Alternatives Should Be Used in Multiple-Choice Items?

There is no magic number of alternatives to use in a multiple-choice item. Typically three, four, or five choices are used. Some favor five-choice items to reduce the chances of guessing the correct answer.

	Chances of a Correct Guess	Chance Score on 100-Item Test
Five-choice items	1 in 5	20
Four-choice items	1 in 4	25
Three-choice items	1 in 3	33

Reducing the chances of guessing the correct answers by adding alternatives enhances reliability and validity, but only if all the distracters are plausible and the items are well constructed. Our preference is for using four-choice items because, with reasonable effort, three good distracters usually can be obtained (a fourth distracter tends to be difficult to devise and is usually weaker than the others). For young students, three-choice items may be preferable in order to reduce the amount of reading.

The number of alternatives can, of course, vary from item to item. You might use a five-choice item when four good distracters are available and a three-choice item when there are only two. Don't give up too soon in constructing distracters, however. It takes time and effort to generate several good ones.

EXAMPLES

Poor: The state of Michigan borders on

    Ⓐ Lake Huron.

    B Lake Ontario.

    Ⓒ Indiana.

    D Illinois.

Better: The state of Michigan borders on

A	Lake Huron.	Ⓣ	F
B	Lake Ontario.	T	Ⓕ
C	Indiana.	Ⓣ	F
D	Illinois.	T	Ⓕ

The second version of this item shows students what type of response is expected. They are to read each alternative and decide whether it is true or false.

Thus, this is not a four-alternative, multiple-choice item, but a series of four statements, each of which has two alternatives—true or false. This second version, which is called a cluster-type true–false item, not only identifies the mental process involved, but simplifies the scoring. Each statement in the cluster can be considered as one point and scored as any other true–false item is scored. In contrast, how would you score a student who selected alternatives A, B, and C in the first version? Would you give two points for the response because two answers were correctly identified? Would you give only one point because one incorrect alternative was also selected? Or would you give no points because the answer as a whole was not completely correct? How would you evaluate the lack of a response to Alternative D? Assume that the student knew Illinois did not border on Michigan and therefore did not select it, or assume that the student was uncertain and left it blank. Fairly complicated and cumbersome scoring rules are required to satisfactorily resolve these problems. Hence, multiple-choice items like the one in the first version should be avoided or converted to the true–false form.

There is another important facet of this rule concerning single-answer multiple-choice items: the answer must be agreed upon by authorities in the area. The best-answer type item is especially subject to variations of interpretation and disagreement concerning the correct answer. Care must be taken to make certain that the answer is clearly the best one. Frequently, rewording the problem in the stem will correct an otherwise faulty item.

In the first version of the following item, different alternatives could be defended as correct, depending on whether the *best* refers to cost, efficiency, cleanliness, or accessibility. The second version avoids this problem by making the criterion of *best* explicit.

EXAMPLES   *Poor:*   Which one of the following is the best source of heat for home use?

A   Coal

B   Electricity

C   Gas

D   Oil

Better: In the midwestern part of the United States, which one of the following is the most economical source of heat for home use?

(A)   Coal

B   Electricity

C   Gas

D   Oil

---

6. *Items used to measure understanding should contain some novelty, but beware of too much.*   The construction of multiple-choice items that measure understanding requires a careful choice of situations and skillful phrasing. The situations must be new to the students, but not too far removed from the examples used in class. If the test items contain problem situations identical with those used in class, the students can, of course, respond on the basis of memorized

answers. On the other hand, if the problem situations contain too much novelty, some students may respond incorrectly merely because they lack necessary factual information about the situations used. Asking students to apply the law of supply and demand to some phase of banking, for example, would be grossly unfair if they had not had a previous opportunity to study banking policies and practices. They may have a good understanding of the law of supply and demand but be unable to demonstrate this because of their unfamiliarity with the particular situation selected.

The problem of too much novelty usually can be avoided by selecting situations from the student's everyday experiences, by including in the stem of the item any factual information needed, and by phrasing the item so that the type of application or interpretation called for is clear.

7. *All distracters should be plausible. The purpose of a distracter is to distract the uninformed from the correct answer.* To the student who has not achieved the learning outcome being tested, the distracters should be at least as attractive as the correct answer and preferably more so. In a properly constructed multiple-choice item, each distracter will be elected by some students. If a distracter is not selected by anyone, it is not contributing to the functioning of the item and should be eliminated or revised.

One factor contributing to the plausibility of distracters is their homogeneity. If all of the alternatives are homogeneous with regard to the knowledge being measured, the distracters are more likely to function as intended. Whether alternatives appear homogeneous and distracters plausible, however, also depends on the students' age level. Note the difference in homogeneity in the following two items:

EXAMPLES　　*Poor:*　Who discovered the North Pole?

　　　　　　　　A　　　　Christopher Columbus

　　　　　　　　B　　　　Ferdinand Magellan

　　　　　　　　Ⓒ　　　　Robert Peary

　　　　　　　　D　　　　Marco Polo

　　　　　Better:　Who discovered the North Pole?

　　　　　　　　A　　　　Roald Amundsen

　　　　　　　　B　　　　Richard Byrd

　　　　　　　　Ⓒ　　　　Robert Peary

　　　　　　　　D　　　　Robert Scott

The first version would probably appear homogeneous to students at the primary level because all four choices are the names of well-known explorers. However, students in higher grades would eliminate alternatives A, B, and D as possible answers because they would know these men were not polar explorers. They might also recall that these men lived several hundred years before the North Pole was discovered. In either case, they could quickly obtain the correct answer by the process of elimination.

The second version includes only the names of polar explorers, all of whom were active at approximately the same time. This homogeneity makes each alternative much more plausible and the elimination process much less effective. It also, of course, increases the item's level of difficulty. See the accompanying "Guidelines" box.

In selecting plausible distracters, the students' learning experiences must not be ignored. In the foregoing item, for example, the distracters in the second version would not be plausible to students if Robert Peary was the only polar explorer they had studied. Obviously, distracters must be familiar to students before they can serve as reasonable alternatives. Less obvious is the rich source of plausible distracters provided by the students' learning experiences. Common misconceptions, errors of judgment, and faulty reasoning that occur during the teaching–learning process provide the most plausible and educationally sound distracters available. One way to tap this supply is to keep a running record of such errors. A quicker method is to administer a short-answer test to students and tabulate the most common errors. This provides a series of incorrect responses that are especially plausible because they are in the students' own language.

8. *Verbal associations between the stem and the correct answer should be avoided.*   Frequently a word in the correct answer will provide an irrelevant clue because it looks or sounds like a word in the stem of the item. Such verbal associations should never permit the student who lacks the necessary achievement to select the correct answer. However, words similar to those in the stem might be included in the distracters to increase their plausibility. Students who depend on rote memory and verbal associations will then be led away from, rather than to, the correct answer. The following item, taken from a fifth-grade test on a weather unit, shows the incorrect and correct use of verbal associations between the stem and the alternatives:

EXAMPLES   *Poor:* Which one of the following agencies should you contact to find out about a tornado warning in your locality?

      A   State farm bureau

      (B)   Local radio station

      C   United States Post Office

      D   United States Weather Bureau

Better: Which one of the following agencies should you contact to find out about a tornado warning in your locality?

      A   Local farm bureau

      (B)   Nearest radio station

      C   Local post office

      D   United States Weather Bureau

In the first version, the association between *locality* and *local* is an unnecessary clue. In the second version, this verbal association is used in two distracters to make them more attractive choices. But if irrelevant verbal associations in the distracters are overused, students will soon catch on and avoid alternatives with pat verbal associations.

> ## GUIDELINES
>
> ### Ways to Make Distracters Plausible
>
> 1. Use the students' most common errors.
> 2. Use important-sounding words (e.g., *significant, accurate*) that are relevant to the item stem. But don't overdo it!
> 3. Use words that have verbal associations with the item stem (e.g., *politician, political*).
> 4. Use textbook language or other phraseology that has the appearance of truth.
> 5. Use incorrect answers that are likely to result from student misunderstanding or carelessness (e.g., forgets to convert from feet to yards).
> 6. Use distracters that are homogeneous and similar in content to the correct answer (e.g., all are inventors).
> 7. Use distracters that are parallel in form and grammatically consistent with the item's stem.
> 8. Make the distracters similar to the correct answer in length, vocabulary, sentence structure, and complexity of thought.
>
>   *Note of Caution:* Distracters should distract the uninformed, but they should not result in trick questions that mislead knowledgeable students (e.g., don't insert *not* in a correct answer to make it a distracter).

9. ***The relative length of the alternatives should not provide a clue to the answer.*** The best we can hope for in equalizing the length of a test item's alternatives is to make them approximately equal. But because the correct answer usually needs to be qualified, it tends to be longer than the distracters unless a special effort is made to control the length of the alternatives. If the correct answer cannot be shortened, the distracters can be expanded to the desired length. Lengthening the distracters also is desirable for another reason. Added qualifiers and greater specificity frequently contribute to their plausibility. The correct answer should not be consistently longer, or consistently shorter, or consistently of medium length. The relative length of the correct answer should vary from one item to another in such a manner that no pattern is discernible to indicate the answer. This means, of course, that sometimes the correct answer will be the longest.

EXAMPLES   *Poor:*   What is the major purpose of the United Nations?

(A)   To maintain peace among the peoples of the world.

B   To establish international law.

C   To provide military control.

D   To form new governments.

Better: What is the major purpose of the United Nations?

Ⓐ   To maintain peace among the peoples of the world.

B   To develop a new system of international law.

C   To provide military control of nations that have recently attained their independence.

D   To establish and maintain democratic forms of government in newly formed nations.

---

10. The correct answer should appear in each of the alternative positions an approximately equal number of times but in random order. Some teachers often bury the correct answer in the middle of the list of alternatives. As a consequence, the correct answer appears in the first and last positions far less often than it does in the middle positions. This, of course, provides an irrelevant clue to the alert student.

In placing the correct answer in each position approximately an equal number of times, care must be taken to avoid a regular pattern of responses. A random placement of correct answers can be attained with the use of any book. For each test item, open the book at an arbitrary position, note the number on the right-hand page, and place the correct answer for that test item as follows:

If Page Number Ends in	Place Correct Answer
1	First
3	Second
5	Third
7	Fourth
9	Fifth

An even simpler method for obtaining an undetectable placement of the correct answer is to place all verbal alternatives in alphabetical order and all numerical answers in numerical order.

11. Use sparingly special alternatives such as "none of the above" or "all of the above." The phrases "none of the above" or "all of the above" are sometimes added as the last alternative in multiple-choice items. This is done to force the student to consider all of the alternatives carefully and to increase the difficulty of the items. All too frequently, however, these special alternatives are used inappropriately. In fact, there are relatively few situations in which their use is appropriate.

The use of "none of the above" is restricted to correct-answer type multiple-choice items and consequently to the measurement of factual knowledge to which absolute standards of correctness can be applied. It is inappropriate in best-answer-type items because the student is told to select the best of several alternatives of varying degrees of correctness.

Use of "none of the above" is frequently recommended for items measuring computational skill in mathematics and spelling ability. But these learning outcomes generally should not be measured by multiple-choice items, because they can be measured more effectively by short-answer items. When "none of the above" is used in such situations, the item may measure nothing more than a student's ability to recognize incorrect answers, a rather inadequate basis for judging computational skill or spelling ability.

The alternative "none of the above" should be used only when the measurement of significant learning outcomes requires it. As with negatively stated item stems, sometimes procedures or practices should be avoided for safety, health, or other reasons. When knowing what not to do is important, "none of the above" might be appropriately applied. When used for this purpose, it also must be used as an incorrect answer a proportionate number of times. See the following box.

The use of "all of the above" is fraught with so many difficulties that it might best be discarded as a possible alternative. When used, some students will note that the first alternative is correct and select it without reading further. Other students will note that at least two of the alternatives are correct and thereby know that "all of the above" must be the answer. In the first instance, students mark the item incorrectly because they do not read all of the alternatives, and in the second instance, students obtain the correct answer on the basis of partial knowledge. Both types of response prevent the item from functioning as intended.

12. Do not use multiple-choice items when other item types are more appropriate. When various item types can serve a purpose equally well, the

---

Examples of Misuse of the Alternative "None of the Above"

Which of the following is *not* an example of a mammal?

Ⓐ   Bird
B   Dog
C   Whale
D   None of the above

(It would be easy to prove that "D" is *not* an example of a mammal.)

When the temperature drops, tire pressure tends to

Ⓐ   Decrease
B   Increase
C   Stay the same
D   None of the above

(There may be something other than A, B, or C, but we can't think of what it might be.)

United States federal law requires that first offenders must be fined or imprisoned if they possess

A   Amphetamine
B   Heroin
C   Marijuana
Ⓓ   None of the above

(Sounds like a very unfair law. If you don't agree, read only the stem and answer "D.")

multiple-choice item should be favored because of its many superior qualities. Sometimes, however, the multiple-choice form is inappropriate or less suitable than other item types. When there are only two possible responses (e.g., fact or opinion), the true–false item is more appropriate. When there are enough homogeneous items but few plausible distracters for each, a matching exercise might be more suitable. In certain problem-solving situations in mathematics and science, for example, supply-type short-answer items are clearly superior. The measurement of many complex achievement goals (such as organizing, integrating, and expressing ideas; the formulation and testing of hypotheses; or the construction of models, maps, or diagrams) requires the use of performance-based assessment tasks. Although we should take full advantage of the wide applicability of the multiple-choice form, we should not lose sight of a principle of test construction cited earlier—select the item type that measures the learning outcome most directly and most effectively.

CHECKLIST

Reviewing Multiple-Choice Items

	Yes	No
1. Is this the most appropriate type of item to use?	____	____
2. Does each item stem present a meaningful problem?	____	____
3. Are the item stems free of irrelevant material?	____	____
4. Are the item stems stated in positive terms (if possible)?	____	____
5. If used, has negative wording been given special emphasis (e.g., capitalized)?	____	____
6. Are the alternatives grammatically consistent with the item stem?	____	____
7. Are the alternative answers brief and free of unnecessary words?	____	____
8. Are the alternatives similar in length and form?	____	____
9. Is there only one correct or clearly best answer?	____	____
10. Are the distracters plausible to nonachievers?	____	____
11. Are the items free of verbal clues to the answer?	____	____
12. Are verbal alternatives in alphabetical order?	____	____
13. Are numerical alternatives in numerical order?	____	____
14. Have *none of the above* and *all of the above* been avoided (or used sparingly and appropriately)?	____	____
15. If revised, are the items still relevant to the intended learning outcomes?	____	____
16. Have the items been set aside for a time before reviewing them?	____	____

13. Break any of these rules when you have a good reason for doing so.   Although these rules provide valuable guidelines for constructing multiple-choice items, you may encounter instances where an exception to the rule may improve the item.

SUMMARY

The multiple-choice item consists of a problem and a list of alternative solutions. The student responds by selecting the alternative that provides the correct or best solution to the problem. The incorrect alternatives are called distracters because their purpose is to distract the uninformed student from the correct response. The problem can be stated as a direct question or an incomplete statement. In either case, it should be a clearly formulated problem that is meaningful without reference to the list of alternatives.

The multiple-choice form is extremely flexible and can be used to measure a variety of learning outcomes at the knowledge and understanding levels. Knowledge outcomes concerned with vocabulary, facts, principles, and methods and procedures all can be measured with the multiple-choice item. Aspects of understanding, such as the application and interpretation of facts, principles, and methods, also can be measured with this item type. Other, more specific uses occur in particular school subjects.

The main advantage of the multiple-choice item is its wide applicability in the measurement of various phases of achievement. It is also free of many of the limitations of other forms of objective items. It tends to present a more well-defined problem than the short-answer item does; it avoids the need for homogeneous material required by the matching item; and it reduces the clues and susceptibility to guessing characteristic of the true–false item. In addition, the multiple-choice item is relatively free from response sets and is useful in diagnosis.

Its limitations are mainly that it is a selection-type paper-and-pencil test and measures problem-solving behavior at the verbal level only. Because it requires selection of the correct answer, it is inappropriate for measuring learning outcomes requiring the ability to recall, organize, or present ideas.

The construction of multiple-choice items involves defining the problem in the stem of the item, selecting one correct or best solution, identifying several plausible distracters, and avoiding irrelevant clues to the answer. Items used to measure learning outcomes at the understanding level must also include some (but beware of too much) novelty.

LEARNING EXERCISES

1. Describe the advantages of the multiple-choice item over each of the other objective-type items. What are the comparative disadvantages?

2. In an area in which you are teaching or plan to teach, construct one multiple-choice item in each of the following areas: knowledge, understanding, and application.

3. Make a checklist for evaluating the plausibility of distracters. Put the criteria in question form so that they can be answered with a simple *yes* or *no*.

4. How does a multiple-choice item designed to measure knowledge outcomes differ from one designed to measure understanding?

5. Describe the relative merits of using correct-answer and best-answer multiple-choice items.

What types of learning outcomes are best measured by each type of multiple-choice item?

FURTHER READING

Bloom, B. S., Madaus, G. F., & Hastings, J. T. (1981). *Evaluation to improve learning.* New York: McGraw-Hill. Chapter 8, "Evaluation Techniques for Knowledge and Comprehension Objectives," and Chapter 9, "Evaluation Techniques for Application and Analysis Objectives," include numerous illustrations of modified forms of multiple-choice items.

Ebel, R. L., & Frisbie, D. A. (1991). *Essentials of educational measurement* (5th ed.). Englewood Cliffs, N.J.: Prentice-Hall. Chapter 9, "Multiple-Choice Test Items," offers numerous sample test items to illustrate desirable and undesirable characteristics of multiple-choice items, as well as suggestions for writing good items.

Gronlund, N. E. (1993). *How to construct achievement tests and assessments* (5th ed.). Boston:

Allyn and Bacon. Chapter 3, "Writing Selection Items: Multiple-Choice," describes and illustrates the use of multiple-choice items for measuring various types of outcomes.

Haladyna, T. M., & Downing, S. M. (1989). A Taxonomy of multiple-choice item-writing rules and Validity of a taxonomy of multiple-choice item writing rules. *Applied Measurement in Education, 2,* 37–50, 51–78. The first of these two companion articles summarizes item-writing rules offered by a wide range of measurement textbooks and other references. The second article reviews results of theoretical and empirical studies that have investigated the validity of the rules.

CHAPTER 8
Measuring Complex Achievement: The Interpretive Exercise

Complex achievement includes those learning outcomes based on the higher mental processes, such as understanding, thinking skills, and various problem-solving abilities. Many aspects of complex achievement can be measured objectively.

We have already had some experience with measuring complex achievement, as this category encompasses all those learning outcomes requiring more than the mere retention of factual knowledge. The use of the short-answer item to measure problem-solving abilities in mathematics and science, the true–false item to measure the ability to recognize cause–effect relationships, and the multiple-choice item to measure various aspects of understanding and application all illustrate the measurement of complex achievement. These illustrations, however, were limited to the use of single, independent test items of the objective type. Greater range and flexibility in measuring complex achievement can be attained by using more complex forms of objective test items.

A variety of learning outcomes are included in complex achievement. Following are some typical examples:

❑ Ability to apply a principle.
❑ Ability to interpret relationships.
❑ Ability to recognize and state inferences.
❑ Ability to recognize the relevance of information.
❑ Ability to develop and recognize tenable hypotheses.
❑ Ability to formulate and recognize valid conclusions.
❑ Ability to recognize assumptions underlying conclusions.
❑ Ability to recognize the limitations of data.

❑ Ability to recognize and state significant problems.

❑ Ability to design experimental procedures.

These and similar learning outcomes have been classified under such categories as understanding, reasoning, critical thinking, scientific thinking, creative thinking, and problem solving. There is general agreement that learning outcomes based on higher-order thinking skills constitute some of the most significant outcomes of education. One of the most promising forms for measuring a variety of complex learning outcomes in school subjects is the interpretive exercise.

NATURE OF THE INTERPRETIVE EXERCISE

An interpretive exercise (also called "classification exercise," "key-type item," or "master-list item") consists of a series of objective items based on a common set of data. The data may be in the form of written materials, tables, charts, graphs, maps, or pictures. The series of related test items may also take various forms but are most commonly multiple-choice or true–false items. Because all students are presented with a common set of data, it is possible to measure a variety of complex learning outcomes. Students can be asked to identify relationships in data, to recognize valid conclusions, to appraise assumptions and inferences, to detect proper applications of data, and the like.

The common set of materials used in interpretive exercises ensures that all students will be confronted with the same task. It also makes it possible to control the amount of factual information given to them. We can give them as much or as little information as we think desirable in measuring their achievement of a learning outcome. In measuring their ability to interpret mathematical data, for example, we can include the formulas needed or require the students to supply them. In other areas, we can supply definitions of terms, meanings of symbols, and other facts or expect students to supply them. This flexibility makes it possible to measure various degrees of proficiency in any particular area.

FORMS AND USES OF THE INTERPRETIVE EXERCISE

As with other objective items, there are so many forms and uses of the interpretive exercise that it is impossible to illustrate all of them. Here we shall present examples of this item type as applied to the measurement of complex learning outcomes in a variety of school subjects at the elementary and secondary levels. Different types of introductory material and different methods of responding also will be used to illustrate the great flexibility of the interpretive exercise. The references at the end of this chapter offer additional illustrative exercises.

Ability to Recognize Inferences

In interpreting written material, it is frequently necessary to draw inferences from the facts given. The following exercise measures the extent to which students are able to recognize warranted and unwarranted inferences drawn from a passage:

EXAMPLE

Directions: Assuming that the information below is true, it is possible to establish other facts using the ones in this paragraph as a basis for reasoning. This is called drawing inferences. There is, of course, a limit to the number of kinds of facts which may be properly inferred from any statement.

By writing the proper symbol in the space provided, indicate that a statement is TRUE, if it may be properly inferred from the information given in the paragraph. Indicate that it is UNTRUE, if the information given in the paragraph implies that it is false. Indicate that NO INFERENCE can be drawn if the statement cannot be inferred one way or the other. Use only the information given in the paragraph as a basis for your responses. . . .

Use the following symbols in writing your answers:

T—if the statement may be inferred as TRUE.

F—if the statement may be inferred as UNTRUE.

N—if no inference can be drawn about it from the paragraph.

Paragraph A

By the close of the thirteenth century there were several famous universities established in Europe, though of course they were very different from modern ones. One of the earliest to be founded was one of the most widely known. This was the University of Bologna, where students from all countries came who wished to have the best training in studying Roman Law. Students especially interested in philosophy and theology went to the University of Paris. Those who wished to study medicine went to the Universities of Montpellier or Salerno.

Questions on Paragraph A

(T)   1. There were law suits between people occasionally in those days.

(N)   2. The professors were poorly paid.

(F)   3. In the Middle Ages people were not interested in getting education.

(T)   4. There were books in Europe at that time.

(N)   5. Most of the teaching in these medieval universities was very poor.

(N)   6. There was no place where students could go to study.

(F)   7. There were no doctors in Europe at this time.

(F)   8. There was no way to travel during the Middle Ages.

(T)   9. If a student wanted to be a priest, he would probably attend the University of Paris.

(N) 10. There were no universities in Europe before the thirteenth century.

(N) 11. There was only one language in Europe at this time.

Source: From "Selected Items for the Testing of Study Skills" by H. T. Morse and G. H. McCune, 1971, *Bulletin, 15,* p. 66. Copyright 1971 by National Council for the Social Studies. Used by permission of the publisher.

Ability to Recognize Warranted and Unwarranted Generalizations

The ability to recognize the validity of generalizations is of central importance in the interpretation of data. At minimum, students should be able to determine which conclusions the data support, which the data refute, and which the data neither support nor refute. The data may be in the form of tables, charts, graphs, maps, or pictures, and the test items may be true-false or multiple-choice items. The use of the true–false format is shown in the following example:

EXAMPLE

Percentage of population between the ages of 25 and 34 who have completed secondary and higher education, by gender, for large industrialized countries: 1989

Country	Males		Females	
	Secondary Education	Higher Education	Secondary Education	Higher Education
United States	85.7	24.9	87.4	23.5
Japan	89.3	34.2	91.8	11.5
Germany	94.5	13.3	88.2	10.3
United Kingdom	79.7	12.8	73.7	9.5
France	65.6	8.1	60.4	7.1
Italy	40.9	6.9	41.2	6.5
Canada	82.1	16.9	84.8	15.2

Source: Data from "The Condition of Education: 1992," Washington, DC: National Center for Education Statistics, U.S. Department of Education, 1992.

Directions: The following statements refer to the data in the table above. Read each statement and mark your answer according to the following key.

Circle: S if the statement is supported by the data in the table.
R if the statement is refuted by the data in the table.
N if the statement is neither supported nor refuted by the data.

Ⓢ R N 1. Across all seven countries, the percentage of men between the ages of 25 and 34 who have completed higher education is greater than the corresponding percentage of women.

S R Ⓝ 2. College admissions policies give preferential treatment to male applicants over female applicants.

S R Ⓝ 3. It is more difficult to get into college in Germany than in Japan.

S Ⓡ N 4. When males and females are combined, the U.S. has the second-highest secondary school completion percentage for young adults between the ages of 25 and 34.

Ability to Recognize Assumptions

Another learning outcome pertinent to the interpretation of various types of information is the ability to identify unstated assumptions that are necessary to a conclusion or course of action. The following item illustrates this type of interpretive exercise.

EXAMPLE

Studies have shown that there is a relationship between vocabulary and crime. Crime rates are higher for people with poorly developed vocabularies and crime rates are lower for people with well-developed vocabularies. Older studies have also shown that there is a positive relationship between the number of years of Latin studied and the size and preciseness of an individual's vocabulary. Conclusion: Crime rates can be lowered by reintroducing the study of Latin in the schools.

Which one of the following assumptions is necessary to reach such a conclusion?

A Correlational methods were used to determine these relationships.

B These reported relationships were statistically significant.

Ⓒ Relationships such as these imply causation.

D Latin scholars have a low crime rate.

Ability to Recognize the Relevance of Information

A learning outcome important to all subject-matter areas and that can be measured at all levels of instruction is the ability to recognize the relevance of information. The exercise presented here was prepared for third-grade students. An example at the high school level may be found in Appendix F.

EXAMPLE

Bill lost his boot on the way to school. He wanted to put a notice on the bulletin board so that the other children could help him find it. Which of the following sentences tell something that would help children find the boot?

Directions: Circle *yes* if it would help. Circle *no* if it would not help.

   (yes)   no   1. The boot was black.

   yes   (no)   2. It was very warm.

   (yes)   no   3. It was for his right foot.

   yes   (no)   4. It was a Christmas present.

   yes   (no)   5. It was nice looking.

   (yes)   no   6. It had a zipper.

   (yes)   no   7. It had a gray lining.

Ability to Apply Principles

The application of principles may be shown in many different ways. In the following example, students are asked to identify principles that explain a situation and to recognize illustrations of a principle:

EXAMPLE

Mary Ann wanted her rose bush to grow faster, so she applied twice as much chemical fertilizer as was recommended and watered the bush every evening. About a month later she noticed that the rose bush was dying.

Directions: Which of the following principles is necessary in explaining why the rose bush is dying? If a principle is necessary, circle N, if unnecessary, circle U.

N (U) 1. A chemical compound is changed into other compounds by taking up the elements of water.

(N) U   2. Semipermeable membranes permit the passage of fluid.

N (U) 3. Water condenses when cooled.

(N) U   4. When two solutions of different concentration are separated by a porous partition, their concentration tends to equalize.

Use of Pictorial Materials

Pictorial materials can serve two useful purposes in interpretive exercises. (1) They can help measure a variety of learning outcomes similar to those already discussed simply by replacing the written or tabular data with a pictorial presentation. This use is especially desirable with younger students and when ideas can be more clearly conveyed in pictorial form. (2) Pictorial materials can also measure the ability to interpret graphs, cartoons, maps, and other pictorial materials. In many school subjects, these are important learning outcomes in their own right.

The following examples illustrate the use of pictorial materials:

EXAMPLE I

What clock shows the time that school starts?   (A)   B   C   D
What clock shows the time closest to lunch time?   A   B   (C)   D   (use oral questions)
What clock shows half past the hour?   A   (B)   C   D

EXAMPLE II

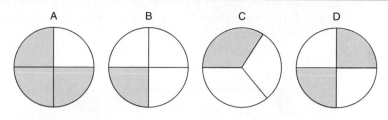

What circle is 1/4 shaded?	A	(B)	C	(D)	
What circle is 1/2 shaded?	A	B	C	(D)	(use oral
What circle is <u>most</u> shaded?	(A)	B	C	D	questions)
What circle is <u>least</u> shaded?	A	(B)	C	D	

EXAMPLE III   At the right is a graph of Bill's weekly allowance distribution.

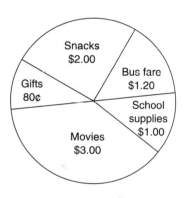

1. What is the ratio of the amount Bill spends
    for school supplies to the amount he spends for
    movies?

    A   7:2

    (B)   1:3

    C   2:7

    D   3:1

2. What would be the best title for this graph?

    A   Bill's weekly allowance.

    B   Bill's money graph.

    (C)   Bill's weekly expenditures.

    D   Bill's money planning.

These Examples I–III were designed for use in lower grades. They illustrate the use of pictorial materials that can be drawn by the teacher and items that are useful for measuring rather simple interpretations of concepts and relationships.

Examples IV–VII are interpretive exercises designed for higher grade levels. They are included here to illustrate the use of various types of pictorial materials, the measurement of different types of learning outcomes, and the use of both multiple-choice and true–false items. As noted in these examples, the pictures and diagrams used in an interpretive exercise frequently can be obtained from published sources. When this is done, care must be taken in reproducing the pictorial elements to make certain that they are clear and detailed enough for proper interpretation. It is also important, of course, to be aware of the copyright laws that govern the use of the material. However, there is seldom a problem in obtaining permission to reproduce copyrighted materials for classroom use.

EXAMPLE IV*

1. The cartoon illustrates which of the following characteristics of the party system in the United States?

    (A)   Strong party discipline is often lacking.

    B   The parties are responsive to the will of the voters.

    C   The parties are often more concerned with politics than with the national welfare.

    D   Bipartisanship often exists in name only.

2. The situation shown in the cartoon is *least* likely to occur at which of the following times?

    A   During the first session of a new Congress

    B   During a political party convention

    C   During a primary election campaign

    (D)   During a presidential election campaign

*Educational Testing Service, *Making the Classroom Test: A Guide for Teachers,* p. 6. Copyright © 1973 by Educational Testing Service (Princeton, N.J.). Used by permission of the publisher.

EXAMPLE V   In the following questions you must make inferences from the data given on the map of the imaginary country, Serendip. The answers will mostly be probabilities rather than certainties. The relative size of towns and cities is not shown. To assist you, the map is divided into squares lettered vertically from A to E and numbered horizontally from 1 to 5.

Which of the following cities would be the best location for a steel mill?

A	Li	(3A)
Ⓑ	Um	(3B)
C	Cot	(3D)
D	Dube	(4B)

Source: From Educational Testing Service, *Multiple-Choice Questions: A Close Look,* p. 5. Copyright © 1973 by Educational Testing Service (Princeton, N.J.). Used by permission of the publisher.

EXAMPLE VI   This question is based on the following situation:

A piece of mineral is placed in a bottle half-filled with a colorless liquid. A two-holed rubber stopper is then placed in the bottle. The system is then sealed by inserting a thermometer and connecting a glass tube to the stoppered bottle and a beaker of limewater as shown in the accompanying diagram:

The following series of observations is recorded:

I. Observations during the first few minutes:

1. Bubbles of a colorless gas rise to the top of the stoppered bottle from the mineral.

2. Bubbles of colorless gas begin to come out of the glass tube and rise to the surface of the limewater.

3. The limewater remains colorless throughout this period of time.

4. The thermometer reads 20° C.

II. Observations at the end of thirty minutes:

1. Bubbles of colorless gas continue to rise in the stoppered bottle.

2. The piece of mineral has become noticeably smaller.

3. There is no apparent change in the level of the liquid in the bottle.

4. The colorless liquid in the bottle remains colorless.

5. The thermometer reads 24° C.

6. The limewater is cloudy.

Which one of the following is the best explanation for the appearance of gas bubbles at the end of the tube in the beaker of limewater?

A   The pressure exerted by the colorless liquid is greater than that exerted by the limewater.

Ⓑ   The bubbles coming from the mineral cause an increased gas pressure in the stoppered bottle.

C   The temperature increase at the end of thirty minutes causes an expansion of gas in the stoppered bottle.

D   The decrease in the size of the piece of mineral causes reduced pressure in the stoppered bottle.

Source: From Educational Testing Service, *Multiple-Choice Questions: A Close Look,* p. 15. Copyright © 1973 by Educational Testing Service (Princeton, N.J.). Used by permission of the publisher.

EXAMPLE VII   Average number of days of school per year for 13-year-olds, by country. School year 1990–91. (From *The Condition of Education,* 1993. National Center for Education Statistics.)

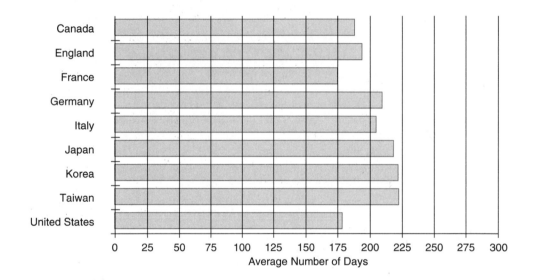

Directions: The following statements refer to the data in the chart above. Read each statement, and mark your answer according to the following key.

   Circle: T - if the data in the chart are sufficient to make the statement true.
           F - if the data in the chart are sufficient to make the statement false.
           I - if the data in the chart are insufficient to determine whether the statement is true or false.

T   (F)   I   1. The number of days per year of school is lower in the U.S. than in any of the other countries shown.

(T)   F   I   2. The average number of days of school is higher in the three Asian countries than in the remaining six.

T   F   (I)   3. U.S. students spend fewer hours in school than students from Japan.

Cartoons like the one in Example IV can be found in newspapers and news magazines. Then simply prepare questions that require the desired interpretations. Either true–false or multiple-choice items might be used with this type of exercise. It is important to select a cartoon that illustrates a concept or principle that is relevant to the learning outcomes to be measured. Interpretive exercises of this type are especially useful in social studies.

Maps like the one in Example V can also be found in published materials, but care must be taken in selecting the map to be sure that is contains the data necessary for preparing questions that measure significant learning outcomes. Maps can also be prepared, of course, but that is a relatively time-consuming task. Drawings and charts like those in Examples VI and VII are typically easy to prepare but may sometimes be found in published sources.

ADVANTAGES AND LIMITATIONS OF INTERPRETIVE EXERCISES

The interpretive exercise has several advantages. First, the introductory material makes it possible to measure the ability to interpret written materials, charts, graphs, maps, pictures, and other communication media encountered in everyday situations. The rapid expansion of knowledge in every subject-matter area has made it impossible to learn all of the important factual information in a given field, which has led to greater dependence on libraries, reference materials, self-study techniques, and interpretive skills. Second, the interpretive exercise makes it possible to measure more complex learning outcomes than can be measured with the single objective item. Some data are usually necessary if students are to demonstrate thinking and problem-solving skills, and the inclusion of such data is awkward in most kinds of test items. Third, by having a series of related test items based on a common set of data, greater depth and breadth can be obtained in the measurement of intellectual skills. Fourth, the interpretive exercise minimizes the influence of irrelevant factual information on the measurement of complex learning outcomes. Students may be unable to demonstrate their understanding of a principle simply because they do not know some of the facts concerning the situation to which they are to be applied. This blocking of response, caused by a lack of detailed factual information not directly pertinent to the purpose of the measurement, can be largely eliminated with the interpretive exercise. In the introductory materials, we can give students the common background of information needed to demonstrate understanding, thinking skills, and problem-solving abilities.

The main advantage of the interpretive exercise over the performance-based assessment task, in measuring complex achievement, is derived from its greater structure. Students are not free to redefine the problem or to demonstrate thinking skills at which they are most proficient. The series of objective items forces them to use only the mental processes called for. This also makes it possible to measure separate aspects of problem-solving ability and to use objective scoring procedures.

As with all forms of test items, the interpretive exercise does have some limitations. Probably the greatest limiting factor, and one that may have occurred to you as you reviewed the sample items, is the difficulty of construction. Selecting printed materials that are new to the students but that are relevant to the instructional outcomes requires considerable searching. When pertinent material is found, it usually must be edited and reworked to make it more suitable for testing purposes.

Next, test items must be constructed that demand the specific behaviors indicated in the learning outcomes being measured. The construction process is often circular (i.e., it goes back and forth between revising the introductory material and revising the test items until a satisfactory product is obtained). This entire procedure is time-consuming and requires much greater skill than that needed to construct single objective test items. But three positive comments can be made regarding the difficulty of constructing interpretive exercises: (1) More and more items of this type now appear in various subject-matter fields. The references at the end of this chapter contain numerous examples that may serve as guides to test construction. (2) The greater instructional emphasis on complex learning outcomes resulting from the use of interpretive exercises offsets the additional effort required in test construction. (3) The task becomes easier with practice and experience.

A second limitation, especially pertinent when the introductory material is in written form, is the heavy demand on reading skill. The poor reader is handicapped by both the difficulty of the reading material and the length of time it takes to read each test exercise. The first problem can be controlled somewhat by keeping the reading level low and the second by using brief passages. Both of these are only partial solutions, however, because the poor reader will still be at a decided disadvantage. In the primary grades and in classes that contain many poor readers, interpretive exercises might be better limited to the use of pictorial materials.

Compared to the performance-based assessment task discussed in Chapter 9, the interpretive exercise has two shortcomings as a measure of complex achievement. First, it cannot measure a student's overall approach to problem solving. It is efficient for measuring specific aspects of the problem-solving process, but it does not indicate whether the student can integrate and use these skills when faced with a particular problem. Thus, it provides a diagnostic view of the students' problem-solving abilities, in contrast with the holistic view of essay questions or other performance assessment tasks. Second, because the interpretive exercise usually uses selection items, it is confined to learning outcomes at the recognition level. To measure the ability to define problems, to formulate hypotheses, to organize data, and to draw conclusions, performance assessment tasks must be used.

SUGGESTIONS FOR CONSTRUCTING INTERPRETIVE EXERCISES

There are two main tasks in constructing interpretive exercises: (1) selecting appropriate introductory material and (2) constructing a series of dependent test items. In addition, care must be taken to construct test items that require analyzing the introductory material in terms of complex learning outcomes. The following suggestions will aid in constructing high-quality interpretive exercises:

1.   *Select introductory material that is relevant to the objectives of the course.*   Interpretive exercises, like other testing procedures, should measure the achievement of specific instructional outcomes. Success in this regard depends to a large extent on the introductory material, as this provides the common basis for the test items. If the introductory material is too simple, the exercise may become a measure of general information or simple reading skill. On the other hand, if the material is too complex or unrelated to instructional goals, it may become a measure of general reasoning ability. Both extremes must be avoided. Ideally, the introductory material should be pertinent to the course content and complex enough to evoke the mental reactions specified in the course objectives.

The amount of emphasis given to the various interpretive skills in the course objectives is also important. Care must be taken not to overload the test with interpretive items in any particular area. The selection of introductory material should be guided by the emphasis to be given to the measurement of complex achievement and each type of interpretive skill.

2.   *Select introductory material that is appropriate to the students' curricular experience and reading level.*   Many complex learning outcomes can be measured with different types of introductory material. The ability to recognize the validity of conclusions, for example, can be measured with written materials, tables, charts, graphs, maps, or pictures. The type used should be familiar to the students so that the nature of the material does not prevent them from demonstrating their achievement of the complex learning outcomes. It would be unfair, for example, to ask students to recognize the validity of conclusions based on data presented in graph form if they had not had experience in interpreting graphs similar to those used in the test.

When various types of introductory material will serve a purpose equally well and all are familiar to the students, we favor material that places the least demand on reading skill. For elementary students, pictorial materials are definitely favored. For higher grade levels, pictorial materials and verbal materials with a low vocabulary load and simple sentences are preferred. Although general reading skill is necessary in all written tests, it can become prominent in interpretive exercises unless efforts are made to minimize its influence.

3.   *Select introductory material that is new to students.*   In order to measure complex learning outcomes, the introductory material must be new. Asking students to interpret materials identical to those used in instruction does not ensure that the exercise will measure anything other than rote memory. Too much novelty, however, must be avoided. Materials that are similar to those used in class but vary slightly in content or form are the most desirable. Such materials can be obtained by modifying selections from textbooks, newspapers, news magazines, and various reference materials pertinent to the course content.

4. *Select introductory material that is brief but meaningful.*   Another method of minimizing the influence of general reading skill on the measurement of complex learning outcomes is to keep the introductory material as brief as possible. Digests of articles are frequently available and are good raw material for interpretive exercises. If digests are unavailable, the summary of an article or a key passage may be sufficient. In some cases, the relevant information is summarized better in a table, diagram, or picture.

In striving for brief introductory material, be careful not to omit elements that are crucial to the interpretive skills being measured. The material also should, of course, be complete enough to be meaningful and interesting to the students.

5. *Revise introductory material for clarity, conciseness, and greater interpretive value.*   Although some materials (for example, graphs) can be used without revision, most selections require some adaptation for testing purposes. Technical articles frequently contain long, detailed descriptions of events. On the other hand, news reports and digests of articles are brief but often present exaggerated reports of events to attract the reader's interest. Although such reports provide excellent material for measuring the ability to judge the relevance of arguments, the need for assumptions, the validity of conclusions, and the like, the material must usually be modified to be used effectively.

Revision of the introductory material and construction of the related test items tend to be interdependent procedures. Rewriting material often suggests questions to be used, and the construction of test questions often necessitates revisions of the material. In revising a description of an experiment, for example, assumptions, hypotheses, or conclusions explicitly stated in the description may be deleted and used as a basis for questions. Likewise, a question calling for application of the experimental findings may require the addition of new material to the selection. Thus, the revision of the introductory material and the construction of test items proceed in a circular fashion until a clear, concise interpretive exercise evolves.

6. *Construct test items that require analysis and interpretation of the introductory material.*   There are two common errors in the construction of interpretive exercises that invalidate them as a measure of complex achievement. One is to include questions that are answered directly in the introductory material; that is, asking for factual information explicitly stated in the selection. Such questions measure simple reading skill. The second error is to include questions that can be answered correctly without reading the introductory material; that is, requiring answers based on general information. These questions measure simple knowledge outcomes.

If the interpretive exercise is to function as intended, it should include only those test items that require students to read the introductory material and to make the desired interpretations. In some instances, the interpretations will require students to supply knowledge beyond that presented in the exercise. In others, the interpretations will be limited to the factual information provided. The emphasis on knowledge and interpretive skill will be determined by the learning outcomes being measured. Regardless of the emphasis, however, the test items should be dependent on the introductory material, while at the same time calling forth mental reactions of a higher order than those related to simple reading comprehension.

7. *Make the number of test items roughly proportional to the length of the introductory material.* It is inefficient to have students analyze a long, complex selection of material and then answer only one or two questions about it. Although it is impossible to specify the exact number of questions that should accompany a given amount of material, the items presented earlier in this chapter show a desirable balance. Other things being equal, we always favor the interpretive exercise that has brief introductory material and a relatively large number of test items.

8. *In constructing test items for an interpretive exercise, observe all pertinent suggestions for constructing objective items.* The form of test item used in the interpretive exercise will determine the rules for construction. If multiple-choice or true–false items are used, the suggestions for constructing these item types should be followed. When modified forms are used, suggestions for constructing each of the various types of objective items should be reviewed for their applicability in construction. Freedom from irrelevant clues and technical defects is as important in interpretive exercises as it is in single, independent test items.

9. *In constructing key-type test items, make the categories homogeneous and mutually exclusive.* The key-type item, which is used frequently in interpretive exercises, is a modified multiple-choice form that uses a common set of alternatives. In this regard, it is also similar to the matching item and so should be constructed in the same way, with special attention devoted to the categories used in the key. All of the categories in any one key should be homogeneous; that is, they all should be concerned with similar types of judgment. At the same time, there should be no overlapping of categories. Each alternative should provide a separate category so that there is a clear-cut system of classification and each item has only one correct answer.

EXAMPLE

The majority of dental scientists agree that fluoridated water reduces tooth decay. A number of cities have fluoridated their water supply, and reports indicate that fluoridated water is both safe and inexpensive. Despite an intensive educational campaign pointing out the benefits of fluoridated water, many cities do not yet have it. Resolved: In the interests of national health, all cities should be required to fluoridate their water supply.

Directions: Read each of the following statements carefully. In front of each statement mark

Key: A   if the statement supports the resolution.

B   if the statement contradicts the resolution.

C   If the statement is a fact.

D   if the statement is an opinion.

_____ 1. The long-range effects of fluoridated water on an individual's health have not been studied.
(Similar items complete the exercise.)

In this example, the key includes two overlapping categories, one concerned with the relationship of each statement to the resolution and the other with the nature of the statement itself. This makes it impossible to have only one correct answer for each statement. Item 1, for example, would have to be marked category B because it contradicts the resolution and category C because it is a statement of fact.

The above key could be improved by limiting the categories to the relevance of the statements to the resolutions, as illustrated in the following key:

EXAMPLE

Key: A   if the statement supports the resolution.
      B   if the statement contradicts the resolution.
      C   if the statement neither supports nor contradicts the resolution.

If judging both the factual nature of a statement and its relevance is important, these two elements can be combined to form discrete categories as follows:

EXAMPLE

Key: A   if it is a statement of fact that supports the resolution.
      B   if it is a statement of opinion that supports the resolution.
      C   if it is a statement of fact that contradicts the resolution.
      D   if it is a statement of opinion that contradicts the resolution.

The main drawback to combining two types of judgment in one category is the greater complexity of the key. This is especially undesirable with younger students.

In mathematics, a key-type item that has been found to be quite efficient is the quantitative comparison item. The use of a fixed-response format for quantitative comparison items, reduces the reading required, and makes it possible for students to respond to a larger number of items in a given period of time.

EXAMPLE*

Directions: Each of the following questions consists of two quantities, one in Column A and one in Column B. You are to compare the two quantities and choose:

Key: A   if the quantity in Column A is greater;
      B   if the quantity in Column B is greater;
      C   if the two quantities are equal;
      D   if the relationship cannot be determined from the information given.

Common Information: In a question, information concerning one or both of the quantities to be compared is centered above the two columns. A symbol that appears in both columns represents the same thing in Column A as it does in Column B.

Sample Items:

				Column A	Column B
(A)	B	C	D	1/3	.30
A	(B)	C	D	4.9	25

$$X + Y = 5$$
$$X - Y = 3$$

				Column A	Column B
A	B	(C)	D	$X^2 - Y^2$	15

$$X - 2Y = 20$$

				Column A	Column B
A	B	C	(D)	X	0

Source: From GRE 1990–91 Information Bulletin, Princeton, NJ: Educational Testing Service, 1990, p.37.

10.   In constructing key-type test items, develop standard key categories where applicable.   Despite the usefulness of the interpretive exercise for measuring complex achievement, classroom teachers have not used it extensively, often because of the difficulty of construction. The popularity of the key-type item in interpretive exercises is probably because it uses a common set of alternatives. This makes it easier to construct than the regular multiple-choice form, which requires a different set of alternatives for each item.

It is often possible to simplify further the construction of key-type interpretive exercises by preparing key categories that can be reused with different content. For example, a learning outcome such as the ability to recognize assumptions might lead to the following key:

EXAMPLE

Key: A   an assumption that is necessary to make the conclusion valid.

B   an assumption that would invalidate the conclusion.

C   an assumption that has no bearing on the validity of the conclusion.

This key could be used with a brief description of a situation, a conclusion based on the situation, and a list of assumptions. Both the key and the form of the item could be used repeatedly, with only the content varying. Although selecting new content material is still a problem, the framework of the standard key categories simplifies the process.

Standard key categories, of course, cannot be used in all areas and their use should not be permitted to determine which learning outcomes receive emphasis. Rather, the time and effort saved by such procedures should free the teacher to explore more creative applications of the interpretive exercise in other areas. See the "Checklist" for reviewing interpretive exercises.

	CHECKLIST		
	Reviewing Interpretive Exercises		
		Yes	**No**
1.	Is this the most appropriate item format to use?	____	____
2.	Is the material to be interpreted relevant to the intended learning outcomes?	____	____
3.	Is the material to be interpreted appropriate to the students' curricular experience and reading level?	____	____
4.	Have pictorial materials been used whenever appropriate?	____	____
5.	Does the material to be interpreted contain some novelty (to require interpretation)?	____	____
6.	Is the material to be interpreted brief, clear, and meaningful?	____	____
7.	Are the test items based directly on the introductory material (cannot be answered without it), and do they call for interpretation (not just recall or simple reading skills)?	____	____
8.	Has a reasonable number of test items been used in each interpretive exercise?	____	____
9.	Do the test items meet the relevant criteria of effective item writing?	____	____
10.	When key-type items are used, are the categories homogeneous and mutually exclusive?	____	____
11.	If revised, are the interpretive exercises still relevant to the intended learning outcomes?	____	____
12.	Have the interpretive exercises been set aside for a time before reviewing them?	____	____

SUMMARY

Complex achievement refers to those learning outcomes based on higher mental processes. Such outcomes are classified under various general headings, including understanding, reasoning, thinking, and problem solving. The attainment of goals in these areas can be measured by both objective and subjective means. The most commonly used objective item is the interpretive exercise.

The interpretive exercise consists of a series of objective questions based on written materials, tables, charts, graphs, maps, or pictures. The questions require students to demonstrate the specific interpretive skill being measured. For example, students might be asked to recognize assumptions, inferences, conclusions, relationships, applications, and the like. The structure of the interpretive exercise makes it possible to obtain independent measures of each aspect of thinking and problem solving. Although it is efficient for measuring such learning outcomes, it does not measure students' ability to integrate and use these skills in a global attack on a problem. Thus, it is limited to a diagnostic analysis of problem-solving skills.

Probably the main reason for not using the interpretive exercise is the difficulty of construction. This process involves (1) selecting appropriate introductory material, (2) revising the material to fit the outcomes to be measured, and (3) constructing a series of dependent test items that call forth the desired behavior. Although these steps are admittedly time-consuming, the rewards in improved teaching–learning practices seem to justify the time and effort.

LEARNING EXERCISES

1. What are the advantages of the interpretive exercise over the performance-based assessment for measuring complex achievement? What are the disadvantages?

2. For which types of learning outcomes is the interpretive exercise most likely to be appropriate? Why?

3. Discuss the relative merits of the interpretive exercise and the single-item multiple-choice question. For which situation would each be most useful? What are the limitations of each?

4. Construct one interpretive exercise for each of the following:
   a. A paragraph of written material.
   b. A picture or cartoon.
   c. A chart or graph.

5. What steps would you follow in examining an interpretive exercise to determine whether it had been properly constructed?

6. What are some of the factors to consider when you are deciding whether to use interpretive exercises in a classroom test?

FURTHER READING

Gronlund, N. E. (1993). *How to make achievement tests and assessments* (5th ed.). Boston: Allyn & Bacon. See Chapter 4 for examples of interpretive exercises and their uses.

Mehrens, W. A., & Lehmann, I. J. (1991) *Measurement and evaluation in education and psychology* (4th ed.). New York: Holt, Rinehart & Winston. See Chapter 7, "Writing Objective Test Items: Multiple-Choice and Context-Dependent," for sample interpretive exercises and suggestions for construction.

Morse, H. T., & McCune, G. H. (1971). *Selected items for the testing of study skills and critical thinking*. Washington, D.C.: National Council for the Social Studies.

Multiple-choice questions: A close look. (1973). Princeton, N.J.: Educational Testing Service. Illustrates the use of the multiple-choice item for measuring complex achievement in a variety of fields. Maps, graphs, pictures, diagrams, and written materials are used. Each item is followed by a statistical and logical analysis of its effectiveness.

Wesman, A. G. (1971). Writing the test item. In R. L. Thorndike (Ed.), *Educational Measurement* (2nd ed.) (pp. 81–129). Washington, D.C.: American Council on Education. An extended treatment of the topic of item writing. See pages 120–128 for the construction of interpretive exercises.

CHAPTER 9

Measuring Complex Achievement: Essay Questions

Some important learning outcomes may best be measured by the use of open-ended essay questions or other types of performance assessments. Essay questions provide the freedom of response that is needed to adequately assess the ability of students to formulate problems; organize, integrate, and evaluate ideas and information; and apply knowledge and skills.

Up to this point, our main concern has been with objective test items. We noted that such items can measure a variety of learning outcomes, from simple to complex, and that the interpretive exercise is especially useful for measuring complex achievement. Despite this wide applicability of objective-item types, there remain significant instructional outcomes for which no satisfactory objective measurements have been devised. These include such outcomes as the ability to recall, organize, and integrate ideas; the ability to express oneself in writing; and the ability to create rather than merely identify interpretations and applications of data. Such outcomes require less structuring of responses than objective test items, and it is in the measurement of these outcomes that written essays and other performance-based assessments are of greatest value.

In this chapter we consider the most familiar form of performance-based assessment—the essay question. Other types of performance-based assessments (which include gathering information, making oral presentations, conducting experiments, repairing or manipulating equipment, etc.) are considered in Chapter 10.

FORMS AND USES OF ESSAY QUESTIONS

We focus our discussion of the essay question on its use in the measurement of complex achievement. We recognize, however, that many teachers use essay questions to measure knowledge of factual information. It certainly can be useful to ask students to generate in their own words, the plot of a story, the causes of an historical event, or the steps in a scientific process, all of which may be provided by a text. Although measuring such knowledge of factual information with essay questions is useful and valid, it does not tap the full potential of essay questions.

The distinctive feature of essay questions is the freedom of response. Students are free to select, relate, and present ideas in their own words. Although this freedom enhances the value of essay questions as a measure of complex achievement, it introduces scoring difficulties that make essays inefficient as a measure of factual knowledge. For most purposes, knowledge of factual information can be more efficiently measured by some type of objective item.

Essay questions should be primarily used to measure those learning outcomes that are not readily measured by objective test items. The special features of essay questions can be utilized most fully when their shortcomings are offset by the need for such measurement. Learning outcomes concerned with the abilities to select, organize, integrate, relate, and evaluate ideas require the freedom of response and the originality provided by essay questions. In addition, these outcomes are of such great educational significance that the expenditure of energy in the difficult and time-consuming task of evaluating the answers can be easily justified.

Essay tests and other performance-based assessments can also be justified on the grounds that the performances required correspond more closely to the larger instructional goals and objectives than discrete factual-knowledge questions. Indeed, the validity of measurement of complex achievement may be enhanced by the use of essay tests and other performance-based assessments. Furthermore, tests send a message of what it is important to learn and be able to do. Just consider how frequently teachers are asked the question: "Will this be on the test?" The form of the assessment provides a model. Thus, it is often argued that if you want students to be able to communicate in writing, then they not only need to be encouraged to write, but have to be required to do so when it counts.

The freedom of response provided by essay questions is not an all-or-nothing affair but, rather, a matter of degree. At one extreme, the response is almost as restricted as that in the short-answer objective item, in which a sentence or two may be all that is required. At the other extreme, students are given almost complete freedom in making their responses, and their answers may require several pages. Although variations in freedom of response tend to fall along a continuum between these extremes, essay questions can be conveniently classified into two types: restricted-response questions and extended-response questions.

Restricted-Response Essay Questions

The restricted-response question usually limits both the content and the response. The content is usually restricted by the scope of the topic to be discussed. Limitations on the form of response are generally indicated in the question.

EXAMPLES   State the main differences between the Vietnam War and previous wars in which the United States has participated.

Why is the barometer one of the most useful instruments for forecasting weather? Answer in a brief paragraph.

Describe two situations that demonstrate the application of the law of supply and demand. Do not use those examples discussed in class.

What is measured on an essay such as the one asking students to state the differences between the Vietnam War and previous wars depends upon a student's previous instructional experiences. If the textbook or recent class presentations have explicitly discussed ways in which the Vietnam War was different from previous wars, then the student's task is simply to demonstrate an understanding of this material and to put it in his or her own words. That is, the essay question is simply a measure of comprehension. If the essay question presents the student with his or her first opportunity to think about the Vietnam War in terms of differences from previous wars, however, then the essay requires analysis and higher-level thinking.

Another way of restricting responses in essay tests is to base the questions on specific problems. For this purpose, introductory material like that used in interpretive exercises can be presented. Such items differ from objective interpretive exercises only by the fact that essay questions are used instead of multiple-choice or true–false items.

EXAMPLE   The majority of dental scientists agree that fluoridating a city's water supply is a safe and inexpensive method of preventing tooth decay. However, many cities have not fluoridated their water because the residents have voted against it. One of the main arguments against fluoridation is that fluoridating a city's water supply violates the individual's freedom of choice.

(A) Indicate whether you agree or disagree with the underlined part of the last statement.

(B) Support your position.

Because the restricted-response question is more structured, it is most useful for measuring learning outcomes requiring the interpretation and application of data in a specific area. In fact, any of the learning outcomes measured by an objective interpretive exercise also can be measured by a restricted-response essay question. The difference is that the interpretive exercise requires students to select the answer, whereas the restricted-response question requires them to supply it. In some instances, the objective interpretive exercise is favored because of the ease and reliability of scoring. In other situations, the restricted-response question is better because of its more direct relevance to the learning outcome (e.g., the ability to formulate valid conclusions).

Although restricting students' responses to essay questions makes it possible to measure more specific learning outcomes, these same restrictions make them less valuable as a measure of those learning outcomes emphasizing integration, organization, and originality. Restricting the scope of the topic to be discussed and indicating the nature of the desired response limit the student's opportunity to demonstrate these behaviors. For higher-order learning outcomes, greater freedom of response is needed.

Extended-Response Essay Questions

The extended-response question allows students to select any factual information that they think is pertinent, to organize the answer in accordance with their best judgment, and to integrate and evaluate ideas as they deem appropriate. This freedom enables them to demonstrate their ability to select, organize, analyze, integrate, and evaluate ideas. If analysis, organization, integration, and evaluation skills are rewarded in the grading of the essays, this form of assessment also makes clear the value that is placed on these higher-order skills. On the other hand, this same freedom that enables the demonstration of higher-order skills makes the extended-response question inefficient for measuring more specific learning outcomes and introduces scoring difficulties.

EXAMPLES   Compare developments in international relations in the administrations of President Bush and President Clinton. Cite examples when possible.

Evaluate the significance of the sea captain's pursuit of the white whale in *Moby Dick*.

Describe the influence of Mendel's laws of heredity on the development of biology as a science.

Write a scientific evaluation of the Copernican theory of the solar system. Include scientific observations that support your statements.

The need to measure a student's global attack on a problem can be easily defended. The thinking and problem-solving skills measured by objective interpretive exercises and restricted-response essay questions seldom function in isolation. In a natural situation they operate together in a manner that includes more than a sum of the skills involved. These skills interact with one another and with the knowledge and understanding the problem requires. Thus, it is not just the skills we are measuring but also how they function together.

Both teachers and test specialists agree that the extended-response question does require complex behaviors that cannot be measured by more objective means. But they often differ in their level of concern about the difficulty of scoring extended written responses in a way that can satisfactorily measure these behaviors. Test specialists point out that unless considerable attention is given to the choice of questions and to scoring procedures, the scoring may be too unreliable to yield defensible measurement. Nevertheless, many teachers continue to use the extended-response question to measure student achievement without adequate attention to the complexities involved in the construction and scoring of such questions. Neither a hard-line measurement position that rejects extended essays as an approach to measurement nor one that ignores the difficulties of scoring seems to contribute much to the valid measurement of student achievement. It seems more sensible to identify the complex behaviors we want to measure, formulate questions that elicit these behaviors, evaluate the results as reliably as we can, and then use these admittedly limited data as the best evidence we have available.

Summary Comparison of Learning Outcomes Measured

The restricted-response essay question can measure a variety of complex learning outcomes similar to those measured by the objective interpretive exercise. The main difference is that the interpretive exercise requires students to select the answer, and the restricted-response question requires the student to supply the answer. In comparison, extended-response essay questions measure more general learning outcomes, such as the abilities to select, organize, integrate, and evaluate ideas. A comparison of the types of complex learning outcomes measured by each of these types of assessment is presented in Table 9.1.

The learning outcomes in Table 9.1, of course, merely suggest the types of learning outcomes that may be measured. With slight modifications, an infinite variety of outcomes can be stated in each area. The freedom of response to essay questions is a matter of degree, and thus, the functions of the restricted-response question and the extended-response question often overlap.

ADVANTAGES AND LIMITATIONS OF ESSAY QUESTIONS

A major advantage of the essay question is that it measures complex learning outcomes that cannot be measured by other means. But the use of essay questions does not guarantee the measurement of complex achievement. To do so, essay questions must be as carefully constructed as objective test items. The course objectives pertinent to complex achievement must be defined in terms of specific learning outcomes, and the essay questions must be phrased in a way that will produce the desired behavior. When a table of specifications is used in planning for the assessment, it is simply a matter of constructing the questions in accordance with the specifications.

A second advantage of the extended-response question is its emphasis on the integration and application of thinking and problem-solving skills. Although objective items such as the interpretive exercise can be designed to measure various aspects of complex achievement, the ability to integrate and apply these skills in a general attack on a problem is best measured by extended-response essay questions.

TABLE 9.1

Types of complex learning outcomes measured by essay questions, and objective interpretive exercises

Type of Test Item	Examples of Complex Learning Outcomes That Can Be Measured
Objective Interpretive Exercises	Ability to— identify cause–effect relationship identify the application of principles identify the relevance of arguments identify tenable hypotheses identify valid conclusions identify unstated assumptions identify the limitations of data identify the adequacy of procedures (and similar outcomes based on the pupil's ability to *select* the answer)
Restricted-Response Essay Questions	Ability to— explain cause–effect relationships describe applications of principles present relevant arguments formulate tenable hypotheses formulate valid conclusions state necessary assumptions describe the limitations of data explain methods and procedures (and similar outcomes based on the pupil's ability to *supply* the answer)
Extended-Response Essay Questions	Ability to— produce, organize, and express ideas integrate learnings in different areas create original forms (e.g., designing an experiment) evaluate the worth of ideas

Another commonly cited advantage of the essay question is its ease of construction. This factor has led to the widespread use of essay questions by classroom teachers. In a matter of minutes, most teachers can formulate several essay questions, an attractive feature for the busy teacher. This apparent advantage can be very misleading, however. Constructing essay questions that require the specific behaviors emphasized in a particular set of learning outcomes takes considerable time and effort. When ease of construction is stressed, it usually refers to the common practice of dashing off questions at the last minute, with little regard for the course objectives. In such cases there is some question whether ease of construction can be considered an advantage. In addition to the invalidity of the measurement, evaluating the answers to carelessly developed questions tends to be confusing and time-consuming.

The most commonly cited limitation of the essay test is the unreliability of the scoring. Over the years various studies have shown that written essays are scored differently by different teachers and that even the same teachers score responses differently at different times. The poor reliability across scorers, however, is frequently the result of failure to identify clearly the learning outcomes being measured and the failure to establish well-defined scoring criteria. Evaluating essays without adequate attention to the learning outcomes being measured and the scoring criteria to be used is like "three blind men appraising an elephant." One teacher stresses factual content; one, organization of ideas; and another, writing skill. With each teacher evaluating the degree to which different learning outcomes are achieved, it is not surprising that scoring diverges. Even variations in scoring by the same teacher can probably be explained to a large extent by inadequate attention to learning outcomes and scoring criteria. When the evaluation of answers is not guided by clearly defined outcomes and scoring criteria, it tends to be based on less stable, intuitive judgments. Although the judgmental scoring of essay questions will always have some degree of unreliability, scoring reliability can be greatly increased by clearly defining the outcomes to be measured, properly framing the questions, carefully following scoring rules, and obtaining practice in scoring.

A closely related limitation of essay questions is the amount of time required for scoring the responses. If the scoring is done conscientiously and helpful feedback is provided to students, even a small number of papers may require several hours of scoring time. If the classes are large and several extended essay questions are used, conscientious scoring becomes practically impossible. Ironically, most of the suggestions for improving the scoring of responses to essay questions require more time; not less, as might be hoped. The only practical solution is to reserve the use of extended essay questions for those learning outcomes that cannot be measured well objectively. With fewer essay questions to score in a given test, more time will be available for evaluating the answers.

Another shortcoming of essay questions is the limited sampling they provide. So few questions can be included in a given test that some areas are measured thoroughly, but many others are neglected. This inadequate sampling makes essay questions especially inefficient for measuring knowledge of factual information. For such outcomes we can use objective test items and reserve essay questions, especially extended-response questions, for measuring complex achievement. This does not eliminate the sampling problem, however, because we would also like an adequate sample of complex behaviors. When we use essay questions, we should try to obtain as representative a sample as possible. One way of doing this is to accumulate evidence from a series of essay questions administered at different times throughout the school year. The collection of the results throughout the year into portfolios of work, as is described in Chapter 13, can serve other important evaluation and communication functions.

SUGGESTIONS FOR CONSTRUCTING ESSAY QUESTIONS

The improvement of the essay question as a measure of complex learning outcomes requires attention to two problems: (1) how to construct essay questions that call forth the desired behavior and (2) how to score the answers so that achievement is reliably measured. Here we shall suggest ways of constructing essay questions, and in the next section, we shall suggest ways of improving scoring, although these two procedures are interrelated.

Some Types of Thought Questions and Sample Item Stems

Comparing

Describe the similarities and differences between . . .

Compare the following two methods for . . .

Relating cause and effect

What are major causes of . . .?

What would be the most likely effects of . . .?

Justifying

Which of the following alternatives would you favor, and why?

Explain why you agree or disagree with the following statement.

Summarizing

State the main points included in . . .

Briefly summarize the contents of . . .

Generalizing

Formulate several valid generalizations from the following data.

State a set of principles that can explain the following events.

Inferring

In light of the facts presented, what is most likely to happen when . . .?

How would Senator X be likely to react to the following issue?

1. Restrict the use of essay questions to those learning outcomes that cannot be measured satisfactorily by objective items.   Other things being equal, objective measures have the advantage of efficiency and reliability. But when objective items are inadequate for measuring the learning outcomes, the use of essay questions can be easily defended, despite their limitations. Some of the complex learning outcomes, such as those pertaining to the organization, integration, and expression of ideas, will be neglected unless essay questions are used. By restricting the use of essay questions to these areas, the evaluation of student achievement can be most fully realized.

2. Construct questions that will call forth the behavior specified in the learning outcomes.   Like objective items, essay questions should measure the achievement of clearly defined instructional objectives. If the ability to apply principles is being measured, for example, the questions should be phrased in such a manner that they call forth that particular behavior. Essay questions should never be hurriedly constructed in the hope that they will measure broad, important (but unidentified) educational objectives. Each essay question should be carefully designed to elicit particular aspects of behavior defined in the desired learning

Classifying

Group the following items according to . . .

What do the following items have in common?

Creating

List as many ways as you can think of for . . .

Make up a story describing what would happen if . . .

Applying

Using the principle of. . .as a guide, describe how you would solve the
  following problem situation.

Describe a situation that illustrates the principle of . . .

Analyzing

Describe the reasoning errors in the following paragraph.

List and describe the main characteristics of . . .

Synthesizing

Describe a plan for proving that . . .

Write a well-organized report that shows. . .

Evaluating

Describe the strengths and weaknesses of . . .

Using the given criteria, write an evaluation of . . .

outcomes. See "Some Types of Thought Questions and Sample Item Stems" for examples of the many types of questions that might be asked; the phrasing of any particular question will vary somewhat from one subject to another.

Constructing essay questions in accordance with particular learning outcomes is much easier with restricted-response questions than with extended-response questions. The restricted scope of the topic and the type of response expected make it possible to relate a restricted-response question directly to one or more of the outcomes. The extreme freedom of the extended-response question makes it difficult to present questions so that the student's responses will reflect the particular learning outcomes desired. This difficulty can be partially overcome by indicating the bases on which the answer will be evaluated.

EXAMPLE Write a two-page statement defending the importance of conserving our natural resources. (Your answer will be evaluated in terms of its organization, its comprehensiveness, and the relevance of the arguments presented.)

Informing students that they should pay special attention to organization, comprehensiveness, and relevance of arguments defines the task, makes the scoring criteria explicit, and makes it possible to key the question to a particular set of learning outcomes. These directions alone will not, of course, ensure that the appropriate behaviors will be exhibited. It is only when the students have been taught the relevant skills and how to integrate them that such directions will serve their intended purpose.

3. Phrase the question so that the student's task is clearly indicated. The purpose a teacher had in mind when developing the question is often not conveyed to the student because of ambiguous phrasing. Students interpret the question differently and give a hodgepodge of responses. Because it is impossible to determine which of the incorrect or off-target responses are due to misinterpretation and which to lack of achievement, the results are worse than worthless: They may actually be harmful if used to measure student progress toward instructional objectives.

One way to clarify the question is to make it as specific as possible. For the restricted-response question, this means rewriting it until the desired response is clearly defined.

EXAMPLES *Poor:* Why do birds migrate?

Better: State three hypotheses that might explain why birds migrate south in the fall. Indicate the most probable one and give reasons for your selection.

The improved version presents the students with a definite task. Although some students may not be able to give the correct answer, they all will certainly know what type of response is expected. Note also how easy it would be to relate such an item to a specific learning outcome such as "the ability to formulate and defend tenable hypotheses."

When an extended-response question is desired, some limitation of the task may be possible, but care must be taken not to destroy the function of the question. If the question becomes too narrow, it will be less effective as a measure of the ability to select, organize, and integrate ideas and information. The best procedure for clarifying the extended-response question seems to be to give the student explicit directions concerning the type of response desired.

EXAMPLES *Poor:* Compare the Democratic and Republican parties.

Better: Compare the current policies of the Democratic and Republican parties with regard to the role of government in private business. Support your statements with examples when possible. (Your answer should be confined to two pages. It will be evaluated in terms of the appropriateness of the facts and examples presented and the skill with which it is organized.)

The first version of the example offers no common basis for responding and, consequently, no frame of reference for evaluating the response. If students interpret the question differently, their responses will be organized differently, because organization is partly a function of the content being organized. Also, some students will narrow the problem before responding, thus giving themselves a much easier task than students who attempt to treat the broader aspects of the problem.

The improved version gives students a clearly defined task without destroying their freedom to respond in original ways. This is achieved both by specifying the scope of the question and by including directions concerning the type of response desired. See "The Importance of Writing Skill."

4. Indicate an approximate time limit for each question. Too often essay questions place a premium on speed, because inadequate attention is paid to reasonable time limits during the test's construction. As each question is constructed, the teacher should estimate the approximate time needed for a satisfactory response. In allotting response time, keep the slower students in mind. Most errors in allotting time needed are in giving of too little time. It is better to use fewer questions and give more generous time limits than to put some students at a disadvantage.

The time limits allotted to each question should be indicated to the students so that they can pace their responses to each question and not be caught at the end of the testing time with "just one more question to go." If the assessment contains both objective and essay questions, the students should, of course, be told approximately how much time to spend on each part of the test. This may be done orally or included on the test form itself. In either case, care must be taken not to create over-concern about time. The adequacy of the time limits might very well be emphasized in the introductory remarks, so as to allay any anxiety that might arise.

5. Avoid the use of optional questions. A fairly common practice when using essay questions is to give students more questions than they are expected to perform and then permit them to select a given number. For example, the teacher may include six essay questions in a test and direct the students to respond to any three of them. This practice is generally favored by students because they can select those questions they know most about. Except for the desirable effect on student morale, however, there is little to recommend the use of optional questions.

The Importance of Writing Skill

Performance on an essay test depends largely on writing ability. If students are to be able to demonstrate the achievement of higher-level learning outcomes, they must be taught the thinking and writing skills needed to express themselves. This means teaching them how to select relevant ideas, how to compare and relate ideas, how to organize ideas, how to apply ideas, how to infer, how to analyze, how to evaluate, and how to write a well-constructed response that includes these elements. Asking students to "compare," "interpret," or "apply" has little meaning unless they have been taught how to do these things. This calls for direct teaching and practice in writing, in an atmosphere that is less stressful than an examination period.

If students answer different questions, it is obvious that they are taking different tests, and so the common basis for evaluating their achievement is lost. Each student is demonstrating the achievement of different learning outcomes. As noted earlier, even the ability to organize cannot be measured adequately without a common set of responses, because organization is partly a function of the content being organized.

The use of optional questions might also influence the validity of the test results in another way. When students anticipate the use of optional questions, they can prepare responses on several topics in advance, commit them to memory, and then select questions to which the responses are most appropriate. During such advance preparation, it is also possible for them to get help in selecting and organizing their response. Needless to say, this provides a distorted measure of the student's achievement, and it also tends to have an undesirable influence on study habits, as intensive preparation in a relatively few areas is encouraged.

Of course, there are learning outcomes that involve in-depth study of topics that are shaped and defined by students. Evaluation of student work on topics of their own choosing is important for such learning outcomes. The assessment of such outcomes, however, is better approached through the assignment of projects than by an essay test.

See the accompanying "Checklist" to evaluate essay questions you construct.

CHECKLIST

Reviewing Essay Questions

	Yes	No
1. Is this the most appropriate type of task to use?	____	____
2. Are the questions designed to measure higher-level learning outcomes?	____	____
3. Are the questions relevant to the intended learning outcomes?	____	____
4. Does each question clearly indicate the response expected?	____	____
5. Are students told the bases on which their answers will be evaluated?	____	____
6. Are generous time limits provided for responding to the questions?	____	____
7. Are students told the time limits and/or point values for each question?	____	____
8. Are all students required to respond to the same questions?	____	____
9. If revised, are the questions still relevant to the intended learning outcomes?	____	____
10. Have the questions been set aside for a time before reviewing them?	____	____

SUGGESTIONS FOR SCORING ESSAY QUESTIONS

Improving the reliability of scoring answers to essay questions begins long before the questions are administered. The first step is to decide what learning outcomes are to be measured. This is followed by phrasing the questions in accordance with the learning outcomes and including explicit directions concerning the types of answers desired. Only when both the students and the teacher understand the task to be performed can reliable scoring be expected. No degree of proficiency in evaluating answers can compensate for poorly designed and phrased questions.

When the necessary preliminary steps have been taken in constructing essay questions, the following suggestions can be used effectively to increase the reliability of the scoring:

1. Prepare an outline of the expected answer in advance. This should contain the major points to be included, the characteristics of the answer (e.g., organization) to be evaluated, and the amount of credit to be allotted to each. For a restricted-response question calling for three hypotheses, for example, a list of acceptable hypotheses would be prepared, and a given number of scoring points would be assigned to each. For an extended-response question, the major points or aspects of the answer would be outlined. In addition, the relative amount of credit to be allowed for such characteristics as accuracy of the factual information, pertinence of examples, skill of organization, and effectiveness of presentation would be indicated.

Preparing a scoring key provides a common basis for evaluating the students' answers and increases the likelihood that our standards for each question will remain stable throughout the scoring. If prepared during the test's construction, such a scoring key also helps us phrase questions that clearly convey the types of answers expected.

2. Use the scoring method that is most appropriate. There are two common methods of scoring essay questions. One is called the analytic method and the other the holistic method. With the analytic method, each answer is compared with the ideal answer in the scoring key, and a given number of points is assigned according to the adequacy of the answer. With the holistic method, each paper is placed in one of a number of piles as the answer is evaluated. These piles represent degrees of quality and determine the credit assigned to each. If eight points are allotted to the question, for example, nine piles might be used ranging in value from eight points to none. Usually between five and ten categories are used with the holistic method.

Restricted-response essay questions can usually be satisfactorily scored by the analytic method. The restricted scope and the limited number of characteristics included in a single response make it possible to define degrees of quality precisely enough to assign point values. The extended-response question, however, usually requires the holistic method. Only global judgments can be made concerning the relevance of ideas, the organization of the material, the effectiveness of the response, and similar qualities of extended-response essays. Classifying such characteristics into ten categories makes our scoring as precise as we can reasonably expect to be.

3.   *Decide how to handle factors that are irrelevant to the learning outcomes being measured.* Several factors influence our evaluations of answers that are not directly pertinent to the purposes of the measurement. Prominent among these are legibility of handwriting, spelling, sentence structure, punctuation, and neatness. We should make an effort to keep such factors from influencing our judgment when evaluating the content of the answers. In some instances, such factors may, of course, be evaluated for their own sake. When this is done, you should obtain a separate score for written expression or for each of the specific factors. As far as possible, however, we should not let such factors contaminate the extent to which our scores reflect the achievement of other learning outcomes.

Another decision concerns the presence of irrelevant and inaccurate factual information in the response. Should you ignore it and score only that which is pertinent and correct? If you do, some students will write everything that occurs to them, knowing that you will sort it out and give them credit for anything correct. This discourages careful thinking and desirable evaluative abilities. On the other hand, if you take off points for irrelevant and inaccurate material, the question of how much to lower the score on a given paper is a troublesome one. Probably the best procedure is to decide in advance approximately how much the score on each question is to be lowered when the inclusion of irrelevant material is excessive. The students should then be warned that such a penalty will be imposed.

4.   *Evaluate all responses to one question before going on to the next one.* One factor that contributes to unreliable scoring of essay questions is a shifting of standards from one paper to the next. A paper with average answers may appear to be of much higher quality when it follows a failing paper than when it follows a near-perfect one. One way to minimize this is to score all answers to the first question, reorder the papers to be evaluated, then score all answers to the second question, and so on, until all of the questions have been scored. A more uniform standard can be maintained with this procedure because it is easier to remember the basis for judging each answer, and answers of various degrees of quality can be more easily compared. When the rating method is used and the responses are placed in several piles on the basis of each answer, shifting standards also can be checked by evaluating each answer a second time and reclassifying it if necessary.

Evaluating all answers to one question at a time helps counteract another type of error that creeps into the scoring of essay questions. When we evaluate all of the answers of a single student, the first few answers create a general impression of the student's achievement that colors our judgment of the remaining answers. Thus, if the first answers are of high quality, we tend to overrate the following answers; if they are of low quality, we tend to underrate them. This "halo effect" is less likely when the answers for a given student are not evaluated in continuous sequence.

5.   *When possible, evaluate the answers without looking at the student's name.* The general impression we form about each student during our teaching is also a source of bias in evaluating essay questions. It is not uncommon for a teacher to give a high score to a poorly written answer by rationalizing that "the student is really capable, even though she didn't express it clearly." A similar response by a student regarded less favorably will receive a much lower score, with the honest conviction that the student deserved the lower score. This halo effect is one of the most serious deterrents to reliable scoring by classroom teachers and is especially difficult to counteract. See "Bluffing: A Special Scoring Problem" for information about a scoring problem unique to essay questions.

When possible, the identity of the students should be concealed until all answers are scored. The simplest way to do this is to have the students put their names on the back of the papers. If a student's identity cannot be concealed because of familiar handwriting, the best we can do is make a conscious effort to eliminate any such bias from our judgment.

Bluffing: A Special Scoring Problem

It is possible for students to obtain higher scores on essay question responses than they deserve by means of clever bluffing. This is usually a combination of writing skill, general knowledge, and common "tricks of the trade." Following are some ways that students might attempt to influence the reader and, thus, inflate their grades.

1. Writing something for every question, even if it is only a restatement of the question. (Students figure they might get some credit. Blank spaces get none.)

2. Stressing the importance of the topic covered by the question, especially when short on facts (e.g., "This battle played a significant role in the Civil War.").

3. Agreeing with the teacher's views whenever it seems appropriate (e.g., "The future of mankind depends on how well we conserve our natural resources.").

4. Being a name-dropper (e.g., "This is supported by the well-known experiment by Smith." The reader assumes that the student knows Smith's "well-known" experiment.).

5. Writing on a related topic and fitting it to the question (e.g., prepared to write on President Harry Truman but asked to write about General Douglas MacArthur, the student might start with: "Harry Truman was the president who fired General MacArthur. From then on, there is more about President Truman than General MacArthur.).

6. Writing in general terms that can fit many situations (e.g., in evaluating a short story, the student might say: "This was an interesting story. The characters were fairly well developed, but in some instances more detail would be welcome. . . ." This might be called the fortune-teller approach.)

Although bluffing cannot be completely eradicated, carefully phrasing the questions and following clearly defined scoring procedures can reduce it.

6. If especially important decisions are to be based on the results, obtain two or more independent ratings. Sometimes essay questions are included in assessments used to select students for awards, scholarships, special training, and the like. In such cases, two or more competent persons should score the responses independently, and their ratings should be compared. After any large discrepancies have been satisfactorily arbitrated (possibly by a third scorer), the independent ratings may be averaged for more reliable results.

SUMMARY

The essay question is especially useful for measuring those aspects of complex achievement that cannot be measured well by more objective means. These include (1) the ability to supply rather than merely identify interpretations and applications of data and (2) the ability to select, organize, and integrate ideas in a general attack on a problem. Outcomes of the first type are measured by restricted-response questions and outcomes of the second type, by extended-response questions.

Although essay questions provide an effective means of measuring significant learning outcomes, they have several limitations: (1) scoring tends to be unreliable; (2) scoring is time consuming; and (3) only a limited sampling of achievement is obtained. Because of these shortcomings, essay questions, especially ones requiring extended responses, should be limited to assessing those outcomes that cannot be measured well by objective items.

The construction and scoring of essay questions are interrelated processes that require attention if a valid and reliable measure of achievement is to be obtained. Questions should be phrased so that they measure the attainment of definite learning outcomes and clearly convey to the students the type of response expected. Indicating an approximate time limit for each question and avoiding the use of optional questions also contribute to more valid results. Scoring procedures can be improved by (1) using a scoring key, (2) adapting the scoring method to the type of question used, (3) controlling the influence of irrelevant factors, (4) evaluating all answers to each question at one time, (5) evaluating without looking at the students' names, and (6) obtaining two or more independent ratings when important decisions are to be made.

LEARNING EXERCISES

1. In an area in which you are teaching or plan to teach, identify several learning outcomes that can be best measured with essay questions. For each learning outcome construct two essay questions.

2. Criticize the following essay questions, and restate them so that they meet the criteria of a good essay question.
   a. Discuss air transportation.

   b. Do you think the government should spend more on environmental protection?
   c. What is your attitude toward health-care reform?

3. For each of the following, would it be more appropriate to use an extended-response question or a restricted-response question?
   a. Compare two periods in history.

b. Describe the procedure for using a dictionary.
c. Indicate the advantages of one procedure over another.
d. Evaluate a short story.

4. What factors should be considered in deciding whether essay questions should be included in a classroom test? Which of the factors are most important?

5. Describe how essay tests might be used to facilitate learning. What types of learning are most likely to be enhanced?

FURTHER READING

Gronlund, N. E. (1993). *How to make achievement tests and assessments* (5th ed.). Boston: Allyn & Bacon. Chapter 5 discusses the construction and use of essay questions.

Mehrens, W. A., & Lehmann, I. J. (1991). *Measurement and evaluation in education and psychology* (4th ed.). New York: Holt, Rinehart & Winston. Chapter 5, "The Essay Test: Preparing the Questions and Grading the Responses," presents suggestions for construction and scoring essay questions.

Payne, D. A. (1992). *Measuring and evaluating educational outcomes.* New York: Macmillan. Chapter 8 describes how to write and score essay questions.

CHAPTER 10

Measuring Complex Achievement: Performance-Based Assessments

Essay tests are the most common example of a performance-based assessment, but there are many others, including artistic productions, experiments in science, oral presentations, and the use of mathematics to solve real-world problems. The emphasis is on doing, not merely knowing; on process as well as product.

Essay tests are an example of one type of performance assessment. But there are many aspects of writing that are not tapped within the constraints of the normal essay test. Choosing a topic, identifying an audience, gathering information, preparing drafts, seeking critiques, and revising are all important aspects of writing that are not measured by the usual essay test. Moreover, writing is not the only type of performance outcome we need to assess. Many highly-valued learning outcomes emphasize the actual performance of tasks in realistic settings. This is obvious in the case of art or music and for vocational or industrial education courses such as auto repair, woodworking, or typing. It is also true for mathematics, science, social studies, and foreign languages. In each case, performance-based assessments are needed to measure some of the desired learning outcomes.

For example, while knowledge of vocabulary and grammar in a foreign language can be measured with the various forms of paper-and-pencil tests, speaking skills cannot. Oral performance is required to assess a student's spoken communication skills in a foreign language. Similarly, the assessment of a student's ability to make observations, formulate hypotheses, collect data, and draw valid scientific conclusions may require the use of performance assessments. The use of mathematics to solve meaningful real-world problems and to communicate solutions to others may also be best assessed by the use of performance tasks in realistic settings.

Performance assessments provide a basis for teachers to evaluate both the effectiveness of the ***process*** or procedure used (e.g., approach to data collection, manipulation of instruments) and the ***product*** resulting from performance of a task (e.g., completed report of results, completed artwork). Unlike simple tests of factual knowledge, there is unlikely to be a single right or best answer. Rather, there may be multiple performances and problem solutions that would be judged to be excellent. Problem formulation, the organization of ideas, the integration of multiple types of evidence, and originality, are all important aspects of performance that may not be adequately assessed by paper-and-pencil tests.

TYPES OF PERFORMANCE-BASED ASSESSMENT

Performance assessments are also sometimes referred to as "authentic assessments" or "alternative assessments." But the terms are not interchangeable. "Alternative assessment" highlights the contrast to traditional paper-and-pencil tests while "authentic assessment" emphasizes the practical application of the tasks in real-world settings. We prefer the label "performance assessment" because it is more descriptive than "alternative assessment" and less pretentious than "authentic assessment."

Authenticity is, obviously, a matter of degree. A highly authentic assessment of communication skills in German, for example, might involve listening to the verbal interactions of a student when visiting Germany. But such an assessment would lack practicality for the teacher of a typical German class. Simulated spoken interactions between the teacher and a student or among students, while not quite as authentic, are much more practical. In either case, the focus of the assessment is on the student's performance in communicating in German.

Although authenticity is usually only approximated, it is an important goal of performance assessment. Providing realistic contexts can make problems more engaging for students, and help the teacher evaluate whether a student who can solve a problem in one context can solve it in another. Hence, it is desirable to increase the authenticity of tasks to whatever extent possible.

Like essay questions, performance assessments should be used primarily to measure those learning outcomes that cannot be measured well by objective test items. Objective test items are generally more efficient and more reliable for measuring factual knowledge and the ability to solve well-structured problems (e.g., solve a quadratic equation). Performance assessments are better suited for applications with less structured problems where problem identification; collection, organization, integration, and evaluation of information; and originality are emphasized (e.g., where is the best place to locate a restaurant?). They are also essential for learning outcomes that involve the creation of a product (e.g., a typed letter, a painting) or an oral or physical performance (e.g., the presentation of a speech, the repair of an engine, the use of a scientific instrument).

Performance tasks can vary substantially in the degree to which performance is restricted. A typing test, for example, might be completely constrained with regard to format and content of a letter to be typed. The task of creating a sculpture might be almost completely unconstrained with regard to the approach a student might take or the nature of the product produced. Most performance tasks fall in between these extremes.

Restricted-Response Performance Tasks

A restricted-response performance task is usually relatively narrow in definition. The instructions are generally more focused than extended-response performance tasks and the limitations on the types of performance expected are likely to be indicated.

EXAMPLES

Type a letter of application for a job.

Read aloud a section of a story.

Use various combinations of five straight pieces of plastic to construct as many different triangles as you can and record the perimeters of each.

Determine which of two liquids contains sugar and explain what results support your conclusion.

Construct graphs of the average amount of rainfall per month for two cities.

Request aloud directions to the train station in French.

Write the names of the countries in the appropriate areas of a blank map of Europe.

Sara knows that half the students in her class were invited to Kim's birthday party. Also, half were invited to Julie's party. Sara thinks that these figures add up to 100 percent, so she thinks she will surely be invited to one of the parties. Explain why Sara is wrong. If possible use a diagram in your explanation.*

*Adapted from a task used in the California Assessment program.

Restricted-response performance tasks sometimes start with a simple multiple-choice or short-answer question such as the one in Figure 10.1. Those questions are then extended by asking for an explanation of the answer, and sometimes, an explanation why the other answers were not selected. Often, different answers in the first part of the task could be given full credit if the explanation provided sound reasoning to defend the choice.

If the explanation parts of the task in Figure 10.1 were omitted, there would be no way to determine the basis for a student's choice of one of the three figures. Even if students selected the preferred choice (B), you would not know whether they did so for a sound reason or simply guessed. Nor would you know whether they were attentive to the fact that Graph C is impossible because it depicts 44 students when there were only 20 students in Mr. Pang's class.

The relative advantages and disadvantages of restricted performance tasks parallel those of restricted essay questions. They are generally more structured and require less time to administer than extended-response performance tasks. The shorter administration time makes it possible to administer more tasks and thereby gain broader

FIGURE 10.1
Example of stimulus material for a mathematics problem administered at Grade 4 in the 1992 National Assessment of Educational Progress

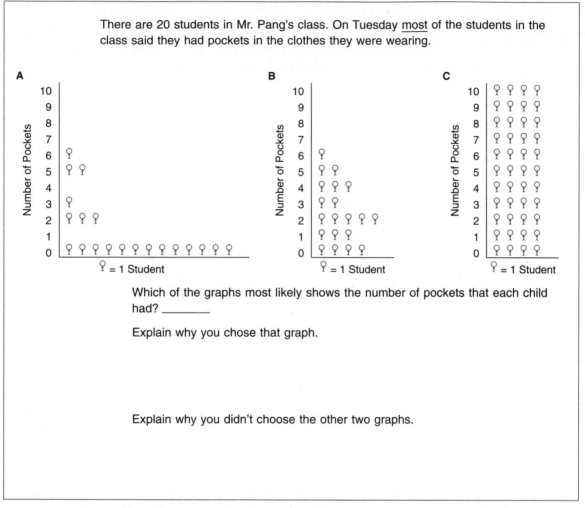

There are 20 students in Mr. Pang's class. On Tuesday <u>most</u> of the students in the class said they had pockets in the clothes they were wearing.

Which of the graphs most likely shows the number of pockets that each child had? _____

Explain why you chose that graph.

Explain why you didn't choose the other two graphs.

Source: From *NAEP 1992: Mathematics Report Card for the Nation and the States* (p. 49) by I. V. S. Mullis, J. A. Dossey, E. H. Owen, and G. W. Phillips, 1993, Washington, D.C.: U.S. Department of Education. Report No. 23–ST02.

coverage of the content domain. The greater degree of structure makes the task easier to score. On the other hand, the structure makes the tasks less valuable for measuring student skills like approaches to ill-structured problems, integration of information, and originality. Extended performance tasks are better suited for such outcomes.

Extended Performance Tasks

The extended performance task may require students to seek information from a variety of sources beyond those provided by the task itself. For example, students may need to use the library, make observations, collect and analyze data in an experiment, conduct a survey, or use a computer or other types of equipment. They may have to identify which aspects of the task are most relevant. The process or procedures that they use may be observed and be an important part of the assessment. The product that is produced may take a variety of forms; e.g., the construction and presentation of graphs or tables, the use of photographs or drawings, or the construction of physical models. Products may be developed over the course of several days and include opportunities for revision or modification. This freedom enables students to demonstrate their ability to select, organize, integrate, and evaluate information and ideas. The price of these gains includes the loss of efficiency, possible loss of breadth of coverage of the content domain, and greater difficulty in rating performance.

EXAMPLES

Prepare and deliver a speech to persuade people to take actions to protect the environment.

Hog is a game played with dice. The goal is to get the largest possible score. You may roll any number of dice out of a large cup. If none of the numbers is a 1, then the score for the roll is the sum of the numbers rolled. If a 1 is obtained on any of the dice, the score for the roll is zero. What number of dice do you think it best to roll? Defend your decision (Mathematical Sciences Education Board, 1993).

Write a computer program in BASIC that will sort a list of words alphabetically.

Design and carry out an investigation to estimate the acceleration, *g,* of a falling object such as a baseball. Describe the procedure used, present the data collected and analyzed, and state your conclusions.

Read an abridged version of the Lincoln–Douglas debates. Imagine that you were living then and heard the debates. Write a letter to a friend explaining the historical issues addressed and their importance in terms of what you know about the problems facing the nation at the time of the debates. (Baker, Aschbacher, Niemi, & Sato, 1992).

Performance assessments require students to demonstrate skills by actually performing. They involve doing rather than just knowing about, and there are sometimes important differences between the two. For example, a guitar player may know which frets to press the strings against for a particular chord without being able to perform the task smoothly to produce the desired sound. Similarly, a computer programmer may know the function of various needed commands without being able to produce a correctly working program to perform a specific task, or a science student may know the parts and functions of an instrument without being able to use it properly to obtain the information needed to solve a problem. Performance assessments are needed to observe and evaluate such skills. They also communicate the message that actual performance is important.

The effective use of performance assessments requires careful attention to task selection and to the ways performances will be rated. Care needs to be taken in the identification of the complex skills we want to measure, in the construction of tasks that will require students to demonstrate those skills, and in the evaluation of the resulting process and/or product. Without careful attention to these aspects of the

TABLE 10.1
Types of performance tasks

Type of Task	Examples of Complex Learning Outcomes That Can Be Measured
Restricted-Response Performance Task	Ability to— read aloud ask directions in a foreign language construct a graph use a scientific instrument type a letter
Extended-Response Performance Task	Ability to— build a model collect, analyze, and evaluate data organize ideas, create visuals, and make an integrated oral presentation create a painting or perform with a musical instrument repair an engine write a creative short story

assessment, it is unlikely that the effort will yield adequately reliable or valid measures of the complex skills that are being sought.

As the name suggests, performance assessments measure the ability of students to perform tasks that correspond to important instructional objectives. Restricted performance tasks generally focus on specific skills (e.g., reading a passage aloud). Extended performance tasks are more likely to involve problem solving and the integration of a variety of skills and understandings. A comparison of the types of complex learning outcomes measured by each of these types of performance tasks is presented in Table 10.1.

ADVANTAGES AND LIMITATIONS OF PERFORMANCE ASSESSMENTS

A major advantage of performance assessments is that they can clearly communicate instructional goals that involve complex performances in natural settings in, and outside of, school. By using tasks that require performances that correspond as closely as is feasible to major instructional objectives, they provide instructional targets and thereby can encourage the development of complex understandings and skills. Often, performance assessment tasks are indistinguishable from good instructional activities.

A second advantage of performance assessments is that they can measure complex learning outcomes that cannot be measured by other means. As has already been stated, knowing how to do something is not the same as being able to do it, much less do it well. Thus, a paper-and-pencil test that measures what a student knows about effective public speaking, for example, does not provide a measure of the student's ability to deliver an effective speech.

A third advantage of performance assessments is that they provide a means of assessing *process* or procedure, as well as the *product* that results from performing a task. For example, by observing students while they are conducting a laboratory experiment, strengths and weaknesses in the use of equipment and in technique can be assessed, as well as success in completing the experiment and the strength of reasoning provided to support conclusions.

A fourth advantage of performance assessments is that they implement approaches that are suggested by modern learning theory. Rather than being recipients of discrete bits of knowledge, modern learning theory conceives of students as active participants in the construction of meaning. According to this view, new information must be actively transformed and integrated with a student's prior knowledge. High quality performance-based assessments take student background knowledge into account and engage students in the active construction of meaning.

The most commonly cited limitations of performance assessments parallel those cited for essay questions. Unreliability of ratings of performances across teachers or across time for the same teacher is clearly a limitation. Careful attention to the learning outcomes that the task is intended to assess and to the criteria that will be used in rating the performances is required both at the time tasks are developed and at the time performances are rated to minimize this limitation. Although the judgmental scoring of complex performances will always include some uncontrollable variations, the rating reliability can be greatly increased by clearly defining the outcomes to be measured, properly framing the tasks, and carefully defining and following criteria for rating performances.

Another limitation of extended performance assessments is their time-consuming nature. Because a substantial amount of time may be required to allow students to have an adequate opportunity to perform each task, relatively few extended performance assessments can be obtained within a reasonable amount of time. There is considerable evidence that performance on one task provides only a relatively weak basis for generalizing to performances on other tasks intended to assess common or related learning outcomes. Thus, solid generalization to a larger domain of outcomes requires the use of multiple tasks. Overcoming the limitation of weak generalization of performance across tasks requires the accumulation of information from performances on different tasks during the course of the year. Justification for the devotion of the required amount of instructional time to the assessments requires that the tasks provide students with good learning opportunities as well as providing assessment results.

SUGGESTIONS FOR CONSTRUCTING PERFORMANCE TASKS

The development of high-quality performance assessments that effectively measure complex learning outcomes requires attention to task development and to the ways in which performances are rated. We shall begin with a consideration of ways to improve the development of tasks, then suggest ways to improve rating.

1. *Focus on learning outcomes that require complex cognitive skills and student performances.* It is important that tasks be interesting, but that is not sufficient. Tasks need to be developed or selected in light of important learning outcomes. Since performance-based tasks generally require a substantial investment of student time, they should be used primarily to assess learning outcomes that are not adequately measured by less time-consuming approaches.

2. *Select or develop tasks that represent both the content and the skills that are central to important learning outcomes.* Current conceptions of learning stress the interdependence of content and skills. Problem-solving in one subject-matter area is not the same as it is in another area. Debating a political issue in social studies is different than debating the effectiveness of a piece of literature. In each case, the content and process are interdependent. Thus, it is important to specify the range of content and resources students can use in performing a task. Past class assignments provide one natural basis for specifying content, but for many tasks it will be desirable to allow students the opportunity to do additional research to expand their knowledge base. In any event, the specification of assumed content understandings is critical in ensuring that a task functions as intended.

3. *Minimize the dependence of task performance on skills that are irrelevant to the intended purpose of the assessment task.* The key here is to focus on the intention of the assessment. Although the ability to read complicated texts and the ability to communicate clearly are both important learning outcomes, they are not necessarily the intent of a particular assessment. Reading ability, for example, might be irrelevant for an assessment that is intended to measure a student's ability to use mathematics to solve a practical problem (e.g., determine how much and what type of lumber to buy to build a clubhouse with specified features). However, if the task is presented in a way that requires substantial reading, then this factor may add to task difficulty for some students but not for others, and thereby reduce the validity of the intended interpretation of the results. This irrelevant source of difficulty would also undermine the fairness of the assessment. On the other hand, writing skills might be an intended part of a mathematics task where a goal of the assessment was to measure a student's ability to communicate mathematical reasoning and results.

4. *Provide the necessary scaffolding for students to be able to understand the task and what is expected.* Challenging tasks often involve ambiguities and require students to experiment, gather information, formulate hypotheses, and evaluate their own progress in solving a problem. However, problems cannot be solved in a vacuum. Students need to have the prior knowledge and skills required to address the problem. These prerequisites can be a natural outcome of prior instruction or may be built into the task. Preassessment activities, for example, can be used not only to introduce a task but to ensure that students have the prior knowledge essential for the task and are familiar with the materials or equipment that they need to use. It is important to ask: what prior knowledge and skills are assumed in order to perform the task?

5. *Construct task directions so that the student's task is clearly indicated.* Vague directions can lead to such a diverse array of performances that it becomes impossible to rate them in a fair or reliable fashion. By design, many performance-based tasks give students a substantial degree of freedom to explore, approach problems in different ways, and come up with novel solutions. Such intended task characteristics, however, are not an excuse for vague directions. In the task shown in Figure 10.2, students need to experiment and decide on the placement of objects into categories on their own. They also have to construct an explanation for the classification they provide. But the task of using the magnet to test the items, the classification of objects into two categories, and the need to explain the difference between the objects in the two categories are made explicit.

> **6. *Clearly communicate performance expectations in terms of the criteria by which the performances will be judged.*** Specifying the criteria to be used in rating performance helps clarify task expectations for a student. Explaining

FIGURE 10.2
Example of performance assessment task in science

Magnet

Task Descriptor

To use a magnet to identify magnetic and non-magnetic items and then to explain the difference between them.

Equipment/Material

A magnet and the following seven objects: plastic button, iron or steel washer, steel paper clip, iron nail, glass marble, plastic rod, and copper coin.

Student Instructions

Test the objects with the magnet and divide them into two groups. List the objects in the two groups and explain what makes the objects in the two groups different.

Scoring Scheme

Credit was given for grouping the objects correctly. Four categories of explanations were recorded: namely, that one group was made of iron or steel, that one group was attracted by the magnet, that one group was made of iron and steel and was attracted by the magnet, and any other explanation.

Source: From *Performance Assessment: An International Experiment* by B. M. Sample, 1992, Princeton, NJ: Educational Testing Service, Report No 22–Caep–06. Copyright 1992 by Educational Testing Service. Reprinted by permission.

the criteria that will be used in rating performances not only provides students with guidance on how to focus their efforts, but helps to convey priorities for learning outcomes.

EXAMPLE   Construct a weather map. Your map will be evaluated for accuracy of information and scale, for appropriate use of symbols, and for the ease with which it can be read.

Listing attributes like appropriate symbol use, accuracy of information and scale, and ease with which the map can be read makes the rating criteria explicit. It also highlights the learning outcomes that are considered important for this task.

Richard Stiggins (1987) has persuasively argued that the specification of performance criteria is the most important aspect of developing effective performance assessments. He suggests imagining the feedback that would be provided to a student who performed poorly before the task is administered. His rationale for focusing on the criteria to be used is straightforward. "If you do not have a clear sense of the key dimensions of sound performance—a vision of poor and outstanding performance—you can neither teach students to perform nor evaluate their performance."

The criteria to be used in judging student performance are critical for reliable, fair, and valid assessment, and the specification of the criteria should begin at the time the tasks are being selected or developed. Both the teacher and the student need to understand the criteria that will be used to judge performance. As was just noted, criteria help clarify the task expectations for students and they communicate learning goals and standards. In addition, they guide the judgment process in ways that enhance reliability, fair treatment of each performance, and the validity of conclusions about each student's achievement.

The two main ways of guiding judgments of both the process used in performing a task and any product resulting from that performance are rating scales and checklists. We begin with rating scales and then turn to a consideration of checklists.

RATING SCALES

Typically, a rating scale consists of a set of characteristics or qualities to be judged and some type of scale for indicating the degree to which each attribute is present. The rating form itself is merely a reporting device. Its value in appraising the learning and development of students depends largely on the care with which it is prepared and the appropriateness with which it is used. As with other assessment instruments, it should be constructed in accordance with the learning outcomes to be assessed, and its use should be confined to those areas in which there is a sufficient opportunity to make the necessary observations. If these two principles are properly applied, a rating scale will serve several important assessment functions: (1) it will direct observation toward specific aspects of behavior; (2) it will provide a common frame of reference for rating the performance of all students on the same set of characteristics; and (3) it will provide a convenient method for recording the observer's judgments.

Types of Rating Scales

Rating scales may take many forms, but most of them belong to one of the types that we shall describe next. Each type will be illustrated by using two dimensions from a scale for rating contributions to class discussion.

Numerical Rating Scale. One of the simplest types of rating scales is that in which the rater checks or circles a number to indicate the degree to which a characteristic is present. Typically, each of a series of numbers is given a verbal description that remains constant from one characteristic to another. In some cases, it is merely indicated that the largest number is high, one is low, and the other numbers represent intermediate values.

The numerical rating scale is useful when the characteristics or qualities to be rated can be classified into a limited number of categories and when there is general agreement concerning the category represented by each number. As commonly used, however, the numbers are only vaguely defined, so the interpretation and use of the scale vary.

EXAMPLES *Directions:* Indicate the degree to which this student contributes to a group problem-solving task by circling the appropriate number. The numbers represent the following values: 4 — consistently appropriate and effective; 3 —generally appropriate and effective; 2 — needs improvement, may wander from topic; and 1—unsatisfactory (disruptive or off topic).

1. To what extent does the student participate in group discussions?

   1 2 3 4

2. To what extent are the comments related to the topic under discussion?

   1 2 3 4

Graphic Rating Scale. The distinguishing feature of the graphic rating scale is that each characteristic is followed by a horizontal line. The rating is made by placing a check on the line. A set of categories identifies specific positions along the line, but the rater is free to check between these points.

EXAMPLES *Directions:* Indicate the degree to which this student contributes to a group problem solving task by placing an *X* anywhere along the horizontal line under each item.

1. To what extent does the student participate in group discussion?

never   seldom   occasionally   frequently   always

2. To what extent are the comments related to the topic under discussion?

never   seldom   occasionally   frequently   always

The scale shown in this example uses the same set of categories for each characteristic and is commonly referred to as a ***constant-alternatives scale.*** When these categories vary from one characteristic to another, the scale is called, quite logically, a ***changing-alternatives scale.***

Although the line in the graphic rating scale makes it possible to rate at intermediate points, using single words to identify the categories has no great advantage over the use of numbers. There is little agreement among raters concerning the meaning of such terms as *seldom, occasionally,* and *frequently.* What is needed are behavior descriptions that indicate more specifically how students behave who possess various degrees of the characteristic being rated.

Descriptive Graphic Rating Scale.   The descriptive graphic rating scale uses descriptive phrases to identify the points on a graphic scale. The descriptions are thumbnail sketches that convey in behavioral terms how students behave at different steps along the scale. In some scales, only the center and end positions are defined. In others, a descriptive phrase is placed beneath each point. A space for comments is also frequently provided to enable the rater to clarify the rating.

EXAMPLES   *Directions:* Make your ratings on each of the following characteristics by placing an *X* anywhere along the horizontal line under each item. In the space for comments, include anything that helps clarify your rating.

1. To what extent does the student participate in group discussions?

Never participates; quiet, passive		Participates as much as other group members		Participates more than any other group member

    Comment:

2. To what extent are the comments related to the topic under discussion?

Comments ramble, distract from topic		Comments usually pertinent, occasionally wanders from topic		Comments are always related to topic

    Comment:

The descriptive graphic rating scale is generally the most satisfactory for school use. It explains to both the teacher and the student the types of behavior that represent different degrees of progress toward desired learning outcomes. The more specific behavior descriptions also contribute to greater objectivity and accuracy during the rating process. To aid scoring, numbers also may be added to each position on the scale.

Use of Rating Scales

Rating scales can be used to assess a wide variety of learning outcomes and aspects of development. As a matter of convenience these uses may be classified into two assessment areas: (1) process or procedure, and (2) product.

Process or Procedure Assessment.   In many areas, achievement is expressed specifically through the student's performance. Examples include the ability to give a speech, manipulate laboratory equipment, work effectively in a group, sing, play a musical instrument, and perform various physical feats. Such activities do not result in a product that can be assessed, and short-answer or fixed response tests are generally inadequate. Consequently, the process or procedures used in the performance itself must be observed and judged.

Rating scales are especially useful in assessing process or procedures because they focus on the same aspects of performance in all students and have a common scale on which to record our judgments. If the rating form has been prepared in terms of specific learning outcomes, it also serves as an excellent teaching device. The dimensions and behavior descriptions used in the scale show the student the type of performance desired.

Two items from a typical rating scale for assessing a speech are presented in Figure 10.3. The first part of the form is devoted to the content of the speech and how well it is organized. The second part is concerned with aspects of delivery such as gestures, posture, appearance, eye contact, voice, and enunciation. In developing such a scale, a teacher must, of course, include those characteristics that are most appropriate for the type of speaking ability to be assessed and for the age level of the student to be judged.

Product Assessment.   When student performance results in some type of product, it is frequently more desirable to judge the product rather than the process or procedures. The ability to write a theme, for example, is best assessed by judging the quality of the theme itself. Little is to be learned by observing the student's performance. In some areas, however, such as typing, conducting work in the laboratory, and woodworking, it might be most desirable to rate procedures during the early phase of learning and products later, after the basic skills have been mastered. In any event, product rating can provide assessment information in many areas. In addition to those already mentioned, it is useful in assessing such things as handwriting, drawings, maps, graphs, notebooks, term papers, book reports, results of laboratory experiments, and objects made in vocational courses.

A rating scale serves somewhat the same purpose in product assessment that it does in process assessment. It helps us judge the products of all students in terms of the same characteristics, and it emphasizes to the students those qualities desired in a superior product.

FIGURE 10.3
Sample items from speech rating scale

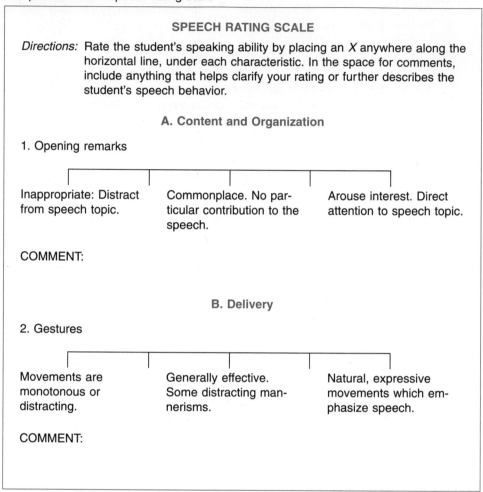

In some instances, it is necessary or desirable to judge a product according to its overall quality rather than its separate features. When this is the case, the products may be simply placed in rank order, or they may be compared to a product scale. A product scale is a series of samples of the product that have been graded to represent different degrees of quality. In assessing handwriting, for example, a sample of handwriting is moved along the scale until the quality of the writing matches. The student's handwriting is then assigned the value indicated on the scale. See Figure 10.4 for a sample of a handwriting scale using a numerical rating from 0 to 10.

Product scales can be used in judging the quality of any product, but in most areas teachers will need to develop their own scales. This can be readily done by selecting samples of student work that represent from five to seven levels of quality and arranging them in order of merit. The levels can then be assigned a value from

FIGURE 10.4
Handwriting scale used with the *Test of Written Language* (copyright 1983 by D. D. Hammill and S. C. Larsen. Used by permission of the publisher, PRO-ED, 5341 Industrial Oaks Blvd., Austin, Texas 78735.)

1 to 7 and each of the remaining student products can be compared to the scale and rated in terms of the quality level it matches most closely. Such a scale might be developed each time a set of products is to be assessed, or a more permanent scale might be developed and made available for student guidance. The latter procedure is favored when the product is fairly complex and difficult to construct.

Common Errors in Rating

Certain types of errors occur so often in ratings that special efforts are needed to counteract them. These include errors due to (1) personal bias, (2) halo effect, and (3) logical error.

Personal bias errors occur when there is a general tendency to rate all individuals at approximately the same position on the scale. Some raters tend to use the high end of the scale only, which is referred to as the ***generosity error.*** Occurring less frequently, but persistently for some raters, is the **severity error,** in which the lower end of the scale is favored. A third type of constant response is shown by the rater who avoids both extremes of the scale and tends to rate everyone as average. This is called the **central tendency error.** It also occurs much less often than the generosity error, but it tends to be a fixed response style for some raters.

The tendency of a rater to favor a certain position on the scale has two undesirable results. First, it puts in doubt a single rating of an individual. A high or low rating might reflect the personal outlook of the rater rather than the actual performance or personal characteristics of the person rated. Second, favoring a certain position on the scale limits the range of any individual's ratings. Therefore, even if we make allowances for a teacher's general tendency to rate students high, the ratings for different students may be so close together that they fail to provide reliable discriminations.

The ***halo effect*** is an error that occurs when a rater's general impression of a person influences the rating of individual characteristics. If the rater has a favorable attitude toward the person being rated there will be a tendency to give high ratings on all traits, but if the rater's attitude is unfavorable, the ratings will be low. This differs from the generosity and severity errors in which the rater tends to rate everyone high or everyone low.

Because the halo effect causes a student to receive similar ratings on all characteristics, it tends to obscure strengths and weaknesses on different traits. This obviously limits the value of the ratings.

Teachers need to guard against the possibility that their ratings might be distorted because of preconceptions based on inappropriate factors such as gender, race, ethnicity, and social background. Halo effects leading to lowered ratings of all performances of some students as the result of such preconceptions are of particular concern. Concealing the identity of the student where feasible when rating products of performance is one good safeguard against halo effects. Awareness of our own personal preferences and prejudices is also important.

A ***logical error*** results when two characteristics are rated as more alike or less alike than they actually are because of the rater's beliefs concerning their relationship. In rating achievement, for example, teachers tend to overrate the achievement of students identified by aptitude tests as gifted because they expect achievement and giftedness to go together. Similarly, teachers who hold the common but false belief that gifted students have poor social adjustment will tend to underrate them on social characteristics. These errors, do not result from biases toward certain students or certain positions on the rating scale, but from the rater's assumption of a more direct relationship among traits than actually exists.

The various types of errors that appear in ratings are rather disconcerting to the classroom teacher who must depend on rating scales for assessing certain aspects of learning and development. Fortunately, however, the errors can be markedly reduced by proper design and use.

Principles of Effective Rating

The improvement of ratings requires careful attention to selection of the characteristics to be rated, design of the rating form, and conditions under which the ratings are obtained. The following principles summarize the most important considerations in these areas. Because the descriptive graphic rating scale is the most generally useful form for school purposes, the principles are directed toward the construction and use of this type of rating scale.

1. Characteristics should be educationally significant. Rating scales, like other assessment instruments, must be in harmony with the school's objectives and desired learning outcomes. Thus, when constructing or selecting a rating scale, the best guide for determining what characteristics are most significant is the list of intended learning outcomes. When these have been clearly stated in performance terms, it is often simply a matter of selecting those that can be most effectively assessed by ratings and then modifying the statements to fit the rating format (see "Guidelines" box).

2. Identify the learning outcomes that the task is intended to assess. The intent of the assessment is critical for determining those characteristics of performance that should determine the ratings. Clear identification of the learning outcomes helps establish priorities for rating, distinguish levels of performance in terms of learning outcomes, and reduce dependence on factors that are irrelevant to the intent of the assessment. When there are multiple learning outcomes associated with the task, separate ratings corresponding to each outcome may be desirable and can enhance the value of the formative feedback that is provided to students.

3. Characteristics should be directly observable. There are two considerations involved in direct observation. First, the characteristics should be limited to those that occur in school situations so the teacher has an opportunity to observe them. Second, they should be characteristics that are clearly visible to an observer. Overt behaviors like participation in classroom discussion, clear enunciation, and use of facts to support an argument can be readily observed and reliably rated. However, less tangible types of behavior such as interest in history, attitude toward literature, and amount of effort expended in library research tend to be unreliably rated because their presence must be inferred from outward signs that are indefinite, variable, and easily faked. Whenever possible, we should confine our ratings to those characteristics that can be observed and judged directly.

4. Characteristics and points on the scale should be clearly defined. Many rating errors arise from the use of vague characterizations and inadequate identification of the scale points. The brief descriptions used with the descriptive graphic rating scale help overcome this weakness. They explain both the points on the scale and each characteristic being rated. When it is infeasible or inconvenient to use a descriptive scale, as on the back of a school report card, a separate sheet of instructions can be used to provide the desired descriptions.

GUIDELINES

Preparing Rating Scales

The same basic principle guiding the construction of test items should be followed in preparing rating scales. That is, the instrument should be designed to measure the student performance described in the instructional objectives. Let us assume, for example, that a science teacher has listed the following outcomes as evidence of skill in one phase of laboratory performance.

Demonstrates Effective Use of Laboratory Equipment

1. Selects proper equipment for a given experiment.
2. Sets up equipment quickly and correctly.
3. Manipulates equipment as needed during the experiment.
4. Measures accurately with each measuring device.
5. Follows safety rules when using equipment.
6. Cleans and returns equipment to its proper place.
7. Interprets results of experiment appropriately.
8. Integrates results with other knowledge in drawing conclusions.

This list of intended outcomes can then serve as the basis for preparing a rating scale to assess skill in using laboratory equipment. Each item in the list becomes an item in the rating form by simply adding some basis for recording degrees of effectiveness, as follows:

Selecting Laboratory Equipment

The same procedure is followed when rating an educational product (theme, graph, painting, shop and home economics projects). The characteristics of a good product are listed and these then become the items in the rating scale. The instrument itself is simply a convenient form for recording observations and judgments concerning the extent to which students are meeting the criteria specified in the objectives.

Detailed descriptions of characteristics or performance corresponding to each point on the scale are known as scoring **rubrics.** A scoring rubric makes explicit the criteria that are used to rate performance. Generic scoring rubrics are available that can be readily adapted for use in rating performance on a variety of tasks. Generic scoring rubrics, such as the one shown in Figure 10.5, provide a useful starting place for many assessments. The distinctions between the levels can be made more specific by considering the specific task and likely features that would distinguish between exemplary performance and competent performance or between satisfactory performance with minor flaws and performance that has serious flaws. For example, lists of minor and major flaws might be constructed for a specific task. In a similar fashion, common misconceptions that are anticipated in response to a particular task might be listed.

5. Select the rating procedure that is most appropriate for the task and the purpose of the assessment. Two general approaches are commonly used in rating performance. These approaches are called *holistic* and *analytic rating procedures.* The rubric illustrated in Figure 10.5 is designed for holistic rating. In **holistic rating,** each performance is given a single rating or score,

FIGURE 10.5

Examples of generalized scoring rubrics for mathematics problems

Quality of Explanation

6 = Excellent explanation (complete, clear, unambiguous).
5 = Good explanation (reasonably clear and complete).
4 = Acceptable explanation (problem completed but may contain minor flaws in explanation).
3 = Needs improvement (on the right track, but may contain serious flaws, demonstrates only partial understanding).
2 = Incorrect or inadequate explanation (shows lack of understanding of problem).
1 = Incorrect without attempt at explanation.

Separate Ratings of Answer and Explanation

Answer

4 = Correct.
3 = Almost correct or partially correct.
2 = Incorrect but reasonable attempt.
1 = Incorrect with no relationship to the problem.
0 = No answer.

Explanation

4 = Complete, clear, logical.
3 = Essentially correct but incomplete or not entirely clear.
2 = Vague or unclear but with redeeming features.
1 = Irrelevant, incorrect, or no explanation.

usually on a scale with four to six points, based on an overall judgment of the quality of the performance in comparison to the criteria specified in the scoring rubric.

The **analytic rating approach** requires the identification of different dimensions or characteristics of performance which are rated separately. For example, a mathematics task might be rated in terms of the accuracy of the calculations and the clarity of the explanation. A written report on the results of a science experiment, might be rated on factual accuracy, quality of analysis, and the degree to which conclusions were justified. A literary criticism might be rated for organization, quality of ideas, clarity of expression, and mechanics. An oral presentation might be rated both for the substantive quality of the report and for the effectiveness of the presentation.

Analytic scoring may have more diagnostic value, because it focuses attention on those aspects of performance where improvement is needed. For analytic scores to be of diagnostic value, the characteristics or dimensions being rated must be sufficiently distinct to allow each to be reliably rated, and not simply be redundant reflections of the same global impression of the performance.

6. Between three and seven rating positions should be provided, and raters should be permitted to mark at intermediate points.   The exact number of points to be designated on a particular scale is determined largely by the judgments to be made. In areas permitting only crude judgments, fewer scale positions are needed. There is usually no advantage in going beyond the seven-point scale. Only rarely can we make finer discriminations than this, and we can provide for those few situations by allowing the rater to mark between points.

7. Rate performances of all students on one task before going on to the next one.   The advantages of rating all performances on one task before starting another task parallel those described for scoring all answers to an essay question before going on to the next question. It is easier to keep the scoring criteria clearly in mind and to apply them more uniformly when considering only a single task at a time than it is when going from task to task for each student. It also reduces the likelihood that judgments of performance on one task will be contaminated by judgments of a student's performance on a preceding task. When responses of a single student to several tasks are considered one after another, there is a strong tendency for the performance on early tasks to create an expectation for performance on later tasks. Those expectations can result in more lenient or more stringent ratings of performance than would otherwise be given.

By rating one task at a time for all students before going to the next task it is also possible to change the order in which student performances are rated. Thus, a student is not rated first or last on all tasks, or right after another student who has exceptionally good performance or exceptionally bad performance on all tasks.

8. When possible, rate performances without knowledge of the student's name.   This suggestion is the same as one given for scoring answers to essay questions. Obviously, it is not possible for all types of performance (e.g., an oral presentation), but it is good practice whenever possible. It is a practice that enhances the fairness of ratings because it reduces the chances that ratings will be influenced by a halo effect rather than only by the actual performance of a student.

*9. **When results from a performance assessment are likely to have long-term consequences for students, ratings from several observers should be combined.***   The pooled ratings of several teachers will generally yield a more reliable description of student performance than that obtained from any one teacher. In averaging ratings, the personal biases of individual raters tend to cancel out one another, but there is still a need to be alert for biases that may be shared due to similarity of background and experiences of teachers doing the rating.

CHECKLISTS

A checklist is similar in appearance and use to the rating scale. The basic difference between them is in the type of judgment needed. On a rating scale, one can indicate the degree to which a characteristic is present or the frequency with which a behavior occurs. The checklist, on the other hand, calls for a simple yes–no judgment. It is basically a method of recording whether a characteristic is present or absent or whether an action was or was not taken. Obviously, a checklist should not be used when degree or frequency of occurrence is an important aspect of the appraisal.

The checklist is especially useful at the primary level, where much of the classroom assessment depends on observation rather than testing. A simple checklist for assessing the mastery of mathematics skills at the beginning primary level is shown in Figure 10.6. If the intended learning outcomes are stated as specifically as this for each learning area, a checklist can be prepared by simply adding a place to check yes or no. As with the rating scales, the stated learning outcomes specify the performance to be assessed, and the checklist is merely a convenient means of recording judgments.

Checklists are also useful in assessing those performance skills that can be divided into a series of specific actions. An example of such a checklist, for the proper application of varnish, is shown in Figure 10.7. The performance has been subdivided into a series of observable steps, and the observer simply checks whether each step was satisfactorily completed. The checklist in Figure 10.7 includes only those actions that are desired in a good performance. In some cases it may be useful to add those actions that represent common errors so that they can be checked if they occur. In Figure 10.7, for example, we might add after Item 4, "Does *not* stir varnish before using." Because stirring paint is a necessary step when painting, some students might incorrectly carry over this action when using varnish. If the checklist is to be used by students, the incorrect actions should, of course, be clearly identified as such.

The following steps summarize the development of a checklist for assessing a procedure consisting of a series of sequential steps.

FIGURE 10.6
Checklist for evaluating student's mastery of beginning skills in mathematics

MATHEMATICS SKILLS CHECKLIST

Primary Level

Directions: Circle YES or NO to indicate whether skill has been demonstrated.

YES	NO	1. Identifies numerals 0 to 10.
YES	NO	2. Counts to 10.
YES	NO	3. Groups objects into sets of 1 to 10.
YES	NO	4. Identifies basic geometric shapes (circle, square, rectangle, triangle).
YES	NO	5. Identifies coins (penny, nickel, dime).
YES	NO	6. Compares objects and identifies bigger–smaller, longer–shorter, heavier–lighter.
YES	NO	7. States ordinals for a series of 10 objects (1st, 2nd, 3rd, etc.).
YES	NO	8. Copies numerals 1 to 10.
YES	NO	9. Tells time to the half hour.
YES	NO	10. Identifies one–half of an area.

1. Identify each of the specific actions desired in the performance.

2. Add to the list those actions that represent common errors (if they are useful in the assessment, are limited in number, and can be clearly stated).

3. Arrange the desired actions (and likely errors, if used) in the approximate order in which they are expected to occur.

4. Provide a simple procedure for checking each action as it occurs (or for numbering the actions in sequence, if appropriate).

In addition to its use in assessment of process, the checklist can also be used to assess products. For this purpose, the form usually contains a list of characteristics that the finished product should possess. In assessing the product, the teacher simply checks whether each characteristic is present or absent. Before using a checklist for product assessment, you should decide whether the quality of the product can be adequately described by merely noting the presence or absence of each characteristic. If quality is more precisely indicated by noting the degree to which each characteristic is present, a rating scale should be used instead of a checklist.

In the area of personal–social development, the checklist can be a convenient method of recording evidence of growth toward specific learning outcomes. Typically, the form lists the behaviors that have been identified as representative of the outcomes to be assessed. In the area of work habits, for

FIGURE 10.7
Checklist for evaluating the proper application of varnish (from N. E. Gronlund, *Stating Objectives for Classroom Instruction,* 3d ed. Copyright 1985, Macmillan Publishing Co., Inc., New York. Used by permission.)

Directions: On the space in front of each item, place a plus (+) sign if performance was satisfactory, place a minus (–) sign if it was unsatisfactory.

_____ 1. Sands and prepares surface properly.

_____ 2. Wipes dust from surface with appropriate cloth.

_____ 3. Selects appropriate brush.

_____ 4. Selects varnish and checks varnish flow.

_____ 5. Pours needed amount of varnish into clean container.

_____ 6. Puts brush properly into varnish (1/3 of bristle length).

_____ 7. Wipes excess varnish from brush on inside edge of container.

_____ 8. Applies varnish to surface with smooth strokes.

_____ 9. Works from center of surface toward the edges.

_____ 10. Brushes with the grain of the wood.

_____ 11. Uses light strokes to smooth the varnish.

_____ 12. Checks surface for completeness.

_____ 13. Cleans brush with appropriate cleaner.

_____ 14. Does *not* pour excess varnish back into can.

_____ 15. Cleans work area.

---

example, a primary teacher might list the following behaviors (to be marked yes or no).

_____ Follows directions.

_____ Seeks help when needed.

_____ Works cooperatively with others.

_____ Waits turn in using materials.

_____ Shares materials with others.

_____ Tries new activities.

_____ Completes started tasks.

_____ Returns equipment to proper place.

_____ Cleans work space.

Although such items can be used in checklist form if only a crude appraisal is desired, they can also be used in rating scale form by recording the frequency of occurrence (e.g., always, sometimes, never).

Although we have described the individual use of checklists, rating scales, and anecdotal records, they are often used in combination when assessing student performance (see Table 10.2).

TABLE 10.2
Combining techniques to assess laboratory performance in science

Types of Proficiency	Examples of Performance to Be Assessed	Assessment Techniques
Knowledge of experimental procedures	Describes relevant procedures. Identifies equipment and uses. Criticizes defective experiments.	Paper-and-pencil testing. Laboratory identification tests.
Skill in designing an experiment	Plans and designs an experiment to be performed.	Product assessment (checklist).
Skill in conducting the experiment	Selects equipment. Sets up equipment. Conducts experiment.	Performance assessment (rating scale).
Skill in observing and recording	Describes procedures used. Reports proper measurements. Organizes and records results.	Product assessment (analysis of report).
Skill in interpreting results	Identifies significant relationships. Identifies weaknesses in data. States valid conclusions.	Product assessment and oral questioning.
Work habits	Manipulates equipment effectively. Completes work promptly. Cleans work space.	Performance assessment (checklist).

STUDENT PARTICIPATION IN RATING

In this chapter, we have limited our discussion to rating scales and checklists used by the teacher. We purposely omitted those checklists and rating scales used as self-report techniques by students because these will be considered in the following chapter. Before closing our discussion here, however, we should point out that most of the devices used for recording the teacher's observations also can be used by students to judge their own progress. From an instructional standpoint, it is often useful to have students rate themselves (or their products) and then compare the ratings with those of the teacher. If this comparison is made during an individual conference, the teacher can explore with each student the reasons for the ratings and discuss any marked discrepancies between the two sets.

Self-rating by a student and a follow-up conference with the teacher can have many benefits. It should help the student (1) understand better the instructional objectives, (2) recognize the progress being made toward the objectives, (3) diagnose more effectively particular strengths and weaknesses, and (4) develop increased skill in self-assessment. Of special value to the teacher is the additional insight gained.

Student participation need not be limited to the use of the assessment instruments. It is also useful to have students help develop the instruments. Through class discussion, for example, they can help identify the qualities desired in a good speech or a well-written report. A list of these suggestions can then be used as a basis for constructing a rating scale or checklist. Involving students in the development of assessment devices has special instructional values. First, it directs learning by causing the students to think more carefully about the qualities to strive for in a performance or product. Second, it has a motivating effect because students tend to put forth most effort when working toward goals they have helped define.

SUMMARY

Performance tasks provide a means of assessing a variety of student skills that cannot be measured by objective tests. To name just a few of the possibilities in addition to written responses, the performances may include oral communication; the construction of models, graphs, diagrams, or maps; or the use of tools and equipment (typewriters, computers, scientific or musical instruments). Unlike objective items, both the *process* and the *product* resulting from the performance can be assessed. Because they are time-consuming both for students to do and for teachers to rate, the emphasis on performance assessment should be on measuring complex achievement that cannot be measured well by objective tests.

Restricted-response tasks are more structured and require less time to administer than extended-response tasks. These features facilitate reliability and wider coverage of a content domain. Extended-response tasks are best suited to the measurement of more complex learning outcomes such as gathering, organizing, synthesizing, evaluating, and presenting information.

Extended performance tasks underscore the importance attached to effective performance and provide an effective means of measuring significant learning outcomes. They are the only feasible approach for measuring some important learning outcomes, they allow for the assessment of process as well as product, and their emphasis on the engagement of students in the active construction of meaning is consistent with modern learning theory. Their limitations are due mainly to the unreliability of judgmental ratings and to the time-consuming nature of the tasks and rating. Careful attention to rating criteria is critical for minimizing the unreliability due to scoring. Because of the limited generalizability of performance across tasks designed to measure the same or similar learning outcomes, it is important to base decisions on evidence accumulated from several tasks.

Rating methods are a systematic procedure for obtaining and recording the observers' judgments. Of the several types of rating scales available, the descriptive graphic scale seems to be the best for school use. In rating procedures, products, and various aspects of personal–social development, certain types of errors commonly occur. These include personal bias, halo effect, and logical errors. The control of such errors is a major consideration in constructing and using rating scales. Effective ratings result when we (1) select educationally significant characteristics, (2) identify the learning outcomes that the task is intended to assess, (3) limit ratings to directly observable behavior, (4) define clearly the characteristics and the points on the scale, (5) select the most appropriate rating procedure, (6) limit the number of points on the scale, (7) rate performances of all students on one task before going on to the next ones, and (8) rate performances without knowledge of the student's name whenever possible, and (9) combine ratings from several raters when results may have long-term consequences for students.

Checklists perform somewhat the same functions as rating scales. They are used in assessing both process and products where assessment is limited to a simple present–absent judgment.

Having students help construct and use rating devices has special values from the standpoint of learning and aids in the development of self-assessment skills.

LEARNING EXERCISES

1. In an area in which you are teaching or plan to teach, identify several learning outcomes that can be best measured with performance-based assessment tasks. For each learning outcome construct two tasks.

2. What factors should be considered in deciding whether extended performance assessment tasks are to be included in a classroom assessment? Which of the factors are most important?

3. Describe how performance assessments might be used to facilitate learning. What types of learning are most likely to be enhanced?

4. Construct a rating scale for one of the following that would be useful for assessing the effectiveness of the performance.
   a. Giving an oral report.
   b. Working in the laboratory.
   c. Participating in group work.
   d. Playing some type of game.
   e. Demonstrating a skill.

5. Construct a rating scale or checklist for one of the following that would be useful for assessing the product.
   a. Constructing a map, chart, or graph.
   b. Writing a personal or business letter.
   c. Writing a theme, poem, or short story.
   d. Making a drawing or painting.
   e. Making a product in home economics.
   f. Making a product in industrial education.

6. Prepare a checklist for assessing the ability to drive an automobile. Would a rating scale be better for this purpose? What are the relative advantages of each?

7. List some of the areas of assessment in which product scales might be used for rating.

REFERENCES

Baker, E. L., Aschbacher, P. R., Niemi, D., & Sato, E. (1992). *CRESST performance assessment models: Assessing content area explanations.* Los Angeles: University of California Center for Research on Evaluation, Standards, and Student Testing.

Mathematical Sciences Education Board. (1993). *Measuring up: Prototypes for mathematics assessment.* Washington, DC: National Academy Press. See pages 141–155 for a discussion of this game and related assessment questions.

Stiggins, R. J. (1987). Design and development of performance assessments. *Educational Measurement: Issues and Practice, 6,* (3), 33–42.

FURTHER READING

Educational Testing Service. (1993). *Performance assessment sampler: A workbook*. Princeton, NJ: Educational Testing Service. This workbook presents examples of performance assessments in various subjects, with examples of student responses and scores assigned.

Gronlund, N. E. (1993). *How to make achievement tests and assessments* (5th ed.). Boston: Allyn & Bacon. Chapter 7 discusses the construction and use of various types of performance assessments.

Hart, D. (1994). *Authentic assessment: A handbook for educators*. Menlo Park, CA: Addison–Wesley. Provides a variety of examples of performance-based assessments and arguments for the importance of this approach to assessment.

Herman, J. L., Aschbacher, P. R., & Winters, L. (1992). *A practical guide to alternative assessment*. Alexandria, VA: Association for Supervision and Curriculum Development. In addition to providing examples of performance assessments and guidelines for rating, the book presents a model for linking assessment and instruction.

Payne, D. A. (1992). *Measuring and evaluating educational outcomes*. New York: Macmillan. Describes a variety of approaches to assessing performance.

Stiggins, R. J. (1987). Design and development of performance assessments. *Educational Measurement: Issues and Practice, 6*(3), 33–42. Part of an instructional series of the National Council on Measurement in Education. It presents helpful guidelines for the construction of performance assessments.

CHAPTER 11

Assessment Procedures: Observational Techniques, Peer Appraisal, and Self-Report

Direct observation is the best means we have for assessing some aspects of learning and development. The use of anecdotal records can turn informal teacher observations into a systematic source of information about student development. Judgments and reports made by students themselves are also a valuable source of information in many areas of learning and development. (1) Peer judgments are especially useful in assessing personal–social development and (2) self-report methods provide a fuller understanding of students' needs, problems, adjustments, interests, and attitudes.

Many outcomes in the cognitive domain, such as those pertaining to knowledge, understanding, and thinking skills can be measured by paper-and-pencil tests or performance-based assessments. However, there also are many important learning outcomes that require informal observation of natural interactions in the classroom, on the playground, or in the lunchroom. In this chapter we focus on procedures for observing and recording student performances in natural settings throughout the school year. These techniques are also useful for assessing important noncognitive outcomes such as attitudes, appreciations, and personal–social development. We also describe procedures for complementing teacher observations of student development with judgments and reports from students. Both peer reports and self-reports are the best sources of information about some aspects of personal–social development and can provide valuable supplements to teacher observations in other areas.

Learning outcomes in skill areas and behavioral changes in personal–social development are especially difficult to assess with paper-and-pencil tests. A list of such outcomes, with representative types of student behavior, is presented in Table 11.1. This list is by no means complete, but it is comprehensive enough to show the

TABLE 11.1

Outcomes requiring assessment procedures beyond the typical paper-and-pencil test

Outcome	Representative Behaviors
Skills	Speaking, writing, listening, oral reading, performing laboratory experiments, drawing, playing a musical instrument, dancing, gymnastics, work skills, study skills, and social skills.
Work habits	Effectiveness in planning, use of time, use of equipment, use of resources, demonstration of such traits as initiative, creativity, persistence, dependability.
Social attitudes	Concern for the welfare of others, respect for laws, respect for the property of others, sensitivity to social issues, concern for social institutions, desire to work toward social improvement.
Scientific attitudes	Open-mindedness, willingness to suspend judgment, sensitivity to cause–effect relations, an inquiring mind.
Interests	Expressed feelings toward various educational, mechanical, aesthetic, scientific, social, recreational, vocational activities.
Appreciations	Feeling of satisfaction and enjoyment expressed toward nature, music, art, literature, physical skill, outstanding social contributions.
Adjustments	Relationship to peers, reaction to praise and criticism, reaction to authority, emotional stability, social adaptability.

great need to supplement paper-and-pencil testing with other methods of assessment. Performance-based tasks of the type discussed in Chapter 10 are well suited for the types of skills illustrated at the top of the table. The other outcomes in the table, however, require the use of informal observation techniques throughout the school year. The use of the observational and recording techniques described in this chapter can improve the assessment of all of these outcomes.

Learning outcomes and aspects of development like those in Table 11.1 can generally be assessed by (1) observing students as they perform and describing or judging that behavior (assessing interactions with other students), (2) asking their peers about them (assessing social relationships), and (3) questioning them directly (assessing expressed interests). Although these observational techniques, peer appraisals, and self-report methods are more subjective than we would like, and their use frequently requires more time and effort than typical assessment procedures, they are the best means available for assessing a variety of important behaviors. Our choice is simple: either we use these techniques to assess each learning outcome and aspect of development as directly and validly as possible, or we neglect learning outcomes that cannot be measured by paper-and-pencil tests.

In this chapter, we shall describe the use of anecdotal records to systematically accumulate information from a teacher's informal observations. We will then describe the use of peer appraisals and self-report techniques to supplement and complement teacher observations.

ANECDOTAL RECORDS

Teachers' daily observations give them a wealth of information concerning the learning and development of their students. For example, a third-grade teacher notices during oral reading that Maria mispronounces several simple words, that George sits staring out the window, and that Carl keeps interrupting the reading with irrelevant questions. Similarly, a high-school chemistry teacher notices during a laboratory period that Bill is slow and inefficient in setting up his equipment, that Juan finishes his experiments early and helps others, and that Sandy handles the chemicals in a careless and dangerous manner despite repeated warnings. Such daily incidents and events have special significance for assessing student learning and development. They enable us to determine how a student typically performs or behaves in a variety of situations. In some instances, this information supplements and verifies data obtained by more objective methods. But in other cases, it is the only means we have for assessing desired outcomes.

Impressions gained through observation are apt to provide an incomplete and biased picture, however, unless we keep an accurate record of our observations. A simple and convenient method of doing this is through anecdotal records.

Anecdotal records are factual descriptions of the meaningful incidents and events that the teacher has observed. Each incident should be written down shortly after it happens. The descriptions may be recorded on separate cards like the one shown in Figure 11.1, or as running accounts, one for each student, on separate pages in a notebook. A good anecdotal record keeps the objective description of an incident separate from any interpretation of the behavior's meaning. For some purposes, it is also useful to keep an additional space for recommendations

FIGURE 11.1
Anecdotal record form

Class 4th Grade   Pupil   Bill Johnson _____

Date 4/25/94   Place   Classroom   Observer   M.G.

Incident

As class was about to start, Bill asked if he could read a poem to the class—one he had written himself—about "spring." He read the poem in a low voice, constantly looked down at the paper, moved his right foot back and forth, and pulled on his shirt collar. When he finished, Jack (in the back row) said "I couldn't hear it. Will you read it again—louder?" Bill said "no" and sat down.

Interpretation

Bill enjoys writing stories and poems and they reflect considerable creative ability. However, he seems very shy and nervous in performing before a group. His refusal to read the poem again seemed to be due to his nervousness.

concerning ways to improve the student's learning or adjustment. Such recommendations are seldom made, however, until several anecdotes have been recorded.

Uses of Anecdotal Records

The use of anecdotal records has frequently been limited to the area of social adjustment. Although they are especially appropriate for this type of reporting, this is a needless limitation. Anecdotal records can be used for obtaining data pertinent to a variety of learning outcomes and to many aspects of personal and social development. The potential usefulness of the anecdotal method is revealed in the various areas of learning outcomes presented earlier in this chapter (see Table 11.1); you will see that many of the behaviors listed there can be appraised by means of direct observation.

The problem in using anecdotal records is not so much what *can* be assessed as what *should* be assessed with this method. It is obvious that we cannot observe and report on all aspects of student behavior, no matter how useful such records might be. Thus, we must be selective in our observations.

What Behaviors to Observe and Record

In general, our objectives and desired outcomes will guide us in determining what behaviors are most worth noting. We must also be alert to those unusual and exceptional incidents that contribute to a better understanding of each student's unique pattern of behavior. Within this general framework, there are several steps we can take to control our observations so that a realistic system of recording can be developed. They are

1. Confining our observations to those areas of behavior that cannot be assessed by other means.
2. Limiting our observations of all students at any given time to just a few types of behavior.
3. Restricting the use of extensive observations of behavior to those few students who are most in need of special help.

There is no advantage in using anecdotal records to derive evidence of learning in areas in which more objective and practical methods are available. Knowledge, understanding, and various aspects of thinking skill can usually be assessed by paper-and-pencil tests. Many learning outcomes of other types that are well suited to the use of performance-based assessment tasks, such as the ability to give a speech, operate a microscope, or write a theme, are most effectively assessed by rating methods or product assessment. Records of actual behavior are best used to assess how a student typically behaves in a natural setting. How does Gary approach a problem? How persistent is Irene in carrying out a task? How willing to listen to the ideas of others is Manuel? What contributions does Paul make to class activities? A student's verbal comments and actions in various natural situations reveal certain clues to attitudes, interests, appreciations, habits, and adjustment patterns that cannot be discovered by any other means. These are the types of behavior on which we should focus when keeping anecdotal records.

The best we can hope to get from anecdotal records is a fairly representative sample of student behavior in the different areas for which we want information. This usually can be obtained more easily if we concentrate our observations on a few areas at a time. For example, an elementary teacher might pay particular attention to reading interests during the free reading period, to signs of appreciation during music and art, and to patterns of social relations during recess. Similarly, a high-school science teacher might concentrate on incidents reflecting scientific attitude during certain class discussions and laboratory periods and on work habits and laboratory skills during others. In some cases the activity itself will indicate the types of observation most fruitful to focus on, whereas in others the emphasis at any given time may need to be determined arbitrarily. Despite the concentration of attention on certain areas at a particular time, however, we should always be alert to other incidents and events that have special significance for understanding a student's learning and development.

In addition to recording some information on all students, there are times when we need more comprehensive information regarding a relative few. The severely retarded reader, the socially rejected child, and the child with a learning disability are typical of those needing special attention. More extensive observations of such students are helpful in understanding their difficulties and in planning effective instructional strategies. The most complete and useful information is obtained when we concentrate our observations on one or two students at a time. During such observations it also may be necessary to restrict our record-keeping on other students.

Some teachers become discouraged when they first use anecdotal records because they attempt to do too much. Limiting observations and reports to specific types of behavior, to specific students, or both is frequently necessary to make the procedure feasible. It is much better to have a clearly delimited and workable observational plan than to end up with an incomplete and atypical collection of unrelated incidents.

Advantages and Limitations of Anecdotal Records

Probably the most important advantage of anecdotal records is that they depict actual behavior in natural situations. The old adage that "actions speak louder than words" has a direct application here. A student may show good knowledge of health practices but violate them in everyday situations, may profess great interest in science but approach laboratory work in a haphazard and uninterested fashion, or may express great concern for the welfare of others but behave in a selfish manner. Records of actual behavior provide a check on other assessment methods and also enable us to determine the extent of change in the student's typical patterns of behavior.

In addition to compiling descriptions of the most characteristic behavior of a student, anecdotal records facilitate gathering evidence on events that are exceptional but significant. Typical examples are the quiet student who speaks in class for the first time, the hostile student who makes a friendly gesture, the extreme conformist who shows a sign of originality, and the apathetic student who shows a spark of interest. These individually significant behaviors are apt to be excluded by other assessment techniques. They are also likely to be overlooked by teachers unless a concerted effort is made to observe such incidents. Keeping anecdotal records makes us more diligent in observation and increases our awareness of such behaviors.

Anecdotal records can be used with very young students and with students who have limited basic communication skills. They are especially valuable in situations where paper-and-pencil tests, performance assessments, self-report techniques, and peer appraisals are likely to be impractical or of limited use. Observational records of younger students are of value for still another reason. Because young children tend to be more spontaneous and uninhibited in their actions, their behavior is easier to observe and interpret.

One limitation of anecdotal records is the amount of time required to maintain an adequate system of records. Though this can be offset somewhat by limiting observations and reports, as suggested earlier, record-keeping is still a time-consuming task. If teachers keep anecdotal records for their own use only, they can work out a realistic plan by starting with a few anecdotes each day and gradually increasing it to a reasonable number. If the entire staff uses anecdotal records, it is good to have all teachers record as many anecdotes as is practical for a period of a few weeks and then hold a staff meeting to discuss the recorded anecdotes and to decide what constitutes a reasonable number. It is generally unwise to set a specific number that must be recorded each week, but an approximate minimum can serve as a general guide. When anecdotal records are used on a school-wide basis, the most time-consuming aspect is summarizing the anecdotes and recording the summaries in the student's cumulative records.

Another serious limitation of anecdotal records is the difficulty of being objective when observing and reporting student behavior. Ideally, we would like a series of verbal snapshots that accurately represent the student's actual behavior. This goal is seldom attained, however, for teachers' own biases, hopes, and preconceived notions inevitably enter into their observations and reports. For example, they will tend to notice more desirable qualities in those students they like best and more undesirable qualities in those they like least. If they are assessing the effectiveness of a new teaching technique in which they have great faith, they may notice positive results and ignore the negative. If they believe that boys are less well coordinated than girls, they will tend to perceive their performance skills as being of lower quality. Training in observation and reporting can reduce such distortions to a minimum, but they cannot be eradicated entirely. In striving to eliminate distortions, it is particularly important that teachers be self-reflective about possible biases in their observations as the result of stereotypes and preconceptions about children on the basis of gender, race, ethnicity, or socio-economic background. They must be on guard against self-fulfilling prophecies, especially in cases where immediate impressions lead to low expectations for individual students.

A related difficulty is obtaining an adequate sample of behavior. When participating in class discussion, some students may be so tense and anxious that they appear cold and unfriendly toward others and their ideas seem disorganized. But when observed in less formal settings, such as in the laboratory or on the playground, their behavior might be quite different. Similarly, a student may appear highly motivated and interested in mathematics class but bored and uninterested during English literature, or a student may be attentive and inquisitive in science one day and apathetic the next. Everyone's behavior fluctuates somewhat from situation to situation and from one time to another. Therefore, to gain a reliable picture of a typical pattern of behavior we need to observe students over a period of time and in a variety of situations. This also implies that general interpretations and recommendations concerning a student's adjustment should be delayed until a fairly adequate sample of behavior is obtained.

Effective Use of Anecdotal Records

In the previous chapters, we stated or implied a number of ways to improve procedures for observing and reporting student behavior. These and other points are listed here as suggestions for the effective use of anecdotal records.

1. Determine in advance what to observe, but be alert for unusual behavior. We are more apt to select and record meaningful incidents if we review objectives and outcomes and decide which behaviors require assessment by direct observation; that is, those that cannot be effectively assessed by other means. We can further focus our observations by looking for just a few types of behavior at any given time. Although such directed observations are valuable for obtaining evidence of student learning, there is always the danger that unique incidents that have special value for understanding a student's development will be overlooked. Consequently, we must be flexible enough to notice and report any unusual behavior in the event that it may be significant.

2. Analyze observational records for possible sources of bias. We should carefully review our initial impressions of each student. We need to consider the possibility that they are influenced by stereotypes based on gender, race, or ethnicity. We can minimize bias by reflecting on these and other factors that may bias our observations. Distinguishing between what is actually observed and the interpretation of that observation can be especially useful in that regard. We should consider, for example, how the same recorded observation might have led to a different interpretation if it had been another student. Different interpretations of the same recorded observation may, of course, be appropriate if they are based on knowledge of different patterns of behavior for two students. But variation in interpretation should not be a consequence of preconceptions based on gender, race, ethnicity, or social background.

3. Observe and record enough of the situation to make the behavior meaningful. It is difficult to interpret behavior apart from the situation in which it occurred. An aggressive action, such as pushing another child, for example, might reflect good-natured fun, an attempt to get attention, a response to direct provocation, or a sign of extreme hostility. Clues to the meaning of behavior frequently can be obtained by directing attention to the actions of the other students involved and the particular setting in which the behavior took place. The record, therefore, should contain a description of those conditions that seem necessary for understanding the student's behavior.

4. Make a record of the incident as soon after the observation as possible.   In most cases it is infeasible to write a description of an incident when it happens. However, the longer we delay in recording observations, the greater the likelihood that important details will be forgotten. Try to make a few brief notes at opportune times following behavioral incidents and complete the records after school.

5. Limit each anecdote to a brief description of a single incident. Brief and concise descriptions take less time to write, less time to read, and are more easily summarized. Just enough detail should be included to make the description meaningful and accurate. Limiting each description to a single incident also simplifies the task of writing, using, and interpreting the records (see "Writing Anecdotal Records").

6. Keep the factual description of the incident and your interpretation of it separate.   The description of an incident should be as accurate and objective as you can make it. This means stating exactly what happened in clear, nonjudgmental words. Avoid such terms as *unhappy, shy, hostile, sad, ambitious, persistent,* and the like. If used at all, reserve such words for the separate section in which you give your tentative interpretations of the incident. There is no need to interpret each incident, but when interpretations are given they should be kept separate and labeled as such.

GUIDELINES

Writing Anecdotal Records

❑ Write brief, specific descriptions.

❑ Include a concise description of what the student said or did and the situation in which it occurred. (Example: On the playground today, Debbie and Kim were choosing sides for softball. Bonnie said, "I want to be on Debbie's team and play first base, or I won't play.")

❑ Do not write generalized descriptive anecdotes. These describe the behavior in general terms, as being typical of the student. (Example: On the playground today, Bonnie again showed that she always wants her own way.)

❑ Do not write evaluative anecdotes. These judge the behavior as acceptable or unacceptable, good or bad. (Example: Bonnie was selfish and disruptive on the playground today.)

❑ Do not write interpretive anecdotes. These explain the reasons for the behavior, usually in terms of a single general cause. (Example: Bonnie can't play well with others because she is an over-protected, only child.)

7. *Record both positive and negative behavioral incidents.* Teachers are often more apt to notice those behaviors that disturb them personally and that interfere with the process in the classroom. The result is that anecdotal records frequently contain a disproportionate number of the incidents that indicate the lack of learning or development. For assessment purposes, it is equally important to record the less dramatic incidents that provide clues concerning the growth that is taking place. Thus, a conscious effort should be made to observe and record more subtle positive behaviors as well as the more obvious negative reactions.

8. *Collect a number of anecdotes on a student before drawing inferences concerning typical behavior.* A single behavioral incident is seldom very meaningful in understanding a student's behavior. We all have our moments of peak performance and extreme error-proneness, elation and despair, confidence and self-doubt. It is only after observing a student a number of times in a variety of settings that the basic pattern of behavior begins to emerge. Consequently, we should generally delay making any judgments concerning learning or development until we have a sufficient sample of behavior to provide a reliable picture of how the student typically behaves in different situations.

9. *Obtain practice in writing anecdotal records.* At first, most teachers have considerable difficulty in selecting significant incidents, in observing them accurately, and in describing them objectively. Some training and practice are therefore desirable before embarking on the use of anecdotal records. If the entire school staff is involved, there should be a regular in-service training program. When one teacher wants to explore the use of anecdotal records, a supervisor or fellow teacher can help appraise the quality of the records. It might be wise to start by observing students' study habits during a study period, as this will allow sufficient time to observe and record significant behavior.

STUDENT JUDGMENTS AND REPORTS

Teachers' observations and judgments of student behavior are of special value in those areas in which the behavior is readily observable and the teachers have special competence to judge. In assessing the ability to conduct and interpret experimental data, the effectiveness of an essay, or the quality of handwriting, for example, the teacher is unquestionably in the best position to make the judgment. The procedure, or the product resulting from the procedure, can be directly observed and the teacher's knowledge in the area contributes to the validity and reliability of the judgments. There are some areas of student development, however, in which the teacher's assessment of behavior is apt to be inadequate unless observations are supplemented and complemented by the students' judgments and reports.

Various aspects of personal–social development can be more effectively assessed by including peer ratings and other peer-appraisal methods in the assessment program. In the realms of leadership ability, concern for others, effectiveness in group work, and social acceptability, for example, students often know better than the teacher one another's strengths and weaknesses. The intimate interactions that occur among peers are seldom fully visible to an outside observer. Some differences between teacher judgment and peer judgment also can be expected because each is using different standards. Children's criteria of social acceptability, for example, are apt to be quite different from adults' criteria.

Self-report techniques are also a valuable adjunct to the teacher's observations of behavior. A complete picture of students' adjustments, interests, and attitudes cannot be obtained without reports from them. Their expressed feelings and beliefs in these areas are at least as important as evidence obtained from observing their behavior. Although expressed feelings and observable behavior do not always completely agree, the self-report provides valuable evidence concerning the students' perceptions of themselves and how they want others to view them. In fact, a discrepancy between reported feelings and actual behavior is, in itself, significant assessment information.

Though peer appraisal and self-report techniques are useful for understanding students better and guiding their learning, development, and adjustment, the results should not be used for marking and reporting or in any manner that interferes with honest responses. The students must be convinced that it is in their own best interests to respond as accurately and frankly as possible. Teachers who have good relations with their students and who have consistently emphasized the positive values of the assessment information should have no difficulty obtaining the students' cooperation in these techniques. When only group results are needed, the students can, of course, respond anonymously.

PEER APPRAISAL

In some instances it is possible to have students rate their peers on the same rating device used by the teacher. At the conclusion of a student's oral report before the class, for example, the other students could rate the performance on a standard rating form. The average of these ratings is a good indication of how the group felt about the student's performance. Except for oral reports, speeches, demonstrations, and similar situations in which one individual performs at a time, however, the usual rating procedures are seldom feasible with students. If we ask students to rate their classmates on a series of personal–social characteristics, each student will be required to fill out thirty or more rating forms. This becomes so cumbersome and time-consuming that we can hardly expect the ratings to be diligently made. When peer ratings and other methods of peer appraisal are used, we must depend on greatly simplified procedures. Some of the techniques are so simple that they can be used effectively with students at the primary school level.

The two most widely used techniques in this area are the (1) guess-who technique and (2) sociometric technique.

Guess-Who Technique

One of the simplest methods of obtaining peer judgments is by means of the guess-who technique. With this procedure, each student is presented with a series of brief behavior descriptions and asked to name those students who best fit each description. The descriptions may be limited to positive characteristics or they may also include negative behaviors. The following items, taken from a form for assessing sociability, are typical of the types of positive and negative descriptions used:

1. Here is someone who is always friendly.
2. Here is someone who is never friendly.

Some teachers prefer to use only the positive behavior descriptions because of the possible harmful effects of negative nominations on group morale. Teachers must make this decision for themselves, however, because they are the only ones who can determine what the effects might be on their students. When good relations have been established among students and between teacher and students, this is not likely to be a problem. But if there is doubt, it is usually better to sacrifice part of the assessment data than to disrupt the morale of the class.

In naming persons for each behavior description, the students are usually permitted to name as few or as many as they wish. Directions and sample items from a form for assessing concern for others are shown in Figure 11.2. The directions and behavior descriptions must, of course, be adapted to the students' age level. With very young students, the technique can be presented as a guessing game, with the items stated as follows: "Here is someone who talks a lot—guess who?" When the technique is used with older students, the guess-who aspect is dropped, and the students are merely told to write the names of those who best fit each behavior description.

The guess-who technique is based on the nomination method of obtaining peer ratings and is scored by simply counting the number of mentions each student receives on each description. If both positive and negative descriptions are used, such as friendly and unfriendly, the number of negative mentions on each characteristic is subtracted from the number of positive mentions. For example, twelve mentions as being friendly and two mentions of being unfriendly would result in a score of ten on friendliness. The pattern of scores indicates each student's reputation in the peer group. This may not completely agree with the teacher's impressions of the student, but it is significant information concerning personal–social development. In fact, one of the great values of this type of peer appraisal is that it makes the teacher aware of feelings and attitudes among students that were undetectable through direct observation.

This nominating method can be used to assess any aspect of personal–social development that students have had an adequate opportunity to observe. It is especially valuable for appraising personality characteristics, character traits, and social skills, but it is not limited to these areas. It is also useful in such areas as creativity, critical thinking, and problem solving. As with other assessment techniques, the items used in any particular guess-who form should be derived directly from the objectives to be assessed.

The items shown in Figure 11.3 were used to assess problem solving at the elementary school level and were derived directly from the stated objectives. More elaborate statements would, of course, be used at higher grade levels.

FIGURE 11.2
Guess-who form for assessing students' "concern for others"

Directions

Listed below are descriptions of what some students in this room are like. Read the descriptions and write the names of the students who *best fit* each description. You may write the names of anyone in this room, including those who are absent. Your choices will not be seen by anyone else. Give first name and initial of last name.

Remember!

1. Write the names of students in this room who best fit each description.
2. Write as many names as you wish for each description.
3. The same person may fit more than one description.
4. You should write the first name and initial of last name.
5. Your choices will *not be seen* by anyone else.

Write the names below each description.

1. Here is someone who enjoys working and playing with others.

2. Here is someone who is willing to share materials with others.

3. Here is someone who is willing to help others with their schoolwork.

4. Here is someone who makes sure others are not left out of games.

5. Here is someone who encourages others to do well.

6. Here is someone who is kind to others who have a problem.

The main advantage of the guess-who technique is its usability. It can be administered in a relatively few minutes to students of all age levels, and scoring is a simple matter of counting the number of nominations received. Its main limitation is the lack of information it provides on the shy, withdrawn student. Such students are frequently overlooked when nomination methods are used. In effect, they have no reputation in their peer group and are simply ignored during the rating process.

FIGURE 11.3
Guess-who items for
evaluating problem solving

> 1. Who is best able to state the problem clearly?
> 2. Who asks the best questions?
> 3. Who is most willing to seek more information?
> 4. Who comes up with the best suggestions?
> 5. Who is most willing to consider the different solutions?
> 6. Who comes up with the most complete plan?

Sociometric Technique

The sociometric technique is a method for assessing the social acceptance of individual students and the social structure of a group. It is also a relatively simple technique, based on students' choices of companions for some group situation or activity. A typical sociometric form is shown in Figure 11.4. This form was used to measure students' acceptance as seating companions, work companions, and play companions at the later elementary school level. The directions illustrate several important principles of sociometric choosing: (1) The choices should be real choices that are natural parts of classroom activities. (2) The basis for choice and the restrictions on the choosing should be made clear. (3) All students should be equally free to participate in the activity or situation. (4) The choices each student makes should be kept confidential. (5) The choices should be actually used to organize or rearrange groups. More spontaneous and truthful responses will be forthcoming when the students know that their choices will be used.

School activities with possibilities for sociometric choosing abound. Students can choose laboratory partners, fellow committee members, companions for group projects, and the like. Although some differences in choice can be expected from one situation to another, a large element of social acceptance runs through all choices. A student who is often chosen for one activity will also tend to be chosen often for other activities. The greatest variation in the choosing is when specific activities are used and skill and knowledge are important to successful performance. Even relatively unpopular students may be chosen as teammates for baseball if they are exceptionally good players. It is unlikely that they would be chosen as seating companions in the classroom, however, because this is almost a pure measure of social acceptance.

Sociometric experts disagree on the desirability of asking students to name those whom they would *not* want as a companion. The arguments in favor of such negative choices are that rejected students can be identified and helped and that interpersonal friction can be avoided in arranging groups. The counterargument is that such questions make students more conscious of their feelings of rejection and that this may disturb both group morale and the emotional development of students. The safest procedure seems to be to avoid using negative choices unless they are absolutely essential to the purpose for which the technique is being used. If their use is essential, the approach should be casual and the students permitted, rather

FIGURE 11.4
Sociometric form

Name_____Date_____

During the next few weeks we will be changing our seats around, working in small
groups and playing some group games. Now that we all know each other by
name, you can help me arrange groups that work and play best together. You can
do this by writing the names of the children you would like *to have sit near you, to
have work with you,* and *to have play with you.* You may choose anyone in this
room you wish, including those students who are absent. Your choices will not be
seen by anyone else. Give first name and initial of last name.

   Make your choices carefully so the groups will be the way you really want them.
I will try to arrange the groups so that each student gets at least two of his
choices. Sometimes it is hard to give everyone his or her first few choices so be
sure to make five choices for each question.

Remember!

1. Your choices must be from students in this room, including those who are ab-
    sent.
2. You should give the first name and the initial of the last name.
3. You should make all five choices for each question.
4. You may choose a student for more than one group if you wish.
5. Your choices will *not be seen* by anyone else.

I would choose to *sit near* these children:

1. _____3. _____

2. _____4. _____

                  5. _____

I would choose to *work with* these children:

1. _____3. _____

2. _____4. _____

                  5. _____

I would choose to *play with* these children:

1. _____3. _____

2. _____4. _____

                  5. _____

than required, to make such choices. A statement like the following will ordinarily suffice: "If there are students you would rather not have in your group, you may also list their names."

It is usually wise to restrict the number of choices each student makes on a sociometric question. For most purposes, five choices for each activity is a suitable number. Sociometric results have been shown to increase in reliability up to five choices, with no increase beyond that number. Also, five choices make it easier to arrange sociometric groups because it is sometimes difficult to satisfy the first several choices for all students. At the lower elementary grades, it is usually necessary to limit the choices to two or three. Very young children find it difficult to discriminate beyond this number.

Tabulating Sociometric Results. The student's sociometric choices must be organized in some fashion if we are to interpret and use them properly. A simple tally of the number of choices each student receives will indicate the degree of social acceptance. This may be all that is needed for some classroom uses, but it will not reveal who made the choices, whether two students chose each other, and what the social structure of the group is like. A complete record of the sociometric results can be made by tabulating the choices in a matrix table like the one shown in Figure 11.5. The students' names are listed down the side of the table and are numbered from 1 to 20. These same numbers, corresponding to the students' names, are then placed across the top of the table so that each student's choices can be recorded in the appropriate column. For example, the choices of John A. were as follows:

Chose	**Rejected**
1. Bill H.	X Steve D.
2. Carlos L.	X Bob F.
3. Mike A.	
4. Donna A.	
5. Pete V.	

These choices were recorded in the table to the right of John A.'s name by placing number 1 in column six to indicate Bill H. as his first choice, number 2 in column seven to indicate Carlos L. as his second choice, and so on. The Xs represent rejection choices, and the circled numbers in the table indicate mutual choices. For example, Mike A. (number 2) chose Jim B. (number 3), and vice versa. Mutual choices are always an equal number of cells from the diagonal line, in each corresponding column and row.

In this particular tabulation form, the boys and girls are listed separately. This divides the main part of the table into four quarters. The boys' choices of boys fall into the upper left-hand quarter of the table, and the girls' choices of girls fall into the lower right-hand quarter. The diagonal line, which goes through the empty cells that are unused because students do not choose themselves, cuts through these two quarters. The upper right-hand quarter and the lower left-hand quarter, then, contain only cross-sex choices. This division of the table makes the number of choices given to the same sex and to the opposite sex readily apparent and easy to summarize.

FIGURE 11.5

Matrix table showing choices and rejections of work companions

	Rejections Given		Choices Given			Students Chosen																			
Name	OS	SS	OS	SS		1	2	3	4	5	6	7	8	9	10	11	12	13	14	15	16	17	18	19	20
John A.	0	2	1	4	1		3		X	X	1	2	4	③	5										
Mike A.	0	2	0	5	2			②	X	X	1	①		④	5										
Jim B.	0	0	0	5	3		③				1	②			5										
Steve D.	0	0	1	4	4					①	2		3		4		5								
Bob F.	1	0	1	4	5						2	3	4				5	⊗							
Bill H.	1	0	3	2	6			④	5	X	①	②	①	③		③	X						⑤		
Carlos L.	0	2	0	5	7		②		5	X	①		X	③	②										
Dick N.	0	0	1	4	8	4	②	③			①	3	X		②		5								
Dale P.	0	1	0	5	9				5	5	4	①	X	3											
Pete V.	0	0	1	4	10					5	2		4	3					4						
Teresa A.	0	0	2	3	11						⑤		4				①	⑤	③		①	③	②		④
Donna A.	0	0	0	5	12					⊗					5	①	②		②				③		
Karen B.	1	1	1	4	13								5			②	①		X			③	4	X	③
Lois C.	0	1	1	4	14											1	2	4					④	X	5
Sharon J.	0	1	0	5	15					5	3					4	2	②	3			①			
Ann K.	0	0	2	3	16										2	4	5	①	③		③		5	X	⑤
Maria M.	0	0	1	4	17						④					②	①		②					X	
Sue R.	0	1	1	4	18						5					2	1	3	②			4	5		
Pat S.	0	0	0	5	19													4	②				③	X	
Carol W.	0	1	1	4	20						5						①	4	②				③	X	
Choices Received					SS	1	4	3	2	3	8	7	5	4	5	7	8	6	5	0	2	3	6	0	4
					OS	0	0	0	0	1	4	0	2	0	2	1	4	0	2	0	0	0	1	0	0
Rejections Received					SS	0	0	0	2	3	0	0	2	0	0	0	0	1	1	0	0	0	0	4	0
					OS	0	0	0	0	1	0	0	0	0	0	0	1	1	0	0	0	0	0	0	0
Mutual Choices					SS	0	3	3	1	1	2	4	2	3	1	3	5	3	4	0	2	2	4	0	3
					OS	0	0	0	0	0	2	0	0	0	0	1	0	0	0	0	0	0	1	0	0

Central (School)
5A (Class)
F.R. Young (Teacher)

Note: SS = Same Sex   OS = Opposite Sex   X = Rejection

In totaling the number of choices received, in Figure 11.5 each choice was given a value of one, regardless of level of choice. Some teachers prefer to weigh the choices so that a first choice counts more than a second choice, and so on, but there is no rational basis for assigning such weights. Various arbitrary weighting systems have been tried, but none has been shown to be superior to the method used here. Although it seems sensible to expect a student's first choice to have greater significance than the second, the degree to which choices differ cannot be predicted. One student may have a strong first preference, whereas another is equally attracted to several friends and finds it difficult to discriminate among the first several choices. Until a weighting system is found that handles such discrepancies, the simpler method of counting one for each choice should be used. The level of choice should still be recorded in the matrix table, however, because it is useful when the choices are used to organize groups.

The number of choices students receive on a sociometric question is used as an indication of their social acceptance by peers. When five choices are used, as in Figure 11.5, students who receive nine or more choices are called stars. A student such as Bill H. (Number 6) who received 8 same-sex and 4 opposite-sex choices and no rejections is obviously popular. A student such as Pat S. (Number 19) who received no choices and 4 same-sex rejections, on the other hand, is not well accepted. Awareness of such results can be useful to teachers in planning activities that may help a child gain greater peer acceptance.

The Sociogram. The matrix table is useful for organizing sociometric data for future use and for determining the social acceptance of individual students. It does not depict the social structure of the group, however. When this is desired, the sociometric results are presented in a sociogram, a graphic picture of the social relations in a group, which may be plotted directly from the data recorded in the matrix table. A typical sociogram is shown in Figure 11.6. The sociometric data depicted here were taken from Figure 11.5.

The concentric circles form a target-type diagram on which to plot the sociometric data. Students who are frequently chosen (nine or more choices in this case) are placed in the center of the target; students who are never chosen are placed in the outer ring; and the remaining students are placed between these extremes according to the number of choices received. The boys are represented by triangles and the girls by circles, with the numbers corresponding to each student's number in the matrix table (see Figure 11.5). The uncluttered appearance of this sociogram is because the use of lines is confined to mutual choices and rejections. Plotting all choices would result in such a maze of lines that the sociogram would be impossible to interpret.

In constructing a sociogram, it is helpful to start with the students chosen most often and work out from the center of the diagram. Students with mutual choices should be placed near each other. The original placement on the chart should be done lightly in pencil, as considerable rearrangement is necessary during the plotting to minimize the number of crossed lines. Plotting boys and girls on separate sides of the diagram also simplifies the process because the number of mutual cross-sex choices is usually small. When all students have been finally arranged on the diagram, check to be certain that each one is still in the proper position between

FIGURE 11.6
Sociogram depicting choices
and rejections of work
companions, based on data in
Figure 11.5

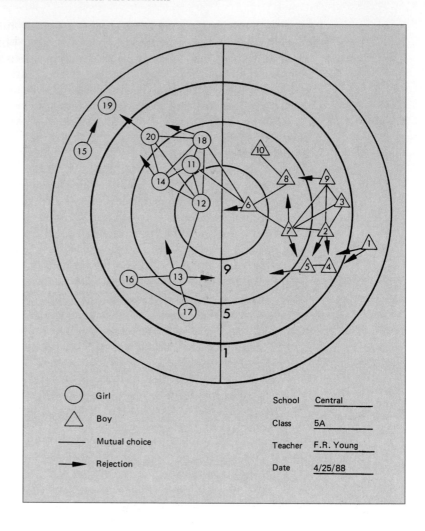

the concentric circles because this indicates the approximate number of choices received.

The sociogram in Figure 11.6 illustrates the common social configurations you can expect in a group structure. Girls 12, 11, 14, 18, and 20 form a very cohesive clique with many mutual choices. The fact that three of the five girls in this clique reject Girl 19 may provide a clue to a source of difficulty. Girls 13, 16, and 17 form a triangle. Boys 10, 8, and 6 form a chain of mutual choices, and Boys 4 and 5 from a mutual pair that reject and, in turn are rejected by several other students. In addition, there seems to be a social cleavage between boys and girls, except for the few mutual cross-sex choices of Boy 6. Students 1, 15, and 19 are isolated from the group, and student 19 is actively rejected by four of her classmates.

Although sociograms depict in graphic form the social relations present in the group, they do not indicate why a particular social structure evolved nor what should be done, if anything, to change it. The sociogram is merely a starting point.

To understand the cliques, cleavages, and social positions of individual students, it is necessary to supplement sociometric data with information obtained from observation, guess-who techniques, and various other assessment methods.

Uses of Sociometric Results. The sociometric technique has been used for a variety of purposes in the school, including (1) organizing classroom groups, (2) improving individual students' social adjustment, (3) improving groups' social structure, and (4) assessing the influence of school practices on students' social relations.

The first step in using sociometric results is to put the choices into effect. For example, if committees are to be formed, they should be patterned as closely as possible to the students' choices. This can usually be done most effectively by starting with the rejected and isolated students and working toward the students receiving the largest number of choices. With five choices, it is usually possible to satisfy at least two choices for each student. By starting with the isolated and rejected, you are able to give them their two highest choices. This places them in contact with the students with whom they may have the best chance for developing social relations. In arranging the groups, the sociometric choices should, of course, not be followed blindly. It may be desirable to place students with different backgrounds together to reduce an undesirable cleavage or to separate the members of a clique that has been disrupting the class. These adjustments can and should be made without violating your promise to give all of the students some of their choices.

Although sociometric results do not indicate how to improve social adjustment, they do help identify those students who are having difficulty in adjusting to the peer group. Isolated and rejected students are not apt to improve their social position without special help. If an isolated student is new to class, arranging opportunities for social contact may be all that is needed. In other cases, it may be a matter of helping isolated students improve their appearance, social skills, and apparent value to the group. In some instances, a student may be so socially withdrawn or aggressive toward others that the assistance of parents, the school counselor, and other special personnel may be required. Specific remedial procedures should be based on the causes of the student's isolation or rejection. The sociometric results merely alert us to the students most in need of further study and possible remedial action.

Sociometric measurement can contribute to the improvement of group structure in two ways. First, it helps pinpoint the cliques, cleavages, and mutual relations present in a group. Second, it provides the basic data for rearranging the group in a manner that is likely to result in a more cohesive social pattern. A disintegrated classroom structure, characterized by an overabundance of cliques, cleavages, and isolated students, commonly results in low group morale and a poor climate for learning. It is not expected that a simple rearrangement will eliminate cleavages along racial, religious, or socioeconomic lines. But it does offer an opportunity for interpersonal contacts, and if accompanied by other efforts to improve relations, these cleavages can be appreciably diminished.

In addition to its more common uses in the classroom, sociometric measurement is also useful in assessing the effect of particular school practices on students' social relations. For example, it can be used to help answer questions like: Are the mainstreamed students with handicapping conditions being accepted by their peers in the regular classroom? Is our method of instructional grouping creating a social cleavage between lower and higher achieving students? Does the competition between boys and girls in our elementary school result in an extreme sex cleavage? How does our activity program, which prevents bus-transported students from participating fully, influence the social relations between the bused and non-bused? The simplicity of the technique makes it usable with an entire school population as well as with a single classroom group.

SELF-REPORT TECHNIQUES

The oldest and best known method of obtaining information directly from an individual is the personal interview. The face-to-face contact has several advantages as a self-report procedure. First, it is flexible. Interviewers can clarify questions, can pursue promising lines of inquiry, and can give the interviewees an opportunity to qualify or expand on their answers. Second, interviewers can observe interviewees, noting the amount of feeling attached to their answers, the topics on which they seem to be evasive, and the areas in which they are most expansive. Third, the interview makes possible not only collecting information from interviewees but also sharing information with them and, as in the counseling interview, using the face-to-face contact as a basis for therapy.

The personal interview would be an almost ideal method of obtaining self-report information from students except for two serious problems. It is extremely time-consuming, and the information gained is not standard from one person to another. Therefore, in the interests of both feasibility and greater comparability of results, the self-report inventory or questionnaire is commonly used in place of the personal interview. An inventory consists of a standard set of questions pertaining to some particular area of behavior, administered and scored under standard conditions. It is a sort of standardized, written interview that enables the collection of a large amount of information quickly and that provides an objective summary of the data collected.

The effective use of self-report inventories assumes that individuals are both willing and able to report accurately. Responses can usually be easily faked if individuals want to present a distorted picture of themselves. Even when they want to be truthful, their recollections of past events may be inaccurate and their self-perceptions biased. These limitations can be partly offset by using self-report inventories only when students have little reason for faking, by emphasizing the value of frank responses for self-understanding and self-improvement and by taking into account the possible presence of distortion when interpreting the results. When these inventories are used for assessing affective behavior in the classroom, it may be wise to have the students respond anonymously.

ATTITUDE MEASUREMENT

One of the areas in which self-report inventories are very useful in the classroom is attitude measurement. In some instances, attitudes may be important instructional outcomes in their own right (e.g., scientific attitude). In other cases, we may wish to obtain measures of students' attitudes toward certain classroom activities, the textbook, laboratory experiences, or our own instruction, so that needed adjustments can be made. Some information concerning attitudes can, of course, be discovered by observation, but a more complete assessment requires that observation be supplemented by reports of the students' feelings and opinions.

One of the simplest self-report devices for measuring attitude is listing the activities or statements the students are expected to respond to and then devising some simple means of responding. The teacher-made form for measuring attitude toward mathematics activities at the lower primary level shown in Figure 11.7 illustrates this type of self-report form. The directions can be given orally and repeated for each activity, as follows: "Put an X in the box under the face that tells how you feel about counting."

Likert Scale

Another simple and widely used self-report method for measuring attitude is to list clearly favorable or unfavorable attitude statements and to ask the students to respond to each statement on the following five-point scale: *strongly agree (SA), agree (A), undecided (U), disagree (D),* and *strongly disagree (SD)*. This is called a **Likert scale,** named after its originator, and it is very easily constructed and scored. The construction involves the following steps:

1. Write a series of statements expressing positive and negative opinions toward some attitude object. For example, in preparing a scale to measure attitude toward school, a number of items like the following might be written.
   ❏ School is exciting.
   ❏ School is a waste of time.

FIGURE 11.7
Teacher-made form for measuring attitude toward mathematics activities at the lower primary level

Things We Do	I like a lot 😊	It's OK 😐	Don't like it ☹️
Counting			
Adding			
Subtracting			
Story problems			
Math games			
Drawing shapes			
Measuring			
Telling time			
Making change			

A good pool of such items can be obtained by having the students in your class each write several positive and negative statements.

2. Select the best statements (at least ten), with a balance of positive and negative opinions, and edit as needed.

3. List the statements, mixing up the positive and negative, and put the letters of the five-point scale (*SA, A, U, D, SD*) to the left of each statement for easy marking. For students at the elementary level, it might be best to list the five points in multiple-choice fashion with the words written out (e.g., *strongly agree*).

4. Add the directions telling students how to mark their answers, and include a key at the top of the page if letters are used for each statement (*SA, A, U, D, SD*).

5. Some prefer to drop the *undecided* category so that respondents will be forced to show agreement or disagreement. Others have expanded the scale by adding the categories *slightly agree* and *slightly disagree*. Although such changes might be useful for some purposes, the five-point scale is quite satisfactory for most uses.

A Likert scale for measuring attitude toward a science course is shown in Figure 11.8. By lengthening the instrument and preparing separate scales, it is possible to

FIGURE 11.8
Illustrative Likert scale for measuring attitude toward a science course

Directions: Indicate how much you agree or disagree with each statement by circling the appropriate letter(s).

	SA—Strongly Agree
	A—Agree
KEY	U—Undecided
	D—Disagree
	SD—Strongly Disagree

SA	A	U	D	SD	1. Science classes are interesting.
SA	A	U	D	SD	2. Science laboratory is dull and boring.
SA	A	U	D	SD	3. It is fun working on science problems.
SA	A	U	D	SD	4. Class activities are good.
SA	A	U	D	SD	5. Reading the textbook is a waste of time.
SA	A	U	D	SD	6. The laboratory experiments are interesting.
SA	A	A	U	SD	7. Most class activities are monotonous.
SA	A	U	D	SD	8. I enjoy reading the textbook.
SA	A	U	D	SD	9. The problems we are studying are unimportant.
SA	A	U	D	SD	10. I am *not* very enthusiastic about science.

obtain a more detailed measure of attitude toward specific parts of the course (e.g., textbook, visual aids, tests, laboratory work). Our example here simply shows the procedure and format.

The scoring of a Likert scale is based on assigning weights from 1 to 5 for each position on the scale. Favorable statements, like Item 1 in Figure 11.8, are weighted 5, 4, 3, 2, 1, going from *SA* to *SD*. Unfavorable statements, like Item 2 in Figure 11.8, have these weights reversed. Thus, they are weighted 1, 2, 3, 4, 5, going from *SA* to *SD*. An individual's total score on this type scale is the sum of the scores on all items, with the higher score indicating a more favorable attitude.

In using attitude scales like the one in Figure 11.8, it is usually best to ask for anonymous responses. This will indicate how the students in class feel about the course and, if separate scales are used, how they view the various activities in it. Such information is useful in making course revisions, and anonymous responses provide greater assurance that the replies will reflect the students' real feelings.

In interpreting the results of attitude scales, it is important to keep in mind that these are verbal expressions of feelings and opinions that individuals are willing to report. Good rapport with the respondents and a sincere belief on their part that frank responses are in their own best interests will help produce valid responses. Even under the most ideal conditions, however, it is wise to supplement attitudes determined by self-report methods with evidence from other sources. For example, if students have reported a favorable attitude toward other ethnic groups, sociometric data can be used to determine how frequently members of those groups are chosen for classroom activities. Similarly, if favorable attitudes toward handicapped persons are reported, this might be checked by observing how the students interact with handicapped students in the classroom.

Published Attitude Scales

A number of published attitude scales are available for school use. An example is the Estes Attitude Scales (Grades 3 through 12), designed to measure attitude toward school subjects. At the secondary level, the scales measure attitude toward English, mathematics, reading, science, and social studies. Items for two of the five subjects are shown in Figure 11.9. There is also an elementary form that measures attitude toward mathematics, reading, and science. Although the complete Likert scale is used at the secondary level, the elementary form uses only three categories (*agree, don't know, disagree*).

The items for each school subject were selected after extensive tryouts and statistical analyses of a larger number of items. The final selection of items resulted in an internally consistent scale for each school subject, with relatively low intercorrelations between the scales. Thus, the scales are fairly independent measures of attitude toward the various school subjects. Studies have also shown that the scores on these scales correlate with other measures of attitude, but the correlations are generally low.

Raw scores can be converted into both T-scores and percentile ranks (based on a limited norm sample).

FIGURE 11.9
Portion of the *Estes Attitude Scales* (Reprinted with permission of PRO-ED)

ESTES ATTITUDE SCALES
(Secondary Form)
© 1981, PRO-ED

DIRECTIONS: These scales measure how you feel about courses taught in school. On the front and back of this sheet are statements about school subjects. Read each statement and decide how you feel about it. Rate each statement on a scale of 1 to 5, as follows:

> 5 will mean "I strongly agree"
> 4 will mean "I agree"
> 3 will mean "I cannot decide"
> 2 will mean "I disagree"
> 1 will mean "I strongly disagree"

Use the separate answer sheet to indicate your feeling toward each statement. Show your answers by putting an X in the proper box. Please be as honest as possible in rating each statement. Your ratings will not affect your grade in any course.

English

1. Work in English class helps students do better work in other classes.
2. The study of English is a waste of time.
3. Writing papers for English class is good practice.
4. Almost any subject is better than English.
5. English courses are some of the worst courses.
6. Studying English is less tiring than studying other subjects.
7. English is a subject with very little real value.
8. English is boring.
9. Studying English in college would be valuable.
10. Students should be required to take English every year.
11. Most literature is dull.
12. English is fun.
13. Time spent in English class is time well spent.
14. English is one class I can do without.
15. English class is too short.

Mathematics

16. People who like math are often weird.
17. Working math problems is fun, like solving a puzzle.
18. It is easy to get tired of math.
19. Working math problems is a waste of time.
20. Studying math in college would be a good idea.
21. Being able to add, subtract, multiply, and divide is all the math the average person needs.
22. It is impossible to understand math.
23. Even though there are machines to work math problems, there is still a reason to study math.
24. Math is boring.
25. Only mathematicians need to study math.
26. Knowledge of math will be useful after high school.
27. Without math courses, school would be a better place.
28. A student would profit from taking math every year.
29. Math is easy.
30. Math is doing the same thing over and over again.

Continued ♦

INTEREST INVENTORIES

As with attitude measurement, information about students' interests can be gathered from simple self-report devices prepared by the teacher. An interest inventory for reading, for example, might be no more than a list of types of books with the students asked to mark whether they like or dislike each type. An example of such an inventory is shown in Figure 11.10. A simpler version of this inventory could be developed for students at the primary level by using broader categories (e.g., animals, people, places).

Various methods of responding can be used with informal interest inventories. The simple like–dislike response method can be expanded to more points, such as *like, indifferent, dislike,* or *strongly like, like, indifferent, dislike, strongly dislike.* When there are relatively few items to respond to, the students can rank them in order from *like most* to *like least,* as in the following example:

Rank	Type of Reading
_____	Fiction
_____	Nonfiction
_____	Poetry
_____	Drama

A simple paired-comparison procedure also might be used to find out the students' reading preferences when there are relatively few items to respond

FIGURE 11.10
Illustrative inventory for surveying reading interests

READING INTEREST INVENTORY

Directions: For each type of book listed below, circle L if you *like* reading that type of book and circle D if you *dislike* reading that type. List any other types of book you like to read on the lines below.

L	D	1. Adventure	L	D	10. Mystery
L	D	2. Animal	L	D	11. Politics
L	D	3. Art	L	D	12. Psychology
L	D	4. Biography	L	D	13. Romance
L	D	5. Boating	L	D	14. Science
L	D	6. Car racing	L	D	15. Science fiction
L	D	7. History	L	D	16. Sociology
L	D	8. Hobbies	L	D	17. Sports
L	D	9. Music	L	D	18. Western

List any others here_____

_____

---

to. Using these same four items, for example, we would have six pairs as follows:

_____Fiction	_____Fiction
_____Nonfiction	_____Drama
_____Fiction	_____Nonfiction
_____Poetry	_____Drama
_____Nonfiction	_____Poetry
_____Poetry	_____Drama

The students are instructed to mark the type of reading that they most prefer in each pair. A simple tally of the number of marks for each type of reading will indicate the students' relative preference.

Using any of the preceding response methods, we can obtain an interest score for each individual student, or we can combine the results for the entire class. Although students can fake responses to informal interest inventories, they seldom do. There are no right or wrong answers, and the results are usually used to plan classroom activities or to develop individual learning programs. In contrast with attitude scales, there is little reason to fear that one's responses to the inventory will influence grades.

Published Interest Inventories

There are a number of published interest inventories, but most of them have been designed for use in educational and vocational guidance. In some cases, however, the results can be used in planning more effective classroom instruction. Low interest scores in art and music, for example, might suggest that special activities are needed in these areas. Similarly, when a number of students have low interest scores in such areas as computation and science, a review of classroom activities and materials may be helpful. As with informal interest inventories, an individual's pattern of interests also may be useful in selecting reading material and planning individual learning programs.

One published interest inventory that has been widely used in the schools and is adaptable to classroom use is the Kuder General Interest Survey. This inventory was designed for Grades 6 to 12 and contains a number of activities arranged in groups of three. The students are forced to decide which one of the three activities they like most and which one they like least. The following items show the item format used in the Kuder General Interest Survey (but the items were not taken from that instrument).

	Most	Least
1. Build model airplanes.	M	L
Draw pictures of airplanes.	M	L
Write stories about airplanes.	M	L
2. Visit a farm.	M	L
Visit a library.	M	L
Visit a science museum.	M	L

CHAPTER 11 ❏ Assessment Procedures   **291**

By marking the activity liked most and the one liked least in each group of three, the individual is, of course, ranking them in order, because the unmarked one will fall in the middle. The same form is used for boys and girls, and the results are profiled using both male and female norms. The inventory can be hand scored by students or machine scored. Special Micro-E software provides for local computer scoring including the printing of a complete narrative report like that shown in Figure 11.11. The various parts of the report are indicated by circled letters and are described as follows:

A   V-score. Verifies that responses were carefully made.

B   Explains the test and its interpretation.

C   Scores are ranked by percentile for each norm group.

D   Each individual is compared to both male and female norms.

E   Graphic results are shown for each percentile.

F   High (above 75%), average, and low (below 25%) are indicated on graph.

G   Student is encouraged to look at both male and female norms.

H   Scores are converted to personality-type codes.

The Kuder General Interest Survey is easy to administer, score, and interpret. Each student receives a narrative report form and an interpretive leaflet that describes the ten areas covered by the Survey. Although the report is designed to be self-interpreting, the aid of a teacher or counselor can contribute to the usefulness of the results.

There is also a Kuder Occupational Interest Survey for use in high school and beyond. It uses the same forced-choice method of responding to triad items (i.e., selecting the most and least liked) and also uses a verification score (V-score) for determining whether the responses were carefully made. The results are reported in terms of 126 specific occupations and 48 college majors. The scores are expressed as correlations between an individual's pattern of interests and the interest pattern of each occupational and college group. The latest form of this instrument provides for both occupational scores and vocational area scores like those in the Kuder General Interest Survey.

Another interest inventory that has been widely used at the high school and college levels is the Strong–Campbell Interest Inventory. This inventory consists of 325 items grouped into seven sections. The items in the first five sections are marked *like* (L), *indifferent* (I), or *dislike* (D) for each item. In Section 6, the individual chooses the preferred activity or marks an equal sign. In Section 7, the rating is *yes, no,* or *?*. The following list of the seven sections includes examples that are not taken from the inventory but are merely illustrative.

1. *Occupations* (131 items)
   Airline pilot
   Animal trainer

2. *School subjects* (36 items)
   Astronomy
   Auto mechanics

FIGURE 11.11

Narrative report form for the Kuder General Interest Survey (Reprinted by permission of Science Research Associates)

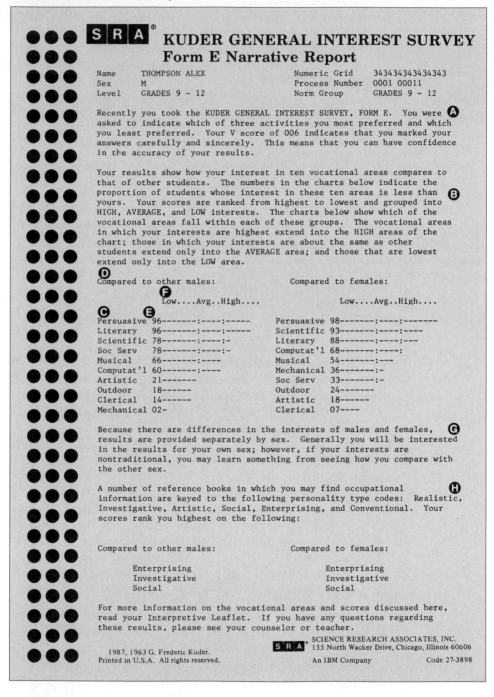

3. *Activities* (51 items)
   Debating
   Woodworking

4. *Leisure Activities* (39 items)
   Swimming
   Watching television

5. *Types of people* (24 items)
   College students
   Submissive people

6. *Preference between two activities* (30 items)
   Ambulance driver–travel agent
   Work with people–work alone

7. *Your characteristics* (14 items)
   Get along well with others
   Can speak effectively to groups

The main part of the Strong–Campbell Interest Inventory is scored and interpreted in terms of the similarity between an individual's expressed interests and those of persons engaged in particular occupations. The answers are placed on answer sheets that must be machine scored. The results are printed out on a profile that contains 207 occupational scales, 23 basic interest scales, and 6 general occupational themes. The same inventory form is used by both males and females, and when scored on all scales, the profile indicates how an individual's interests compare to those of both sexes on each scale.

As with other self-report techniques, responses to published interest inventories can be easily faked. This is seldom a problem, however, where the emphasis is on self-understanding and educational and vocational planning. Students are anxious to find out about their interests and the inventories consist of items that tend to be psychologically nonthreatening.

The instability of students' interests during elementary and high school years suggests that we should use interest inventories with extreme caution at these levels. Interests typically are not very stable until approximately age seventeen. This does not mean that we must wait until this age to measure interests but that our interpretations must be highly tentative. In one sense the instability of interests among children and adolescents is highly encouraging, for it indicates that our efforts to broaden and develop interests through school activities have some chance of succeeding. It is mainly when we are attempting to use them in career planning that stability poses a serious problem. For vocational decisions, we should rely most heavily on interest measures obtained during the last two years of high school and later.

Another precaution to keep in mind is not to confuse interest scores with measures of ability. A strong interest in science, for example, may or may not be accompanied by the verbal and numerical abilities needed to pursue successfully a course of study or career in science. A scientific interest may be satisfied by collecting butterflies or by discovering a cure for cancer. Interest measures merely indicate whether an individual is apt to find satisfaction in a particular type of activity. Measures of ability determine the level of activity at which the individual can expect to function effectively.

PERSONALITY MEASURES

Classroom assessments of students' personality characteristics and adjustment problems are probably best made through the use of anecdotal records, rating scales, and other observational and peer-appraisal techniques. However, there are two types of personality measures that classroom teachers should know about: personality inventories and projective techniques. These will be briefly described for general information only. To use them effectively requires special training in counseling or clinical psychology.

Personality Inventories

The typical personality inventory presents students with a series of questions like those used in a psychiatric screening interview. For example, an inventory might include items like the following:

❑ Do you daydream often?

❑ Are you frequently depressed?

❑ Do you have difficulty making friends?

❑ Do you usually feel tired?

Responses to such questions are commonly indicated by circling *yes, no,* or *?* (for uncertain). In some instances a forced-choice procedure is used, where the items are paired and the respondent must indicate which of the two statements is more characteristic of him.

Personality inventories vary considerably in the type of score provided. Some provide a single adjustment score, others have separate scores for particular adjustment areas (e.g., health, social, emotional) or for specific personality traits (e.g., self-confidence, sociability, ascendancy). In general, research has not supported the validity of separate scores for assessing adjustment by means of inventories. Even using the total score for distinguishing between adjusted and maladjusted individuals is open to question.

All of the limitations of the self-report technique tend to be accentuated in the personality inventory. (1) The replies can be easily faked, and the threatening nature of many of the questions encourages presenting a distorted picture. Some inventories have "control keys" to detect faking, and others reduce faking by means of the forced-choice procedure, but it cannot be entirely eliminated. (2) In addition to honesty, accurate responses require good self-insight. But this is the very characteristic that poorly adjusted individuals are apt to lack, as they are prone to excessive use of adjustment mechanisms that tend to distort their perceptions of themselves and their relations with others. (3) The ambiguity of the items is also likely to distort the results. Questions like "Are you frequently depressed?" do not mean the same thing to different individuals. Although some ambiguity may be desirable in these inventories (as we are seeking perceptions rather than facts), words like *frequently* have such a broad range of meanings that error is likely to be introduced. In addition to these technical shortcomings, there is the invasion of privacy issue. Congressional investigators, parents, and others have raised the question of the school's right to ask students such personal questions. Primarily because of the invasion of privacy issue, the routine use of personality and adjustment inventories in schools has declined to near zero.

Psychologically trained counselors may find personality inventories useful for beginning counseling interviews. The client can be asked to fill out the inventory early in the counseling session, and the response to individual items can serve as a starting point for discussion. Even if the responses are not completely frank or insightful, this can be dealt with in the counseling sessions. When used in this way, the inventory serves as an ice-breaker. Invasion of privacy is not an issue here because the client has voluntarily sought out a relationship in which revelation of inner feelings is a known requisite for obtaining help.

Projective Techniques

Projective techniques are another method of assessing personal–social adjustment with which the classroom teacher should be familiar. Because they generally require clinical training to administer and interpret, it is not expected that teachers will use them directly. It is more than likely, however, that they will encounter some clinical reports of students that contain interpretations of projective test results.

In contrast with the highly structured personality inventory, projective techniques provide almost complete freedom of response. Typically, individuals are presented with a series of ambiguous forms or pictures and asked to describe what they see. Their responses are then analyzed to determine what content and structure they have "projected" onto the ambiguous stimuli.

Two of the best known projective techniques are the Rorschach Inkblot Test and the Thematic Apperception Test (TAT). The Rorschach consists of ten inkblot figures on cards, and the TAT includes a series of pictures. These tests are usually administered to one individual at a time, and the individual's responses are recorded during the testing. Analysis of the results requires both systematic scoring and impressionistic interpretation, with emphasis on the total personality pattern revealed. Projective techniques are used primarily as part of a complete clinical study of those individuals who are experiencing adjustment difficulties.

SUMMARY

Observational techniques are especially useful in assessing performance skills and certain aspects of personal–social development. In addition, observation supplements and complements paper-and-pencil testing and performance-based assessments by indicating how students typically behave in natural situations.

The least structured observational technique is the anecdotal record. This is simply a method of recording factual descriptions of student behavior. To make anecdotal record-keeping feasible, it is desirable to restrict observations at any given time to a few types of behavior or to a few students. Anecdotal records have the advantages of (1) describing behavior in natural settings, (2) highlighting evidence of exceptional behavior apt to be overlooked by other techniques, and (3) being usable with the very young. Their limitations are (1) the time and effort required to maintain an adequate record system, (2) the difficulty of writing objective descriptions of behavior, and (3) the problem of obtaining an adequate sample of behavior. These disadvantages can be minimized by following specific procedures for observing and recording the behavioral incidents. Suggestions for improving anecdotal records include (1) determining in advance what to observe, (2) analyzing observational records for possible sources of bias, (3) describing the setting in which the behavior occurred, (4) making the record as soon as possible after observing the behavior, (5) confining each anecdote to a single incident, (6) separating factual description from interpretation, (7) recording both positive and negative incidents, (8) collecting a number of anecdotes before drawing inferences, and (9) obtaining practice in observing and recording student behavior.

In some areas of learning and development, it is desirable to supplement the teacher's observations with information obtained directly from the students. We can ask the students to rate or judge their peers and to report on their own feelings, thoughts, and past behavior. Several peer-appraisal methods and self-report techniques have been developed for this purpose.

Peer appraisal is especially useful in assessing personality characteristics, social relations skills, and other forms of typical behavior. The give-and-take of social interaction in the peer group provides students with a unique opportunity to observe and judge the behavior of their fellow students. Because these peer ratings are based on experiences that are seldom fully visible to adult observers, they are an important adjunct to teachers' observations.

Peer-appraisal methods include the guess-who technique and the sociometric technique. The first of these techniques for obtaining peer ratings requires students to name those classmates who best fit each of a series of behavior descriptions. The number of nominations students receive on each characteristic indicates their reputation in the peer group. This nominating procedure can be used to assess any aspect of behavior that is observable to fellow students. The sociometric technique also calls for nominations, but here the students indicate their choice of companions for some group situation or activity. The number of choices students receive serves as an indication of their social acceptance, and the network of choices can be used to plot the social structure of the group. The results also can be used to rearrange groups, to improve the social adjustment of individual students, and to assess the influence of school practices on students' social relations.

Self-report techniques are used to obtain information that is inaccessible by other means, including reports on the student's attitudes, interests, and personal feelings. Such information can be obtained by means of a personal interview, but a self-report inventory is more commonly used. The inventory is a sort of standardized written interview that produces comparable results from one person to another. The effective use of self-report techniques assumes that the respondent is both willing and able to report accurately. Thus, special efforts must be made to ensure these conditions.

Attitude scales can be used to gather information concerning students' feelings and opinions toward various classroom activities, situations, groups, and special events. Interest inventories contribute to a better understanding of students' preferences and are useful in educational and vocational planning. Personality inventories and projective techniques aid in assessing students' personal–social adjustment but they are not recommended for use by the classroom teacher.

Both peer ratings and self-report inventories can provide useful information for understanding students better and for guiding their learning, development, and adjustment. These purposes are best served, however, when this information is combined with test results, observational data, and all other information concerning the students.

LEARNING EXERCISES

1. Observe a child at play and write an anecdotal record. Give both your descriptive account of the child's behavior and your interpretation of the behavior, but place these under separate headings.

2. What are the advantages and disadvantages of using observational techniques for assessing student learning?

3. Briefly describe the steps you would follow if you were going to have students help assess the effectiveness of their class discussion.

4. What types of behavior are best assessed by peer appraisal? What are some of the necessary precautions in using peer-appraisal methods?

5. List several positive and negative statements that might be used on a guess-who form for assessing ability to work effectively in a group.

6. List three positive statements and three negative statements that might be used in a sociometric test for assessing students' social acceptance by their peers. What are the advantages and disadvantages of using negative choices?

7. Describe the advantages and limitations of self-report inventories. What can be done to increase the validity of the results?

8. Write several statements that might be useful in a Likert-type attitude scale for assessing students' attitudes toward homework.

9. What are the advantages and disadvantages of using each of the following for assessing attitudes toward school?
   a. Attitude scale
   b. Teacher observation
   c. Guess-who technique

10. Why have so few interest inventories been developed for use at the elementary level? How might interest inventories contribute to the instructional program?

11. What types of peer-appraisal and self-report methods might be used to determine whether ability grouping adversely affects student development? How would you develop each instrument?

FURTHER READING

Anastasi, A. (1988). *Psychological Testing* (5th ed.). New York: Macmillan. Chapter 17, "Self-Report Inventories," and Chapter 18, "Measuring Interests, Values, and Attitudes," discuss the development and use of inventories and describe widely used instruments.

Boehm, A. E., & Weinberg, R. A. (1987). *The Classroom Observer: A Guide to Developing Observation Skills* (2d ed.). New York: Teachers College Press. A brief guide to help pre-service and in-service teachers make systematic observations of classroom situations and individual students at the preschool and grade-school levels.

Cohen, D. H., Stern, V., & Balaban, N. (1983). *Observing and Recording the Behavior of Young Children* (3rd ed.). New York: Teachers College Press. Describes methods of studying children in various classroom situations. Includes numerous checklists and examples for preschool and primary levels.

Cronbach, L. J. (1990). *Essentials of Psychological Testing* (4th ed.). New York: Harper & Row. See Chapter 12, "Interest Inventories," Chapter 13, "General Problems in Studying Personality," and Chapter 14, "Personality Measurement Through Self-Report," for a comprehensive discussion of self-report measures, their validity, and the ethical issues involved.

Ebel, R. L., & Frisbie, D. A. (1991). *Essentials of Educational Measurement* (5th ed.). Englewood Cliffs, N.J.: Prentice-Hall. Chapter 14, "Nontest and Informal Evaluation Methods" describes the use of observational techniques and rating scales.

Harmon, L. W. (1992). Interest measurement. In M. C. Alkin, (Ed.), *Encyclopedia of Educational Research* (6th ed.), (Vol. 2). New York: Macmillan. Provides an overview of the measurement of interests and the use of interest measurement in education.

Kifer, E. (1992). Attitude measurement. In M. C. Alkin, (Ed.), *Encyclopedia of Educational Research* (6th ed.), (Vol 1). New York: Macmillan. Describes the techniques of attitude measurement and discusses the validity and reliability of attitude measures.

Krug, S. E. (1992). Personality measurement. In M. C. Alkin, (Ed.), *Encyclopedia of Educational Research* (6th ed.), (Vol. 3). New York: Macmillan. Provides an introduction to personality measurement.

Mehrens, W. A., & Lehmann, I. J. (1987). *Using standardized tests in education* (4th ed.). New York: Longman. See Chapter 9, "Interest, Personality, and Attitude Inventories," for a discussion of the problems of using self-report inventories and a description of representative instruments.

Mueller, D. J. (1986). *Measuring social attitudes: A handbook for researchers and practitioners*. New York: Teachers College Press. Describes and illustrates various methods of attitude scale construction. Includes an annotated bibliography of various sources of attitude scales.

CHAPTER 12

Assembling, Administering, and Appraising Classroom Tests and Assessments

Care in preparing an assessment plan and constructing relevant test items and assessment tasks should be followed by similar care in reviewing and editing the items and tasks, preparing clear directions, and administering and appraising the results. Classroom assessments also can be improved by using simple methods to analyze student responses, and building a file of effective items and tasks.

Effective classroom assessment begins with an assessment plan that specifically describes the instructional objectives and content to be measured and the relative emphasis to be given to each intended learning outcome. This is followed by the selection of the most appropriate item and task formats (e.g., multiple choice, essay, hands-on performance assessment) and the preparation of items and tasks that are relevant to the learning outcomes specified in the plan. These steps have received considerable attention in the preceding chapters because they are crucial to the validity of the assessment. The only way we can ensure that a classroom test will serve its intended purpose is to identify the learning outcomes we want to measure and then to construct test items and assessment tasks that call forth the specific performance described in the learning outcomes. We must also assemble the items and tasks, prepare directions, administer the instrument, score the student responses, and interpret and appraise the results.

Our goal throughout the preparation and use of classroom tests and assessments is to obtain valid evidence of student learning. In the final analysis, valid measurement of achievement is the product of a systematically controlled series of steps, beginning with the identification of instructional objectives and ending with the scoring and interpretation of results. Although validity is built-in during the construction of the items and tasks, systematic procedures of assembly, administration, and scoring will provide greater assurance that the items and tasks will function as intended. Appraising the test items and assessment tasks after they have been administered can also help improve their quality. Procedures for analyzing student responses provide information for evaluating the functional effectiveness of each item or task and for detecting weaknesses that should be corrected. This information is useful when reviewing the results with students, and it is indispensable when building a file of high-quality items and tasks for future use.

Performance-based assessments typically involve a relatively small number of tasks because each task requires a substantial amount of time. Thus, some of the issues addressed in this chapter apply more to classroom tests that involve a substantial number of items and/or restricted response tasks. For example, if a single extended-response, performance-based task is to be administered the issues of test assembly and some aspects of item analysis are not relevant. Hence, in this chapter we will focus on classroom tests and make note where the same or related considerations apply to performance-based assessments.

ASSEMBLING THE CLASSROOM TEST

The preparation of test items for use in a test is greatly facilitated if the items are properly recorded, if they are written at least several days before they are to be used, and if extra items are constructed.

Recording Test Items

When constructing the test items, it is desirable to write each one on a separate index card, or, if a computer is used, in a form that makes it possible to easily address and retrieve individual items. In addition to the test item, the card should contain information concerning the instructional objectives, the specific learning outcome, and the content measured by the item. A space should also be reserved for item-analysis information, usually on the back of the card, to allow room to record the data each time the item is used. A card containing this information is presented in Figure 12.2.

Item cards provide flexibility. As the items are reviewed and edited, they can be eliminated, added, or revised with very little difficulty. The same holds true when arranging the items for the test: They can be arranged and rearranged merely by sorting the cards. The flexibility of this recording system also makes it easy to add the items to a computer item bank.

Reviewing Test Items and Assessment Tasks

No matter how carefully items or tasks have been prepared, defects inadvertently creep in during construction. As we concentrate on the clarity and conciseness of a question, a verbal clue slips in unnoticed. As we attempt to construct more challenging items, we unwittingly introduce some ambiguity. As we rework a multiple-choice item to make the incorrect choices more plausible, the behavior called forth by the item is unintentionally modified. As we attempt to increase the authenticity of a task for problems faced outside the classroom, we introduce unintended reliance on access to resources that put students from families with limited resources at an unfair disadvantage. In short, we focus so closely on some aspects of item or task construction that we overlook others. This results in an accumulation of unwanted errors that may distort the function of the item or task. Such technical defects can be most easily detected by (1) reviewing the items and tasks after they have been set aside for a few days and (2) asking a fellow teacher to review and criticize them.

In reviewing test items and tasks, we should try to view them from the student's viewpoint, as well as from that of the teacher. From these two vantage points, each item or task should be read carefully and its effectiveness judged. The following questions will help you analyze the quality of each item or task.

1. Is the format appropriate for the learning outcome being measured? If the learning outcome calls for the definition of a term, for example, a supply-type item (e.g., short-answer item) would be appropriate, and a selection-type item (e.g., multiple choice) would be clearly inappropriate. If the learning outcome calls for the ability to collect, organize, integrate, and present information in the form of a coherent argument, then nothing short of a performance-based task will suffice. On the other hand, if the intended outcome was simply the identification of the correct definition, then a selection-type item would be adequate. Thus, the first step is to check whether the format is suitable for the type of student performance described in the testing and assessment plan. The action verb in the statement of each specific learning outcome (e.g., *defines, describes, identifies*) indicates which item format is more appropriate.

2. Does the knowledge, understanding, or thinking skill called forth by the item or task match the specific learning outcome and subject-matter content being measured? When a table of specifications has been used as a basis for constructing items and tasks, this is merely a matter of checking to see whether the item or task is still relevant to the same cell in the table. If, for example, an item's functioning content has shifted during construction, the item either should be modified so that it serves its original purpose or reclassified in light of the new purpose. In any case, the response called forth by an item or task should agree with the purpose for which it is to be used.

3. Is the point of the item or task clear? A careful review of items and tasks often reveals ambiguity, inappropriate vocabulary, and awkward sentence structure that were overlooked during their construction. Returning to items and tasks after they have been set aside for a few days provides a fresh outlook that makes such defects more apparent. The difficulty of the vocabulary and the complexity of the sentence structure must, of course, be judged in terms of the students' maturity level. At all levels, however, ambiguity should be removed. In its final form, each item or task should be so clearly worded that all students understand what is called for. The quality of student responses should be determined solely by whether they possess the knowledge, understanding, or skill being measured.

4. Is the item or task free from excessive verbiage? Often, items become excessively wordy because of awkward sentence structure or the inclusion of nonfunctional material. Some teachers justify the use of an item by including a statement or two concerning the problem's importance. Others expand a simple question into an elaborate story situation to make the item more interesting. Although adding such nonfunctional material may be useful in some instances, items and tasks are generally more effective when the problem is stated as concisely as possible. When reviewing items, the content of each item should be analyzed to determine the functional elements leading to the correct response. If there are any elements that the students may disregard entirely and still respond correctly, they probably should be removed. See "Reviewing and Revising Test Items."

5. Does the item have an answer that would be agreed upon by experts? How well would experts agree about the degree of excellence of task performances? This is seldom a problem with factual material, which usually can be judged as correct or incorrect. It is more of a problem with selection-type items that ask for the best reason, the best method, or the best interpretation. The problem is greatest with tasks requiring extended performances where qualified judges may differ in their evaluation of performances. If experts agree on the best response, fine, but do not include items that require students to endorse someone's unsupported opinion (even if it happens to be yours) and don't evaluate performances on tasks simply in terms of your own personal preferences.

6. Is the item or task free from technical errors and irrelevant clues? The checklists for reviewing each of the item and types, presented in Chapters 6 through 9, list points to consider in searching out technical errors and irrelevant clues. As noted earlier, an irrelevant clue for a selection-type item is any element that leads the poor achiever to the correct answer and thereby prevents the item from functioning as intended. These include (1) grammatical inconsistencies, (2) verbal associations, (3) specific determiners (e.g., words such as *always* and *never*), and (4) some mechanical features, such as correct statements tending to be longer than incorrect ones. Most of these clues can be removed merely by trying to detect them during the item review. They somehow seem more obvious after the items have been set aside for a while.

7. Is the item or task free from racial, ethnic, and sexual bias? A final check should be made to make certain that the vocabulary and problem situation in each item or task would be acceptable to the members of all groups and would have a similar meaning to them. An effort should be made to remove any type of stereotyping, such as always portraying minorities in subservient roles, women in homemaking roles, and the like. A judicious and balanced use of different roles for minorities and males and females should contribute to more effective assessment.

When possible, it can be useful to get fellow teachers to review your test items and assessment tasks. With right–wrong or best-answer items, they should be asked to read each item, indicate the answer, and note any technical defects. If an answer does not agree with the key, it may be because the question is ambiguous. Asking another teacher to "think out loud" when deciding on the answer will usually reveal

Reviewing and Revising Test Items

1. Matching the learning outcome.
   Specific Learning Outcome: Identifies the use of weather instruments.
   Item: Describe how the hygrometer works.
   Improved: The hygrometer is used to measure
   - A. Air pressure.
   - *B. Humidity.
   - C. Rainfall.
   - D. Wind velocity.

2. Clarifying the point of the item and the desired response.
   Item: Earthquakes are detected by _____ .
   Improved: Earthquakes are detected by an instrument called a(n) (seismo-
   graph).

3. Removing excessive verbiage from multiple-choice stems.
   Item: In which one of the following regions of the United States
   can we expect annual rainfall to be the greatest?
   Improved: In which region of the United States is yearly rainfall greatest?
   - A. Midwest
   - B. New England
   - *C. Pacific Northwest
   - D. Southwest

4. Removing excessive verbiage from multiple-choice alternatives.
   Item: In which direction do tornadoes move?
   - *A. They move toward the Northeast.
   - B. They move toward the Northwest.
   - C. They move toward the Southeast.
   - D. They move toward the Southwest.

   Improved: Tornadoes move toward the
   - *A. Northeast.
   - B. Northwest.
   - C. Southeast.
   - D. Southwest.

5. Keeping the reading level low.
   Item: *T F There is a dearth of information concerning the possi-
   bility that life exists on Mars.
   Improved: *T F There is a lack of information concerning life on Mars.

6. Removing verbal clues.
   Item: Evaporation is shown by water changing to
   - A. Dew.
   - B. Ice.
   - *C. Water vapor.

   Improved: Evaporation is shown by water changing to
   - A. Dew.
   - B. Ice.
   - *C. Steam.

the misinterpretation of the question and the source of the ambiguity. For performance tasks requiring extended responses, reviewers identify the nature of the performances that they would expect and the qualities they would look for in evaluating the performances as well as possible defects in the task itself. This is how other persons can be most useful. Reviewers will be less helpful in evaluating the types of responses called forth by the items because this requires a knowledge of what the students have been taught. Only the teacher who prepared the item or task knows for sure whether it is likely to measure understanding or merely the recall of a previously learned response.

When items or tasks have been revised and those to be included in the test or assessment have been tentatively selected, the following questions should be asked:

1. Does the set of items and tasks measure a representative sample of the learning outcomes and course content included in the assessment plan?
2. Are there enough items or tasks for each interpretation to be made?
3. Is the difficulty of the items and tasks appropriate for the measurement purpose and for the students for whom the test or assessment is intended?
4. Are the test items free from overlapping so that the information in one does not provide a clue to the answer in another?

The first question can be answered by comparing the final selection of items and tasks with the table of specifications or other assessment plan. Answers to the last three are determined by reviewing the items and tasks in each content area and as a total set. Affirmative answers to these questions mean the items and tasks are ready to be assembled for administration. See "Review of Test Items Selected from Item Banks" for guidelines on selecting items from published sources.

Arranging Items in the Test

There are various methods of grouping items in an achievement test, and the method will vary somewhat with the use to be made of the results. For most classroom purposes, the items can be arranged by a systematic consideration of (1)

Review of Test Items Selected from Item Banks

Test items selected from workbooks, teachers' guides, instructors' manuals, and item banks are seldom appropriate for use without modification. Thus, before they are used in a classroom test, they should be screened and modified to fit the local instructional program. Both the checklists for reviewing test items and tasks, presented in Chapters 6 through 9, and the list of review questions in this chapter are guides for this purpose. Our aim when selecting items for classroom use should be the same as when constructing them. We want the items to be both technically sound and relevant to what has been taught during the instruction.

the types of items used, (2) the learning outcomes measured, (3) the difficulty of the items, and (4) the subject matter measured.

First and foremost, the items should be arranged in sections by item type. That is, all true–false items should be grouped together, then all matching items, then all multiple-choice items, and so on. This arrangement requires the fewest sets of directions; it is the easiest for the students because they can retain the same mental set throughout each section; and it greatly facilitates scoring. When two or more item types are included in a test, there is also some advantage in keeping the simpler item types together and placing the more complex ones in the test, as follows:

1. True–false or alternative-response items.
2. Matching items.
3. Short-answer items.
4. Multiple-choice items.
5. Interpretive exercises.
6. Restricted-response essay questions.

It is not expected that all item types will appear in the same test. Seldom are more than a few types used, but this is the general order.

Arranging the sections of the test in this order produces a sequence that roughly approximates the complexity of the learning outcomes measured, ranging from the simple to the complex. It is then merely a matter of grouping the items within each item type. For this purpose, items that measure similar outcomes should be placed together and then arranged in order of ascending difficulty. For example, the items in the multiple-choice section might be arranged in the following order: (1) knowledge of terms, (2) knowledge of specific facts, (3) knowledge of principles, and (4) application of principles. Keeping together items that measure similar outcomes is especially helpful in determining the types of learning outcomes causing students the greatest difficulty.

If, for any reason, it is not feasible to group the items by the learning outcomes measured, it is still desirable to arrange them in order of increasing difficulty. Beginning with the easiest items and proceeding gradually to the most difficult has a motivating effect on students. Also, encountering difficult items early in the test often causes students to spend a disproportionate amount of time on such items. If the test is long, they may be forced to omit later questions that they could easily have answered.

With the items classified by item type, the sections of the test and the items within each section can be arranged in order of increasing difficulty. Some shifts in the first four item types may be warranted by the difficulty of the items used, but the interpretive exercises and essays items certainly should be last.

In constructing classroom achievement tests, there is little to be gained by grouping test items according to content. When it appears desirable to do so, such as in separating historical periods, these divisions should be kept to a minimum.

Extended-response essay questions, by their very nature require separate administration. Performance-based tasks or oral presentations requiring extended time or access to such resources as the library, laboratory equipment or a computer for construction of a response, also obviously need to be assigned as separate units rather than as part of a classroom test.

To summarize, the most effective method for organizing items in the typical classroom test is to (1) form sections by item type, (2) group the items within each section by the learning outcomes measured, and (3) arrange both the sections and the items within sections in an ascending order of difficulty. Use subject-matter groupings only when needed for some specific purpose.

Preparing Directions for the Test or Assessment

Teachers sometimes devote considerable time and attention to the construction and assembly of test items or a challenging performance-based assessment and then dash off directions with very little thought. In fact, many teachers include no written directions with their tests, assuming either that the items are self-explanatory or that the students are conditioned to answering the types of items used in the test. Some teachers also use oral directions, but they frequently leave much to be desired. Whether written, oral, or both, the directions should include at least the following points (Gronlund, 1993):

1. Purpose of the test or assessment.
2. Time allowed for completing the test or performing the task.
3. Basis for responding.
4. Procedure for recording the responses.
5. What to do about guessing for selection-type test items.
6. The basis for scoring open-ended or extended responses.

The amount of detail for each of these points depends mainly on the students' age level, the comprehensiveness of the test or assessment, the complexity of the items or tasks, and the students' experience with the testing or assessment procedure used. Using new item types and separate answer sheets, for example, requires much more detailed directions than do familiar items requiring students merely to circle or underline the answer.

Purpose of the Test or Assessment.   The purpose of the test or assessment is usually indicated when the test is announced or at the beginning of the semester when the evaluation procedures are described as a part of the general orientation to the course. Should there be any doubt whether the purpose is clear to all students, however, it could be explained again at the time of testing or assessment. This is usually done orally. The only time a statement of the purpose of the test or assessment needs to be included in the written directions is when it is to be administered to several sections taught by different teachers. Then a written statement of purpose ensures greater uniformity.

Time Allowed for Completing the Test or Performing the Task.   It is helpful to tell the students how much time they will have for the whole test or performance task and how to distribute their time among the parts. When essay questions are included, it is also good to indicate approximately how much time should be allotted to each question. This enables the students to use their time most effectively and prevents less able students from spending too much time on questions that are particularly difficult for them.

Classroom tests or assessments of achievement should generally have liberal time allowances. Except for special computational skills, speed is not important. Our main concern is the level of achievement each student has attained. Were it not for practical considerations like the length of class periods and the pressure of other school activities, there would be no need for any time limits with most classroom achievement tests or assessment tasks.

Judging the amount of time that students will need to complete a given test or assessment task is not simple. It depends on the types of items and tasks used, the age and ability of the students, and the complexity of the learning outcomes measured. As a rough guide, the average high school student should be able to answer two true–false items, one multiple-choice item, or one short-answer item per minute of testing time. Interpretive test items take much more time; the exact amount depends on the length and complexity of the introductory materials. The time required for essay questions and other performance-based assessment tasks can vary anywhere from a few minutes each to several class periods. Also, elementary school students generally require more time per item than high school students, and reading skill is an important determiner of the amount of time needed by a specific group. Experienced teachers familiar with the ability and work habits of a given group of students are in the best position to judge time allotments. It is better to err in the direction of allotting too much time than to deprive some of the slower students from demonstrating their maximum levels of achievement.

Basis for Responding. The directions for each section of the test should indicate the basis for selecting or supplying the answers. With true–false, matching, and multiple-choice items, this part of the directions can be relatively simple. For example, a statement like "select the choice that best completes the statement or answers the question" might be sufficient for multiple-choice items. When interpretive exercises are used, however, more detailed directions are necessary because the basis for the response is much more complex. The directions must clearly indicate the type of interpretation expected. As stated in Chapter 8, each interpretive exercise usually requires its own directions.

It is sometimes good to include sample test items correctly marked so that students can check their understanding of the basis for answering. This practice is especially helpful to elementary school students and to students at other levels when complex item types are used.

As noted earlier, essay questions and other performance-based assessment tasks frequently require special directions concerning the type of response expected. If the selection and organization of ideas are emphasized, for example, this should be indicated to the students so that they have a more adequate basis for responding.

Procedure for Recording Responses. Answers may be recorded on the test form itself or on separate answer sheets. If the test is short, the number of students taking the test is small, or the students are relatively young, answers are generally recorded directly on the test paper. For most other situations, separate answer sheets are preferred because they reduce the time needed for scoring, and they make it possible to use the test papers over again. The latter feature is especially useful when the test is to be given to students in different sections of the same course.

Directions for recording the answer on the test paper itself can be relatively simple. With selection items, it is merely a matter of instructing the students to circle, underline, or check the letter indicating the correct answer. For students in the primary grades, it is usually better to ask them to mark the answer directly by drawing a line under it. With supply items, the directions should indicate where to put the answer and the units in which it is to be expressed if the answer is numerical.

Separate answer sheets are easily constructed, and the directions for their use can be placed on the test paper or on the answer sheet itself. A common type of teacher-made sheet is shown in Figure 12.1. The directions on this sheet are rather general, as they must cover instructions for recording various types of answers. Students are instructed to cross out rather than circle the letters indicating the correct

FIGURE 12.1
Top portion of a teacher-made answer sheet

Course_____   Name _____

Section_____   Date _____

Test _____   Score: Part I_____

                                        Part II _____

                                        Total _____

DIRECTIONS: Read all directions on the test paper carefully and follow them exactly. For each test item, indicate your answer on this sheet by crossing out the appropriate letter (x) or filling the appropriate blank. Be sure that the number on the answer sheet is the same as the number of the test item you are answering.

True-False		Multiple-Choice		Short-Answer	
Item	Answer	Item	Answer	Item	Answer
1	T F	21	A B C D E	41	_____
2	T F	22	A B C D E	42	_____
3	T F	23	A B C D E	43	_____
4	T F	24	A B C D E	44	_____

answers, to facilitate scoring with a stencil key. Circled letters cannot be readily seen through holes in a stencil.

Special answer sheets for machine scoring can be used with classroom tests, but there is no advantage in using them unless machine scoring facilities are readily available and the number of papers to be scored warrants the expense. When machine scoring is used, special directions should be obtained from the company supplying the scoring service.

What to Do About Guessing for Selection-Type Items.

When selection-type items are used, the directions should tell students what to do when they are uncertain of the answer. Should they guess or omit the item? If no instructions are given on this point, the bold students will guess freely, whereas others will answer only those items of which they are fairly certain. The bold students will select some correct answers just by lucky guesses, and thus their scores will be higher than they should be. On the other hand, if the students are instructed "Do not guess" or "Answer only those items of which you are certain," the more timid students will omit many items they could answer correctly. Such students are not very certain about anything, which prevents them from responding even when they are reasonably sure of the answers. With these directions, the bold students will continue to guess, although possibly not quite so wildly.

As Cronbach (1990) pointed out, the tendency to guess or not to guess when in doubt about an item is determined by personality factors and cannot be entirely eliminated by directions that caution against guessing or that promise penalties to those who do guess. The only way to eliminate variations in the tendency to guess is to instruct students to answer every item. When this is done, no student is given a special advantage, and it is unnecessary to correct for guessing in the scoring. Directions such as the following are usually sufficient to communicate this to the students: "Because your score is the number right, be sure to answer every item."

Some teachers object to such directions on the grounds that encouraging guessing is undesirable from an educational standpoint. Most responses to doubtful items are not wild guesses, however, but are guided by some information and understanding. In this respect, they are not too different from the informed guesses we make when we predict weather, judge the possible consequences of a decision, or choose one course of action over another. Problem solving always involves a certain amount of this type of informed guessing.

A more defensible objection to directions that encourage guessing is that the chance errors introduced into the test scores lower the accuracy of measurement. Although this is certainly objectionable, it probably has less influence on the validity of the results than does the systematic advantage given to the bold guessers by the "do not guess" directions.

For liberally timed classroom tests, the "answer every item" directions are favored. But for speed tests and when teachers want to discourage guessing, directions such as the following are a good compromise:

"Answer all items for which you can find some reasonable basis for answering, even though you are not completely sure of the answer. Do not guess wildly, however, because there will be a correction for guessing."

The Basis for Scoring Extended Responses.   For tasks requiring extended written responses, it is important to tell students the basis for scoring. If there are several essay questions, for example, the number of points possible for the response to each question should be indicated. The importance attached to factors such as factual accuracy, organization, comprehensiveness, persuasiveness, and originality can be indicated. Students should also be informed if their responses will be graded for mechanics. (See the accompanying "Guidelines" box.)

Reproducing the Test

In preparing the test materials for reproduction, it is important that the items be spaced and arranged so that they can be read, answered, and scored with the least amount of difficulty. Cramming too many test items onto a page is poor economy. What little paper is saved will not make up for the time and confusion that results during the administration and scoring of the test.

GUIDELINES

Helping Students Prepare for Tests and Assessments

General Preparation

1. Suggest ways of studying.
2. Give practice tasks like those to be used.
3. Teach test-taking skills.
4. Teach how to write well-organized essay answers.
5. Stress the value of tests and assessments for improving learning.

Preparation for Each Test or Assessment

1. Announce in advance when the test or assessment will be given.
2. Describe the conditions of administration (e.g., one hour, closed book).
3. Describe the length and the types of items or tasks to be used (e.g., twenty multiple-choice, three essay items, one extended-response performance task).
4. Describe the content and type of performance to be covered (a table of specifications is useful for this).
5. Describe how the test or assessment will be scored and how the results will be used.
6. Give the students sample items and tasks similar to those to be used (use a short practice test or present items orally and discuss responses).
7. Relieve anxiety by using a positive approach in describing the test or assessment and its usefulness.

All test items should have generous borders. Multiple-choice items should have the alternatives listed in a vertical column beneath the stem of the item, rather than across the page. Items should not be split, with parts of the item on two different pages. With interpretive exercises, the introductory materials can sometimes be placed on a facing page or separate sheet, with all of the items referring to it on a single page.

Unless a separate answer sheet is used, the space for answering should be down one side of the page, preferably the left. The most convenient method of response is circling the letter of the correct answer. With this arrangement, scoring is simply a matter of placing a strip scoring key beside the column of answers.

Test items should be numbered consecutively throughout the test. Each test item will need to be identified during discussion of the test and for other purposes such as item analysis. When separate answer sheets are used, consecutive numbering is, of course, indispensable.

It is desirable to proofread the entire test or assessment before it is administered. Charts, graphs, and other pictorial material must be checked to ensure that the reproduction has been accurate and the details clear.

ADMINISTERING AND SCORING CLASSROOM TESTS AND ASSESSMENTS

The same care that went into the preparation of the test or assessment should be carried over into its administration and scoring. Here we are concerned with (1) providing optimum conditions for obtaining the students' responses and (2) selecting convenient and accurate procedures for scoring the results.

Administration

The guiding principle in administering any classroom test or assessment is that all students must be given a fair chance to demonstrate their achievement of the learning outcomes being measured. This means a physical and psychological environment conducive to their best efforts and the control of factors that might interfere with valid measurement.

Physical conditions such as adequate work space, quiet, proper light and ventilation, and comfortable temperature are sufficiently familiar to teachers to warrant little attention here. Of greater importance, but frequently neglected, are the psychological conditions influencing results. Students will not perform at their best if they are tense and anxious during testing. Some of the things that create excessive test anxiety are

1. Threatening students with tests if they do not behave.
2. Warning students to do their best "because this test is important."
3. Telling students they must work fast in order to finish on time.
4. Threatening dire consequences if they fail.

The antidote to test anxiety is to convey to the students, by both word and deed, that the test and assessment results are to be used to help them improve their learning. They also should be reassured that the time limits are adequate to allow them to complete the test or assessment tasks. This, of course, assumes that the test and assessment results will be used to improve learning and that the time limits are adequate.

The time of testing can also influence the results. If tests are administered just before the "big game" or the "big dance," the results may not be representative. Furthermore, for some students, fatigue, the onset of illness, or worry about a particular problem may prevent maximum performance. Arranging the time of testing accordingly and permitting its postponement when appropriate can enhance the validity of the results.

Actual administration is relatively simple, because a properly prepared test or assessment is practically self-administering. Oral directions, if used, should be presented clearly. Any sample problems or illustrations put on the blackboard should be kept brief and simple. Beyond this, suggestions for administration consist mainly of things to avoid.

1. *Do not talk unnecessarily before letting students start working.* When a teacher announces that there will be "a full forty minutes" to complete the test and then talks for the first ten minutes, students feel that they are being unfairly deprived of testing time. Besides, just before a test is no time to make assignments, admonish the class, or introduce next week's topic. Students are mentally set for the test and will ignore anything not pertaining to the test for fear it will hinder their recall of information needed to answer the questions. Thus, the well-intentioned remarks merely increase anxiety toward the test and create hostility toward the teacher.

2. *Keep interruptions to a minimum.*   At times, a student will ask to have an ambiguous item clarified, and it may be beneficial to explain the item to the entire group at the same time. Such interruptions are necessary but should be kept to a minimum. All other distractions outside and inside the classroom should, of course, also be eliminated when possible. It is sometimes helpful to hang a "Do not disturb—TESTING" sign outside the door.

3. *Avoid giving hints to students who ask about individual items.*   If the item is ambiguous, it should be clarified for the entire group, as indicated earlier. If it is not ambiguous, refrain from helping the student answer it. Refraining from giving hints to students who ask for help is especially difficult for beginning teachers. But giving unfair aid to some students (the bold, the apple polishers, and so on) decreases the validity of the results and lowers class morale.

4. *Discourage cheating, if necessary.*   When there is good teacher–student rapport and the students view tests as helpful rather than harmful, cheating is usually not a problem. Under other conditions, however, it might be necessary to discourage cheating by special seating arrangements and careful supervision. Receiving unauthorized help from other students during a test has the same deleterious effect on validity and class morale as does receiving special hints from the teacher. We are interested in students' doing their best; but for valid results, their scores must be based on their own unaided efforts. See "Steps to Prevent Cheating."

Steps to Prevent Cheating

1. Take special precautions to keep the test secure during preparation, storage, and administration.
2. Have students clear off the tops of their desks (for adequate work space and to prevent use of notes).
3. If scratch paper is used (e.g., for math problems), have it turned in with the test.
4. Proctor the testing session carefully (e.g., walk around the room periodically and observe how the students are doing).
5. Use special seating arrangements, if possible (e.g., leave an empty row of seats between students).
6. Use two forms of the test and give a different form to each row of students (for this purpose, use the same test but simply rearrange the order of the items for the second form).
7. Prepare tests that students will view as relevant, fair, and useful.
8. Create and maintain a positive attitude concerning the value of tests for improving learning.

Scoring the Test

Procedures for scoring performance-based assessments were described in Chapter 10. Here we shall discuss scoring objective items.

If the students' answers are recorded on the test paper itself, a scoring key can be made by marking the correct answers on a blank copy of the test. Scoring then is simply a matter of comparing the columns of answers on this master copy with the columns of answers on each student's paper. A strip key, which consists merely of strips of paper on which the columns of answers are recorded, may also be used if more convenient. These can easily be prepared by cutting the columns of answers from the master copy of the test and mounting them on strips of cardboard cut from manila folders.

When separate answer sheets are used, a scoring stencil is most convenient. This is a blank answer sheet with holes punched where the correct answers should appear. The stencil is laid over each answer sheet, and the number of answer checks appearing through the holes are counted. When this type of scoring procedure is used, each test paper should also be scanned to make certain that only one answer was marked for each item. Any item containing more than one answer should be eliminated from the scoring.

As each test paper is scored, mark each item that is answered incorrectly. With multiple-choice items, a good practice is to draw a red line through the correct answer of the missed items rather than through the student's wrong answers. This will indicate to the student those items missed and at the same time will indicate the correct answers. Time will be saved and confusion avoided during discussion of the test. Marking the correct answers of missed items is especially simple with a scoring stencil. When no answer check appears through a hole in the stencil, a red line is drawn across the hole.

In scoring objective tests, each correct answer is usually counted as one point, because an arbitrary weighing of items makes little difference in the students' final scores. If some items are counted two points, some one point, and some one-half point, the scoring will be more complicated without any accompanying benefits. Scores based on such weightings will be similar to the simpler procedure of counting each item one point. When a test consists of a combination of objective items and a few, more time-consuming, essay questions, however, more than a single point is needed to distinguish several levels of response and to reflect the disproportionate time devoted to each of the essay questions.

When students are told to answer every item on the test, a student's score is simply the number of items answered correctly. There is no need to consider wrong answers or to correct for guessing. When all students answer every item on a test, the rank of the students' scores will be same whether the number right or a correction for guessing is used.

See "Correction for Guessing" for a simple formula that is sometimes used. The formula is based on the questionable assumption that students either know the

Correction for Guessing

Correcting for guessing is usually done when students do not have sufficient time to complete all items on the test and when they have been instructed that there will be a penalty for guessing. The most common formula used for this purpose is the following:

$$\text{Score} = \text{Right} - \frac{\text{Wrong}}{n - 1}$$

In this formula, n is the number of alternatives for an item. Thus, the formula applies to various selection-type items as follows:

True–False Items

$$S = R - \frac{W}{2 - 1}$$

(or)

$$S = R - W$$

Multiple-Choice Items

A. Three alternatives $S = R - \dfrac{W}{2}$

B. Four alternatives $S = R - \dfrac{W}{3}$

C. Five alternatives $S = R - \dfrac{W}{4}$

answer or they guess it at random. It is not needed when students are allowed sufficient time to respond to all the items on the test. Thus, it is recommended that it *not* be used with the ordinary classroom test. The only exception is when the test is speeded to the extent that students complete different numbers of items. Here its use is defensible because students can increase their scores appreciably by rapidly (and blindly) guessing at the remaining untried items just before the testing period ends.

APPRAISING CLASSROOM TESTS AND ASSESSMENTS

Before a classroom test or assessment has been administered, it should be evaluated according to the points discussed earlier. The most important of these points are listed in the "Checklist for Evaluating the Classroom Test." Most of these questions also apply to a performance-based assessment. A *yes* response to each of these questions indicates that the test or the assessment has been carefully prepared and will probably function effectively.

After a test or assessment has been scored and the students have discussed the results it is often simply discarded. Except for the students' criticism during class discussion, which helps identify some of the defective items or ambiguities in a task, the teacher has little evidence concerning the quality of the test or assessment that was used. Much of the careful planning and hard work that went into the preparation of the test or assessment is wasted. A better procedure is to appraise the effectiveness of the test items and assessment tasks and to build a file of high-quality items and tasks for future use.

Determining Item and Task Effectiveness

The effectiveness of each test item can be determined by analyzing student responses to it. Item analysis is generally associated with a norm-referenced perspective. This is natural, because the results of an item analysis can be used to select items of desired difficulty that best discriminate between high- and low-achieving students. Selection on these grounds is not relevant from a criterion-referenced perspective. From both perspectives, however, the results of an item analysis can be useful in identifying faulty items and can provide information about student misconceptions and topics that need additional work.

Item analysis is usually designed to answer questions such as the following:

1. Did the item function as intended?
2. Were the test items of appropriate difficulty?
3. Were the test items free of irrelevant clues and other defects?
4. Was each of the distracters effective (in multiple-choice items)?

Answers to all but Question 2 are relevant in constructing future tests based on either a norm-referenced or a criterion-referenced perspective. The answer to Question 2 is only relevant when planning future norm-referenced tests; however, it is relevant in instructional planning regardless of perspective.

	CHECKLIST

Evaluating the Classroom Test

Adequacy of Test Plan

	Yes	No
1. Does the test plan adequately describe the instructional objectives and the content to be measured?	_____	_____
2. Does the test plan clearly indicate the relative emphasis to be given to each objective and each content area?	_____	_____

Adequacy of Test Items

	Yes	No
3. Is the format of each item suitable for the learning outcome being measured (*appropriateness*)?	_____	_____
4. Does each test item require pupils to demonstrate the performance described in the specific learning outcome it measures (*relevance*)?	_____	_____
5. Does each test item present a clear and definite task to be performed (*clarity*)?	_____	_____
6. Is each test item presented in simple, readable language and free from excessive verbiage (*conciseness*)?	_____	_____
7. Is each test item of appropriate difficulty for the type of test constructed (*ideal difficulty*)?	_____	_____
8. Does each test item have an answer that would be agreed upon by experts (*correctness*)?	_____	_____
9. Is each test item free from technical errors and irrelevant clues (*technical soundness*)?	_____	_____

Answers to such questions are of obvious value in selecting or revising items for future use. The benefits of item analysis are not limited to the improvement of individual test items, however. There are a number of fringe benefits of special value to classroom teachers. The most important of these are the following:

1. Item-analysis data provide a basis for efficient class discussion of the test results.   Knowing how effectively each item functioned in measuring achievement makes it possible to confine the discussion to those areas most helpful to students. Easy items that were answered correctly by all students can be omitted from the discussion, and the concepts in those items causing students the greatest difficulty can receive special emphasis. Similarly, misinformation and

Adequacy of Test Items, Continued

	Yes	No
10. Is each test item free from racial, ethic, and sexual bias (*cultural fairness*)?	_____	_____
11. Is each test item independent of the other items in the test (*independence*)?	_____	_____
12. Is there an adequate number of test items for each learning outcome (*sample adequacy*)?	_____	_____

Adequacy of Test Format and Directions

	Yes	No
13. Are test items of the same type grouped together in the test (or within sections of the test)?	_____	_____
14. Are the test items arranged from easy to more difficult within sections of the test and the test as a whole?	_____	_____
15. Are the test items numbered in sequence?	_____	_____
16. Is the answer space clearly indicated (on the test itself or on a separate answer sheet), and is each answer space related to its corresponding test item?	_____	_____
17. Are the correct answers distributed in such a way that there is no detectable pattern?	_____	_____
18. Is the test material well spaced, legible, and free of typographical errors?	_____	_____
19. Are there directions for each section of the test and the test as a whole?	_____	_____
20. Are the directions clear and concise?	_____	_____

misunderstandings reflected in the choice of particular distracters can be corrected. Item analysis will also expose technical defects in items. During discussion, defective items can be pointed out to students, saving much time and heated discussion concerning the unfairness of these items. If an item is ambiguous and two answers can be defended equally well, both answers should be counted correct and the scoring adjusted accordingly.

2. Item-analysis data provide a basis for remedial work. Although discussing the test results in class can clarify and correct many specific points, item analysis frequently brings to light general areas of weakness requiring more extended attention. In an arithmetic test, for example, item analysis may reveal that the students are fairly proficient in arithmetic skills but are having difficulty with problems requiring the application of these skills. In other subjects, item analysis may indicate a general weakness in knowledge of technical vocabulary, in an understanding of principles, or in the ability to interpret data. Such information makes it possible to focus remedial work directly on the particular areas of weakness.

3.   Item-analysis data provide a basis for the general improvement of classroom instruction.   In addition to the preceding uses, item-analysis data can assist in evaluating appropriateness of the learning outcomes and course content for the particular students being taught. For example, material that is consistently too simple or too difficult for the students might suggest curriculum revisions or shifts in teaching emphasis. Similarly, errors in student thinking that persistently appear in item-analysis data might direct attention to the need for more effective teaching procedures. In these and similar ways, item-analysis data can reveal instructional weaknesses and clues for improvement.

4.   Item-analysis procedures provide a basis for increased skill in test construction.   Item analysis reveals ambiguities, clues, ineffective distracters, and other technical defects that were missed during the test's preparation. This information is used directly in revising the test items for future use. In addition to the improvement of the specific items, however, we derive benefits from the procedure itself. As we analyze students' responses to items, we become increasingly aware of technical defects and what causes them. When revising the items, we gain experience in rewording statements so that they are clear, rewriting distracters so that they are more plausible, and modifying items so that they are at a more appropriate level of difficulty. As a consequence, our general test construction skills improve.

Simplified Item-Analysis Procedures

A simplified form of item analysis is all that is necessary or warranted for classroom tests. Because most classroom groups consist of 20 to 40 students, an especially useful procedure is to compare the responses of the ten highest-scoring students with the responses of the ten lowest-scoring students. As we shall see later, keeping the upper and lower groups at ten students each simplifies the interpretation of the results. It also is a reasonable number for analysis in groups of 20 to 40 students. For example, with a small classroom group, like that of 20 students, it is best to use the upper and lower halves to obtain dependable data, whereas with a larger group, like that of 40 students, use of the upper and lower 25 percent is quite satisfactory. For more refined analysis, the upper and lower 27 percent is often recommended, and most statistical guides are based on that percentage.

To illustrate the method of item analysis, suppose that we have just finished scoring 32 test papers for a sixth-grade science unit on weather. Our item analysis might then proceed as follows:

1. Rank the 32 test papers in order from the highest to the lowest score.
2. Select the 10 papers within the highest total scores and the 10 papers with the lowest total scores.

3. Put aside the middle 12 papers as they will not be used in the analysis.
4. For each test item, tabulate the number of students in the upper and lower groups who selected each alternative. This tabulation can be made directly on the test paper or on the test item card, as shown in Figure 12.2.
5. Compute the difficulty of each item (percentage of students who got the item right).
6. Compute the discriminating power of each item (difference between the number of students in the upper and lower groups who got the item right).
7. Evaluate the effectiveness of distracters in each item (attractiveness of the incorrect alternatives).

The first steps of this procedure are merely a convenient tabulation of student responses from which we can readily determine item difficulty, item discriminating power, and the effectiveness of each distracter. This latter information can frequently be obtained simply by inspecting the item-analysis data. Note that in Figure 12.2, for

FIGURE 12.2
Test item card with item-analysis data recorded on back

COURSE _____Science_____ UNIT _____Weather_____

OBJECTIVE _____Identifies use of instruments_____

ITEM

Which of the following is most useful in weather forecasting?
   A. Anemometer
   B. Barometer
   C. Thermometer
   D. Rain gauge

(Back of Item Card)

		ITEM ANALYSIS DATA							
Dates		Alternatives						Indexes	
Used	Pupils	A	Ⓑ	C	D	E	Omits	Diff.	Disc.
4/25/95	Upper 10	0	10	0	0		0	70%	.60
	Lower 10	2	4	1	3		0		
	Upper								
	Lower								
	Upper								
	Lower								
Comment:									

example, ten students in the upper group and four students in the lower group selected the correct alternative, *B*. Thus, 14 of the 20 students got the item right, indicating that the item has a fairly low level of difficulty. Because more students in the upper group than in the lower group got the item right, it is discriminating positively. That is, it is distinguishing between high and low achievers (as determined by the total test score). Finally, because all the alternatives were selected by some of the students in the lower group, the distracters (Alternatives *A, C,* and *D*) appear to be operating effectively.

From a norm-referenced perspective the fact that all ten students with the highest test scores but only four of the ten with the lowest scores answered the item correctly makes this item a good candidate for use in the future because it helps discriminate between high and low achieving students. Although this would not be a basis for selecting an item for a criterion-referenced test, it does provide an indication that the item is not miskeyed or being misinterpreted by the higher-achieving students. It also provides an indication that some students do not understand the uses of instruments listed.

Although item analysis by inspection will reveal the general effectiveness of a test item and is satisfactory for most classroom purposes, it is sometimes useful to obtain a more precise estimate of item difficulty and discriminating power. This can be done by applying relatively simple formulas to the item-analysis data.

Computing Item Difficulty.   The difficulty of a test item is indicated by the percentage of students who get the item right. Hence, we can compute item difficulty (*P*) by means of the following formula, in which *R* equals the number of students who got the item right, and *T* equals the total number of students who tried the item.

$$P = \frac{R}{T} \times 100$$

Applying this formula to the item-analysis data in Figure 12.2, our index of item difficulty is 70 percent, as follows:

$$P = \frac{14}{20} \times 100 = 70 \text{ percent}$$

In computing item difficulty from item-analysis data, our calculation is based on the upper and lower groups only. We assume that the responses of students in the middle group follow essentially the same pattern. This estimate of difficulty is sufficiently accurate for classroom use and is easily obtained because the needed figures can be taken directly from the item-analysis data.

Note that because our item analysis is based on ten in the upper group and ten in the lower group, all we need to do to obtain item difficulty is to divide the number getting it right by two (14/2 = 7), move the decimal point one place to the right (70), and add the percent sign (70%). In other words, 14 out of 20 is the same as 7 out of 10, which is 70 percent. If 13 students were to get the item right, item difficulty would be 6.5 out of 10 (13/2 = 6.5), or 65 percent. This may seem a bit confusing at first, but once you grasp the idea, you can compute item difficulty very quickly. As noted earlier, the ease of interpreting item statistics is one of the advantages of using ten in each group. If more (or fewer) than ten are used, the formula for computing item difficulty is the same, but it is much more difficult to compute the results mentally.

Computing Item Discriminating Power. As we have already stated, an item discriminates positively if more students in the upper group than the lower group get the item right. Positive discrimination indicates that the item is discriminating in the same direction as the total test score. Because we assume that the total test score reflects achievement of desired objectives, we would like all of our test items to show positive discrimination.

The discriminating power of an achievement test item refers to the degree to which it discriminates between students with high and low achievement. Item discriminating power (D) can be obtained by subtracting the number of students in the lower group who get the item right (R_L) from the number of students in the upper group who get the item right (R_U) and dividing by one-half the total number of students included in the item analysis ($.5T$). Summarized in formula form, it is:

$$D = \frac{R_U - R_L}{.5T}$$

Applying this formula to the item-analysis data in Figure 12.2, we obtain an index of discriminating power of .60, as follows:

$$D = \frac{10 - 4}{10} = .60$$

This indicates approximately average discriminating power. An item with maximum positive discriminating power is one in which all students in the upper group get the item right and all the students in the lower group get the item wrong. This results in an index of 1.00, as follows:

$$D = \frac{10 - 0}{10} = 1.00$$

An item with no discriminating power is one in which an equal number of students in both the upper and lower groups get the item right. This results in an index of .00, as follows:

$$D = \frac{10 - 10}{10} = .00$$

When our item analysis is based on 10 in the upper group and 10 in the lower group, the index of discriminating power, like item difficulty, can be computed easily and quickly. All we need to do is subtract the number in the lower group getting it right from the number in the upper group getting it right ($10 - 4 = 6$), move the decimal point one to the left (.6), and add a zero after it (.60). With ten in each group the index of discrimination is essentially the difference between the number getting it right in the two groups with the decimal point moved one to the left. The zero is added simply because the index of discrimination is usually carried to two decimal places. With more than ten in each group, we could not make these simple mental calculations but would have to resort to use of the formula.

Evaluating the Effectiveness of Distracters.   How well each distracter is operating can be determined by inspection, and so there is no need to calculate an index of effectiveness, although the formula for discriminating power can be used for this purpose. In general, a good distracter attracts more students from the lower group than the upper group. Thus, it should discriminate between the upper and lower groups in a manner opposite to that of the correct alternative. An examination of the following item-analysis data will illustrate the ease with which the effectiveness of distracters can be determined by inspection. Alternative A is the correct answer.

Alternatives	A	B	C	D	Omits
Upper 10	5	4	0	1	0
Lower 10	3	2	0	5	0

First, note that the item discriminates positively, because five in the upper group and three in the lower group got the item right. The index of discriminating power is fairly low however (D = .20), and this may be partly due to the ineffectiveness of some of the distracters. Alternative B is a poor distracter because it attracts more students from the upper group than from the lower group. This is most likely due to some ambiguity in the statement of the item. Alternative C is evidently not a plausible distracter because it attracted no one. Alternative D is functioning as intended, for it attracts a larger proportion of students from the lower group. Thus, the discriminating power of this item can probably be improved by removing any ambiguity in the statement of the item and revising or replacing Alternatives B and C. The specific changes must, of course, be based on an inspection of the test item itself; item-analysis data merely indicate poorly functioning items, not the cause of the poor functioning.

In some cases, an examination of the test item will reveal no obvious error in the structure of the item and it may be best to try it with a second group. The number of cases involved is so small that considerable variation in student response can be expected from one group to another. A casual comment by the teacher, or some other classroom event, may cause students to select or reject a particular alternative.

Recording Item-Analysis Data on the Test Paper.   There is some advantage in recording item-analysis data directly on the test paper that was used as a scoring key, as shown in Figure 12.3, and making the calculations mentally. These mental calculations for the two items in Figure 12.3 are summarized in Figure 12.4. Thus, during discussion of the test results, you can quickly judge the difficulty and discriminating power of each item and the effectiveness of the distracters. This will help determine how much discussion to devote to any particular item, the types of misconceptions students may have (by the distracters selected), and which items are so defective that they might be discounted. See "Item Analysis by Computer" for a look at another way to analyze test items.

FIGURE 12.3
Sample test scoring key with item analysis data added (U = upper 10 pupils, L = lower 10 pupils)

WEATHER UNIT

Name _____ Date _____

Directions. This test will measure what you have learned during the unit on weather. There are 40 objective questions in the test. You will have the entire class period to complete it.

For each question there are several possible answers. Select the *best* answer and indicate it by encircling the letter of your answer.

Your score will be the number of questions answered correctly, so *be sure to answer every question.*

KNOWLEDGE OF FACTS

U	L	
0	1	1. Which of these instruments is used to measure humidity?
		A. Anemometer
0	1	B. Barometer
10	8	©Hygrometer
0	0	D. Thermometer

U	L	
1	2	2. What does the Beaufort scale indicate on a weather map?
		A. Air pressure
0	1	B. Air temperature
0	1	C. Precipitation
9	6	ⒹWind velocity

FIGURE 12.4
Illustrative item analysis calculations from data in Figure 12.3

Item Difficulty Index

Steps (using numbers to left of answer)	*Item 1*	*Item 2*
1. Add U + L and divide by 2.	18/2 = 9	15/2 = 7.5
2. Move decimal point one to the right.	90	75
3. Add the percent sign.	90%	75%

Item Discrimination Index

Steps (using numbers to left of answer)	*Item 1*	*Item 2*
1. Subtract U − L.	10 − 8 = 2	9 − 6 = 3
2. Move decimal point one to the left.	.2	.3
3. Add a zero after the number.	.20	.30

Item Analysis by Computer

Many schools now have computers (or have access to them) that can both score and analyze tests. The computer printout will provide item-analysis information, a reliability coefficient, standard error of measurement for the test, and various other types of information concerning the performance of the individuals tested and the characteristics of the test. The nature of the information depends on the sophistication of the computer and the program that is used.

When item analysis is done by computer, the scores of the entire group are usually used rather than just the scores of the upper and lower groups. The total set of scores might be divided into two, three, four, or five levels, depending on the size of the group and the types of analyses. Item-analysis data on a computer printout based on 50 pupils might appear as follows, for each item:

Item Response Pattern

Item 1	A	B	C	D	E	Omit	Total	Item Statistics
Upper 30%	1	1	12	1	0	0	15	Difficulty 60%
Middle 40%	2	2	12	3	1	0	20	Discrimination .40
Lower 30%	2	3	6	3	1	0	15	
Total	5	6	30	7	2	0	50	

The item-response data indicate how many pupils, at each level, selected the correct answer (C) and how many selected each of the distracters. The item statistics at the right indicate the index of difficulty and the index of discrimination for this item. Some computer programs report only the item statistics, but the item-response pattern is especially valuable for evaluating the effectiveness of the distracters and planning for item revision. Alternative E, for example, should be examined to determine whether it can be replaced by a more effective distracter.

Cautions in Interpreting Item-Analysis Results

Item analysis is a quick, simple technique for appraising the effectiveness of individual test items. The information from such an analysis is limited in many ways, however, and must be interpreted accordingly. The following are some of the major cautions to observe:

1. *Item discriminating power does not indicate item validity.* In our description of item analysis, we used the total test score as a basis for selecting the upper group (high achievers) and the lower group (low achievers). This is the most common procedure because comparable measures of achievement are usually not available. Ideally, we would examine each test item in relation to some independent measure of achievement. However, the best measure of the particular achievement we are interested in assessing is usually the total score on the achievement test we have constructed because each classroom test is related to specific instructional objectives and course content. Even standardized tests in the same content area are usually inadequate as independent criteria, because they are aimed at more general objectives than those measured by a classroom test in a particular course.

Using the total score from our classroom test as a basis for selecting high and low achievers is perfectly legitimate as long as we remember that we are using an internal criterion. In doing so, our item analysis offers evidence concerning the internal consistency of the test rather than its validity. That is, we are determining how effectively each test item is measuring whatever the whole test is measuring. Such item-analysis data can be interpreted as evidence of item validity only when the validity of the total test has been proven or can be legitimately assumed. This is seldom possible with classroom tests so we must be satisfied with a more limited interpretation of our item analysis data.

2. *A low index of discriminating power does not necessarily indicate a defective item.* Items that discriminate poorly between high and low achievers should be examined for the possible presence of ambiguity, clues, and other technical defects. If none is found and the items measure an important learning outcome, they should be retained for future use. Any item that discriminates in a positive direction can contribute to the measurement of student achievement, and low indexes of discrimination are frequently obtained for reasons other than technical defects.

Classroom achievement tests are usually designed to measure several different types of learning outcomes (knowledge, understanding, application, and so on). When this is the case, test items that represent an area receiving relatively little emphasis will tend to have poor discriminating power. For example, if a test has forty items measuring knowledge of facts and ten items measuring understanding, the latter items can be expected to have low indexes of discrimination. This is because the items measuring understanding have less representation in the total test score and there is typically a low correlation between measures of knowledge and measures of understanding. Low indexes of discrimination here merely indicate that these items are measuring something different from what the major part of the test is measuring. Removing such items from the test would make it a more homogeneous measure of knowledge outcomes, but it would also damage the test's validity because it would no longer measure learning outcomes in the understanding area. Because most classroom tests measure a variety of types of learning outcomes, low positive indexes of discrimination are the rule rather than the exception.

Another factor that influences discriminating power is the difficulty of the item. Those items at the 50 percent level of difficulty make maximum discriminating power possible, because only at this level of difficulty can all students in the upper half of the group get the item right, and all students in the lower half get it wrong. The 50 percent level of difficulty does not guarantee maximum discriminating power, but merely makes it possible. If half the students in the upper group and half the students in the lower group got the item right, the level of difficulty would still be 50 percent, but the index of discrimination would be zero. As we move away from the 50 percent level of difficulty toward easier or more difficult items, the index of discriminating power becomes smaller. Thus, items that are very easy or very difficult have low indexes of discriminating power. Sometimes it is necessary or desirable to retain such items, however, in order to measure a representative sample of learning outcomes and course content.

To summarize, a low index of discriminating power should alert us to the possible presence of technical defects in a test item but should not cause us to discard an otherwise worthwhile item. A well-constructed achievement test will, of necessity, contain items with low discriminating power; to discard them would result in a less, rather than more, valid test.

3.   *Item-analysis data from small samples are highly tentative.*   Item-analysis procedures focus our attention so directly on a test item's difficulty and discriminating power that we are commonly misled into believing that these are fixed, unchanging characteristics. This, of course, is not true. Item-analysis data will vary from one group to another, depending on the students' level of ability, educational background, and type of instruction they have had. Add to this the small number of students available for analyzing the items in our classroom tests, and the tentative nature of our item-analysis data becomes readily apparent. If just a few students change their responses, our indexes of difficulty and discriminating power can be increased or decreased by a considerable amount.

The tentative nature of item-analysis data should discourage us from making fine distinctions among items on the basis of indexes of difficulty and discriminating power. If an item is discriminating in a positive direction, all of the alternatives are functioning effectively, and it has no apparent defects, it can be considered satisfactory from a technical standpoint. The important question then is *not* how high the index of discriminating power is, but, whether the item measures an important learning outcome. In the final analysis, the worth of an achievement test item must be based on logical, rather than statistical, considerations.

When used with norm-referenced classroom tests, item analysis provides us with a general appraisal of the functional effectiveness of the test items, a means for detecting defects, and a method for identifying instructional weaknesses. For these purposes, the tentative nature of item-analysis data is relatively unimportant. When we record indexes of item difficulty or discriminating power on item cards for future use, we should interpret them as rough approximations only. As such, they are still superior to our unaided estimates of item difficulty and discriminating power.

Application of Item Analysis Principles with Performance-Based Assessments

Item analysis procedures have somewhat limited applicability with performance-based assessments, primarily because such assessments generally contain a relatively small number of tasks. If the assessment has several tasks, however, the general principles can be readily adapted for use. One necessary modification results from the fact that scores on performance-based tasks almost always involve more than a simple 0 or 1. For example, each task might have possible scores of 0, 1, 2, 3, or 4. Still, a comparison of the individual task scores for the 10 highest and 10 lowest scoring students can be useful.

Suppose, for example, that a performance assessment consisted of five separate tasks, each of which had possible scores ranging from low of 0 for no response or a response that was unrelated to the task to a 4 for a complete and well-elaborated response. Possible total scores for the set of five tasks would range from 0 to 20. As before, the total scores would be ranked to identify the ten highest and the ten lowest scores. The individual task scores for these two groups of students would then be summarized as illustrated in Figure 12.5.

The ten highest-achieving students generally have higher scores on each item than the ten lowest-achieving students. The higher average score on Task 1 for the upper ten students than for the lower ten indicates that the task discriminates between these two groups. The equal means on Task 2 for the two groups of students indicate that the latter task does not discriminate.

A number of possible reasons for results such as those shown in Figure 12.5 need to be considered. It is possible that Task 2 simply has less similarity than does Task 1 to the remaining tasks. That is, it calls for different skills and abilities than the other four tasks. Or it may be that the type of performance expected on Task 2 is ambiguous. If careful review of the task in comparison to the other four tasks leads to the first conclusion, then there is no need to revise or discard the task. If a review leads to the second conclusion, however, then the task would need to be either discarded or revised to clarify what is intended.

FIGURE 12.5
Illustrative analysis of scores on two tasks

Task 1

Score	0	1	2	3	4	Average
Upper 10	0	0	1	4	5	3.4
Lower 10	1	3	4	2	0	1.7

Task 2

Score	0	1	2	3	4	Average
Upper 10	2	2	3	1	1	1.5
Lower 10	3	2	2	3	0	1.5

BUILDING A FILE OF EFFECTIVE ITEMS AND TASKS

A file of effective items and tasks can be built and maintained easily if items and tasks are recorded on cards like the one shown in Figure 12.2. By indicating on the card both the objective and the content area being measured, it is possible to file the cards under both headings. Course content can be used as major categories, with the objectives forming the subcategories. For example, the item in Figure 12.2 measures knowledge of weather instruments, so it is placed in the first category under weather instruments, as follows:

Weather Instruments

> Knowledge
>
> Understanding
>
> Application

This type of filing system makes it possible to select items or tasks in accordance with any table of specifications in the particular area covered by the file. See "Item Banking by Computer" for a description of another way to build an assessment bank.

Item Banking by Computer

Some schools use computers to maintain item files (or item pools) for each of the various subjects and grade levels. The items are coded and stored by the test builder for easy retrieval. The code includes such things as instructional level, subject area, instructional objective, content topic, and item statistics (e.g., difficulty and discrimination indexes). This makes it possible to select items and build a test that matches a particular set of test specifications. The coded information concerning each item also aids in arranging the items in the test (e.g., by objective, order of difficulty).

The computer will print out these custom-designed tests and will also score, report, and analyze them. Some test publishers provide microcomputer programs that include item banking, test generation, scoring, and related functions (e.g., *SRA Micro Test Administration System* by Science Research Associates). See test publishers' catalogues for details on the microcomputer programs each offers. Publishers' addresses are listed in Appendix C.

Computer item banks are like any other item pool—*you get out only what you put in*. If you store ineffective items, you will get back ineffective items. Thus, item banking by computer requires careful screening of the items before they are entered. This is usually done by a committee of teachers in each department or instructional area, using checklists like those presented earlier in this book.

Building a file of effective items and tasks is a little like building a bank account. The first several years are concerned mainly with making deposits; withdrawals must be delayed until a sufficient reserve is accumulated. Thus, items and tasks are recorded on cards as they are constructed; information from analyses of student responses is added after the items and tasks have been used; and then the effective items and tasks are deposited in the file. At first it seems to be additional work, with very little return. However, in a few years it is possible to start using some of the items and tasks from the file and supplementing these with newly constructed items and tasks. As the file grows, it becomes possible to select the majority of the items and tasks from the file for any given test or assessment without repeating them too frequently. To prevent using a test item or assessment task too often, record on the card the date it is used.

A file of effective items and tasks assumes increasing importance as we shift from test items that measure knowledge of facts to items and tasks that measure understanding, application, and thinking skills. Items and tasks in these areas are difficult and time-consuming to construct. With all of the other demands on our time, it is nearly impossible to construct effective test items or assessment tasks in these areas each time we prepare a new test or assessment. We have two alternatives: Either we neglect the measurement of learning outcomes in these areas (which, unfortunately, has been the practice), or we slowly build a file of effective items and tasks in these areas. If quality of student learning is our major concern, the choice is obvious.

SUMMARY

Some of the topics considered in this chapter are more relevant to traditional classroom tests involving right–wrong or single-best-answer items than to complex, performance-based tasks involving extended responses and more complicated scoring procedures. Test assembly and item analysis, for example, are more relevant for a classroom test containing many items than for a performance assessment involving a single task for a class period. At a conceptual level, however, the general principles considered in this chapter apply to complex performance-based assessments as well as to classroom tests involving only objective items.

The same care that goes into the construction of individual test items and assessment tasks should be carried over into the final stages of development and use. Attending to the procedures for assembling, administering, scoring, and appraising the results will increase assurance that results are valid.

The preliminary steps in preparing the test will be simpler if items are recorded on cards. This facilitates the task of editing and arranging the items. Editing includes checking each item to make certain that its format is appropriate, that it is relevant to the specific learning outcome it measures, and that it is free from ambiguity, irrelevant clues, and nonfunctioning material. The final group of items selected for the test also should be checked against the table of specifications, or other test plan, to make sure that a representative sample of the learning outcomes and course content is being measured. In arranging the items in the test, all items of one type should be placed together in a separate section. The items within each section should be organized by the learning outcome measured and then placed in order of ascending difficulty.

The directions for the test or assessment should convey clearly the purpose of the measurement, the time allowed to finish, the basis for responding, and the procedure for recording the responses. The directions should indicate what to do about guessing for selection-type items. For performance-based tasks the directions should describe the scoring procedure.

The procedures for administering the test or assessment should give all students a fair chance to demonstrate their achievement. Both the physical and the psychological atmosphere should be conducive to maximum performance. Unnecessary interruptions and unfair aid from other students or the teacher should be avoided.

Scoring the test can be facilitated by a scoring key or scoring stencil if separate answer sheets are used. Counting each right answer as one point is usually satisfactory. A correction for guessing is unnecessary on a typical classroom test for which students have sufficient time. Because assumptions underlying the use of correction-for-guessing formulas are debatable, it is recommended that they be used only with speeded tests. For most classroom tests, it is satisfactory to tell students to answer every question and then simply count the number of correct answers.

After the test has been scored, you should appraise the effectiveness of each item by means of item analysis. Use simple statistical procedures for determining the index of item difficulty (percentage of students who got the item right), item discriminating power (the difference between high and low achievers), and the effectiveness of each distracter (degree to which it attracts more low achievers than high achievers). Item analysis indexes can be computed quickly and easily if the data are based on the ten highest-scoring and ten lowest-scoring students (for class sizes ranging from twenty to forty students). Because criterion-referenced mastery tests are designed to describe the learning tasks that students can perform, rather than to discriminate among students, traditional indexes of item analysis are not used to select items for future tests, but they are relevant for detecting faulty items and for planning instruction. The results of item analysis are valuable in discussing the test with students, in planning remedial work, in improving teaching and testing skills, and in selecting and revising items for future use. Item-analysis data must always be interpreted cautiously because of their limited and tentative nature.

Building a file of effective test items and assessment tasks involves recording the items or tasks on index cards, adding information from analyses of student responses, and filing the cards by both the content area and the objective that the item or task measures. Such a file is especially valuable in areas of complex achievement, when the construction of test items and assessment tasks is difficult and time-consuming. When enough high-quality items and tasks have been assembled, the burden of preparing tests and assessments is considerably lightened. Computer item banking makes the task even easier and soon will be available in most schools.

LEARNING EXERCISES

1. What are the advantages of recording items on separate index cards during test construction?

2. List as many things as you can think of that might prevent a test item or assessment task from functioning as intended. Compare your list with the checklist on pages 316–317.

3. In what ways might poorly arranged items in a test adversely influence the validity of test results? What arrangement is best for valid results? Why?

4. What factors should be included in the general directions for a comprehensive departmental examination? How would the directions for a teacher's unit test differ?

5. What special precautions might be taken to avoid ambiguity, irrelevant clues, and other errors in objective test items?

6. Under what conditions should a correction for guessing be used to score a test?

7. If item analysis data showed that an item was answered correctly by seven out of ten students in the upper group, and three out of ten students in the lower group, what would the index of item difficulty be? What would the index of discriminating power be? Would this item be considered effective or ineffective? Why?

8. How can you increase the discriminating power of a norm-referenced test?

9. What are some of the advantages of maintaining a file of items and tasks? What precautions are necessary in using such a file?

REFERENCES

Cronbach, L. J. (1990). *Essentials of psychological testing* (5th ed.). New York: Harper & Row.

Gronlund, N. E. (1993). *How to make achievement tests and assessments* (5th ed.). Boston: Allyn & Bacon.

FURTHER READING

Anastasi, A. (1988). *Psychological testing* (6th ed.). New York: Macmillan. Chapter 8, "Item Analysis," describes item-analysis procedures for norm-referenced tests with a brief introduction to item-response theory.

Baker, F. A. (1989). Computer technology in test construction and processing. In R. L. Linn (Ed.), *Educational measurement* (3rd ed.). New York: Macmillan. Describes the use of microcomputers for item writing, item banking, test construction, scoring, and reporting.

Crocker, L. (1992). Item analysis. In M. C. Alkin (Ed.), *Encyclopedia of educational research: Vol. 1* (6th ed.). New York: Macmillan. Provides an overview of item-analysis procedures and uses of the results.

Ebel, R. L., & Frisbie, D. A. (1991). *Essentials of educational measurement* (5th ed.). Englewood Cliffs, N.J.: Prentice-Hall. Chapter 13, "Using Item Analysis to Evaluate and Improve Test Quality," describes item analysis and illustrates its use in item revision.

Mehrens, W. A., & Lehmann, I. J. (1991). *Measurement and evaluation in education and psychology* (4th ed.). New York: Holt, Rinehart & Winston. Chapter 8, "Assembling, Reproducing, Administering, Scoring, and Analyzing Classroom Achievement Tests," presents a discussion of topics like those covered in this chapter.

CHAPTER 13
Marking and Reporting

Marking and reporting student progress is one of the more frustrating aspects of teaching—there are so many factors to consider, and so many decisions to be made. This chapter will remove some of the complexity by describing the various types of marking and reporting systems and providing guidelines for their effective use.

The task of reporting student progress cannot be separated from the procedures used in assessing student learning and development. If instructional objectives have been clearly defined in performance terms and relevant tests and other assessment procedures have been properly used, marking and reporting become a matter of summarizing the results and presenting them in understandable form. The task is still a perplexing one, however, because the evidence of learning and development must be presented on a very brief report form that is understandable to a variety of users (students, parents, teachers, counselors, administrators).

Reporting student progress becomes especially difficult when the vast array of assessment data must be summarized as a single letter grade (e.g., *A, B, C, D, F*) or numerical value. Should the assigned grade represent achievement only or should effort and work habits be included? How should the various aspects of achievement (e.g., tests, daily assignments, reports, lab work, response to oral questioning) be weighted and combined? Should the achievement be judged in relation to other students, some absolute standard, or the individual's learning potential? What distribution of grades (i.e., *A, B, C, D, F*) should be used and how should this be determined? How can student work be displayed to illustrate progress, strengths, and weaknesses to students and parents? There are no simple answers to these questions.

Although some schools provide guidelines for assigning marks, practices vary from school to school and from teacher to teacher within the same school. Many schools have circumvented the problems of using a single letter grade by supplementing it with a more elaborate reporting system. Some of these systems will be described here, but first let us consider some of the functions served by a marking and reporting system.

FUNCTIONS OF MARKING AND REPORTING SYSTEMS

School marking and reporting systems are designed to serve a variety of functions in the school. These include instructional uses, reports to parents, and administrative and guidance uses.

Instructional Uses

The focus of the marking and reporting system should be the improvement of student learning and development. This is most likely to occur when the report (1) clarifies the instructional objectives, (2) indicates the student's strengths and weaknesses in learning, (3) provides information concerning the student's personal–social development, and (4) contributes to the student's motivation. These functions require a much more comprehensive report than the single letter grade.

The improvement of student learning is probably best achieved by the day-to-day assessments of learning and the feedback from tests and other assessment procedures. However, students also seem to need a periodic summary of their learning progress. They find it difficult to integrate test scores, ratings, and other assessment results into a summary of how they are doing. A well-designed report form, together with a portfolio of student work that contains carefully selected examples, can provide this systematic summary of learning progress. If they are sufficiently detailed, the report and portfolio of work can pinpoint strengths and weaknesses in learning with implications for corrective action. They also can help communicate desired learning outcomes.

Periodic progress reports can contribute to student motivation by providing short-term goals and knowledge of results. Both are essential features of effective learning. How motivating the reports are likely to be, however, depends on the nature of the report and how it is used. If a single letter grade is used and students are threatened with low grades unless they study harder, the results are likely to be negative. However, if a comprehensive report of learning strengths and weaknesses is used and the report is presented as an opportunity to check on progress, motivation toward improved learning is likely to result.

The involvement of students in the selection of examples of work to include in a portfolio can encourage reflection on standards of performance. One common practice, for example, is to ask students to select their best piece of writing and to explain why they chose that piece. The inclusion of examples that show early efforts, teacher feedback, and final products can illustrate progress and help students internalize performance standards.

Well-designed progress reports can also aid in evaluating instructional procedures by identifying areas needing revision. When a majority of students have reports showing poor learning progress in a particular area, there may be a need to modify the instructional objectives or the classroom activities. In other cases, the reports may indicate that some special instructional activities would be beneficial for small groups or individuals.

Reports to Parents/Guardians

Informing parents (or guardians) of their children's school progress is a basic function of a marking and reporting system. These reports should help parents understand the objectives of the school and how well their children are achieving the intended learning outcomes of their particular program. This information is important from several viewpoints. First, by knowing what the school is attempting to do, parents are better able to cooperate with the school in promoting their children's learning and development. Second, information concerning their children's successes, failures, and special problems enables parents to give them the emotional support and encouragement needed. Third, knowing their children's strengths and weaknesses in learning provides a basis for helping them make more sound educational and vocational plans. To serve these purposes adequately, the reports and portfolios of student work should contain as much information and detail as parents can comprehend and use. At the elementary level, the report form is frequently supplemented by parent–teacher conferences.

Administrative and Guidance Uses

Marks and progress reports serve a number of administrative functions. They are used for determining promotion and graduation, awarding honors, determining athletic eligibility, and reporting to other schools and prospective employers. For most administrative purposes, a single letter grade tends to be preferable, because such marks are compact and can be easily recorded and averaged.

There is little doubt that the convenience of the single letter grade in administrative work has been a major factor in retarding the development of more comprehensive and useful progress reports. This need not be the case, however. Where a new reporting system is being developed, it is possible to retain the use of letter grades for administrative purposes and supplement them with the type of information needed by students, parents, teachers, and counselors. At the high school level, the retention of letter grades is almost mandatory because most college admission officers insist on them.

Counselors use reports on student achievement and development, along with other information, to help students make realistic educational and vocational plans. Reports that include ratings on personal and social characteristics are also useful in helping students with adjustment problems. These guidance functions are best served by a reporting system that is both comprehensive and detailed.

In summary, the diverse functions to be served by a marking and reporting system indicate that more elaborate reports are needed than the traditional single letter grade. This does not mean that letter grades should be discarded. They are convenient, easily averaged, useful for administrative functions, and required for college admissions. Instead, letter grades should be supplemented by the type of information needed by the various users of the reports. When this is done, the letter grade can be retained as a pure measure of achievement, and such factors as effort, attitude, work habits, and personal–social characteristics can be reported separately.

TYPES OF MARKING AND REPORTING SYSTEMS

Throughout the history of education, letter grades have been the primary method of reporting student progress in school. Various studies have indicated that approximately 50 to 90 percent of all schools use letter grades. In some cases, especially at the elementary level, the report form also includes a series of work habits and personal–social characteristics to be checked by the teacher. Various attempts have been made to replace or improve the traditional report form. The modifications typically represent some type of compromise between the need for detailed information and the need for simplicity and conciseness.

Traditional Letter-Grade System

The traditional use of the letter-grade system is to assign a single letter grade (e.g., *A, B, C, D, F*) for each subject. In some cases a single number (e.g., *5, 4, 3, 2, 1* or *100, 95, 90*, etc.) is used instead of a letter, but the marking system is essentially the same. This system is concise and convenient, the marks are easily averaged, and they are useful in predicting future achievement. However, they have several shortcomings when used as the sole method of reporting:

1. They typically are a combination of achievement, effort, work habits, and good behavior.
2. The proportion of students assigned each letter grade varies from teacher to teacher.
3. They do not indicate a student's strengths and weaknesses in learning.

These limitations of the single letter grade make them difficult to interpret and use. A grade of *C,* for example, may represent good achievement but poor work habits and disruptive behavior or poor achievement accompanied by attentiveness, strong effort, and good behavior. In reacting to criticisms that the letter-grade system fosters unfair competition among students, some schools have reduced the number of marks to two (e.g., *S* = satisfactory, *U* = unsatisfactory) or three (e.g., by adding *H* = honors). These changes, of course, provide even less information than the traditional letter grade system.

Pass–Fail System

A two-category system (e.g., satisfactory–unsatisfactory, pass–fail) has been used in some elementary schools for many years. More recently, it has also found widespread use in high schools and colleges. At these levels, it typically serves as an option to the traditional letter grade in a limited number of courses. It permits students to take some courses, usually elective courses, under a pass–fail option that is not included in their grade-point average. The intent is to encourage students to explore new areas, even those for which they are not fully prepared. It also permits students to focus on those aspects of a course that relate most directly to their major field of study and to neglect those areas of little interest or relevance. Removing the fear of a lower grade-point average gives students greater freedom to select their learning experiences.

Like any two-category system, the pass–fail option is easy to use but it offers less information than the traditional *A, B, C, D, F* system. It provides no indication of the level of learning and, thus, its value for describing present performance or predicting future achievement is lost. Also, study effort is frequently directed toward merely passing rather than a higher level of achievement. Despite its shortcomings, however, the pass–fail option can serve the purposes for which it is intended if its use is restricted to a minimum number of courses.

A pass–no grade marking system is often used for courses taught under a pure mastery learning approach. Here, where students are expected to demonstrate mastery of all course objectives before receiving credit for a course, a simple *pass* is all that is needed to indicate mastery. The practice of assigning a letter grade of *A* to all students who complete a course under mastery conditions, as is frequently done, simply adds greater confusion to the meaning of letter grades. When the pass–no grade system is used, nothing is recorded on a student's school record until mastery of the course is demonstrated. The mastery learning approach presupposes that each student will be given as much time as needed to attain mastery of the course objectives. Thus, the school record remains a blank until the course is successfully completed.

Checklists of Objectives

To provide more informative progress reports, some schools have replaced or supplemented the traditional marking system with a list of objectives to be checked or rated. These reports, which are most common at the elementary school level, typically include ratings of progress toward the major objectives in each subject-matter area. The following statements for reading and arithmetic illustrate the nature of these reports.

Reading

1. Reads with understanding
2. Works out meaning and use of new words
3. Reads well to others
4. Reads independently for pleasure

Arithmetic

1. Uses fundamental processes
2. Solves problems involving reasoning
3. Is accurate in work
4. Works at a satisfactory rate

The symbols used to rate students on each of these major objectives vary considerably. In some schools the traditional *A, B, C, D, F* lettering system is retained, but more commonly there is a shift to fewer symbols, such as *O* (outstanding), *S* (satisfactory), and *N* (needs improvement).

The checklist form of reporting has the obvious advantage of providing a detailed analysis of the student's strengths and weaknesses so that constructive action can be taken to help improve learning. It also provides students, parents, and others with a frequent reminder of the objectives of the school. The main difficulties encountered with such reports are in keeping the list of statements down to a workable number and in stating them in such simple and concise terms that they are readily understood by all users of the reports. These difficulties are probably best overcome by obtaining the cooperation of parents and students during the development of the report form.

Letters to Parents/Guardians

Some schools have turned to the use of letters to provide for greater flexibility in reporting student progress to parents (or guardians). Letters make it possible to report on the unique strengths, weaknesses, and learning needs of each student and to suggest specific plans for improvement. In addition, the report can include as much detail as is needed to make clear the student's progress in all areas of development.

Although letters to parents might provide a good supplement to other types of reports, their usefulness as the sole method of reporting progress is limited by several factors.

1. Comprehensive and thoughtful written reports require an excessive amount of time and skill.
2. Descriptions of a student's learning weaknesses are easily misinterpreted by parents.
3. Letters fail to provide a systematic and cumulative record of student progress toward the objectives of the school.

The flexibility of this method, which is one of its major strengths, limits its usefulness in maintaining systematic records. Because different aspects of development are likely to be stressed from one report to another, the continuity in reporting is lost.

When used in connection with a more formal reporting system, the informal letter can serve a useful role in clarifying specific points in the report and in elaborating upon various aspects of student development. Letters can also be an effective supplement to a portfolio of student work by providing an overview of the portfolio entries and calling attention to particular things that the parent might consider in reviewing the portfolio. In general, letters probably should be restricted to this supplementary role, however, and be used only as needed for clarification. See "Tactful Remarks for Reporting to Parents" for some extreme examples that illustrate the touchiness of reporting to parents.

Portfolios of Student Work

Portfolios of student work are most common in writing and art, but are being used with increasing frequency in other areas. A carefully constructed portfolio can be an

---

Tactful Remarks for Reporting to Parents

A teacher listed tactful ways of reporting to parents concerning their children's misbehavior in school. It included items like the following:

❑ *Lying:* "Presents interesting oral reports but has difficulty in differentiating between factual and imaginary material."

❑ *Cheating:* "Uses all available resources in obtaining answers but needs help in controlling resourcefulness during testing."

❑ *Bullying:* "Has leadership qualities but needs to redirect them into more constructive activities."

❑ *Laziness:* "Works on school tasks when given ample supervision but needs to develop independent work habits."

---

effective means of showing student progress, illustrating strengths, and identifying areas where greater effort is needed. The process of identifying products for the portfolio and commenting on the entries can help students gain a better understanding of expectations and standards of excellence. The portfolio is also an effective means of making grades and other summary reports more concrete for parents and guardians by illustrating both progress and current levels of student achievement.

An effective portfolio is more than simply a file into which student work products are placed. It is a purposefully selected collection of work that often contains commentary on the entries by both students and teachers. The entries in the portfolio need to be selected to illustrate the range of student work (e.g., types of writing, types of mathematical problems, or results of laboratory experiments). The entries also need to be selected to illustrate progress during the year (e.g., products from different parts of the school year) and, in some cases, progress from early to later stages of completing a project (e.g., drafts, revisions, and final versions of a project).

Parent–Teacher Conferences

To overcome the limited information provided by the traditional report card and to establish better cooperation between teachers and parents (or guardians), some schools use regularly scheduled parent–teacher conferences. This reporting method is most widely used at the elementary level, with its greatest use in the primary grades.

The parent–teacher conference is a flexible procedure that provides for two-way communication between home and school. Besides receiving a report from the teacher, parents have an opportunity to present information concerning the student's out-of-school life. The conference permits teachers and parents to ask questions, discuss their common concerns in helping the student, and cooperatively plan a program for improving the student's learning and development. The give and take in such a conference makes it possible to avoid, or overcome, any misunderstandings concerning the student's progress.

The parent–teacher conference is an extremely useful tool, but it shares two important limitations with the informal letter: (1) it requires an excessive amount of time and skill and (2) it does not provide a systematic record of student progress. In addition, some parents (or guardians) are unwilling or unable to come for conferences. Thus, it is most useful as a supplementary method of reporting.

MULTIPLE MARKING AND REPORTING SYSTEMS

Schools have used traditional letter grades (*A, B, C, D, F*) to report student progress for more than seventy years, despite efforts to replace them with a more meaningful report. Their continued use indicates that they are serving some useful functions in the school (e.g., administrative). They are a simple and convenient means of maintaining permanent school records. Thus, rather than replace letter (or number) grades, it seems more sensible to try to improve the letter-grade system and supplement it with more detailed and meaningful reports of student learning progress. Some schools already use multiple marking and reporting systems.

The typical multiple reporting system retains the use of traditional marking (letter grades or numbers) and supplements the marks with checklists of objectives. In some cases, two marks are assigned to each subject: one for achievement and the other for effort, improvement, or growth. An example of a high school report form used for multiple marking is shown in Figure 13.1.

The report form in Figure 13.1 uses separate marks for achievement, effort, and ratings on two lists of objectives. At left is a list of common school objectives appearing on all the report forms. The list of objectives at right is of those pertaining to the particular subject being marked, in this case social studies. This report form makes it possible to assign an achievement grade that solely measures achievement because effort and other personal characteristics are marked separately. It also informs both the student and parents of the progress being made toward the school's objectives and each subject's objectives. This report form was developed by committees of students, parents, teachers, and other school personnel and thus reflects the types of information these groups considered most useful.

Guidelines for Developing a Multiple Marking and Reporting System

No marking and reporting system is likely to be equally satisfactory in all schools. Each school system must develop methods that fit its particular needs and circumstances. The following principles for devising a multiple marking and reporting system are guidelines for this purpose:

1. The development of the marking and reporting system should be guided by the functions to be served.   The type of information most needed by the report's users should be included. This typically requires a study of the functions for which the reports are to be used by students, parents, teachers, counselors, and administrators. Although it is seldom possible to meet all of their

PROGRESS REPORT   SOCIAL STUDIES
University of Illinois High School
Urbana, Illinois

_____ 1st quarter–November   _____ 3rd quarter–April

_____ Semester–February   _____ Final Report–June

RATING SCALE: + Outstanding   S–Satisfactory   U–Unsatisfactory   O–Inadequate basis for judgment

S	U	O	+	Respects rights, opinions, and abilities of others
S	U	O	+	Accepts responsibility for group's progress
S	U	O	+	Is careful with property
S	U	O	+	Uses time to advantage
S	U	O	+	Is attentive
S	U	O	+	Makes regular preparations as directed
		O	+	Evidences independent thought and originality
		O	+	Seeks more than superficial knowledge
		O	+	Evidences growth in orderly and constructive group discussion
		O	+	Keeps informed on current affairs
		O	+	Discriminates in the selection and use of social studies materials
		O	+	Demonstrates growth in the skills of critical thinking
		O	+	Places people and events in their chronological and cultural setting
		O	+	Demonstrates social responsibility

ACHIEVEMENT

The grade is a measure of achievement with respect to what
is expected of a student of this class in this school and in relation
to what is expected in the next higher course in this subject.

_____ 5 excellent   _____ 2 passing, but weak
_____ 4 very good   _____ 1 failing
_____ 3 creditable   _____ 0 inadequate basis for judgment

EFFORT

The grade below is an estimate, based on evidence available
to the teacher, of the individual student's effort.

_____ 5 excellent   _____ 2 weak
_____ 4 very good   _____ 1 very weak
_____ 3 creditable   _____ 0 inadequate basis for judgment

COMMENTS: Teacher: _____

341

needs, a satisfactory compromise is more likely if they are known. It is helpful to supplement letter grades in each subject with separate reports on course objectives, effort, personal and social characteristics, and work habits. The letter grade should be retained as a pure measure of achievement, and any marks for improvement, effort, or growth should be made separately.

2. The marking and reporting system should be developed cooperatively by parents, students, and school personnel. School reports are apt to be most useful when all users have some voice in their development. This is usually done by organizing a committee consisting of representatives of parent groups, student organizations, elementary and secondary school teachers, counselors, and administrators. Ideas and suggestions are fed into the committee through the representatives, and the members carry back to their own respective groups, for modification and final approval, the committee's tentative plans. This cooperative participation not only will result in a more adequate reporting system but also increases the likelihood that the reports will be understood by those for whom they are intended.

3. The marking and reporting system should be based on a clear statement of educational objectives. The same objectives that have guided instruction and assessment should serve as a basis for marking and reporting. Some of these will be general school objectives and others will be unique to particular courses or areas of study. Nevertheless, when devising a reporting system, the first question should be, "How can we best report student progress toward these particular objectives?" The final report form will be limited and modified by a number of practical considerations, but the central focus should be on the objectives of the school and course and the types of performance that represent the achievement of these objectives.

4. The marking and reporting system should be based on adequate assessment. Teachers should not be expected to report on aspects of student performance when evidence is lacking or is very unreliable. By the same token, including items on a report form assumes that the performance will be assessed as objectively as possible. Ratings on such items as critical thinking, for example, should be the product of testing, assessment, and controlled observation, rather than snap judgments or hazy recollections of incidental happenings. Therefore, in planning a marking and reporting system, it is necessary to take into account the types of assessment data needed. The items included in the final report form should be those on which teachers can obtain reasonably reliable and valid information.

5. The marking and reporting system should be detailed enough to be diagnostic and yet compact enough to be practical. For guiding students' learning and development, we should like as comprehensive a picture of their strengths and weaknesses as possible. This desire for detail, however, must be balanced by such practical demands as (1) a reasonable amount of time required to prepare and use the reports; (2) reports that are understandable to students, parents, employers, and school personnel; and (3) reports that are easily summarized for school records. As noted earlier, a compromise between comprehensiveness and practicality is probably best obtained by supplementing the letter-grade system with more detailed reports on other aspects of student development.

6. The marking and reporting system should provide for parent–teacher conferences, as needed. At the elementary school level, regularly scheduled conferences with parents might constitute part of the reporting system. At the high school level, such conferences are typically arranged as needed, to deal with specific problems. At both levels, however, such conferences should supplement a more formal report form, rather than replace it. A uniform method of reporting student progress is needed for school records, and this is difficult to obtain from conference notes.

In summary, a multiple marking and reporting system takes into account the varied needs of students, parents, teachers, and other school personnel. The letter-grade system (*A, B, C, D, F*) provides a simplified method of keeping a record of student achievement. The checklist of objectives provides a detailed report of student strengths and weaknesses in learning and development. The carefully constructed portfolio provides concrete examples of both progress and level of achievement. The parent–teacher conference helps maintain cooperation between home and school. When letter grades are supplemented by these other methods of reporting, the grades become more meaningful. Rather than being a conglomerate of achievement, effort, improvement, and personal behavior, letter grades can be confined to measuring achievement only. Multiple marking makes this possible by reporting separately on the other aspects of student development.

ASSIGNING LETTER GRADES

Because most schools use the *A, B, C, D, F* marking system, most teachers will be faced with the problem of assigning letter grades. This involves questions such as the following:

1. What should be included in a letter grade?
2. How should achievement data be combined in assigning letter grades?
3. What frame of reference should be used in grading?
4. How should the distribution of letter grades be determined?

Each of these issues will be discussed in turn.

Determining What to Include in a Grade

As noted earlier, letter grades are likely to be most meaningful and useful when they represent achievement only. If they are contaminated by such extraneous factors as effort, amount of work completed (rather than quality of the work), personal conduct, and so on, their interpretation will become hopelessly confused. When letter grades combine various aspects of student development, they lose their meaningfulness as a measure of achievement and suppress other important aspects of development. A letter grade of *B,* for example, may represent average achievement with outstanding effort and excellent conduct or high achievement with little effort and some disciplinary infractions. Only by making the letter grade as pure a measure of achievement as possible and reporting on these other aspects separately can we hope to improve our descriptions of student learning and development.

Teachers often are comfortable with the notion that grades should be based strictly on achievement for students that they judge to be highly able. But they feel that effort should be considered along with achievement for students that they judge to be less able (Stiggins, Frisbie, and Griswold, 1989). Although this position seems reasonable on the surface, it has some major drawbacks: (1) it is difficult, if not impossible, for a teacher to adequately assess a student's effort or potential, (2) it is difficult to distinguish between aptitude and achievement even with the most sophisticated measures; both depend on student learning, and (3) using different bases of marking for different students sends a mixed message and may be unfair to students who are perceived as being more able than they are.

If letter grades are to be valid indicators of achievement, they must be based on valid measures of achievement. This involves the process described earlier in this book—defining the course objectives as intended learning outcomes and developing or selecting tests and assessments that measure these outcomes most directly. How much emphasis should be given to tests, ratings of performances, written reports, and other measures of achievement in the letter grades is determined by the nature of the course and the objectives being stressed. Thus, a grade in English might be determined largely by tests and writing projects, a grade in science by tests and assessments of laboratory performance, and a grade in music by tests and ratings on performance skills. The types of assessment data to include in a course grade and the relative emphasis to be given to each type of evidence are determined primarily by examining the instructional objectives. Other things being equal, the more important the objective is, the greater the weight it should receive in the course grade. In the final analysis, letter grades should reflect the extent to which students have achieved the learning outcomes specified in the course objectives, and these should be weighted according to their relative importance.

Combining Data in Assigning Grades

When the aspects of achievement (e.g., tests, written reports, performance ratings) to be included in a letter grade and the emphasis to be given to each aspect have been decided, the next step is to combine the various elements so that each element receives its intended weight. If we decide, for example, that the final examination should count 40 percent, the midterm 30 percent, laboratory performance 20 percent, and written reports 10 percent, we will want our course grades to reflect these emphases. A typical procedure is to combine the elements into a composite score by assigning appropriate weights to each element, and then use these composite scores as a basis for grading.

Combining data into a composite score in order to produce the desired weighting is not as simple as it may appear at first glance. This can be illustrated by a simple example. Let us assume that we want to combine scores on a final examination and a term report and that we want them to be given equal weight. Our range of scores on the two measures are as follows:

Range of Scores

Final examination	80 to 100
Term report	10 to 50

In practice, we would want to combine more than two assessment results before assigning grades, but the use of just two elements is sufficient for illustration. Because the two sets of scores are to be given equal weight, we may be inclined simply to add together the final examination score and the term report score for each student. We can check on the effectiveness of this procedure by comparing the composite score of a student who is highest on the final examination and lowest on the term report ($100 + 10 = 110$) with a student who is lowest on the final examination and highest on the term report ($80 + 50 = 130$). It is obvious from this comparison that simply adding together the two scores will not give them equal representation.

Another common but erroneous method of equating scores is to make the maximum possible score the same for both sets of scores. For our scores, this would mean multiplying the scores on the term report by 2, so that the top score on both measures would equal 100. Applying this procedure to the same two extreme cases we considered earlier, our first student would have a score of 120 ($100 + 20$) and our second student a score of 180 ($80 + 100$). It is obvious that this procedure does not equate the scores. In fact, there is now an even larger difference between the two composite scores. This is due to the fact that the influence each component has on the composite score depends on the variability, or spread, of scores, not on the total number of points. Thus, to properly weight the components in a composite score, the variability of the scores must be taken into account.

The range of scores in our example provides a measure of score variability, or spread, and this can be used to equate the two sets of scores. We can give the final examination and the term report equal weight in the composite score by using a multiplier that makes the two ranges equal. Because the final examination scores have a range of 20 ($100 - 80$) and the term report scores a range of 40 ($50 - 10$), we would need to multiply each final examination score by 2 to obtain the desired equal weight. Note that this weighting is the reverse of the incorrect weighting procedure based on making the maximum possible scores equal. We can check on the effectiveness of this procedure by using the same two cases we considered earlier. The student highest on the final examination and lowest on the term report would now have a score of 210 ($200 + 10$), and the student lowest on the final examination and highest on the term report would also have a score of 210 ($160 + 50$). Our check shows that the procedure gives the two sets of scores equal weight in the composite score. If we wanted our final examination to count twice as much as the term report, it would be necessary to multiply each final examination score by 4 rather than by 2.

A more refined weighting system can be obtained by using the standard deviation as the measure of variability (Ebel and Frisbie, 1991). For teachers with access to computers, this is a simple matter of converting scores on each test or assessment to T-scores (see Chapter 17). The T-scores can then be multiplied by whatever weights are desired and summed to yield a composite score for which grades are assigned (see the accompanying box). However, the range is satisfactory for most classroom purposes.

Selecting the Proper Frame of Reference for Grading

Letter grades are typically assigned on the basis of one of the following frames of reference:

1. Performance in relation to other group members (relative grading).
2. Performance in relation to specified standards (absolute grading).
3. Performance in relation to learning ability or amount of improvement.

Example of Using T-Scores to Compute Composite Score

Assessment Component	Mean	Standard Deviation	Desired Weight	$T = 50 + 10((X{-}M)/S)$
Midterm (X_1)	30	10	20%	$T_1 = 50 + 10((X_1 - 30)/10)$
Project (X_2)	20	4	40%	$T_2 = 50 + 10((X_2 - 20)/4)$
Final (X_3)	65	20	40%	$T_3 = 50 + 10((X_3 - 65)/20)$

	Raw Scores			T-Scores			Weighted Composite
Students	X_1	X_2	X_3	T_1	T_2	T_3	$.2T_1 + .4T_2 + .4T_3$
Bob	20	16	55	40	40	45	42
Carla	20	18	45	40	45	40	42
Donna	40	24	85	60	60	60	60
Ed	30	20	95	50	50	65	56

X = raw score, M = Mean, S = Standard Deviation. Note that Bob and Carla have the same weighted composite T-score and that Donna has a slightly higher weighted composite T-score than Ed. If the difference in standard deviations had been ignored and the same weights were applied to raw scores, the weighted composite raw scores would give Bob a higher score (32.4) than Carla (29.2) because he had his best performance on the component with the largest standard deviation while she had her best performance on the component with the smallest standard deviation. Consider why Donna's weighted composite raw score (51.6) is slightly lower than Ed's (52), while their T-scores show the opposite pattern.

Assigning grades on a relative basis involves comparing a student's performance with that of a reference group, typically one's classmates. With this system, the grade is determined by the student's relative ranking in the total group, rather than by some absolute standard of achievement. Because the grading is based on relative performance, the grade is influenced by both the student's performance and the performance of the group. Thus, one will fare much better, gradewise, in a low-achieving group than in a high-achieving group.

Although relative grading has the disadvantage of a shifting frame of reference (i.e., grades depend on the group's ability), it is widely used in the schools, because much of classroom testing is norm-referenced. That is, the tests are designed to rank students in order of achievement, rather than to describe achievement in absolute terms. Although position in the group is the key element in a relative system of grading, the actual grades assigned are also likely to be influenced to some extent by achievement expectations the teacher has acquired from teaching other groups. Thus, a high-achieving group of students is likely to receive a larger proportion of good grades than a low-achieving group will.

Assigning grades on an absolute basis involves comparing a student's performance to specified standards set by the teacher. These standards are usually concerned with the degree of mastery to be achieved by students and may be specified as (1) tasks to be performed (e.g., type 40 words per minute without error) or (2) the percentage of correct answers to be obtained on a test designed to measure a clearly defined set of learning tasks. Thus, with this system, letter grades are assigned on the basis of an absolute standard of performance rather than a relative one. If all students demonstrate a high level of mastery, all will receive high grades.

The absolute system of grading is much more complex than it first appears. To use absolute level of achievement as a basis for grading requires that (1) the domain of learning tasks be clearly defined, (2) the standards of performance be clearly specified and justified, and (3) the measures of student achievement be criterion-referenced. These conditions are difficult to meet except in a mastery learning situation. When complete mastery is the goal, the learning tasks tend to be more limited and easily defined. In addition, percentage-correct scores, which are widely used in setting absolute standards, are most meaningful in mastery learning because they indicate how far a student is from complete mastery. All too frequently, schools use absolute grading based on percentage-correct scores (e.g., $A = 95-100$, $B = 85-94$, $C = 75-84$, $D = 65-74$, $F =$ below 65) but the domain of learning tasks has not been clearly defined and the standards have been set in a completely arbitrary manner. To fit the grading system, teachers attempt to build norm-referenced tests with scores in the 60 to 100 range. If the test turns out to be too difficult or too easy, they somehow adjust the scores to fit the absolute grading scale. But such grades are difficult to interpret because they represent an adjusted level of performance on some ill-defined conglomerate of learning tasks.

Although reporting student performance in relation to learning ability or amount of improvement shown is fairly widespread at the elementary school level, this type of grading is fraught with difficulties. Making reliable estimates of learning ability, with or without tests, is a formidable task, because judgments or measurements of ability are likely to be contaminated by achievement to some unknown degree. Similarly, improvement (i.e., growth in achievement) over short spans of time is extremely difficult to estimate reliably with classroom measures of achievement. Thus, the lack of reliability in judging achievement in relation to ability and in judging degree of improvement will result in grades of low dependability. If used at all (e.g., to motivate low-ability students), such grades should be supplementary. In dual marking, for example, one letter grade might indicate level of achievement (relative or absolute), and the second letter grade might be used to represent achievement in relation to ability, or the degree of improvement shown since the last marking period.

Determining the Distribution of Grades

As noted in the previous section, there are two ways of assigning letter grades to measure the level of student achievement: the relative grading system based on relative level of achievement and the absolute grading system based on absolute level of achievement.

Relative Grading.   The assignment of relative grades is essentially a matter of ranking the students in order of overall achievement and assigning letter grades on the basis of each student's rank in the group. This ranking might be limited to a single classroom group or might be based on the combined distributions of several classroom groups taking the same course. In any event, before letter grades can be assigned, the proportion of *A*'s, *B*'s, *C*'s, *D*'s, and *F*'s to be used must be determined.

One method of grading that has been widely used in the past is to assign grades on the basis of the normal curve. Grading on the normal curve results in an equal percentage of *A*'s and *F*'s, and *B*'s and *D*'s. Thus, regardless of the group's level of ability, the proportion of high grades is balanced by an equal proportion of low grades. Such grading is seldom defensible for classroom groups because (1) the groups are usually too small to yield a normal distribution and (2) classroom assessment instruments are usually not designed to yield normally distributed scores. It is only when a course or combined courses have a relatively large and unselected group of students that grading on the normal curve might be defended. Even then, however, one might ask whether the decision concerning the distribution of grades should be left to a statistical model (i.e., normal curve) or should be made on a more rational basis.

The most sensible approach in determining the distribution of letter grades to be used in a school is to have the school staff set general guidelines for the approximate distribution of marks. This might involve separate distributions for introductory and advanced courses, for gifted and slow learning classes, and the like. In any event, the distributions should be flexible enough to allow for variation in the caliber of students from one course to another and from one time to another in the same course. Indicating ranges rather than fixed percentages of students who should receive each letter grade offers this flexibility. Thus, a suggested distribution for an introductory course might be stated as follows:

A = 10 to 20 percent of the students

B = 20 to 30 percent of the students

C = 30 to 50 percent of the students

D = 10 to 20 percent of the students

F = 0 to 10 percent of the students

These percentage ranges are presented for illustrative purposes only; there is no simple or scientific means of determining what these ranges should be for a given situation. The decision must be made by the local school staff, taking into account the school's philosophy, the student population, and the purposes of the grades. All staff members must understand the basis for assigning grades, and this basis must be clearly communicated to users of the grades.

In setting an approximate distribution of grades for teachers to follow, the distribution should provide for the possibility of *no* failing grades. Whether students pass or fail a course should be based on their absolute level of learning, rather than their relative position in some group. If all low-ranking students have mastered enough of the material to succeed at the next highest level of instruction, they all probably should pass. On the other hand, if some have not mastered the minimum essentials needed at the next highest level, these students probably should fail. Whether minimum performance has been attained can be determined by reviewing the low-ranking students' performance on tests and other assessment instruments or by administering a special mastery test on the course's minimum essentials. Thus, even when grading is done on a relative basis, the pass–fail decision must be based on an absolute standard of achievement if it is to be educationally sound.

Absolute Grading. If the course's objectives have been clearly specified and the standards for mastery appropriately set, the letter grades in an absolute system may be defined as the degree to which the objectives have been attained, as follows:

A = *Outstanding.* Student has mastered all of the course's major and minor instructional goals.

B = *Very Good.* Student has mastered all of the course's major instructional goals and most of the minor ones.

C = *Satisfactory.* Student has mastered all of the course's major instructional goals but just a few of the minor ones.

D = *Very Weak.* Student has mastered just a few of the course's major and minor instructional goals and barely has the essentials needed for the next highest level of instruction. Remedial work would be desirable.

F = *Unsatisfactory.* Student has not mastered any of the course's major instructional goals and lacks the essentials needed for the next highest level of instruction. Remedial work is needed.

If the tests and other assessment instruments have been designed to yield scores in terms of the percentage of correct answers, absolute grading then might be defined as follows:

A = 95 to 100 percent correct

B = 85 to 94 percent correct

C = 75 to 84 percent correct

D = 65 to 74 percent correct

F = below 65 percent correct

As noted earlier, defining letter grades in this manner is defensible only if the necessary conditions of an absolute grading system have been met. Using percentage-correct scores when the measuring instruments are based on some undefined hodgepodge of learning tasks produces uninterpretable grades.

With absolute grading systems such as these, the distribution of grades is not predetermined. If all students demonstrate a high level of mastery, all will receive high grades. If some students demonstrate a low level of performance, they will receive low grades. See the following "Guidelines box."

The absolute grading system for reporting on student progress seldom uses letter grades alone. A comprehensive report generally includes a checklist of objectives to inform both student and parent which objectives have been mastered and which have not been mastered by the end of each marking period. In some mastery learning programs, letter grades (or numbers) are assigned to each objective to indicate the level of mastery that has been achieved. An example of such a report

GUIDELINES

Effective Grading

1. Describe your grading procedures to students at the beginning of instruction.

2. Make clear to students that the course grade will be based on achievement only.

3. Explain how other elements (effort, work habits, personal–social characteristics) will be reported.

4. Relate the grading procedures to the intended learning outcomes (i.e., instructional goals and objectives).

5. Obtain valid evidence (e.g., tests, assessments, reports, ratings) as a basis for assigning grades.

6. Take precautions to prevent cheating on tests and assessments.

7. Return and review all test and assessment results as soon as possible.

8. Properly weight the various types of achievement included in the grade.

9. Do not lower an achievement grade for tardiness, weak effort, or misbehavior.

10. Be fair. Avoid bias, and when in doubt (as with a borderline score) review the evidence. If still in doubt, assign the higher grade.

FIGURE 13.2

Illustrative report form used for mastery learning (Reproduced by permission of Roselle School District No. 12, Roselle, Illinois.)

ROSELLE SCHOOL DISTRICT NO. 12
ROSELLE JUNIOR HIGHSCHOOL

PROGRESS REPORT TO PARENTS 19___ –19___

Student _____ __Math__ Teacher _____

Basic Skills–Blank indicates skill not covered or evaluated

	HAS ACQUIRED	NOT ACQUIRED
1. Addition (whole, decimal, fraction)		
2. Subtraction (whole, decimal, fraction)		
3. Multiplication (whole, decimal, fraction)		
4. Division (whole, decimal, fraction)		
5. Four operations applied to new work		
6. Knowledge of math formulas		
7. Ability to see relationships		
8. Ability to follow procedures		
9. Ability to formulate problems from word context		
10.		

Social Growth, Work Habits, Attitudes
+ indicates strength
Blank indicates acceptable development
− indicates need for improvement

1. Self-discipline
2. Acceptance of responsibility
3. Positive attitude toward authority
4. Class participation
5. Independence in doing assignments
6. Completion of assignments
7. Positive influence in class
8. Positive effort
9. School work affected by frequent absences
(✓) if applicable

If a parent desires a conference, call the school for an appointment – 529-1600

---

form, designed for use in a junior high school, is shown in Figure 13.2. On this report form, a numerical rating is assigned to each objective as follows:

Has Acquired

1 = Skill well developed, good proficiency.

2 = Skill developed satisfactorily, proficiency could be improved.

3 = Basic skill developed, low proficiency, needs additional work.

Not Acquired

   4 = Basic skill not acquired.

   As with other types of absolute grading, the number of *1*'s, *2*'s, *3*'s, and *4*'s to be assigned to each objective is not predetermined but depends entirely on the absolute level of performance achieved by each student. If all students achieve good proficiency on a particular objective, all will receive *1*'s on that objective.

CONDUCTING PARENT–TEACHER CONFERENCES

Regardless of the type of marking and reporting system used in the school, the parent–teacher conference is an important supplement to the written report of student progress. The face-to-face conference makes it possible to share information with parents (or guardians), to overcome any misunderstanding between home and school, and to plan cooperatively a program of maximum benefit to the student. At the elementary school level, where parent–teacher cooperation is most important, conferences with parents are regularly scheduled. At the secondary level, the parent–teacher conference is typically used only when some special problem situation arises.

   Conferences with parents are most likely to be productive when they are preceded by careful planning and the teacher has skill in conducting such conferences. Many schools offer in-service training for teachers to help them develop effective conference techniques. Typically, such training includes knowledge of how to conduct a parent–teacher conference and role playing to practice the use of conference skills. The following points provide helpful reminders when preparing for and conducting parent–teacher conferences.

   1. Make plans for the conference.   Determine ahead of time the goals of the conference. Your main purpose may be to inform parents of their student's progress, but you may also want to obtain information from parents, make suggestions for home study, or discuss how to solve a particular problem. It is helpful to review the student's record, organize the information you are going to present, and make a list of points you want to cover and questions you plan to ask. Portfolios can provide a good basis for highlighting topics for discussion, but only if the entries are carefully selected and reviewed.

   2. Begin the conference in a positive manner.   Starting the conference by making a positive statement about the student sets the tone for the meeting. Saying something like "Kimberly really enjoys helping others," "Ruben is an expert on dinosaurs," or "Marie is always smiling" tends to create a cooperative and friendly atmosphere. Once established, this positive attitude should be maintained throughout the conference.

   3. Present the student's strong points before describing the areas needing improvement.   It is helpful to present examples of the student's work when discussing the student's performance. A brief review of portfolio entries before the conference is useful in identifying appropriate examples. The work examples help keep the focus on what the student can do and what he or she has yet to learn. Showing an arithmetic test to a parent is much more effective than simply saying the student "does addition problems well but has difficulty with division problems" or "is good with simple computation but needs help with story problems." Similarly, showing examples of an essay written in September alongside one written the following February makes the statement that the student's writing "has shown great improvement" much more concrete.

*4.   **Encourage parents to participate and share information.*** Although as a teacher you are in charge of the conference, you must be willing to listen to parents and share information rather than "talk at" them. They may have questions and concerns about the school and about their child's behavior that need to be brought out before constructive, cooperative action can be taken.

*5.   **Plan a course of action cooperatively.*** The discussion should lead to what steps can be taken by the teacher and the parent to help the student. A brief summary at the end of the conference should review the points discussed and the action to be taken at home and school.

*6.   **End the conference with a positive comment.*** At the end of the conference, thank the parents for coming and say something positive about the student, like "Erik has a good sense of humor and I enjoy having him in class." Any such statement should, of course, fit the student, and not be a vague generality that is used repeatedly.

*7.   **Use good human relation skills during the conference.*** Some of these skills can be summarized by the following *do*'s and *don't*s.

Do's
❑ Be friendly and informal.
❑ Be positive in your approach.
❑ Be willing to explain in understandable terms.
❑ Be willing to listen.
❑ Be willing to accept parents' feelings.
❑ Be careful about giving advice.

Don'ts
❑ Don't argue or get angry.
❑ Don't ask embarrassing questions.
❑ Don't talk about other students, teachers, or parents.
❑ Don't bluff if you don't know an answer.
❑ Don't reject parents' suggestions.
❑ Don't be a know-it-all, with pat answers.

Although one cannot expect to conduct an effective conference by reading about how to do it, these points serve as a helpful reminder of things to do and to avoid when preparing for a conference.

REPORTING STANDARDIZED TEST RESULTS TO PARENTS

Standardized test results are sometimes reported to parents during a parent–teacher conference. Although parents may have a legal right to all information the school has concerning their children, it should be presented to them in an understandable and usable form. This means avoiding technical jargon and presenting test results to parents in language that is meaningful to them. There also will be less chance of misunderstanding and more chance of being viewed in proper perspective if the test results are presented as part of the total pattern of information about the student.

In preparing to report to parents, review the test results, and decide when and how they will be introduced into the conference. The meaningful communication of test results to parents includes:

1. Describing what the test measures.
2. Explaining the meaning of the test scores.
3. Clarifying the accuracy of the test scores.
4. Discussing the use of the test results.

The amount of detail you give in each of these areas will, of course, depend on the time available for the conference and the parents' ability to understand the test results. In general, it is best to keep the explanations brief and simple. Do not overwhelm parents with more test information than they can grasp in the short span of time that is typically available for presenting test information.

Describing What the Test Measures

In reporting on the results of an aptitude or learning ability test, saying something like "this test measures skills and abilities useful in school learning" may be sufficient. If the test contains several scores (e.g., verbal, quantitative, and nonverbal), each section of the test may be described in similarly general terms. Test manuals usually contain general descriptions of the tests and subtests that can be used to explain the test to parents. The following list of things to avoid should help prevent misinterpretation.

1. Do not refer to aptitude or learning ability tests as intelligence tests. The term *intelligence* is emotionally charged and often misunderstood.
2. Do not describe aptitude or learning ability tests as measures of fixed abilities. They are not! They measure learned abilities.
3. Do not say, "These test scores predict how well your child will do in school." They won't! Predictions for individuals are hazardous at best, and many factors determine school success. It is better to say something like "Students with scores like these usually do well in school," or, for low scores, ". . . usually find learning difficult."

Achievement tests are easily described in terms of the test content, and the names of the subtests usually indicate what the test measures. To say that a reading test measures "vocabulary and reading comprehension" or that a math test measures "computation and problem solving" is frequently sufficient. In some cases it may be desirable to describe the test results by objective or item clusters, and these are typically identified on the student's individual report form. When narrative report forms are used, the test content is included as part of the narrative report.

Interpretations of vocational interest inventories, personality inventories, and other guidance-oriented assessment devices are best interpreted by the school counselor or other guidance personnel. Parents should be referred to the appropriate staff member if they have questions about scores on these instruments.

Explaining the Meaning of Test Scores

More detailed discussion of standardized tests and the meaning of various types of scores is provided in Chapters 14 through 17. In this section we will just provide a broad overview of issues in explaining standardized test results to parents. In making norm-referenced interpretations of test scores, both the meaning of the score and the nature of the norm group should be explained to parents, both simply and understandably. Percentile ranks, grade equivalent scores, and stanines are widely used in reporting to parents because they are easy to explain and misinterpretations are less likely to occur. Saying something like the following will usually suffice with these scores:

EXAMPLES

Interpreting percentile ranks: "On the reading vocabulary test, Mary scored higher than 85 percent of a national group of fourth-grade students." (It might also be necessary to point out that the 85 percent does not refer to the percentage of items answered correctly, but only to the percentage of students scoring lower.)

Interpreting grade equivalent scores: "On the reading vocabulary test, Mary scored as well as the typical student in a national group did in the spring of the fifth grade. That is well above the national average for fourth-grade students. The score does not necessarily mean that Mary can do all aspects of fifth-grade work, however, only that she does fourth-grade work better than most in the fourth grade and about as well as the typical fifth-grade student."

Interpreting stanines: "On a scale of 1 to 9, on which the average score is 5, Mary received a score of 7 on the reading vocabulary test, when compared with a national group of fourth-grade students." (In some cases it may be desirable to use verbal descriptions such as *above average* [7, 8, 9], *average* [4, 5, 6], or *below average* [1, 2, 3] in place of numbers.)

Figure 13.3 shows the relation of stanines, percentile ranks, and broad verbal descriptions that can be used in reporting to parents.

FIGURE 13.3
Relation of stanines, percentile ranks, and broad verbal descriptions in a normal distribution

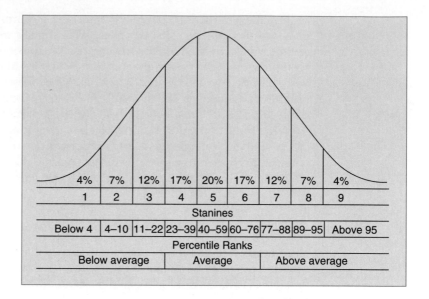

4%	7%	12%	17%	20%	17%	12%	7%	4%
1	2	3	4	5	6	7	8	9

Stanines

Below 4	4–10	11–22	23–39	40–59	60–76	77–88	89–95	Above 95

Percentile Ranks

Below average	Average	Above average

It is wise to report all test results in terms of the same type of score (e.g., percentile ranks, grade equivalents, or stanines). This makes it easier to explain the scores to parents and makes comparisons among tests more understandable.

Although parents are interested in how their child's test performance compares with that of other children, they also want to know what the child has learned and has yet to learn. This type of criterion-referenced interpretation is more readily understood by parents and is typically reported in terms of relative degree of mastery. If you use percentage-correct scores, you may want to distinguish between percentile scores and percentage-correct scores. If you use mastery–nonmastery designations, describe the standard of mastery and explain how it was determined.

Clarifying the Accuracy of Test Scores

It is important to communicate to parents that all test scores contain some error. This can be done most easily if confidence bands (i.e., error bands) are used in interpreting test scores. Profiles using percentile rank frequently include confidence bands. If these are not available, percentile ranks should be interpreted as estimates that may vary up or down by several points on retesting.

Stanines contain broad units that allow for measurement error. Because each stanine is at least one-half standard deviation wide, a difference of two stanines usually represents a significant difference in test performance. Thus, if we had scores like these:

Mathematics   8

Reading   6

Science   5

we could make the following interpretation, "Performance is higher in mathematics than reading and science, but there is no real difference in performance between reading and science." Parents should be told that a difference of one stanine is so small that it can be accounted for by errors of measurement alone.

When interpreting test results by objective or by item cluster, attention should be paid to the number of items on which each interpretation is based. If the number of items is small (say less than 10), make only tentative interpretations, and explain to the parents that these are simply clues to be verified by further study. When combined with the results of teacher-made tests and other classroom work, more dependable interpretations may be possible. It is always good practice to interpret test scores to parents in light of the other available data concerning the student.

Discussing Use of the Test Results

The interpretation of test results should be accompanied by an explanation of how the test results are to be used in the instructional program and a discussion of what action should be taken by both teacher and parent to improve the student's learning and development. This discussion, of course, should not be limited to the test results but should be based on all of the evidence concerning the student's learning and development. The value of test scores becomes clearer to parents when they are coordinated with all of the other information about the student, and when they are seen as contributing to plans for constructive action.

SUMMARY

School marks and progress reports serve various functions in the school. They provide information that is helpful to students, parents, and school personnel. Students find them useful as summary appraisals of learning progress that serve somewhat the same functions as other assessment results. Parents, teachers, and counselors use the information in guiding learning and development and in helping students make realistic future plans. Administrators use the information to determine promotion, athletic eligibility, honors, and graduation. The reports also provide a basis for reporting to other schools and prospective employers.

The diverse functions of progress reports make it difficult to find a universally satisfactory reporting method. Some of the methods that have been tried include (1) the traditional marking system (e.g., A, B, C, D, F), (2) the pass–fail system, (3) checklists of objectives, (4) informal letters, (5) portfolios of selected examples of student work, and (6) parent–teacher conferences. Each method has rather severe limitations when used alone. Probably the best reporting system combines a concise mark for administrative functions with a more detailed report and portfolio for teaching and guidance purposes. In any event, some combination of methods seems most appropriate.

The letter-grade system of marking (A, B, C, D, F) continues to be the most widely used system at both the elementary and secondary levels, despite attempts to replace it with a more meaningful report. This is probably because such grades are easily assigned and averaged and serve many useful administrative functions. Thus, it seems sensible to retain letter grades as a pure measure of achievement and to supplement them with more detailed and meaningful reports of learning progress. Such a multiple marking and reporting system should be developed cooperatively by parents, students, teachers, and other school personnel. Efforts should be made to develop a system that is in harmony with the functions to be served, the school's objectives, and the assessment data available. Ideally, the report form should be as comprehensive and detailed as is practical and should be supplemented by parent–teacher conferences as needed.

Whether or not a multiple marking and reporting system is used in a school, most teachers will be responsible for assigning letter grades to students. This involves such considerations as determining what to include in the letter grade, how to combine the various achievement data into a composite, what frame of reference to use, and what distribution of letter grades to use. The letter grade is most likely to provide a meaningful measure of achievement (1) when it reflects the extent to which students have attained the learning outcomes specified in the instructional goals and objectives, (2) when it is based on valid measures of achievement, and (3) when each component of achievement is weighted in terms of its relative importance. Assigning weights to each component requires that the variability (i.e., spread) of scores be taken into account.

Letter grades may be used to indicate a student's relative level of achievement or absolute level of achievement. When assigning relative grades, the normal curve is seldom an appropriate model for determining the distribution of grades. A more sensible approach is to have the school staff set up suggested distributions of grades that take into account the school's philosophy, the student population, and the purposes to be served by the grades. In absolute grading the letter grades represent the degree to which the instructional goals have been achieved. With this system, no predetermined distribution of letter grades is specified. If all students achieve a high degree of mastery, all will receive high grades.

Even when students are assigned grades on a relative basis, the pass–fail decision should be based on a student's absolute level of achievement. The important consideration is whether the student has the minimum knowledge and skills needed to succeed at the next highest level of instruction.

Letter grades are sometimes assigned on the basis of performance in relation to learning ability or amount of improvement. The problems of adequately judging learning ability apart from achievement and of reliably measuring learning gain over short spans of time restrict the use of these marking methods. If used at all (e.g., for motivation purposes), such grades should supplement grades based on the student's relative or absolute level of achievement.

Parent–teacher conferences are an important method of sharing information with parents. Such conferences should supplement the more formal written report of student progress, however, rather than replace it. Effective conferences with parents require careful planning and sound conference techniques. Portfolios of student work can help make both student progress and level of achievement concrete for parents. Since reports of standardized test results also may be expected to be part of some conferences, teachers should know how to report test results to parents. Although guidelines are useful in preparing for conferences with parents, in-service training is usually needed to develop adequate conference skills.

LEARNING EXERCISES

1. What are the advantages and limitations of each of the following marking systems?
   a. Letter-grade system (*A, B, C, D, F*).
   b. Pass–fail system.
   c. Checklist of objectives.

2. What types of information are most useful in a marking and reporting system designed to support the instructional program of the school? Why?

3. What are the advantages and limitations of a multiple marking and reporting system?

4. What are some of the uses of portfolios of student work? How are portfolios different than simple files of student work?

5. If you were to help set up a marking and reporting system for the level at which you plan to teach, what types of marks and reports would you want included? Why?

6. What procedures are involved in using an absolute basis for grading? What are some of the problems in using this system?

7. What are the advantages and limitations of assigning grades on a relative basis?

8. Describe the procedure for combining two test scores into a composite score where one of the scores is given twice the weight of the other.

9. List as many ways as you can think of for improving marking and reporting in the school.

10. What factors should be considered when deciding whether to pass or fail a student? Do you think the decision should be based on a relative standard or an absolute standard? Why?

11. What types of information should you have at hand during the parent–teacher conference? How would you explain to parents that their child was performing poorly in school? Describe the general approach that you would use in explaining test scores to parents.

REFERENCES

Ebel, R. L, & Frisbie, D. A. (1991). *Essentials of educational measurement* (5th ed.). Englewood Cliffs, N.J.: Prentice-Hall.

Stiggins, R. J., Frisbie, D. A., & Griswold, P. A. (1989). Inside high school grading practices: Building a research agenda. *Educational Measurement: Issues and Practice, 8*(2), 5–14.

FURTHER READING

Airasian, P. W. (1994). *Classroom assessment* (2nd ed.). New York: McGraw-Hill, Chapter 9, "Grading Pupil Performance," provides a detailed discussion of grading and gives examples of report cards currently being used.

Arter, J. R., & Spandel, V. (1992). Using portfolios of student work in instruction and assessment. *Educational Measurement: Issues and Practice, 11*,(1), 36–44. Describes characteristics of portfolios and provides suggestions on their design.

The article is part of an instructional module series of the National Council on Measurement in Education.

Ebel, R. L., & Frisbie, D. A. (1991). *Essentials of educational measurement* (5th ed.). Englewood Cliffs, N.J.: Prentice-Hall. Chapter 15, "Grading and Reporting Student Achievement," discusses the problems of grading and describes various grading systems. Also describes the procedure for weighting components when assigning grades.

Mehrens, W. A., & Lehmann, I. J. (1991). *Measurement and evaluation in education and psychology* (4th ed.). New York: Holt, Rinehart and Winston. Chapter 19, "Marking and Reporting the Results of Measurement," describes the procedures for marking and reporting, including the reporting of test results.

Ory, J. C., & Ryan, K. E. (1993). *Tips for improving testing and grading*. Newbury Park, CA: Sage Publications. Chapter 7, "Assigning Grades," discusses the purposes of grading and provides suggestions for developing and implementing a grading strategy.

Terwilliger, J. S. (1989). Classroom standard-setting and grading practices. *Educational Measurement: Issues and Practice, 8*(2), 15–19. Presents a model of grading that combines features of normative and absolute grading approaches.

PART III

Selecting and Using Published Tests

CHAPTER 14

Achievement Tests

There are hundreds of published achievement tests available for use. Some consist of a battery of tests, whereas others measure an individual subject or skill; some provide a general survey of learning outcomes, whereas others provide descriptive and diagnostic information. Becoming familiar with these basic types of achievement tests and principles of selection and use should provide helpful guidelines for effective achievement testing.

Achievement testing plays an important role in the school program, and published achievement tests are widely used at both the elementary and secondary school levels. Most published achievement tests are called standardized achievement tests. These typically are norm-referenced tests that measure the students' level of achievement in various content and skill areas by comparing their test performance with the performance of other students in some general reference group (e.g., a nationwide sample of students at the same grade level). Quite a few criterion-referenced achievement tests also have been published.

In recent years, a number of states and districts have introduced their own testing and assessment systems or have contracted with publishers to develop assessments to their specifications. Many of these assessments have included open-ended performance assessment tasks. Test publishers also market writing assessments and other types of open-ended performance assessments as supplements to their standardized tests. Nevertheless, standardized tests are still widely used either as part of a broader assessment system or alone, in part because they provide an efficient and relatively inexpensive means of measuring broad achievement goals. Hence, it is important to understand the strengths and weaknesses of these tests.

Although norm-referenced achievement tests and criterion-referenced achievement tests can be considered distinct test types, test publishers often attempt to incorporate elements of each in the same test. For example, most newly developed standardized achievement tests provide for both norm-referenced interpretation and interpretation by objective or by skill area. Caution is needed when interpreting by objective or skill area, however, because standardized tests usually cover such a broad area of achievement that there may be relatively few items for each objective or skill being measured. On the other hand, some criterion-referenced achievement tests provide norms for further interpretation.

Because norm-referenced standardized achievement tests still dominate the field of educational testing, we shall discuss them first. We shall begin by examining their characteristics and showing how they compare with teacher-made achievement tests. We then shall discuss the major types of published achievement tests used in schools. Although we shall give examples of some of the more widely used tests, there are many other published achievement tests of high quality. We hope that the tests referred to here will simply serve as a starting point for exploring the many achievement tests available. At minimum, you should become familiar with some of the better published tests in your teaching area. See Appendix D for a selected list of published tests.

CHARACTERISTICS OF STANDARDIZED ACHIEVEMENT TESTS

A standardized achievement test has certain distinctive features, including a fixed set of test items designed to measure a clearly defined achievement domain, specific directions for administering and scoring the test, and norms based on representative groups of individuals like those for whom the test was designed. Standard content and procedure make it possible to give an identical test to individuals in different places at different times. The norms enable us to compare an individual's test score with those of known groups who also have taken the test. Thus, test norms provide a standard frame of reference for determining an individual's relative level of test performance on a particular test and for comparing test performance on several different tests (providing all were standardized on the same group).

Equivalent forms are included in many standardized achievement tests, which make it possible to repeat the test without fear that the test takers will remember the answers from the first testing. Because equivalent forms of a test are built according to the same specifications, they measure the same domain of achievement with different sets of test items. They therefore can be used interchangeably for such purposes as measuring educational growth, checking on questionable test results from an earlier testing, and the like.

Comparable forms are also included in some standardized tests. These are forms that measure the same aspects of behavior, but at different grade levels. For example, one form will cover Grades 1 to 3, and other forms will cover Grades 4 to 6, 7 to 9, and 10 to 12. Such forms are especially useful for maintaining continuity of measurement in a schoolwide testing program or for studying long-term trends in educational growth.

In summary, the characteristics of a carefully constructed standardized achievement test include the following:

1. The test items are of a high technical quality. They have been developed by educational and test specialists; tried out experimentally (pretested); and selected on the basis of difficulty, discriminating power, and relationship to a clearly defined and rigid set of specifications (see "How Publishers Select Test Items").

2. Directions for administering and scoring are so precisely stated that the procedures are standard for different users of the test.

How Publishers Select Test Items

Iowa Tests of Basic Skills, Levels 9–14:
Selection Process for Test Questions

1. **Research:** Writing teams study curriculum guides, textbooks, latest professional literature and research to identify the skills to be tested and new ways of testing these skills.

2. **Writing:** Four times as many test questions are produced as will eventually be used.

3. **Editing for Tryouts:** Questions are checked for length, reading level, vocabulary, art, and space requirements; and changed or dropped as necessary.

4. **Editing after Tryouts:** Iowa Testing Program tries out questions on school population of over 300,000. Each question is tried out on at least 200 students. Those questions that do not measure well (almost half) are dropped.

5. **Author Reviews:** Test authors review questions' relationship to skills categories, review balance between skills categories, and check for freedom from bias, eliminating where necessary.

6. **Publisher Reviews:** Test editors review questions for all factors, especially balance (geographical, urban/rural, sex, race, etc.) and recommend further changes, which are made.

7. **Independent Reviews:** National team of professionals, representing five ethnic and racial groups, review questions for all factors, particularly cultural fairness. More changes are made following their recommendations.

8. **Final Editing for Standardization:** Editors and authors make final reviews for all factors, and final choice of questions is made for national norming.

Reproduced by permission of The Riverside Publishing Company.

3. Norms based on national samples of students in the grades where the test is intended for use are provided as aids in interpreting the test scores. Separate norms are usually provided for different parts of the school year (e.g., fall, spring). Norms for regions, states, or special groups, such as private schools, also might be supplied.

4. Equivalent and comparable forms of the test are usually provided, as well as information concerning the degree to which the forms are comparable.

5. A test manual and other accessory materials are included as guides for administering and scoring the test, evaluating its technical qualities, and interpreting and using the results.

Despite the common characteristics of standardized tests, no two are exactly alike. Each test measures somewhat different aspects of content and skill. Also, there is wide variation in the completeness and quality of materials from one test to another. To further complicate test selection, some tests with similar titles measure objectives that differ markedly. Thus, the intelligent selection of standardized achievement tests from among the hundreds of tests available in each area requires studying the test content and the test materials in light of the objectives to be measured and the uses to be made of the results.

STANDARDIZED TESTS VERSUS INFORMAL CLASSROOM TESTS

Standardized achievement tests and carefully constructed classroom tests are similar in many ways. Both are based on a table of specifications and both provide clear directions to the students. The main differences between the two types are (1) the nature of the learning outcomes and content measured, (2) the quality of the test items, (3) the reliability of the tests, (4) the procedures for administering and scoring, and (5) the interpretation of scores. Comparative advantages of standardized and informal classroom tests of achievement are shown in Table 14.1.

A review of the comparative advantages of the two types of tests indicates that each is superior for certain purposes and inferior for others. The broader coverage of the standardized test, its more rigidly controlled procedures of administering and scoring, and the availability of norms for evaluating scores make it especially useful for the following instructional purposes:

1. Evaluating students' general educational development in the basic skills and in those learning outcomes common to many courses of study.

2. Evaluating student progress during the school year or over a period of years.

3. Determining students' relative strengths and weaknesses in broad subject or skill areas.

4. Comparing students' general level of achievement with their scholastic aptitude.

The standardized test's inflexibility makes it less valuable for those purposes for which the informal classroom test is so admirably suited.

TABLE 14.1
Comparative advantages of standardized and informal classroom tests of achievement

	Standardized Achievement Tests	Informal Achievement Tests
Learning outcomes and content measured	Measure outcomes and content common to majority of United States schools. Test of basic skills and complex outcomes adaptable to many local situations; content-oriented tests seldom reflect emphasis or timeliness of local curriculum.	Well adapted to outcomes and content of local curriculum. Flexibility affords continuous adaptation of measurement to new materials and changes in procedure. Adaptable to various-sized work units. Tend to neglect complex learning outcomes.
Quality of test items	General quality of items high. Written by specialists, pretested, and selected on basis of effectiveness.	Quality of items is unknown unless test item file is used. Quality typically lower than standardized because of teacher's limited time and skill.
Reliability	Reliability high, commonly between .80 and .95; frequently is above .90.	Reliability usually unknown; can be high if carefully constructed.
Administration and scoring	Procedures *standardized;* specific instructions provided.	Uniform procedures favored but may be flexible.
Interpretation of scores	Scores can be compared with those of norm groups. Test manual and other guides aid interpretation and use.	Score comparisons and interpretations limited to local school situation, can be interpreted in light of known instructional history.

1. Evaluating the learning outcomes and content unique to a particular class or school.

2. Evaluating students' day-to-day progress and their achievement on work units of varying sizes.

3. Evaluating knowledge of current developments in rapidly changing content areas such as science and social studies.

   The complementary functions of the two types of tests indicate that both can contribute to a sound instructional program. Each provides a specific type of information regarding the students' educational progress. In both cases, however, the value of the information depends on the extent to which the tests are related to the instructional objectives of the school and the ways in which the results are used. Standardized achievement tests, like informal classroom tests, can serve the many worthwhile instructional purposes attributed to them only when they measure the particular outcomes and content deemed important by those responsible for the instructional program. In addition, the test results must be used appropriately.

Much of the criticism of standardized tests can be related to misuses of results. Too often standardized tests are expected to serve functions for which they were never intended or for which they are poorly suited. Rigid tracking of students based only on standardized test results, for example, places too much reliance on a single source of information and frequently results in inferior instructional opportunities for students placed in the lower tracks. Overemphasis on test results as a primary means of teacher accountability can also lead to distortions of instruction by narrowing the curriculum to the content of the standardized tests at the expense of other important instructional goals that are not measured by the test.

STANDARDIZED ACHIEVEMENT TEST BATTERIES

Standardized achievement tests are frequently used in the form of survey test batteries. A battery consists of a series of individual tests all standardized on the same national sample of students. This makes it possible to compare test scores on the separate tests and thus determine the students' relative strengths and weaknesses in the different areas covered by the test. With an elementary school test battery, for example, it is possible to determine that a student is strong in language skills but weak in arithmetic skills, good in reading but less proficient in spelling, and so on. Such comparisons are not possible with separate tests that have been standardized on different groups of students because the base for comparison is not uniform.

One limitation of test batteries is that all parts of the battery are usually not equally appropriate for measuring a particular school's objectives. When a test battery is constructed, it is based on the objectives and the content considered important by the specialists building the test. Although a particular school's goals probably will agree with some sections of the battery, it is fairly certain that they will not agree with all sections. Variations in subject-matter content from one curriculum to another and differences in grade placement of instructional materials make it unlikely that the various sections of a test battery will be uniformly applicable to the instructional program of any given school. This limitation is especially pronounced in content-oriented test batteries. It is less important in batteries designed to measure basic skills and general educational development.

Achievement batteries are used most often at the elementary school level. Most schools use an achievement battery in Grades 3 through 6, and many also use a battery in Grades 1 and 2. This extensive usage is understandable because there is considerable uniformity in the learning outcomes sought.

Elementary school batteries focus on the basic skills and usually include sections on reading, language, mathematics, and study skills. To allow for increasing difficulty and for varying emphasis from one grade level to another, a series of comparable forms has been developed to cover the various grade levels. Each form in the series covers one or two grades at the primary level and two or more grades beyond Grade 4.

The basic skills in an achievement battery are measured by a number of subtests. Although the names of the subtests vary somewhat from one test publisher to another, and the batteries at the primary level usually contain fewer subtests, there is considerable uniformity in the outcomes measured by the various basic skill batteries. The following subtests are typical of those used in each basic skill area:

Reading
❏ Decoding skills (discrimination, analysis)
❏ Vocabulary (meaning of words)
❏ Comprehension (meaning of paragraphs and other written material)

Language
❏ Mechanics (capitalization, punctuation)
❏ Expression (correctness, effectiveness)
❏ Spelling (from dictation or identifying misspelled words)

Mathematics
❏ Computation (fundamental operations)
❏ Concepts (meaning of concepts)
❏ Problem solving (solving story problems)

Study Skills
❏ Library and reference skills
❏ Reading maps, graphs, and tables

A list of skill objectives and two sample test items for the mathematics concepts and applications subtest of a widely used basic skill battery is shown in Figure 14.1. Notice that each test item is designed to measure a specific skill objective. A similar set of objectives is used in the construction of each of the other subtests, which are included in the teachers' guide that accompanies the battery.

In addition to the traditional basic skills, some achievement batteries at the elementary school level include tests in listening comprehension and in the content areas of science and social studies. Some batteries also offer writing supplements requiring students to write essays in response to standard prompts. For these batteries it is usually possible also to obtain a separate partial battery limited to the measurement of basic skills. Batteries confined to the basic skills are generally preferred because content-oriented tests become outdated more quickly and are seldom well suited to the objectives of the local instructional program.

Achievement batteries are less widely used at the high school level. The wide diversity of course offerings and the variations in course content within the same subject area have made it difficult to find a common core on which to base the tests. Most high school batteries focus on the same basic skills of reading, mathematics, language, and study skills that are covered by the elementary batteries (with the optional science and social studies tests). This provides for the continuous measurement of the basic skills throughout all grade levels.

Some high school batteries, such as the *Iowa Tests of Educational Development,* were designed to measure general educational development in intellectual

FIGURE 14.1
Objectives, subskills, and sample items (From the *Mathematics Concepts and Applications Subtest of the Comprehensive Tests of Basic Skills,* 4th edition, © 1990. Used by permission of CTB, Macmillan/McGraw–Hill.)

MATHEMATICS CONCEPTS AND APPLICATIONS OBJECTIVES

OBJECTIVE AND SUBSKILL	LEVEL*

55 NUMERATION   K–21/22
  Subskills may include comparison; cardinality; correspondence; sets; ordinality; recognize numbers; fractional part; place value; expanded notation; round, estimate; Roman numeral; number line; root; exponential notation.

56 NUMBER THEORY   10–21/22
  Subskills may include sequence; properties; equivalent form; odd, even numbers; divisibility; multiples; factors; prime, composite numbers.

57 DATA INTERPRETATION   10–21/22
  Subskills may include graph; table, chart, diagram; strategy application; pre-solution; probability, statistics.

58 PRE-ALGEBRA   11–21/22
  Subskills may include number sentence; function, pattern; missing element; ratio, proportion; percent; inequality.

59 MEASUREMENT   K–21/22
  Subskills may include comparison; money; calendar; time; appropriate instrument; length; mass; capacity; temperature; perimeter; area; volume; circumference.

60 GEOMETRY   K–21/22
  Subskills may include spatial relationships; logical reasoning; pattern, shape; symmetry; plane figure; solid figure; congruency; geometric elements; coordinate geometry; triangles; similarity; parts of circle; angles; constructions; transformation; visualization; Pythagorean theorem.

* Level K is for use in kindergarten; Levels 10 through 22 are used in Grades 1 through 12.

55 NUMERATION   Levels K–21/22
Levels K–12 Examiner reads problem. Skills include applying concepts such as cardinal and ordinal numbers, fractional parts, place value as well as comparing and ordering.

Find the group of coins that has one coin for each bank.

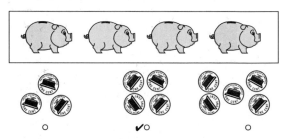

57 DATA INTERPRETATION   Levels 10–21/22
Levels 10–12 Examiner reads problem. Skills include interpreting graphs, tables, and charts; applying concepts of statistics and probability; and using problem solving strategies.

The table shows how many inches long five different objects are. Find the two objects that together are as long as the pencil.

skills and abilities that are not dependent on any particular series of courses. Instead, they assess analytical and evaluative skills that are needed in everyday life. The complete battery contains the following seven tests:

❑ Correctness and Appropriateness of Expression
❑ Ability to Do Quantitative Thinking
❑ Analysis of Social Studies Materials
❑ Analysis of Natural Science Materials
❑ Ability to Interpret Literary Materials
❑ Vocabulary
❑ Use of Sources of Information

Interpretive-type exercises are used throughout the test battery. Sample items representing two of the tests are shown in Figure 14.2. In both tests, Part 1 focuses on understandings and thinking skills gained from the content area, and Part 2 stresses the ability to analyze and evaluate various types of material.

A list of widely-used achievement batteries is shown in Table 14.2. The grade range covered by each test series is indicated in the table. In some of the test series (e.g., *Stanford*), the tests at various levels have different names, but they are all part of a coordinated series that provides for continuous assessment throughout the grade range. Also, although *Tests of Achievement and Proficiency (TAP)* is listed separately, it is used in conjunction with the *Iowa Tests of Basic Skills* to form a coordinated program covering Grades K–12. *TAP* covers the same basic skill and content areas, with emphasis on ability to use information rather than on specific course content.

Although the batteries of tests designed to measure the basic skills are all somewhat similar in terms of the areas of skill covered, they vary considerably in terms of the nature of the test materials used and the specific abilities measured within each skill area. Therefore, in selecting an achievement battery, it is important to appraise carefully the specific test items to be certain that the abilities measured are relevant to the learning outcomes stressed in the school program. Any achievement battery will, of course, measure only some of the important outcomes of the school program. Other tests and assessment procedures will be needed for comprehensive coverage of a school's objectives.

Supplements to Standardized Tests

Some test publishers provide performance assessments as supplements to their standardized tests. The most common form of supplement is a direct writing assessment. The Stanford Writing Assessment Program, for example, includes standard prompts that are designed to elicit written responses in four different modes of writing. (1) Descriptive: students are asked to write about a place or thing based upon their own experiences. (2) Narrative: the prompt presents a brief scenario and students are asked to write a story. (3) Expository: students are asked to state an opinion or position regarding a topic and defend it. (4) Persuasive:

FIGURE 14.2

Sample items like those in the *Iowa Tests of Educational Development* (Copyright © 1988 by The Riverside Publishing Company. Used by permission.)

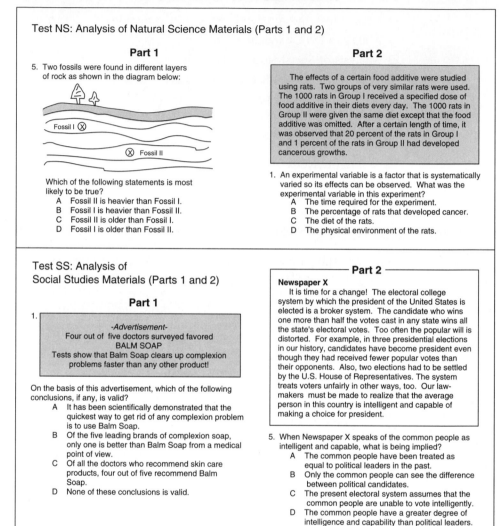

students are asked to write about an issue from their own point of view in a way that would persuade a particular audience. A central scoring service provides both holistic scores for the overall quality of the essay and analytical scores for writing mechanics, sentence formation, and usage.

Assessment instruments with open-ended questions in other content areas have become increasingly common in recent years. *GOALS™: A Performance-Based Measure of Achievement* is an example of such a supplement. *GOALS* is published by the Psychological Corporation and is intended to complement one of their two

TABLE 14.2
Representative list of achievement batteries

Achievement Batteries	Grade Levels Covered														
	K	1	2	3	4	5	6	7	8	9	10	11	12	13
California Achievement Tests	X	X	X	X	X	X	X	X	X	X	X	X	X	
Comprehensive Tests of Basic Skills	X	X	X	X	X	X	X	X	X	X	X	X	X	
Iowa Tests of Basic Skills	X	X	X	X	X	X	X	X	X	X				
Metropolitan Achievement Tests	X	X	X	X	X	X	X	X	X	X	X	X	X	
Sequential Tests of Educational Progress (STEP + CIRCUS)	X	X	X	X	X	X	X	X	X	X	X	X	X	
SRA Achievement Series	X	X	X	X	X	X	X	X	X	X	X	X	X	
SRA Survey of Basic Skills	X	X	X	X	X	X	X	X	X	X	X	X	X	
Stanford Achievement Test Series	X	X	X	X	X	X	X	X	X	X	X	X	X	X
Iowa Tests of Educational Development										X	X	X	X	
Tests of Achievement and Proficiency (TAP)										X	X	X	X	

achievement test batteries. Five content areas (reading, language, mathematics, science, and social studies) are assessed by *GOALS*. In each content area students are required to generate a response to each of ten open-ended questions by writing, drawing diagrams, completing charts, or editing text. A sample Grade 7 mathematics question is shown in Figure 14.3.

Responses to sets of open-ended tasks provided by publishers can usually be scored locally or sent to a central scoring service. When the latter option is used the scores can be compared to normative information provided by the publishers.

Diagnostic Batteries for Instructional Use

Achievement test batteries traditionally were designed as survey tests. That is, they provided a general, overall measure of the various areas of the curriculum. Typically, however, there were too few items measuring each skill to provide much help in making instructional decisions. The results might indicate a student's performance was low in reading or mathematics, for example, but were of limited value for identifying the specific areas of strength and weakness. The few items in each area served as indicators of achievement but they were insufficient for describing what individual students had learned, what they had yet to learn, and the types of errors they were making.

Test publishers have taken steps to make the test results of achievement batteries more useful to classroom teachers. Some test batteries, for example, consist

FIGURE 14.3
Sample open-ended mathematics problem for Grade 7 (From *GOALS™: A Performance-Based Measure of Achievement, Mathematics Preview Booklet,* © 1992. Used by permission of The Psychological Corporation, Harcourt Brace Jovanovich, Inc.)

A magic square of numbers is a square in which the sum of all the numbers of every row, column, and the two main diagonals is the same, and this sum is called the magic sum. Find the magic sum and complete the magic square below. Show your work.

		1
	$\dfrac{5}{4}$	$\dfrac{3}{4}$
$\dfrac{3}{2}$	$\dfrac{1}{4}$	2

of an integrated series of survey tests and group-administered diagnostic tests covering the same areas of basic skills. The survey battery provides information about the students' relative performance in each of the areas, and the diagnostic tests in reading, mathematics, and language provide a more detailed description of the students' strengths and weaknesses in each skill area. This is accomplished, in part by including a larger number of items in the diagnostic tests, using more subtests, and providing for criterion-referenced interpretation. The tests covered in each of the diagnostic tests associated with *Metropolitan Achievement Tests* are presented in Table 14.3. The number of items in each test ranges from 15 to 60, but more commonly falls between 30 and 45. Sample items from four of the reading tests are shown in Figure 14.4.

In addition to the direct interpretation of strengths and weaknesses by subscores and instructional objectives, several special features were built into the *Metropolitan Achievement Tests* to aid instructional decisions.

1. An instructional reading level can be determined by comparing the criterion-referenced reading comprehension score to graded basal readers.
2. An instructional mathematics level can be determined by comparing criterion-referenced mathematics scores to graded levels of mathematics books.

TABLE 14.3
Tests included in the diagnostic batteries of the *Metropolitan Achievement Tests*

Reading	Mathematics	Language
Visual Discrimination	Numeration	Listening Comprehension
Letter Recognition	Geometry and Measurement	Punctuation and Capitalization
Auditory Discrimination	Problem Solving	Usage
Sight Vocabulary	Computation: Whole Numbers	Written Expression
Phoneme/Grapheme:	Computation: Decimals and	Spelling
Consonants	Fractions	Study Skills
Phoneme/Grapheme: Vowels	Graphs and Statistics	
Vocabulary in Context		
Word Part Clues		
Rate of Comprehension		
Skimming and Scanning		
Reading Comprehension		

Note: Diagnostic batteries have six levels for Grades K–9.9, but, of course, not all diagnostic tests are used at each level.

3. Various comparisons between mathematics scores can be made to determine whether low problem-solving performance is due to lack of computational skills, low reading ability, or carelessness.

4. A research skills score is obtained from items imbedded in various subject matter tests.

5. A higher-order thinking skills score is obtained from critical thinking items used in several subject-matter tests.

6. Specific information is provided for instructional planning for those students needing remediation, as well as for those performing at or above average levels.

Similar diagnostic batteries in reading and mathematics are provided as separate components of the *Stanford Achievement Tests,* the *California Achievement Tests,* and the *Comprehensive Tests of Basic Skills.* This two-component system of survey and diagnostic tests, which are statistically linked, provides a sound approach for meeting both administrative and instructional needs. The survey tests provide a general measure of achievement for comparisons among schools and the diagnostic tests provide a more detailed measure of achievement for assessing the learning of individual students.

Although some achievement test batteries do not have a separate series of diagnostic tests, they typically aid instructional use by providing for analysis of results by objective, by specific skill area, or both. Whenever achievement test batteries (or any other test) provide for interpretation by objective or specific skill, it is important to note the number of test items involved. It is not uncommon to base interpretation on as few as two or three test items. A lucky guess or careless error may be the deciding factor in determining whether success or failure is

FIGURE 14.4

Sample items illustrating *Metropolitan Achievement Tests: Reading Diagnostic Tests,* Intermediate Level (Copyright © 1986, Harcourt Brace Jovanovich. Used by permission.)

Phoneme/Grapheme: Consonants
(Choose the word that has the <u>same silent letter</u> as the underlined part of the key word)

<u>k</u>nee

    A king

    B pink

    C knit

    D keen

Phoneme/Grapheme: Vowels
(Choose the word that has the <u>same sound</u> as the underlined part of the key word)

b<u>oa</u>t

    E hole

    F land

    G shoe

    H got

Vocabulary in Context
(Choose the word that best completes the sentence)

Terry _____ to the park today.

A went   C home

B likes   D fast

Word Part Clues
(Choose the word that best completes the sentence)

Barry was very _____ when it rained on Saturday.

E nonhappy   G dishappy

F unhappy   H rehappy

indicated. In such cases, it would be wiser to base instructional decisions on larger item clusters formed by combining items measuring similar objectives or skills.

Group-administered survey and diagnostic batteries are useful for identifying students who could benefit from remedial teaching and individual help. More serious learning problems, however, typically require the use of individually administered diagnostic tests and a careful study of the student's total development. The diagnosis and remediation of severe learning disabilities are best left to the skilled clinician. See "Selecting Achievement Batteries" for more guidelines.

| GUIDELINES |

Selecting Achievement Batteries

1. Achievement batteries that focus on the basic skills measure important outcomes of the elementary school program, but these constitute only a portion of the outcomes of a modern curriculum.

2. At the high-school level, basic skill batteries may serve both as learning readiness tests and as measures of learning outcomes in remedial basic skill programs. However, they provide only a limited measure of the many intended outcomes of the secondary school program.

3. Content-oriented tests in basic achievement batteries have broad coverage but limited sampling in each content area and may tend to become more quickly outdated than basic skills tests.

4. Achievement batteries differ in their emphasis on the various areas of basic skills, the different areas of content, and the specific types of learning outcomes measured. Thus, the selection of a battery should be based on its relevance to the school's objectives.

5. Diagnostic batteries should contain a sufficient number of test items for each type of interpretation to be made.

ACHIEVEMENT TESTS IN SPECIFIC AREAS

In addition to achievement batteries, there are literally hundreds of separate tests designed to measure achievement in specific areas. The majority of these can be classified as tests of course content or reading tests of the general survey type. A limited number of tests also have been developed for use in determining learning readiness.

A separate test has certain advantages over a test battery. First, it is easier to select a test that fits the instructional objectives of a particular area. The difficulty of relating an entire battery of tests to instructional objectives was pointed out earlier. Second, a separate test is usually longer than a battery's subtests. This provides a more adequate sample of performance and more reliable part scores for instructional purposes. Third, the separate test's flexibility makes it easier to adapt to classroom instruction. Teachers can administer separate tests when they best fit their instructional needs, rather than following the rigid schedule of the school testing program.

One disadvantage of separate tests is that each one is usually standardized on a different group of students. Because norm groups are not comparable, relative achievement of students in different areas cannot be compared. For example, it is not possible to determine whether a student has achieved more in science than in mathematics or in social studies than in English, if the tests were not standardized on the same representative group of students.

Separate Content-Oriented Tests

There are many achievement tests at the secondary level designed to measure the outcomes of specific courses. In fact, there are over a hundred separate tests in each of the major content areas of English, mathematics, science, and social studies. There are also separate tests in foreign language, business, and fine arts but not as many as those designed for the basic courses. All of these tests of specific course content are intended as end-of-course tests and thus are used primarily to measure the students' final levels of achievement. Although the tests vary in quality, many of them require students to demonstrate understanding and application as well as knowledge of factual information. See "Selecting Separate Tests in Specific Content Areas" for general guidelines. For a complete listing of the separate tests available for use in schools, consult the catalogues of the test publishers in Appendix C. For critical reviews of the tests, see the latest *Mental Measurements Yearbook* or *Test Critiques.*

Because of its flexibility and timeliness, an informal teacher-made test is frequently better suited to the measurement of instructional objectives in a particular course than a standardized achievement test. However, when carefully selected according to course content and learning outcomes, the standardized test can serve as a valuable check on the teacher's informal classroom tests.

GUIDELINES

Selecting Separate Tests in Specific Content Areas

1. Because separate tests are content oriented, the date of construction is especially important. Developments in some content areas, such as science and social studies, take place at such a rapid rate that some are soon out of date.

2. In addition to timeliness of test content, attention should be directed toward its appropriateness for the particular course in which it is to be used. Because a standardized test includes only the content common to many school systems, it may lack comprehensiveness and at the same time include questions on material that has not been covered in the local instructional program.

3. Many content-oriented tests emphasize the measurement of knowledge outcomes, although there are a number of exceptions. Standardized tests of specific knowledge are seldom as relevant and useful as well-constructed teacher-made tests in the same area.

4. When a content-oriented test measures a variety of learning outcomes beyond those of specific knowledge (e.g., understanding, application, interpretation), it is important that the learning outcomes measured by the test complement those emphasized in the local instructional program.

Reading Tests

One of the most widely used tests at all levels of instruction is the reading test. It occupies a prominent position in achievement test batteries and receives special emphasis in tests of general educational development. In addition, there are well over a hundred separate tests of reading ability.

Many reading tests are of the survey type, designed to measure a student's general level of reading ability. Such tests commonly measure vocabulary, reading comprehension, and rate of reading. The following list of reading skills is typical of those that reading survey tests attempt to measure.

❑ Identifies the meaning of given words.

❑ Identifies the meaning of words when used in context.

❑ Identifies details directly stated in a passage or selection.

❑ Identifies ideas implied in a passage or selection.

❑ Identifies relationships (e.g., time, cause and effect) in a passage or selection.

❑ Identifies the main thought or purpose of a passage or selection.

❑ Identifies inferences drawn from a passage or selection.

❑ Identifies conclusions drawn from a passage or selection.

❑ Identifies the writer's tone, mood, and intent.

Reading tests differ greatly in the extent to which they cover these skills and in the degree of emphasis given to each. Some tests focus on the lower levels of comprehension (e.g., identifying directly stated details), whereas others stress the more complex interpretive skills (e.g., identifying relationships, inferences, and conclusions). Moreover, the last two reading skills in this list are more likely to be found in reading tests for high school than elementary school.

Reading tests also differ widely in the material to be read by the student. Some tests use short passages of a sentence or two, whereas others use extended passages. Some use stories only, and others use stories, letters, poems, and scientific articles. Still another source of difference among reading tests is the extensiveness with which each type of reading material and each reading skill is sampled. One test, for example, may have a relatively large number of test items measuring the ability to draw conclusions from scientific articles, whereas another test has just a few such items. These differences highlight the importance of defining what reading abilities are to be measured before selecting a test.

Reading tests may be selected for any of the following uses: (1) to evaluate the effectiveness of reading instruction, (2) to identify those students needing remedial work in reading, (3) to predict success in subject-matter courses, (4) to determine whether poor reading ability can account for low scores on scholastic aptitude tests, and (5) to help locate the causes of learning problems. Although a single reading test may not serve all of these uses equally well, how the results are to be used is an important consideration in test selection. The ideal reading test for a particular program is the one that best measures the instructional objectives and most

GUIDELINES

Selecting Reading Tests

1. No two reading tests are exactly alike. Although reading survey tests usually measure vocabulary, reading comprehension, and rate of reading, they differ in the material that the reader is expected to comprehend, in the specific reading skills tested, and in the adequacy with which each skill is measured.

2. Reading survey tests measure only some of the outcomes of reading instruction. The mechanics of reading (e.g., perceptual skills, word analysis) are typically measured by diagnostic reading tests. Some specialized reading skills (e.g., reading maps, graphs, charts) are more commonly measured by tests of study skills. Attitude toward reading and interest in reading, both of which are extremely important outcomes of reading instruction, must be determined by observation or other means.

3. Reading tests can serve many purposes in the school program. Thus, in addition to matching the objectives of instruction, test selection should take into account all of the possible uses to be made of the results.

effectively fulfills the uses to which the results will be put. See "Selecting Reading Tests" for more guidelines, and Appendix D for a list of reading tests.

Readiness Tests

Some tests have been designed to determine student readiness for learning school tasks. At the elementary level, reading readiness tests are probably the most familiar, but other types of tests are also used. Although readiness tests are essentially specialized scholastic aptitude tests, they are considered here because their test items are drawn from specific achievement areas. This gives them the advantage of providing diagnostic as well as predictive information. Thus, in addition to predicting learning success in a particular achievement area, test performance can provide information concerning the specific skills that students need to improve if their learning is to be effective.

In the 1980s many school districts started making wider use of early school readiness tests, not for the instructional planning purposes that the tests are intended to serve, but for screening children before they are allowed to start kindergarten or first grade. That is, children with low scores are often forced to delay starting kindergarten for a year, are retained a second year in kindergarten, or are placed for a year in a transitional class before starting the first grade. Unfortunately, none of the available readiness tests has sufficiently high predictive validity to support this type of use. They are more appropriately used to make instructional decisions regarding skills a child needs to develop.

Early School Readiness and Achievement Tests. Several tests have been developed to measure those basic concepts and skills considered essential for effective learning in the early school years. The tests are intended to be useful in instructional planning. The tests are usually designed for preschool use (kindergarten or sooner) but also can be used in the early primary grades. A typical example is the *Boehm Test of Basic Concepts–Revised.* This test is based on a selection of verbal concepts (e.g., *biggest, nearest, several*) that are needed to understand oral communication and to profit most from school experiences. The test items are read to the students, and they answer by placing an X on the pictures designed to measure the concepts.

Somewhat similar in makeup and purpose are the *Cooperative Preschool Inventory,* the *Stanford Early School Achievement Test,* and *Tests of Basic Experience.* These tests emphasize basic concepts, but they also tap other types of preschool learning (e.g., knowledge of environment). Although these tests are broader in scope than the *Boehm Test,* their intended use is the same—to determine the students' achievement of important concepts and skills and to detect deficiencies for which appropriate learning experiences might be supplied. These tests should be useful in planning for and evaluating preschool instruction and in designing remedial programs for individual students.

Reading Readiness Tests. Tests of reading readiness are used at the kindergarten and first-grade level to help identify skills that have been mastered and those that need to be learned and to help plan beginning reading instruction. The following functions are commonly measured by reading readiness tests:

1. Visual discrimination. Identifying similarities and differences in words, letters, numbers, geometric figures, or pictures.

2. Auditory discrimination. Identifying similarities and differences in spoken words or sounds.

3. Verbal comprehension. Demonstrating or understanding the meaning of words, sentences, and directions.

4. Recognition of letters, words, and numbers. Identifying letters of the alphabet, words, and numerals.

5. Recognition of words in sample lessons. Identifying words that have been taught in sample lessons.

6. Memory. Reproducing a geometric figure, following instructions, or selecting a picture from memory.

7. Drawing or copying. Demonstrating skill in drawing or copying geometric forms, objects, letters, or numbers.

Not all reading readiness tests provide comprehensive coverage of the above areas. Some tests cover only a few readiness skills, whereas others include tasks from four or five of the areas. Thus, as in all types of testing, the first step is to decide what is to be measured. In this particular case, it means deciding what reading readiness skills are most relevant to the reading program. A clear description of the skills to be measured is a prerequisite to valid test selection and use. (See "Selecting Readiness Tests.")

A typical example of a widely used readiness test is the *Metropolitan Readiness Test*. It is available in two levels: Level 1 is used up to the middle of kindergarten, and Level 2 is used in the second half of kindergarten and the first half of first grade. Level 2 contains the following eight tests:

1. Beginning Consonants.

2. Sound-Letter Correspondence.

3. Visual Matching.

4. Finding Patterns.

5. School Language.

6. Listening.

7. Quantitative Concepts.

8. Quantitative Operations.

Sample items for some of the tests are shown in Figure 14.5. The items are orally administered with elaborate directions. The very abbreviated directions used here are simply to illustrate the nature of the task. If a test user is interested in reading readiness only, separate scoring and norms are available for Tests 1 through 6.

Readiness for beginning reading involves more than the skills measured by readiness tests. Such factors as mental ability, physical development, experiential background, social and emotional adjustment, and desire to read also must be considered. The readiness test focuses on important prerequisite skills, but test performance must be interpreted in light of the student's total readiness for learning.

GUIDELINES

Selecting Readiness Tests

1. Because these tests are predictive instruments, the test manual should be examined concerning the effectiveness with which they predict success in the given area. Validity coefficients should be at least as high as those obtained with general scholastic aptitude tests and preferably higher.

2. In addition to their predictive value, these tests also have some general diagnostic value. Thus, the test's content should be evaluated in light of the type of readiness information desired and the uses to be made of the results.

3. These tests provide just a fraction of the information needed to determine readiness for learning in a given area. The pupil's social and emotional adjustment, past achievement in the area, motivation to learn, and cultural background also must be taken into account.

4. Readiness tests do not have sufficient predictive validity to be used alone to screen children out of kindergarten or delay entry into first grade.

FIGURE 14.5
Sample items illustrating the *Metropolitan Readiness Test, Level 2* (Copyright © 1986, Harcourt Brace Jovanovich. Used by permission.)

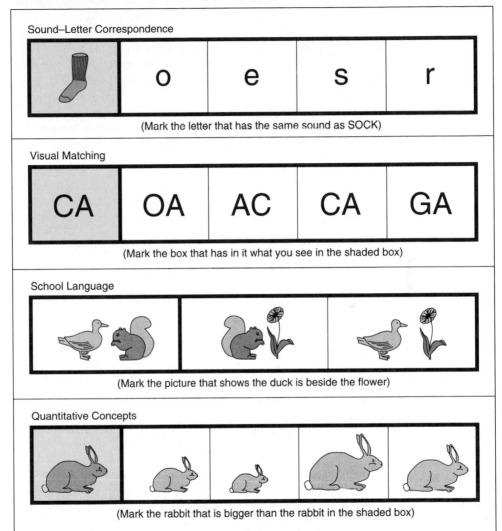

Sound–Letter Correspondence

(Mark the letter that has the same sound as SOCK)

Visual Matching

(Mark the box that has in it what you see in the shaded box)

School Language

(Mark the picture that shows the duck is beside the flower)

Quantitative Concepts

(Mark the rabbit that is bigger than the rabbit in the shaded box)

CUSTOMIZED ACHIEVEMENT TESTS

Banks of objectives and related test items are maintained by most large test publishers and by some other organizations. These item banks are used for computer generation of customized tests. In some cases the tests are prepared by the test publisher. In others, the publisher will sell or lease computer software that includes banks of items keyed to objectives and a program for constructing and printing locally prepared customized tests.

When using publisher-prepared customized achievement tests, the test user typically selects the objectives to be measured from an objective catalogue and specifies the number of items to be used for measuring each objective. The test publisher then assembles and prints the test by taking from the item banks those items that measure the selected objectives. Scoring and reporting services are also available from the publisher for these tests. A typical example of such a customized program is the *Multiscore System,* by The Riverside Publishing Company. Currently it offers approximately 1,500 objectives and more than 5,500 test items in reading and language arts, mathematics, science, social studies, and life skills. The objectives are arranged by unit clusters in three catalogues, with the recommended grade level indicated for each objective. See Figure 14.6 for a sample listing. The service includes customized test booklets (either machine scorable or reusable), scoring,

FIGURE 14.6
Sample performance objectives from *Multiscore, Criterion-Referenced Testing Service Catalog* (Copyright © 1985 by The Riverside Publishing Company. Used by permission.)

Scientific Methods
Grades 1 – 12(9 objectives)
A SCIENCE

UNIT CLUSTERS	PERFORMANCE OBJECTIVES	PERFORMANCE OBJECTIVE CODES	GRADE RANGE
Scientific Procedures A5A3	The student:		
	. . . classifies pictures by shape, sequence, function, symmetry, or other features.	5A01 5A02	3 - 4 7 - 8
	. . . identifies an object from various perspectives.	5A03	5 - 6
	. . . draws conclusions based on elapsed time, descriptions, and tabular data.	5A04	9 - 12
	. . . forms a hypothesis about an outcome.	5A05	3 - 4
	. . . forms a hypothesis or identifies a test for a hypothesis.	5A06 5A07 5A08	5 - 6 7 - 8 9 - 12
	. . . interprets visual or tabular data.	5A09 5A10 5A11	1 - 2 3 - 4 7 - 8
	. . . measures length in arbitrary units and/or solves problems involving measurement.	5A12 5A13 5A14	3 - 4 7 - 8 9 - 12

and reports (including class reports by objective and test item). Other test publishers have similar programs.

Locally produced customized achievement tests can be prepared using microcomputer-based software products available from test publishers. An example of this type of program is the *Academic Instructional Measurement System (AIMS)* by The Psychological Corporation. This is a large bank of objectives and test items in mathematics and reading and language arts developed from texts and curriculum materials used nationally. The preparation of locally constructed customized tests can be done manually, from camera-ready printed materials, or by use of an optional microcomputer software system (see "Academic Instructional Measurement Systems (AIMS))." The system makes possible local test printing, scoring, and reporting of results.

Customized tests prepared by test publishers, or prepared locally, are especially useful for classroom testing because they can be designed to yield measurements of the specific knowledge and skills covered in the instructional program. Locally controlled microcomputer systems have the added advantage of being able to prepare tests as needed, without the time lag created when ordering customized tests from the publisher. In addition, a microcomputer system makes it easy to add locally prepared objectives and test items to the bank. In using customized tests, however they are prepared, it is important to select the objectives carefully and to include enough items for each instructional objective or skill cluster to provide for

Academic Instructional Measurement Systems (AIMS)

AIMS is a test development system for preparing locally developed tests for Grades 1 to 12. It includes 989 objectives and 7,000 related test items in mathematics and reading and language arts. Steps in using the system include:

1. Selecting objectives that were taught in the classroom.
2. Selecting from among the 6 to 8 items for each objective.
3. Producing test booklets using camera-ready copy or the optional computer software system.
4. Producing answer keys and administration manuals.

AIMS Software Option

AIMS tests can be constructed by microcomputer with the *AIMS* software system. Objectives, test items, item statistics, and related materials are included on microcomputer diskettes. The program permits retrieval of text from the item bank for tests, administration manuals, and scoring keys. It also allows the deletion of items and the integration of locally written items and objectives into the bank. A demonstration disk with a tutorial booklet is available to show how *AIMS* software can make local test construction efficient and easy.

Note: Adapted from The Psychological Corporation catalogue (1992).

reliable interpretations. It is also necessary, of course, to make certain that the individual items are relevant to the instructional objectives they are to measure.

Information concerning customized test development and microcomputer software can be obtained from test publishers' catalogues. See Appendix C for test publishers' addresses and a list of banks of items keyed to objectives, that are available for school use.

INDIVIDUAL ACHIEVEMENT TESTS

Because of the increased number of handicapped children in the regular classroom, it would seem desirable for classroom teachers to become familiar with some of the individual tests that are available for measuring achievement. These tests are administered to one student at a time and the questions are typically answered orally or by pointing, although some writing may be required. Some of the tests provide for norm-referenced interpretation, some use criterion-referenced interpretation, and still others provide for both types of interpretation. Typical examples of individual achievement tests include the following:

❑ *Basic Achievement Skills Individual Screener* (Grades 1 to A)
❑ *Peabody Individual Achievement Test—Revised* (K to adult)
❑ *KeyMath Diagnostic Arithmetic Test—Revised* (K to Grade 6) (see Figure 14.7)
❑ *Woodcock Reading Mastery Tests—Revised* (K to adult)

Each of these tests can be administered in 30 to 60 minutes, with much of the scoring completed during the administration. Other individual achievement tests can be obtained from test publishers' catalogues (see Appendix C). For reviews of these and other achievement tests discussed in this chapter, see the latest *Mental Measurements Yearbook* or *Test Critiques* described in Chapter 16.

SUMMARY

Standardized achievement tests measure the common objectives of a wide variety of schools, have standard procedures for administration and scoring, and provide norms for interpreting the scores. A test manual and other accessory materials are typically provided to aid in the administration of the test and the interpretation and use of the results. The test items are generally of high quality because they have been prepared by specialists, pretested, and selected on the basis of their effectiveness and their relevance to a rigid set of specifications.

Despite their high technical quality, standardized achievement tests complement rather than replace teachers' informal classroom tests. They are especially useful for measuring general educational development, determining student progress from one year to the next, grouping students, diagnosing learning difficulties, and comparing achievement with learning ability. They are of less value for measuring learning outcomes unique to a particular course, the day-to-day progress

FIGURE 14.7
Sample items from *KeyMath Diagnostic Arithmetic Test* illustrating use of Easel-Kit for individual testing (Used by permission of AGS, American Guidance Service.)

When open, the Easel-Kit® is a freestanding easel, simultaneously displaying test items to the subject and directions to the examiner.

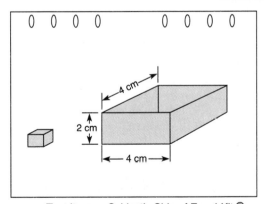

Test Item on Subject's Side of Easel-Kit ®

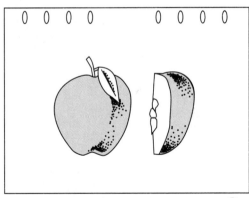

Test Item on Subject's Side of Easel-Kit ®

S-25 Point to the small block and say: **The small block is a one-centimeter cube. How many of these cubes can be put into the box?** (32)

Test Item on Examiner's Side of Easel-Kit ®

B-1 Say: **Here is an apple** (point to the whole apple).
What part of an apple is this (point to the half apple)? ($\frac{1}{2}$)

Test Item on Examiner's Side of Easel-Kit ®

of students, and knowledge of current developments in rapidly changing fields. These purposes are more effectively served by informal classroom tests.

Achievement test batteries are widely used at the elementary school level. They cover the basic skills (i.e., reading, language, mathematics, and study skills), and some batteries also include sections on listening comprehension and science and social studies. Test batteries are less widely used at the high-school level because of the difficulty of identifying a common core of content. Batteries at this level are confined to the basic skills, to content included in the basic high-school subjects, or to measures of general educational development. The main advantage of a test battery is that a student's strengths and weaknesses in different areas can be determined. Most test batteries provide for both norm-referenced interpretation and interpretation by objective or skill area. The complete test battery seldom fits all of the instructional objectives of the school, however, and this must be taken into account when one is interpreting the results.

Some test publishers offer open-ended assessment exercises to supplement their standardized tests. Writing supplements are the most common addition, but sets of open-ended assessment tasks are also offered in different content areas. Typically, the responses can be scored locally or by means of a central scoring service. When the central scoring option is used the scores can be compared to national norms.

The instructional use of achievement batteries has been enhanced by the publishing of sets of diagnostic batteries that are statistically linked to the survey batteries. The larger number of items and subtests in the diagnostic batteries make it possible to obtain a more detailed description of each student's strengths and weaknesses in learning.

In addition to achievement test batteries, there are many separate published tests designed to measure achievement in specific areas. These include tests on course content, reading tests, and readiness tests. Although these can be more readily adapted to the instructional program than complete batteries, the following cautions should be kept in mind during their selection and use: (1) published tests with similar titles may differ radically in terms of the type of test content and in terms of the emphasis given to the various skills measured; (2) published tests measure only a portion of the knowledge, skills, and abilities needed to evaluate, predict, or diagnose learning progress; (3) published tests are effective to the extent that they measure the instructional objectives and serve the intended uses of the particular school program in which they are administered.

To more adequately meet the needs of classroom teachers for individualized instruction and mastery learning, test publishers are now making available customized achievement tests. Some publishers also provide item banks and software programs that enable schools to produce their own customized tests with microcomputers. These customized achievement tests measure student mastery of locally selected instructional objectives and thus describe what learning tasks a student can and cannot perform in the local instructional program. The interpretations must be made with great caution, however, because there are frequently a small number of test items measuring each objective or skill.

There are now many students with handicaps in regular classrooms. In testing these students, an individual achievement test may be more appropriate. These are administered on a one-to-one basis, and the questions are typically answered orally or by pointing. There are a number of such tests available for school use.

LEARNING EXERCISES

1. What are the similarities and differences in the making of a classroom test and a standardized test of achievement? How are the uses of the two tests likely to differ?

2. What are the advantages of using an achievement battery rather than separate achievement tests? What are the disadvantages?

3. Describe how a survey achievement battery and a related diagnostic battery differ in makeup and use.

4. If possible, study the manual of an achievement test battery. Review the information on how it was constructed. How complete is the information?

5. Examine two standardized achievement tests in an area you are teaching or plan to teach. How do the tests differ in terms of the learning outcomes and content each measures? What types of interpretations are suggested?

6. What are the advantages of using school readiness tests? What are some possible disadvantages?

7. For what situations might you use a customized achievement test instead of a standardized test?

8. What are the advantages of providing both norm-referenced interpretations and objective-referenced interpretations of published achievement tests? What are some of the cautions to be observed in making both types of interpretation for the same test?

FURTHER READING

Anastasi, A. (1988). *Psychological testing* (6th ed.). New York: Macmillan. Chapter 14, "Educational Testing," describes common types of achievement tests used in education with illustrative test items.

Ebel, R. L., & Frisbie, D. A. (1991). *Essentials of educational measurement* (5th ed.). Englewood Cliffs, NJ: Prentice-Hall. Chapter 16, "The Nature of Standardized Tests" describes the characteristic features of standardized tests.

Linn, R. L. (1992). Achievement testing. In M. C. Alkin, (Ed.), *Encyclopedia of educational research* (6th ed.), (Vol. 1). New York: Macmillan. Provides a discussion of contemporary issues in achievement testing.

Mehrens, W. A., & Lehmann, I. J. (1991). *Using standardized tests in education* (4th ed.). New York: Holt, Rinehart & Winston. Chapter 8, "Standardized Achievement Tests," describes various types of achievement tests used in the schools and the uses of achievement test results.

Shepard, L. A. (1990). Readiness testing in local schools: An analysis of backdoor policy. *Politics of Education Association Yearbook,* 159–179.

CHAPTER 15
Aptitude Tests

Aptitude tests are designed to predict future performance in some activity. Those used in schools range from traditional scholastic aptitude tests to more comprehensive differential aptitude tests. Attempts have also been made to develop special culture-fair tests. In this chapter, typical examples of aptitude tests used in schools will be discussed and illustrated.

Because one of the school's major aims is to help students achieve the maximum of which they are capable, it is not surprising that standardized aptitude tests are widely used. Aptitude tests can provide information that is useful in determining learning readiness, individualizing instruction, organizing classroom groups, identifying underachievers, diagnosing learning problems, and helping students with their educational and vocational plans. Although the results of achievement tests are also useful for these purposes, aptitude tests make a special contribution.

To avoid misinterpretations and misuses it is important to understand the limitations as well as the strengths of aptitude tests. Contrary to popular belief, aptitude tests do not measure a fixed capacity. Rather, they provide an indication of present level of learned abilities and can be useful in predicting future performance. Performance on aptitude tests is influenced by previous learning experiences, but it is less directly dependent on specific courses of instruction than is performance on achievement tests.

ACHIEVEMENT AND APTITUDE TESTS

Before we discuss the various types of aptitude tests, we shall consider some similarities and differences between achievement tests and aptitude tests. A common distinction is that achievement tests measure what a student has learned, and aptitude tests measure the ability to learn new tasks. Although this appears to be a clear distinction, it oversimplifies the problem and covers up some important similarities and differences. Actually both types measure what a student has learned, and both are useful for predicting success in learning new tasks. The main differences lie in (1) the types of learning measured by each test and (2) the types of prediction for which each is most useful.

Types of Learning Measured: The Ability Spectrum

The various types of learning measured by achievement and aptitude tests can be best depicted if they are arranged along a continuum, as shown in Table 15.1. In this spectrum of ability tests, achievement tests fall at Levels A and B and aptitude tests fall at Levels C, D, and E. The spectrum classifies the various types of tests according to the degree to which the test content depends on specific learning experiences. At one extreme (Level A) is the content-oriented achievement test that measures knowledge of specific course content. At the other extreme (Level E) is the culture-oriented nonverbal aptitude test that measures a type of learning not influenced much by typical school experiences. Thus, as we move through the different levels of the spectrum from A to E, the test content becomes less dependent on any particular set of learning experiences.

The closer two tests are to each other in the spectrum, the more nearly alike will be the types of learning measured. Achievement tests designed to measure

TABLE 15.1
Spectrum of ability tests according to types of learning measured.

Level	General Test Type	Types of Learning Measured
A	Content-oriented achievement tests (e.g., *Tests of Achievement and Proficiency*)	Knowledge of subject matter in courses such as social studies, English, mathematics, and science.
B	Tests of general educational development (e.g., *Iowa Tests of Educational Development, ITBS*)	Basic skills and complex learning outcomes common to many courses, such as the application of principles and interpretation of data.
C	School-oriented aptitude tests (e.g., *School and College Ability Tests, SCAT*)	Verbal, numerical, and general problem-solving abilities similar to those learned in *school,* such as vocabulary, reading, and arithmetic reasoning.
D	Culture-oriented verbal aptitude tests (e.g., *Cognitive Abilities Test, Verbal Battery, and Quantitative Battery*)	Verbal, numerical, and general problem-solving abilities derived more from the *general culture* than from common *school experiences.*
E	Culture-oriented nonverbal aptitude tests (e.g., *Cognitive Abilities Test, Nonverbal Battery*)	Abstract reasoning abilities based on figure analogies, figure classification, and other nonverbal tasks unrelated to school experience.

Source: Adapted from L. J. Cronbach, *Essentials of Psychological Testing,* 4th ed. (New York: Harper & Row, 1984).

general educational development (Level B) and scholastic aptitude tests based on school-learned abilities (Level C), for example, both measure somewhat similar abilities, and can be expected to correlate highly. Likewise, the farther apart two tests are in the spectrum, the less they will have in common and the lower the correlation will be between them. This information is useful in selecting and using aptitude tests. For instance, we can expect aptitude tests at Levels C and D to provide a better prediction of school achievement than those at Level E. On the other hand, if we are primarily interested in identifying students with undeveloped learning potential, tests at Level E will be more useful. When using this spectrum, however, remember that these are merely convenient categories for classifying the different types of ability tests and that some tests will cover two or more categories. Several wide-spectrum scholastic aptitude tests, for example, include a range of test content covering Levels C, D, and E in a single test score.

Types of Predictions Made with Achievement and Aptitude Tests

Achievement and aptitude tests also can be distinguished according to the types of predictions for which each is most useful. Because past achievement is frequently the best predictor of future achievement, both types of achievement tests are useful in predicting future learning. In general, the content-oriented achievement test (Level A) can predict how well a student will learn new knowledge in the same content area, but it is of less value in predicting future learning in other areas. For example, a test of first-semester English will be a good predictor of second-semester English but not of second-semester mathematics, science, or social studies. In other words, its value as a predictor of future learning depends largely on the relationship between the content being measured and the content in the future learning situation. Tests measuring general educational development (Level B) are much more effective predictors of future achievement than are content-oriented tests because they measure intellectual skills and abilities common to a variety of content areas.

If achievement tests are such good predictors of future learning, then why do we use aptitude tests (Levels C to E) in schools? There are several good reasons. (1) An aptitude test can be administered in a relatively short time (some as short as twenty minutes), whereas a comprehensive battery of achievement tests takes several hours. (2) In addition to time saved, aptitude tests can be used with students of more widely varying educational backgrounds. Because the type of learning measured is common to most students, an individual is less apt to be penalized because of specific weaknesses in past instruction. (3) Aptitude tests can be used before a student has had any training in a particular area. For example, success in a French course cannot be predicted by an achievement test in French until the person has had some instruction in it. (4) Another reason applies more to the culture-oriented aptitude test (Levels D and E). Because these measures of aptitude are least influenced by school-learned abilities, they can be used to distinguish low achievers working up to their ability from those with the potential for higher achievement. Identifying such underachievers with aptitude tests that depend heavily on school-learned abilities (Level C) is possible but less effective because the achievement skills required to respond to the test are those in which the underachiever is most apt to be weak.

In summary, both achievement tests and aptitude tests measure learned abilities, but achievement tests measure those that are more directly dependent on specific school experiences, whereas aptitude tests measure those based on a wide range of both in-school and out-of-school experiences. This is a matter of degree, however, and it is possible to arrange both types of tests on a continuum, ranging from the measurement of specific course content (Level A) to the measurement of more broadly based abilities (Levels D and E). Achievement tests and aptitude tests become very much alike near the center of the continuum (Levels B and C). Achievement and aptitude tests are also similar in that they both are useful for predicting future achievement. In general, aptitude tests are a more convenient measure and one that predicts over a wide range of future experiences. As with types of learning outcomes measured, these differences are less pronounced near the center of the continuum.

SCHOLASTIC APTITUDE AND LEARNING ABILITY

Tests designed to measure learning ability traditionally have been called "intelligence tests." This terminology is still used for some individually administered tests and for some group tests, but its use is declining. There are a number of reasons for this. (1) Many people have come to associate the concept *intelligence* with inherited capacity. (2) There is increasing controversy over the meaning of intelligence and the factors that should be included in the concept. (3) Tests in this area have been increasingly used for predicting achievement and describing learning abilities. In place of the term *intelligence test* have come such terms as *learning ability tests, school ability tests, cognitive ability tests,* and *scholastic aptitude tests*. All of these terms emphasize the fact that these tests measure developed abilities useful in learning and not innate capacity or undeveloped potential.

Students' scores on scholastic aptitude tests or ability tests are best interpreted as a measure of present learning ability. Test performance is influenced by such factors as inherited characteristics, experiential background, motivation, particular skills (e.g., reading, test taking), attention, persistence, self-confidence, and emotional adjustment. These factors are all a part of an individual's present ability to perform and, as such, affect both test scores and school achievement. Many of these factors can be modified by educational experiences, however, and therefore both learning ability and school achievement can be improved. It is when we interpret the test scores as unmodifiable measures of learning potential that we are apt to misuse the results.

GROUP TESTS OF LEARNING ABILITY

The majority of tests of learning ability administered in the schools are group tests. These are tests that, like standardized achievement tests, can be administered to many students at one time by persons with relatively little training in test administration. Some group tests yield a single score; others yield two or more scores based on measures of separate aspects of ability. Here we shall briefly describe and illustrate the various types of group tests. Critical reviews of these and other ability tests can be found in the *Mental Measurements Yearbooks* and *Test Critiques.*

Single-Score Tests

Tests that yield a single score are sometimes designed to measure students' general learning ability. Typically, such a variety of types of items is included in the test that no particular ability or skill receives undue emphasis in the total score. Thus, the specific aspects of ability (such as verbal, numerical, and abstract reasoning) are blended together into one global measure of ability. These are sometimes called wide-spectrum tests and cover Levels C through E in the spectrum of abilities described earlier (see Table 15.1).

The single-score test based on a mixture of general verbal and nonverbal items is less common than it once was. Even one of the most widely used tests of this type, the *Otis–Lennon School Ability Test (OLSAT),* has moved away from a single score. The fifth edition of the *OLSAT,* which is still available, provides a single general score. The sixth edition, published in 1989, reports separate verbal and nonverbal scores as well as a total score.

It is now more common for single-score tests to focus on verbal abilities. Like the *Boehm Test of Basic Concepts—Revised* that was discussed in Chapter 14, single ability tests are typically used to measure readiness for school learning and to predict success in future schoolwork. They are highly verbal in nature and this, of course, contributes to their predictive value because school learning is largely verbal. There are exceptions, however, to this general emphasis on verbal abilities. The *Matrix Analogies Test—Short Form,* for example, is a test of nonverbal reasoning that presents abstract designs with missing elements or matrices containing a progression of elements. Students are asked to select the missing element or the next element in the progression.

Whether a test contains a mixture of verbal and nonverbal items or focuses on only one of these abilities, single-score tests do not provide for differential prediction for various types of schoolwork. They are intended only as a general measure of current learning readiness. Thus, a low score will indicate a lack of readiness to perform well on school tasks, but will reveal neither the nature nor the cause of the poor performance. Single-score ability tests provide a quick, effective, general measure of present learning ability.

Tests Yielding Separate Scores

A number of tests of learning ability yield two or more part-scores as well as the total score. Some tests, like the *Otis–Lennon School Ability Test,* Sixth Edition (Grades K to 12), have both verbal and nonverbal scores as well as a total score. The nonverbal score provides a check on the verbal score for those students who are deficient in verbal skills (e.g., poor readers). Other tests, like the *School and College Ability Tests (SCAT)* (Grades 3.5 to 12), provide verbal and quantitative scores. The purpose of these is to obtain differential prediction of school success between courses stressing verbal concepts and those emphasizing mathematical concepts. Predictive studies indicate that verbal scores tend to be the best predictor of success in most courses, however, so interpretations concerning differential prediction must be cautiously made. A relatively large difference between verbal and quantitative scores is needed before it is meaningful. The test manual will indicate what size score difference is significant.

The *Cognitive Abilities Test* (Grades K through 12) provides a measure of all three types of reasoning ability important in school learning. It provides scores for each of three different test batteries: verbal, quantitative, and nonverbal. The test includes two primary levels for testing in kindergarten through Grade 3, and eight higher levels for use in Grades 3 through 12. These later eight levels are published in a single multilevel booklet that contains all three batteries. With the multilevel format, the items in each subtest are arranged in order of increasing difficulty and the examinees start and stop at different places, depending on their grade level. If the assigned level is inappropriate for a particular group (e.g., extremely good or poor readers) it is simply a matter of shifting to a higher or lower level within the test.

The primary levels of the *Cognitive Abilities Test* include the following six tests:

Verbal Battery

❑ *Oral Vocabulary*. Mark a picture that illustrates a word or phrase read aloud (e.g., "the one that is round").

❑ *Verbal Classification*. Mark a picture that belongs with three other pictures that are alike in some way (e.g., all are toys).

Quantitative Battery

❑ *Quantitative Concepts*. Mark a picture illustrating a concept (e.g., half a pie).

❑ *Relational Concepts*. Mark a picture illustrating a relation (e.g., tallest tree).

Nonverbal Battery

❑ *Figure Matrices*. Mark the figure that completes a four-cell matrix containing three geometric figures and one empty cell.

❑ *Figure Classification*. Mark the figure that belongs with three other figures that are alike in some way (e.g., all are triangles).

Tests at the primary level are all administered with oral directions and a predetermined pattern of testing is followed. The order alternates tests from different batteries to maintain interest and attention. Time limits are suggested but they are power tests, not speed tests. The test administrator reads the instructions for each item and allows sufficient time for all children to try the item. No reading is involved.

The multilevel edition for Grades 3–12 contains three tests in each of the three batteries—verbal, quantitative, and nonverbal. The three tests in the verbal battery are illustrated by the sample items shown in Figure 15.1. The items in all three tests include verbal tasks that have not been directly taught in school but require the use of verbal concepts that have been learned both in and out of school. The instructions for our illustrative items are very abbreviated.

FIGURE 15.1

Sample items from the verbal battery of the *Cognitive Abilities Test,* Multilevel edition (Copyright © 1986 by The Riverside Publishing Company. Used by permission.)

Verbal Classification (Pick the word that is like the three words in **dark** type)

dog   rabbit   lion

A zoo   B cat   C wild   D pet   E feed

Sentence Completion (Pick the one word that makes a complete, sensible sentence)

We sailed the ——————— in the bathtub.

A dog   B doll   C boat   D towel   E rock

Verbal Analogies (Pick the word that is related to the third word in the same way that the second word is related to the first)

fire ⟶ hot: ice ⟶

A cream   B melt   C box   D cold   E freeze

The quantitative battery contains three tests that require students to solve quantitative tasks that have not been directly taught in school. The sample items in Figure 15.2 illustrate the nature of these tests. Like the verbal battery, the emphasis is on reasoning abilities that require the use of concepts that have been learned both in and out of school.

The nonverbal battery consists of three tests using geometric shapes and figures, as illustrated in Figure 15.3. The concepts needed to solve the problems in these items are learned primarily from experiences out of school. Because the tests use neither words nor numbers, the nonverbal battery provides a poorer prediction of school success than the other two batteries. However, the nonverbal tests provide a more accurate measure of the reasoning abilities of poor readers and those deficient in language skills.

The scores on all batteries of the *Cognitive Abilities Test* are expressed as a standard age score (SAS) that has a mean of 100 and a standard deviation of 16. Separate verbal, quantitative, and nonverbal scores are reported, but no total score is reported for the combined batteries. It was felt that a total score could be misleading where skill development in the three areas was very uneven. For instructional purposes, it is better to focus on the strengths and weaknesses in cognitive skills than to conceal them with a total score.

In keeping with the current trend in ability testing, the authors make explicit that this test measures developed abilities that are modifiable by experience.

All users of the *Cognitive Abilities Test* should recognize that it measures developed abilities, not innate abilities. The cognitive skills measured by the test reflect the cog-

FIGURE 15.2

Sample items from the quantitative battery of the *Cognitive Abilities Test,* Multilevel edition (Copyright © 1986 by The Riverside Publishing Company. Used by permission.)

nitive strategies and general cognitive control processes that an individual has developed, from experience both in and out of school, that enable him or her to learn new tasks or solve problems when instruction is absent or incomplete. Research has clearly shown that these skills change as individuals get older and as their experiences both in and out of school become broader and more varied (Thorndike and Hagen, 1986).

The use of standard age scores, in place of the outmoded deviation IQ used in some older tests, helps avoid the many misinterpretations associated with IQ scores.

The *Cognitive Abilities Test* was described and illustrated in considerable detail because it shows the variety of item types used in group ability tests and it includes some of the current trends in testing (e.g., use of a multilevel format, elimination of the terms *intelligence* and *IQ scores,* and emphasis on power rather than speed of work). There are, of course, many other good tests of learning ability. See Appendix D for representative examples.

Choosing the Appropriate Test

The decision as to which type of test to select depends largely on the use to be made of the results. If the test is to be used only for an overall prediction of school success, a single-score test would suffice. However, if we want to obtain a more accurate measure of the reasoning abilities of poor readers or want to detect students weak in quantitative reasoning, then a test yielding separate scores would be favored. The single-score test provides a quick, easy-to-administer, global measure of reasoning

FIGURE 15.3

Sample items from the nonverbal battery of the *Cognitive Abilities Test,* Multilevel edition (Copyright © 1986 by The Riverside Publishing Company. Used by permission.)

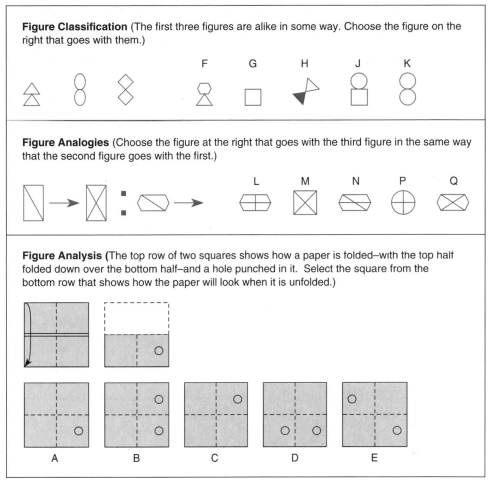

ability, but multiscore tests provide information concerning several separate types of reasoning ability.

If the ability test is to be used in conjunction with an achievement test battery, it is important that the ability test and achievement battery both be standardized on the same population. This makes it possible to compare directly the two sets of scores, and thus obtain a more complete description of educational progress and the factors affecting it. Most publishers of achievement test batteries publish a corresponding ability test, covering the same grade levels, and administer both to the same standardization groups. A list of such ability and achievement tests is presented in Table 15.2.

In some cases, it may be desirable to select the achievement battery first and then use the ability test that has been standardized on the same groups.

TABLE 15.2
Representative ability tests and corresponding achievement batteries standardized on the same populations

Ability Test	Grade Levels	Achievement Batteries
Otis–Lennon School Ability Test (OLSAT)	1–12	Metropolitan Achievement Tests Stanford Achievement Tests
Educational Ability Series	K–12	SRA Achievement Series SRA Survey of Basic Skills
Cognitive Abilities Test (CogAT)	K–12	Iowa Tests of Basic Skills (K–9) Tests of Achievement and Proficiency (9–12)
School and College Ability Tests (SCAT)	3.5–12.9	Sequential Tests of Educational Progress
Tests of Cognitive Skills	2–12	California Achievement Tests (K–12) Comprehensive Tests of Basic Skills (K–12)

INDIVIDUAL TESTS

Learning abilities are also measured by individual tests. These are typically called intelligence tests or intelligence scales but a broader interpretation is more defensible. Like the group tests, they measure present abilities that have been acquired through both in-school and out-of-school experiences.

Individual tests are administered to one examinee at a time in a face-to-face situation. The problems are presented orally by the examiner and the examinee responds by pointing, giving an oral answer, or performing some manipulative task. The administration of individual tests requires extensive training. This is typically obtained in a special course in individual testing. A basic part of the course is extensive practice in test administration under supervision. No one should attempt to use individual tests without this special training.

Group tests provide a satisfactory estimate of learning abilities for the majority of students. However, individual tests have some special advantages over a group test. Because the individual test is administered to one student at a time, it is possible to control more carefully such factors as motivation and to assess more accurately the extent to which disabling behaviors are influencing the score. The influence of reading skill is deemphasized because the tasks are presented orally to the student. In addition, clinical insights concerning the student's method of attacking problems and persistence in solving them are more readily obtained with individual testing. These advantages make the individual test especially useful for testing young children, for retesting students whose scores on group tests are questionable, and for testing students with special problems. For example, in planning individualized programs for students with mental handicaps, the more dependable and informative individual measure of ability is preferred.

The two most highly regarded individual tests for use with school children are the *Stanford–Binet Intelligence Scale* and the *Wechsler Intelligence Scales*. Each of these will be briefly described. Although teachers would not be expected to administer such tests, some familiarity with the testing procedures should contribute to more effective interpretation and use of the test scores.

Stanford–Binet Scale, Fourth Edition

The fourth edition of the *Stanford–Binet Scale* changed considerably from earlier editions. In the former editions (from 1908 on), the tests were arranged by age levels and the examiner presented a variety of item types as he or she moved from one age level to the next. The resulting measure of ability was expressed as a mental age that was then converted to a deviation IQ with a mean of 100 and a standard deviation of 16. The deviation IQ represented a highly verbal measure of general ability.

In the fourth edition, the grouping of items by age level has been replaced by the grouping of items into fifteen separate tests. Each test consists of the same type items arranged in order of increasing difficulty, with two items at each level having approximately the same difficulty. The fifteen tests include many of the item types of earlier editions but provide broader coverage of memory, quantitative, and spatial tasks. Six of the tests cover the full range of the scale, from age 2 to adult, but seven of the tests start above age 2 and two tests end below the adult level. The 15 tests are arranged into four cognitive areas, as follows:

Verbal Reasoning
❑ *Vocabulary:* Defining terms.
❑ *Comprehension:* Identifying and giving reasons for events.
❑ *Absurdities:* Explaining what is wrong or silly about pictures.
❑ *Verbal Relations:* Telling how three things are alike and differ from a fourth.

Quantitative Reasoning
❑ *Quantitative:* Counting, computation, and problem solving.
❑ *Number Series:* Completing the next two items in a number sequence.
❑ *Equation Building:* Arranging numbers and symbols to form an equation.

Abstract/Visual Reasoning
❑ *Pattern Analysis:* Reproducing patterns using a form board and cubes.
❑ *Copying:* Copying designs using blocks and drawings.
❑ *Matrices:* Completing matrices that have portions missing.
❑ *Paper Folding and Cutting:* Identifying pictures of unfolded paper after viewing it folded and cut.

Short-Term Memory
❑ *Bead Memory:* Identifying beads and bead patterns.
❑ *Memory for Sentences:* Repeating sentences verbatim.
❑ *Memory for Digits:* Repeating digits forward and backward.
❑ *Memory for Objects:* Identifying proper sequences of pictures.

The tests are grouped under these four areas for scoring and profiling but are not administered in that order. The examiner follows a scheduled sequence that mixes the order of tests to maintain the examinee's interest. The examiner begins with the vocabulary test, using chronological age for determining the entry level (i.e., where to begin the test). The vocabulary test, along with chronological age, is then used as a routing test to determine the entry level on all other tests. On each test, the basal level is established (when all four items on two consecutive levels are passed) and then the test is continued until a ceiling level is reached (when three or more items are failed at two consecutive levels). This adaptive testing procedure, a carryover from earlier editions, eliminates the items that are too easy and too difficult for the examinee and administers only those of appropriate difficulty (see Figure 15.4).

The raw score for each test is obtained by subtracting the number of items failed from the sequential number (or value) of the highest item administered. This procedure, of course, gives credit for those items below the basal level that were not administered. An individual's raw score on each test is converted, by means of

FIGURE 15.4

Adaptive testing procedure like that used in the *Stanford–Binet,* Fourth Edition (Adapted from the *Stanford–Binet,* Fourth Edition, scoring form.)

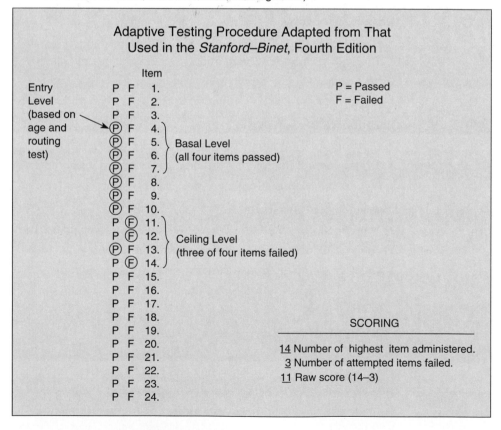

tables, to standard scores with a mean of 50 and a standard deviation of 8. These scores are then combined to obtain Standard Age Scores (SAS^s) for each of the four cognitive areas and for the total scale. These SAS^s are normalized standard scores with a mean of 100 and a standard deviation of 16. The SAS units are the same as those used with the deviation IQ of earlier editions, and thus provide for continuity of records. The elimination of the term *IQ* is a desirable move and one that is typical of newer ability tests.

An individual typically does not take all fifteen tests. There are only eight tests suitable for the youngest ages and only thirteen tests suitable for the highest level. Also, in addition to the normal testing procedure, there are a number of abbreviated batteries for special purposes (e.g., quick screening, selecting gifted, assessing learning problems) and modifications in procedure for testing special populations (e.g., deaf, visually impaired, motor impaired, limited English proficiency). The changes from earlier editions make this fourth edition a more flexible and useful instrument.

In summary, the fourth edition of the *Stanford–Binet Scale* includes a variety of ability tests grouped into four cognitive areas. It is administered to one person at a time using an adaptive testing procedure. It provides four area scores and a full-scale score, called Standard Age Scores, that have a mean of 100 and a standard deviation of 16. The comprehensive coverage of the fourth edition and its flexibility make it an excellent measure of cognitive abilities when administered by a skillful and experienced examiner.

Wechsler Scales

The *Wechsler Scales* include three tests that collectively cover all ages, from age 4 through adult:

1. *Wechsler Preschool and Primary Scale of Intelligence (WPPSI—R)* (ages 4 to 6.5).
2. *Wechsler Intelligence Scale for Children (WISC—R)* (ages 6.5 to 16.5).
3. *Wechsler Adult Intelligence Scale (WAIS—R)* (age 16 to adult).

The Wechsler tests are organized by subtests. Each test consists of a verbal scale made up of five or six subtests and a performance scale made up of five subtests. Although the subtests vary slightly from one level to another, the following subtests from the *WISC—R* exemplify the test content in the *Wechsler Scales*. The sample questions in parentheses were not taken from the *WISC—R* but are similar to items in the *WISC—R*.

Verbal Scale

1. *Information:* Answer questions based on general information (e.g., "How many legs does a cat have?").
2. *Similarities:* Explain in what way a series of paired things are alike (e.g., apple and orange).
3. *Arithmetic:* Solve problems similar to those used in school (e.g., "If two pencils cost a nickel, how many could you buy for a quarter?").

4. *Vocabulary:* Tell the meaning of words from a master list of 32, arranged in order of increasing difficulty.

5. *Comprehension:* Answer questions requiring common-sense comprehension (e.g., "Why should people tell the truth?").

Digit Span (alternate test): Repeat series of digits forward and backward after hearing them once (e.g., 493). This test may substitute for any of the others in the verbal scale.

Performance Scale

6. *Picture Completion:* Tell what part is missing in incomplete pictures.

7. *Picture Arrangement:* Arrange sets of cartoon panels in proper sequence so that they tell a story.

8. *Block Design:* Arrange sets of blocks (colored red and white) so that they match pictures of designs on examiner's cards.

9. *Object Assembly:* Put together jigsaw puzzles based on parts of objects (e.g., car).

10. *Coding:* Match numbers and symbols by referring to a simple code that is kept in front of the examinee.

Mazes (alternate for the coding test): Trace on a paper maze, within a set time limit.

Each subtest in the *WISC—R* is administered and scored separately. The tests are administered by alternating between the verbal and performance scales (test order is 1, 6, 2, 7, etc.) to maintain greater interest and attention. The raw scores on the individual tests are converted to scaled scores with a mean of 10 and a standard deviation of 3. They are then combined to produce a verbal IQ, a performance IQ, and a total IQ. These are deviation IQ^s with a mean of 100 and a standard deviation of 15 (*Stanford–Binet* SAS^s use 16).

The three *Wechsler Scales* are similar in test content and organization, and all three provide the same deviation IQ^s for the verbal, performance, and total scales. Like the *Stanford–Binet,* a number of abbreviated scales also can be used for various screening purposes.

Both the *Stanford–Binet* and the *Wechsler Scales* have been widely used for the individual testing of school children. Both yield highly reliable results (.90+ for the full-scale scores) when administered by competent examiners, and they are probably equally good for predicting success in school. However, the fourth edition of the *Stanford–Binet,* because of its broader coverage, is likely to be more useful for analyzing learning problems and testing special populations.

CAUTIONS IN INTERPRETING AND USING LEARNING ABILITY SCORES

There are a number of cautions to keep in mind when interpreting and using learning ability tests. Here we shall highlight some of the main ones.

1. Allow for normal variation in the test scores. Learning ability or scholastic aptitude tests are some of our most reliable psychological tests. A reliability coefficient of .90 (which is typical), however, results in a standard error of measurement of approximately 5 points (SD = 16). Thus, a score of 100 should be interpreted as a band of scores ranging from 95 to 105, rather than as a precise point. When scores from different tests are compared we can expect differences larger than 5 points because the tests measure different aspects of ability and they are standardized on different populations. The largest variations in scores can be found at the elementary school levels because abilities are less stable during their formation and testing conditions are more difficult to control with elementary students.

2. Seek the causes of low scores. The scores on learning ability tests are based on the use of concepts acquired from both in-school and out-of-school experiences. Thus, inadequate motivation to do school tasks, a language handicap, or a barren home environment can prevent the learning of concepts required in the test. Similarly, poor reading ability, lack of test-taking skills, anxiety, and low self-esteem can lower scores by adversely influencing test performance. Many of these factors can be detected by simply looking for possible causes of low scores. Following up low scores on a group test with an individual test is also helpful. This reduces the influence of reading ability and provides for more careful observation of test-taking skills, language skills, motivation, and other relevant personal characteristics.

3. Verify test results by comparison with other information. More effective interpretation of learning ability test scores is likely to result when test performance is checked against teachers' observations, achievement test scores, and other evidence of learning and development. Discrepancies between the test scores and other information may suggest retesting or clarify the nature of the factors influencing test performance.

4. Use the test results to improve learning. Learning ability tests provide a fairly good prediction of school success. Correlations between these test scores and school marks typically fall between .40 and .60. When correlated with scores on achievement test batteries, correlations of .60 to .80 are common. Unfortunately, the relationship between learning ability test scores and achievement is all too frequently used as a rationalization for inadequate school performance. For example, we might hear comments like, "These students aren't doing well in school because of their poor learning ability." Instead, teachers should alter the instruction for these children; slow the pace, introduce programs that build up their verbal and quantitative concepts, and provide more direction and practice in problem solving. The same factors that lower school achievement (e.g., poor verbal and quantitative development) also lower scores on learning ability tests and both types of performance are modifiable. Thus, learning ability scores can be used, in conjunction with other information, to facilitate plans for improved learning rather than as an excuse for lack of school success.

5. Be cautious in identifying students as underachievers. Comparing a student's scores on a learning ability test and an achievement test and labeling the student as an underachiever if the achievement test scores are lower is fraught with difficulties. Because both are measuring developed abilities, these discrepancies typically can be accounted for by such factors as the measurement error in both tests, the differences in content measured by the two tests, and variations in attitude and attention during test taking. If the two tests are normed on different populations, another basis for deviation is introduced. Discrepancies between learning ability and achievement test scores simply reflect the fact that the correlation between them is far from perfect. The safest procedure is to consider only very large discrepancies as possible signs of underachievement and then confirm these judgments by examining other types of information.

CULTURE-FAIR TESTING

Because all tests are measures of learned abilities, special problems arise when testing the aptitudes of individuals from different cultures and subcultures. There are numerous cultural differences that are likely to influence test performance. In addition to the more obvious one of language, there are such differences as motivation, attitude toward testing, competitiveness, speed, practice in test taking, and opportunity to learn the knowledges and skills measured by the test. Culture-fair testing is an attempt to obtain a measure of ability that is relatively free of all or most of these differences. Although various approaches have been used to accomplish this, the following procedures are typical: (1) The test materials are primarily nonverbal and include diagrams or pictures familiar to the various cultural groups for whom the test is intended. Sometimes translated verbal tests are used. (2) Attempts are made to use materials and methods that are interesting to the examinees, in order to encourage motivation. (3) Liberal time limits are typically provided to deemphasize speed as a factor. (4) The test procedures are kept simple in order to rule out differences in test-taking experience. (5) Test content is based on those intellectual skills common to the cultural groups being tested. Of course, culture-fair testing is an ideal, not a reality. Most attempts to remove cultural influences from tests have fallen short of their goal.

One of the best-known tests in this area is R. B. Cattell's *Culture-Fair Intelligence Tests*. These are short, nonverbal tests that use pictures and diagrams common to many cultures. There are three scales available for different age levels. Scale 1 is for ages 4 to 8 and older retardates. It includes eight subtests, four of which must be administered individually. Scales 2 and 3 (age 8 to adult) each contain four subtests, involving the following perceptual tasks (see sample items in Figure 15.5):

1. *Series:* Select the item that comes next in a series.
2. *Classification:* Select the item that does not belong with the others.
3. *Matrices:* Select the item that completes a matrix.
4. *Conditions:* Match the conditions in a sample design by placing a dot in the appropriate place on one of several alternate designs. In the item in Figure 15.5, the dot must be in the circle but not in the small square.

Scales 2 and 3 can be administered individually or as group tests. They have been given to individuals in a number of countries with mixed results. In general, test performance tended to differ most where the cultural differences were greatest.

FIGURE 15.5
Sample items from the
Culture-Fair Intelligence Tests
(Reproduced by permission of
the copyright owner, Institute of
Personality and Ability Testing.)

When used in schools in the United States, the *Culture-Fair Intelligence Tests* can be expected to produce results similar to those of the *Nonverbal Battery of the Cognitive Abilities Test.*

DIFFERENTIAL APTITUDE TESTING

The work of Guilford (1967) has been a major influence in moving testing from the measurement of a limited number of general mental abilities to the measurement of numerous specific abilities. On the basis of years of research, using the method of factor analysis, he proposed a three-dimensional model to provide a complete "structure of intellect." His theoretical model is shown in Figure 15.6. The model contains 120 cells (5 × 6 × 4), and each cell represents an ability that can be described by (1) what the person does (operation), (2) the nature of the material on which the operation is performed (content), and (3) the type of outcome or product involved (product). For example, a test based on figure analogies, like that in the nonverbal battery of *Cognitive Abilities Test* (see Figure 15.3), would be classified in the Cognition–Figural–Relations cell because it calls for the recognition of figure relations. Similarly, a test using verbal analogies, such as those in the verbal battery of *Cognitive Abilities Test* (see Figure 15.1), would be classified in the Cognition–

FIGURE 15.6
Guilford's structure of intellect model (From J. P. Guilford, *The Nature of Human Intelligence.* New York: McGraw-Hill, 1967. Reproduced by permission.)

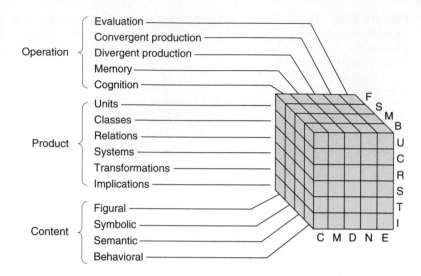

Semantic–Relations cell because it calls for recognition of the relations between word meanings.

Tests have not been developed for each of the cells in the structure of intellect, but the model has served as a guide to Guilford and his coworkers in their search for specific abilities. Although it was assumed that someday there will be tests for all 120 cells, many of the distinctions between cells are so minor that they are unlikely to be reliably measured or be of practical importance. Broader dimensions that would span several cells are generally of greater utility in practical applications.

The experimental search for multiple abilities by Guilford and others, combined with the increasing emphasis on educational and vocational guidance since World War II, has resulted in a number of multi-aptitude batteries. Although such batteries are intended primarily for guidance purposes, they also can be useful in individualizing instruction and in planning courses that utilize a broader range of human abilities. As noted earlier, school learning is largely verbal learning, regardless of the name of the course. The differential testing of abilities provides an opportunity to develop learning experiences that take advantage of each individual's total pattern of aptitudes.

Multi-aptitude batteries that measure both educational and vocational aptitudes have been designed primarily for the high school level and beyond. Among the most widely used tests of this type are the *Differential Aptitude Tests (DAT)* (Grades 8–12), the *Armed Services Vocational Aptitude Battery (ASVAB),* and the *General Aptitude Test Battery (GATB).* The *ASVAB* is used in screening and counseling enlisted personnel for the military services. It is also made available for use in high school counseling programs. The *GATB* was developed by the federal government for use in offices of the United States Employment Service (USES). It can be given in high schools, however, by special arrangement with USES. The *GATB* contains more vocationally-oriented tests than the *DAT* or *ASVAB*.

Here we shall describe the *DAT* in order to illustrate the nature and content of multi-aptitude batteries. Information concerning other batteries available for use in the schools can be obtained from the *Mental Measurements Yearbooks* and *Test Critiques* (see Chapter 16).

Differential Aptitude Tests (DAT)

The first edition of the *DAT* battery was published shortly after World War II (1947) by the Psychological Corporation. The most recent version, the fifth edition, was published in 1990. The fifth edition includes eight tests, each measuring a separate set of abilities. Although some of the tests measure abilities specific enough to fit a particular cell in Guilford's model (see Figure 15.6), most measure a composite of abilities that have been found useful in educational and vocational guidance. The eight tests are Verbal Reasoning (VR), Numerical Reasoning (NR), Abstract Reasoning (AR), Perceptual Speed and Accuracy (PSA), Mechanical Reasoning (MR), Space Relations (SR), Spelling (S), and Language Usage (LU). In addition to separate scores for each of these tests, a combined Verbal Reasoning and Numerical Reasoning score (VR + NR) provides an index of scholastic aptitude similar to that obtained with group tests of learning ability. The Verbal Reasoning and Numerical Reasoning subtests are also available for administration alone in what is called the partial battery. Sample items from the eight tests are shown in Figure 15.7.

Using a battery of aptitude tests like the *DAT* has several advantages over using a series of separate tests covering the same areas. First, because all tests have been standardized on the same population, it is possible to compare a student's strengths and weaknesses on the various measures of aptitude. Second, because all tests are built for the same population of users, they are matched in difficulty and appropriateness for the grade levels for which they are intended. Separate tests covering the same areas are apt to range widely in difficulty, especially the vocational tests. Third, using a common test format and uniform testing procedures for all tests simplifies test administration.

The tests in the DAT tend to be internally consistent (split-half reliabilities average about .90), and the intercorrelations between tests are low enough (average about .50) to indicate that each test measures a relatively independent ability. The evidence of differential prediction, however, is rather disappointing. One might expect the Verbal Reasoning scores to best predict English achievement, the Numerical Reasoning scores to best predict mathematics and science achievement, the Space Relations scores to best predict achievement in mechanical drawing, and so on. A review of the extensive data presented in the test manual, however, reveals only slight differences in prediction from one area to another. The best predictor of school marks in all courses turned out to be the general ability measure, VR + NR.

Computerized *DAT Adaptive* Edition

The computerized adaptive edition of the *Differential Aptitude Tests (DAT Adaptive)* is administered and scored by microcomputer. The "adaptive" feature permits each student to answer only the items appropriate for his or her ability level. Items that are too easy or too difficult for the individual are not administered. This individually tailored version reduces testing time. Although the *DAT Adaptive* is untimed,

FIGURE 15.7
Sample items from the *Differential Aptitude Tests (DAT),* fifth edition (Reproduced by permission. Copyright © 1990 by the Psychological Corporation, San Antonio, Texas. All rights reserved.)

Verbal Reasoning* (25 min.)
Measures the ability to see relationships among words; may be useful in predicting success in business, law, education, journalism, and the sciences.

> **SAMPLE ITEM**
> Which answer contains the missing words to complete this sentence?
>
> ... is to fin as bird is to ...
>   A water – – feather
>   B shark – – nest
> ★ C fish – – wing
>   D flipper – – fly
>   E fish – – sky

Numerical Reasoning* (30 min.)
Measures the ability to perform mathematical reasoning tasks; important in jobs such as bookkeeping, lab work, carpentry, and toolmaking.

> **SAMPLE ITEM**
> Which number should replace R in this correct addition example?
>
>
>
> $$\begin{array}{r} 7R \\ + \ \ R \\ \hline 88 \end{array}$$
>   ★ A 9   D 3
>   B 6   E None of these
>   C 4

Abstract Reasoning (20 min.)
A nonverbal measure of the ability to reason using geometric shapes or designs; important in fields such as computer programming, drafting and vehicle repair.

> **SAMPLE ITEM**
> Choose the Answer Figure that should be the next figure (or fifth one) in the series.

Perceptual Speed and Accuracy (6 min.)
Measures the ability to compare and mark written lists quickly and accurately; helps predict success in performing routine clerical tasks.

> **SAMPLE ITEM**
> Look at the underlined combination of letters or numbers and find the same one on the answer sheet. Then fill in the circle under it.
> 1 XY Xy XX YX Yy
> 2 6g 6G G6 Gg g6
> 3 nm mn mm nn nv
> 4 Db BD Bd Bb BB

Mechanical Reasoning (25 min.)
Understanding basic mechanical principles of machinery, tools, and motion is important for occupations such as carpentry, mechanics, engineering, and machine operations.

> **SAMPLE ITEM**
> Which load will be easier to pull through soft sand?
> A   B   C

Space Relations (25 min.)
Measures the ability to visualize a three-dimensional object from a two-dimensional pattern, and to visualize how this object would look if rotated in space; important in drafting, architecture, design, carpentry, and dentistry.

> **SAMPLE ITEM**
> Choose the one figure that can be made from the pattern.
> 20
> F   ★ G   H   I

Spelling (10 min.)
Measures one's ability to spell common English words; a useful skill in many academic and vocational pursuits.

> **SAMPLE ITEM**
> Decide which word is not spelled correctly in the group below.
>
> ★ A paragraf
>   B dramatic
>   C circular
>   D audience

Language Usage (15 min.)
Measures the ability to detect errors in grammar, punctuation, and capitalization; needed in most jobs requiring a college degree.

> **SAMPLE ITEM**
> Decide which of the four parts of the sentence below contains an error. If there is no error, mark the space on your answer sheet for the letter next to No Error.
>
> Jane and Tom / is going / to the office / this morning.
>   A   ★B   C   D
> E No Error

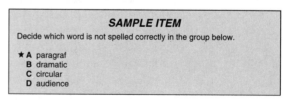

* Also available in the DAT *Partial Battery*

administration time is approximately half of that required for the paper-and-pencil edition. It has the added feature of providing a complete score report immediately following the completion of the testing.

An optional career planning questionnaire (also available with the paper-and-pencil edition) can be administered and scored by computer, along with the *DAT Adaptive.* This questionnaire has students indicate their interest in school subjects and activities, their educational and career plans, their level of academic performance, and their interest in fields of work and specific occupations. A computer-generated career planning report compares each student's interests and plans to the *DAT* scores and interprets and explains areas of agreement and disagreement. When a student's choices of occupation do not match the *DAT* scores, educational plans, and school subject preferences, a list of three occupational areas that do match them is added to the report. Thus, the *DAT Adaptive* can provide both a profile of *DAT* scores and a narrative report describing how the scores relate to the student's educational and career plans. With the aid of a school counselor, such reports should assist students in their vocational planning.

SUMMARY

Standardized aptitude tests are designed to predict future performance in some activity, such as school learning. Like achievement tests, aptitude tests measure learned abilities. They differ from achievement tests, however, in that the test content is broader in scope, and test performance is less dependent on any specific set of learning experiences. This makes it possible to use the tests with students of varying educational backgrounds and to predict performance over a wide range of learning activities.

Group tests of learning ability (or scholastic aptitude) may yield a single score, separate verbal and nonverbal scores, separate verbal and quantitative scores, or several scores based on a series of specific aptitudes. The single-score test is designed to measure general learning ability only. In tests using verbal and nonverbal scores, the nonverbal score serves as a check on the learning ability of the poor reader. Tests with separate verbal and quantitative scores are used primarily for differential prediction. Which type of test to choose depends largely on the type of information desired and the use for which it is intended. For straightforward prediction of school success, a single-score test may suffice, but for helping students with learning problems and educational choices, tests with two or more scores are desirable.

Individual tests of learning ability deemphasize reading skill and provide more carefully controlled testing conditions. Thus, the individual test is especially valuable for testing young children and for checking on questionable scores obtained with group tests. Although extensive training and experience are required to administer individual tests, classroom teachers will likely encounter the scores on school records. It is therefore desirable to know the nature of the test content and the types of scores that are commonly used.

Most group and individual tests of learning ability report test performance in terms of standard scores with a mean of 100 and a standard deviation of 16 (15 for

Wechsler tests). In interpreting and using the scores, it is important to allow for normal variation due to error, to seek causes of low scores, to verify the scores by comparison to other information, to use the results to improve learning, and to interpret underachievement cautiously.

Various attempts have been made to develop culture-fair tests by using nonverbal materials that are interesting and common to many cultures and by using simple procedures and liberal time limits. Although the instruments have not lived up to expectations, they have helped clarify the problems involved.

Comprehensive aptitude batteries, such as the *Differential Aptitude Tests* (*DAT*), have also been developed for school use. These tests include reasoning ability tests as well as vocationally-oriented tests. The computerized adaptive edition of the *DAT* is administered and scored by microcomputer and permits each student to answer only those items appropriate for his or her ability level. When combined with an optional career planning questionnaire, a computer-generated profile of scores and a narrative report for career guidance is provided.

LEARNING EXERCISES

1. List the similarities and differences between achievement tests and aptitude tests.

2. What are the relative advantages and disadvantages of using group tests of learning ability rather than individual tests?

3. What are the main factors that might account for a difference in scores between two different group tests of learning ability?

4. List the similarities and differences between the *Stanford–Binet Scale* and the *Wechsler Scales*.

5. What cautions are necessary in interpreting and using group ability tests?

6. A student from a culturally different home received a verbal score of 80 and a nonverbal score of 90 on the *Otis–Lennon School Ability Test*. What additional information would help you interpret the scores? If you could have the student take another test, what type of test would you want him or her to take? Why?

7. What tests in the *Differential Aptitude Tests* are most similar to the *Cognitive Abilities Test*?

8. What are the advantages of using the *Differential Aptitude Tests* instead of a group test like the *Cognitive Abilities Test?* What are the disadvantages?

REFERENCES

Guilford, J. P., (1967). *The nature of human intelligence*. New York: McGraw-Hill.

Thorndike, R. L. & Hagen, E. (1986). *Examiners Manual, Cognitive Abilities Test* Multilevel Edition. Boston: Riverside Publishing Company.

FURTHER READING

Anastasi, A. (1988). *Psychological testing* (6th ed.). New York: Macmillan. Chapters 9–13 include descriptions of widely used individual, group, and multiple aptitude tests.

Pellegrino, J. (1992). Intelligence and aptitude testing. In M. C. Alkin, (Ed.), *Encyclopedia of educational research* (6th ed.), (Vol. II). New York:

Macmillan. Provides an overview of contemporary issues in intelligence and aptitude testing.

Salvia, J., & Ysseldyke, J. (1991). *Assessment* (5th ed.). Boston: Houghton Mifflin. See Chapters 9–11 for descriptions of group and individual ability tests and difficulties of using them in current practice.

Sattler, J. M. (1988). *Assessment of children* (3rd ed.). San Diego: Jerome M. Sattler. Chapters 6–11 describe the administration and interpretation of the *Stanford–Binet* and the *Wechsler Scales*.

Thorndike, R. M., Cunningham, G. K., Thorndike, R. L., & Hagen, E. P. (1991). *Measurement and evaluation in psychology and education* (5th ed.). New York: Macmillan. Chapter 12, "Aptitude Tests", gives examples from several aptitude tests including illustrative items from the *Wechsler Intelligence Scale for Children—Revised* and the *General Aptitude Test Battery*.

CHAPTER 16

Test Selection, Administration, and Use

Published tests play an important role in the instructional program of the school. They supplement and complement informal classroom tests and aid in many instructional decisions. The task for schools is to locate and select those tests that are most suitable, administer and score them under carefully controlled conditions, and make effective use of the results.

There are many published tests available for school use. The two types of most value to the instructional program of the school are the achievement tests and aptitude tests discussed in the last two chapters. There are hundreds of tests of each type, so great care is needed in selecting those tests that are most relevant to the objectives of the school program and most appropriate for the uses to be made of the results.

Some published tests are selected by individual teachers, but more frequently the tests are selected in accordance with the school testing program. In the latter case, teachers still should have a voice in the selection process, either through direct service on a test committee or through departmental and general staff meetings.

It is important that teachers participate actively in the selection of published tests. Their participation provides greater assurance that the tests are in harmony with the objectives of the instructional program and that the results will serve the various instructional uses for which they are intended. Although published tests can serve a variety of administrative and guidance functions, of central concern to any testing program is the effective use of tests in the instructional program.

In addition to familiarity with the procedures for selecting tests, teachers must also know the procedures for administering tests. In some schools they participate directly in these functions, while in others special personnel is used. In either case, however, the teacher's understanding of the procedures contributes to more effective interpretation and use of test results.

OBTAINING INFORMATION ABOUT PUBLISHED TESTS

There are many available resources that are useful for locating and evaluating published tests in specific areas. These will aid in selecting tests that are most suitable and that are technically sound.

Buros Institute of Mental Measurements Guides

A basic source of information about tests is the *Mental Measurements Yearbook (MMY),* first published in 1938. The *MMY* was started and edited by Oscar K. Buros for many years and is now published by the Buros Institute of Mental Measurements of the University of Nebraska—Lincoln. The *MMYs* are published periodically but on no definite schedule. Each *Yearbook* typically includes the following types of material:

1. Descriptive information concerning each test.
2. Critical reviews written by test specialists for the *MMY.*
3. Excerpts from test reviews published in professional journals.
4. Comprehensive bibliographies for many specific tests.
5. Listing of measurement books and book reviews.

The test reviews in the *Yearbooks* provide especially valuable information for evaluating the quality of published tests. Each test is typically reviewed by two or more specialists qualified by training and experience to evaluate the test. The reviewers often point out test weaknesses as well as any exaggerated claims made by test publishers. They also indicate the strengths of a test and the uses for which it is best suited.

Another useful Buros Institute guide for locating tests and information about tests is *Tests in Print.* This publication includes a descriptive listing of published tests, with extensive bibliographies for some. Although test reviews are not included, each is indexed to those editions of the *Mental Measurements Yearbooks* that contain reviews of the test.

As aids for locating tests for a particular use, *Tests in Print* provides an excellent guide to available tests, and the *Mental Measurements Yearbooks* provide the information needed to evaluate them. The cross-references to the *Yearbooks* in *Tests in Print* make it possible to locate numerous reviews for each test.

Tests in Print has been published less frequently than the *Mental Measurements Yearbooks* and in the event a recent edition is not available, tests can be located by going directly to the *Yearbooks.* They are fully indexed and contain descriptions of the tests, as well as the test reviews. The *Yearbooks* can also be used, of course, for evaluating tests that have been located through test publishers' catalogues or other sources.

The Buros Institute of Mental Measurements also provides test information through a *Mental Measurements Yearbooks* database. This computer database is updated monthly and thus provides the most recent information available (see the accompanying box).

Test Corporation of America Guides

Another useful source for locating and evaluating tests is in the publications of the Test Corporation of America (4050 Pennsylvania, Suite 310, Kansas City, MO 64111) One, titled *Tests: A Comprehensive Reference for Assessments in Psychology, Education, and Business,* describes more than 3,000 tests published in English. For each entry, there is a statement of the instrument's purpose, a brief description, and information concerning cost, scoring, and the publisher. *Tests* does not include evaluations of the instruments but serves as an excellent guide for locating tests. This is enhanced by the classification of tests into various categories and the use of numerous indexes.

Evaluations of tests in psychology, education, and business are provided in a series of volumes entitled *Test Critiques*. Each critique is written by a measurement specialist and includes a detailed description of the test, practical applications of the test, technical information concerning the test, and a summarizing critique. There is special emphasis on aiding the test user, such as guidelines for administration, scoring, and interpretation. Technical terms are explained to make the information understandable to readers with little experience in testing. A separate publication, titled *Test Critiques Compendium,* contains reviews of the sixty most-used psychology and education tests in a single volume.

Educational Testing Service (ETS) Test Collection

Educational Testing Service (Princeton, New Jersey) maintains a Test Collection that contains more than 14,000 tests. Annotated bibliographies are available in various areas that describe each test in detail. As new tests are added to the ETS Test

---

Mental Measurements Yearbooks
and On-line Computer Service

The Buros Institute of Mental Measurements (University of Nebraska—Lincoln) produces a database that is part of the on-line computer service offered by Bibliographic Retrieval Services, Inc. (BRS). The institute's database began with test descriptions and reviews from *The Eighth Mental Measurements Yearbook* and includes updated descriptions and reviews of tests published after the eighth *MMY* (search label *MMYD*). The institute's database is especially useful for obtaining current information on new and revised tests that appear between editions of the *Mental Measurements Yearbooks*. Computer searches of the database can be made through libraries that offer the BRS service.

Collection holdings, they are briefly described in a monthly newsletter, titled *News on Tests*. This newsletter provides a good source for locating new and recently revised tests. It also includes references to test reviews, lists of new publications, announcements of testing conferences, changes in publishers' addresses, and other news about testing.

The ETS Test Collection has established a database of its records that is part of the on-line computer service offered by Bibliographic Retrieval Services, Inc. (BRS). Computer searches for test information can be made through libraries that provide the BRS service. The ETS Test Collection will also provide computer searches for clients.

Test Publishers' Catalogues

Recent information concerning tests available for school use also can be obtained from test publishers' catalogues. These usually contain brief descriptions of each test, including possible uses of the test, cost, administration time, and similar information. If a publisher's claims for its tests are checked by independent reviews such as those presented in the *Mental Measurements Yearbooks* and *Test Critiques,* test catalogues provide a good source of information. They are especially useful for locating new tests and recent editions of earlier tests. A brief list of test publishers who will send catalogues upon request is included in Appendix C.

Testing Standards

An especially useful aid in evaluating and using published tests is the *Standards for Educational and Psychological Testing* (American Psychological Association, 1985). This set of standards was prepared by a joint committee of the American Psychological Association, the American Educational Research Association, and the National Council on Measurement in Education. The most recent version of the *Standards* was published in 1985. A joint committee of the three sponsoring organizations began work on a revision of the *Standards* in late 1993 and it is likely that the revision of the *Standards* will be published in 1996.

The 1985 *Standards* includes recommendations intended for both test publishers and test users. Part I contains standards for the technical aspects of test instrumentation (validity, reliability, test development, norming, scaling, and related issues). Part II provides standards for the use of tests in various situations (clinical, educational, counseling, employment, professional licensure, and program evaluation). Part III covers standards for particular applications (linguistic minorities and handicapped). Part IV provides standards for test administration, scoring, reporting, and the rights of test takers.

Each recommendation in the *Standards* is classified as primary (to be met by all tests), secondary (desirable), or conditional (classification depending on the conditions of testing). Comments following these standards are used to clarify or justify the recommendation or to describe the conditions under which the standard would apply (see "Illustrative Test Standard from the 'Validity' Section").

Illustrative Test Standard from the "Validity" Section

Standard 1.1

Evidence of validity should be presented for the major types of inference for which use of the test is recommended. A rationale should be provided to support the particular mix of evidence presented for the intended uses. (Primary)

Comment

Whether one or more kinds of validity evidence are appropriate is a function of the particular question being asked, the context, and the extent of previous evidence.

Source: From *Standards for Educational and Psychological Testing* by American Psychological Association, 1985, Washington D.C.: Copyright 1985 by American Psychological Association.

A review of the standards in Part I provides a good background for selecting and evaluating tests and the specific recommendations in Parts II, III, and IV provide excellent guidelines for effective test use.

Code of Fair Testing Practices in Education

The *Code of Fair Testing Practices in Education* was prepared by a Joint Committee on Testing Practices, a group that was formed in cooperation with several professional associations. The *Code* is intended to apply to a wide range of published tests and tests used in formal administrations that may be developed and required by school districts or states. The code is not intended to apply to tests developed by individual teachers for use in their own classrooms.

The *Code* is intended for two primary audiences: test users and test developers. Test users are defined as "people who select tests, commission test development services, or make decisions on the basis of test scores." The *Code* presents standards in four areas (A) developing/selecting tests, (B) interpreting scores, (C) striving for fairness, and (D) informing test takers. Each of these sections of the *Code* will be discussed in subsequent sections of this chapter and Chapter 17.

Other Sources of Test Information

Test reviews and information concerning the nature and use of particular tests can frequently be found in professional journals (see list in Appendix B). Journal articles can be most easily located through the use of such bibliographic sources as the *Current Index to Journals in Education,* the *Education Index,* and *Psychological Abstracts.* In using these guides it is usually necessary to search under many different headings, such as *aptitude testing, achievement testing, psychological tests, reading tests, tests and scales,* and *testing programs.* In locating information on tests in a specific content area, it also may be necessary to look under that subject in a specific content area (e.g., English, science). Test reviews in professional journals can be most easily located by a computerized literature search.

Some textbooks in educational and psychological measurement include descriptions and evaluations of widely used tests and contain selected lists of tests in an appendix. Also, some textbooks in particular areas (e.g., reading, special education) describe tests that are especially useful in those areas. Although textbooks provide descriptive information concerning representative tests, this is mainly useful for orientation to the field of testing. Test selection for a particular situation includes a study of the situation to determine testing needs, searching for possible tests, consulting test reviews, and examining the test manuals and other test materials of the most likely prospects.

SELECTING APPROPRIATE TESTS

Published tests play an important role in the educational program of the school and therefore should be selected with utmost care. When carefully selected and appropriately used, they can make a valuable contribution to instructional planning and student learning. On the other hand, hastily or casually selected tests seldom are in harmony with the objectives of the instructional program, and thus may provide inadequate or inappropriate information on which to base educational decisions.

TABLE 16.1

Sources for locating and evaluating published tests

Publisher	Sources	Test Descriptions	Technical Information	Test Reviews
Buros Institute of Mental Measurements	*Mental Measurements Yearbooks,*	X	X	XX
	Tests in Print	X		
Test Corporation of America	*Tests,*	X		
	Test Critiques	X	X	XX
Educational Testing Service	*Test Collection,*	X		X(S)
	News on Tests	X(N)		
(See publishers in Appendix C)	Test Publishers' Catalogues	X(N)		
American Psychological Association	*Standards for Educational and Psychological Testing*		XX	
(Varies)	Test Manuals	XX	XX	
(See list in Appendix B)	Professional Journals	X(N)	X(S)	X(S)
(Varies)	Measurement Textbooks	X(S)	X(S)	X(S)

Note: XX = Most useful, X = Useful, X(N) = Useful for new tests, X(S) = Useful for some tests.

Even when selected with care, however, the value of the information depends on the way in which it is used. Misinterpretations (e.g., assuming that performance on an aptitude test is an indication of innate capacity) and misuses (e.g., placement of students in remedial programs based solely on low test performance) can have serious negative consequences. The following sequence of steps provides general guidelines for a systematic approach to test selection. Issues regarding the use and interpretation of results are considered in a subsequent section of this chapter.

Defining Testing Needs

The first task in selecting published tests is to define specifically the purpose of testing and the type of information being sought through testing. As is emphasized by the first standard for test users in the *Code of Fair Testing Practices in Education* (see Figure 16.1), it is critical that purpose be clearly defined and that the test match the purpose. In selecting achievement tests, for example, it is insufficient to search for a test to evaluate "achievement in social studies" or to measure "reading comprehension." There are numerous tests in any given content area, and each measures somewhat different aspects of knowledge, understanding, and skill. To make a proper selection, we must first identify the objectives and specific learning outcomes of our instructional program. This is necessary in choosing relevant tests, whether selecting a single test for a particular course or a battery of tests for a schoolwide testing program.

Clarifying the type of information needed is equally necessary in selecting aptitude tests. It makes a difference whether we are going to use the results for determining reading readiness, for grouping students, for vocational planning, or for predicting success in science and mathematics courses. Each function requires different information and consequently a different type of aptitude measure. Thus, selection must be preceded by an analysis of the intended use of the results and the type of test data most appropriate for each use.

Narrowing the Choice

The need for published tests is usually considered in relation to the total measurement program. This makes it possible to choose tests that supplement and complement the other means of assessing students. It is desirable to choose a test of general educational development, for example, if certain learning outcomes in the knowledge area already are being adequately measured by informal classroom tests and assessments. Similarly, if a scholastic aptitude test is to be used at a particular grade level for identifying students needing extra help in learning to read, it is best to replace the aptitude test with a diagnostic reading test. Such decisions can be made only when the need for testing is viewed in terms of the total measurement program.

Other factors in the school situation also help narrow the choice. If, for instance, the school lacks a person with the training and experience required to administer individual tests, only group tests should be considered. If the tests are to be administered by teachers without experience in test administration, tests with

FIGURE 16.1

Standards for developing/selecting appropriate tests (From the *Code of Fair Testing Practices in Education,* 1988, Washington, D.C.: Joint Committee on Testing Practices. [Mailing Address: Joint Committee on Testing Practices, American Psychological Association, 1200 17th Street, NW, Washington, D.C. 20036.])

Test developers should provide the information that test users need to select appropriate tests.

Test users should select tests that meet the purpose for which they are to be used and that are appropriate for the intended test-taking populations.

Test Developers Should:

1. Define what each test measures and what the test should be used for. Describe the population(s) for which the test is appropriate.

2. Accurately represent the characteristics, usefulness, and limitations of tests for their intended purposes.

3. Explain relevant measurement concepts as necessary for clarity at the level of detail that is appropriate for the intended audience(s).

4. Describe the process of test development. Explain how the content and skills to be tested were selected.

5. Provide evidence that the test meets its intended purpose(s).

6. Provide either representative samples or complete copies of test questions, directions, answer sheets, manuals, and score reports to qualified users.

7. Indicate the nature of the evidence obtained concerning the appropriateness of each test for groups of different racial, ethnic, or linguistic backgrounds who are likely to be tested.

8. Identify and publish any specialized skills needed to administer each test and to interpret scores correctly.

Test Users Should:

1. First define the purpose for testing and the population to be tested. Then, select a test for that purpose and that population based on a thorough review of the available information.

2. Investigate potentially useful sources of information, in addition to test scores, to corroborate the information provided by tests.

3. Read the materials provided by test developers and avoid using tests for which unclear or incomplete information is provided.

4. Become familiar with how and when the test was developed and tried out.

5. Read independent evaluations of a test and of possible alternative measures. Look for evidence required to support the claims of test developers.

6. Examine specimen sets, disclosed tests or samples of questions, directions, answer sheets, manuals, and score reports before selecting a test.

7. Ascertain whether the test content and norms group(s) or comparison group(s) are appropriate for the intended test takers.

8. Select and use only those tests for which the skills needed to administer the test and interpret scores correctly are available.

*Many of the statements in the *Code* refer to the selection of existing tests. However, in customized testing programs test developers are engaged to construct new tests. In those situations, the test development process should be designed to help ensure that the completed tests will be in compliance with the *Code*.

simple directions are best. If the same type of achievement battery is desired for both the elementary and high-school levels, only those batteries with tests at all grade levels need to be examined. Considerations such as these offer additional criteria for determining the types of tests to seek.

Although reputable test publishers work hard to eliminate materials that are offensive to different groups of test takers, avoid stereotypes, and in other ways make the material as fair as possible for test takers of different races, gender, or ethnic backgrounds, it is also important that test users review potential tests for possible sources of unfairness. Useful guidelines in this regard from the *Code of Fair Testing Practices in Education* are reproduced in Figure 16.2.

Locating Suitable Tests

When the needs for testing have been identified, a list of possible tests can be compiled from test publishers' catalogues and the most recent edition of the *Mental*

FIGURE 16.2

Standards for striving for fairness (From the *Code of Fair Testing Practices in Education*, 1988, Washington, D.C.: Joint Committee on Testing Practices. [Mailing Address: Joint Committee on Testing Practices, American Psychological Association, 1200 17th Street, NW, Washington, D.C. 20036.])

Test developers should strive to make tests that are as fair as possible for test takers of different races, gender, ethnic backgrounds, or handicapping conditions.

Test Developers Should:

14. Review and revise test questions and related materials to avoid potentially insensitive content or language.

15. Investigate the performance of test takers of different races, gender, and ethnic backgrounds when samples of sufficient size are available. Enact procedures that help to ensure that differences in performance are related primarily to the skills under assessment rather than to irrelevant factors.

16. When feasible, make appropriately modified forms of tests or administration procedures available for test takers with handicapping conditions. Warn test users of potential problems in using standard norms with modified tests or administration procedures that result in non-comparable scores.

Test users should select tests that have been developed in ways that attempt to make them as fair as possible for test takers of different races, gender, ethnic backgrounds, or handicapping conditions.

Test Users Should:

14. Evaluate the procedures used by test developers to avoid potentially insensitive content or language.

15. Review the performance of test takers of different races, gender, and ethnic backgrounds when samples of sufficient size are available. Evaluate the extent to which performance differences may have been caused by inappropriate characteristics of the test.

16. When necessary and feasible, use appropriately modified forms of tests or administration procedures for test takers with handicapping conditions. Interpret standard norms with care in the light of the modifications that were made.

Measurements Yearbook and *Test Critiques*. The reviews in these guides are sufficiently detailed to weed out those tests that are clearly inappropriate or that have obvious technical weaknesses. Further evaluative information also can be found in other sources, such as those described earlier.

Obtaining Specimen Sets

When the list of tests has been reduced to a reasonable number, specimen sets should be obtained so that test manuals and the test items themselves can be evaluated. Test publishers generally supply specimen sets for each test they publish.

These can be purchased at relatively low cost and include a test manual, a test booklet, and scoring keys. Many universities, colleges, and large school systems maintain a file of such specimen sets.

Reviewing Test Materials

The test manual (sometimes accompanied by a technical manual and related aids) usually provides the most complete information for judging the appropriateness and the technical qualities of a test. A good test manual includes the following types of information:

1. Uses for which the test is recommended.
2. Qualifications needed to administer and interpret the test.
3. Evidence of validity for each recommended use.
4. Evidence of reliability for recommended uses and an indication of equivalence for any equivalent forms provided.
5. Directions for administering and scoring the test.
6. Adequate norms (including a description of the procedures used in obtaining them) or other bases for interpreting the scores.

Some test manuals (or supplements to the manuals) also contain suggestions and guides for interpreting and using the results. These are especially helpful for determining the functions for which the test is best suited.

In addition to reviewing the test manual, it is also wise to study the individual test items. The best method of doing this is to try to answer each item, as if you were taking the test. For achievement tests, it is also helpful to classify the items by means of a previously prepared table of specifications or other test plan. Although the process is time consuming, there is no better means of determining how appropriate a test is for measuring the knowledge, skills, and understanding emphasized in the instructional program.

Using a Test Evaluation Form

Gathering information about specific tests is made easier if a test evaluation form is used. This provides a convenient means of recording significant data; it increases the likelihood that pertinent information will not be overlooked; and it provides for a summary comparison of each test's strengths and weaknesses (see "Test Evaluation Form").

Although a test evaluation form provides a useful summary of information concerning tests, no test should be selected on the basis of this information alone. How well a test fits the school program and the particular uses for which it is being considered are always the main considerations.

Test Evaluation Form

Test title _____ Authors _____

Publisher _____ Publication date _____

Purpose of test _____

For grades (ages) _____ Forms _____

Scores available _____ Types of scoring _____

Administration time _____ Cost _____

Technical Features

Validity: Nature of evidence (content-, construct-, criterion-related).

Reliability: Nature of evidence (stability, internal consistency, equivalence). Standard error of measurement (size, type).

Norms: Type, adequacy, and appropriateness to local situation.

Criterion-referenced interpretation: Describe (if available).

Practical Features

Ease of administration (procedure and timing).

Ease of scoring and interpretation.

Adequacy of test manual and accessory materials.

General Evaluation

Comments of reviewers (see *MMY* and *Test Critiques*).

Summary of strengths.

Summary of weaknesses.

Recommendations concerning local use.

◾◾◾◾◾ # ADMINISTERING PUBLISHED TESTS

Most group tests of achievement and scholastic aptitude can be successfully administered by any conscientious teacher. The main requirement is that the testing procedures prescribed in the test manual be rigorously followed. To do this, it is necessary to shift from being a teacher and helper to being an impartial test examiner who will not deviate from the test directions.

Teachers sometimes wonder why it is important to follow the test procedures so closely. What harm is there in helping students if they do not understand particular questions? Why not give the students a little more time if they are almost finished? Aren't some of the directions nit-picking, anyway? The answer is

> A published test must be administered under standard conditions if the results are to be meaningfully interpreted.

When a published, norm-referenced test is given to a national sample of students to establish norms, it is administered in exact accordance with the procedures prescribed in the test manual. Unless teachers adhere strictly to the same procedures, the standard conditions of measurement will be violated, and the test norms cannot legitimately be used to interpret scores. Although not all published criterion-referenced tests have norms, the interpretation of the results according to an absolute standard (e.g., mastery–nonmastery) also depends on controlled conditions of administration. In short, when we alter the procedures for administering a published test, we lose the basis for a meaningful interpretation of the scores.

Test Administration

The administration of group tests is relatively simple: (1) motivate the students to do their best, (2) follow the directions closely (3) keep time accurately, (4) record any significant events that might influence test scores, and (5) collect the materials promptly.

1. *Motivate the students.* In testing, our goal should be to obtain maximum performance within the standard conditions set forth in the testing procedures. We want all students to earn as high a score as they are capable of achieving. This obviously means that they must be motivated to put forth their best effort. Although some students will respond to any test as a challenge to their ability, others will not work seriously at the task unless they are convinced that the test results will be beneficial to them.

In school testing, we can stimulate students to put forth their best effort by convincing them that the test results will be used primarily to help them improve their learning. We can also explain to them the value of the test results for understanding themselves better and for planning their future. But these need to be more than hollow promises. Test results must be used in such a way that these benefits are clearly evident to the students.

Before administering a particular test, the teacher should explain to students the purpose of the test and the uses to be made of the results (see Figure 16.3). At

FIGURE 16.3
Standards for informing test-takers (From the *Code of Fair Testing Practices in Education,* 1988, Washington, D.C.: Joint Committee on Testing Practices. [Mailing Address: Joint Committee on Testing Practices, American Psychological Association, 1200 17th Street, NW, Washington, D.C. 20036.])

Under some circumstances, test developers have direct communication with test takers. Under other circumstances, test users communicate directly with test takers. Whichever group communicates directly with test takers should provide the information described below.

Test Developers or Test Users Should:

17. When a test is optional, provide test takers or their parents/guardians with information to help them judge whether the test should be taken, or if an available alternative to the test should be used.

18. Provide test takers the information they need to be familiar with the coverage of the test, the types of question formats, the directions, and appropriate test-taking strategies. Strive to make such information equally available to all test takers.

Under some circumstances, test developers have direct control of tests and test scores. Under other circumstances, test users have such control. Whichever group has direct control of tests and test scores should take the steps described below.

Test Developers or Test Users Should:

19. Provide test takers or their parents/guardians with information about rights test takers may have to obtain copies of tests and completed answer sheets, retake tests, have tests rescored, or cancel scores.

20. Tell test takers or their parents/guardians how long scores will be kept on file and indicate to whom and under what circumstances test scores will or will not be released.

21. Describe the procedures that test takers or their parents/guardians may use to register complaints and have problems resolved.

---

this time, the teacher should emphasize the advantages of obtaining a score that represents the students' best efforts, but should not make the students overly anxious. Verbal reassurance that the size of the score is not as important as the fact that it represents one's best effort is usually helpful. The judicious use of humor can also offset test anxiety. The most effective remedy, however, is a positive attitude toward test results. When the students are convinced that valid test scores are beneficial to their own welfare, both their test anxiety and motivation tend to become minor problems.

*2. **Follow directions strictly.*** The importance of following the directions given in the test manual cannot be overemphasized. Unless the test is administered in exact accordance with the standard directions, the test results will contain an indeterminate amount of error and thereby prevent proper interpretation and use.

The test directions should be read word for word in a loud, clear voice. They should never be paraphrased, recited from memory, or modified in any way. The oral reading of directions will usually be more effective if the directions have been practiced beforehand.

After the directions have been read and during the testing period, some students are likely to ask questions. It is usually permissible to clarify the directions and to answer questions concerning mechanics (for example, how to record the answer), but the test manual must be your guide. If it is permissible to clarify the directions, you should not change or modify the directions in any way during your explanation.

Some teachers find it hard to refrain from helping students who are having difficulty answering items on a published test. When questioned about a particular test item, they are tempted to say, "You remember, we discussed that last week," or give similar hints to the students. This merely distorts the results. When asked about a particular test item during testing, the teacher should quietly tell the student: "I'm sorry, but I cannot help you. Do the best you can."

3. Keep time accurately. If a series of short subtests must be timed separately, it is desirable to use a stopwatch when giving the test. For most other purposes, a watch with a second hand is satisfactory. To ensure accurate timing, keep a written record of the starting and stopping times, the exact hour, minute, and second as follows:

	Hour	Minute	Second
Starting Time	2	10	0
Time Allowed		12	
Stopping Time	2	22	0

4. Record significant events. The students should be carefully observed during testing and a record made of any unusual behavior or event that might influence the test scores. If, for example, a student appears overly tense and anxious, sits staring out of the window for a time, or seems to be marking answers randomly without reading the questions, a description of the behavior should be recorded. Similarly, if there are interruptions during the testing (despite your careful planning), a record should be made of the type and length of the interruption and whether it did or did not alter the testing conditions.

A record of unusual student behavior and significant events provides valuable information for determining whether test scores are representative of the students' best efforts and whether standard conditions have been maintained during testing. Questionable test scores should, of course, be rechecked by administering a second form of the test.

5. Collect test materials promptly. When the test has ended, all test materials should be collected promptly so that students cannot work beyond the time limits and so that all materials can be accounted for and secured.

For those responsible for the testing program, from the ordering of the tests to their administration, the "Test Giver's Checklist" summarizes the points that need to be considered (see box).

Test Giver's Checklist

1. Order and check test materials well in advance of the testing date.
   a. Were correct forms of the test sent?
   b. Is there the right number of tests and answer sheets?
   c. Have all needed materials been assembled (pencils, watch, etc.)?
   d. Have all test materials been securely stored until the testing date?

2. Select a suitable location for testing.
   a. Is there adequate work space?
   b. Is the lighting, heat, and ventilation satisfactory?
   c. Is the room in a quiet location?
   d. Is the seating arrangement satisfactory?

3. Take steps to prevent distractions.
   a. Will a "Testing in Progress" sign be posted on the door?
   b. Will all needed materials be on hand before starting?
   c. Have arrangements been made to terminate distractions (e.g., bells)?
   d. Has the test been scheduled to avoid major school events?

4. Study the test materials and practice giving the test.
   a. Did you carefully read the test manual?
   b. Did you take the test yourself?
   c. Did you practice reading the directions?
   d. Did you anticipate questions students might ask?

5. Motivate the students.
   a. Was the purpose of the test explained to the students?
   b. Were the students told how the results would be used?
   c. Were the students encouraged to put forth their best effort?
   d. Has care been taken not to create test anxiety?

6. Follow test directions strictly and keep time accurately.
   a. Did you read the test directions word for word?
   b. Did you refrain from helping students (except with mechanics)?
   c. Did you make a written record of starting and stopping times?
   d. Did you stick to the exact time schedule?

7. Record significant events.
   a. Did students do anything that might affect the test results?
   b. Were there any interruptions that might affect the scores?

8. Collect the test materials promptly when the testing has ended.
   a. Were all test materials collected immediately?
   b. Were the collected materials counted, checked, and secured?

Improving Students' Test-Taking Skills

Our suggestions for test administration, as summarized in the "Test Giver's Checklist", emphasize the importance of establishing the most suitable environment for the test taker and using methods that motivate the students to put forth their best efforts. Despite these procedures, however, some students might not perform at the level of which they are capable because they lack skill in test taking. It has been suggested by Sarnacki (1971) that all students be given training in test-taking skills to prevent such deficiencies from lowering their test scores. This seems to be a sensible suggestion and one that could be easily handled in the regular classroom or through the use of programmed materials. Among the skills important in test taking are the following:

1. Listening to or reading directions carefully.
2. Listening to or reading test items carefully.
3. Setting a pace that will allow time to complete the test.
4. Bypassing difficult items and returning to them later.
5. Making informed guesses rather than omitting items.
6. Eliminating as many alternatives as possible on multiple-choice items before guessing.
7. Following directions carefully in marking the answer sheet (e.g., darken the entire space).
8. Checking to be sure the item number and answer number match when marking an answer.
9. Checking to be sure that the appropriate response was marked on the answer sheet.
10. Going back and checking the answers if time permits.

Test-taking skills such as these can be easily mastered, but students need practice to develop them. Fortunately, many test publishers now provide practice tests that can be given before the regular test. This is of some help, but special training in test taking will provide even greater assurance that a student's test scores are not depressed by deficiencies in test-taking skills.

Unsound and Unethical Test Preparation Practices

Although it is important to take steps such as those discussed above to help students be ready to do their best when taking tests, it is easy to go overboard. Especially in high-stakes testing situations, where teachers are under great pressure to get their students to score high, it is natural to focus more and more attention on the contents of the test. Unfortunately, this can lead to poor instructional practices and inflated test scores.

In some schools teachers devote the majority of their instructional time for several weeks to practice for the high-stakes test. Such practice ignores important learning objectives that are not on the test and is not even a sound pedagogical approach for the objectives that are covered. Moreover, when the practice materials match the actual test too closely, the result can be improved test scores without improved achievement. As a consequence, the scores give an inflated impression of the students' overall achievement.

Occasionally, the actual items that appear on a test become the focus of instruction. Providing practice on the actual test items prior to administration of a standardized test invalidates the results. It is an unethical practice.

USING RESULTS OF PUBLISHED TESTS

Published achievement and learning ability tests can serve many different purposes in the school's educational program. Here, we will describe briefly some of the possible uses and misuses of published tests that are of special interest to teachers.

Possible Uses of Published Tests

If they are selected and used with discretion, published tests of achievement and ability can play an important role in the school's evaluation program. Tests should be selected in accordance with the school's objectives and the purposes for which the results are to be used. When selected in this manner, they can contribute to more effective educational decisions in a number of areas.

Instructional Planning.   Published tests of achievement and learning ability can aid instructional planning in a particular school or course in the following ways:

1. Identifying the level and range of ability among students.   Among other things, instructional plans must take into account the students' learning ability and their present levels of achievement. Published tests can provide objective evidence on both of these points.

2. Identifying areas of instruction needing greater emphasis.   If the published tests have been selected in accordance with the school's objectives, instructional weaknesses will be revealed by those areas of the test in which the students do poorly. Published tests are especially helpful in appraising strengths and weaknesses in learning (see Table 16.2).

3. Identifying discrepancies between learning ability and achievement.   Although differences between learning ability and achievement must be interpreted with caution, large discrepancies can aid in identifying students who may be underachieving. In this as well as other areas, however, the results of published tests should be verified by other available evidence.

4. Diagnosing learning errors and planning remedial instruction.   Published diagnostic tests are especially useful for pinpointing the learning errors that are handicapping a student's learning progress. Published tests provide a more systematic approach than informal methods, and the manuals typically provide suggestions for remediation. Unfortunately, these tests are limited almost entirely to the basic skills of reading and arithmetic.

TABLE 16.2
Percentage of teachers using standardized achievement test results in various ways

Teachers Were Asked to Indicate Which of These Uses They Made	Percentage Reporting Each Use
Diagnosing strengths and weaknesses	74
Measuring student "growth"	66
Individual student evaluation	65
Instructional planning	52
Class evaluation	45
Reporting to parents	42
Evaluation of teaching methods	37
Reporting to students	24

Source: Adapted from "Attitudes toward Standardized Tests: Students, Teachers, and Measurement Specialists" by J. P. Stetz and M. D. Beck, *NCME Measurement in Education* (Washington, D.C.: National Council on Measurement in Education, 12(1), 1981).
Note: Based on a survey of 3,306 teachers, Grades K through 12.

5. Clarifying and selecting instructional objectives. The use of published tests aids in the clarification and selection of objectives in several ways. First, selecting the tests forces us to identify and state our objectives as clearly as possible. Second, an examination of the items in published tests tells us how different objectives function in testing. As we go back and forth (during test selection) between our objectives and the items in the tests under consideration, what a particular objective looks like in operational terms becomes clearer. Third, the results of published tests provide evidence that helps in selecting objectives at a particular grade level or in a particular course. If fall test results indicate that students in the sixth grade are weak in study skills, for example, sixth-grade teachers may want to include an objective in this area, even though they had not originally planned to devote much attention to study skills. Similarly, published test results might indicate that a particular objective is unnecessary because it has been satisfactorily achieved at an earlier grade level.

Individualizing Instruction. In any classroom there are substantial individual differences in aptitude and achievement. Thus, it is necessary to study the strengths and weaknesses of each student in class so that instruction can be adapted as much as possible to individual learning needs. For this purpose (1) scholastic aptitude tests provide clues concerning learning ability; (2) reading tests indicate the difficulty of material the student can read and understand; (3) norm-referenced achievement tests point out general areas of strength and weakness; (4) criterion-referenced achievement tests describe how well specific tasks are being mastered; and (5) diagnostic tests aid in detecting and overcoming specific learning errors.

Criterion-referenced tests are especially well adapted to individualizing instruction because each set of test items is keyed to a specific objective. This makes it possible for a student to proceed through a given learning sequence by demonstrating mastery of the objectives one by one. Many publishers also provide references to books and other learning aids to guide the individual study of students who have failed to master a particular objective.

Identifying the Needs of Exceptional Children.   Some students deviate so markedly from the group of normal students at their grade or age level that special instructional programs are needed. The gifted, mentally retarded, emotionally disturbed, physically handicapped, and similar exceptional children fall into this category. For this student, published tests are helpful in identifying their problems of learning and development so that special provisions can be made for meeting their exceptional needs. This use of tests is growing in importance now that mainstreaming (placing children with handicapping conditions in the least restrictive environment) has increased the number of exceptional children in regular classrooms. Mainstreaming requires that a detailed *individualized educational program* be written for each handicapped student.

Monitoring of Educational Progress over Extended Periods.   Published tests are especially useful in measuring learning progress over a given number of years. Comparable forms make it possible to measure the same learning outcomes annually and thus obtain a long-range picture of the students' educational development. Teacher-made tests are not as useful for this purpose because of the lack of uniformity from one year to the next.

In using published tests as a basis for determining students' educational development, care must be taken not to overgeneralize from the results. Tests that yield comparable measures of general educational progress throughout the school years must, of necessity, be confined to learning that is continuously developing and that is common to diverse curricula. In the main, this means the basic skills and critical abilities used in the interpretation and application of ideas that cut across subject-matter lines. Although these are significant learning outcomes, they are only a partial indication of total educational development. Knowledge and understanding of specific content, skills unique to each subject field, attitudes and appreciation, and similar learning outcomes that cannot be measured by survey tests of educational development are equally important.

Providing Parents with an Independent Source of Information.   Teacher reports regarding student achievement and grades assigned provide parents with the most important information about the educational progress of their children. Standardized test results, however, are a useful supplement to teacher reports. They have the advantage of being independent of teacher opinions. Normative information also provides a comparison against a wider context than that provided by an individual classroom or school.

Helping Students Make Educational and Vocational Choices.   At the high-school level, published test results can contribute to more intelligent educational and vocational decisions. In deciding which curriculum to pursue, which courses to take, whether to plan for college, or which occupations to consider, students can be aided greatly by knowing their aptitudes and their strengths and weaknesses in achievement. Published tests are especially useful in educational and vocational planning because they indicate to students how they compare with persons beyond the local school situation. This is important because these are the persons with whom they will be competing after leaving high school.

Supplementary Uses.   In addition to the preceding uses of published tests, all of which are directly concerned with improving students' instruction and guidance, there are a number of supplementary uses to which they can be put, including (1) placing students transferred from other schools, (2) appraising the general effectiveness of the school program in developing basic skills, (3) identifying areas in the educational program in which supervisory aid and in-service training can be used most effectively, (4) evaluating new educational programs, (5) providing evidence for interpreting the school program to the public, and (6) gathering information for reports to other schools, colleges, and prospective employers. When published test results are presented to individuals and groups outside the school, it should be emphasized that these tests measure only some of the objectives of the school program.

Misuses of Published Tests

Published tests can be misused in any of the preceding areas if (1) there is inadequate attention to the educational objectives being measured; (2) there is a failure to recognize the limited position of tests in the total assessment program; (3) there is unquestioning faith in the test results; or (4) the group tested is markedly different from the group for whom the test was intended. These factors contribute to the misapplication and misinterpretation of published test results in any situation. In addition, there are three misuses that warrant special attention.

Assignment of Course Grades.   Some teachers use the scores from published tests as a basis for assigning course grades. This is undesirable for at least two reasons: (1) published tests are seldom closely related to the instructional objectives of a particular course, and (2) they measure only a portion of the desired learning outcomes emphasized in instruction. Using these tests for grading purposes tends to overemphasize a limited number of ill-fitting objectives. In addition to the unfairness to the student, this practice encourages both teachers and students to neglect those objectives that are not measured by the tests.

In borderline cases, especially when promotion or retention is being decided, published test results can be a valuable supplement. Knowing a student's scholastic aptitude and general level of educational development contributes to a more intelligent decision concerning the best grade placement. Except for such special uses, however, published tests should play a minor role, if any, in determining course grades.

Assignment of Remedial Track or Retention in Grade Solely on the Basis of a Test Score.   Although test results can contribute to informed decisions regarding student placement in special programs, they are not adequate for such decisions when used in isolation. Information about a student's background and prior learning experiences needs to be considered. Teacher observations of classroom behavior and performance are also relevant considerations. Moreover, there should be compelling reasons to believe that students placed in special instructional programs or required to repeat a grade will be likely to learn more than they would in a normal class and sequence. It should be noted that research suggests remedial tracks frequently *do not* lead to improved learning and students who are retained in grade seldom benefit more than they would if promoted (Shepard and Smith, 1989).

Evaluation of Teaching Effectiveness. In some schools, teacher effectiveness is judged by the scores students make on published tests. This is an extremely unfair practice because so many factors other than teaching effectiveness influence test scores. Many of these, such as the class's level of ability, the students' cultural background, the students' educational experiences, and the relative difficulty of learning different course materials, cannot be controlled or equated with sufficient accuracy to justify inferring that the results are solely, or even largely, based on the teacher's efforts. Even if such factors could be controlled, published test results would be a poor criterion of teaching success because they are not closely related to the instructional objectives of particular courses and they measure only a portion of the learning outcomes teachers strive for in their instruction. At most, they should play only a minor role in teacher evaluation.

An especially undesirable side effect of using published tests as the sole or main measure of teaching effectiveness is that some teachers will obtain copies of the test and start teaching students the answers to specific test items. Although this unprofessional practice may begin with a few unethical teachers, subtle pressures (to avoid looking ineffective by comparison) soon cause the practice to spread. Such "teaching for the test," of course, not only distorts the measures of teaching effectiveness but also invalidates the test scores for other school uses.

SUMMARY

Teachers should know how to locate, select, administer, interpret, and use published tests. This contributes to more effective use of the test results in the instructional program. Two of the most useful sources for locating and evaluating tests are provided by the Buros Institute for Mental Measurements (*Mental Measurements Yearbooks* and *Tests in Print*) and Test Corporation of America (*Tests* and *Test Critiques*). Both sets of publications provide comprehensive coverage of available tests. Other sources include the ETS Test Collection, *News on Tests,* test publishers' catalogues, and various professional journals and textbooks. The testing *Standards* helps determine what to look for in evaluating a test; the test manual provides useful information for the evaluation; and the *Yearbooks* and *Test Critiques* provide critical reviews by measurement experts.

To ensure that the most appropriate tests are selected, a systematic procedure should be followed. This includes (1) defining the specific type of testing information needed, (2) appraising the role of published tests in relation to other measurement procedures and to the practical constraints of the school situation, (3) locating suitable tests through the various guides and test publishers' catalogues, (4) obtaining specimen sets of those tests that seem most appropriate, (5) reviewing the test materials in light of their intended uses, and (6) summarizing the data and making a final selection. A summary of data concerning each test under consideration is simplified if a standard evaluation form is used when compiling the information.

Administration of published tests involves careful preparation beforehand and strict adherence to the set procedures during testing. In preparing for testing (1) order and check the materials well in advance; (2) select a suitable location for testing; (3) make provisions to prevent distractions; and (4) practice administering the test. During test administration, (1) closely follow the directions and time limits; (2) encourage the students to do their best; and (3) keep a record of any event during the testing period that might affect the test scores. Test results are more likely to be valid if questionable scores are checked by administering a second form of the test and students are given training in test-taking skills.

Published test results can serve a number of useful purposes in the school. They can aid in instructional planning, individualizing instruction, identifying the needs of exceptional children, monitoring educational progress over extended periods, reporting to parents, making educational and vocational decisions, and appraising and reporting on the effectiveness of the school program. In general, they should not be used for assigning course grades, as the sole basis for assignment to remedial programs or retention in grade, or as the sole or main basis for evaluating teaching effectiveness. Published tests are not closely enough related to the instructional objectives of particular courses and they measure too limited a sampling of the intended learning outcomes to be useful for these purposes. Using published test results to judge a teacher's effectiveness may lead to "teaching for the test" and invalidate the test scores for other school uses.

LEARNING EXERCISES

1. List the steps you would follow in locating and selecting the most recent suitable test in one of your teaching areas.

2. What types of information would you expect to find in each of the following: (a) *Mental Measurements Yearbooks,* (b) *Test Critiques,* (c) test manual?

3. Why is it important to follow the directions strictly when administering a published test?

4. Describe some of the ways published tests might be used for instructional planning in one of your teaching areas.

5. Consult a test publisher's catalogue and read the descriptions of one achievement test and one scholastic aptitude test. What type of information is provided?

6. Consult the latest *Mental Measurements Yearbook* and study the reviews for one achievement battery, one reading test, and one scholastic aptitude test. What strengths and weaknesses do the reviewers emphasize?

7. Consult the *Standards for Educational and Psychological Testing* and review the types of validity and reliability information that test manuals should contain. Compare a recent test manual against the *Standards* and evaluate its strengths and weaknesses.

8. Why shouldn't published achievement tests be used as the main basis for assigning course grades, retention in grade, or determining teaching effectiveness?

REFERENCES

American Psychological Association. (1985). *Standards for Educational and Psychological Testing*. Washington, D.C.: Author.

Sarnacki, R. E. (1979). An examination of testwiseness in the cognitive domain. *Review of Educational Research, 49,* (Spring, 1979), 252–279.

Shepard, L. A., & Smith, M. L. (Eds.). (1989). *Flunking grades: Research and policies on retention*. New York: The Falmer Press.

FURTHER READING

American Psychological Association. (1985). *Standards for educational and psychological testing*. Washington, D.C.: Author. Presents recommendations for (1) the preparation of tests, manuals, and reports and (2) the selection and use of tests. An excellent set of guidelines for evaluating test materials and for using tests effectively.

Anastasi, A. (1988). *Psychological testing* (6th ed.). New York: Macmillan. For an orientation to psychological testing see: Chapter 1, "Functions and Origins of Psychological Testing," Chapter 2, "Nature and Use of Psychological Tests," and Chapter 3, "Social and Ethical Considerations in Testing."

Keyser, D. J., & Sweetland, R. C. (Eds.). (1987). *Test critiques compendium*. Kansas City: Test Corporation of America. Descriptions and critiques of sixty widely used educational and psychological tests with special emphasis on practical user information. See also the various volumes of *Test Critiques*.

Kramer, J. J. (Ed.). (1993). *Tests in Print IV*. Lincoln, NE: Buros Institute of Mental Measurements. Includes brief descriptions of published tests, references on specific tests, and a directory of test publishers with an index to their tests. The test entries are cross-referenced to reviews in the *Mental Measurements Yearbooks*.

Kramer, J. J., & Conoley, J. C. (Eds.). (1992). *The eleventh mental measurements yearbook*. Lincoln, NE: Buros Institute of Mental Measurements. Provides test descriptions, critical reviews by measurement specialists, and references. Plans are to publish new editions periodically with supplements published in between.

Salvia, J., & Ysseldyke, J. (1991). *Assessment* (5th ed.). Boston: Houghton Mifflin. For an orientation to the selection, administration, and use of tests with elementary and secondary students with special problems, the entire book should be reviewed. Written for beginners.

Sweetland, R. C., & Keyser, D. J. (Eds.). (1986). *Tests: A comprehensive reference for assessments in psychology, education, and business* (2nd ed.). Kansas City: Test Corporation of America. Provides brief descriptions of 3,000 tests in psychology, education, and business. The easy-to-read entries include title, age or grade range, purpose, test description, time, scoring, cost, and publisher. Look for supplements or new editions of this reference.

Thorndike, R. M., Cunningham, G. K., Thorndike, R. L., & Hagen, E. P. (1991). *Measurement and evaluation in psychology and education* (5th ed.). New York: Macmillan. Chapter 10, "Sources of Information About Tests" and Appendix 4, "Commercially Available Psychological and Educational Tests and Inventories" provide a discussion of sources of information about a wide range of tests and a brief description of some of the more widely used ones.

CHAPTER 17

Interpreting Test Scores and Norms

Test results can be interpreted in terms of the types of tasks that can be performed (criterion reference) or the relative position held in some reference group (norm reference). Both types of interpretation are useful. The first describes what a person can do, and the second describes how the performance compares with that of others. Standardized tests traditionally emphasized norm-referenced interpretation, but many now include both types. Interpreting test scores with the aid of norms requires an understanding of the various methods of expressing test scores, and a clear grasp of the nature of the norm group. Criterion-referenced interpretation requires analysis by objective or content cluster.

Test interpretation would be greatly simplified if we could express test scores on scales like those used in physical measurement. We know, for example, that "5 feet" means the same height whether we are talking about the height of a boy or a picket fence; that a 200-pound football player weighs exactly twice as much as a 100-pound cross-country runner, and that 8 minutes is exactly one-third as long as 24 minutes, whether we are timing a standardized test or a basketball game. This ability to compare measurements from one situation to another and to speak in terms of "twice as much as" or "one third as long as" is possible because these physical measures are based on scales that have a true zero point and equal units.

The ***true zero point*** (e.g., the point at which there is no height at all or no weight at all) indicates precisely where measurement begins. The equal units (e.g., feet, pounds, minutes) provide uniform meaning from one situation to another and from one part of the scale to another. Ten pounds indicates the same weight to a doctor, a grocer, a farmer, or a homemaker. The difference between 15 and 25 pounds is exactly the same as the difference between 160 and 170 pounds.

Unfortunately, the properties of physical measuring scales with which we all are so familiar, are generally lacking in educational measurement. A student who receives a score of zero on a history test does not have zero knowledge of history; there are probably many simple questions that could be answered correctly but were not included in the test. A true zero point in achievement, where there is no achievement at all, cannot be clearly established. Even if it could, it would be impractical to start from that point each time we tested. What we do in actual practice is assume a certain amount of basic knowledge and measure from there. This arbitrary starting point, however, prevents us from saying that a zero score indicates no achievement at all or that a score of 100 represents twice the achievement of a score of 50. Because we are never certain how far the zero score on our test is from the true zero point (i.e., the point of no achievement at all), test scores cannot be interpreted in the same way as physical measurements. We can speak of more or less of a given characteristic, but not twice as much as or half as much as.

The interpretation of test results is additionally handicapped by the inequality of our units of measurement. Sixty items correct on a simple vocabulary test does not have the same meaning as sixty items correct on a more difficult one; nor does either of the scores represent the same level of achievement as sixty items correct on a test of arithmetic, science, or study skills. Test items simply do not represent equal units like feet, pounds, and minutes.

To overcome this lack of a definite frame of reference in educational measurement, a variety of methods of expressing test scores have been devised. As we shall see shortly, the methods vary considerably in the extent to which they provide satisfactory units of measurement. Much of our difficulty in the interpretation and use of test results is because we have so many different scoring systems—each with its own peculiar characteristics and limitations.

METHODS OF INTERPRETING TEST SCORES

Raw Scores

If a student responds correctly to 65 items on an objective test in which each correct item counts one point, the raw score will be 65. Thus, a **_raw score_** is simply the number of points received on a test when the test has been scored according to the directions. It does not make any difference whether each item is counted as one point, whether the items are weighted in some way, or whether a correction for guessing is applied; the resulting point score is still known as a raw score. We all are familiar with raw scores from our many years of taking classroom tests.

Although a raw score is a numerical summary of a student's test performance, it is not very meaningful without further information. If we are told that Michael Adams answered 35 items correctly on an arithmetic test, and therefore has a raw score of 35, our response is likely to be a question: "What does a 35 mean?" or "Is that a good score?" We might also have a list of more specific questions. "How many items were on the test?" "What kinds of arithmetic problems (e.g., addition of integers, multiplication of fractions, story problems) were presented?" "How difficult was the test?" "How does a score of 35 compare with the scores received by other students in Michael's class?"

Answers to these or similar questions are needed to make any raw score meaningful. In general, we can provide meaning to a raw score either by converting it into a description of the specific tasks that the student can perform (criterion-referenced interpretation) or converting it into some type of derived score that indicates the student's relative position in a clearly defined reference group (norm-referenced interpretation). Questions such as the one about the specific kind of arithmetic problems that are on the test are directed at a desire for criterion-referenced interpretations; while those such as the one asking for a comparison with the performance of other students are directed at the desire for norm-referenced interpretations. Often both types of interpretation are appropriate and useful.

Criterion-Referenced Interpretation

Criterion-referenced test interpretation permits us to describe an individual's test performance without referring to the performance of others. Thus, we might describe student performance in terms of the speed with which a task is performed (e.g., types 40 words per minute without error), the precision with which a task is performed (e.g., measures the length of a line within one-sixteenth of an inch), or the percentage of items correct on some clearly defined set of learning tasks (e.g., identifies the meaning of 80 percent of the terms used to describe fractions). The percentage-correct score is widely used in criterion-referenced test interpretation. Standards for judging whether a student has mastered each of the instructional objectives or achievement domains measured by a criterion-referenced test are frequently set in these terms. The key, however, is in providing a clear description of what a student can and cannot do rather than in the use of a percentage-correct score. Knowing, for example, that Michael Adams' raw score of 35 corresponds to a percentage-correct score of 70 because there were 50 items on the arithmetic test provides little help in understanding the meaning of the score. We still need to have a clear description of the domain of arithmetic items that the test represents in order to make a criterion-referenced interpretation of Michael's score.

Criterion-referenced interpretation of test results is most meaningful when the test has been specifically designed for this purpose (see Chapter 14). This typically involves designing a test that measures a set of clearly stated learning tasks. Enough items are used for each interpretation to make it possible to describe test performance in terms of a student's mastery or nonmastery of the tasks. The value of these descriptions of test performance is enhanced by the fact that the domain of measured achievement is delimited and clearly specified, the test items are selected on the basis of their relevance to the domain being measured, and there are enough test items to make dependable judgments concerning the types of tasks a student can and cannot perform.

Criterion-Referenced Interpretation of Standardized Tests. Although standardized tests have been typically designed for norm-referenced interpretations, it is possible to attach criterion-referenced meaning to the test results. This simply involves analyzing each student's test responses by item content and summarizing the results with descriptive statements (e.g., Michael solved all of the addition problems involving no carrying but solved only two of the ten problems requiring carrying). Some test publishers aid this type of interpretation by (1) providing the list of objectives measured by the test, with each item keyed to the appropriate objective, and (2) arranging the items into larger homogeneous content clusters for easy analysis.

Later in this chapter we shall describe and illustrate how criterion-referenced interpretations have been added to the norm-referenced interpretations of standardized tests. Because these tests are usually designed for norm-referenced testing, however, the criterion-referenced interpretations must be made with considerable caution (see "Guidelines" box).

Expectancy Tables.   The use of expectancy tables, as discussed in Chapter 3, also falls within the province of criterion-referenced interpretation. The expectancy table makes it possible to interpret raw scores in terms of expected performance on some

GUIDELINES

Making Criterion-Referenced Interpretations of Standardized Tests

1. Are the achievement domains (objectives or content clusters) homogeneous, delimited, and clearly specified? If not, avoid specific descriptive statements.

2. Are there enough items (say ten) for each type of interpretation? If not, make tentative judgments and/or combine items into larger content clusters for interpretation.

3. In constructing the test, were the easy items omitted to increase discrimination among individuals? If so, remember that the descriptions of what low achievers can do will be severely limited.

4. Does the test use selection-type items only? If so, keep in mind that a proportion of correct answers may be based on guessing (this is especially crucial when only a few items are used to measure a specific content domain).

5. Do the test items provide a directly relevant measure of the objectives? If not, base interpretation on what the items actually measured (e.g., "ability to identify misspelled words" rather than "ability to spell." They are related but are not the same process).

Grouping items in standardized tests by objective and by larger content clusters enhances the instructional use of the results, but criterion-referenced interpretations must be made cautiously.

measure other than the test itself. As illustrated in Chapter 3, the scores on an aptitude test can be used to predict the probability of earning a particular letter grade (*A, B, C, D, F*) in a course. Similarly, expectancy tables can be used to predict the probability of success in a training program, on a job, or in any other situation of interest. The use of an expectancy table makes it possible to interpret a raw score simply and directly without the aid of test norms.

Norm-Referenced Interpretation

Norm-referenced test interpretation tells us how an individual compares with other persons who have taken the same test. The simplest type of comparison, one that is used in classroom testing, is to rank the scores from highest to lowest and to note where an individual's score falls. Noting whether a particular score is third from the top, about average, or one of the lowest scores in class provides a meaningful report to teacher and student alike. If a student's test score is third from the top in a classroom group of thirty students, it is a high score, whether it represents 90 percent of the items correct or 60 percent correct. The fact that a test is relatively easy or difficult for the students does not alter our interpretation of test scores in terms of relative performance. All that is required is a sufficient spread of test scores to provide a reliable ranking.

Derived Scores. Although the simple ranking of raw scores may be useful for reporting the results of a classroom test, it is of limited value beyond the immediate situation because the meaning of a given rank depends on the composition of the group and on the number of group members. To obtain a more general framework for norm-referenced interpretation, raw scores are converted into some type of derived score. A derived score is a numerical report of test performance on a score scale that has well-defined characteristics and yields normative meaning. The most common types of derived scores are grade equivalents, percentile ranks, and standard scores. Grade equivalent scores, which are sometimes described as an example of a developmental score scale, report test performance in terms of the grade group in which an individual's raw score is just average. Percentile ranks and standard scores indicate the individual's relative standing within some particular group (see Table 17.1). Converting raw scores to derived scores is simple with standardized tests. Frequently the test publisher performs the conversions before reporting the scores. If not, however, all we need to do is consult the table of norms in the test manual and select the derived score that corresponds to the individual's raw score. Some derived scores are so easily computed that we can also develop local norms if desired.

There are, as we shall see, a variety of ways of expressing standard scores (e.g., T-scores, normal-curve equivalent scores, and standard age scores), but they are based on a common logic. They differ only in terms of the numerical values used and whether they are based on a normal distribution. There are also a number of approaches other than grade equivalents (e.g., age equivalents or publisher-specific extended score scales) to the definition of a developmental score scale. However, grade equivalents are by far the most common for educational achievement tests.

TABLE 17.1
Most common types of test norms

Type of Test Norm	Name of Derived Score	Meaning in Terms of Test Performance
Grade norms	Grade equivalents	Grade group in which student's raw score is average.
Percentile norms	Percentile ranks (or percentile scores)	Percentage of students in the reference group who fall below student's raw score.
Standard score norms	Standard scores	Distance of student's raw score above or below the mean of the reference group in terms of standard deviation units.

Norms.   Tables of norms in test manuals merely present scores earned by students in clearly defined reference groups. The raw scores and derived scores are presented in parallel columns so that the conversion to derived scores can be easily made. These scores do not represent especially good or desirable performance but, rather, normal or typical performance. They were established at the time the test was standardized by administering the test to representative groups of students for whom the test was constructed. Thus, they indicate the typical performance of students in these standardization groups and nothing more. They should not be viewed as standards or goals to be achieved by other students.

Test norms enable us to answer questions such as the following:

1. How does a student's test performance compare with that of other students?
2. How does a student's performance on one test (or subtest) compare with performance on another test (or subtest)?
3. How does a student's performance on one form of a test compare with performance on another form of the test, administered at an earlier date?

These comparisons of test scores make it possible to predict a student's probable success in various areas, to diagnose strengths and weaknesses, to measure educational growth, and to use the test results for other instructional and guidance purposes. Such functions of test scores would be severely curtailed without the use of the derived scores provided by test norms.

A summary of the most common types of test norms is presented in Table 17.1. To interpret and use test results effectively, we need a good grasp of the characteristics, advantages, and limitations of each of these types of norms.

GRADE NORMS

Grade norms have been widely used with standardized achievement tests, especially at the elementary school level. The grade equivalent that corresponds to a particular raw score identifies the grade level at which the typical student obtains that raw score. Grade equivalents are based on the performance of students in the norm group in each of two or more grades. For example, suppose the arithmetic test that Michael Adams took had been administered to fourth- and fifth-grade students in the norm group in October and in May. We would expect that the group who took the test in May of the fifth grade would generally get higher scores than the group who took the test in October of the fourth grade.

As we see in Table 17.2, this expected pattern is obtained. In October of Grade 4, 50 percent of the students have raw scores below the median score of 28, but this value goes up to 35 in May of Grade 4, to 37 in October of Grade 5, and to 41 in May of Grade 5. Thus, Michael would need to have a higher raw score (41) to obtain a grade equivalent of 5.8 (which corresponds to the typical performance of the Grade 5 student in May) than he would to obtain a grade equivalent of 4.1 (the typical performance of the Grade 4 student in October). Since Michael's raw score was actually 35, he would receive a grade equivalent score of 4.8: the grade at which the typical student receives a raw score of 35.

As is suggested by this example, grade equivalents are expressed by two numbers; the first indicates the year and the second, the month. Grade equivalents for the fifth grade, for example, range from 5.0 to 5.9, or if the decimal point is omitted, as is the practice for some tests, from 50 to 59. This division of the calendar year into tenths, starting with September = .0 and ending with June = .9, is based on the traditional school year and assumes little or no growth in achievement test performance during the summer vacation months.

Table 17.2 provides all that is needed to convert Michael's raw score to a grade equivalent because he happened to get a raw score equal to the median of one of the grade norm groups. To obtain grade equivalents for Bob Brown who got a raw score of 31 and Teresa Chavez who got a raw score of 45, however, we would need some more information. We could see that Bob should have a grade equivalent somewhere between 4.1 and 4.8, but to determine a specific score we would need to interpolate (that is, decide how far to go above 4.1 toward 4.8) to account for the fact that Bob did better than the typical fourth-grade student did in October but not as well as the typical fourth-grade student in May. Similarly, we could see that Teresa's raw score of 45 should be converted to a grade equivalent score above 5.8, but would have to extrapolate (that is, project the rate of increase with grade

TABLE 17.2
Illustration of the construction of grade equivalent scores

Time of Administration		Median* Raw Score	Grade Equivalent
Grade	Month		
4	October (.1)	28	4.1
4	May (.8)	35	4.8
5	October (.1)	37	5.1
5	May (.8)	41	5.8

*50 percent of the students in the norm group score below and 50 percent score above the median raw score (see Appendix A).

level beyond the point where data were collected) to give Teresa a specific grade equivalent.

Fortunately, we don't need to know the details of interpolation and extrapolation to convert Bob's and Teresa's raw scores to grade equivalents. Test publishers perform those operations and produce tables showing the grade equivalent corresponding to each possible raw score. To convert to grade equivalents with a table of grade norms, all one needs to do is find the students' raw scores in the table and read off the corresponding grade equivalents. Using this procedure, for example, we might find that Bob's grade equivalent is 4.4 and that Teresa's grade equivalent is 6.5.

Grade norms are popular, largely because test performance is expressed in units that are easy to understand and interpret. To illustrate, assume that we obtained the following grade equivalents for Jennifer, who is in the middle of the fifth grade:

❑ Arithmetic 5.5

❑ Language 6.5

❑ Reading 9.0

In examining these scores, teachers, parents, and students alike would recognize that Jennifer is exactly average in arithmetic, one year advanced in language, and three and a half years advanced in reading. Grade equivalents provide a common unit with which we all are familiar. The only difficulty is that this familiarity leads those who are unaware of the numerous limitations of grade norms to misleading or inaccurate interpretations. Concern about misinterpretations of grade equivalents has led to sharp criticisms of the scores. Indeed, an earlier version of the *Standards* (American Psychological Association, 1974) suggested that the use of grade equivalent scores should be discouraged. On the other hand, some measurement experts (Hoover, 1984) have argued that grade equivalents are useful and no more subject to misinterpretation than other types of scores. In any event, there is no indication that their popularity is declining. It is important to understand their limitations so that misinterpretations can be avoided.

Six possible misinterpretations of grade equivalents are worthy of consideration. Each of these misinterpretations is based upon an unjustified assumption about the meaning of the scores. These inappropriate assumptions are: (1) assuming that norms are standards of what should be, (2) assuming that grade equivalents indicate the appropriate grade placement for a student, (3) assuming that all students should be expected to grow one grade equivalent unit per year, (4) assuming that the units are equal throughout the score range, (5) assuming that grade equivalents for different tests are comparable, and (6) assuming that the scores that are based on extrapolations to grades well above or below the test level are meaningful. Let's briefly consider each of these faulty assumptions and the resulting misinterpretation of grade equivalents.

1. Don't confuse norms with standards of what should be.
For any particular grade equivalent, 50 percent of the students in the standardization group are above this norm, and 50 percent are below. Consequently, we should not interpret a particular grade norm as something all of our students should attain. If half of our students are above norm and half are below, we may conclude that our

students compare favorably with the students in the norm group. Whether this is good or bad depends on a number of factors, such as our students' ability, the extent to which the learning outcomes measured by the test reflect our curriculum emphasis, and the quality of the educational facilities at our disposal. If we are teaching students with above-average ability under conditions comparable to those of schools in the norm group, merely matching the norm would be cause for concern. On the other hand, if our students have a history of low achievement in previous grades, reaching the norm might call for considerable pride. In any case, it is well to remember that the norm is merely an average score made by the students in the standardization group. As such, it represents the typical performance of average students in average schools and should not be considered a standard of excellence to be achieved by others.

2. Don't interpret a grade equivalent as an estimate of the grade where a student should be placed. One potential misinterpretation of grade norms, although not because of weaknesses in the scoring system itself, is to assume that students who earn certain grade equivalent scores are ready to do work at that level. For example, we might conclude that a fourth-grade student should be doing sixth-grade work in language skills if she earns a grade equivalent of 6.0 on a language skills test. This assumption overlooks the fact that she can obtain a grade equivalent score well above her grade level by doing the less-difficult test items more rapidly and accurately than the average fourth-grade student. The grade equivalent score of 6.0 may represent nothing more than a thorough mastery of language skills taught in the first four grades. Thus, grade equivalents should never be interpreted literally; at best, they are only rough guides to the level of test performance. Students at different grade levels who earn the same grade equivalent score are apt to be ready for quite different types of instruction.

3. Don't expect that all students should gain 1.0 grade equivalent each year. It seems natural to think that if Jane and Sara had grade equivalents of 4.7 and 2.5, respectively, at the end of Grade 3, they should be expected to each gain 1.0 and have scores of 5.7 and 3.5 at the end of Grade 4. This expectation is inappropriate, not only because norms should not be confused with standards, but because a gain of 1.0 per year is only typical of students scoring close to the average for their grade. On average, students who score well above their grade placement gain more than 1.0 grade equivalents per year, while students who score well below the norm gain less than 1.0 per year. Thus, if students in a remedial reading program show an average gain of 1.0 in a year's time, that actually would be better than is typical of students with low initial scores.

4. Don't assume that the units are equal at different parts of the scale. A year of growth in arithmetic achievement from Grade 2.0 to 3.0, for example, might represent a much greater improvement than an increase from Grade 4.0 to 5.0 or Grade 8.0 to 9.0. Thus, being advanced or behind in terms of grade units has a different meaning on different parts of the grade scale. Students who earn grade equivalents several grades above their grade placement might be demonstrating either vastly superior achievement or performance just slightly above average.

5. *Don't assume that scores on different tests are comparable.* A grade equivalent score of 8.0 on one test publisher's fifth-grade reading comprehension test may not represent the same degree of superior performance as an 8.0 on another publisher's fifth-grade reading comprehension test. We know that in both cases an 8.0 is well above the average for a fifth grader. However, an 8.0 might be one of the highest possible scores for one publisher's test, while the scores provided by the other publisher might go considerably higher.

The lack of comparability also applies to a single publisher's tests in different subjects. Patterns of growth vary from subject to subject, and so our grade equivalent units stretch and contract at different points on the scale for different subjects. Although it would be tempting to conclude that a fourth-grader who received a grade equivalent of 7.2 in reading and a grade equivalent of 6.3 in mathematics was better at reading than mathematics, such a conclusion is likely to be inappropriate. In comparison with other fourth-grade students, the two scores may actually represent equally superior performance because the range of grade equivalent scores for fourth-grade students is generally greater in reading than in mathematics.

6. *Don't interpret extreme scores as dependable estimates of students' performance level.* Grade equivalent scores that are several years above or below the student's actual grade placement and the grade levels where the test is normally used are based on extrapolation. This results in artificial units that do not correspond to the achievement of students in any particular group. Estimating these grade equivalents is frequently necessary because the younger students do not have the needed skills to take the test and because growth in the basic skills tends to level off in the eighth and ninth grades. In interpreting grade equivalents at the extremes, therefore, it is well to keep in mind that they do not represent the actual performance of students at these levels.

In summary, grade norms are based on the average performance of students at various grade levels. They are widely used at the elementary school level, largely because of the ease with which they can be interpreted. As we have seen, however, grade equivalents have a number of limitations that can lead to misinterpretations. In general, grade norms are most useful for reporting growth in the basic skills during the elementary school period. They are least useful for comparing a student's performances on different tests. For whatever purpose grade norms are used, however, the inequality of grade units must be considered during interpretation of the results.

PERCENTILE RANK

One of the most widely used and easily understood methods of describing test performance is percentile rank. A percentile rank (or percentile score) indicates a student's relative position in a group in terms of the percentage of students scoring lower. Thus, if we consult a table of norms and find that a student's raw score of 29 equals a percentile rank of 70, we know that 70 percent of the students in the reference group obtained a raw score lower than 29. Stating it another way, this student's performance surpasses that of 70 percent of the group. Percentile rank is sometimes interpreted as the percentage of individuals receiving scores equal or lower than a given score. The specific interpretation depends on the methods of computation used, but for all practical purposes the meaning is the same.

One method of presenting percentile norms is shown in Table 17.3. These norms are for the three mathematics subtests of the *Stanford Achievement Test, Eighth Edition.* Percentile norms for other subtests and for the Mathematics Total score are presented in similar tables. The raw scores for each subtest are listed in the first column and the corresponding percentile rank is listed in the second column under the subtest heading. Corresponding stanine scores, grade equivalent scores, and scaled scores are also listed in the third, fourth, and fifth columns under each subtest. Grade equivalent scores have already been discussed and stanine and scaled scores will be described below.

A student with raw scores of 20 on the Concepts of Number subtest and 25 on the Mathematics Computation subtest would have percentile ranks of 53 and 47, respectively, on those two subtests. It is not surprising that the higher raw score converts to a lower percentile rank in this example because there are fewer items on the Concepts of Number subtest than on the Mathematics Computation subtest. Note that these two percentile ranks of 53 and 47 for a test administered in the spring of Grade 7 convert to a grade equivalent scores slightly above (8.1) and slightly below (7.6) grade level.

Several points are worth noting about the example in Table 17.3. (1) The conversion of raw scores to percentile scores is specific to each subtest (a raw score of 20 corresponds to a percentile rank of 53 on Concepts of Number but only 33 on Mathematics Computation). (2) The conversion is specific to the particular level and form of the test (see table title, Advanced Level 1, Form J). (3) The conversion is specific to a particular grade and time of year (spring of grade 7). Different tables would be needed if another form of the test had been administered or if the test had been administered at another time of year or grade. (4) The percentile ranks are for a particular norm group. In this case these are the national norms for students tested in the spring of 1988. Different percentile ranks would be obtained for specialized norms (large city norms, private schools) or for different norming years. (5) As can be seen in Table 17.3, conversions on the Mathematics Applications subtest depend on whether or not the students used a calculator when taking this section of the test. A Mathematics Applications raw score of 25, for example, yields a percentile rank of 52 for a student who took the test without a calculator but a percentile rank of only 44 for a student who was tested using a calculator.

A desirable feature of percentile norms is that we can interpret a student's performance in terms of various groups. Most commonly, performance is reported in terms of relative standing in the student's own grade or age group. In some instances, however, we are more interested in how a student compares with those who have completed second-year French, are majoring in home economics, or are enrolled in the college-preparatory program. Such comparisons are possible with percentile norms. The interpretations of a particular score are limited only to the types of decisions we want to make and the availability of the appropriate sets of norms.

TABLE 17.3
Partial norms for the *Stanford Achievement Tests*, Advanced Level 1, Form J, for students tested in the spring of Grade 7

Concepts of Number

Raw Score	%-ile Rank	Sta-nine	Grade Equiv.	Scaled Score
34	99	9	PHS	818
33	99	9	PHS	794
.	.	.	.	.
20	53	5	8.1	676
19	50	5	7.8	672
18	45	5	7.5	667
17	41	5	7.2	663
16	36	4	6.8	658
15	31	4	6.5	653
.	.	.	.	.
2	1	1	2.7	558
1	1	1	2.2	532
.	.	.	.	.

Mathematics Computation

Raw Score	%-ile Rank	Sta-nine	Grade Equiv.	Scaled Score
44	99	9	PHS	818
43	99	9	PHS	795
.	.	.	.	.
30	62	6	8.7	687
29	59	5	8.5	683
28	56	5	8.3	679
27	53	5	8.1	675
26	50	5	7.9	672
25	47	5	7.6	668
.	.	.	.	.
5	1	1	3.5	579
4	1	1	3.2	570
3	1	1	2.8	559
2	1	1	2.5	543
1	1	1	2.0	518

Mathematics Applications

Raw Score	%-ile Rank	Sta-nine	Grade Equiv.	Scaled Score
40	99	9	PHS	814
39	99	9	PHS	791
.	.	.	.	.
26	55	5	8.3	679
25	52	5	8.0	675
24	48	5	7.7	671
23	44	5	7.4	667
22	41	5	7.1	663
21	37	4	6.7	659
.	.	.	.	.
4	1	1	3.1	572
3	1	1	2.7	561
2	1	1	2.4	545
1	1	1	1.9	520
.	.	.	.	.

Mathematics Applications*

Raw Score	%-ile Rank	Sta-nine	Grade Equiv.	Scaled Score
40	99	9	PHS	808
39	99	9	PHS	785
.	.	.	.	.
26	48	5	7.7	671
25	44	5	7.4	667
24	41	5	7.1	663
23	37	4	6.7	659
22	34	4	6.5	655
21	30	4	6.2	651
.	.	.	.	.
4	1	1	2.8	563
3	1	1	2.6	552
2	1	1	2.3	536
1	1	1	1.7	511
.	.	.	.	.

Source: From *Stanford Achievement Test, 8th ed.* Copyright © 1989 by Harcourt Brace & Company. Reproduced by permission. All rights reserved.
*For students tested using calculators

The wide applicability of percentile norms is not without its drawbacks. When interpreting a percentile rank, we must always refer to the norm group on which it is based. A student does not have a percentile rank of 80, but a percentile rank of 80 in some particular group. A raw score on a scholastic aptitude test, for example, may be equivalent to a percentile rank of 80 in a general group of high school seniors, 63 in a group of college-bound seniors, and 25 in a group of college freshmen in a highly selective college. Relative standing varies with the ability of the reference group used for comparison.

A related inconvenience with percentile norms is that numerous sets of norms are usually required. We need a set of norms for each group with which we wish to compare a student. This is not especially troublesome at the elementary school level where a student's own grade and age mates provide a suitable basis for comparison. At the high-school level, however, where the curriculum becomes diversified and students pursue different courses, it becomes rather difficult. Here we need sets of norms for students who have completed varying numbers of courses in each subject area.

The main limitation of percentile norms is that percentile units are not equal on all parts of the scale. A percentile difference of ten near the middle of the scale (e.g., 45 to 55) represents a much smaller difference in test performance than the same percentile difference at the ends (e.g., 85 to 95), because a large number of students receive scores near the middle, whereas relatively few students have extremely high or low scores. Thus, a student whose raw score is near average can surpass another 10 percent of the group by increasing the raw score just a few points. But a student with a relatively high score will need to increase the raw score by a great many points in order to surpass another 10 percent, simply because there are so few students at that level.

The inequality of units requires special caution when using percentile ranks. First, a difference of several percentile points should be given greater weight at the extremes of the distribution than near the middle. In fact, small differences near the middle of the distribution generally can be disregarded. Second, percentile ranks should not be averaged arithmetically. The appropriate average when using percentile norms is the 50th percentile. This is the midpoint of the distribution and is called the median, or counting average.

In summary, percentile norms are widely applicable, easily determined, and readily understood. A percentile rank describes a student's performance in terms of the percentage of students in some clearly defined group that earn a lower score. This might be a grade or age group, or any other group that provides a meaningful comparison (e.g., college freshmen). More than one set of norms is usually required, and percentile ranks must be interpreted in terms of the norm group on which they are based. The most severe limitation of percentile ranks is that the units are unequal. This can be offset somewhat by careful interpretation, however, because the inequality of units follows a predictable pattern.

STANDARD SCORES

Another method of indicating a student's relative position in a group is by showing how far the raw score is above or below average. This is the approach used with standard scores. Basically, standard scores express test performance in terms of standard deviation units from the mean. The mean (M) is the arithmetical average, which is determined by adding all of the scores and dividing by the number of scores. The standard deviation (SD) is a measure of the spread of scores in a group. Because the method of computing the standard deviation is not especially helpful in understanding it, the procedure will not be presented here (see Appendix A for computation). The meaning of standard deviation and the standard scores based on it can best be explained in terms of the normal probability curve (also called the normal distribution curve or simply the normal curve).

The Normal Curve and the Standard Deviation Unit

The normal curve is a symmetrical bell-shaped curve that has many useful mathematical properties. One of the most useful from the viewpoint of test interpretation is that when it is divided into standard deviation units, each portion under the curve contains a fixed percentage of cases. This is shown in the idealized normal curve presented in Figure 17.1. (For the moment, disregard the raw scores beneath the figure.) Note that 34 percent of the cases fall between the mean and +1 SD, 14 percent between +1 SD and +2 SD, and 2 percent between +2 SD and +3 SD. (All percentages have been rounded.) The same proportions, of course, apply to the standard deviation intervals below the mean. Only 0.13 percent of the cases fall below −3 SD or above +3 SD. Thus, for all practical purposes, a normal distribution of scores falls between −3 and +3 standard deviations from the mean.

To demonstrate the value of standard deviation units for expressing relative position in a group, raw scores from two different tests have been placed beneath the row of deviations along the baseline of the curve in Figure 17.1. The tests have the following means and standard deviations:

FIGURE 17.1
Normal curve, indicating the approximate percentage of cases falling within each standard deviation interval

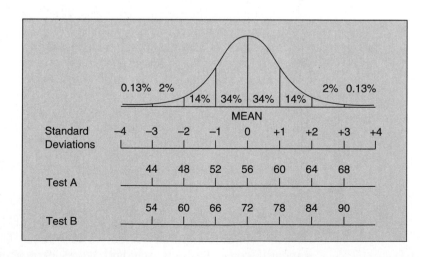

	Test A	**Test B**
M	56	72
SD	4	6

In Figure 17.1 the mean raw scores of both tests have been placed at the zero point on the base line of the curve. Thus, they have been arbitrarily equated to zero. Notice that +1 SD is equivalent to 60 (56 + 4) on Test A and 78 (72 + 6) on Test B, and −1 SD is equivalent to 52 (56 − 4) on Test A and 66 (72 − 6) on Test B. If we convert all of the raw scores on the two tests to the standard deviation units in this manner, we can directly compare performance on the tests. For example, a raw score of 62 on Test A and 81 on Test B are equal because both are 1.5 standard deviation units *above* the mean. When converted to standard deviation units, the raw scores are, of course, no longer needed. A +2.5 SD on Test A is superior to a +2.0 SD on Test B, regardless of the size of the raw scores from which they were derived. The only restriction for such comparisons is that the conversion to standard deviation units must be based on a common group.

The utility of the standard deviation is that it permits us to convert raw scores to a common scale that has equal units and that can be readily interpreted in terms of the normal curve. At this point, it should be helpful to review a few of the characteristics that make the normal curve so useful in test interpretation.

Referring to Figure 17.1 again, note that 68 percent (approximately two thirds) of the cases fall between −1 and +1 standard deviations from the mean. This provides a handy bench mark for interpreting standard scores and the standard error of measurement, as both are based on standard deviation units. The fixed percentages in each interval make it possible to convert standard deviation units to percentile ranks. For example, −2 SD equals a percentile rank of 2 because 2 percent of the cases fall below that point. Starting from the left of the figure, each point on the base line of the curve can be equated to the following percentile ranks:

$$-2 \text{ SD} = 2\%$$

$$-1 \text{ SD} = 16\% \ (2 + 14)$$

$$0 \text{ (M)} = 50\% \ (16 + 34)$$

$$+1 \text{ SD} = 84\% \ (50 + 34)$$

$$+2 \text{ SD} = 98\% \ (84 + 14)$$

This relationship between standard deviation units and percentile ranks enables us to interpret standard scores in simple and familiar terms. When used for this purpose, we must, of course, be able to assume a normal distribution. This is not a serious restriction in using standard score norms, however, because the distribution of scores on which they are based usually closely approximates the normal curve. In many instances the standard scores are normalized; that is, the distribution of scores is made normal by the process of computing percentiles and converting directly to their standard score equivalents. Although it is generally safe to assume a normal distribution when using standard scores from tables of norms in test manuals, it is usually unwise to make such an assumption for standard scores computed directly from a relatively small number of cases, such as a classroom group.

Types of Standard Scores

There are numerous types of standard scores used in testing. Because they all are based on the same principle and are interpreted in somewhat the same manner, only the most common types will be discussed here.

Z-Score.   The simplest of the standard scores, and the one on which others are based, is the z-score. This score expresses test performance simply and directly as the number of standard deviation units a raw score is above or below the mean. The formula for computing a z-score is:

$$\text{z-score} = \frac{X - M}{SD}$$

where

X = any raw score

M = arithmetic mean of raw scores

SD = standard deviation of raw scores

You can quickly become familiar with this formula by applying it to various raw scores in Test A or Test B of Figure 17.1 and then visually checking your answer along the baseline of the curve. For example, z-scores for the raw scores of 58 and 50 on Test A (M = 56, SD = 4) would be computed as follows:

$$z = \frac{58 - 56}{4} = .5 \qquad z = \frac{50 - 56}{4} = -1.5$$

A z-score is always negative when the raw score is smaller than the mean. Forgetting the negative sign can cause serious errors in test interpretation. For this reason, z-scores are seldom used directly in test norms but are usually transformed into a standard score system that uses only positive numbers.

T-Score.   The term *T-score* was originally given to a type of normalized score based on a group of unselected twelve-year-old children. However, it has come to refer to any set of normally distributed standard scores that has a mean of 50 and a standard deviation of 10. T-scores (linear conversion) can be obtained by multiplying the z-score by 10 and adding the product to 50. Thus,

$$\text{T-score} = 50 + 10(z)$$

This formula will provide T-scores only when the original distribution of raw scores is normal, because with this type of conversion (linear), the distribution of standard scores retains the same shape as the original raw score distribution. Some people call any set of scores derived from this formula T-scores; others call them linear T-scores or Z-scores, to distinguish them from normalized T-scores. Applying this formula to the two z-scores computed earlier (z = .5, z = −1.5), we would obtain the following results:

$$T = 50 + 10(.5) = 55 \qquad T = 50 + 10 (−1.5) = 35$$

One reason that T-scores are preferred to z-scores for reporting test results is that only positive integers are produced. It seems preferable, for example, to report a person's test performance as a T-score of 33 than to report the same performance as a z-score of −1.7. The two scores are equivalent, however. Because T-scores always have a mean of 50 and a standard deviation of 10, any T-score is directly interpretable. A T-score of 55, for example, always indicates one-half standard deviation above the mean, and so on. Once the concept of T-scores is grasped, interpretation is relatively simple.

Normalized Standard Scores. Normalized T-scores are calculated by (1) converting the distribution of raw scores into percentile ranks, (2) looking up the z-score each percentile rank would have in a normal distribution and assigning these z-scores to the corresponding raw scores, and (3) converting the z-scores to T-scores, using the formula presented earlier. The procedure of going from raw score to percentile to the corresponding z-score in a normal distribution is called an ***area conversion*** and yields normalized z-scores, which are then transformed directly into normalized T-scores. This results in a normally distributed set of standard scores, regardless of the shape of the original distribution of raw scores. Normalizing is used by test publishers to remove minor irregularities in the raw score distributions.

Many other normalized standard scores are computed in the same way that normalized T-scores are determined, but different values are used for the mean and standard deviation. For example, standard scores with a mean of 100 and a standard deviation of 15 are used with some aptitude tests. Consequently, on these tests a score of 115 means one standard deviation above the mean, the same as a T-score of 60. Standard scores can be assigned any arbitrarily selected mean and standard deviation, and the interpretation will be the same because the basic frame of reference is the standard deviation unit.

Stanines. Stanines (pronounced *stay-nines*) are a simple type of normalized standard score that illustrates the process of normalization. Stanines are single digit scores ranging from 1 to 9. This system of scores is so named because the distribution of raw scores is divided into nine parts (standard nines). Stanine 5 is precisely in the center of the distribution and includes all cases within one-fourth of a standard deviation on either side of the mean. In a normal distribution, percentile ranks of 40 and 60 correspond to one-fourth of a standard deviation below and above the mean. Any score with a percentile rank of at least 40 but less than 60 is converted to a stanine score of 5. Thus raw scores corresponding to percentile ranks between 40 and 59 all convert to stanine scores of 5.

The remaining stanines are evenly distributed above and below Stanine 5. Each stanine, with the exception of Stanines 1 and 9, which cover the tails of the distribution, includes a band of raw scores the width of one-half of a standard deviation unit. Thus, for all practical purposes, stanines present test norms on a nine-point scale of equal units. These standard scores have a mean of 5 and a standard deviation of 2. The conversion from percentile ranks to stanines is straightforward for a normal distribution. See "Correspondence of Percentile Ranks and Stanine Scores in a Normal Distribution."

The following points summarize the major strengths of stanine scores.

1. The stanine system uses a nine-point scale, in which 9 is high, 1 is low, and 5 is average. Thus, the system is easily explained to students and parents, and they can readily visualize where test performance (e.g., 7) falls on a scale of 1 to 9.

2. Stanines are normalized standard scores that make it possible to compare a student's performance on different tests (if based on a common group). Typically a difference of two stanines represents a significant difference in performance between tests (assuming test reliability is satisfactory). Thus, a student with a stanine of 7 in arithmetic and 5 in spelling is probably demonstrating superior performance in arithmetic.

3. The stanine system makes it easy to combine diverse types of data (e.g., test scores, ratings, ranked data) because stanines are computed like percentile ranks but are expressed in standard score form. Thus, the conversion to stanines is simple, and the standard score feature makes it possible to add stanine scores from various measures to obtain a composite score. A simple summing of stanines will give equal weight to each measure in the composite.

Correspondence of Percentile Ranks and Stanine Scores in a Normal Distribution

Range of Percentile Ranks	Stanine
96 or higher	9
89 to 95	8
77 to 88	7
60 to 76	6
40 to 59	5
23 to 39	4
11 to 22	3
4 to 10	2
Below 4	1

4. Because the stanine system uses a single-digit score, it is easily recorded and takes up less space than other scores. (It was originally developed to fit into a single column on an IBM card.)

The main limitation of stanine scores is that growth cannot be shown from one year to the next. If a student's progress matches that of the norm group, the same position in the group will be retained and the same stanine will be assigned. Percentile ranks and other standard scores used to indicate relative position in a particular group share this shortcoming. To determine growth, we need to examine the increase in the raw scores or in developmental scale scores (e.g., grade equivalents).

Stanines are sometimes criticized on the grounds that they are rather crude units, because they divide a distribution of scores into only nine parts. On the plus side, however, these crude units prevent the overinterpretation of test scores. Although greater refinement might be desirable for some special purposes (e.g., identifying gifted students), stanines provide satisfactory discrimination for most educational purposes. With a more refined scoring system, there is always the danger that minor, chance differences in scores will be interpreted as significant differences.

Normal-Curve Equivalent (NCE). The normal-curve equivalent (NCE) is another normalized standard score which was introduced in order to avoid some of the pitfalls of grade equivalent scores. Because school districts need NCE scores to fulfill the requirements of some federally supported compensatory education programs, publishers of the major standardized achievement tests have added this score to their list of score reporting options.

Like T-scores, NCE scores have a mean of 50. However, the standard deviation of NCE scores is 21.06, rather than the 10. This seemingly strange choice for a standard deviation was selected so that NCE scores would range from 1 to 99. As can be seen from the following list of a few NCE scores and their corresponding percentile ranks, NCE scores of 1, 50, and 99 are equivalent to percentile ranks of the same numerical values. At other points on the scale, however, NCE scores have different numerical values than the corresponding percentile ranks. Compared to percentile ranks, they are more spread out at the extremes (e.g., an NCE difference of 90 to 99 corresponds to a percentile rank difference of only 97 to 99) and less spread out near the middle (e.g., an NCE difference of 50 to 75 corresponds to a percentile rank difference of 50 to 88).

NCE Score	Corresponding Percentile Rank	Percentile Rank	Corresponding NCE Score
99	99	99	99
90	97	90	77
75	88	75	64
50	50	50	50
25	12	25	36
10	3	10	23
1	1	1	1

Standard Age Scores.   Another widely used standard score for ability tests is the Standard Age Score (SAS). Here the mean is set at 100 and the standard deviation at 16. Thus, a student with an SAS of 84 has scored one standard deviation below the mean (T-score = 40), and a student with an SAS of 116 has scored one standard deviation above the mean (T-score = 60). Scores on ability tests could just as easily be expressed as T-scores or NCEs. However, in the past these tests reported scores as deviation IQ scores with a mean of 100 and a standard deviation of 16 (15 on some tests). The SAS (or similar scales such as the Cognitive Skills Quotient or School Ability Index) has replaced deviation IQ scores in an attempt to avoid some of the misinterpretations associated with the terms *intelligence* and *IQ.*

Comparison of Score Systems

The equivalence of scores in various standard score systems and their relation to percentiles and the normal curve are presented in Figure 17.2. This figure illustrates the interrelated nature of the various scales for reporting relative position in a normally distributed group. A raw score one standard deviation below the mean, for example, can be expressed as a z-score of −1.0, a percentile rank of 16, a T-score of 40, an NCE score of 29, a deviation IQ of 85, an SAS of 84, or a stanine of 3. Thus, the various scoring systems are merely different ways of saying the same thing, and we can easily convert from one scale to another if we assume a normal distribution and comparable norm groups.

The relationships among the scoring systems shown in Figure 17.2 are especially helpful in understanding a particular standard score scale. Until we fully understand T-scores, for example, it is helpful to convert them, mentally, into percentile ranks. A T-score of 60 becomes meaningful when we note that it is equivalent to a percentile rank of 84. This conversion to percentile ranks, which are more easily understood, is also useful for interpreting standard scores to parents and students.

In summary, standard scores indicate a student's relative position in a group in terms of standard deviation units above or below the mean. In a normal distribution, the various standard score scales and the percentile scale are interrelated, making it possible to convert from one to another. Standard scores have the special advantage of providing roughly equal units. Thus, unlike percentiles, ten standard score points represent approximately the same difference in test performance anywhere along the scale. In addition, standard scores can be averaged arithmetically. One drawback of standard scores is that they are not readily understood by students and parents. A more serious limitation is that interpretation is difficult unless the scores are normally distributed. This is not a problem in using standard score norms, however, because norm tables are generally based on normalized standard scores.

One of the best ways to become familiar with the various scoring systems and the relationships among them is to review the corresponding scores below a selected point in Figure 17.2.

FIGURE 17.2

Corresponding standard scores and percentiles in a normal distribution

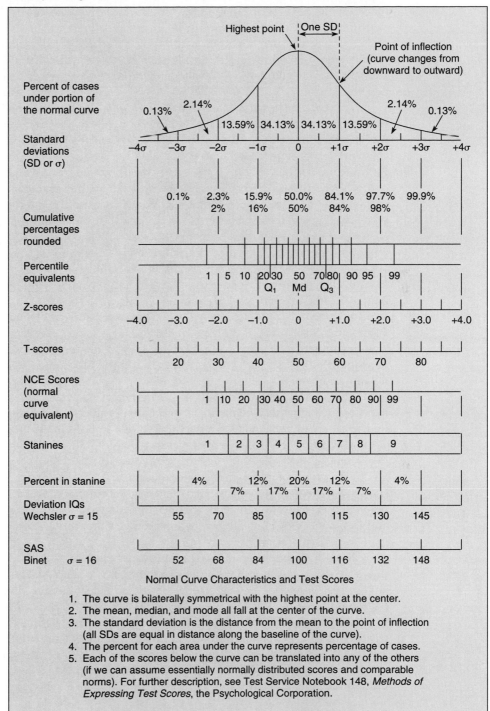

Normal Curve Characteristics and Test Scores

1. The curve is bilaterally symmetrical with the highest point at the center.
2. The mean, median, and mode all fall at the center of the curve.
3. The standard deviation is the distance from the mean to the point of inflection (all SDs are equal in distance along the baseline of the curve).
4. The percent for each area under the curve represents percentage of cases.
5. Each of the scores below the curve can be translated into any of the others (if we can assume essentially normally distributed scores and comparable norms). For further description, see Test Service Notebook 148, *Methods of Expressing Test Scores*, the Psychological Corporation.

PROFILES

One advantage of converting raw scores to derived scores is that a student's performance on different tests can be compared directly. This is usually done by means of a test profile, like the one presented in the top half of Figure 17.3. Such a graphic representation of test data makes it easy to identify a student's relative strengths and weaknesses. Most standardized tests have provisions for plotting test profiles.

The profile shown in the top half of Figure 17.3 indicates a desirable trend in profile construction. Instead of plotting test scores as specific points on the scale, test performance is recorded in Section D by means of bands that extend one standard error of measurement above and below the student's obtained scores. Recall from our discussion of reliability that there are approximately two chances out of three that a student's true score will fall within one standard error of the obtained score. Thus, these confidence bands indicate the ranges of scores within which we can be reasonably certain of finding the student's true standings. Plotting them on the profile enables us to take into account the inaccuracy of the test scores when comparing performance on different tests. Interpreting differences between tests is simple with these score bands. If the bands for two tests overlap, we can assume that performance on the two tests does not differ significantly, and if the bands do not overlap, we can assume that there is probably a real difference in performance. Thus, performance on Verbal Reasoning, Numerical Reasoning, Perceptual Speed and Accuracy, and Language Usage subtests does not differ significantly for the example in Figure 17.3. The performance on the Abstract Reasoning subtest is clearly higher than that on the Mechanical Reasoning or Spatial Relations subtests.

The score bands used with the *Differential Aptitude Tests* can be plotted by hand or by computer. The computer-produced profile shown in Figure 17.3 is based on the same-sex percentiles. These are recorded in Section C of the form, under the column heading "PR". Also shown, under the column head "S," are the corresponding stanine scores. The opposite-sex percentiles and stanines as well as those for the combined group of males and females are listed down the right side of the report to show how the scores compare with the female norms and to total group norms. The difference in male and female percentiles for some tests (e.g., Mechanical Reasoning and Language Usage) highlights the importance of reporting scores in terms of both male and female norms.

Not all test publishers make provisions for plotting score bands, but more will probably do so in the future. In the meantime, it is possible to plot these bands for any test for which we have a standard error of measurement. All we need to do is determine the error band in raw score points and refer to the norm table with these figures. For example, if a student has earned a raw score of 74 and the standard error of measurement is 3, the error band in raw score points will range from 71 to 77. By locating these two numbers in the norm table we can obtain the corresponding range in percentiles, standard scores, or whatever derived score is being used, and plot the results directly on the profile. The use of such bands minimizes the

FIGURE 17.3

DAT Student profile and narrative summary (Reproduced from *The Differential Aptitude Tests,* 5th edition, by permission. Copyright 1990, The Psychological Corporation. All rights reserved.)

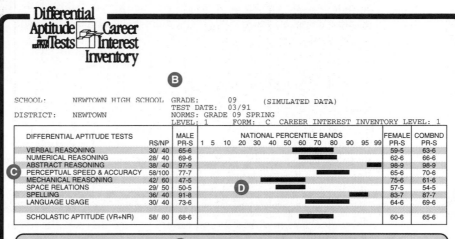

Differential Aptitude Tests ▪ Career Interest Inventory

B

SCHOOL: NEWTOWN HIGH SCHOOL   GRADE: 09   (SIMULATED DATA)
                                    TEST DATE: 03/91
DISTRICT: NEWTOWN   NORMS: GRADE 09 SPRING
                                    LEVEL: 1   FORM: C   CAREER INTEREST INVENTORY LEVEL: 1

DIFFERENTIAL APTITUDE TESTS	RS/NP	MALE PR-S	NATIONAL PERCENTILE BANDS	FEMALE PR-S	COMBND PR-S
VERBAL REASONING	30/ 40	65-6		59-5	63-6
NUMERICAL REASONING	28/ 40	69-6		62-6	66-6
ABSTRACT REASONING	38/ 40	97-9		98-9	98-9
PERCEPTUAL SPEED & ACCURACY	58/100	77-7		65-6	70-6
MECHANICAL REASONING	42/ 60	47-5		75-6	61-6
SPACE RELATIONS	29/ 50	50-5		57-5	54-5
SPELLING	36/ 40	91-8		83-7	87-7
LANGUAGE USAGE	30/ 40	73-6		64-6	69-6
SCHOLASTIC APTITUDE (VR+NR)	58/ 80	68-6		60-6	65-6

(National percentile band scale: 1 5 10 20 30 40 50 60 70 80 90 95 99)

C   **D**

E EDUCATIONAL PLANS

The Scholastic Aptitude score gives you some information about your ability to learn the subjects taught in school. Your score is in the average range. When you took the DAT, you indicated that you have not decided on an educational plan beyond graduating from high school. Because you are capable of doing well in school, you might want to think about attending a college, a university, or some other type of school or training program.

F UNDERSTANDING YOUR DAT RESULTS

Recently, you took the <u>Differential Aptitude Tests</u> (DAT). This brief description of the scores presented above tells how you did compared with other male students in the same grade from across the country.

You scored in the average range on the Verbal Reasoning and Numerical Reasoning tests. Verbal Reasoning measures your ability to see relationships among words, and Numerical Reasoning measures your ability to perform mathematical reasoning tasks. Both abilities are important to success in school, and your scores show that you are capable of doing well.

G Your score on the Abstract Reasoning test is in the highest range. People who have this ability can recognize relationships that do not depend on language or numbers.

You scored in the above-average range on the Spelling test. Many courses and careers require good spelling skills.

You scored in the above-average range on the Perceptual Speed & Accuracy test. The ability measured by this test is important in jobs that involve filing, coding, or keypunching.

Your Language Usage score is in the average range. People who do well in this area are usually very good at writing and using correct English. Because many courses and careers require this ability, you may want to improve your ability by taking courses in English grammar or writing.

Your score on the Mathematical Reasoning test is in the average range. Mechanical Reasoning measures the ability to figure out how things work and how to fix them.

Your score on the Space Relations test is in the average range. Space Relations measures the ability to do well when the task involves using patterns to build things.

It is important to remember that DAT scores give only one indication of your aptitudes at this time. Aptitudes can change as you learn and do more things. Keep this in mind as you think about what courses to take and what plans to make for the future.

tendency of test profiles to present a misleading picture. Without the bands we are apt to attribute significance to differences in test performance that can be accounted for by chance alone.

When profiles are used to compare test performance, it is essential that the norms for all tests be comparable. Many test publishers provide for this by standardizing a battery of achievement tests and a scholastic aptitude test on the same population.

Profile Narrative Reports

Narrative reports that describe how well the student is achieving are also available from publishers of many tests. As illustrated in Figure 17.3, profile reports are frequently accompanied by a narrative report. The graphic profile provides a quick view of the student's strengths and weaknesses, and the narrative report aids in interpreting the scores and identifying areas in which instructional emphasis is needed.

Narrative reports are especially useful in communicating test results to parents. They are, of course, also helpful to those teachers who have had little or no training in the interpretation and use of scores from published tests.

SKILL ANALYSIS

Some test publishers provide profiles that include reports for skill objectives as well as for full subtests. An example of such a report is shown in Figure 17.4. The objectives performance scores shown on the bottom of Figure 17.4 are based on the *Comprehensive Tests of Basic Skills,* Fourth Edition. It presents a comprehensive, detailed description of each individual's test results. The norm-referenced scores and profile (using percentile bands) are shown in the top half of the report for the full subtests, and the criterion-referenced skill analysis by "Objective Performance Index" is shown in the bottom half.

Report forms like this yield a wealth of information for the instructional use of test results. The norm-referenced scores indicate how the student's test performance compares with that of others; the subtest profile identifies strengths and weaknesses in each general content area; and the objectives performance scores and profile, by detailed objectives, identify strengths and weaknesses in specific skills in each general content area. As noted earlier in this chapter, however, caution is necessary when interpreting performance on content clusters based on a small number of test items. In these instances, the results are best interpreted as clues for further study.

In addition to detailed reports for individuals, many publishers also offer profile and skill analysis by class, school, and school system. By using computer scoring and reporting services, test results can be obtained in almost any form desired.

FIGURE 17.4

Illustrative score report for the *Comprehensive Tests of Basic Skills,* Fourth Edition. (Reproduced by permission. Copyright 1990, CTB Macmillan/McGraw–Hill. All rights reserved.)

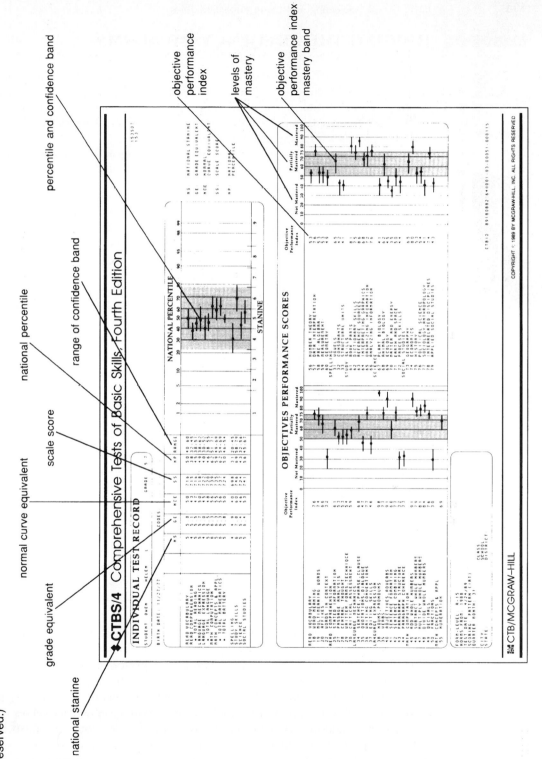

JUDGING THE ADEQUACY OF NORMS

As noted earlier, test norms can be expressed in terms of several different types of derived scores. Regardless of the type of derived score used, the main purpose is to make possible an interpretation of students' test performance in terms of a clearly defined reference group. This should not be just any reference group, however, but one that provides a meaningful basis for comparison.

The adequacy of test norms is a basic consideration during test selection and a factor to be reckoned with during the interpretation of test scores. The following criteria indicate the qualities most desired in norms:

1. ***Test norms should be relevant.***   Test norms are based on various types of groups. Some represent a national sample of all students at certain grade or age levels, whereas others are limited to samples from a given region or state. For special purposes, the norms also might be confined to a limited group such as high school students in independent schools, girls who have completed secretarial training in a commercial high school, or college freshmen in engineering. The variety of groups available for comparison makes it necessary to study the norm sample before using any table of norms. We should ask whether these norms are appropriate for the students being tested and for the decisions to be made with the results.

If we merely want to compare our students with a general reference group in order to diagnose strengths and weaknesses in different areas, national norms may be satisfactory. Here our main concern is with the extent to which our students are similar to those in the norm population on such characteristics as scholastic aptitude, educational experience, and cultural background. The more closely our students approximate those in the norm group, the greater will be our certainty that the national norms are a meaningful basis for comparison.

But when we are trying to decide such things as which students should be placed in an accelerated group, who should be encouraged to select the college preparatory curriculum, or whether a particular student should pursue a career in engineering, national norms are much less useful. For such decisions, we need norms for each of the specific groups involved. A student can have an above-average aptitude and achievement when compared with students in general and still fall short of the ability needed to succeed in highly select groups. When decisions involve predictions of future success in a particular area, comparing a student with potential competitors is more meaningful than comparisons with grade or age mates.

2. ***Test norms should be representative.***   Once we are satisfied that a set of test norms is based on a group with which comparisons are desired, it is appropriate to ask whether the norms are truly representative of that group. Ideally, the norms should be based on a random sample of the population they represent. This is extremely difficult and expensive, however, so we must usually settle for something less. At minimum, we should demand that all significant subgroups of the population be adequately represented. For national norms, it is desirable to have a proper proportion of students from such subgroups as boys and girls, geographic regions, rural and urban areas, socioeconomic levels, racial groups, and schools of

varying size. The most adequate representation in these areas is obtained when the norm sample closely approximates the population distribution reported by the United States Census Bureau.

   3. *Test norms should be up to date.*   One factor that is commonly neglected in judging the adequacy of norms is whether they are currently applicable. The age of norms became a major issue in the late 1980s when John Cannell (1988; also Linn, Grave, and Sanders, 1990) reported that all states and most school districts where norm-referenced tests were used were reporting scores above the national average in the elementary grades. This result came to be known as the "Lake Wobegon Effect"—a reference to Garrison Keillor's radio program and book about a fictitious place where all the children are above average. The Lake Wobegon Effect led to the charge that the public was being misled and caused a minor scandal in the popular press. One of the major reasons for this effect—though not the only one—was the use of old norms. When achievement is going up, a given raw score will yield a higher percentile rank when compared to old norms than when compared to new norms. With the rapid changes that are taking place in education, we can expect test norms to become out of date much sooner than they did in the past.

   It is generally unsafe to use the copyright date on the test manual as an indication of when the norms were obtained, as this date may be changed whenever the manual is altered, no matter how slightly. To find the year in which the norm groups were tested, consult the description of the procedures used in establishing norms. When a test has been revised, make certain that the norms are based on the new edition.

   4. *Test norms should be comparable.*   It is often necessary or desirable to directly compare scores from different tests, such as when we make profile comparisons of test results to diagnose a student's strengths and weaknesses, or when we compare aptitude and achievement test scores to detect underachievers. Such comparisons can be justified only if the norms for the different tests are comparable. We can be assured of comparability when all tests have been normed on the same population. This is routinely done with the tests in an achievement battery, and test publishers also usually administer a scholastic aptitude test to the same norm group. Whenever the scores from different tests are to be compared directly, the test manuals should be checked to determine whether the norms are based on the same group and, if not, whether they have been made comparable by other means.

   5. *Test norms should be adequately described.*   It is difficult to determine whether these norms provide a meaningful basis of comparison unless we know something about the norm group and the norming procedures used. The type of information we might expect to find in a test manual includes (1) method of sampling; (2) number and distribution of cases in the norm sample; (3) characteristics of the norm group with regard to such factors as age, sex, race, scholastic aptitude, educational level, socioeconomic status, types of schools represented, and geographic location; (4) extent to which standard conditions of administration and motivation were maintained during the testing; and (5) date of the testing (i.e., whether in the fall or the spring). Other things being equal, we should always favor the test for which we have detailed descriptions of these and other relevant factors. Such information is needed if we are to judge the appropriateness of test norms for our particular purposes.

USING LOCAL NORMS

In some cases it may be desirable to compare students with local norms. If our students deviate markedly from those in the published norms on such characteristics as scholastic aptitude, educational experience, or cultural background, for example, comparison with a local group may be more meaningful. Local norms can also be useful for making within-class comparisons in special groups (e.g., remedial class in reading) and for determining how well particular children (e.g., handicapped children being mainstreamed) are succeeding in the regular classroom group. When we wish to make profile comparisons of scores obtained from tests standardized on different populations, local norms can also be used to obtain comparable scores by administering all tests to a common local group. Local norms can, of course, also be computed for classroom tests and are especially useful for departmental examinations used in several sections of a course.

Local norms are typically prepared using either percentile ranks or stanines. Most test publishers will provide local norms if requested, but they also can be prepared locally.

CAUTIONS IN INTERPRETING TEST SCORES

Interpreting test scores with the aid of norms requires an understanding of the type of derived score used and a willingness to study the characteristics of the norm group. The standards listed in Figure 17.5 provide good advice that can increase the likelihood that scores will be interpreted correctly. In addition, keep in mind the following general cautions that apply to the interpretation of any test score.

1. A test score should be interpreted in terms of the specific test from which it was derived.   No two scholastic aptitude tests or achievement tests measure exactly the same thing. Achievement tests are especially prone to wide variation, and the differences are seldom reflected in the test title. For example, one arithmetic test may be limited to simple computational skills, whereas another may contain a number of reasoning problems. Similarly, one science test may be confined largely to items measuring knowledge of terminology, whereas another with the same title stresses the application of scientific principles. With such variation it is misleading to interpret a student's test score as representing general achievement in any particular area. We need to look beyond test titles and evaluate the student's performance in terms of what the test actually does measure.

2. A test score should be interpreted in light of all of the student's relevant characteristics.   Test performance is influenced by the student's aptitudes, educational experiences, cultural background, emotional adjustment, health,

FIGURE 17.5
Standards for interpreting scores (From the *Code of Fair Testing Practices in Education,*
1988, Washington, D.C.: Joint Committee on Testing Practices. [Mailing Address: Joint
Committee on Testing Practices, American Psychological Association, 1200 17th Street,
NW, Washington, D.C. 20036.])

Test developers should help users interpret scores correctly.

Test Developers Should:

9. Provide timely and easily understood score reports that describe test performance clearly and accurately. Also explain the meaning and limitations of reported scores.

10. Describe the population(s) represented by any norms or comparison group(s), the dates the data were gathered, and the process used to select the samples of test takers.

11. Warn users to avoid specific, reasonably anticipated misuses of test scores.

12. Provide information that will help users follow reasonable procedures for setting passing scores when it is appropriate to use such scores with the test.

13. Provide information that will help users gather evidence to show that the test is meeting its intended purpose(s).

Test users should interpret scores correctly.

Test Users Should:

9. Obtain information about the scale used for reporting scores, the characteristics of any norms or comparison group(s), and the limitations of the scores.

10. Interpret scores taking into account any major differences between the norms or comparison groups and the actual test takers. Also take into account any differences in test administration practices or familiarity with the specific questions in the test.

11. Avoid using tests for purposes not specifically recommended by the test developer unless evidence is obtained to support the intended use.

12. Explain how any passing scores were set and gather evidence to support the appropriateness of the scores.

13. Obtain evidence to help show that the test is meeting its intended purpose(s).

---

and the like. Consequently, when a student performs poorly on a test, first consider factors such as language background, prior educational experiences, improper motivation, or similar factors that might have interfered with the student's response to the test.

3. A test score should be interpreted according to the type of decision to be made.   The meaningfulness of a test score is determined to a considerable extent by the use to be made of it. For example, a *Scholastic Aptitude* stanine score of 4 on the *DAT* would have quite different meaning if we were wanting to predict achievement in the senior year of high school than if we were counseling a student about submitting an application to a highly selective college. We will find test scores much more useful when we stop considering them as high or low in general and begin evaluating their significance in relation to the decision to be made.

4. A test score should be interpreted as a band of scores rather than as a specific value. Every test score is subject to error that must be allowed for during test interpretation. One of the best means of doing this is to consider a student's test performance as a band of scores one standard error of measurement above and below the obtained score. For example, if a student earns a score of 56 and the standard error is 3, the test performance should be interpreted as a band ranging from score 53 to score 59. Such bands were illustrated in the profiles presented earlier. Even when they are not plotted, however, we should make allowances for these error bands surrounding each score. This will prevent us from making interpretations that are more precise than the test results warrant. Treating small chance differences between test scores as though they were significant can lead to erroneous decisions.

5. A test score should be verified by supplementary evidence. When interpreting test scores, it is impossible to determine fully the extent to which the basic assumptions of testing have been met (i.e., maximum motivation, equal educational opportunity, and so on) or to which the conditions of testing have been precisely controlled (i.e., administration, scoring, and so on). Consequently, in addition to the predictable error of measurement, which can be taken into account with standard error bands, a test score may contain an indeterminate amount of error caused by unmet assumptions or uncontrolled conditions. Our only protection against such errors is not to rely completely on a single test score. As Cronbach (1970) pointed out:

> The most helpful single principle in all testing is that test scores are data on which to base further study. They must be coordinated with background facts, and they must be verified by constant comparison with other available data. (p. 381)

The misinterpretation and misuse of test scores would be substantially reduced if this simple principle were more widely recognized. But this caution should not be restricted to test scores; it is merely a specific application of the more general rule that no important educational decision should ever be based on one limited sample of performance.

SUMMARY

Test interpretation is complicated because the raw scores obtained for a test lack a true zero point (point where there is no achievement at all) and equal units (such as feet, pounds, and minutes). In an attempt to compensate for these missing properties and to make test scores more readily interpretable, various methods of expressing test scores have been devised. In general, we can give meaning to a raw score either by converting it into a description of the specific tasks that the student can perform (criterion-referenced interpretation) or by converting it into some type of derived score that indicates the student's relative position in a clearly defined reference group (norm-referenced interpretation). In some cases both types of interpretation can be made.

Criterion-referenced test interpretation permits us to describe an individual's test performance without referring to the performance of others. This is typically done in terms of some universally understood measure of proficiency (e.g., speed, precision) or the percentage of items correct in some clearly defined domain of learning tasks. The percentage-correct score is widely used in criterion-referenced test interpretation, but it is primarily useful in mastery testing where a clearly defined and delimited domain of learning tasks can be most readily obtained. Although criterion-referenced interpretation is frequently possible with standardized tests, such interpretations must be made with caution because these tests were typically designed to discriminate among individuals rather than describe the specific tasks they can perform. Test publishers are attempting to produce tests that are more amenable to criterion-referenced interpretation.

Expectancy tables also provide a type of criterion-referenced interpretation. Instead of describing an individual's performance on the test tasks, it indicates expected performance in some situation beyond the test (e.g., success in college). Expectancy tables provide a simple and direct means of interpreting test results without the aid of test norms.

Standardized tests typically have been designed for norm-referenced interpretation, which involves converting the raw scores to derived scores by means of tables of norms. These derived scores indicate a student's relative position in a particular reference group. They have the advantage of providing more uniform meaning from one test to another and from one situation to another than raw scores.

Test norms merely represent the typical performance of students in the reference groups on which the test was standardized and consequently should not be viewed as desired goals or standards. The most common types of norms are grade norms, percentile norms, and standard score norms. Each type has its own characteristics, advantages, and limitations, which must be taken into account during test interpretation.

Grade norms describe test performance in terms of the particular grade group in which a student's raw score is just average. These norms are widely used at the elementary school level, largely because of the ease with which they can be interpreted. Depicting test performance in terms of grade equivalents can often lead to unsound decisions, however, because of the inequality of the units and the invalid assumptions on which they are based. Grade equivalent scores must be interpreted with caution.

Percentile norms and standard score norms describe test performance in terms of the student's relative standing in some meaningful group (e.g., own grade or age group). A percentile rank indicates the percentage of students falling below a particular raw score. Percentile units are unequal, but the scores are readily understood by persons without special training. A standard score indicates the number of standard deviation units a raw score falls above or below the group mean. It has the advantage of providing equal units that can be treated arithmetically, but persons untrained in statistics find it difficult to interpret such scores. Some of the more common types of standard scores are z-scores, stanines, T-scores, NCE scores, and standard age scores.

With a normal distribution of scores, we can readily convert between standard scores and percentiles, utilizing the special advantages of each. Standard scores can be used to draw on the benefits of equal units, and we can convert to percentile equivalents when interpreting test performance to students, parents, and those who lack statistical training.

A student's performance on several tests that have comparable norms may be presented in the form of a profile, making it possible to readily identify areas of strength and weakness. Profile interpretation is apt to be more accurate when standard error bands are plotted on the profile. Some test profiles also include narrative reports and/or detailed analysis of the results by content or skill clusters. This criterion-referenced analysis is especially useful for the instructional use of test results.

The adequacy of test norms can be judged by determining the extent to which they are (1) relevant, (2) representative, (3) up to date, (4) comparable, and (5) adequately described. In some instances, it is more appropriate to use local norms than published norms. When local norms are desired, percentile and stanine norms can be easily computed.

In addition to a knowledge of derived scores and norms, the proper interpretation of test scores requires an awareness of (1) what the test measures, (2) the student's characteristics and background, (3) the type of decision to be made, (4) the amount of error in the score, and (5) the extent to which the score agrees with other available data. No important educational decision should ever be based on test scores alone.

LEARNING EXERCISES

1. Describe the cautions needed in making criterion-referenced interpretations of standardized achievement tests.

2. Describe the meaning of raw scores and derived scores.

3. A fifth-grade student received an average grade equivalent score of 6.8 on a standardized achievement battery administered in the fall of the year. What arguments might be presented for and against moving the student ahead to the sixth grade?

4. What advantages do stanines have over T-scores? What disadvantages?

5. Explain each of the following statements:
   a. Standard scores provide approximately equal units.
   b. Percentile scores provide systematically unequal units.
   c. Grade equivalent scores provide unequal units that vary unpredictably.

6. Assuming that all of the following test scores were obtained from the same normally distributed group, which score would indicate the highest performance? the lowest performance?
   a. z-score = .65.
   b. T-score = 65.
   c. NCE score = 65.
   d. Percentile score = 65.

7. Consult the section on norms in *Standards for Educational and Psychological Testing* (American Psychological Association, 1985), and review the types of information that test manuals should contain. Compare a recent test manual with the *Standards*.

8. What is the difference between a norm and a standard? Why shouldn't test norms be used as standards of good performance?

9. What is the value of using national norms? Under what conditions is it desirable to use local norms?

10. What are the relative advantages and disadvantages of using local norms for disadvantaged students? For what purposes are more general norms (e.g., national) useful with these students?

REFERENCES

American Psychological Association. (1974). *Standards for educational and psychological tests.* Washington, D.C.: Author.

Cannell, J. J. (1988). Nationally normed elementary achievement testing in America's schools: How all 50 states are above the national average. *Educational Measurement: Issues and Practice,* 7 (2), 5–9.

Cronbach, L. J. (1970). *Essentials of psychological testing* (3rd ed.). New York: Harper & Row.

Hoover, H. D. (1984). The most appropriate scores for measuring educational development in elementary schools: GE's. *Educational Measurement: Issues and Practice,* 3 (4), 8–14.

Linn, R. L. Graue, M. E. & Sanders, N. M. (1990). "Comparing state and district test results to national norms: The validity of claims that everyone is above average," *Educational Measurement: Issues and Practice,* 9 (3), 5–14 for for a discussion of reasons behind the Lake Wobegon Effect.

FURTHER READING

American Psychological Association. (1985). *Standards for educational and psychological testing.* Washington, D.C.: Author. See Part I for what to look for in test manuals and Parts II and III for material on the effective interpretation and use of tests in various areas.

Anastasi, A. (1988). *Psychological testing* (6th ed.). New York: Macmillan. Chapter 4, "Norms and the Interpretation of Test Scores," describes the various types of norms, computer interpretation of test scores, and criterion-referenced testing.

Gronlund, N. E. (1993). *How to make achievement tests and assessments,* (5th ed.). Boston: Allyn and Bacon. Chapter 8, "Interpreting Test Results,"

describes simplified methods for use with classroom tests.

Lyman, H. B. (1991). *Test scores and what they mean,* (5th ed.). Englewood Cliffs, N.J.: Prentice-Hall. A well-written and interesting description of the various types of test scores and how to interpret them, with emphasis on norm-referenced interpretation.

Petersen, N. S., Kolen, M. J., & Hoover, H. D. (1989). Scaling, norming, and equating. In R. L. Linn (Ed.), *Educational measurement* (3rd ed.). New York: Macmillan. A comprehensive and technically advanced treatment of scales, norms, and equating scores.

PART IV

Current Issues in Teaching and Assessment

CHAPTER 18

Externally Mandated Testing and Assessment: Trends and Issues

Accountability demands; state, national, and international assessment programs; national content and performance standards; and workforce requirements and global competition—all contribute to increased demands for student assessment as well as the assessment of teachers. All have both stimulated and reflected new trends in educational measurement. The increased reliance on testing and assessment as an educational reform tool has also raised issues concerning the nature, quality, and use of tests and assessments.

The emphasis in most of this book has been on teacher-constructed or teacher-selected tests and assessments. Tests and assessments that are designed and controlled by teachers are most readily integrated with instruction and, when well designed and properly used, can make substantial contributions to student learning. Students also spend considerably more time taking teacher-made tests and assessments than they do taking ones that are externally mandated. Nevertheless, it is externally mandated tests and assessments that attract the greatest attention of policymakers, the media, and the general public and that are a source of considerable controversy.

Attention to externally mandated tests and assessments is nothing new. The United States has a long history of expecting a great deal of such tests and assessments. A 1992 report prepared for Congress by the Office of Technology Assessment states,

> From the earliest days of the public school movement, American educators, parents, policymakers, and taxpayers have turned to these tests as multipurpose tools: yardstick of individual progress in classrooms, agent of school reform, filter of educational opportunity, and barometer of the national educational condition. (p. 3)

There are many variations in both the nature of the tests and assessments and in the uses that have been made of them. But as the OTA report indicates, there have been some consistent themes. Educational reformers have used results of mandated tests and assessments to document shortcomings, but more importantly, they have used them as instruments of educational reform.

Minimum-competency testing (MCT) programs were the major test-based reform movement of the 1970s and early 1980s. MCT programs that required students to pass tests for grade-to-grade promotion or for high school graduation swept the nation during that period. As the name suggests, MCT programs focused on basic skills that were considered to be the minimal essentials for the next grade level or a high-school diploma. The recognition of the need to consider more than minimum levels of performance soon led to other testing and assessment demands.

ACCOUNTABILITY AND REFORM

Another wave of test-based reforms followed closely on the heels of the MCT movement. This round of reform efforts stressed school-level accountability and attempted to push beyond minimums. The test-based reforms of the mid- and late 1980s were encouraged by a number of reports on the status of education that were completed in 1983. *A Nation at Risk: The Imperative for Educational Reform,* issued by the National Commission on Excellence in Education, was probably the best known and most influential of these.

A Nation at Risk featured testing in two ways. Test scores, especially the decline in scores on college admissions tests that occurred between the early 1960s and 1980, were used to make the case that "the educational foundations of our society are presently being eroded by a rising tide of mediocrity that threatens our very future as a Nation and a people" (National Commission on Excellence in Education, p. 5). *A Nation at Risk* also stressed the importance of tests as instruments to improve education through their use to "(a) certify the student's credentials; (b) identify the need for remedial intervention; and (c) identify the opportunity for advanced work" (National Commission on Excellence in Education, p. 28).

All fifty states attempted some type of educational reform in the wake of *A Nation at Risk.* Consistent with the emphasis of the report, testing was central in the majority of state-legislated reform efforts. Indeed, in many cases, externally mandated tests were relied on as the major instrument of reform.

Building and District Report Cards

Building and district "report cards" showing student test performance were used to make educators more accountable for student achievement. As intended, test-based comparisons of schools and districts placed considerable pressure on school superintendents, principals, and teachers to "get the scores up." Test preparation became a major component in the instructional programs of many schools. Teachers reported in surveys that, as the result of the pressure, they focused their instruction on the skills tested, taught test-taking skills, and used the format of the externally mandated test in their own tests. The focus sometimes narrowed to the specific topics known to be on the mandated test and practice was provided on items similar to those in the test. Under high-stakes testing conditions, topics corresponding to important instructional objectives not included on the test often were found to fall by the wayside as the testing date approached (See, for example, Nolan, Haladyna and Hass, 1992; Smith and Rottenberg, 1991).

The Lake Wobegon Effect, which was briefly mentioned in Chapter 17, received considerable publicity. This finding, that almost all states using standardized tests in the elementary grades were reporting that the majority of their students were above the national average, has generally been attributed to a combination of placing great pressure on getting scores up and the reuse of the same test with old norms year after year (Linn, Graue, and Sanders, 1990). The Lake Wobegon Effect raised serious questions about the credibility of test results and about the possible negative side-effects of high-stakes accountability uses of standardized test results.

The degree to which the increased pressure helped or hurt education, however, remains controversial. Proponents of high-stakes testing argue that the tests measure objectives that are important for students to learn and that it is desirable for teachers to focus their attention on those objectives. They point with pride to the increases in test scores that were observed in state and district testing programs during late 1980s and early 1990s.

Critics of the increased emphasis on test results argue that an over-reliance on test results distorts education. They argue that important objectives are ignored when they are not included on the tests that count. Moreover, they claim that the increased scores paint a misleading picture because teachers teach the specifics of the tests rather than more general content domains.

The proper role of externally mandated tests and assessments in directing instruction is an issue you will have to struggle with, especially if the current emphasis on holding educators accountable for results on these instruments continues. What sort of preparation for taking tests or assessments should students have? How much time should be spent in test preparation activities such as taking practice tests and learning test-taking strategies? To what degree should tested objectives be given emphasis at the expense of objectives that are not tested? These are important educational questions that have no simple answers. They require thought and reflection on the part of individual teachers and principals.

Consider, for example, the seemingly simple issues of "teaching to the test" and "teaching the test itself." We are almost always interested in making inferences that go beyond the specific test that is used. We would like, for example, to be able to say something about the degree of a student's understanding of mathematical concepts based on the score that is obtained on a math concepts test. Because the items on a test only sample the domain of interest, the test score and the inference about the degree of understanding are not the same. A generalization is required, and it is the generalization, not the test score, *per se,* that is important. When the specific items on the test are taught, the validity of the inference about the student's level of achievement is threatened. Teaching the specific test items is apt to result in an exaggerated view of student achievement in the overall domain of interest.

Teaching to the test—that is, emphasizing the objectives that are on the test without teaching the specific test items—has both advantages and disadvantages. Inasmuch as the objectives on the test are important, then emphasizing those objectives provides a desirable focus. On the other hand, multiple-choice, standardized tests do not cover all the important learning objectives. Hence, narrowing to only those objectives that are covered would be detrimental for education as a whole.

In summary, WYTIWYG (what you test is what you get) has both positive and negative aspects. Focusing on important instructional objectives that are on the test can help ensure that they are achieved but, as has been stressed in a number of places in this book, some important objectives are not well measured by traditional test items. Thus, the converse of WYTIWYG—you don't get what you don't test—is a cause of concern for any high-stakes testing or assessment program.

NATIONAL EMPHASIS ON ASSESSMENT

High-stakes testing and assessment requirements have traditionally been put in place by states and local school districts rather than by the federal government. However, the role of the federal government in testing and assessment has expanded and there are indications that it may continue to grow. Until recently, the strongest influence of the federal government on testing and assessment came through the testing requirements that were put in place to provide a means of evaluating several national educational programs. The most notable of these is Chapter I (formally Title I), the Elementary and Secondary Education Act of 1965.

Chapter I is the largest federal educational aid program. It provides funds to almost all school districts in the country for supplementary services for low achieving students. Each school year, almost five million children receive some services paid for by Chapter I funds. Thus, the testing requirements of Chapter I have had a strong influence on local testing programs. Prior to the most recent reauthorization, most districts satisfied program evaluation requirements by administering norm-referenced tests to Chapter I students each year. For many districts with large numbers of Chapter I students, the testing done for Chapter I was simply expanded and became by default the primary testing program for all students.

National Assessment of Educational Progress

In addition to influencing local and state testing through testing requirements of Chapter I and other federal education programs, the federal government has been involved directly in assessment through its support of the *National Assessment of Educational Progress (NAEP)* and the participation of the United States in international assessments. *NAEP* is a nationwide assessment program designed to obtain nationally representative data to report to the public on the educational attainment of children and young adults in this country. Testing began in 1969 and has been continued periodically, with reports through the news media, professional associations, and various publications.

During the first twenty years of operation, assessments were administered to national samples of students in reading, writing, mathematics, science, citizenship, literature, social studies, career and occupational development, art, music, history, geography, and computer competence. In each area, test exercises are designed to measure specific objectives so that criterion-referenced interpretation of the data is possible. The exercises measure knowledge, understanding, skills, and attitudes and include a variety of item types. In addition to short-answer and essay questions, the exercises include performance tasks, observations, interviews, questionnaires, and sample products (e.g., art).

In the early days of *NAEP,* assessment exercises in one or more of the content areas were given to samples of 9-, 13-, and 17-year-old children each year. Exercises were also given to samples of young adults from age 26 to 35 on a regular basis. Since 1980 the assessments have taken place every other year, and in recent years samples have been selected to represent students in selected grades (3, 7, and 11 before 1988 and 4, 8, and 12 since that time) as well as age levels.

To determine changes in performance over time, some of the exercises in each area are repeated after a period of several years. Some of these items are used to report results after each assessment, while others are maintained as secure items for use in future assessments.

Prior to the 1984 assessment, results were reported separately by item. The reports simply indicated the percentage of individuals in each age group that gave the correct and incorrect answers to each exercise. Since 1984, the item level results have been supplemented by results on scales in each content area. Graphs of trends such as the one shown in Figure 18.1 plot the changes in typical performance of 9-, 13-, and 17-year-old children throughout the nation. Trends are also reported separately by geographic region, gender, and race/ethnicity. No results are given for individual students (each student completes only a sample of the exercises) or for individual schools.

In 1990 the first state-by-state comparisons on *NAEP* were started for mathematics in Grade 8 on a voluntary basis. The state-by-state comparisons were expanded to include reading and mathematics in Grade 4 in the 1992 assessment and have become a regularly established part of *NAEP* in the most recent reauthorization. Figure 18.2 illustrates the type of state-by-state comparison data that was reported for the 41 states participating in the 1992 state administrations of *NAEP.*

The intent of the program is not to compare individuals or schools, but to report to the public, policymakers, and the profession on (1) what level of educational achievement is being attained by various age groups, (2) what changes in achievement have taken place over time, and (3) what differences there are in achievement and in changes in achievement for major regions of the country, gender, and racial/ethnic groups. Similar information is also available for states that volunteer to participate in *NAEP* state-level administrations. The addition of the state level option has increased the size and visibility of *NAEP.* As is discussed below, its importance has also been increased by the reliance on *NAEP* results as a major means of monitoring the progress of the nation's students toward meeting the National Education Goals established in 1989.

FIGURE 18.1
National trends in average mathematics proficiency for 9-, 13-, and 17-year-olds: 1973 to 1990 (From *Trends in Academic Progress:* Washington, DC: National Center for Education Statistics, 1991.)

	1973	1978	1982	1986	1990
Age 17	304(1.1)	300(1.0)*	299(0.9)*†	302(0.9)	305(0.9)
Age 13	266(1.1)*	264(1.1)*	269(1.1)	269(1.2)	270(0.9)†
Age 9	219(0.8)*	219(0.8)*	219(1.1)*	222(1.0)*	230(0.8)†

95 percent confidence interval. [---] Extrapolated from previous *NAEP* analyses. *Statistically significant difference from 1990 and † statistically significant difference from 1973, as determined by an application of the Bonferroni procedure, where alpha equals .05 per set of 7 comparisons. The standard errors of the estimated proficiencies appear in parentheses. It can be said with 95 percent certainty that for each population of interest, the value for the whole population is within plus or minus two standard errors of the estimate for the sample.

International Assessments

The increased awareness of the need to compete in a global economy has stimulated ever-growing interest not only in state and national assessments of student progress, but in international comparisons. International assessments of achievement are fraught with many difficulties. Comparisons are complicated by differences in the selectivity of the educational systems of different countries, variations in the quality of the samples obtained, and differences in definitions of educational levels. In addition, it is difficult to agree on the content to be included in the assessment, and even after reaching an agreement on content, there is the challenge of translation. It is well known that the difficulty of a test item can be altered substantially by subtle changes in wording when working in a single language. This problem is compounded when items must be translated from one language to another. All these factors threaten the validity of international assessments of student achievement.

FIGURE 18.2

Distributions of overall reading proficiency for states participating in the 1992 Grade 4 reading assessment of *NAEP* (organized by average proficiency). (From *NAEP 1992 Reading Report Card for the Nation and the States.* Washington, DC: National Center for Education Statistics, 1993.)

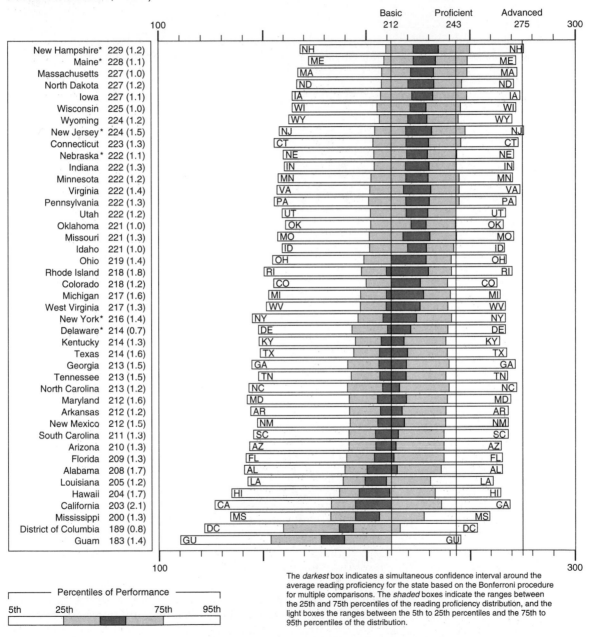

The *darkest* box indicates a simultaneous confidence interval around the average reading proficiency for the state based on the Bonferroni procedure for multiple comparisons. The *shaded* boxes indicate the ranges between the 25th and 75th percentiles of the reading proficiency distribution, and the light boxes the ranges between the 5th to 25th percentiles and the 75th to 95th percentiles of the distribution.

Despite the many limitations, international assessments results such as those illustrated in Figure 18.3 attract considerable attention. The relatively poor performance of United States students in comparison to their counterparts in other industrialized nations has been used repeatedly to argue that students in this country are not doing well enough and to push for higher standards of student performance.

FIGURE 18.3
Distribution of proficiency scores on mathematics assessment by age and country: 1991. (From *The Condition of Education 1993.* Washington, DC: National Center for Education Statistics, 1993.)

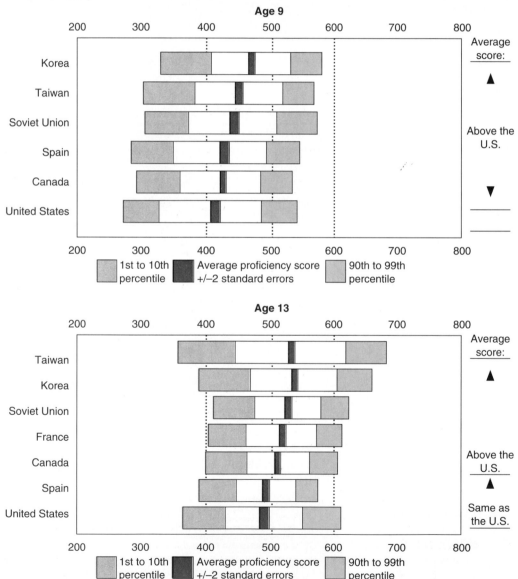

Note: The scale for proficiency scores ranges from 0—1,000. The mean proficiency score for all participating populations, 9- and 13-year-olds together, is 500. The standard deviation is 100.

National Education Goals 3 and 4

Goal 3: Student Achievement and Citizenship

By the year 2000, American students will leave Grades four, eight, and twelve having demonstrated competency in challenging subject matter including English, mathematics, science, history, and geography, and every school in America will ensure that all students learn to use their minds well, so they may be prepared for responsible citizenship, further learning, and productive employment in our modern economy.

Goal 4: Mathematics and Science

By the year 2000, U.S. students will be the first in the world in science and mathematics achievement.

Source: National Education Goals Panel

New National Testing and Assessment Initiatives

NAEP and international assessments serve a monitoring function. They provide information on current status and progress. Several developments at the national level, however, reflect a desire to use testing and assessment, not just to record progress, but as an instrument of educational reform.

In 1989 the President and the nation's governors agreed to a set of six national education goals. Two of the goals are concerned with subject-matter achievement and lead to demands for assessment (see accompanying box). The National Education Goals Panel was created and charged with the responsibility of monitoring progress toward those goals. In addition to assembling data from the *National Assessment of Educational Progress* and other sources for its annual reports, the goals panel argued for the establishment of national standards and "a voluntary national system of examinations (not a single test)" in its first *Goals Report*. (National Education Goals Panel, 1991) With encouragement from the Goals Panel, Congress established the National Council on Education Standards and Testing and charged the Council with the responsibility of evaluating the desirability and feasibility of creating such a system. In its 1992 report, the Council concluded that it was both desirable and feasible to develop a voluntary national system of assessments tied to national content standards. (National Council on Education Standards and Testing, 1992)

The first education legislation put forward by the Clinton administration and enacted by Congress is known as the "Goals 2000: Educate America Act". That legislation strengthened the role of the National Education Goals Panel and called for the development of national content standards and a voluntary system of assessments that could be certified to be consistent with those standards. The impact of these new national testing and assessment initiatives remains to be seen. As was true with requirements put in place with the enactment of the Elementary and Secondary Education Act of 1965, however, it seems likely that the effects on local and state testing and assessment practices may be both substantial and long-lasting.

CURRENT MEASUREMENT TRENDS AND ISSUES

In recent years, numerous changes have taken place in educational measurement. In some instances, the various educational testing and assessment programs that we have been discussing have helped create or hasten these changes, whereas in others they have simply made the changes more visible. The rapidly expanding role of testing and assessment in education has also been paralleled by mounting criticisms of testing and its possible hazards to individuals and groups. In this section, we shall briefly describe some of the more important trends and issues accompanying current developments in educational measurement.

Some Apparent Trends

Describing trends in any area is hazardous, and it is especially so in education. There seem to be so many new developments in education that turn out to be fads that rise quickly and fall even more quickly. The following changes in educational measurement seem to have enough breadth and staying power to represent trends. Significant changes are taking place in approaches to assessment, in the technology of testing, in the assessment of teachers, and in the public concern about testing and assessment.

Performance-Based Assessment.   The interest in placing increased reliance on performance-based assessment grew at an extraordinary rate in the early 1990s. That interest was stimulated by a combination of factors. WYTIWYG (what you test is what you get) and its converse helped focus attention on the content and nature of tests and assessments. Concerns in the late 1980s and early 1990s that the standardized achievement tests being used in high-stakes programs overemphasized low-level skills at the expense of higher-order skills, deep understanding, and problem solving contributed to the demand for alternative forms of assessment. Increased emphasis on performance-based assessments was also fostered by changing views of learning and instruction that stress the need to engage students in the process of thinking about, and trying to make sense of, new information in terms of current understanding and in the organization and reorganization of knowledge.

Direct writing assessments were the first form of performance-based assessment introduced by a number of states. Written essays were hardly a new form of measurement, but they were not a part of many mandated testing requirements in the early and mid-1980s. By the early 1990s, a number of states had not only included direct writing as a part of their assessment programs, but had also added performance-based assessment tasks in other content areas.

The increased reliance on performance-based assessments is motivated by a number of considerations. WYTIWYG has already been mentioned in this regard. Proponents of performance-based assessments take as a given that assessments influence what does and does not get taught and argue that we should therefore make assessments that are worth teaching to. Such assessments must use tasks that are worthwhile instructional activities in their own right. In addition, assessments are expected to serve as models for instruction and curriculum reform and to provide a mechanism for staff development.

Although the movement toward performance-based assessments is not motivated primarily by the desire for more dependable measurement, considerations of the technical quality of the assessments from a measurement perspective become crucial when they are used for high-stakes purposes. Issues of consistency of ratings of performance from one rater to another and across different tasks become increasingly important when performance-based assessments are used to make decisions about individual teachers or students. A key issue that will need to be addressed with the widespread use of performance-based assessments is the degree to which it is feasible to meet rigorous measurement requirements without excessive cost or time being devoted to assessment.

Computerized Test Administration. With the rapid growth in the availability and power of relatively low-cost microcomputers, it is not surprising that the use of computers to administer tests is becoming increasingly common. Indeed, some readers of this text may have taken, or be planning to take, a computer-based version of the *Graduate Record Examination (GRE),* which was introduced in 1993. Using a computer to administer items from a paper-and-pencil test can have several advantages. Rather than having to take the test on a scheduled national administration day, for example, test-takers can make an appointment to take the test according to their own schedule. Rather than waiting several weeks to receive test results, scores can be obtained immediately. Computer-based tests also make possible the separation of speed and accuracy of responses. Although these advantages can be substantial in some cases, the potentially more significant changes depend on using the computer to do things that cannot be reasonably accomplished with paper-and-pencil tests.

The change that has the most potential to improve both the efficiency with which information is handled and the quality of that information is the use of the computer to administer adaptive tests; that is, tests in which the choice of the next item to administer is based upon previous responses of the test-taker. The design of an adaptive test usually starts with the administration of an item that is expected to be of middle difficulty. The second and subsequent items to be administered are determined by the responses of the test-taker. In general, if a test-taker answers an item correctly, then the computer will select a somewhat more difficult item to administer next. Conversely, a somewhat easier item is administered following an incorrect response. Testing is stopped when the estimates of the individual's performance reach some predetermined level of precision or when some pragmatic maximum number of items has been administered.

It has been demonstrated that adaptive testing can enhance the efficiency and the precision with which certain types of knowledge, skills, and abilities are measured. In some cases, adaptive tests can obtain the same level of reliability of measurement in just over half the time required for a conventional paper-and-pencil test. But if adaptive tests just administer items of the type already in use in a better way, the full potential of the use of computers for the administration of tests will not be realized. The appeal of computers as testing devices is not limited to doing better what we already do. Their potential to measure proficiencies that are not measured well by conventional paper-and-pencil tests is even more appealing.

Simulations can be used to present test-takers with problems that have greater realism and more apparent relevance than problems that are commonly found on paper-and-pencil tests. Computer-based examinations that have been used for some time in medical education and in certification testing for physicians provide an illustration of the type of simulation tests that are apt to be seen in the future as computerized test administration becomes more common. Computer problems simulate aspects of the job of a physician. The test-taker is initially presented with a limited set of information about a patient, such as a verbal description of symptoms of the type that a patient might provide at the start of a visit. The test-taker then has a variety of options such as getting a patient history, ordering laboratory tests, or deciding on a course of treatment. Requested information is provided and new options can be followed by the test-taker until a diagnosis is made and a course of treatment is prescribed.

Computer-administered problem simulations along these lines have a number of potential advantages over current paper-and-pencil tests in many content areas. They provide a means of going beyond the sort of factual recall that is sometimes overemphasized on paper-and-pencil tests. They focus attention on the use of information to solve realistic problems. They can help assess not only the product of a student's thinking, but the process that the student uses to solve a problem, including the way in which the problem is attacked, the efficiency of the solution, and the number of hints that may be needed to solve the problem.

Evolving Issues in the Assessment of Teachers.   Test requirements for prospective teachers were common in the 1920s and 1930s but fell out of favor and were rarely used for a number of years. They came back into favor as part of the educational reform movement of the 1980s. Within a few years, what was once a practice of only a few states became the norm, and by 1987 all but two states had either implemented or enacted plans to require teacher testing of some kind. (Rudner, 1988)

Tests used for teacher certification are mandated by states and, consequently, they vary in content coverage. Typically, however, the tests are intended to provide three general types of measures: basic skills, professional knowledge, and subject-matter knowledge. Basic skills tests are generally required for all prospective teachers in a state and usually cover general communication skills (e.g., reading, arithmetic, and writing). The professional knowledge tests usually cover topics such as instructional planning, student assessment, and legal and professional standards affecting classroom practice. The subject-matter tests are tailored to the prospective teacher's area of certification (e.g., mathematics, reading specialist).

Traditionally, the intent of the certification tests, like that of certification tests in other professions, has been rather modest. They are intended to protect the public from teachers who lack the knowledge necessary to teach. Justification that the tests satisfy that goal depends almost entirely on content-related evidence of validity that is obtained by asking panels of teachers and teacher educators to judge the degree to which test objectives and item content assess knowledge that is necessary for a minimally qualified teacher to know.

Not even proponents of teacher testing claim that paper-and-pencil tests of basic skills, professional knowledge, and subject-matter knowledge measure all that is required to be a successful teacher. Paper-and-pencil certification tests do not assess critical characteristics of good teachers like dedication, caring, and integrity. Nor do they assess how well teachers can manage a classroom or how good they are at instilling a love of learning in their students.

Just as concern that important instructional objectives were not being measured by traditional standardized tests given to students led to demands for expanded forms of assessment, the recognition that paper-and-pencil tests do not measure many important aspects of teaching has led to demands for an expanded range of assessment approaches for teachers. A number of states have instituted a wider array of approaches for the appraisal of teacher performance. At the national level, the most notable effort in this regard is that of the National Board of Professional Teaching Standards.

The National Board of Professional Teaching Standards was formed for the purpose of upgrading the profession of teaching by encouraging and recognizing outstanding performance. Toward this end, the Board has undertaken the development of systems of assessments designed for experienced teachers. The assessments are intended to provide accomplished teachers with an opportunity to demonstrate high levels of professional performance. Candidates who meet the Board's standards receive certification, which it is expected will be recognized and rewarded by states and districts.

The assessments include understanding of subject matter that is taught, but go far beyond that. They rely on a variety of approaches to the assessment of performance in the classroom. Videotapes of a candidate's teaching, for example, are assembled into a portfolio. The portfolios may also include examples of student work together with the teacher's analyses and commentary on the work. The portfolios and results of responses to other performance-based tasks are complemented by classroom observations.

Public Concern About Testing and Assessment.   Decisions about the selection, administration, and use of educational tests and assessments are no longer left to the educator alone: The public has become an active and vocal partner. At the state level, externally mandated assessment programs have been imposed on the schools as a result of the public demand for evidence of the school programs' effectiveness. In some states, the public at large has participated, through selected groups, in determining the objectives and standards of the statewide assessment programs. In states where testing and assessment has been made the responsibility of the local school district, parent groups often help shape the programs. It is interesting to note that the concern of state legislators and the general public with the quality of school programs has created a demand for more testing and assessment in the schools—not less.

During the expansion of testing programs, there also has been some concern that there is too much testing in the schools. In addition to taking the tests in the local school program, high-school students, for example, may also have to take one or more state competency tests and several college admissions tests. It is feared that the heavy demand on their time and energy might detract from their schoolwork and that the external testing programs may cause undesirable shifts in the school's curriculum. When teachers and schools are judged by how well students perform on state tests and assessments and by how many students are accepted by leading colleges, direct preparation for the test and assessments is likely to enter into classroom activities and thereby distort the curriculum.

Probably the greatest public concern has been with the social consequences of testing, especially perceived threats to the rights and opportunities of individuals and groups. This concern has shown up in the form of attacks on standardized tests and the testing industry, new legislation affecting testing, calls for a moratorium on standardized testing, and charges that tests are biased and discriminatory. Although there is certainly some justification for the public's concern with the social consequences of testing, much of the furor has been caused by the misinterpretation and misuse of test scores. Some of the current issues surrounding the testing controversy will be discussed in the following section.

Concerns and Issues

Although educational testing always has had its friendly and unfriendly critics, in recent years there has been increasing concern about the role of testing in the schools, especially the use of standardized tests. Critical issues concern the nature and quality of the tests, the possible harmful effects of testing on students, the fairness of the tests to minorities, and the potential hazards of testing to the individual's right to privacy.

Nature and Quality of Tests.   A long-standing criticism of standardized tests is directed primarily at the use of multiple-choice items. In the early 1960s, critics such as Hoffmann (1962) contended that the multiple-choice item penalized the more intelligent original thinkers. He supported his claims by reviewing items from standardized tests and showing how the more brilliant and creative students were likely to see implications in the items and, thus, question the correctness of the keyed answers. Although Hoffman obviously was able to discover some defective items that appeared in standardized tests, his criticisms seemed to go well beyond the evidence presented. But he did encourage test publishers to supplement statistical item analysis with a more careful, logical analysis of test items.

Multiple-choice questions continue to bear the brunt of criticisms made by both specialists in educational measurement who seek ways of improving educational tests and critics who would like to eliminate standardized testing. Frederiksen (1984), a major contributor to the field of measurement, for example, has argued that multiple-choice items place too much emphasis on "well structured problems" when problems of greatest interest both in and out of school are often "ill structured," and where skills such as problem identification and hypothesis generation are often as important as problem solution. Such criticisms have led to increased emphasis on open-ended questions and the design of computer simulation tests.

Critics such as Owen (1985), on the other hand, are more sweeping in their criticism. Owen's focus of criticism is frequently on Educational Testing Service and the *Scholastic Aptitude Test,* a test that he thinks lacks educational value and is more a measure of the degree to which the test-taker knows the tricks of the test constructors and can think like they do than it is a measure of scholastic aptitude. To prove his point, he provides advice on how to beat the test by using various test-taking strategies, without evidence of effectiveness. Owen's criticisms of multiple-choice items do not add much to the earlier criticisms by Hoffmann and others, but they are more strident in tone.

Another type of criticism, that tests measure only limited aspects of an individual, has also received considerable attention. This criticism is well founded. Tests do measure specific and limited samples of behavior. Aptitude tests typically measure samples of verbal and quantitative skills useful in predicting school success, and achievement tests measure samples of student performance on particular learning tasks useful in assessing educational progress. Both fulfill their limited functions quite well, but the difficulty arises when we expect more of them than was intended. For example, both the advocates and critics of college admissions testing sometimes assume that the tests measure all that is needed for success in college and beyond. This tendency to read into test scores more than they really tell has been called the "whole person fallacy" by W. W. Trunbull, the former president of the Educational Testing Service. A quotation from one of its publications makes clear the limited nature of these tests:

> Ability and academic achievement occupy an Olympian perch on the prestige ladder. Yet it is widely agreed that motivation, creativity, personal honesty, intuition, even the degree of social consciousness play significant roles in the struggle for the most cherished of American ideals—"success in life." Admission tests thus measure a relatively narrow segment of the human potential. (*ETS Developments,* 1979)

Much of the misinterpretation and misuse of test scores would be avoided if the limited nature of the information tests provide was more widely recognized. In college admission decisions, as well as in all other educational decisions, test scores provide just one type of information and always should be supplemented by past records of achievement and other types of assessment data. No major educational decision should ever be based on test scores alone.

The reliability and validity of tests also have been subject to criticism. This usually has been by uninformed critics who mistakenly believe that tests should be completely reliable and provide perfect predictions. These, of course, are unrealistic expectations. All measurement is subject to error, and predictions in all areas are fallible. Rather than compare the tests' reliability and validity with nonexistent ideal standards, they should be compared with the alternatives. Would our judgments of aptitude and achievement be more reliable without test results? Would our predictions of future school or occupational success be more valid without the additional information supplied by tests? Would our educational decisions be improved if we stopped using tests? We doubt it! Qualified users of tests take into account the possible error in test scores during interpretation and use, and they combine test scores with other relevant information when making educational decisions. To argue that better educational decisions would be made without tests scores is to argue that better decisions are made when less information is available. Test scores are certainly fallible, but probably less so than most of the other types of information that enter into educational decisions. See "What Are the Consequences of Not Testing?"

What Are the Consequences of Not Testing?

If the use of educational tests were abandoned, the encouragement and reward of individualized efforts to learn would be more difficult. Excellence in programs of education would become less tangible as a goal and less demonstrable as an attainment. Educational opportunities would be extended less on the basis of aptitude and merit and more on the basis of ancestry and influence; social-class barriers would become less permeable. Decisions on important issues of curriculum and method would be made less on the basis of solid evidence and more on the basis of prejudice or caprice. These, it seems to us, are likely to be the more harmful consequences, by far. Let us not forgo the wise use of good tests.

Source: *Practical Problems in Educational Measurement* (pp. 34–35) by R. L. Ebel, 1980, Lexington, MA: Heath. Copyright 1980 by Heath. Reprinted by permission.

Effects of Testing on Students.   Critics of testing charge that testing is likely to have a number of undesirable effects on students. Some of the most commonly mentioned charges directed toward the use of aptitude and achievement tests are listed here with brief comments.

Criticism 1: Tests create anxiety.   There is no doubt that anxiety increases during testing. For most students, it motivates them to perform better. For a few, test anxiety may be so great that it interferes with test performance. These typically are students who are generally anxious, and the test simply adds to their already high level of anxiety. A number of steps can be taken to reduce test anxiety, such as thoroughly preparing for the test, taking practice exercises, and using liberal time limits. Fortunately, many test publishers in recent years have provided practice tests and shifted from speed tests to power tests. This should help, but it is still necessary to observe students carefully during testing and to discount the scores of overly anxious students. There is little likelihood, however, that test anxiety has any lasting influence on a student's mental health.

Criticism 2: Tests categorize and label students.   Categorizing and labeling individuals is a serious problem in education, just as it is in society. It is all too easy to place individuals in pigeonholes and apply labels that determine, at least in part, how they are viewed and treated. Classifying students in terms of levels of mental ability has probably caused the greatest concern in education. Critics contend that when students are classified as mentally retarded, for example, it influences how teachers and peers view them, how they view themselves, and the kind of school program they are provided. When students are mislabeled as mentally retarded, as has been the case with some racial and ethnic minorities, the problem is compounded. At least some of the support for mainstreaming handicapped students has come from the desire to avoid the categorizing and labeling that accompanies special education classes.

Classifying students into various types of learning groups can more efficiently use the teacher's time and the school's resources. However, any grouping needs to take into account that tests measure only a limited sample of a student's abilities and that students are continuously changing and developing. Keeping the groupings tentative and flexible and regrouping for different subjects (e.g., reading, math) can avoid most of the undesirable features of grouping. It is when the categories are viewed as rigid and permanent that labeling becomes a serious problem. In such cases, it is not the test that should be blamed, but the user of the test.

Criticism 3: Tests damage students' self-concepts.   This is one of the most serious charges against testing and requires the attention of teachers, counselors, and other users of tests. The improper use of tests may indeed contribute to distorted self-concepts. The stereotyping of students is one misuse of tests that is likely to have an undesirable influence on a student's self-concept. Another is the inadequate interpretation of test scores that may cause students to overgeneralize from the results. It is certainly discouraging to receive low scores on tests, and it is easy to see how students might develop a general sense of failure unless the results are properly interpreted. Low-scoring students need to be made aware that aptitude and achievement tests are limited measures and that the results can change. In addition, the possibility of overgeneralizing from low test scores will be lessened if the student's positive accomplishments and characteristics are mentioned during the interpretation. When properly interpreted and used, tests can help students develop a realistic understanding of their strengths and weaknesses and, thereby, contribute to improved learning and a positive self-image.

Criticism 4: Tests create self-fulfilling prophecies.   This criticism has been directed primarily toward intelligence or scholastic aptitude tests. The argument is that test scores create teacher expectations concerning the achievement of individual students; the teacher then teaches in accordance with those expectations, and the students respond by achieving to their expected level—a self-fulfilled prophecy. Thus, those who are expected to achieve more do achieve more, and those who are expected to achieve less *do* achieve less. This so-called Pygmalion effect received strong support from a widely heralded study by Rosenthal and Jacobsen (1968), even though the study was later challenged by other researchers (Elashoff and Snow, 1971; West and Anderson, 1976). The belief that teacher expectations enhance or hinder a student's achievement is widely held, and the role of testing in creating these expectations is certainly worthy of further research.

In summary, there is some merit in the various criticisms concerning the possible undesirable effects of tests on students. But these criticisms should be directed at the users of the tests rather than the tests themselves. The same persons who misuse test results are likely to misuse alternative types of information that are even less accurate and objective. Thus, the solution is not to stop using tests, but to start using tests and other data sources more effectively. When tests are used in a positive manner—that is, to help students improve their learning and development—the consequences are likely to be desirable rather than undesirable.

Fairness of Tests to Minorities.   The issue of test fairness to racial and ethnic minorities has received increasing attention over the years. Concern with the fairness of tests has paralleled the general public concern with providing equal rights and opportunities to all United States citizens. Critics have charged that tests are biased and discriminatory and impede educational and occupational opportunities for minorities. The charge of test bias or unfairness can be examined from two viewpoints: (1) the possible presence of bias in the test content and (2) the possible unfair use of test results. These factors are undoubtedly related, but we shall discuss them separately.

Much of the concern with bias in test content focuses on the fact that some minorities frequently earn lower test scores than their more advantaged peers. As Gardner pointed out, however, low test scores do not necessarily indicate test bias:

> Lower scores alone on an achievement test do not signify bias. If they did, then every spelling test would be biased against poor spellers, every vocabulary test against persons who had poor vocabularies, and every shorthand test against persons who had never learned shorthand. (Gardner, 1978)

Thus, in evaluating the possible presence of bias in test content, it is important to distinguish between the performance the test is intended to measure and factors that may distort the scores unfairly. In testing arithmetic skills with story problems, for example, it is important to keep the reading level low so that the test scores are not contaminated by reading ability. If the reading level is too difficult, poor readers will obtain lower scores than warranted, and the test will be biased against them. Because a particular minority group may have a disproportionately large number of poor readers, the test may be biased against that minority group. But if the test of arithmetic skill is not contaminated by reading or other factors, low scores will simply indicate lack of arithmetic skills. Such a test is fair to everyone even if the test scores indicate group differences in the mastery of arithmetic.

In the past, standardized tests typically emphasized content and values that were more familiar to white middle-class students than to racial or ethnic minorities and students of lower socioeconomic status. Thus, the content of some scholastic aptitude tests contained vocabulary, pictures, and objects that minorities had less opportunity to learn. Similarly, some reading tests contained stories and situations that were unrelated to their life experiences. Racial and ethnic minorities were seldom represented in pictures, stories, and other test content and when they were, it was sometimes in an offensive manner. How much these types of bias might have lowered the scores of individual students is impossible to say, but most persons familiar with testing would acknowledge some adverse effect. Fortunately, test publishers have taken steps to correct the situation. Test publishers now employ staff members representing various racial and cultural minorities, and new tests are routinely reviewed for content that might be biased or offensive to minority groups. Statistical analysis is also being used to detect and remove test items that function differently for different groups of test takers. (See, for example, Cole and Moss, 1989.)

The most controversial problems concerning the fair use of tests with minority groups are encountered when aptitude tests are used as a basis for educational and vocational selection. Much of the difficulty here is with the definition of fair test use. One view is that a test is fair or unbiased if it predicts as accurately for minority groups as it does for the majority group. This traditional view, which favors a common cutoff score for selection, has been challenged as being unfair to minority groups because they often earn lower test scores, and thus, a smaller proportion of qualified individuals tends to be selected. Alternative definitions of test fairness favor some type of adjustment such as separate cutoff scores or bonus points for some minorities.

Ultimately, the decision as to whether minority group membership is to be ignored or given special consideration in selection will not be made by educators or psychologists. The fair use of tests in selection is part of a larger issue that must be settled by society through court rulings. Stated in simplified form, the issue is how equal educational and occupational opportunities can be best provided for members of minority groups without infringing on the rights of other individuals.

Sex Bias. In recent years, considerable attention also has been given to the possibility of sex bias in tests. Critics have objected to the excessive use of masculine pronouns and to the portrayal of women mainly in such traditional roles as homemaker, nurse, and secretary. Although there is no question that such bias has been present in tests (as it has been in textbooks and other educational materials), the effect of the bias on test performance is unclear. A study of the influence of male and female references in reading passages, for example, showed no effect on test performance (Moss and Brown, 1979). Despite such negative results, the removal of sex bias from all educational materials is desirable on other grounds, and test and book publishers are making concerted efforts to correct the situation.

The use of scores on tests such as the *Preliminary Scholastic Aptitude Test (PSAT)* and the *Scholastic Aptitude Test (SAT)* as the basis of awarding college scholarships has focused attention on the issue of sex bias in tests in recent years. On the mathematics section of the *PSAT* or the *SAT,* the average score for males has been higher than the average score for females, and there have been more males than females with very high scores, for many years. In recent years, the average score for males is also slightly higher than the average for females on the verbal section of these tests. As a consequence, a substantially larger percentage of scholarships are awarded to males than to females.

As in the case of differences in scores of racial/ethnic groups, the existence of a difference in average scores for males and females does not necessarily imply that the test is biased. There are, for example, differences in the amount of mathematics taken by females and males in high school and these differences may lead to differences in the scores on the mathematics tests. Whatever the cause of the differences, however, it does not change the fact that use of the tests alone results in a larger proportion of scholarships being awarded to males than to females, despite the fact that females earn higher grades in school than males on average. Judgments about the proper use of test scores must rest on more than technical evaluations of the tests or the degree to which the scores reflect real differences in knowledge, skills, and developed abilities rather than unintentional biases. Such judgments also involve questions of social values and social policy.

Although not a minority group, women have had some of the same problems as minorities have in attempting to obtain equal educational and occupational opportunities. Thus, in the use of test results in career planning, care needs to be taken so that test scores are not unfairly used to direct females away from certain occupations. For example, females tend to score lower than males on mechanical comprehension tests and to have lower mechanical interest scores. Although these differences probably reflect cultural influences rather than sex bias in the tests, it would be unfortunate if such results were used to limit the occupations females might consider as possible careers.

Invasion of Privacy.   The most frequently expressed concern with invasion of privacy has been with personality and adjustment inventories. Many of these instruments ask individuals to respond to questions concerning family relationships, sexual attitudes and behavior, and religious beliefs. Such questions are viewed as an invasion of privacy, as questions the school has no right to ask. The problem is most serious when such inventories are routinely administered to all students, as was once the practice in schools. The problem is less serious when the student is seeking help from a qualified counselor and is asked to respond to an inventory as part of the counseling process. Ever since the 1965 United States congressional investigations into the use of personality inventories in government, industry, and education, the routine use of personality inventories in schools has practically disappeared. Their use is now restricted primarily to counseling situations, where they can be interpreted and used by psychologically trained counselors. In such cases, it is recommended that the completed inventory and scores be destroyed when they are no longer needed in counseling, to prevent them from falling into the hands of unqualified persons who might misinterpret or misuse the results.

The invasion of privacy issue is not limited to personality inventories but also affects personal information obtained for school records, college admission programs, and other external testing and data-gathering programs. When invasion of privacy is considered a possibility, informed consent should be obtained from students or parents. This involves making the interested persons aware of the purpose for which the information is being obtained, the nature of the information sought, and the ways in which the information might be used.

In protecting student privacy, it is also necessary to keep test scores and other personal information confidential. Test scores, grades, and other assessment data should not be posted. They should be shared only with the student, the student's parents, and other qualified professionals in the school district who have a legitimate need for the information. Federal law states that information from school records must not be released to persons other than those mentioned without the written permission of parents, or student if eighteen years of age or older. The law also gives parents, and students eighteen or older, the right to examine a student's school records and to challenge the contents. This legal right to review and dispute school records should aid in detecting errors in recording test scores and other evaluation data. It should also help remove biased, irrelevant, and obsolete material. Teachers and other school personnel are now under pressure to make sure that the information entered in students' records is objective, accurate, and relevant. Let us hope that the law does not inhibit teachers from entering useful information in students' files.

SUMMARY

There are a number of externally mandated testing and assessment programs that you are likely to encounter in the school. As a teacher you may be directly involved in some of the programs. Others you may simply need to know about so that you can serve as an informed professional in dealing with students, parents, and the general public. These programs have generally contributed to expanded testing and assessment in the schools, which in turn have created new trends and raised concerns.

Demands for accountability have led to substantial increases in the amount of testing and assessment in the schools and in the importance that is attached to the scores. Minimum-competency testing programs that required students to pass tests to receive high-school diplomas or to be promoted to the next grade grew rapidly throughout the country in the late 1970s. Demands for comparisons of schools, school districts, and states in terms of student achievement test scores led to the introduction of still more testing and assessment requirements and increased the stakes for teachers and school administrators.

The *National Assessment of Educational Progress (NAEP)* periodically tests a sample of children and young adults to obtain representative data concerning the nation's educational progress. The tests measure the attainment of specific objectives in all major areas of school learning, and the results are reported to the public through the news media, professional associations, and various publications. Since 1990, *NAEP* has also allowed for state-by-state comparisons on a voluntary basis, a practice that may increase the importance of *NAEP* in the future.

Many factors, such as difficulty in translation and differences in sampling, make international assessment results difficult to interpret. The results of international assessments continue to attract considerable attention and to be used to argue for improvements in education in this country.

Several recent initiatives at the national level are likely to further increase the importance of testing and assessment. The adoption of national educational goals by the President and the nation's governors, the development of national standards, and the emphasis on certification of state assessments in terms of those standards, have all placed heavy emphasis on assessment both for purposes of monitoring progress and as an instrument of educational reform.

A number of changes in educational measurement have been broad enough and persistent enough to be identified as trends. In addition to the expanded uses of tests that have just been summarized, developments are changing the nature of testing and assessment. Most notable of these developments is the increased emphasis on performance-based assessment. Concerns that tests and assessments strongly influence what gets taught have led to increased emphasis on making assessments that correspond as closely as possible to complex learning objectives that are not readily measured by conventional tests. Demands for new forms of assessment have led to changes in approaches being used to measure teacher performance as well as student performance.

Technological developments also promise to change the nature of testing and assessment. Computers provide a means of making tests adaptive to the individual test-taker and constructing realistic simulations to test problem-solving skills.

Critics of testing have raised a number of issues concerning the possible consequences of testing in the schools. Most of the criticism has been directed toward standardized tests, including such issues as the nature and quality of the tests, the possible harmful effects of testing on students, the fairness of tests to minorities and women, the hazards of testing to the individual's right to privacy. Although most of the criticisms of testing have some merit, most problems are not caused by the use of tests, but by the misuse of tests. In most cases, tests provide results that are more objective, accurate, and relevant than alternative sources of information. What is needed is a more professional use of tests, with greater emphasis on ways they can be used to improve student learning and development.

LEARNING EXERCISES

1. Discuss the potential effects of the pressure to compare schools, districts, and states in terms of student achievement test scores on instruction and student learning.

2. Discuss the pros and cons of teaching to the specific content of externally mandated tests and assessments.

3. Describe the purpose and function of the *National Assessment of Educational Progress*. In what ways might this program influence school instruction?

4. What types of testing and assessment do you think should be increased or decreased in the schools? Why?

5. List possible advantages and disadvantages for each of the apparent trends in educational measurement cited in this chapter.

6. Which criticisms of testing do you consider to be most serious? What steps should be taken to correct them?

7. What are advantages of the legal requirement that parents and students be given access to school records? What problems might arise from this, and what solutions would you suggest?

REFERENCES

Cole, N. S. & Moss, P. A. (1989). Bias in test use. In R. L. Linn (Ed.) *Educational measurement* (3rd ed.). New York: Macmillan.

Educational Testing Service. (1979). *ETS Developments, 26.* Princeton, N.J.: Author.

Elashoff, J. D., & Snow, R. E. (Eds.). (1971). *Pygmalion reconsidered.* Worthington, OH: Charles A. Jones

Frederiksen, N. (1984). The real test bias. *American Psychologist, 39* 193–202.

Gardner, E. F. (1978). Bias. *NCME Measurement in Education, 9.*

Hoffman, B. C. (1962). *The tyranny of testing.* New York: Crowell–Collier.

Linn, R. L., Graue, M. E., & Sanders, N. M. (1990). Comparing state and district test results to national norms: The validity of claims that everyone is above average. *Educational Measurement: Issues and Practice, 9*(3), 5–14.

Moss, J. D., & Brown, F. G. (1979). Sex bias and academic performance: An empirical study. *Journal of Educational Measurement, 16,* 197–201.

National Commission on Excellence in Education. (1983). *A nation at risk: The imperative for educational reform.* Washington, D.C.: U.S. Government Printing Office.

National Council on Education Standards and Testing. (1992). *Raising standards for American education: A report to Congress, the Secretary of Education, the National Education Goals Panel, and the American people.* Washington, DC: U.S. Government Printing Office.

National Education Goals Panel. (1991). *The national education goals report, 1991: Building a nation of learners. Executive summary.* Washington, DC: Author.

Nolan, S. B., Haladyna, T. M., & Hass, N. S. (1992). Uses and abuses of achievement test scores. *Educational Measurement: Issues and Practice, 11*(2), 9–15.

Owen, D. (1985). *None of the above: Behind the myth of scholastic aptitude.* Boston: Houghton Mifflin.

Rosenthal, R., & Jacobsen, L. (1968). *Pygmalion in the classroom.* New York: Holt, Rinehart & Winston.

Rudner, L. M. (1988). Teacher testing—An update. *Educational Measurement: Issues and Practice, 7*(2), 16–19.

Smith, M. L., & Rottenberg, C. (1991). Unintended consequences of external testing in elementary schools. *Educational Measurement: Issues and Practice, 10*(4), 7–11.

United States Congress, Office of Technology Assessment. (1992). *Testing in American schools: Asking the right questions* (OTA-SET-519). Washington, DC: U.S. Government Printing Office p. 3.

West, C. K., & Anderson, T. H. (1976). The question of preponderant causation in teacher expectancy research. *Review of Educational Research, 46* 613–630.

FURTHER READING

Baker, E. L., O'Neil, H. F., Jr., & Linn, R. L. (1993.) Policy and validity prospects for performance-based assessment. *American Psychologist, 48,* 1210–1218. Discusses the rationale for the use of performance-based assessments and need for evaluations of the degree to which expectations can be met by new forms of assessment.

Bunderson, C. V., Inouye, D. K., & Olsen, J. B. (1989). The Four Generations of Computerized Educational Measurement. In R. L. Linn, (Ed.), *Educational Measurement* (3rd ed.). New York: Macmillan. Discusses uses of computers to administer tests.

Cole, N. S., & Moss, P. A. (1989). Bias in test use. In R. L. Linn, (Ed.), *Educational measurement* (3rd ed.). New York: Macmillan. Discusses a wide range of issues related to bias in test use and interpretation.

U.S. Congress, Office of Technology Assessment. (1992). *Testing in American schools: Asking the right questions* (OTA–SET–519). Washington, DC: U.S. Government Printing Office. A comprehensive report on the role of externally mandated educational testing and assessment in American education. Presents a discussion of policy issues and arguments for and against various approaches to assessment.

Widgor, A. K., & Garner, W. R. (Eds.). (1982). *Ability testing: Uses, consequences, and controversies, Part I.* Washington, D.C.: National Academy Press. A report by the Committee on Ability Testing convened by the National Academy of Sciences to study the role of testing in American life. Covers the controversies surrounding testing, the nature of ability testing, the use of tests in education and industry, and the social and legal issues in testing. The final chapter is a summary and review of the role of ability testing.

Appendixes

APPENDIX A
Elementary Statistics

Statistics is concerned with the organization, analysis, and interpretation of test scores and other numerical data. At minimum, teachers should know those statistical techniques that enable them to (1) analyze and describe the results of measurement obtained in their own classrooms, (2) understand the statistics used in test manuals and research reports, and (3) interpret the various types of derived scores used in testing.

Many teachers shy away from statistics because they think it requires advanced mathematics and tedious calculations. However, the elementary statistical concepts and skills we shall deal with require neither. The calculations that can be quite tedious if conducted by hand can be done quite readily with a simple, inexpensive, hand-held calculator. Calculators costing $20 or so cannot only do all of the intermediate calculations but often have built-in procedures for all of the statistics we shall discuss. Computation of the statistics we consider as well as much more complicated ones obviously can also be readily performed on a personal computer with easy-to-use statistical software. Hence, we have reduced the emphasis on calculation that was present in previous editions. We also have kept the mathematics to a minimum and will emphasize interpretation.

The statistics that we shall be concerned with here are known as descriptive statistics. As the term suggests, the emphasis is on describing a set of scores. The description may take the form of tables, graphs, or a single number (e.g., an average). Some of these modes of description are seen routinely in newspapers, magazines, and the evening television news. The purpose of these statistics is to summarize sets of numbers so that interesting features may be seen and understood more easily. For example, given a list of the high and low temperatures for each of the 365 days of a year, it would be possible to read them all and get a sense of how temperate the climate was and of seasonal changes. However, a graph of the average high and low temperatures for each of the twelve months of the year could convey the information much more efficiently and effectively.

We shall begin with a brief discussion of organizing data and displaying results in tables and graphs. We shall then turn to a discussion of three types of statistical measures. These are

1. Measures of central tendency (averages).
2. Measures of variability (spread of scores).
3. Measures of relationship (correlation and regression).

The first two measures provide a convenient means of analyzing and describing a single set of test scores, and the third category of measures can be used to indicate the agreement between two sets of test scores obtained for the same students. All three are widely used in educational measurement and should be mastered by anyone working with test data.

ORGANIZING AND DISPLAYING SCORES

When test scores are obtained for a group of students they are usually in haphazard order as shown in Table A.1.

After careful inspection of the scores on the midterm exam for the 24 students we see that scores in the 70s and 80s are fairly common, that only 3 students had scores in the 90s, and that one student had a score less than 50. Similar statements might be made after inspecting the scores on the final exam. We might even note that there is a tendency for the scores on the final to be slightly higher than those on the midterm and that there is a tendency for students with high scores on the midterm to receive relatively high scores on the final, though the relationship is far from perfect. For example, Student E, who had the highest score on the midterm, had the fourth highest score on the final, while Student W, who had the fifth highest score on the midterm, had the highest score on the final.

From our detailed inspection of the scores in Table A.1 we could actually get a rough idea of all three of the statistical concepts that we are concerned with here.

TABLE A.1
Set of scores for a class of 24 students

Student	Midterm	Final	Student	Midterm	Final
A	78	85	M	65	80
B	67	71	N	92	93
C	88	78	O	53	69
D	74	71	P	65	75
E	97	91	Q	83	76
F	84	88	R	79	74
G	57	76	S	45	63
H	65	68	T	95	80
I	81	94	U	62	58
J	58	67	V	74	80
K	70	72	W	85	96
L	81	87	X	76	81

These are the *central tendency,* or the score obtained by the average student, the *variability of the scores* (e.g., the midterm scores range from a high of 97 to a low of 45, but most of the students have scores between 60 and 90), and the *relationship between performance on the midterm and performance on the final.* None of these characteristics of the scores is very easy to see from the haphazard arrangement of the scores, however, nor are they very precise. If we were working with 200 scores for all seventh-grade students at a junior high school or 3,000 scores for all third-grade students in a school district, the difficulty of seeing interesting characteristics and communicating them in a precise way would be much greater than it was for our class of 24 students. But even for our 24 students, we need to organize and display the scores to see these characteristics more easily and we need to do some simple calculations to quantify the information in a more precise fashion.

Simple Ranking

For some uses, it may be sufficient to arrange a set of scores in order of size and to assign a rank to each score. This will indicate the relative position of each score in the group. Ordinarily, the largest score is given a rank of 1, the second largest a rank of 2, and so on until all scores are ranked. The midterm scores from Table A.1 have been rearranged in order of size and assigned ranks to illustrate the procedure. The results are presented in Table A.2.

Note that when two or more students have the same score (the two 81s, the two 74s, and the three 65s) the average of the ranks for those students is given to each. Thus, the two students who received scores of 81 on the midterm would have been ranked 8 and 9. They are both given the average of these two ranks (8.5) because there is no basis for giving one of the students a rank of 8 and the other one a rank of 9.

Using Table A.2, it is obviously much easier to find the highest and lowest midterm scores, the number of students with scores above 90 or below 70, and to

TABLE A.2
Ranking test scores

Midterm	Rank		Midterm	Rank	
97	1		74	13.5	⎫ Tied ranks
95	2		74	13.5	⎬ 13 and 14
92	3		70	15	
88	4		67	16	
85	5		65	18	⎫ Tied ranks
84	6		65	18	⎬ 17, 18,
83	7		65	18	⎭ and 19
81	8.5	⎫ Tied ranks	62	20	
81	8.5	⎬ 8 and 9	58	21	
79	10		57	22	
78	11		53	23	
76	12		45	24	

see that scores in the 70s are obtained by students who rank close to the middle of the class than it was with Table A.1. It is also easy to see that half the students score above 75 and half of them score below 75. Creating a rank order list for the final exam scores would make it easy to see similar characteristics of those scores. For example, it would make it easier to see that while nine students had scores below 70 on the midterm, only five had scores below 70 on the final.

With only 24 scores there is not a great need to go beyond a rank order display of scores. With more scores, however, it is often helpful to construct grouped frequency distributions and graphs of the score distributions. Grouped frequency distributions of the midterm and final scores are shown in Table A.3. Note that the scores have been grouped into *class intervals,* the number of scores falling in each interval has been tallied, and the tallies have been counted to obtain the *frequency,* or number of scores in each interval. Thus, there were two students with midterm scores in the interval 95–99, one student with a score in the interval 90–94, and so on. The total number (N) is the sum of the numbers in the frequency column. In the finished table the tally column is usually omitted as it has been for the final exam scores.

To construct a grouped frequency distribution it is conventional to choose a class interval that is an odd number and that will result in approximately 10 to 12 intervals. This makes the midpoint of each interval an integer. For our example the class interval is 5 (e.g., 95, 96, 97, 98, and 99 in the highest interval) and the midpoint of each interval is an integer (e.g., 97 is the midpoint of the highest interval). The lower bound of each interval starts with a multiple of the width of the interval (e.g., the lowest interval starts with 45, the next with 50, and so on). All class intervals should be the same size.

TABLE A.3
Frequency distributions of midterm and final scores

Midterm			Final	
Class Interval	Tally	Frequency	Class Interval	Frequency
95–99	//	2	95–99	1
90–94	/	1	90–94	3
85–89	//	2	85–89	3
80–84	////	4	80–84	4
75–79	///	3	75–79	4
70–74	///	3	70–74	4
65–69	////	4	65–69	3
60–64	/	1	60–64	1
55–59	//	2	55–59	1
50–54	/	1	50–54	0
45–49	/	1	45–49	0
		N = 24		N = 24

To decide on the width of the interval that will result in a reasonable number of intervals, the range can be divided by 12 and the nearest odd number used as the width of the class interval. For example, the highest midterm score is 97 and the lowest is 45 for a range of 52 (97 − 45 = 52). Since 52/12 = 4.33 the class interval was set at 5, the nearest odd number. Note that applying the same process for the final scores would have suggested that a class interval of 3 be used. However, using the same interval makes it easier to compare the two sets of scores.

The grouped frequency distributions provide a good summary of the results. Features of the two distributions that already have been mentioned can be easily seen. However, there is some loss of information. For example, from the grouped frequency distribution we see that two students had scores in the interval 95–99 on the midterm, but we can no longer tell that one of these students had a 95, while the other one had a score of 97.

Graphic Presentations of Frequency Distributions

A frequency distribution presents test data in a clear, effective manner, and it is satisfactory for most classroom purposes. But if we want to study the distribution of scores more carefully or to report the results to others, a graphic representation may be more useful. The two most commonly used graphs are the *histogram* (or bar graph) and the *frequency polygon* (or line graph). Both graphs are presented in Figure A.1, based on the midterm scores in Table A.3. The scores are shown along the base line, or horizontal axis, and are grouped into the same class intervals used in Table A.3. The vertical axis, to the left of the graphs, indicates the number of students earning each score and thus corresponds to the frequency column in Table A.3.

The *histogram* presents the data in the form of rectangular columns. The base of each column is the width of the class interval, and the height of the column indicates the frequency, or the number of students falling within that interval. It is as if each student earning a score within a given class interval were standing on the shoulders of the student beneath, to form a human column.

FIGURE A.1
Histogram and frequency polygon plotted from midterm exam scores in Table A.3

The *frequency polygon* is constructed by plotting a point at the midpoint of each class interval at a height corresponding to the number of students, or frequency, within that interval and then joining these points with straight lines. As can be seen in Figure A.1, the frequency polygon and histogram are simply different ways of presenting the same data. In actual practice we would use only one of the graphs, the choice being somewhat arbitrary.

Histograms or frequency polygons allow us to see the shape of the distribution of scores as well as some of the features we have seen before. With a small number of students, such as the 24 in our example, the shape of the distribution is often jagged, going up and down and up again as you go from left to right. With a large number of scores, however, distributions of scores generally look smoother than the one shown in Figure A.1. Distributions of scores for many students on standardized tests often appear smooth and bell shaped, not unlike the shape of a normal distribution, and in many cases normal distribution is assumed or used as an approximation. See Chapter 17 for a description of the normal distribution and illustrations of some of its uses.

Stem-and-Leaf Display

An approach to displaying data that has become increasingly popular in recent years is the stem-and-leaf display. Like grouped frequency distributions, frequency polygons, and histograms, stem-and-leaf displays show the shape of a distribution of scores. In addition, they preserve all the information about the individual scores that is lost when scores are grouped into class intervals.

Tables A.4 and A.5 show two versions of stem-and-leaf displays for the midterm and final exam scores in Table A.1. The "stem" in Table A.4 is simply the tens digit for each score and the "leaf" is the units digit. On the midterm there were three scores in the 90s (92, 95, and 97). These three scores all have a stem of 9, and the individual scores are represented by the string of numbers 257 for the three leaves of 2, 5, 7. Similarly, six students with scores in the 80s (81, 81, 83, 84, 85, and 88) are represented by the common stem of 8 and the string of numbers 113458 for the six leaves. The numbers in the columns labeled "count" simply record the

TABLE A.4
Stem-and-leaf displays of midterm and final exam scores (data from Table A.1)

	Midterm Exam			Final Exam	
Stem	Leaf	Count	Stem	Leaf	Count
9	257	3	9	1346	4
8	113458	6	8	0001578	7
7	044689	6	7	11245668	8
6	25557	5	6	3789	4
5	378	3	5	8	1
4	5	1	4		
		N = 24			N = 24

TABLE A.5
Stem-and-leaf displays of midterm and final exam scores (data from Table A.1)

Midterm Exam			Final Exam		
Stem	Leaf	Count	Stem	Leaf	Count
9*	57	2	9*	6	1
9:	2	1	9:	134	3
8*	58	2	8*	578	3
8:	1134	4	8:	0001	4
7*	689	3	7*	5668	4
7:	044	3	7:	1124	4
6*	5557	4	6*	789	3
6:	2	1	6:	3	1
5*	78	2	5*	8	1
5:	3	1	5:		
4*	5	1	4*		
		N = 24			N = 24

number of scores with a given stem. As can be seen, the stem-and-leaf displays retain the detail that two students received a score of 81 while giving a general summary of the type provided by a grouped frequency distribution or frequency polygon.

The stem-and-leaf displays in Table A.5 show exactly the same information as is shown in Table A.4. The stem now corresponds to five-point intervals, however. Thus *9** represents a stem for the numbers 95–99, *9:* represents the stem for the numbers 90–94, and so on. By using two stems for each tens digit, the shape of the distribution can be seen more easily.

Scatterplots

The graphs and displays we have presented have highlighted all but one of the features that was discussed concerning the data in Table A.1. Since the tables, graphs, and displays have focused on one type of score at a time, they have not done anything to make it easier to see the relationship between scores on the midterm and the final. To see the relationship better than can be seen from a simple listing of the scores, we need to construct a plot that displays pairs of numbers. Such a plot is called a scatterplot (or scattergram). The scatterplot for the scores in Table A.1 is shown in Figure A.2.

Each dot in Figure A.2 represents a pair of scores for an individual student. Thus, there are 24 dots corresponding to the students. A student's score on the midterm is shown on the horizontal, or X, axis and the student's score on the final is shown on the vertical, or Y axis. For example, Student A had a score of 78 on the midterm and a score of 85 on the final. That student's score is represented by the dot that is shown by the arrow and the letter A. It is directly above the point on the horizontal line corresponding to a score of 78 and directly to the right of the point on

FIGURE A.2

Scatterplot of midterm and final exam scores (scores from Table A.1)

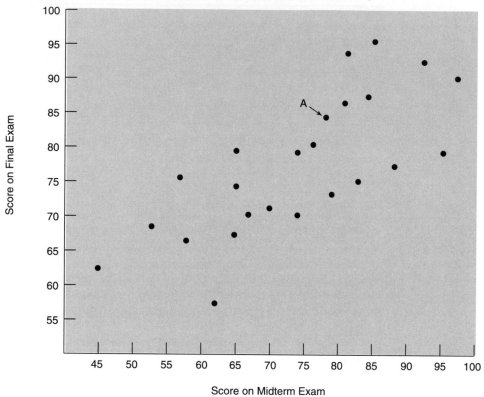

the vertical axis corresponding to a score of 85. Points representing the remaining 23 students are plotted in a similar fashion.

By looking at the plot we see that there is a swarm of dots that tends to run from the lower left-hand corner to the upper right-hand corner of the figure. This shows that there is a positive relationship between the scores on the midterm and the scores on the final. That is, students with relatively low scores on one test tend to have relatively low scores on the other test while students with relatively high scores on one test tend to have relatively high scores on the other test. For example, there are 9 dots to the right of 80 on the horizontal axis. These represent the 9 students with midterm scores higher than 80. We see that all 9 of these points are above 75 on the vertical scale, indicating that no student who had a score of 80 or higher on the midterm had a score of 75 or less on the final. On the other hand, we can see by looking at the lower left-hand corner of the scatterplot that 6 of the 8 students who had midterm scores of 65 or less had scores of 75 or less on the final.

Although there clearly is a relationship between scores on the two tests, it is also clear that the relationship is far from perfect. That is, a student who has the highest or one of the highest scores on one test is not always ranked as highly on the other test. Indeed, the four students with scores of 90 or higher on the final had scores ranging all the way from 81 to 97 on the midterm, while one of the three students who had scores of 90 or higher on the midterm received a score of only 80 on the final.

Scatterplots and the graphs considered above can be produced easily with a personal computer. The version of the scatterplot shown in Figure A.3, for example, was produced using *SPSS/PC+*, one of a number of statistical packages available for personal computers. The scores on the midterm and final examinations were in a data file called *APPEND.DOC* which was on a disk in Drive A of the computer. The first two columns of each row of data contain the score on the midterm and the fourth and fifth columns contain the score on the final. The *SPSS/PC+* DATA statement gets that data and the PLOT command produces the scatterplot.

FIGURE A.3
Example of *SPSS/PC+* commands to get scatterplot of midterm and final scores

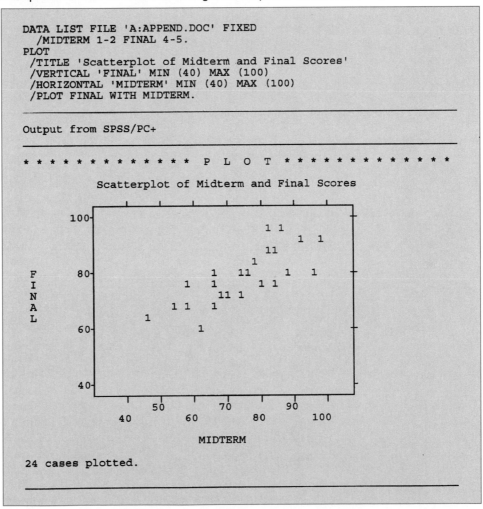

```
DATA LIST FILE 'A:APPEND.DOC' FIXED
  /MIDTERM 1-2 FINAL 4-5.
PLOT
  /TITLE 'Scatterplot of Midterm and Final Scores'
  /VERTICAL 'FINAL' MIN (40) MAX (100)
  /HORIZONTAL 'MIDTERM' MIN (40) MAX (100)
  /PLOT FINAL WITH MIDTERM.
```

Output from SPSS/PC+

```
* * * * * * * * * * * *  P L O T  * * * * * * * * * * * * *
            Scatterplot of Midterm and Final Scores
```

24 cases plotted.

MEASURES OF CENTRAL TENDENCY

A measure of central tendency is simply an average or typical value in a set of scores. We all are familiar with the *arithmetic average* obtained by adding all of the scores in a set and dividing this sum by the number of scores. In statistics this type of average is called the *mean* and is represented by the letter M (or $\overline{X}$). Two other commonly used measures of central tendency are the *median* (represented by Mdn or P_{50}) and the *mode*. The median is the midpoint of a set of scores, that is, the point on either side of which half the scores occur. The mode (fashion) is the score that occurs most frequently. Because the mean, median, and mode are different types of averages the word *average* should be avoided when describing data. Preciseness requires that the specific type of average be indicated.

The method of determining each measure of central tendency will be described next and is illustrated in Table A.6.

TABLE A.6
Measures of central
tendency

Midterm Score (X)			Final Score (Y)		
	97			96	
	95			94	
	92			93	
	88			91	
	85			88	
50% of	84			87	50% of
scores	83			85	scores
	81			81	
	81			80	
	79			80	} Mode = 80
	78			80	
	76			78	
Median = 75→				←Median = 77	
	74			76	
	74			76	
	70			75	
	67			74	
	65			72	
50% of	65	} Mode = 65		71	50% of
scores	65			71	scores
	62			69	
	58			68	
	57			67	
	53			63	
	45			58	
Sum of X = 1,774			Sum of Y = 1,873		
Mean = (1,774/24)			Mean = (1,873/24)		
= 73.92			= 78.04		

Note: Scores are rank ordered separately for the midterm and the final.

The Mean (M or $\overline{X}$)

The *mean,* or arithmetic average, is the most widely used measure of central tendency. Because it is calculated by adding a series of scores and then dividing this sum by the number of scores, the computation can be represented by the following formula:

$$\overline{X} = \frac{\text{Sum of all scores}}{\text{Number of scores}}$$

$$\overline{X} = \frac{\sum X}{N}$$

where

$\sum$ = the sum of

X = any score

N = number of scores

Applying this formula to the scores in Table A.6 produces a mean of 73.92 for the midterm and 78.04 for the final. The mean takes into account the value of each score, and so one extremely high or low score could have an appreciable effect on it.

The Median (*Mdn* or P_{50})

The *median* is a *counting average*. It is determined by arranging the scores in order of size and counting up to (or down to) the midpoint of the set of scores. If the number of scores is *even* (as in Table A.6) the median will be halfway between the two middlemost scores. When the number of scores is *odd,* the median is the middle score.

The median is a *point* that divides a set of scores into equal halves, and thus the same number of scores falls above the median as below the median, regardless of the size of the individual scores. Because it is a counting average, an extremely high or low score will not affect its value.

The Mode

The *mode* is simply the most frequent or popular score in the set and is determined by inspection. In Table A.6 the mode is 65 for the midterm because the largest number of persons made that score. The mode is the least reliable type of statistical average and is frequently used merely as a preliminary estimate of central tendency. A set of scores sometimes has two modes and is called *bimodal.*

MEASURES OF VARIABILITY

A set of scores can be more adequately described if we know how much they spread out above and below the measure of central tendency. For example, we might have two groups of students with a mean test score of 70 but in one group, the span of scores is from 60 to 80, and in the other the span is from 50 to 100. These represent quite different spreads of performance. We can identify such differences by numbers that indicate how much scores spread out in a group. These are called measures of variability, or dispersion. The three most commonly used measures of variability are the *range,* the *quartile deviation,* and the *standard deviation.*

The Range

The simplest and crudest measure of variability is the range, calculated by subtracting the lowest score from the highest score. In the preceding example, the range of scores in the first group is 20 points and in the second, 40 points. The range provides a quick estimate of variability but is undependable because it is based on the position of the two extreme scores. The addition or subtraction of a single score can change the range significantly. In the preceding example, the ranges of the two groups would become equal if we added two students to the first group: one with a score of 50 and another with a score of 100. It is obvious that a more stable measure of variability would be desirable. For our example with the midterm and final exam scores, however, the smaller range for the final (96 − 58 = 38) than for the midterm (range = 97 − 45 = 52) accurately reflects the smaller variability in scores on the final exam that we have previously noted and that will be quantified by the other measures of variability.

The Quartile Deviation (Q)

The quartile deviation is based on the range of the middle 50 percent of the scores, instead of the range of the entire set. The middle 50 percent of a set of scores is called the *interquartile range,* and the *quartile deviation* is simply half of this range. The quartile deviation is also called the *semi-interquartile range.*

The middle 50 percent of the scores is bounded by the 75th percentile and the 25th percentile. These points are called *quartiles* and are indicated by Q_3 and Q_1, respectively. Quartiles are merely *points* that divide a set of scores into quarters. The middle quartile, or Q_2, is the median.

To compute the quartile deviation, we simply determine the values of Q_3 and Q_1 and apply the following formula:

$$Q = \frac{Q_3 - Q_1}{2}$$

We use the same counting procedure to locate Q_3 and Q_1 that we used to find the median. With the scores arranged in order of size, we start from the lowest score, and count off 25 percent of the scores to locate Q_1 and 75 percent of the scores to locate Q_3. Since we have 24 students in our example, Q_1 is equal to the score that is higher than that achieved by 6 students (25%) and lower than that achieved by 18 students (75%). For the midterm, $Q_1 = 65$ and for the final $Q_1 = 71.5$. Note that Q_1 is 71.5 on the final because it falls halfway between 71, the 6th lowest score, and 72, the 7th lowest score. The values of Q_3 are 83.5 for the midterm (halfway between 83 and 84) and 86 for the final (halfway between 85 and 87).

Given the 75th and 25th percentiles (Q_1 and Q_3), the quartile deviation (Q) is easily computed. As would be expected from what we have already seen, Q is larger for the midterm scores ($Q = [83.5 - 65]/2 = 9.25$) than it is for the final scores ($Q = [86 - 71.5]/2 = 7.25$). These quartile deviation values simply quantify the fact that the midterm scores are more variable than the final scores.

Although quartiles are *points* on the scale (like averages and percentiles), the quartile deviation represents a distance on the scale. It indicates the distance we need to go above and below the median to include approximately the middle 50 percent of the scores.

The Standard Deviation (*SD*, s, or σ)

The most useful measure of variability, or spread of scores, is the *standard deviation*. The computation of the standard deviation does not make its meaning readily apparent, but essentially it is an average of the degree to which a set of scores deviates from the mean. Because it takes into account the amount that each score deviates from the mean, it is a more stable measure of variability than either the range or quartile deviation.

Because the procedure for calculating a standard deviation involves squaring each score, summing the scores and the squares of the scores, as well as taking a square root, the help of a hand-held calculator is highly desirable for any reasonably sized problem. Better yet, a calculator with built-in statistical procedures or a microcomputer with a simple statistical package is recommended for anyone who wants to compute statistics such as standard deviations and correlations on a routine basis. To perform the calculations by hand or with a hand-held calculator that does not offer statistical procedures, however, the following steps are involved.

1. Find the sum of the scores (ΣX) as was done to compute the mean.
2. Square each score (X^2).
3. Find the sum of the squared scores (ΣX^2).
4. Square the sum of the scores obtained in Step 1; that is, multiply (ΣX) times (ΣX).
5. Divide the square obtained in Step 4 by N, the number of students, (ΣX)(ΣX)/N.
6. Subtract the result in Step 5 from the sum of the squared scores obtained in Step 3, $[\Sigma X^2 - (\Sigma X)(\Sigma X)/N]$.
7. Divide the result in step 6 by ($N - 1$), one less than the number of students, $[\Sigma X^2 - (\Sigma X)(\Sigma X)/N]/(N - 1)$.
8. Find the square root of the result of Step 7. This number is the standard deviation (*SD*) of the scores. Thus, the formula for the *SD* is

$$SD = \sqrt{\frac{\sum X^2 - (\sum X)(\sum X)/N}{N-1}}$$

The square of each midterm score and the square of each final score is listed in Table A.7. Also shown are the sums of the scores and of the squared scores. The last column of the table lists the product of the midterm score times the final score for each student. Those numbers are not used for calculating standard deviations but will be used later to calculate the correlation. Using the numbers for the midterm exam in the eight steps just listed, the standard deviation is obtained as follows.

1. From Table A.7, $\sum X = 1,774$.
2. See Table A.7 for a listing of X^2 for each student.
3. From Table A.7, $(\sum X^2 = 135,342)$.
4. $(\sum X)(\sum X) = (1,774)(1,774) = 3,147,076$.
5. $(\sum X)(\sum X)/N = 3,147,076/24 = 131,125.1667$.
6. $[\sum X^2 - (\sum X)(\sum X)/N] = 135,342 - 131,125.1667 = 4,213.8333$.
7. $[\sum X^2 - (\sum X)(\sum X)/N]/(N-1) = 4,213.8333/23 = 183.2101$.
8. $SD = \sqrt{183.2101} = 13.54$.

Applying the same steps to the scores on the final exam we find that the *SD* for the final is 10.04. What do these standard deviations of 13.54 on the midterm and 10.04 tell us? First, it should be no surprise that the midterm scores have a larger standard deviation than the final scores. We have already noted that the midterm scores are more spread out. The midterm scores have a larger range and a larger quartile deviation than the final scores. The larger standard deviation is one more way of quantifying the fact that the midterm scores have greater variability than the final scores do.

The standard deviation, like other measures of variability, represents a distance. If we move the distance equal to one *SD* above and below the mean we will find that somewhere between 60 and 75 percent of the scores fall in that region for most distributions of scores. In a normal distribution, 68 percent of the scores are included between the mean minus one *SD* and the mean plus one *SD*. For example, the midterm had a mean of 73.92 and a standard deviation of 13.54. Thus, the mean minus one *SD* is 73.92 − 13.54 = 60.35 and the mean plus one *SD* is 73.92 + 13.54 = 87.46. Looking at Table A.7, we see that 16 of the 24 students (67 percent) have midterm scores between these two limits. Although the distribution of midterm scores is not the same shape as a normal distribution, the percentage of cases that fall between the mean plus and minus one *SD* is very close to the 68 percent that would be found for a true normal distribution. This result is not unusual and it is reasonable to expect that roughly two thirds of the cases will have scores between the mean minus one *SD* and the mean plus one *SD*.

TABLE A.7
Intermediate calculations for standard deviation (*SD*) and product–moment correlation coefficient (*r*)

| Student | Midterm Score | | Final Score | | |
	(X)	X²	(Y)	Y²	XY
E	97	9409	91	8281	8827
T	95	9025	80	6400	7600
N	92	8464	93	8649	8556
C	88	7744	78	6084	6864
W	85	7225	96	9216	8160
F	84	7056	88	7744	7392
Q	83	6889	76	5776	6308
I	81	6561	94	8836	7614
L	81	6561	87	7569	7047
R	79	6241	74	5476	5846
A	78	6084	85	7225	6630
X	76	5776	81	6561	6156
D	74	5476	71	5041	5254
V	74	5476	80	6400	5920
K	70	4900	72	5184	5040
B	67	4489	71	5041	4757
H	65	4225	68	4624	4420
M	65	4225	80	6400	5200
P	65	4225	75	5625	4875
U	62	3844	58	3364	3596
J	58	3364	67	4489	3886
G	57	3249	76	5776	4332
O	53	2809	69	4761	3657
S	45	2025	63	3969	2835
Sum = 1,774		135,342	1,873	148,491	140,772
SD on midterm = 13.54			SD on final = 10.04		r = .74

Finding the mean and standard deviation is quite easy with a microcomputer. The commands in Figure A.4 and resulting output illustrate the process using *SPSS/PC+*. As in the earlier example of the scatterplot, the DATA command gets the scores and the DESCRIPTIVES command tells the computer what to compute. Additional statistics could also have been computed adding other numbers after the /STATISTICS statement, but we only asked for ones that we have discussed.

Which Measure of Dispersion to Use

The quartile deviation is used with the median and is satisfactory for analyzing a small number of scores. Because these statistics are obtained by counting and thus

FIGURE A.4

Example of *SPSS/PC+* commands to get simple descriptive statistics. The mean, standard deviation, range, minimum, and maximum values are requested by the DESCRIPTIVES command followed by the STATISTICS 1 5 9 10 11 statement. The VARIABLES statement indicates that the requested statistics should be computed for both the midterm and the final scores.

```
DATA LIST FILE 'A:APPEND.DOC' FIXED
  /MIDTERM 1-2 FINAL 4-5.
DESCRIPTIVES
  /VARIABLES MIDTERM FINAL
  /STATISTICS 1 5 9 10 11.
```

Output from SPSS/PC+

Number of Valid Observations (Listwise) =   24.00

Variable	Mean	Std Dev	Range	Minimum	Maximum	N
MIDTERM	73.92	13.54	52.00	45	97	24
FINAL	78.04	10.04	38.00	58	96	24

are not affected by the value of each score, they are especially useful when one or more scores deviate markedly from the others in the set.

The standard deviation is used with the mean. It is the most reliable measure of variability, and is especially useful in testing. In addition to describing the spread of scores in a group, it serves as a basis for computing standard scores, the standard error of measurement, and other statistics used in analyzing and interpreting test scores.

COEFFICIENT OF CORRELATION

The next statistical measure that we shall consider is the *correlation coefficient*. The meaning of the correlation coefficient and its use in describing the validity and reliability of test scores can be found in Chapters 3 and 4. Basically, a coefficient of correlation expresses the degree of relationship between two sets of scores by numbers ranging from −1.00 to +1.00. A perfect positive correlation is indicated by a coefficient of +1.00 and a perfect negative correlation by a coefficient of −1.00. A correlation of .00 indicates no relationship between the two sets of scores. Obviously, the larger the coefficient (positive or negative), the higher the degree of relationship expressed.

Recall that from the scatterplot shown in Figure A.2 it was concluded that there was a positive relationship between scores on the midterm and scores on the final exam. The relationship was far from perfect, however. Thus, we should expect from an inspection of the scatterplot that the correlation coefficient should be greater than .00 but less than +1.00. As we shall see, the correlation between the midterm and final scores is .74. This value reflects a relatively strong but less than perfect relationship between these two sets of scores.

Just as there are several measures of central tendency and several measures of variability, there are several different measures of relationship expressed as correlation coefficients. We shall consider only one of these, the *product–moment correlation coefficient*. This is by far the most commonly used and most useful correlation coefficient. It is the one that is most likely to be reported in test manuals and research studies. Indeed, if it is not specified otherwise when a correlation coefficient is reported, it is ordinarily assumed to be a product–moment correlation. The product–moment correlation coefficient is indicated by the symbol r.

As was true of a standard deviation, computation of a product–moment correlation coefficient is best done by a calculator or computer. Fortunately, much of the work for our example of 24 students with scores on a midterm and a final exam has already been done in Table A.7 because many of the intermediate values needed to compute the standard deviations of the two sets of scores are also used to compute the correlation coefficient. The following steps are involved in computing the correlation coefficient, r.

1. Begin by writing the pairs of scores to be studied in two columns, as was done in the columns labeled X and Y in Table A.7. Make certain that the pair of scores for each student is in the same row.

2. Square each of the entries in the X column and enter the result in the X^2 column, as was done to compute a standard deviation.

3. Square each of the entries in the Y column and enter the result in the Y^2 column.

4. In each row, multiply the entry in the X column by the entry in the Y column, and enter the result in the XY column (see the right-hand column of Table A.7).

5. Sum the entries in each column and note the number (N) of pairs of scores. From Table A.7, then:

$$\sum X = 1,774$$

$$\sum X^2 = 135,342$$

$$N = 24$$

$$\sum Y = 1,873$$

$$\sum Y^2 = 148,491$$

$$\sum XY = 140,772$$

6. Substitute the obtained values in the formula:

$$r = \frac{[\sum XY - (\sum X)(\sum Y)/N]}{\sqrt{[\sum X^2 - (\sum X)(\sum X)/N][\sum Y^2 - (\sum Y)(\sum Y)/N]}}$$

This formula looks complex, but it requires only simple arithmetic. For the scores in Table A.7, the most tedious part of the calculations has already been done. All that remains is to substitute numerical values for the appropriate symbols in the previous formula for r and do the arithmetic operations. The substitutions and intermediate steps are illustrated by the following.

The numerator for r is

$$[\sum XY - (\sum X)(\sum Y)/N] = 140{,}772 - (1{,}774)\,(1{,}873)/24$$
$$= 140{,}772 - 3{,}322{,}702/24$$
$$= 140{,}772 - 138{,}445.9167$$
$$= 2{,}326.0833$$

The part of the denominator involving X already has been used as part of the calculation of the standard deviation. It is

$$[\sum X^2 - (\sum X)(\sum X)/N] = 135{,}342 - (1{,}774)(1{,}774)/24$$
$$= 135{,}342 - 3{,}147{,}076/24$$
$$= 135{,}342 - 131{,}125.1667$$
$$= 4{,}213.8333$$

The part of the denominator involving Y is

$$[\sum Y^2 - (\sum Y)(\sum Y)/N] = 148{,}491 - (1{,}873)(1{,}873)/24$$
$$= 148{,}491 - 3{,}508{,}129/24$$
$$= 148{,}491 - 146{,}172.0417$$
$$= 2{,}318.9583$$

Putting these three parts together in the formula for r we have

$$r = \frac{2{,}326.0833}{\sqrt{(4{,}213.8333)(2{,}318.9583)}}$$
$$= .74$$

Although it is not readily apparent from the preceding formula, the computations involve most of the steps needed to find the mean and the standard deviation of each set of scores (X and Y). Thus, the formula also can be written

$$r = \left(\frac{\dfrac{\sum XY}{N} - (\overline{X})(\overline{Y})}{(SD_X)(SD_Y)} \right) \left(\frac{N}{N-1} \right)$$

where

$\overline{X}$ = mean of scores in X column

$\overline{Y}$ = mean of scores in Y column

SD_X = standard deviation of scores in X column

SD_Y = standard deviation of scores in Y column

Thus, for the same data

$$r = \left(\frac{5{,}865.5 - (73.92)(78.04)}{(13.54)(10.04)} \right) \left(\frac{24}{23} \right)$$

$$= .74$$

If the means and standard deviations are already available for the two sets of scores, this latter formula will be easier to apply. If they are not available, the first formula can be used, and the means and standard deviations of the two sets of scores can also be computed during the process, if needed.

As was already stated, it is obviously much easier to compute a correlation with the help of a calculator with statistical functions or with a microcomputer. The commands to compute the correlation as well as obtain the means and standard deviations using *SPSS/PC+* are shown together with resulting output in Figure A.5.

FIGURE A.5

Example of *SPSS/PC+* commands to get the correlation between the midterm and final scores as well as the mean and standard deviation for each set of scores

```
DATA LIST FILE 'A:APPEND.DOC' FIXED
  /MIDTERM 1-2 FINAL 4-5.
CORRELATIONS /VARIABLES MIDTERM FINAL /OPTIONS 3 /STATISTICS 1.
```

Output from SPSS/PC+

Variable	Cases	Mean	Std Dev
MIDTERM	24	73.9167	13.5355
FINAL	24	78.0417	10.0411

Correlations:	MIDTERM	FINAL
MIDTERM	1.0000	.7441**
FINAL	.7441**	1.0000

N of cases: 24   2-tailed Signif: * - .01 ** - .001

LINEAR REGRESSION COEFFICIENTS

Correlation coefficients provide an indication of the strength of relationship between two sets of scores. In many situations, however, we are interested in using one set of scores to predict the scores that would be obtained on another measure. For example, we might want to predict the grades that students will obtain from their test scores. Or we might want to predict scores on an achievement test from scores obtained on an aptitude test. In the example used in this appendix, we can show how linear regression is used to make such predictions.

The linear regression equation for predicting Y (the final) from X (the midterm) is:

$$\hat{Y} = a + b(X)$$

where a and b are the regression coefficients. The caret ($\wedge$) over the Y indicates that is the predicted Y score rather than the one that is actually achieved. The coefficient b is known as the slope, and the coefficient a is known as the intercept. They can be computed using the following formulas.

$$b = \frac{r(SD_Y)}{SD_X}$$

and

$$a = \overline{Y} - b(\overline{X})$$

where

r is the correlation coefficient,

SD_X and SD_Y are the standard deviations of X and Y, and

$\overline{X}$ and $\overline{Y}$ are the means of X and Y, respectively.

For the midterm and final scores the coefficients are

$$b = \frac{(.7441)(10.0411)}{(13.5355)} = .5520$$

and

$$a = 78.0417 - (.5520)(73.9167)$$

$$= 37.24$$

Hence, the predicted scores on the final from scores on the midterm are given by the following equation.

$$\hat{Y} = 37.24 + .552(X)$$

Using this formula for Students A, B, and C, who had midterm scores of 78, 67, and 88 respectively, yields the following predicted scores on the final.

$$\text{Student A:} \quad \hat{Y} = 37.24 + .552(78) = 80.3$$

$$\text{Student B:} \quad \hat{Y} = 37.24 + .552(67) = 74.2$$

$$\text{Student C:} \quad \hat{Y} = 37.24 + .552(88) = 85.8$$

The actual final exam scores for Students A, B, and C are 85, 71, and 78, respectively. Thus, Students A and B did somewhat better on the final than predicted while Student C did somewhat worse than predicted. The difference between the actual Y scores and the predicted ones is known as the error of prediction. The errors of prediction get smaller in comparison to the standard deviation of Y as the correlation increases. Thus, the higher the correlation, the more accurate the prediction will be.

Of course, if we already know the scores on Y there is no need to predict them, other than to see who did better or worse than would have been predicted from previous performance. A more common use of the regression equation for making predictions occurs when the equation that is obtained for one group of students (e.g., the freshman class of 1995) is used to predict the performance of another group (e.g., the applicants for freshman class of 1996). For example, we could use the regression of freshman grades on test scores obtained for the 1995 freshman class to predict the grade that 1996 applicants would obtain if they are admitted.

Figure A.6 illustrates the use of *SPSS/PC+* to compute the regression coefficients, the predicted scores on the final, and the residuals (i.e., the difference between the actual score on the final and the predicted scores). The letters identifying the students are contained in Column 6 of the data file and read in together with the midterm and final scores by the ID command. The output reports the *Multiple R* and *R Square*, which in this case, with just one predictor, are simply the correlation between the midterm and the final (.74412) and the squared correlation. The regression coefficients are listed in Column B. The slope, b is listed first and then the intercept, a (referred to as the *constant*) is listed. We have not discussed the statistics in the SE B, Beta, T, or Sig T columns. For our purposes, those statistics can be ignored. The plot shows the residuals in standardized form, which we have not discussed, but the actual predicted and residual scores are listed for each student under the columns labeled *PRED and *RESID, respectively.

A FINAL CAUTION

Correlation indicates the degree of relationship between two sets of scores, but not causation. If X and Y are related, there are several possible explanations: X may cause Y, Y may cause X, or X and Y may be the result of a common cause. For example, the increase in incidence of juvenile delinquency during the past decade has been paralleled by a corresponding increase in teachers' salaries. Thus, the correlation between these two sets of figures would probably be quite high. Obviously, further study is needed to determine the cause of any particular relationship.

FIGURE A.6

Example of *SPSS/PC+* commands to get of regression of final scores on midterm scores as well as predicted and residual scores for each case

```
DATA LIST FILE 'A:APPEND.DOC' FIXED
 /MIDTERM 1-2 FINAL 4-5 ID 6 (A).
REGRESSION /VARIABLES MIDTERM FINAL/DEPENDENT FINAL
 /METHOD ENTER MIDTERM/RESIDUALS ID(ID).
 /CASEWISE ALL DEPENDENT PRED RESID.
```

Partial Output from SPSS/PC+

```
          * * * *   M U L T I P L E   R E G R E S S I O N   * * * *

Equation Number 1    Dependent Variable..   FINAL

Variable(s) Entered on Step Number
  1..    MIDTERM

Multiple R          .74412
R Square            .55371

------------------ Variables in the Equation ------------------

Variable            B          SE B        Beta         T    Sig T

MIDTERM          .552011     .105659     .744115      5.224  .0000
(Constant)     37.238836    7.934454                  4.693  .0001

     Casewise Plot of Standardized Residual

   *: Selected   M: Missing

           -3.0        0.0        3.0
  Case ID  O:........:........:O   FINAL    *PRED      *RESID
    1  A   .          . *       .     85   80.2957     4.7043
    2  B   .         *.         .     71   74.2236    -3.2236
    3  C   .       * .          .     78   85.8158    -7.8158
    4  D   .       * .          .     71   78.0877    -7.0877
    5  E   .          *         .     91   90.7839      .2161
    6  F   .          . *       .     88   83.6078     4.3922
    7  G   .          .  *      .     76   68.7035     7.2965
    8  H   .        * .         .     68   73.1196    -5.1196
    9  I   .         .    *     .     94   81.9517    12.0483
   10  J   .         *.         .     67   69.2555    -2.2555
   11  K   .        * .         .     72   75.8796    -3.8796
   12  L   .          . *       .     87   81.9517     5.0483
   13  M   .          .  *      .     80   73.1196     6.8804
   14  N   .          . *       .     93   88.0239     4.9761
   15  O   .          .*        .     69   66.4954     2.5046
   16  P   .          .*        .     75   73.1196     1.8804
   17  Q   .       * .          .     76   83.0558    -7.0558
   18  R   .       * .          .     74   80.8477    -6.8477
   19  S   .         *          .     63   62.0793      .9207
   20  T   .      *  .          .     80   89.6799    -9.6799
   21  U   .    *     .         .     58   71.4635   -13.4635
   22  V   .         .*         .     80   78.0877     1.9123
   23  W   .         .   *      .     96   84.1598    11.8402
   24  X   .         .*         .     81   79.1917     1.8083
  Case   ID   O:........:........:O   FINAL       *PRED      *RE
              -3.0        0.0        3.0
```

522

REFERENCES

Coladarci, A., & Coladarci, T. (1979). *Elementary descriptive statistics: For those who think they can't*. Belmont, Calif.: Wadsworth. A witty and precise introduction to the basic concepts and procedures in elementary statistics.

Downie, N. M., & Heath, R. W. (1984). *Basic statistical methods* (5th ed.). New York: Harper & Row. An introductory textbook designed for nonmathematics majors.

Hopkins, K. D., Glass G. V., & Hopkins, B. R. (1987). *Basic statistics for the behavioral sciences* (2nd ed.). Englewood Cliffs, NJ: Prentice-Hall. Provides an introduction to statistics with a good discussion of interpretations of correlation coefficients and factors that influence them.

Jaeger, R. (1990). *Statistics: A spectacular sport* (2nd ed.). Newbury Park, CA: Sage Publications. Explains what statistics are, what they mean, and how they are used and interpreted. Emphasizes understanding rather than computation.

Townsend, E. A., & Burke, P. J. (1975). *Using statistics in classroom instruction*. New York: Macmillan. Offers step-by-step directions and practice in using simple descriptive statistics with test scores.

APPENDIX B

Professional Journals for Locating Measurement and Assessment Articles

Articles on educational and psychological measurement and assessment appear in many different types of professional journals. List A includes those journals that focus most directly on measurement and assessment articles. List B contains journals that sometimes have relevant articles.

List A

❑ *Applied Measurement in Education*

❑ *Applied Psychological Measurement*

❑ *Educational Assessment*

❑ *Educational Measurement: Issues and Practice*

❑ *Educational and Psychological Measurement*

❑ *Journal of Educational Measurement*

❑ *Journal of Personality Assessment*

❑ *Measurement and Evaluation in Counseling and Development*

List B

❑ *American Educational Research Journal*

❑ *Educational Leadership*

❑ *Educational Researcher*

❑ *Journal of Applied Psychology*

❑ *Journal of Counseling Psychology*

❑ *Journal of Educational Psychology*

❑ *Journal of School Psychology*

❑ *Journal of Special Education*

❏ *Psychology in the Schools*
❏ *Phi Delta Kappan*
❏ *Review of Educational Research*

APPENDIX C

Test Publishers and Objective-Item Banks

TEST PUBLISHERS

The following is a list of the test publishers and distributors whose tests are mentioned in this book (the tests are listed in Appendix D, with the publisher's number that appears here in boldface). All will provide catalogues of their current tests.

The names and addresses of other test publishers and distributors can be obtained from the latest volume of the *Mental Measurements Yearbook.*

1. American Guidance Service, Inc.
4201 Woodland Rd.
Circle Pines, MN 55014

2. C.P.S., Inc.
P.O. Box 83
Larchmont, NY 10538

3. CTB/McGraw-Hill
20 Ryan Ranch Rd.
Monterey, CA 93940

4. Consulting Psychologists Press, Inc.
3803 E. Bayshore Rd.
Palo Alto, CA 94303

5. Educational Testing Service
Princeton, NJ 08540

6. Institute for Personality and Ability Testing
P.O. Box 188
Champaign, IL 61820

7. Psychological Assessment Resources (PAR)
P.O. Box 998
Odessa, FL 33556

8. PRO–ED
8700 Shoal Creek Blvd.
Austin, TX 78757

9. Psychological Corporation
555 Academic Ct.
San Antonio, TX 78204

10. Riverside Publishing Co.
8420 Bryn Mawr Ave.
Chicago, IL 60631

11. Scholastic Testing Service
480 Meyer Road
Bensenville, IL 60106

12. Science Research Associates
155 N. Wacker Drive
Chicago, IL 60606

OBJECTIVE-ITEM BANKS

Collections of instructional objectives and related test items are maintained by test publishers and others. These are usually in the form of a customized test development service, a complete test development system that has computer software for sale or lease, or both. Some of the larger item banks that cover all grade levels are listed below.

❑ CTB/McGraw-Hill: CTB/McGraw-Hill Item Bank; and
   Objective-Referenced Bank of Items and Tests (ORBIT)

❑ Psychological Corporation: Academic Instructional Measurement System (AIMS)

❑ Riverside Publishing Company: MULTISCORE

❑ Tescor, Inc. (461 Carlisle Drive, Herndon, VA 22070): First National Item Bank & Test Development System

Objective-item banks are also maintained by some state departments, colleges, public schools, and private organizations. For a list and descriptions of a large number of objective-item banks, see Richard W. Naccarato, *A Guide to Item Banking in Education,* 3rd ed., 1988 (Northwest Regional Education Laboratory, 101 S.W. Main Street, Suite 500, Portland, Oregon 97204). This volume consists of a detailed item bank data sheet for each system that describes the objective-item collection and how the system functions.

APPENDIX D
Selected Published Tests

Test Name (Publisher's No.)[1]	Grade[2] Level Covered
Achievement Batteries	
California Achievement Tests (3)	K–12
Comprehensive Tests of Basic Skills (3)	K–12
Iowa Tests of Basic Skills (10)	K–9
Iowa Tests of Educational Development (10)	9–12
Metropolitan Achievement Tests (9)	K–12
Sequential Tests of Educational Progress (3)	K–12
Stanford Achievement Tests (9)	1–12
Tests of Achievement and Proficiency (10)	9–12
The 3-Rs Test (10)	K–12
Diagnostic Tests	
California Diagnostic Mathematics Tests (3)	1–12
California Diagnostic Reading Tests (3)	1–12
Metropolitan Achievement Tests	
Language Diagnostic Tests (9)	1–9.9
Mathematics Diagnostic Tests (9)	1–9.9
Reading Diagnostic Tests (9)	K.5–9.9

---

[1]The publisher's number in parentheses refers to the list in Appendix C.
[2]Gives total span only, not the number of separate levels available (p = preschool, K = kindergarten, A = adult).

Stanford Diagnostic Mathematics Test (9)	1.5–12
Stanford Diagnostic Reading Test (9)	1.5–12

Individual Achievement Tests

Basic Achievement Skills Individual Screener (9)	1–A
Peabody Individual Achievement Test—R (1)	K–A
KeyMath Diagnostic Arithmetic Test—R (1)	P–6
Woodcock Reading Mastery Test—R (1)	K–adult

Criterion-Referenced Tests

DMI Mathematics System (3)	K–8.9
National Proficiency Survey Series (10)	8–12
PRI Reading Systems (3)	K–9

(For Customized Testing, see objective item banks in Appendix C.)

Reading Tests

Gates–McGinitie Reading Tests (10)	K–12
Iowa Silent Reading Tests (9)	6–14
Nelson Reading Skills Test (10)	3–9
Nelson–Denny Reading Test (10)	9–16, A

(See also Achievement Batteries and Diagnostic Tests.)

Learning Ability Tests

Cognitive Abilities Test (10)	K–12
Culture-Fair Intelligence Test (6)	4–16, A
Henmon–Nelson Tests of Mental Ability (10)	K–12
Otis–Lennon School Ability Test (9)	K–12
School and College Ability Tests, SCAT (3)	3.5–12.9
Tests of Cognitive Skills (3)	2–12

Multiaptitude Batteries

Differential Aptitude Tests (9)	8–13, A

Readiness Tests

Boehm Test of Basic Concepts (9)	K–2
Cooperative Preschool Inventory (3)	P–K
Metropolitan Readiness Test (9)	K–1
Stanford Early School Achievement Test (9)	K–1
Tests of Basic Experience (3)	P–1

Attitude Scales

Estes Attitude Scales (8)	3–12
School Interest Inventory (10)	7–12
Survey of School Attitudes (9)	1–8

Interest Inventories

Kuder General Interest Survey (12)   6–12

Kuder Occupational Interest Survey (12)   10–A

Strong–Campbell Interest Inventory (9)   11–A

APPENDIX E

Taxonomy of Educational Objectives

TABLE E.1
Major categories in the cognitive domain of the taxonomy of educational objectives
(Bloom 1956)

Descriptions of the Major Categories in the Cognitive Domain

1. **Knowledge.** Knowledge is defined as the remembering of previously learned material. This may involve the recall of a wide range of material, from specific facts to complete theories, but all that is required is the bringing to mind of the appropriate information. Knowledge represents the lowest level of learning outcomes in the cognitive domain.

2. **Comprehension.** Comprehension is defined as the ability to grasp the meaning of material. This may be shown by translating material from one form to another (words or numbers), by interpreting material (explaining or summarizing), and by estimating future trends (predicting consequences or effects). These learning outcomes go one step beyond the simple remembering of material and represent the lowest level of understanding.

3. **Application.** Application refers to the ability to use learned material in new and concrete situations. This may include the application of such things as rules, methods, concepts, principles, laws, and theories. Learning outcomes in this area require a higher level of understanding than those under comprehension.

4. **Analysis.** Analysis refers to the ability to break down material into its component parts so that its organizational structure may be understood. This may include the identification of the parts, analysis of the relationships between parts, and recognition of the organizational principles involved. Learning outcomes here represent a higher intellectual level than comprehension and application because they require an understanding of both the content and the structural form of the material.

5. **Synthesis.** Synthesis refers to the ability to put parts together to form a new whole. This may involve the production of a unique communication (theme or speech), a plan of operations (research proposal), or a set of abstract relations (scheme for classifying information). Learning outcomes in this area stress creative behaviors, with major emphasis on the formulation of *new* patterns or structures.

6. **Evaluation.** Evaluation is concerned with the ability to judge the value of material (statement, novel, poem, research report) for a given purpose. The judgments are to be based on definite criteria. These may be internal criteria (organization) or external criteria (relevance to the purpose) and the student may determine the criteria or be given them. Learning outcomes in this area are highest in the cognitive hierarchy because they contain elements of all of the other categories plus value judgments based on clearly defined criteria.

TABLE E.2
Examples of general instructional objectives and clarifying verbs for the
cognitive domain of the taxonomy

Illustrative General Instructional Objectives	Illustrative Verbs for Stating Specific Learning Outcomes
Knows common terms Knows specific facts Knows methods and procedures Knows basic concepts Knows principles	Defines, describes, identifies, labels, lists, matches, names, outlines, reproduces, selects, states
Understands facts and principles Interprets verbal material Interprets charts and graphs Translates verbal material to mathematical formulas Estimates consequences implied in data Justifies methods and procedures	Converts, defends, distinguishes, estimates, explains, extends, generalizes, gives examples, infers, paraphrases, predicts, rewrites, summarizes
Applies principles to new situations Applies theories to practical situations Solves mathematical problems Constructs charts and graphs Demonstrates correct usage of a procedure	Changes, computes, demonstrates, discovers, manipulates, modifies, operates, predicts, prepares, produces, relates, shows, solves, uses
Recognizes unstated assumptions Recognizes logical fallacies in reasoning Distinguishes between facts and inferences Evaluates the relevancy of data Analyzes the organizational structure of a work (art, music, writing)	Breaks down, diagrams, differentiates, discriminates, distinguishes, identifies, illustrates, infers, outlines, points out, relates, selects, separates, subdivides
Writes a well-organized theme Gives a well-organized speech Writes a creative short story (or poem) Proposes a plan for an experiment Integrates learning from different areas into a plan for solving a problem Formulates a new scheme for classifying objects (or events or ideas)	Categorizes, combines, compiles, composes, creates, devises, designs, explains, generates, modifies, organizes, plans, rearranges, reconstructs, relates, reorganizes, revises, rewrites, summarizes, tells, writes
Judges the consistency of written material Judges the adequacy with which conclusions are supported by data Judges the value of a work (art, music, writing) by use of internal criteria Judges the value of a work (art, music, writing) by use of external standards	Appraises, compares, concludes, contrasts, criticizes, describes, discriminates, explains, interprets, justifies, relates, summarizes, supports

TABLE E.3
Major categories in the affective domain of the taxonomy of educational objectives
(Krathwohl 1964)

Descriptions of the Major Categories in the Affective Domain

1. **Receiving.** Receiving refers to the student's willingness to attend to particular phenomena or stimuli (classroom activities, textbook, music, etc.). From a teaching standpoint, it is concerned with getting, holding, and directing the student's attention. Learning outcomes in this area range from the simple awareness that a thing exists to selective attention on the part of the learner. Receiving represents the lowest level of learning outcomes in the affective domain.

2. **Responding.** Responding refers to active participation on the part of the student. At this level he not only attends to a particular phenomenon but also reacts to it in some way. Learning outcomes in this area may emphasize acquiescence in responding (reads assigned material), willingness to respond (voluntarily reads beyond assignment), or satisfaction in responding (reads for pleasure or enjoyment). The higher levels of this category include those instructional objectives that are commonly classified under *interest;* that is, those that stress the seeking out and enjoyment of particular activities.

3. **Valuing.** Valuing is concerned with the worth or value a student attaches to a particular object, phenomenon, or behavior. This ranges in degree from the more simple acceptance of a value (desires to improve group skills) to the more complex level of commitment (assumes responsibility for the effective functioning of the group). Valuing is based on the internalization of a set of specified values, but clues to these values are expressed in the student's overt behavior. Learning outcomes in this area are concerned with behavior that is consistent and stable enough to make the value clearly identifiable. Instructional objectives that are commonly classified under *attitudes* and *appreciation* would fall into this category.

4. **Organization.** Organization is concerned with bringing together different values, resolving conflicts between them, and beginning the building of an internally consistent value system. Thus, the emphasis is on comparing, relating, and synthesizing values. Learning outcomes may be concerned with the conceptualization of a value (recognizes the responsibility of each individual for improving human relations) or with the organization of a value system (develops a vocational plan that satisfies his need for both economic security and social service). Instructional objectives relating to the development of a philosophy of life would fall into this category.

5. **Characterization by a Value or Value Complex.** At this level of the affective domain, the individual has a value system that has controlled his behavior for a sufficiently long time for him to have developed a characteristic *life style.* Thus, the behavior is pervasive, consistent, and predictable. Learning outcomes at this level cover a broad range of activities, but the major emphasis is on the fact that the behavior is typical or characteristic of the student. Instructional objectives that are concerned with the student's general patterns of adjustment (personal, social, emotional) would be appropriate here.

TABLE E.4
Examples of general instructional objectives and clarifying verbs for the affective domain of the taxonomy

Illustrative General Instructional Objectives	Illustrative Verbs for Stating Specific Learning Outcomes
Listens attentively Shows awareness of the importance of learning Shows sensitivity to social problems Accepts differences of race and culture Attends closely to the classroom activities	Asks, chooses, describes, follows, gives, holds, identifies, locates, names, points to, selects, sits erect, replies, uses
Completes assigned homework Obeys school rules Participates in class discussion Completes laboratory work Volunteers for special tasks Shows interest in subject Enjoys helping others	Answers, assists, complies, conforms, discusses, greets, helps, labels, performs, practices, presents, reads, recites, reports, selects, tells, writes
Demonstrates belief in the democratic process Appreciates good literature (art or music) Appreciates the role of science (or other subjects) in everyday life Shows concern for the welfare of others Demonstrates problem-solving attitude Demonstrates commitment to social improvement	Completes, describes, differentiates, explains, follows, forms, initiates, invites, joins, justifies, proposes, reads, reports, selects, shares, studies, works
Recognizes the need for balance between freedom and responsibility in a democracy Recognizes the role of systematic planning in solving problems Accepts responsibility for own behavior Understands and accepts own strengths and limitations Formulates a life plan in harmony with his abilities, interests, and beliefs	Adheres, alters, arranges, combines, compares, completes, defends, explains, generalizes, identifies, integrates, modifies, orders, organizes, prepares, relates, synthesizes
Displays safety consciousness Demonstrates self-reliance in working independently Practices cooperation in group activities Uses objective approach in problem solving Demonstrates industry and self-discipline Maintains good health habits	Acts, discriminates, displays, influences, listens, modifies, performs, practices, proposes, qualifies, questions, revises, serves, solves, uses, verifies

TABLE E.5
A classification of educational objectives in the psychomotor domain (Simpson 1972)

Description of the Major Categories in the Psychomotor Domain

1. **Perception.** The first level is concerned with the use of the sense organs to obtain cues that guide motor activity. This category ranges from sensory stimulation (awareness of a stimulus), through cue selection (selecting task-relevant cues), to translation (relating cue perception to action in a performance).

2. **Set.** Set refers to readiness to take a particular type of action. This category includes mental set (mental readiness to act), physical set (physical readiness to act), and emotional set (willingness to act). Perception of cues serves as an important prerequisite for this level.

3. **Guided Response.** Guided response is concerned with the early stages in learning a complex skill. It includes imitation (repeating an act demonstrated by the instructor) and trial and error (using a multiple-response approach to identify an appropriate response). Adequacy of performance is judged by an instructor or by a suitable set of criteria.

4. **Mechanism.** Mechanism is concerned with performance acts where the learned responses have become habitual and the movements can be performed with some confidence and proficiency. Learning outcomes at this level are concerned with performance skills of various types, but the movement patterns are less complex than at the next higher level.

5. **Complex Overt Response.** Complex overt response is concerned with the skillful performance of motor acts that involve complex movement patterns. Proficiency is indicated by a quick, smooth, accurate performance, requiring a minimum of energy. This category includes resolution of uncertainty (performs without hesitation) and automatic performance (movements are made with ease and good muscle control). Learning outcomes at this level include highly coordinated motor activities.

6. **Adaptation.** Adaptation is concerned with skills that are so well developed that the individual can modify movement patterns to fit special requirements or to meet a problem situation.

7. **Origination.** Origination refers to the creating of new movement patterns to fit a particular situation or specific problem. Learning outcomes at this level emphasize creativity based upon highly developed skills.

TABLE E.6
Examples of general instructional objectives and clarifying verbs for the psychomotor domain

Illustrative General Instructional Objectives	Illustrative Verbs for Stating Specific Learning Outcomes
Recognizes malfunction by sound of machine Relates taste of food to need for seasoning Relates music to a particular dance step	Chooses, describes, detects, differentiates, distinguishes, identifies, isolates, relates, selects, separates
Knows sequence of steps in varnishing wood Demonstrates proper bodily stance for batting a ball Shows desire to type efficiently	Begins, displays, explains, moves, proceeds, reacts, responds, shows, starts, volunteers
Performs a golf swing as demonstrated Applies first aid bandage as demonstrated Determines best sequence for preparing a meal	Assembles, builds, calibrates, constructs, dismantles, displays, dissects, fastens, fixes, grinds, heats, manipulates, measures, mends, mixes, organizes, sketches
Writes smoothly and legibly Sets up laboratory equipment Operates a slide projector Demonstrates a simple dance step	(Same list as for Guided Response)
Operates a power saw skillfully Demonstrates correct form in swimming Demonstrates skill in driving an automobile Performs skillfully on the violin Repairs electronic equipment quickly and accurately	(Same list as for Guided Response)
Adjusts tennis play to counteract opponent's style Modifies swimming strokes to fit the roughness of the water	Adapts, alters, changes, rearranges, reorganizes, revises, varies
Creates a dance step Creates a musical composition Designs a new dress style	Arranges, combines, composes, constructs, creates, designs, originates

REFERENCES*

Bloom, B. S., *et al.* (Eds.). 1956. *Taxonomy of Educational Objectives: Handbook I, Cognitive Domain*. New York: D. McKay. Describes the cognitive categories in detail and presents illustrative objectives and test items for each.

Harrow, A. J. (1972). *A Taxonomy of the Psychomotor Domain*. New York: D. McKay. Provides a model for classifying learning outcomes in the psychomotor domain and presents illustrative objectives.

Krathwohl, D. R., *Et Al.* (Eds.). 1964. *Taxonomy of Educational Objectives: Handbook II, Affective Domain*. New York: D. McKay. Describes the affective categories in detail and presents illustrative objectives and test items for each.

Simpson, E. J. (1972). The Classification of Educational Objectives in the Psychomotor Domain. *The Psychomotor Domain* (Vol. 3.). Washington: Gryphon House. Describes the psychomotor domain in detail and presents illustrative objectives.

---

*Tables E.1 through E.6 are reprinted from N. E. Gronlund, *Stating Objectives for Classroom Instruction,* 3d ed.(New York: Macmillan, 1985).

APPENDIX F

Relating Assessment Procedures to Instructional Objectives

Instructional objectives encompass a variety of learning outcomes, and assessment includes a variety of procedures. The key to effective assessment of student learning is to relate the assessment procedures as directly as possible to the intended learning outcomes. This is easiest to accomplish if the general instructional objectives and the specific learning outcomes have been clearly stated in terms of student performance. It is then simply a matter of constructing or selecting assessment instruments that provide the most direct evidence concerning the attainment of the stated outcomes.

The sequence of steps shown in Figure F.1 summarizes the general procedure for relating assessment techniques to instructional objectives.

FIGURE F.1
Relation of assessment techniques to objectives

General Instructional Objectives
Intended outcomes that direct our teaching
↓
Specific Learning Outcomes
Types of student performance we are willing to accept as evidence of the attainment of objectives
↓
Assessment Techniques
Procedures for obtaining samples of student performance like those described in the specific learning outcomes

RELATING TEST ITEMS TO INSTRUCTIONAL OBJECTIVES

Preparing test items that are directly relevant to the instructional objectives to be measured requires matching the performance measured by the test items to the types of performance specified by the intended outcomes. Stating the outcomes as specifically as possible is useful in this regard, but good judgment is still needed. If the intended learning outcomes call for *supplying* the answers (e.g., *name, define*), the test items should also require that the answers be supplied rather than selected. If the intended learning outcomes call for *identifying* a procedure, the test items should be concerned only with identifying, rather than with more complex outcomes. If the intended learning outcomes call for *performing* a procedure, the test items should require actual performance rather than a verbal description of how to do it. Issues such as these highlight the care needed in determining whether there is a good match between the stated outcomes and the expected responses to the test items.

Constructing relevant test items was considered in earlier chapters. Here we are simply pointing out the importance of matching test items and assessment tasks as closely as possible to the learning outcomes they are intended to measure. The following examples, from various content areas, show reasonably good matches between intended outcomes and test items. In each example, the specific learning outcome describes the performance the student is to demonstrate, and the test item presents a task that demands that type of performance.

EXAMPLES

Specific Learning Outcome: Defines common terms. (Elementary Mathematics)

Directions: In one or two sentences, define each of the following words:

1. Interest
2. Premium
3. Dividend
4. Collateral
5. Profit

Specific Learning Outcome: Identifies procedure for converting from one measure to another. (Elementary Mathematics)

1. The area of a rug is given in square yards. How should you determine the number of square feet?

   A   Multiply by 3
   Ⓑ   Multiply by 9
   C   Divide by 3
   D   Divide by 9

Specific Learning Outcome: Differentiates between relative values expressed in fractions. (Elementary Mathematics)

1. Which of the following fractions is smaller than one half?

   A 2/4

   B 4/6

   Ⓒ 3/8

   D 9/16

Specific Learning Outcome: Distinguishes fact from opinion. (Elementary Social Studies)

Directions: Read each of the following statements carefully. If you think the statement is a *fact,* circle the F. If you think the statement is an *opinion,* circle the O.

   Ⓕ O 1. George Washington was the first president of the United States.

   F Ⓞ 2. Abraham Lincoln was our greatest president.

   Ⓕ O 3. Franklin Roosevelt was the only president elected to that office three times.

   Ⓕ O 4. Alaska is the biggest state in the United States.

   F Ⓞ 5. Hawaii is the most beautiful state in the United States.

Specific Learning Outcome: Identifies common uses of weather instruments. (Elementary Science)

1. Which one of the following instruments is used to determine the speed of the wind?

   A Wind vane

   Ⓑ Anemometer

   C Altimeter

   D Radar

Specific Learning Outcome: Identifies cause-and-effect relationships. (Elementary Science)

Directions: In each of the following statements, both parts of the statement are true. Decide whether the second part explains *why* the first part is true. If it does, circle Yes. If it does not, circle No.

Examples:

   Ⓨes No 1. People can see   *because*   they have eyes.

   Yes Ⓝo 2. People can walk   *because*   they have arms.

In the first example, the second part of the statement explains *why* "people can see," and so Yes was circled. In the second example, the second part of the statement does *not* explain *why* "people can walk," and so No was circled. Read each of the following statements and answer in the same way.

   Yes Ⓝo 1. Some desert snakes   *because*   the weather is hot in
                   are hatched   the desert.
                   from eggs

(Yes)	No	2. Spiders are very useful	*because*	they eat harmful insects.
(Yes)	No	3. Some plants do not need sunlight	*because*	they get their food from other plants.
Yes	(No)	4. Water in the ocean evaporates	*because*	it contains salt.
(Yes)	No	5. Fish can get oxygen from the water	*because*	they have gills.

Specific Learning Outcome: Identifies reasons for an action or event. (Biology)

1. Which one of the following best explains why green algae give off bubbles of oxygen on a bright sunny day?

  A Transpiration

  B Plasmolysis

  (C) Photosynthesis

  D Osmosis

Specific Learning Outcome: Identifies the relevance of arguments. (Social Studies)

Directions: The items in this part of the test are to be based on the following resolution:

Resolved: The legal voting age in the United States should be lowered to eighteen. Some of the following statements are arguments *for* the resolution, some are arguments *against* it, and some are *neither* for nor against the resolution. Read each of the following statements and circle

F if it is an argument *for* the resolution.
A if it is an argument *against* the resolution.
N if it is *neither* for nor against the resolution.

  (F) A N 1. Most persons are physically, emotionally, and intellectually mature by the age of eighteen.

  F A (N) 2. Many persons are still in school at the age of eighteen.

  F A (N) 3. In most states it is legal to drive an automobile by the age of eighteen.

  F (A) N 4. The ability to vote intelligently increases with age.

  F A (N) 5. The number of eighteen-year-old citizens in the United States is increasing each year.

These examples are sufficient to show how test items should be related to specific learning outcomes. Although not all subject-matter areas and all types of learning outcomes are represented, the basic principle is the same. State the desired learning outcomes in measurable terms, and select or develop test items that demand that specific type of performance.

RELATING PERFORMANCE ASSESSMENT TASKS TO INSTRUCTIONAL OBJECTIVES

There are many areas in which testing procedures are not useful. In assessing some performance skills (e.g., singing, dancing, speaking), it is necessary to observe the students as they perform and to judge the effectiveness of the performance. In other instances it is possible to assess students' skill by judging the quality of the product resulting from the performance (e.g., a theme, a painting, a typed letter, a baked cake). In assessing students' social adjustment it may be necessary to observe the students in formal and informal situations in order to judge their tendencies toward aggression or withdrawal, relations with peers, and the like. In fact, whenever we assess how students typically behave in a situation, some type of observational procedure is usually called for.

As with testing procedures, the selection or development of a performance-based assessment task or an observational technique should evolve from the objectives and specific learning outcomes. In the case of rating scales or checklists, the specific learning outcomes become the dimensions to be observed. In the following examples, note how the specific learning outcomes require only a slight modification to become items in a rating scale.

EXAMPLES

Speech

Specific Learning Outcome: Maintains good eye contact with audience.

Rating Scale Item: How effective is the speaker in maintaining eye contact with the audience?

1	2	3	4	5
Ineffective	Below average	Average	Above average	Very effective

Theme Writing

Specific Learning Outcome: Organizes ideas in a coherent manner.

Rating Scale Item: Organization of ideas.

1	2	3	4	5
Poor organization		Fair organization		Clear, coherent organization

Group Work

Specific Learning Outcome: Contributes worthwhile ideas to group discussion.

Rating Scale Item: How often does the student contribute worthwhile ideas to group discussion?

1	2	3	4	5
Never	Seldom	Occasionally	Fairly often	Frequently

More complete rating scales and checklists are presented in Chapter 15. It is our purpose here merely to illustrate how assessment tasks and other observational procedures can be related to the learning outcomes we wish to assess. The specific learning outcomes specify the characteristics to be observed, and the rating scale provides a convenient method of recording our judgments. Such judgments are, of course, still subjective, but we have made them as objective as possible by defining the samples of student responses we wished to observe and then observing those responses.

RELATING ASSESSMENT PROCEDURES USING AN EXPANDED TABLE OF SPECIFICATIONS

When using multiple techniques to assess classroom learning, it is usually desirable to expand the table of specifications used in test construction to include both test and nontest procedures. This provides an overall plan that clarifies how each assessment technique relates to the instructional objectives. Including all objectives and assessment procedures in a single table makes clear the relative emphasis given to each objective and each method of assessment and prevents an overemphasis on testing procedures. A simplified version of such a table is presented in Table F.1.

TABLE F.1

Table of specifications for evaluation of a weather unit in junior high school science

Content	Objectives						Total Number of Items
	Knows		Understands	Interprets	Skill in		
	Symbols and Terms	Specific Facts	Influence of Each Factor on Weather Formation	Weather Maps	Using Measuring Devices	Constructing Weather Maps	
Air pressure	2	3	3	3	Observe pupils using measuring devices (rating scale)	Evaluate maps constructed by pupils (checklist)	11
Wind	4	2	8	2			16
Temperature	2	2	2	2			8
Humidity and precipitation	2	1	2	5			10
Clouds	2	2	1				5
Total number of items	12	10	16	12			50
Percentage of evaluation	12%	10%	16%	12%	25%	25%	100%

Name Index

Subject Index

Ability spectrum, 392–393
Ability tests. *See* Aptitude tests
Absolute grading, 346, 347, 349–352
Academic Instructional Measurement System (AIMS), 385
Accountability, 476–478
Achievement batteries, 368–377, 399–400, 529
Achievement tests. *See* Classroom tests; Standardized achievement tests
Action verbs, 40, 43, 535, 537, 539
Adaptive testing, 402, 409, 485–486
Adjustment outcomes, 32
Administration of tests
   checklist on, 429
   classroom tests, 311–312, 367
   computerization of, 485–486
   procedures for, 415, 429
   standardized achievement tests, 365, 367, 426–431
   usability and, 106–108
   validity and, 76
Affective domain, 32, 536–537
AIMS. *See Academic Instructional Measurement System*
Alternate forms method. *See* Equivalent forms method
Alternative assessment, 238
Alternative-response test items, 127, 157–165
Alternatives, 173, 189, 193–195

Ambiguity, 74, 137, 162
Analytic rating, 256
Analytic scoring method, 231
Anecdotal records
   advantages of, 269–271
   behavior types, 268–269
   defined, 267
   form for, 267
   guidelines for, 272
   improving effectiveness of, 271–273
   limitations of, 269–271
   uses of, 268
Answer sheets, 308–309
Anxiety, 311–312, 427, 490
Application outcomes, 31, 134, 179–181
Appreciation outcomes, 32
Aptitude tests
   ability spectrum and, 392–393
   achievement tests and, 391–394, 529–530
   choosing, 398–400
   culture-fair tests, 406–407
   describing, 354
   differential, 407–411
   individual, 400–404
   learning ability, 346, 347–348, 394–406, 530
   multi-aptitude batteries, 408–411, 530
   predictions made with, 393–394
   purpose of, 12

results of, 431–435
   scholastic, 55, 394–406, 432, 530
   school-oriented, 392
   separate scores, 395–398
   single-score, 395, 398–399
   standard age scores and, 397, 403
   vocational choice and, 492–493
Area conversion, 455
Armed Services Vocational Aptitude Battery (ASVAB), 408
Assessment. *See also* Observational techniques; Peformance-based assessments; Personal-social development; Reliability; Tests and testing; Usability; Validity
   categories of, 18–20
   cognitive research and, 30
   complex performance, 13–14, 19
   consistency of, 48
   defined, 3, 5–6
   diagnostic, 15, 19, 117, 119, 432
   difficulty of, 99
   fixed-choice, 13–14
   formative, 14–15, 19, 117, 119
   instructional decisions and, 4
   instructional objectives and, 25–44, 299–300, 541–546
   instructional process and, 8–11
   international, 480, 481–482
   learning outcomes and, 25
   maximum versus typical performance, 12